SuperVision and Instructional Leadership

A Developmental Approach

FIFTH EDITION

Carl D. Glickman

The University of Georgia

Stephen P. Gordon

University of South Florida

Jovita M. Ross-Gordon

University of South Florida

Allyn and Bacon

Boston • London • Toronto • Sydney • Tokyo • Singapore

Vice President: *Paul A. Smith*
Series Editor: *Arnis E. Burvikovs*
Editorial Assistant: *Patrice Mailloux*
Marketing Managers: *Brad Parkins and Kathleen Morgan*
Editorial Production Service: *Marbern House*
Manufacturing Buyer: *Julie McNeill*
Cover Administrator: *Linda Knowles*
Electronic Composition: *Omegatype Typography, Inc.*

A Pearson Education Company
160 Gould Street
Needham Heights, MA 02494

Previous editions were published under the title *Supervision of Instruction:
A Developmental Approach.* Copyright 1998, 1995, 1990, 1985 by Allyn & Bacon

Internet: www.abacon.com

Library of Congress Cataloging-in-Publication Data
Glickman, Carl D.
    Supervision and instructional leadership : a developmental approach / Carl D.
Glickman, Stephen P. Gordon, Jovita M. Ross-Gordon.—5th ed.
        p.   cm.
    Rev. ed. of: Supervision of instruction. 4th ed. c1998.
    Includes bibliographical references and indexes.
    ISBN 0-205-32202-6
    1. School supervision.   I. Gordon, Stephen P., 1948–   II. Ross-Gordon, Jovita M.
III. Glickman, Carl D.   Supervision of instruction.   IV. Title.

LB2806.4 .G56 2001
371.2'03—dc21   00-041626

Printed in the United States of America

10 9 8 7 6 5 4 3 2 1   RRD-VA   05 04 03 02 01 00

Contents

PART III • *Interpersonal Skills*   *123*

6 *Supervisory Behavior Continuum: Know Thyself*   *125*

7 *Developmental Supervision: An Introduction*   *136*

14   *Observing Skills   250*

15   *Research and Evaluation Skills   276*

PART V • *Tasks of SuperVision*   *313*

16 *Direct Assistance to Teachers*   *315*

17 *Group Development*   *334*

Preface

In 1984, an emergency meeting was called between the editor and the first author about whether this book should be published. Prepublication reviews of the manuscript had been quite negative. Established education authorities had criticized the manuscript as really not about the traditional domain of supervision. It was too comprehensive, too complex, and too much about leadership and school change. The editor was in a quandary. However, the decision was made to proceed—without any further changes to the text—and to wait and see what the response would be. In 1985, the first edition of *Supervision of Instruction: A Developmental Approach* was published.

The book immediately found a warm reception among practitioners, graduate students, and college faculties. Within a few years, the book became a leading text and now, after fifteen years and four editions, it continues to retain a major part of the graduate course market in the United States. The critics were, in fact, correct—the book was not solely about what a supervisor in a formal position of authority does to or with a classroom teacher, but, rather, it was as Jack Frymier, scholar activist at Ohio State University wrote in the 1985 foreword about "the confinements, the pressures, the conflicts, the purposes, the materials, the relationships, (and) the opportunities...what teaching and learning are all about." Frymier went on to say, "[T]his book is clearly different" and that it is one of the rare books that may "actually reconceptualize the field." (Frymier, 1985, xii and xiii)

The challenge now in the fifth edition is to continue the quest of redefinition. The three of us as co-authors bring our perspectives of change, classroom practice, instructional leadership, adult development, staff development, evaluation, and political and social theory into the everyday life of schools. To us, the lines between supervision and instructional leadership in successful schools are nonexistent. Successful school educators often do not use the term *supervision* in their work. Instead, words such as *collegiality, critical friends, moral leadership,* and *leadership teams* hold sway.

So what we have created is a new title—SuperVision and Instructional Leadership—to more aptly capture the broader vision and reality of teaching and learning success.* We hope that this book will continue to find a home in super-

---

*SuperVision in the title reflects a paradigm shift in this text and the field from a managerial focus to a much broader educational leadership orientation.

vision courses and that it will also be useful for courses in leadership and school and educational change.

Instructors familiar with previous editions will note updating of the following topics:

- The relationship between school culture and classroom instruction
- The linkage of adult learning and adult development with teacher development
- The theory of developmental supervision, including four alternative supervisory approaches (directive control, directive informational, collaboration, nondirective)
- A wide variety of quantitative and qualitative classroom observation methods
- Models for evaluating specific instructional programs as well as the school's overall program
- The five tasks of instructional supervision (direct assistance, group development, professional development, curriculum development, and action research)
- Relating instructional supervision and leadership to shared governance and democratic education

And new material includes:

- SuperVision: a new name for a new paradigm (Chapter 1)
- From effective schools to school improvement (Chapter 3)
- The role of gender in adult and teacher development (Chapter 4)
- Changing views: emphasis on constructivist teaching and learning (Chapter 5)
- Summative and formative teacher evaluation (Chapter 14)
- Integrating clinical supervision with developmental supervision (Chapter 16)
- Role plays on dealing with dysfunctional group members and conflict within groups (Chapter 17)
- Effects of state mandated curriculum and higher stakes tests on teachers and instruction (Chapter 19)
- Chaos theory: implications for school and instructional improvement (Chapter 21)

We hope that this fifth edition signals the need for all of us—writers and readers—to think, challenge, and practice the promise of schools, education, and democracy (Glickman, 1998).

Acknowledgments

It is impossible to acknowledge all those who have contributed to the development of this book. A host of colleagues—school practitioners, graduate students, and university faculty members—have provided us with settings, collaborations, and discussion for field-testing developmental and democratic propositions about supervision. Special mention is given to Lew Allen for his work on the action research chapter and to Barbara Lunsford, Emily Calhoun, Ed Pajak, Jo Blase, Frances Hensley, Dale Rogers, Maude Glanton, and Russ Yeany for their assistance in developing long-term, instructionally focused collaborations with schools as part of The University of Georgia, League of Professional Schools.

We also acknowledge the support of our colleagues in the College of Education at Southwest Texas State University, including Dean John Beck and Educational Administration and Psychological Services Department Chair Sue McCullough, as well as, in the Developmental and Adult Education Program, Barbara Lyman and Emily Payne, and in the Educational Administration Program, Mike Boone, Marla McGhee, Marianne Reese, Trinidad San Miguel, Grant Simpson, Charles Slater, and Duncan Waite.

We thank the following reviewers for their helpful comments: Janet E. Alleman, Michigan State University; L. Nan Restine, Oklahoma State University; and Pamela Curtiss, Drake University.

Finally, many thanks to Heather Pereira, graduate assistant, for her research and general assistance with this text, and to Marisa Polviriyakij, student worker, for typing and proofing revisions to the fifth edition.

We know there are others we have unwittingly left out; for that, we are sorry. Those who have helped us are not responsible for any faults and limitations of this book. Any errors are ours alone. Many have extended our vision about supervision and human development. All of you have helped to show us the light of school success and inspired us to devote our careers to understanding the journey.

To the Instructor

At the end of each chapter, you will find exercises that might be assigned to your graduate students. The first four editions of this text have been used in universities and colleges throughout the United States and Canada. Based on the experience of many colleagues who have used the text with their supervision classes, we would like to offer some suggestions. For those who teach on a semester system, the first three chapters are relatively brief and can be read as one assignment; students can then complete one or two chapters for each subsequent week. For those who teach on a quarter system, it is recommended that the first three chapters be assigned the first week, and two or three chapters each subsequent week.

Exercises are categorized as academic, field, and developmental. *Academic exercises* are those done primarily through library research, reading, writing, and constructing. *Field exercises* are those done in practice within school settings and with other professionals. Academic exercises are suitable for graduate students who do not hold supervisory positions and/or are seeking more knowledge of theory and research. Field exercises are suitable for practitioners who wish to make immediate improvements in their professional situations. Whether or not students are in supervisory positions, we suggest that students do both field and academic exercises at a ratio weighted toward their interest, situation, and needs. Students periodically can be asked to choose and complete one academic or field exercise from a set of related chapters. A short sharing session is useful at the beginning of the subsequent class, to give students an opportunity to discuss the results of their exercises.

Developmental exercises are done as sustained projects that can be used as a term or an extra-credit project. Developmental exercises are written with the purpose of encouraging students to continue their professional growth. If used as a term assignment, please allow students during the first week of classes to scan *all* the developmental activities in each chapter before asking them to make a choice for the academic term.

The exercises (academic, field, and developmental) are numerous and provide students a wide arena of choice. Likewise, we encourage the instructor to make his or her own choices according to his or her own expertise and experience. The sequence of chapters is consistent with the proposed model of supervision, but an individual instructor might find another order more suitable. Similarly, the instructor might wish to adapt, revise, or discard suggestions for using chapter exercises. Our purpose in writing this book was to increase supervisory success in schools. However an instructor can use this book to bring about such success will make our efforts worthwhile.

References

Frymier, J. Foreword to Glickman, C. D. 1985. *Supervision of instruction: A developmental approach.* Newton, MA: Allyn & Bacon.

Glickman, C. D. 1998. *Revolutionizing American Schools.* San Francisco: Jossey-Bass.

Part I

Introduction

1

SuperVision for Successful Schools

Take a walk with us. First, let's step into Finnie Tyler High School, with a student body of 1,200, in a lower- to middle-class urban neighborhood. A sign by the entrance tells all visitors to report to the office. In the halls, we see students milling around, boys and girls talking in groups, couples holding hands, one couple intertwined romantically in a corner. The bell rings and students scurry to the next class. We find the school office and introduce ourselves to the secretary and school principal, who are expecting our visit. They welcome us and assure us that we may move around the school and talk to students, teachers, and other staff. The school population has been notified of our visit and understands that we have come to see how Tyler High School operates. The principal tells us we will find Tyler a pleasant place. Equipped with a floor plan of classrooms and other facilities, we continue on our way.

The principal's description is accurate: Students seem happy and uninhibited, socializing easily with each other even during instruction time. Teachers joke with students. In the faculty lounge, we hear laughter that rises, falls, and then rises again. Several teachers have told us about the traditional Friday after-school gatherings at the local pizza parlor, where teachers and administrators socialize over a drink.

Classrooms vary considerably from each other; teachers tell us they can teach however they wish. Most teachers stand at the front of the room, lecturing, asking questions, and assigning seatwork. Some, however, take a less structured approach, allowing students to work alone or in small groups. There is an unhurried atmosphere. Students move at a leisurely pace, and classes seldom start on time. Teachers of the same subjects use the same textbooks but otherwise seem to have discretion to function as they please. As one seven-year veteran teacher at this school sums it up: "We have an ideal situation. We like each other, and the administration leaves us alone. I am observed once a year. I have one faculty meeting a month to attend. I love the other teachers and we have a great time together. The kids are fine, not as academic as they should be, but this school is a nice place for them. I wouldn't want to teach anyplace else."

Now let's drive across town to Germando Elementary School, with 600 students, located in a wealthy, suburban part of the city. Again, we follow the sign to the office. A few students are standing with their noses against the wall by their classroom doors. Otherwise, the halls are vacant and still; all classroom doors are shut. In the principal's office sit two students with tears in their eyes, obviously fearful of their impending conference with the principal. The principal welcomes us and hands us a preplanned schedule of times to visit particular teachers. She tells us not to visit any classroom during instructional time. "I think you will find that I run a tight ship," she says. "Teachers and students know exactly what is expected of them and what the consequences are for ignoring those expectations. Teachers are here to teach, and I see to it that it happens."

Moving down the halls, we are struck by the similarity of the classrooms. The desks are in rows; the teacher is in front; the school rules are posted on the right of the chalkboard. At the first recess time, the students seem to erupt onto the playground. Expecting to find a group of teachers in the faculty lounge, we are surprised to find only two people. One is knitting and the other is preparing a cup of coffee. All the other teachers have remained in the classrooms, either alone or with one other teacher.

Continuing our observation after recess, we find that teachers at each grade level not only work with the same textbooks but are on the same pages as well. When we ask about this, one teacher tells us that the principal has standardized the entire curriculum and knows what is being taught in every classroom at each moment of the day. At the first faculty meeting in August, the principal lays out materials, schedules, and time lines developed by the central office. We ask how the principal can enforce such procedures, and the teacher replies, "She asks for weekly lesson plans, visits my room at least once every two weeks, and has other central office personnel visit and report back to her."

In the classrooms we visit, students are generally quiet but restless. They appear attentive; those who are not are disciplined. Teachers are mostly business-like; some show warmth toward their students, others do not. We conclude our visit with three separate interviews of teachers. It seems that teaching in Germando is perceived as a job to do. Whether one likes them or not, the principal's rules and regulations are to be followed. Teachers mention that when they have attempted to make modest changes in their instruction, they have been told to drop the changes and return to the school plan. All three mention the teacher who last year refused to follow the reading textbook and was subsequently forced to resign.

Finnie Tyler High School and Germando Elementary School are examples of real schools. Which is the successful school? Which has better attendance, attitudes, and achievement? *Neither does!* Both are ineffective, mediocre schools. The successful schools in the same system are quite different from either. Our first conclusion might be that these schools are very different. Tyler High School appears to have little supervision of instruction, whereas Germando has too much.

According to the definition of instructional supervision presented in this book, however, *neither* school has effective instructional supervision. It also might appear that Tyler meets teachers' individual needs, whereas Germando meets organizational goals set by the principal. In successful schools, however, individual needs are fulfilled through organizational goals. In these two schools, *neither* need is being met. Finally, the working environments in these two schools only appear to be dissimilar; soon we will see how similar they really are.

The last school on our tour is Progress Middle School. Our first stop at Progress is the school office, where we are informed by the school secretary that the principal will meet with us at the end of the period. The principal is teaching Mr. Simmons's class while Simmons observes another teacher as part of a peer coaching program involving a number of teachers. The secretary invites us to wait for the principal in the teachers' lounge, where several teachers are spending their preparation period. As we relax with a soda, we listen to an animated discussion among the teachers concerning an interdisciplinary unit of instruction they are planning. The teachers are brainstorming alternative teaching and assessment strategies for the unit, and discussing how these strategies could be connected to the unit's theme.

Soon the principal joins us and invites us on a tour of the school. During the tour, we note that classroom environments are work oriented, as well as warm and supportive. In some classrooms, students are involved in hands-on inquiry. In other classrooms, cooperative learning is taking place. In still others, teachers are challenging students to reflect on lesson content by using higher-level questioning and inviting student opinions on the lesson topic. A commonality across all classrooms is students engaged in active learning. Teachers give students feedback on their performance, and provide alternative learning opportunities and special attention to those experiencing difficulties.

After school, we attend a meeting of the school leadership council, made up primarily of teachers. The council is considering action research proposals submitted by faculty liaison groups. Each proposal is focused on improvement of curriculum and instruction. Much of the debate among council members is concerned with whether or not the proposed research will assist in meeting the school's vision, mission, and goals agreed upon two years earlier by the entire faculty. At times the debate becomes heated. Clearly the council is taking its decision making seriously. The principal is a voting member of the council, but does not have veto power over council decisions, which are made by majority rule.

Germando Elementary is an example of a *conventional school*—characterized by dependency, hierarchy, and professional isolation. Finnie Tyler is an example of a *congenial school*—characterized by friendly social interactions and professional isolation. A successful school like Progress Middle School is a *collegial school*—characterized by purposeful adult interactions about improving schoolwide teaching and learning. Professional respect is a by-product of discussing issues with candor, accepting disagreements as integral to change, and respecting the wisdom and care of all for arriving at educational decisions for students.

Collegial schools establish learning goals for all students consistent with the responsibility of education in a democratic society. These schools are always studying teaching and learning, setting common priorities, making decisions about internal changes and resource allocations, and assessing effects on student learning. These schools are driven by (1) a covenant of learning—mission, vision, and goals; (2) a charter for schoolwide, democratic, decision making; and (3) a critical study process for informing decisions and conducting action research (Glickman 1993). In effect, successful schools create a "SuperVision" of instruction, democratically derived and studied, that gives purpose and direction to the common world of adults.

SuperVision: A New Name for a New Paradigm*

Like schools, supervision can be conventional, congenial, or collegial. Throughout most of its history supervision has operated from within a conventional paradigm (world view), attempting to control teachers' instructional behaviors. From the 17th to the late 19th century, supervision took the form of committees of lay persons conducting inspections of schools, teachers, and student learning (Cooper, 1982). During the first part of the 20th century—the age of scientific management—lay committees were replaced by professional supervisors. These supervisors demonstrated how subjects were to be taught and visited classrooms to recommend ways that teachers could improve instruction. Inspection and control by lay committees became inspection and control by bureaucrats (Cooper, 1982). The following quote from a 1917 address by Coffman typifies the scientific management approach to supervision:

> The four duties—the laying out and prescribing of materials of instruction, the thinking of teachers and teaching in terms of efficiency levels, the use of standardized tests and scales, and the improvement of the teaching act through the criticism of instruction—constitute the scope of supervision. (cited in Barr & Burton, 1926, p. 2)

From the 1930s through the late 1950s a new paradigm, "human relations supervision" attempted to break the grip of conventional supervision. The basic premise of human relations supervision was that by improving interpersonal relationships and meeting personal needs the supervisor and teachers could improve instruction. Because of its emphasis on meeting personal needs and de-emphasis on organizational goals, this form of supervision, when practiced sincerely, tended to result in congenial schools like Finnie Tyler. More often, attention to the individual actually never went beyond the superficial. In many schools human relations theory was co-opted by conventional supervision and thus became artificial and manipulative (Smyth, 1993).

---

*This discussion includes excerpts from S. P. Gordon, 1992, Paradigms, Transitions, and the New Supervision, *Journal of Curriculum and Supervision*, 8(1), pp. 64–65. Reprinted with permission from ASCO. All rights reserved.

In the 1960s, instructional supervision came under the sway of the behavioral science approach, another form of conventional supervision. Direct supervisory control through inspection and criticism become indirect control through "teacher-proof" curriculum and materials developed by outside researchers and publishers, with implementation mandated by school districts and monitored by supervisors.

The neo-scientific management of the last third of the 20th century saw a shift of external control from researchers and publishers to state legislators and state departments of education. Narrowly defined student performance objectives, standardized achievement tests, and evaluation systems requiring the display of externally defined teacher competencies were legislated by the majority of states. The task of conventional supervision became that of assisting and monitoring "legislated learning" (Wise, 1979, 1988).

As we've stated above, based on what we know about successful schools, the time has come to move from conventional schools (still dominant in the United States) and congenial schools (less prevalent but still present throughout the nation) toward collegial schools (growing in number and success). *A "paradigm shift" toward the collegial model, if it is to succeed, must include a shift away from conventional or congenial supervision toward collegial supervision.* This view of supervision includes all of the following:

1. A collegial rather than a hierarchical relationship between teachers and formally designated supervisors.
2. Supervision as the province of teachers as well as formally designated supervisors.
3. A focus on teacher growth rather than teacher compliance.
4. Facilitation of teachers collaborating with each other in instructional improvement efforts.
5. Teacher involvement in ongoing reflective inquiry. (Gordon, 1997, p. 116).

Jo Blase captures the spirit of this new, collegial approach to supervision in the following description:

> Leadership is shared with teachers, and it is cast in coaching, reflection, collegial investigation. study teams, explorations into the uncertain, and problem solving. It is position-free supervision wherein the underlying spirit is one of expansion, not traditional supervision. Alternatives, not directives or criticism, are the focus, and the community of learners perform professional—indeed, moral—service to students. (cited in Gordon, 1995).

Collegial supervision, then, stands in sharp contrast to traditional approaches to supervision.

Given the fact that the historic role of supervision has been inspection and control, it is not surprising that most teachers do not equate supervision with collegiality. When teachers have been asked to make word associations with the term *instructional supervision*, most of the associations have been negative, as indicated by the following list (Gordon, 1997, p. 118):

Control	Directive
Step-by-step	Irrelevant
Lack of creativity	Waste of time
Lack of free choice	Restricting
Evaluation	Rules
Negative	Dog and pony show
Nonexistent	Big brother
Jumping through hoops	Intimidating
Boring	Constantly under watch
Paperwork	Anxiety
Bureaucrat	Boss
Monitoring instruction	Stress
Guidelines for testing	Need for detailed lesson plans
Authority	Administrative micro management
Unrealistic	Yuck!

Considering the dictionary definition of supervision (to "watch over," "direct," "oversee," "superintend"), the history of instructional supervision as an instrument for controlling teachers, and negative teacher perceptions of conventional supervision, it seems that a new term for describing the collegial model of instructional leadership espoused in this book is in order. Therefore the first word in the title of this new edition is *SuperVision*. This term denotes a common vision of what teaching and learning can and should be, developed collaboratively by formally designated supervisors, teachers, and other members of the school community. The word also implies that these same persons will work together to make their vision a reality—to build a democratic community of learning based on moral principles calling for all students to be educated in a manner enabling them to lead fulfilling lives and be contributing members of a democratic society.

Supervisory Glue as a Metaphor for Success

We can think of supervision as the *glue* of a successful school. Supervision is the function in schools that draws together the discrete elements of instructional effectiveness into whole-school action. Research shows that those schools that link their instruction and classroom management with professional development, direct assistance to teachers, curriculum development, group development, and action research under a common purpose *achieve their objectives* (MacKenzie, 1983). In other words, when teachers accept common goals for students and therefore complement each other's teaching, and when supervisors work with teachers in a manner consistent with the way teachers are expected to work with students, then—and only then—does the school reach its goals. Regardless of a school's grade span, socioeconomic setting, or physical characteristics, successful schools have a common glue that keeps a faculty together and creates consistency among a school's various elements. The glue is the process by which some person or group of people is responsible for providing a link between individual teacher needs and organizational goals so that individuals within the school can work in harmony toward their vision of what the school *should* be.

This harmony does not happen by chance; those schools or systems in which the responsibility for applying the glue is not assigned to specific persons, through job descriptions and allocations of time, simply do not achieve. Unfortunately, there are more "glueless" than "glued" schools. Research findings on the effectiveness of schools paint a dismal picture. Most schools simply do not make much difference in their students' lives. Research focused on those rare schools that do make a difference, however, has much to tell us about how all schools could be changed for the better.

Thus, the primary function of effective supervision is to take responsibility for putting more "glue" into the school. However, before you run down to the nearest hardware store for buckets of glue to spill on your school floors and corridors (which, it's true, might cut down on student discipline problems and teacher absenteeism, particularly if the glue hardened during a recess period or between classes), let's caution that the adhesive under discussion is of a particular nature.

Effective supervision requires knowledge, interpersonal skills, and technical skills. These are applied through the supervisory tasks of direct assistance to teachers, curriculum development, professional development, group development, and action research. This adhesive pulls together organizational goals and teacher needs and provides for improved learning.

James McDonald (1981) has written about understanding a person's world view by the language and, particularly, the metaphors he or she uses. *Glue* is a good metaphor for effective, fully functioning school supervision. Glue is not glamorous; neither is supervision. When glue is doing its work properly—for example, by keeping a chair together—it goes largely unnoticed; so does supervision, when a school is functioning well. Glue does get attention when the legs of a chair collapse, just as supervision does when a school fragments and fails. With success, both glue and supervision are taken for granted; with failure, they are both held responsible. This is as it should be: Teachers are in the forefront of successful instruction; supervision is in the background, providing the support, knowledge, and skills that enable teachers to succeed. When improved instruction and school success do not materialize, supervision should shoulder the responsibility for not permitting teachers to be successful.

Who Is Responsible for SuperVision?

Mark Zelchack, an experienced teacher, has been appointed as a mentor for a beginning teacher in his elementary school. At the beginning of the school year, Mark oriented the new teacher to the school, the curriculum, and the new teacher's responsibilities. Mark visits the new teacher's classroom on a regular basis, has conferences with his mentee, and is helping him to carry out an instructional improvement plan that they designed collaboratively.

Jane Simmons is a school principal. She has recently initiated a clinical supervision program with a group of volunteer teachers. In a typical clinical cycle, Jane holds a preconference with a teacher in which they discuss the teacher's plan for a future lesson. They also discuss nonjudgemental data that the teacher wishes Jane to collect while observing the lesson. After observing the class and collecting the desired data, Jane shares the data with the teacher during a postconference. The postconference is nonevaluative, aimed at interpreting the data and helping the teacher to plan improvement goals and strategies for reaching those goals.

Michele Carver is a lead teacher. She is released from teaching for three periods a day to help other teachers improve their instruction. This year Michele has conducted professional development programs on cooperative learning and teaching thinking skills, and has provided expert coaching to teachers who are attempting to transfer their new instructional skills to their classrooms. Recently, Michele has been elected chairperson of her school's instructional improvement committee.

Briget Myers is a first-grade teacher. She is a member of a collegial peer-coaching triad. This week she is scheduled to observe two other first-grade teachers who are attempting to use some of the same balanced literacy strategies that Briget is trying out with her own first-graders. She hopes not only to provide her colleagues with useful observation data, but also to pick up ideas on how she can better implement balanced literacy in her own classroom.

The educators discussed here carry out a variety of roles within their schools. However, they all participate in supervision during at least part of their working day. Our definition of supervision is that SuperVision is identical to leadership for the improvement of instruction. This definition allows for instructional leadership to be viewed as a function and process rather than a role or position. Educators throughout the school system—from the top to the bottom of its organizational chart—can engage in the function and process of supervision.*

Typical supervisors are school principals, assistant principals, instructional lead teachers, department heads, master teachers, teachers, program directors, central office consultants and coordinators, and associate or assistant superintendents. Research on effective schools documents that such schools have in common staff members who attend to the function of improving instruction. The formal titles vary from school to school, however (Schneider, 1982–1983; Purkey and Smith, 1982). Therefore, what is crucial is not a person's title but rather his or her responsibilities. Ben Harris (1975) clarified the supervisor's role further by stating that supervision is related directly to helping teachers with instruction but only indirectly to instructing students. Supervision is not the act of instructing students—that is, teaching—but rather the actions that enable teachers to improve instruction for students.

The reason we emphasize the process and function of supervision rather than the title or position is that the titles *supervisor* and *administrator* are used indiscriminately in public schools. For example, a school system may have science

---

*To avoid awkwardness of writing, from here on we will use the spelling of SuperVision only in particular headings. But the point is that SuperVision and instructional leadership are integrated and interchangeable concepts.

supervisors, elementary supervisors, or high school supervisors who function mainly as record keepers, inventory clerks, and proposal writers and do not work directly to improve instruction. Despite the title of supervisor, they do not function in the realm of supervision. On the other hand, persons with titles such as principal, lead teacher, or superintendent may be heavily involved in supervision through direct assistance to teachers, curriculum development, professional development, group development, and action research. Of course, some titled supervisors do function in supervision, but the point is that what a person does in his or her job is the only key to whether or not he or she is involved in supervision. In this book, the term *supervisor* will refer to any person involved with supervision, not to a particular title or position.

Schools vary with respect to who carries out supervisory responsibilities. Some schools assign responsibilities to department heads, assistant principals, guidance counselors, lead teachers, or central office personnel; in such schools, the principal focuses on overall administration—the budget, community matters, schedules and reports, and the physical plant. In other schools, the principal might be largely responsible for supervision, with others attending to administrative matters. Again, a characteristic of successful schools is that someone, somewhere is responsible for and committed to the process, function, and tasks of supervision. Behind every successful school is an effective supervision program.

Organization of This Book

Figure 1.1 demonstrates the scope and organization of this book. For those in supervisory roles, the challenge to improving student learning is to apply certain knowledge, interpersonal skills, and technical skills to the tasks of direct assistance, group development, curriculum development, professional development, and action research that will enable teachers to teach in a collective, purposeful manner uniting organizational goals and teacher needs. As the supervisor allows teachers to take greater control over their own professional lives, a school becomes a dynamic setting for learning.

To facilitate such collective instructional improvement, those responsible for supervision must have certain prerequisites. The first is a *knowledge* base. Supervisors need to understand the exception—what teachers and schools can be—in contrast to the norm—what teachers and schools typically are. They need to understand how knowledge of adult and teacher development and alternative supervisory practices can help break the norm of mediocrity found in typical schools. Second, there is an *interpersonal skills* base. Supervisors must know how their own interpersonal behaviors affect individuals as well as groups of teachers and then study ranges of interpersonal behaviors that might be used to promote more positive and change-oriented relationships. Third, the supervisor must have *technical skills* in observing, planning, assessing, and evaluating instructional improvement. Knowledge, interpersonal skills, and technical competence are three complementary aspects of supervision as a developmental function.

Supervisors have certain educational tasks at their disposal that enable teachers to evaluate and modify their instruction. In planning each task, the supervisor

| Prerequisites | Function | Tasks | Unification | Product |

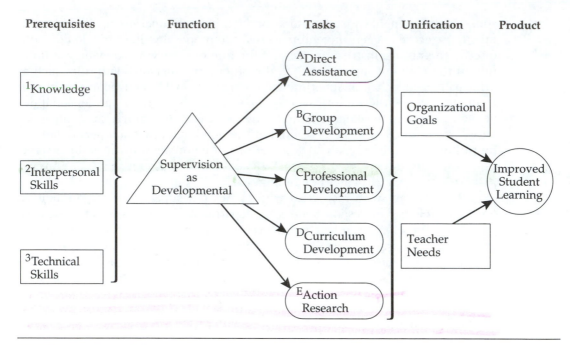

FIGURE 1.1   *SuperVision for Successful Schools*

needs to plan specific ways of giving teachers a greater sense of professional power to teach students successfully. Those supervisory tasks that have such potential to affect teacher development are direct assistance, group development, professional development, curriculum development, and action research. Direct assistance *(A)* is the provision of personal, ongoing contact with the individual teacher to observe and assist in classroom instruction. Group development *(B)* is the gathering together of teachers to make decisions on mutual instructional concerns. Professional development *(C)* includes the learning opportunities for faculty provided or supported by the school and school system. Curriculum development *(D)* is the revision and modification of the content, plans, and materials of classroom instruction. Action research *(E)* is the systematic study by a faculty of what is happening in the classroom and school with the aim of improving learning.

By understanding how teachers grow optimally in a supportive and challenging environment, the supervisor can plan the tasks of supervision to bring together organizational goals and teacher needs into a single fluid entity. The unification of individual teacher needs with organizational goals in "a cause beyond oneself" has been demonstrated to promote powerful instruction and improved student learning.

Figure 1.1, therefore, presents the organization of this textbook in a nutshell. Part II will be devoted to essential knowledge. Part III will deal with interpersonal skills. Part IV will explain technical skills the supervisor needs, and Part V will discuss the application of such knowledge and skills to the tasks of supervision. Finally, Part VI will suggest ways of applying knowledge, skills, and tasks to integrate individual needs with organizational goals to achieve needed change and instructional success.

The Agony of Thought and Feeling

This book promises to provide a deep and comprehensive understanding of supervision, instruction, and school improvement. Treatment of the knowledge, the technical and interpersonal skills, and the tasks of supervision will be explained from theoretical, philosophical, empirical, and experiential premises, from ideology to case studies. Such understandings, however, are ours, formed from our own beliefs about desirable goals of schools and supervision. The details of practice are not intended to be taken as scientific prescriptions to be learned and followed. We concur with Wiggins (1979), who wrote:

> I entertain the unfriendly suspicion that [the reason some people]…want a scientific theory of rationality [is]…because they hope and desire, by some conceptual alchemy, to turn such a theory into…a system of rule by which to spare themselves some of the agony of thinking and all the torment of feeling and understanding all that is involved. (p. 150)

You will not be spared! As you finish this first chapter, please be prepared to read and react with your own "agony of thinking" and "torment of feeling" in formulating your own theory of supervision.

Exercises

Academic

1. Compare this chapter's definition of instructional supervision with at least four definitions of instructional supervision found in other supervision texts.

2. This chapter lists five tasks of instructional supervision. Rank these tasks according to what you consider their order of importance. Write a rationale for your ranking.

3. Several recent national studies have cited shortcomings in U.S. public education and have called for educational reforms. After reviewing one of these studies, discuss the major educational problems the study cites and the major reforms it recommends.

4. This chapter describes two ineffective schools: Finnie Tyler High School and Germando Elementary School. For both schools, discuss at least three instructional problems likely to result from the type of supervision practiced by the respective principals. Discuss how each probable instructional problem could be avoided or better managed through more appropriate supervision.

5. Review three journal articles that deal with the tasks, roles, or responsibilities of instructional supervision. Write a summary of each article.

Field

1. Prepare five questions to be asked during an interview with a school supervisor, focusing on problems the supervisor confronts in his or her attempts to facilitate instructional improvement and how he or she attempts to manage such problems. Conduct the interview and write a brief report on the supervisor's responses.

2. Arrange to visit a school that has a reputation for being exemplary. If possible, include visits to the school office, a few classrooms, the teachers' lounge, the cafeteria, and the school playground. Write a description of the learning climate of the school, including examples of how the type of supervision present in the school affects the learning climate.

3. Ask three supervisors and three teachers to list what they consider the five most important tasks of instructional supervision. Write a report comparing supervisors' perceptions and teachers' perceptions with the five tasks of supervision outlined in Chapter 1.

4. Ask two supervisors, two teachers, two students, and two parents to write one or two paragraphs on "What Makes a Successful School." After reviewing the responses, write a report discussing and comparing the respondents' perceptions.

5. Arrange a panel interview of four persons on the topic "What Makes a Successful School." The panel might include supervisors, teachers, parents, students, and perhaps business and community leaders. Record the discussion on a tape recorder.

Developmental

1. Write down any questions concerning instructional supervision that you have raised while reading Chapter 1. Refer to these questions as you read appropriate chapters in the remainder of this book.

2. Review Figure 1.1 and the model of instructional supervision it implies. As you continue to explore this book and other readings in supervision, begin to formulate your own proposed model of educational supervision.

3. Begin a file (to be kept throughout your reading of this book) on knowledge, skills, and procedures gained from the text and related activities that can be used by you as a supervisor—either now or in the future—to help teachers improve their instructional performance.

References

Barr, A. S., and Burton, W. H. 1926. *The Supervision of Instruction.* New York: Appleton and Company.

Cooper, J. M. 1982. Supervision of teachers. In H. E. Mitzel, (Ed.), *Encyclopedia of Educational Research,* 2nd ed., pp. 1824–1834. New York: The Free Press.

Glickman, C. D. 1993. *Renewing America's schools: A guide for school-based action.* San Francisco, CA: Jossey-Bass.

Gordon, S. P. 1992. Paradigms, transitions, and the new supervision. *Journal of Curriculum and Supervision, 8*(1), 62–76.

Gordon, S. P. (Ed.). 1995, April. *Newsletter of the Instructional Supervision Special Interest Group of the American Educational Research Association.*

Gordon, S. P. 1997. Has the field of supervision evolved to a point that it should be called something else? *Yes.* In J. Glanz and R. F. Neville (Eds.), *Educational Supervision: Perspectives, issues, and controversies,* pp. 114–123. Norwood, MA: Christopher-Gordon Publishers.

Harris, B. M. 1975. *Supervisory behavior in education* (2nd ed.). Englewood Cliffs, NJ: Prentice Hall.

MacKenzie, D. E. 1983. Research for school improvement: An appraisal of some recent trends. *Educational Researcher 12*(4):8.

McDonald, J. 1981. *Hermeneutics and curriculum.* Address to a meeting on curriculum development, Athens, GA, May.

Purkey, S. C., and Smith, M. S. 1982. Too soon to cheer? Synthesis of research on effective schools. *Educational Leadership 40*(3):64–69.

Schneider, E. J. 1982–1983. Stop the bandwagon, we want to get off. *Educational R and D Report 5*(1):7–11.

Smyth, J. W. 1983, March. *Towards a critical consciousness in the instructional supervision of experienced teachers.* Paper presented at the Annual Meeting of the Council of Professors of Instructional Supervision, Houston.

Wiggins, D. 1979. Deliberation and practical reason. In J. Raz (Ed.), *Practical reasoning.* New York: Oxford University Press.

Wise, A. A. 1979. *Legislated learning: The bureaucratization of the American Classroom.* Berkeley, CA: University of California Press.

Wise, A. A. 1988. Two conflicting trends in school reform: Legislated learning revisited. *Phi Delta Kappa, 69,* 328–333.

Suggested Readings

Glanz, J., and Neville, R. (Eds.) 1997. *Educational supervision: Perspectives, issues, and controversies.* Norwood, MA: Christopher Gordon.

Glickman, C. D. (Ed.). 1992. *Supervision in transition.* Alexandria, VA: Association for Supervision and Curriculum Development.

Gordon, S. P. 1992. Paradigms, transitions, and the new supervision. *Journal of Curriculum and Supervision 8*(1), 62–76.

Pajak, E. 1993. Conceptions of supervision and leadership: Change and continuity. In Gordon Cawelti (Ed.), *Challenges and achievements of American education.* 1993 ASCD Yearbook. Alexandria, VA: Association for Supervision and Curriculum Development.

Sergiovanni, T. J., and Starratt, R. J. 1993. *Supervision: A redefinition.* New York: McGraw-Hill.

Part II

Knowledge

Part II examines the prerequisite knowledge for supervision. Chapter 2 will consider the pessimistic news—why schools are typically ineffective. The causes of ineffectiveness will be traced to the teaching career and the school environment. Chapter 3 will explain the optimistic news found in school research on characteristics of successful schools, with particular attention to those work environment factors within the province of supervision. Chapter 4 will explain how optimal adult development contrasts with the teaching career. Chapter 5 will look at how supervisory practices might respond to helping teachers develop and eliminate the causes of ineffectiveness. While moving from pessimism to optimism to realism, we will be riding through highly explosive grounds. Reactions of delight, anger, chagrin, hope, and disagreement are to be expected as current research challenges us to rethink current supervisory practices.

2

The Norm

Why Schools Are as They Are

Dan Lortie (1986) wrote about the concept of structural strain, describing teachers of today who still work under school conditions of long ago (see Kottkamp, Provenzo, and Cohn, 1986). He and others have studied the work environment of schools and how work conditions promote or inhibit teacher development and instructional improvement. Our eyes must be wide open as we examine historical aspects of schools, teachers, and leadership. We must acknowledge that schools cannot be left alone to do business as usual, if we are serious about lasting instructional improvement.

The Work Environment or Culture of Schools

The study of values, beliefs, myths, rituals, symbols, heroes, shamans, and story-tellers in organizations is well documented in the literature (Deal, 1985). It may seem technically incorrect to apply the term *culture* to professional settings; the term is appropriated from the anthropological studies of largely intact and isolated communities of people. However, the concept of culture helps us reexamine schools as places of human community with peculiar histories and stories. When we grasp the underlying values of our particular school as a work environment, we can consciously act to reshape the organization into a purposeful collection of individuals who believe that schools are for students, for learning, and for improvement rather than for insularity, self-protection, and complacency.

How does it happen that in the same school district, teachers in two schools view their work so differently from each other? In Meadow Valley Middle School, teachers come to school within 15 minutes of the required arrival time and leave school 15 minutes after the last bell. If a teacher arrives earlier or stays later, other teachers' questions and glances make that teacher feel as if he or she shouldn't be working more than the required time. To do so is to violate an unspoken norm that teachers have come to accept about the proper amount of time to spend in school. Yet, one and a half miles across town, at the other middle school in the same district, the norms about proper time are different. At Mountain View Middle School, teachers are in their classrooms 45 minutes ahead of time, sharing coffee with each other, organizing materials, and conferring with individual students. One hour after school each day, the majority of staff are still there, working industriously in their own rooms, conducting tutorials, calling parents, and checking on tomorrow's plans. If a teacher arrives later or leaves earlier, the questions and glances of other teachers make him or her feel that a taboo is being violated.

Teachers in both schools work under the same district regulations, yet their expectations about work in their particular school are quite different. Why is this so? How does this come about? What have been the enduring norms of schools and how have they been established? The answers to these questions are quite important if we are to know how to intervene in our own schools so as to minimize resistance and capitalize on school beliefs that give impetus to student learning.

The Legacy of the One-Room Schoolhouse

Discussing the present work environment of schools without discussing the one-room schoolhouse would be comparable to talking about issues in Western democracies without acknowledging the Magna Carta. Much of what exists in beliefs and expectations about schools can be traced to the idyllic-looking, clapboard, one-room schoolhouses of pioneer times. The teacher was responsible for the total instruction of all students, the maintenance of the building, keeping the stove filled with wood, and cleaning the floors. Our first schoolteachers were seen as working in an honorable but menial profession, poorly paid but second only to the preacher in prestige (Lortie, 1975).

Many readers who currently teach may think of hall and bus duty, taking attendance, and straightening venetian blinds and immediately identify with the honorable but menial status of their predecessors. In the one-room schoolhouse, the teacher was responsible for all that transpired within its four walls; therefore, collective action in a school was automatic. What the teacher wanted to do about curriculum and instruction was what the school did! This legacy of independence, isolation, and privatization of teaching remains alive and well in many schools today. Instead of having physically separated one-room schoolhouses, we often see the one-room schoolhouses repeated every few yards down a school corridor. Each teacher sees his or her students, within the four walls, as his or her own school. Although the old one-room school is physically gone, it still holds a pervasive grip on the minds and actions of many teachers and schools.

The sense of classrooms as being private places is in direct contrast to the research on norms of improving schools.

Research suggests that the schools with the greatest student learning going on are those which do not isolate teachers, but instead encourage professional dialogue and collaboration. Teaching in effective schools is a collective, rather than individual enterprise. (Freiberg and Knight, 1987, p. 3)

However, Willower and Smith (1986) observed the following in a study of two secondary schools:

> Many of the features of the typical school organization appear to be stacked against the formation of a peculiar school culture devoted to educational aims.... A number of the norms in the teacher group such as that for autonomy and non-interference in a colleague's teaching activities encourage the kind of fragmentation we found. (p. 15)

The one-room schoolhouse of pioneer times has spawned a deep-seated institutional belief among educators that is characterized by isolation, psychological dilemmas, routine, inadequate induction of beginning teachers, lack of career stages, lack of professional dialogue, lack of involvement in school decisions, lack of a shared technical culture, and conservatism. Many educators accept that these characteristics are simply part of a school culture, and there is little doubt that they pervade the minds and beliefs of most teachers and administrators. However, instructional leaders question whether beliefs and practices acceptable in the past are appropriate for the present, when we need to initiate a new culture based on purposeful and collective beliefs about school, students, and teaching. Let's look at the characteristics of today's education that are derived from the one-room schoolhouse of bygone days.

Isolation

The isolation and individualism of teachers has been observed in all major studies of their work environment. As an example of this isolation, Dreeben (1973) noted:

> Perhaps the most important single property of classrooms, viewed from a school-wide perspective, is their spatial scattering and isolation throughout school buildings; and because teachers work in different places at the same time, they do not observe each other working...the implications of this spatial isolation are far reaching. (p. 468)

Dreeben further wrote:

> Unlike hospitals and law firms, for example, where new recruits to medicine and law learn their trade as apprentices by performing work tasks of gradually increasing difficulty under close supervision, schools provide a less adequate setting—the classroom—for work and training activities to occur simultaneously. (p. 470)

As Dreeben pointed out, classrooms are set up structurally in such a way that teachers are difficult to supervise, do not receive feedback from others, and cannot work collaboratively. During a typical workday, a teacher will talk to only a few other adults—on the way to the classroom in the morning, for 20 minutes or so at lunch and recess, and at the end of the day on the way out of the building. While teaching, teachers in most schools are invisible to each other and lack any concrete knowledge of what other teachers are doing in their classrooms.

Sarason (1996) points out that *physical* teacher isolation can lead to *psychological* isolation:

> What does it mean to go through a work day with no sustained personal contact with another adult? Being and talking with children is not psychologically the same as being and talking with peers....When one is almost exclusively with children—responsible for them, being vigilant in regard to them, "giving" to them—it must have important consequences. *One of the consequences is that teachers are psychologically alone even though they are in a densely populated setting.* It is not only that they are alone, but they adapt to being alone. (p. 133; emphasis in original)

Teachers who have experienced long-term psychological isolation tend to view their work environment as limited to *their* classroom, *their* students, and *their* teaching. Although their isolation was initially involuntary, over time they have adapted to and accepted the tradition of isolation (Sarason, 1996); they now resist opportunities for professional dialogue and collaboration with other teachers that might arise. To see just how strong this tradition of classroom isolation is, think of schools built in the 1970s according to an open-space design. Within a few years, in almost every school, portable partitions were erected to wall off each classroom. It is little wonder, then, that most school faculties do not work well together on common goals that transcend their individual self-interests. They do not talk with each other about professional matters, and they seldom see what others are doing.

Suppose members of a surgical staff were given separate cubicles to perform their specific parts of the common function of saving a patient. The patient would be wheeled first into the anesthesiologist's cubicle for drugs, then into the technician's room for monitoring of vital signs, then to the surgeon's room for the first incision, back to the technician's room for monitoring vital signs, to the surgeon's assistant's room for cleaning the incision, to the surgeon's room for the second incision—an absurd notion of how to save the patient! This is the work environment of teaching—more comparable to that of a piecework garment factory, where no one except top management needs to know what each person is doing. In high-status professions, by contrast, success depends on professionals working together to combine, review, and share their knowledge, skills, and practices.

Psychological Dilemma and Frustration

The teacher's work environment is marked by incessant psychological encounters. In just a few minutes of observation, one might see a teacher ask a question, reply with a smile to a student's answer, frown at an inattentive student, ask a student to be quiet, put a hand on a student's shoulder, and begin to lecture. Teachers have thousands of such psychological encounters in a normal schoolday (Jackson, 1968). A look, a shrug, and a word all have intended meanings between teacher and students.

Each day an elementary teacher meets with 25 to 35 students for six and one-half hours. A secondary teacher meets with 100 to 150 students for five to seven 50-minute periods. All this human interaction takes place in a 900 square-foot room, where a teacher must instruct, manage, discipline, reinforce, socialize, and attend to multiple occurrences. This crowded professional life makes teachers wish for smaller classes to reduce the psychological demand of constant decision making. Sarason (1996) described this incessant demand as a psychological dilemma:

> The teacher feels, and is made to feel, that one's worth as a teacher will be judged by how much a class learns in a given period of time. The strong feeling that teachers have about the complexity of their tasks stems from the awareness that they are expected to bring their children (if not all, most) to a certain academic level by a time criterion in regard to which they have no say. Faced with numbers and diversity of children and the pressure to adhere to a time schedule presents the teacher not with a difficult task but an impossible one. *I say impossible because I have never met a teacher who was not aware of and disturbed by the fact that he or she had not the time to give to some children in the class the kind of help they needed.* (p. 187; emphasis in original)

Hargreaves (1994) describes how in recent years teachers have been working under additional stress because of increasing accountability demands:

> Form filling, meetings, interviews with parents, more extensive reporting systems, more tightly defined curriculum guidelines are all said to have expanded and proliferated. Increasingly, teachers are having to attend more conscientiously to external expectations of growing stringency and they must also do this for a wider range of often competing publics and interest groups. (pp. 148–149)

Hargreaves (1994) also points out that increased accountability has been accompanied by what he refers to as *intensification* of teachers' work:

> The time demands of teaching have become more densely packed, multiple innovations have had to be accommodated, the integration of special needs students into ordinary classes has required additional planning, and shared decision making has also called for extra investments of time. (p. 149)

To maintain their own sanity in the face of an overload of psychological encounters and an inability to attend to the psychological needs of each student in a confined and regulated workplace, teachers often cope by routinizing classroom activity. The classroom routine for students becomes similar to the outside routine for teachers. For example, a science teacher might have students listen to a 20-minute presentation, followed by a 10-minute question-and-answer period and then by 20 minutes of seatwork. An elementary teacher might have three reading groups who rotate to him or her for 15 minutes each; each group reads aloud, responds to teacher questions, and then does worksheets. By routinizing what happens within the classroom, a teacher avoids making hundreds of decisions. The routinization of teaching allows the teacher to avoid the inherent conflict between being overwhelmed psychologically by the responsibility for teaching a large number of students, and being aware of neglecting the personal needs of individual students. In interpersonal terms, teaching closely resembles clinical psychology, but it takes place in an environment more like that of factory production.

Routine

The routine of the teaching day is imposed by administrative fiat, school board policy, and state guidelines. Every classroom teacher is required to be at school before students enter and to remain until they have departed. In primary or elementary schools, a teacher has specific times for recess and lunch, as well as approximate time allocations for teaching a given subject (for example, 45 minutes for reading, 30 minutes for mathematics, 30 minutes twice a week for social studies). The teacher is assigned a certain number of students and has responsibility for them for the entire day and school year. He or she is expected to remain physically in the assigned classroom for the entire schoolday, with the exception of recess, lunch, or special classes. Outside the classroom, teachers also have scheduled responsibilities for lunch, recess, and dismissal. In middle schools, junior high schools, and senior high schools, the schoolday is different from that of elementary schools but still has a set routine. A secondary teacher will have four to seven different classes of students meeting at specific times each day for an extended period (11, 18, or 36 weeks). Again, the teacher begins and dismisses each class at a prescribed time and has regular duties outside the classroom (for example, monitoring the lunchroom, halls, or bathrooms).

Regardless of grade level, teachers do not schedule their own time or determine the number or type of students. Unlike more autonomous professionals, teachers do not put up a shingle on the door, ask clients to arrange for appointments, or take Wednesday mornings off. Teachers do not have the right to make changes in their schedule. Imagine a teacher asking the school secretary to clear his or her schedule for several hours so he or she can attend to other business. School goes on, students keep coming, the bells keep ringing, and teachers cannot make individual readjustments of their professional time.

Of course, elementary and secondary teachers often do make readjustments within the assigned time, within their four walls, with their assigned students, and with instruction. School time, however, is imposed. Starting and ending times, numbers of students, physical locations for teaching, and extra duties are set for the duration, and a teacher has little control. The routines the school as a workplace imposes are more like those of the factory than like those of high-status professions. The punch-in, punch-out clock may not be visible in the entering hallway of the school, but nonetheless it exists.

Sarason (1996) raises a critical question concerning the effects of routine on teachers and students:

> *If teaching becomes neither terribly interesting nor exciting to many teachers, can one expect them to make learning interesting or exciting to children?* If teaching becomes a routine, predictable experience, does this not have inevitable consequences for life in the classroom? The model classroom does not allow me other than to conclude that children and teachers show most of the effects of routinized thinking and living. (p. 200; emphasis in original)

Inadequate Induction of Beginning Teachers

Teaching has been a career in which the greatest challenge and most difficult responsibilities are faced by those with the least experience—a strange state of affairs indeed! Beginning teachers in many schools are faced with a number of environmental difficulties: inadequate resources, difficult work assignments, unclear expectations, a sink-or-swim mentality, and reality shock (see Gordon, 1991).* As we describe these difficulties, we invite you to reflect on your own first year of teaching and to recall if they were part of your entrance to the profession.

Inadequate Resources. If a teacher makes known that he or she will not be returning in the fall, then after the last day of school other teachers will often descend on the vacant classroom and remove materials that will be useful to them. Not only are instructional materials removed but also desks, tables, and chairs! In their place are put those discarded items and furniture that no one else wants. Additionally, teachers may jockey around for the more spacious, better lighted classrooms. Thus, for the incoming year, the neophyte teacher with the least amount of experience often steps into the physically least desirable classroom in the school, with discards for furniture and equipment, and few instructional materials.

Difficult Work Assignments. Experienced staff and administration will often arrange for the "problem" children and/or lowest-achieving groups of students to be assigned to the newest teacher. In addition, the least interesting and most difficult courses usually are assigned to beginners (Kurtz, 1983). New teachers are often given larger classes and more duties than experienced teachers (Romatowski, Dorminey, and Van Voorhees, 1989).

Unclear Expectations. A common complaint among first-year teachers is that they are never sure what is expected of them as professionals (Kurtz, 1983). Administrators, other teachers, parents, and students express conflicting expectations

---

*Parts of this section are adapted from Stephen P. Gordon, *How to Help Beginning Teachers Succeed*, pp. 1–6. Reprinted by permission of the Association for Supervision and Curriculum Development, Alexandria, VA. Copyright c 1991 by the Association for Supervision and Curriculum Development. All rights reserved.

of the beginner, leaving the neophyte in a quandary about whose expectations he or she should try to meet. A failure to socialize novice teachers into a professional community leads to what Corcoran (1981) has called the "condition of not knowing" (p. 20).

Sink-or-Swim Mentality.   For a variety of reasons, beginning teachers are left on their own to "sink or swim." Administrators and experienced teachers tend to view the first year of teaching as a necessary "trial by fire" through which all neophytes must pass. Many experienced colleagues are reluctant to provide assistance to beginning teachers. Some veterans think it is only fair that new teachers should pass through the same trials and tribulations that they navigated when they were beginners. Some see it as a process that "weeds out" weak teachers, allowing only the strong to survive. Other experienced teachers are reluctant to assist beginners because of the norms of individualism and privacy that pervade the school culture.

Beginners often are reluctant to ask the principal or colleagues for help when they are experiencing management or instructional problems. This is due to the fact that teaching is the only profession in which a novice is expected to assume the same (or more) responsibilities at the same level of competence as experienced colleagues. Novice teachers often do not ask for help because they fear that a request for assistance will call into question their professional competence. In fact, neophytes often go to great lengths to conceal their classroom problems (Newberry, 1978).

Reality Shock.   Veenman defined *reality shock* as "the collapse of the missionary ideals formed during teacher training by the harsh and rude reality of classroom life" (1985, p. 143). Individuals tend to enter teaching with idealized visions of what it will be like. Classroom management problems, student learning difficulties, and the environmental difficulties already discussed tend to destroy those ideals rather quickly. Moreover, neophytes are faced with the numbing realization that they are unprepared to deal with the harsh realities of teaching. This realization can lead to disillusionment and professional paralysis (Corcoran, 1981).

Effects of Environmental Difficulties.   The environmental problems just discussed can cause tremendous stress and eventually lead to physical and emotional problems. Novice teachers tend to have more negative attitudes about themselves, their teaching, their profession, and students at the end than at the beginning of their first year of teaching (Gordon, 1991). Between one-third and one-half of teachers drop out of the profession within their first seven years of teaching (Metropolitan Life, 1985), with up to 15 percent leaving each of the first two years (Schlechty and Vance, 1983). Many of the most promising teachers are the ones who leave the profession early in their careers (Harris and Collay, 1990; Schlechty and Vance, 1983). Finally, as a result of their initial negative experiences, many teachers who stay in the profession develop a survival mentality, a narrow set of teaching methods, and resistance to experimentation and change that may last throughout their teaching careers (Romatowski, Dorminey, and Van Voorhees, 1989; Huling-Austin, 1986).

Is there truth in this depiction? Many of us, looking back at our first year, would concur that it was the most difficult teaching experience we ever encountered. Many of us also need to admit, sheepishly, that teaching did improve in following years because we could use seniority to our benefit by creating a better teaching situation—to the distinct detriment of new teachers. We didn't see the norms of our work as creating "a cause beyond oneself" in looking at a common good—which would mean giving the first-year teachers the least-difficult students and best physical and material conditions. Instead, we saw the norms of teaching as protecting us, in our four walls, so as to keep our one-room schoolhouse intact. The message conveyed by such actions is that teaching is not a supportive career that eases neophytes into graduated responsibilities; rather, it's a case of "do unto others as they've done unto you."

In recent years many school districts have initiated beginning teacher assistance programs (sometimes called teacher induction programs) in an effort to address the problems discussed above. These programs often include the assignment of experienced teachers as mentors of novice teachers. Chapter 18 includes a description of a successful beginning teacher assistance program.

Unstaged Career

More prestigious professions avoid such an abrupt transition from student to full professional. Physicians, lawyers, engineers, and scientists all experience several transition years of apprenticeship, internship, and junior membership on the job before they qualify for full rights and responsibilities in the profession.

This set of circumstances leads to the negative characteristic of the teaching profession that perhaps most significantly differentiates it from others—an unstaged career. More prestigious occupations have rigorous screening and requirements. Furthermore, they have a transitional or proving-ground stage; only when an aspirant has been judged competent by senior members does the junior member step into the next stage of the career, which provides high visibility, greater challenge, a substantial increase in salary, and responsibility for monitoring and judging the next wave of junior members. For example, a law school graduate must pass the bar exam and then serve as a clerk, as a legal aide, or as a junior member of a law firm. He or she works behind the scenes on writing and research that are credited to his or her superior. After proving competence over time, however, the lawyer then becomes a partner in a firm, a public prosecutor or defender, or an independent attorney. This movement brings visibility and stature in the profession and the right to have one's own apprentices to do the less challenging, less exciting work.

This apprenticeship period has persisted because aides, interns, or assistants are willing to endure the long hours and hard work in view of the ultimate benefits. It is not unusual for the salary of a legal assistant, a medical intern, a junior engineer, or a graduate assistant to double upon promotion to full membership in the profession. The public appears to recognize and approve this long, arduous, and selective process as a requirement for membership in a high-status profession.

Teaching, on the other hand, has been unstaged from entry to exit. Education majors take courses, spend time in schools, perform as student teachers, and then graduate from college into their own classrooms as teachers. After that, no matter how many years they continue to teach, they do not move into another stage. The 20 year veteran teacher has the same classroom space, number of students, and requirements as the first-year teacher. Furthermore, for each year of experience, a teacher realizes a salary increase identical to that received by all others of comparable experience.

Lack of Dialogue about Instruction

Generally, people in schools do not talk about their work—teaching—with each other. DeSanctis and Blumberg (1979) found that the length of instruction-related discussion among teachers in a typical schoolday in a high school in New York was two minutes. Little's (1982) study of schools, Rosenholtz's (1985) review of effective schools, and Pajak and Glickman's (1987) study of 15 exemplary elementary and secondary schools in three improving districts pointed to one essential dimension of successful schools: Professionals constantly talk with each other, in a problem-solving, action-oriented way, about teaching. This talk is generated through faculty and committee meetings, in-service workshops, observations and conferences, faculty lounge contacts, and other informal occasions. This talk is of a specific nature: teaching and learning of students. Of course, teachers talk with each other in all schools, but the talk is of a more social nature—telling stories about students, parents, administrators, community, and school events.

For teachers to talk often and seriously with each other about the core of their job—instruction and curriculum—is a rarity in many schools. Time is not planned for it to occur. Faculty meetings are information giving, and when school concerns are raised, they are often deflected to noninstructional matters such as schedules, district policies, extracurricular responsibilities, and building maintenance.

The public school as a work institution is unique in that a collection of adults can be employed as professionals within the same physical setting, with a common responsibility for providing their particular services to the same group of clients (students), and not be frequently and intensively engaged with each other in discussions on how to improve their services. Again, the lack of such dialogue is related to the one-room schoolhouse legacy, which accepts isolation, privacy, and lack of career stages as the norms of teaching.

Lack of Involvement in Schoolwide Curriculum and Instructional Decisions

If teachers don't see each other at work, don't talk with each other about their work, and see teaching as what goes on within their own four walls, it is not surprising that they are not given the opportunity, time, or expectations to be involved in decisions about curriculum and instruction beyond their four walls. Goodlad's (1984) study of schooling found that teachers' involvement in decisions about curriculum and instruction was virtually nil. Blumberg (1987) has referred to one of the basic problems with public schools as "institutions premised on having mature, competent adults as employees, yet treating these same adults as children when it comes to deciding and operationalizing their work." Boyer (1983) has been even more adamant, referring to schools as impoverished intellectual climates for adults. The norm in most schools is that teachers are not expected to contribute experience, knowledge, and wisdom to decisions about the common good of educating students.

Lack of a Shared Technical Culture

Colleagues within a shared technical culture possess common purpose, expertise, and methods for analyzing and solving problems. They have developed sophisticated performance standards and communicate through a shared technical language. Imagine that a team of surgeons is about to perform a heart transplant operation. Each member of the team shares extensive knowledge of the cardiovascular system as well as state-of-the-art surgical procedures that will be used during the operation. The purpose of the surgery, as well as the technical means for achieving that purpose, are clear to each team member. Both in planning and performing the operation, the surgeons communicate in a complex technical language, much of which would be difficult for a layperson to understand. During the operation, the surgeons receive precise feedback from advanced technology and each other on the patient's condition. Should complications arise during the operation, the surgeons will rely on their expertise and each other to analyze the problem and take corrective action. The patient's survival is never assured, but the shared technical culture of the surgical team greatly enhances the patient's chances for recovery.

Unlike advanced professional communities, most schools are not characterized by shared technical cultures. Isolation, lack of dialogue, inadequate induction, and lack of involvement in schoolwide decisions all inhibit the development of such cultures among teachers. Based on his classic sociological study of schools and teachers, Lortie's (1975) description of school culture is in sharp contrast to the shared technical culture we have been discussing.

> There is little "state of the art"….The image projected is more individualistic, teachers are portrayed as an aggregate of persons each assembling practices consistent with his experience and peculiar personality. It is not what "we the colleagues" know and share which is paramount, but rather what I have learned from experience. (p. 79)

Lortie concluded that the lack of a shared technical culture means that "the teacher's craft…is marked by the absence of concrete models for emulation, unclear lines of influence, multiple and controversial criteria, ambiguity about assessment timing, and instability in the product" (p. 136). Lortie's seminal research about nontechnical school cultures and their effects on teachers was carried out in the mid-1970s. Unfortunately, more recent studies have found that most schools still lack sophisticated technical cultures and are still characterized by unclear goals, uncertainty about what constitutes effective instruction, idiosyncratic teaching, and ambiguous assessment (Rosenholtz, 1989).

Conservatism

The lack of a shared technical culture and the resulting ambiguity and uncertainty foster teacher conservatism. One aspect of this conservatism is a set of restricted, teacher-centered instructional methods. After reviewing data from observations of more than 1,000 classrooms, John Goodlad (1984) concluded the following:

> The domination of the teacher is obvious in the conduct of instruction. Most of the time the teacher is engaged in either frontal teaching, monitoring, students' seat work, or conducting quizzes. Relatively rarely are students actively engaged in learning directly from one another or in initiating processes of interaction with teachers. When students work in smaller groups, they usually are doing the same thing side by side, and these things tend to be determined by the teacher. (pp. 123–124)

Beyond reliance on traditional teaching methods, less obvious aspects of conservatism can be observed in most schools, including the following:

- An emphasis on short-range rather than long-range instructional goals
- Satisfaction with successes with individual lessons, students, and projects rather than with the continuous growth of all students
- Reliance on personal experience rather than educational research
- Narrow limits on the types and degree of collegiality and collaboration in which teachers are willing to engage
- A reflexive resistance to curricular or instructional innovations

Such conservatism is not surprising considering the isolation and psychological dilemma found in the traditional school environment. The irony is that conservatism, which results largely from the other environmental problems we have described, tends to hinder efforts to solve those very same problems!

Blaming the Victim and Structural Strain

A Nation at Risk (National Commission on Education, 1983) intensified a long era of legislated school reform that enforced more rigorous teacher selection, teacher evaluation, standardization of curriculum, and testing of students. Arthur Wise (1988) noted that the previous 16 years of school reform had been predicated on the assumption that teachers are the problem or reason for mediocre school performance and therefore need to be carefully controlled and monitored. Lee Shulman (1987) has referred to this 16-year period as one of "teacher bashing," in which the wrongs of education were attributed to incompetent, inconsiderate, and self-serving teachers and administrators.

Myriad critical reports on the status of teaching have been published. For example, Schlechty and Vance (1981) wrote of a longitudinal seven-year study of teachers in North Carolina. They concluded, "There is considerable evidence that those who choose to major in teacher education are, as a group, less academically able than most other college majors. There is some strong evidence that graduates of teacher education institutions are not as academically proficient as most other categories of college graduates" (p. 106). Their study of characteristics of teachers who remain in the profession, compared with those who decide to leave the profession, concluded, "There is a strong negative relationship between measured academic ability and retention in teaching....Year after year, those North Carolina teachers who scored highest on a test of academic ability (the NTE) are the most likely to leave education" (pp. 110, 112).

In the same year, Milton Goldberg, director of the National Institute of Education, after reviewing national statistics about teachers, reported to the U.S. House Subcommittee on Post Secondary Education that those entering teaching were not terribly promising and that those leaving were among the best in the profession. Teaching seemed to be attracting, in his words, "the least academically able students."

The result of such criticisms of teachers has been the establishment of more rigorous, liberal-arts-based teacher education programs; many required five-year teacher education degree programs (Holmes Group, 1986); a National Center for Teacher Licensing (Carnegie Task Force, 1986); the development of career ladders that pay teachers more for experience combined with increased responsibility; merit pay to reward those who attain higher teacher evaluation rankings; scholarship incentives to attract more academically proficient students into teaching; and general pay scale increases to be competitive with pay scales in comparable private professions, in order to attract and retain competent teachers.

Although some of these attempts to retain, attract, and reverse the loss of bright and capable teachers are worthwhile, laudable, and essential, they do not deal directly with the school as a culture or a workplace. It is the workplace of teaching that supports or stifles intellectual vitality and is a major factor in the ability of public schools to retain the "best and brightest."

The studies of Barbara Tye (1987) and Linda McNeil (1986, 1988) have shown that most school environments are predicated on control—control of students and control of teachers. The feminist literature helps us to understand why schools as controlling workplaces have been resistant to change. Historically, teachers' work has been equated with a sexist view of women's work—servile yet smiling. Administrators' work has been equated with a similarly prejudiced view of men's work—controlling and paternalistic. As Grambs (1987) wrote, "Men have organized the structure of the school environment which suits their perceptions of what is appropriate. Yet, since most teachers are women, the lack of it has been ignored; women teachers themselves may be unaware of what in school makes them uncomfortable" (p. 61). The parallels are clear. Administrators prize conformity, privacy, dependency, quietness, and routine in their teachers and consider unconventionality, public attention, creativity, assertiveness, spontaneity, and collective action among teachers to be threatening and "unschool-like." As a result,

teachers are rewarded for conforming and penalized for being intellectually critical. Critics then bemoan the statistics that show the majority of teachers to be con-
formist, dependent, and not of the highest academic caliber as compared to those
who do not choose to enter or who decide to leave teaching. It takes no great insight to know that inquisitive and thoughtful people are drawn to work cultures
that value, reward, and encourage inquisitiveness and thoughtfulness. Those who
are less inquisitive and thoughtful about their work are not the villains of school
improvement, but the victims of institutional work environments that demand
compliance and conformity. We then blame teachers for being what most schools
force them to be. What if we changed the work culture of schools?

Ted Sizer (1984) poignantly argued that the fine high school teacher named
Horace could never become a great teacher under the existing structure of
schools. Neither he nor his colleagues are encouraged to rethink and restructure
how students could learn in their schools. As a result, Horace has learned to compromise his beliefs about how students should receive instruction in English
against the realities of the work environment.

> Horace is a gentle man. He reads the frequent criticism of his profession in the press
> with compassion. Johnny can't read. Teachers have low Graduate Record Examina-
> tion scores. We must vary our teaching to the learning styles of our pupils. We must
> relate to the community. We must be scholarly, keeping up with our fields. English
> teachers should be practicing, published writers. If they aren't all these things, it is
> obvious that they don't care. Horace is a trouper; he hides his bitterness.
>   Nothing can be gained by showing it. The critics do not really want to hear
> him or to face facts. He will go with the flow. What alternative is there? (Sizer,
> 1984, p. 19)

We believe that people have quickly reached the point of structural strain
with the Horaces of public education. Either the work environment of schools
must be altered or we must accept that, regardless of extrinsic rewards, schools
are not the place for our best teachers and thinkers. Supervision of instruction
can play a strong role in reshaping the work environment to promote norms of
collegiality and collective action, or supervision can remain another control apparatus "to keep teachers in their place." We can then continue to blame the victims
for not shaking the institutional chains that shackle every attempt to work together in the instructional interest of all students.

To Qualify, Summarize, and Propose

If supervision is to improve instruction in a school, then it must be an active force
that provides focus, structure, and time for matters of curriculum and instruction.
Supervision is intended to reduce the norms of the one-room schoolhouse—
isolation, psychological dilemma, routine, inadequate teacher induction, inverted
beginner responsibilities, lack of career stages, and absence of shared technical

culture—and increase the norms of public dialogue and action for the benefit of all students. If supervision is to improve instruction, it must reshape norms and beliefs about the work culture of schools, as in the following propositions:

- Proposition 1: *Supervision cannot rely on the existing work environment of schools to stimulate instructional improvement.* Since the work environments of schools are routinized, isolated, and psychologically tense, teachers become private and regulated in their work rather than open to improvement.
- Proposition 2: *Supervisors cannot assume that teachers will be reflective, autonomous, and responsible for their own development.* Since teachers as a group have been conditioned to conform rather than to be involved as initiators of change, change will not automatically occur if left solely to teacher initiative.
- Proposition 3: *Supervisors who hold formal leadership roles will have to redefine their responsibilities—from controllers of teachers' instruction to involvers of teachers in decisions about school instruction.* Since successful schools are communities of professional colleagues rather than hierarchies of power and status, formal supervisors will need to view teachers as worthy of making decisions about their work.

These three bold propositions have a basis in research but nevertheless need further qualification. For the most part, schools have been portrayed as operating in a culture of fragmentation and control and teachers have been portrayed as operating in a professional world of isolation and dependency. Obviously, this is more true of some schools than others. Historically, this has been the state of affairs, but there have always been teachers and schools that do not fit such portrayals.

In fact, there are increasing numbers of teachers and schools that have established autonomous, collective, and intellectually challenging work environments. That is the very point of this book. *Those schools whose staff members knowingly combat the inertia of their profession and environment are most successful.* In the most successful schools, supervision works to break up the routine, lack of career stages, and isolation of teaching and to promote intelligent, autonomous, and collective reason in order to establish a cause beyond oneself and to shape a purposeful and productive body of professionals achieving common goals for students.

The best response to structural strain today is to move away from patching and reinforcing the old school vessel and instead remake it with a broader base, greater flexibility, and more adaptations so as to challenge teachers to take an increasingly intellectual and active role.

Exercises

Academic

1. Choose a period of American history (for example, the colonial period or the early twentieth century) and research the state of teaching as a profession during that

era. Prepare a report comparing the role, functions, working conditions, and status of teachers in the selected era and the current era.

2. Research the state of teaching as a profession in an industrialized nation other than the United States. Prepare a report comparing the role, functions, working conditions, and status of teachers from the selected nation with those of U.S. teachers.

3. The chapter lists routine, psychological dilemma, and isolation as three factors associated with the work environment of teachers. Interview a supervisor about the work environment of teachers in his or her school. How does he or she attempt to improve conditions? Write a summary of your interview.

4. In most school systems, a teacher's career is unstaged. Outline a plan for a staged teaching career. Include recommended entry requirements, screening methods, a description of an apprenticeship period (other than student teaching), and suggested requirements and rewards for promotion to full membership in the teaching profession. Suggest ways in which teachers who have attained full professional status can be presented with new challenges and rewarded for meeting such challenges.

5. Write an autobiographical essay in which you discuss your experiences with the daily routine, psychological encounters, and isolation you have confronted as a teacher or observed as a visitor in a school.

Field

1. Interview three teachers of various experience levels about why they chose teaching as a career. Write a report that includes a brief description of each teacher, a summary of his or her reasons for becoming an educator, and a comparison of the various teachers' responses.

2. Conduct interviews with a veteran and a first-year teacher in which you ask them to compare their written job descriptions with the duties they actually carry out. During both interviews, write out a list of duties the teacher carries out that are not listed on the formal job description. Prepare a report summarizing your findings and drawing conclusions.

3. Interview a member of a graded profession (physician, attorney, college professor, scientist, engineer, or the like) who has reached full professional status. Ask the professional about the stages and challenges he or she had to pass through to attain such status, the extent to which having to pass through these grades increased his or her professional performance, and the rewards of reaching full professional status. Prepare a report summarizing the interviewee's responses and giving your opinion of whether aspects of such a graded career could be adapted to the teaching profession.

4. Interview a veteran instructor or supervisor in a teacher preparation program. Ask him or her to compare students who are preparing for a career in education today with teacher candidates of 10 years ago in terms of academic preparation, performance, and commitment to a teaching career. If the interviewee perceives significant differences between present and past teacher candidates, ask for his or her

perceptions of why such differences exist and how they are likely to affect the future of education. Prepare a report summarizing the interview and drawing your own conclusions.

5. Interview an individual who was a teacher for at least five years and voluntarily left teaching for a new career. Request (a) his or her reasons for entering the teaching field, (b) his or her reasons for leaving teaching, and (c) a comparison of the teaching profession with his or her present career. Prepare a written report on the interview.

Developmental

1. As you read the remainder of this book, note the propositions on page 33. Examine the remaining chapters for proposals, implicit in the propositions, for dealing with instructional problems. Keep a written journal of major propositions, proposals, and actions you would take to change your own school.

2. Begin a diary of how the major characteristics of your work environment affect your job performance over a period of time.

3. Begin a notebook of ideas for breaking up the inertia of the teaching profession and environment. Over time, note your own ideas and also record the ideas and actions of teachers and supervisors you observe attempting to counter the routine, psychological dilemma, and isolation of the teaching environment. Include ideas for promoting teacher autonomy and encouraging teachers and supervisors to focus on a cause beyond oneself.

References

Blumberg, A. 1987. *A discussion on the effects of local, state, and federal mandates on supervisory practices.* Annual conference of the Council of Professors of Instructional Supervision, Philadelphia, November.

Boyer, E. L. 1983. *High school: A report on secondary education in America.* New York: Harper & Row.

Carnegie Task Force on Teaching as a Profession. 1986. *A nation prepared: Teachers for the 21st century.* New York: Carnegie Forum on Education and the Economy.

Corcoran, E. 1981. Transition shock: The beginning teacher's paradox. *Journal of Teacher Education* 32(3):19–23.

Deal, T. E. 1985. The symbolism of effective schools. *Elementary School Journal* 85(5):601–620.

DeSanctis, M., and Blumberg, A. 1979. *An exploratory study into the nature of teacher interactions with other adults in the schools.* Paper presented at the annual meeting of the American Educational Research Association, San Francisco, April.

Dreeben, R. 1973. The school as a workplace. In R. M. Travers (Ed.), *Second handbook of research on teaching.* Chicago: Rand McNally, pp. 450–473.

Freiberg, H. J., and Knight, S. 1987. *External influences of school climate.* Paper presented at the annual meeting of the American Educational Research Association, Washington, DC, April.

Goodlad, J. I. 1984. *A place called school.* New York: McGraw-Hill.

Gordon, S. P. 1991. *How to help beginning teachers succeed.* Alexandria, VA: Association for Supervision and Curriculum Development.

Grambs, J. D. 1987. *Are older women teachers different? Journal of Education* 169(1):47–65.

Hargreaves, A. 1994. *Changing teachers, changing times: Teacher work and culture in the postmodern age:* London: Cassel.

Harris, M. M., and Collay, M. P. 1990. Teacher induction in rural schools. *Journal of Staff Development 11*(4):44–48.

The Holmes Group. 1986. *Tomorrow's teachers: A report of the Holmes Group.* East Lansing, MI: Holmes Group.

Huling-Austin, L. 1986. What can and cannot reasonably be expected from teacher induction programs. *Journal of Teacher Education 37*(1):2–5.

Jackson, P. W. 1968. *Life in classrooms.* New York: Holt, Rinehart & Winston.

Kottkamp, R. B., Provenzo, E. F., Jr., and Cohn, M. M. 1986. Stability and change in a profession: Two decades of teacher attitudes. 1964–1984. *Kappan 67*(8):559–567.

Kurtz, W. H. 1983. Identifying their needs: How the principal can help beginning teachers. *NASSP Bulletin 67*(459):42–45.

Little, J. W. 1982. Norms of collegiality and experimentation: Workplace conditions of school success. *American Educational Research Journal 19*(3):325–340.

Lortie, D. C. 1975. *School teacher: A sociological study.* Chicago: University of Chicago Press.

Lortie, D. C. 1986. Teacher status in Dade County: A case of structural strain. *Kappan 67*(8):568–575.

McNeil, L. M. 1986. *Contradictions of control: School structure and knowledge.* New York: Methuen/Routledge and Kegan Paul.

McNeil, L. M. 1988. Contradictions of reform, Part I: Administrators and teachers. *Kappan 69*(5):333–339.

Metropolitan Life. 1985. *Former teachers in America.* New York: Author.

National Commission on Education. 1983. An open letter to the American people. A nation at risk: The imperative for educational reform. *Education Week 2*(31):12.

Newberry, J. 1978. The barrier between beginning and experienced teachers. *The Journal of Educational Administration 16*(1):46–56.

Pajak, E., and Glickman, C. 1987. *Dimensions of improving school districts.* Presentation to the annual conference of the Association for Supervision and Curriculum Development, New Orleans, March.

Romatowski, J. A., Dorminey, J. J., and Van Voorhees, B. 1989. *Teacher induction programs: A report.*(ERIC ED 316 525)

Rosenholtz, S. J. 1985. Effective schools: Interpreting the evidence. *American Journal of Education 93*(3):352–388.

Rosenholtz, S. J. 1989. *Teachers' workplace: The social organization of schools.* New York: Longman.

Sarason, S. B. 1996. *Revisiting the culture of the school and the problem of change.* New York: Teachers College Press.

Schlechty, P. C., and Vance, V. S. 1981. Do academically able teachers leave education? The North Carolina case. *Kappan 63*(2):106–112.

Schlechty, P. C., and Vance, V. 1983. Recruitment, selection, and retention: The shape of the teaching force. *The Elementary School Journal 83*(4):469–487.

Shulman, L. S. 1987. *Teaching alone, learning together: Needed agendas for the new reforms.* Paper presented at Conference on Restructuring Schooling for Quality Education, San Antonio, August.

Sizer, T. 1984. *Horace's compromise.* Boston: Houghton Mifflin.

Tye, B. T. 1987. The deep structure of schooling. *Kappan 69*(4):281–284.

Veenman, S. 1984. Perceived problems of beginning teachers. *Review of Educational Research 54*(2):143–178.

Willower, D. J., and Smith, J. P. 1986. *Organizational culture in schools: Myth and creation.* Paper presented at the annual meeting of the American Educational Research Association, San Francisco, April.

Wise, A. E. 1988. The two conflicting trends in school reform: Legislated learning revisited. *Kappan 69*(5):328–333.

Suggested Readings _____

Hargreaves, A. 1994. *Changing teachers, changing times: Teachers work and culture in the postmodern age.* London: Cassel.

Reyes, P. (Ed.). 1990. *Teachers and their workplace.* Newbury Park, CA: Sage.

Sarason, S. B. 1996. *Revisiting "The culture of the school and the problem of change."* New York: Teachers College Press.

Sashkin, M., and Walberg, H. 1993. *Educational leadership and school culture.* Berkeley, CA: McCutchan.

Smith, S. C. 1990. *The collaborative school: A work environment for effective instruction.* Eugene, OR: ERIC Clearinghouse on Educational Management.

Yee, S. M. 1990. *Careers in classroom: When teaching is more than a job.* New York: Teachers College.

Zehm, S. J., and Kottler, J. A. 1993. *On being a teacher.* Newbury Park, CA: Sage.

3

The Exception

What Schools Can Be

At the most general level, the primary characteristic of a successful organization is apparent. Whether it be a school, a potato chip manufacturer, an airline company, or a civic club, there exists a certain commonality to their success. William James, the philosopher, once mentioned that characteristic when he wrote about his concern with men involved in war. During World War I, he was disturbed by his admiration for the qualities that war brought out in humans. As a Quaker and a pacifist, he could not condone the activities involved in waging war, yet he couldn't help but be impressed by the loyalty, support, and courage soldiers gave to their comrades, even to the point of sacrificing their own lives to advance the cause of their division (Stone, 1986).

As James pondered his ambivalence, he rendered an observation that the challenge of our times was to find those domestic causes that are "the moral equivalent of war." In that statement, James identified what has been the essential point made by researchers and writers about successful organizations. Whether it be found in the best-selling book, *In Search of Excellence* (Peters and Waterman, 1982), about corporate success, or in interpretive writings about effective schools (Rosenholtz, 1985), what is conveyed is that successful organizations have a collection of individuals who work together on a common goal that transcends their own self-interests. As a result, they willingly sacrifice their own immediate gain in pursuit of the common goal because it is perceived as far more important. Later, the concept of educators being involved in a cause beyond themselves will be discussed in greater detail, from a moral, social, and cognitive developmental perspective.

The "common cause" and the "moral equivalent of war" are critical concepts for understanding school success. However, when we analyze the definitions of school success, we find great divergence in goals and practices. What do we mean by school success, and how do we measure it? Is the measure of school success short term—higher achievement scores on standardized basic-skills tests? Is school success measured by improved student attitudes toward learning, social behavior, displays of creative work, critical writing or thinking, attendance, grades, promotion, retention, or community or extracurricular participation? The instructional goals that a school sets and how these goals are measured reflect how the staff members collectively understand and prioritize their beliefs about education. A successful school is foremost an organization that defines good education for itself, through its goals and desired practices, and then engages in the "moral equivalent of war" in achieving that vision (Glickman, 1987).

Background to School Effectiveness Studies

The research of the late 1960s and early 1970s reported that most schools are not effective. James Coleman's assessment of equality in 1966 was the second-largest school study ever done in the United States. He and his staff canvassed schools across the country in rural, urban, and suburban settings. He considered the contributions to school quality of a wide range of characteristics—teacher academic credentials, district per-pupil expenditures, instructional materials, socioeconomic background of students, racial mix of students, structure and age of physical plant, and size of the school. He found that most school variables had little or no relationship to student achievement. Performance on standardized tests was not affected by teacher credentials, per-pupil cost, materials, or curriculum. Instead, the variable that had the greatest relationship with student achievement was the composition of the student population. Students from low-income populations did significantly better when they attended schools where a majority of students came from middle- or upper-income populations. When school composition was mostly low income, students did not perform as well. Coleman concluded that the strongest variable accounting for student achievement was parents' socioeconomic class. He observed further that this variable was beyond the control of the school. Children of middle- or upper-income families entered schools substantially ahead of students of low-income families; as they continued in school, the achievement gap between socioeconomic levels grew larger. Wealthy students stayed ahead, and poor students fell further behind. Regardless of the school's physical plant, teachers, materials, or finances, the gap enlarged. Most interpretations of Coleman's study indicate that schools made no difference in student achievement.

In 1972, Christopher Jencks and colleagues reanalyzed Coleman's data and issued a report entitled *Inequality: A Reassessment of the Effect of Family and Schooling in America*. Instead of using achievement test results to measure school effectiveness, Jencks looked at what employment students secured after leaving public school. He studied factors that contributed to students going into different careers or vocations, such as higher education, white-collar work or blue-collar work, or remaining unemployed. First, the reassessment of Coleman's data reaffirmed that school success was largely a result of socioeconomic status, not of teachers or schools. Second, a student's job success in terms of status and pay was similar to the parents' occupational status. Those who obtained high-status jobs were children of parents with high-status jobs. Finding a specific job was a matter of chance and included being at the right place at the right time. It was socioeconomic background, however, that influenced students to use behavior, language, and manners appropriate for specific job opportunities. Students of low-income parents usually mirrored the conditions of their parents and either secured low-status and low-paying jobs or went onto the unemployment and welfare rolls. Jencks concluded that public schools not only did not help alleviate inequality in the United States but, in fact, contributed to such inequality. He concluded that the solutions to unequal opportunity in adult life were not to be found in the schools, but rather in the redistribution of wealth in the larger society.

During the time of these studies, another distinguished researcher was moving across the country, visiting schools to observe classrooms and interview teachers, principals, and administrators. He and his staff were studying classroom practices and what students were learning. In his 1971 book *Crisis in the Classroom*, Charles Silberman concluded from his lengthy studies that schools were not only ineffective but mindless as well. When he asked teachers and principals to articulate the reasons they organized their schools or classes in certain ways, used particular instructional materials, or grouped their students as they did, the reply was more often than not an incredulous "I don't know—we've always done it this way." When he sought to establish the priorities or objectives of each school, Silberman found little consistency between the response and what actually transpired in the classrooms. He found that schools were operating in a confused manner, without specific purpose, commitment, understanding, or shared belief.

Silberman's study, together with those of Coleman and Jencks, left a haze over the landscape of public education—one that has yet to lift. Books such as Jonathan Kozol's *Death at an Early Age* and Ivan Illich's *Deschooling Society* have further weakened confidence in school effectiveness. The media have focused on declining achievement scores and the continued erosion of public confidence. The National Commission on Excellence in Education, in its "Open Letter to the American People" (1983), reported that U.S. students ranked considerably below those of other nations on achievement tests, that 23 million Americans were functionally illiterate, that average achievement scores of students were lower than those of 1957, that only 20 percent of 17-year-olds could write a persuasive essay, and that only one-third could solve multistep problems in mathematics.

Early Effective Schools Research

Researchers, including Edmonds as well as Brookover and colleagues, have demonstrated that there *are* effective schools and school systems. The large normative studies of the mid-1960s and early 1970s were concerned with schools as monolithic institutions. A researcher who pulls together data from many schools looks for the overall influences schools have on students. If the overwhelming majority of schools are ineffective, the group results would wash out those individual schools that might have results to the contrary.

Beginning in the mid-1970s, research began to focus on individual schools that are exceptional, that consistently achieve results far superior to those of schools in general. In composition of student body, location, socioeconomic setting, and per-pupil expenditure, these schools do not differ from schools in general. Yet whether they are in poor urban areas or in wealthy suburbs, they succeed while others fail.

Ronald Edmonds, after discovering that the results of his own research were consistent with those of other independent investigations, was confident enough to predict that *all schools could be effective.*

> It seems to me, therefore, that what is left of this discussion are three declarative statements: (a) We can, whenever and wherever we choose, successfully teach all children whose schooling is of interest to us; (b) We already know more than we need to do that; and (c) Whether or not we do it must finally depend on how we feel about the fact that we haven't so far. (1979, p. 22)

How can one make such bold statements? What are these findings that so contradict the gloomy assessments of Coleman, Jencks, Silberman, and the National Commission on Excellence in Education? Effective schools have faculties with a clear, collective purpose toward which they work. They believe in "a cause beyond oneself." Let's look at how such a phrase has been derived from the research. Edmonds (1979) conducted three different studies. His first study was of 2 inner-city schools in Detroit; the second was of 55 effective schools in the Northeast (discovered by reanalyzing the Coleman study); and the third included 20 schools in inner-city New York. Edmunds's findings were consistent with those of other early effective schools studies. He found that effective schools were distinguished by the presence of:

- Strong leadership
- A climate of expectation
- An orderly but not rigid atmosphere
- Communication to students of the school's priority on learning the basics
- Diversion of school energy and resources when necessary to maintain priorities
- Means of monitoring student (and teacher) achievement

The Second Wave of Effective Schools Research

Beginning in the latter half of the 1980s a new wave of effective schools research was carried out. These new studies, relying on more sophisticated research designs and new statistical analysis techniques (Creemers, 1996), tended to result in longer lists of correlates than the early effects research (Mortimore and associates, 1988; Levine and Lezotte, 1990; Teddlie and Stringfield, 1993). After reviewing "second wave" effective schools research generated in a number of countries, Autin and Reynolds (1990, pp. 168–174) reported the following characteristics of effective schools:

- Site Management
- Leadership
- Staff Stability
- Curriculum and Instructional Articulation and Organization
- Staff Development
- Maximized Learning Time
- Widespread Recognition of Academic Success
- Parental Involvement and Support
- Collaborative Planning and Collegial Relationships
- Sense of Community
- Clear Goals and Expectations Commonly Shared
- Order and Discipline

Although agreeing with the early effective schools research on the need for such things as strong leadership, order, and agreed upon priorities, the second wave of research introduced new correlates such as site-based management, professional development, parental involvement, and teacher collaboration and collegiality.

Context Studies in Effective Schools Research

Traditional effective schools research has been criticized for reporting characteristics common to effective schools while ignoring differences between schools from various contexts (Hannaway and Talbert, 1993). Examples of context include location (urban, suburban, rural), socioeconomic status (SES), students' ethnicity and race, and school level (elementary, middle, or high school). In response to this criticism, a number of researchers have studied school effects in context. An example is a study reported by Teddlie and Stringfield (1993) in which middle and low SES status schools were compared. The researchers found that effective middle SES schools were characterized by high present *and* future expectations, teacher instructional leadership, an expanded curriculum, increased community contact, and experienced teachers. Conversely, effective low SES schools were characterized by high present expectations, principals who are initiators and overall instructional leaders, external rewards for academic achievement, an initial focus on basic skills with other offerings after basics have been achieved, buffering from negative external influences, and younger, idealistic teachers.

Makedon (1992) maintains that schools identified as effective have not closed the achievement *gap* between students of low and middle socioeconomic status. Cook, Semmel, and Gerber (1995) reported that in schools seeking to apply effectiveness research, general student achievement increased, but special education student achievement decreased. Pierce (1991) concluded that implementation of factors identified in effective schools research has failed to bring about significant achievement gains for language minority students. The fact that implementation of "traditional" effective schools correlates has often failed to raise the achievement of low-income, minority, and special needs students has led to effectiveness research aimed specifically at these groups. Stedman's (1987) research synthesis focused on case studies of schools that had demonstrated grade-level academic success for low-income students over several years. Contrary to the conclusions of many studies on effective schools, he found that emphasis on basic skills and time on task had little impact. Instead, he concluded that there were nine broad categories related to effectiveness (1987, p. 218):

1. Emphasis on ethnic and racial pluralism
2. Parent participation
3. Shared governance with teachers and parents
4. Academically rich programs
5. Skilled use and training of teachers
6. Personal attention to students
7. Student responsibility for school affairs
8. An accepting and supportive environment
9. Teaching aimed at preventing academic problems

Pierce (1991) reanalyzed studies of effective schools serving language-minority students. Common characteristics of these schools included the following:

- A healthy respect for cultural pluralism
- Staff development aimed at enabling teachers to deal with the special needs of linguistically and culturally different children
- A curriculum which went beyond basic skills to the integration of these skills in the content areas
- Encouraging student collaboration and coordination in lesson planning and preparation between all teachers serving these students
- Shared school governance between students, parents, and teachers. (p. 35)

Finally, Reyes, Scribner, and Scribner conducted case studies of eight high-performing Hispanic schools. They found that these schools were organized around four dimensions:

- Establishing a caring community, governing for student success, and empowering the school community to foster collaborative governance and leadership.

- Building collaborative relationships with parents and empowering the surrounding community.
- Creating a culture of caring—an inclusive student-centered classroom culture—and cultivating funds of knowledge to nurture a culturally responsive pedagogy
- Conducting advocacy-oriented assessments for appropriate and relevant language/ psychoeducational evaluations of high poverty, linguistically diverse students (Scribner 1999, p.16).

Has Effective Schools Research Outlived its Usefulness?

Soon after publication of the first effective schools studies, school districts across the nation began to plan and implement programs designed to apply the research to their own schools. By the early 1990s over half of the school districts in America were implementing programs based on effective schools research (Reynolds and Stoll, 1996). Such efforts are still going on today. Yet many educators have raised concerns about using the effective schools research as the basis of school reform. One concern is that effective schools have usually been identified by student scores on standardized literacy and mathematics tests, despite the fact researchers have warned against using such tests to judge a school's performance (Cuban, 1998). Another concern is that effective schools research is *correlational;* there is a significant positive correlation between the identified characteristics and the chosen measure of school effectiveness, but the research has not shown that these characteristics *cause* the effectiveness they have been associated with. Yet another problem with the effectiveness research is discussed by Hill (1998):

> School effectiveness research has not found a satisfactory way of dealing with the fact that schools and school education are essentially about growth, progress, and change. Researchers have been reduced to taking snapshots of phenomena, to focusing on achievement rather than rates of progress of students, and on measuring current status rather than charting change over time. (p.428)

For the above reasons as well as continuing problems in research design and methodology, many experts believe that effective schools research has outlived its usefulness and that it is time to base school reform efforts on a new research paradigm (Cuban, 1998; Hill, 1998).

The Legacy of Effective Schools Research

Despite criticism of effects research, it has left a positive legacy. It has disproven the earlier conclusions by Coleman, Jencks, and others that socioeconomic status determines student achievement and that schools and teachers have little effect on student learning. Larry Cuban (1998) points out that basic values of Effective Schools reformers of the early 1970s—that all children can learn, the importance of academic achievement, the need for accountability—have now been adopted by those who make and influence public policy.

Joseph Murphy (1992) suggests that since effective schools correlates tend to change in different studies and contexts, educators need to move beyond a narrow interpretation of school effectiveness to a set of broad principles that underlie the various correlates. Murphy maintains that these principles constitute the real legacy of the effective schools research and include the following:

1. All students can learn.
2. Schools should focus on student outcomes and rigorously assess progress toward reaching those outcomes.
3. Schools should assume a fair share of the responsibility for student learning.
4. Schools should be structurally, symbolically, and culturally linked, providing for consistency and coordination throughout the school community (pp. 165–168).

Although the legacy of effective schools research is secure, the prevalent opinion of researchers is that this body of research, *by itself,* provides an insufficient basis for school reform. Additional research beyond the effects studies is necessary. This leads us to the topic of school improvement research.

From Effective Schools to School Improvement

Although effective schools research is still being carried out, over the last several years *school improvement research* has taken center stage. Before reviewing the research in this area, let's discuss differences between the two types of research. As noted by Bennett and Harris, effects research asks the question "What do effective schools look like?" and school improvement research asks "How do schools improve over time?" Effects research examines inputs, throughputs, and outputs and emphasizes organizational structure, while school improvement research is focused on school culture and the change process (Bennett and Harris, 1997). Effects research takes statistical snapshots of performance measures and their correlates, while school improvement research is concerned with long-term growth, often examined through case studies (Bollen, 1996). In short, school improvement research is concerned with the *how* of successful schools. The summaries below include the results of specific studies as well as lists of characteristics of improving schools compiled by experts who have carried out a variety of improvement studies.

Little (1982) studied work conditions in three elementary and three urban desegregated schools. Based on aggregate standardized achievement test scores over a three-year period, four "relatively successful" and two "relatively unsuccessful" schools were studied. Little found that professional development and school improvement in the successful schools were fostered by norms (shared expectations) of *collegiality* (working together) and *continuous improvement* (ongoing analysis, evaluation, and experimentation). She further concluded that four types of interactions are crucial to achieving norms of collegiality and continuous improvement:

- Teachers engage in frequent, continuous, and increasingly concrete and precise talk about teaching practice.
- Teachers are frequently observed and provided with useful (if potentially frightening) critiques of their teaching.
- Teachers plan, design, research, evaluate, and prepare teaching materials together.
- Teachers teach each other the practice of teaching. (Little, 1982, p. 331)

Rosenholtz (1989) collected quantitative and qualitative data on a random sample of elementary schools in Tennessee. Of the 78 schools that were examined, 65 were classified as "learning impoverished" or "stuck" and 13 were classified as "learning enriched" or "moving." Characteristics of the learning-enriched schools included the following:

- Teachers shared instructional goals
- Teachers collaborated with each other
- There was a spirit of continuous learning and growing among teachers
- Teachers had a sense of certainty about technical knowledge and instructional practice
- Teachers possessed commitment and optimism

Pajak and Glickman (1989) studied *school districts* with improved student achievement sustained for three consecutive years. They found three major dimensions concerning the "how" of school improvement present in all three school systems:

- *An instructional dialogue:* Teachers were engaged in a continuous cycle of discussing, planning, implementing, and reviewing curriculum and instruction.
- *An infrastructure of support:* Each superintendent had set up an organizational structure and designated staff responsible for fostering dialogue about improving instruction and student learning.
- *Varied sources of instructional leadership:* Although principals supported instructional improvement efforts, they usually were secondary instructional leaders. The primary instructional leaders varied from system to system. They included central office supervisors, assistant principals for instruction, department chairs, grade-level leaders, and teams of teachers.

Levine (1991, pp. 390–392) presented nine guidelines for creating effective schools based on successful districtwide effective schools projects:

1. Substantial staff development time must be provided for participating faculty, at least part of the time during the regular teacher workday.
2. Faculties engaged in effective schools projects must not wait very long before beginning to address issues involving the improvement of instruction.
3. Faculties embarking on effective schools projects must avoid getting bogged down in elaborate schemes to train all staff members in the details of a particular instructional technique or approach at the beginning of a project.
4. Improvement goals must be sharply focused to avoid overloading teachers and schools.
5. Significant technical assistance must be made available to faculties participating in effective schools projects.
6. Effective schools programs should be "data-driven" in the sense that appropriate information should be collected and used to guide participants in preparing and carrying out plans for improvement.
7. Effective schools projects must avoid reliance on bureaucratic processes that stress forms and checklists, as well as on mandated components rigidly applied in participating schools and classrooms.
8. Effective schools projects should seek out and consider using materials, methods, and approaches that have been successful in schools and projects elsewhere.
9. The success of an effective schools program depends on a judicious mixture of autonomy for participating faculties and control from the central office, a kind of "directed autonomy."

Teddlie and Stringfield (1993) have examined several cases of schools improving dramatically. Based on these cases, they make the following recommendations for school-level improvement:

- Perform a context analysis (including SES, any inequities in service to students, geographic-demographic context, school organization, sociological and historic factors)
- Develop a plan unique to the school
- Implement instructional and school improvement plan simultaneously
- Assess improvement plan using many indicators
- Include a teacher induction process (pp. 224–226)

After reviewing the research literature, Hopkins, Ainscow, and West (1994) derived the following messages for those embarking on school improvement:

- Improvement efforts should be directed toward student outcomes, with student progress defined by the school rather than by scores on achievement tests alone.
- Characteristics of an effective school are dependent to some extent on the climate and culture of the particular school and are open to modification by the school staff.

- The primary focus of school improvement should be teaching and learning.
- Staff development for school improvement should include both workshops to learn new skills and immediate, sustained classroom and school implementation characterized by collaborative support, peer coaching, and study of the improvement effort.
- School improvement should focus on school development as a whole rather than either processes with little substantive content *or* isolated curriculum innovations or teaching practices.

After in-depth study of five schools, each involved in reform for at least seven years, Wasley, Hampel, and Clark (1997) developed seven "clues" for school improvement:

- Clue 1. Schools able to use re-visioning as a continuous activity are more likely to move forward. (p. 692)
- Clue 2. Schools with a coherent sense of their ongoing efforts at reform are better equipped to achieve their goals. A coherent sense of the interconnectedness of all reform efforts under way in a building is a rare but enabling factor in the school's ability to make changes that positively affect students. (p. 693)
- Clue 3. Schools able to deal directly with difficult and often controversial issues are more likely to continue to involve the whole school community. (pp. 693–694)
- Clue 4. Schools regularly able to receive and act on good critical feedback from external sources made more progress than those that worked autonomously. (p. 694)
- Clue 5. A faculty's ability to develop skills in rigorous self-analysis that focused on student gains was a critical tool to broaden and deepen teachers' efforts. (p. 694)
- Clue 6. Staff members who can attend simultaneously to multiple aspects of school redesign—curriculum, pedagogy, assessment, and school culture—are more likely to see the kind of results for which they hope. (pp. 694–695)
- Clue 7. Schools that involve parents in substantive ways in their efforts to change are better able to gain the support they need to continue. (p. 695)

In addition to their seven clues for school improvement, Wasley, Hampel, and Clark (1997) recommend two ways for schools to investigate their own progress in school reform. One way is *civil discourse;* extended, thoughtful dialogue characterized by mutual respect. The other is *rigorous analysis;* critical examination of improvement efforts in light of students' learning.

Finally, Joyce, Calhoun, and Hopkins (1999) have developed seven hypotheses, based on the numerous studies of school improvement in which they have participated.

- Hypothesis 1: Restructuring the job assignments of educators so that time for collective inquiry is built into the workplace will increase school improvement activity. (p. 11)
- Hypothesis 2: Active, living democracy, including community members, engaged in collective inquiry, creates the structural condition in which the process of school improvement is nested. (p .11)
- Hypothesis 3: An information-rich environment will enhance inquiry. Learning to study the learning environment will increase inquiry into ways of helping students learn better. (p. 12)
- Hypothesis 4: Connecting the responsible parties to the knowledge base on teaching and learning will increase the development of successful initiatives for school improvement. (p. 13)
- Hypothesis 5: Staff development, embedded in the workplace, increases inquiry into new practices and the implementation of school improvement initiatives. (p. 13)
- Hypothesis 6: Staff development, structured as inquiry, both fuels energy and results in initiatives that have greater effects. (p. 13)
- Hypothesis 7: Building small work groups connected to the larger community but responsible for one another will increase the sense of belonging that reduces stress, isolation, and feelings of alienation. (p. 14)

Although the specific characteristics of successful school improvement efforts vary somewhat across the above reviews, a consensus has emerged on the most important factors. Figure 3.1 provides a composite list of these characteristics.

After reviewing both the effective schools and the school improvement research, it becomes clear that these are not entirely separate types of research. Rather, effects research has informed and provided a foundation for school

FIGURE 3.1 *Characteristics of Improving Schools*

- Varied sources of leadership, including teacher leadership
- Consideration of individual school context and culture
- Parental involvement
- Shared vision, and continuous revisioning
- External and internal support, including time, moral, and technical support
- Focus on teaching and learning
- Ongoing professional development, including continuous analysis, reflection, and growth
- Instructional dialogue
- Teacher collaboration
- Democratic, collective inquiry, including action research
- Integration of improvement efforts into a coherent program
- Data-based feedback on improvement efforts using multiple measures

improvement research. Together, the two types of studies provide us with a knowledge base for developing successful schools.

Studies have pointed out that a successful school can vary considerably from other successful schools in the degree of community involvement, school leadership, and change initiation (Hallinger and Murphy, 1987; Purkey and Smith, 1983). There is ample research on school improvement to inform us of the different paths, factors, and actors of school success. However, we can say with confidence that participants in successful schools show a remarkable tendency to see themselves as being involved in "a moral equivalent of war" or "a cause beyond oneself."

A Cause Beyond Oneself

Later chapters on observation, direct assistance, professional development, and curriculum development will explain how a supervisor can use the research on effective classroom practice with teachers. For now, however, the outside-the-classroom but within-the-school factors that correlate with or predict school success provide the more significant issue. All the research on successful schools has cited a particular type of social organization, which Edmonds referred to as a "climate of expectation." Brookover called it "teacher belief that students could learn and not being satisfied with less," and Goodlad cited it as "goal participation and agreement." Rutter and colleagues (1979, p. 184) identified this social organization as a "concept of ethos...the well-nigh universal tendency for individuals in common circumstances to form social groups with their own rules, values and standards of behavior." Where ethos was developed around a clear educational purpose, a successful school emerged:

> It should be emphasized that the more successful schools were not unduly regimented. Rather, good morale and the routine of people working harmoniously together as part of an efficient system meant that both supervision and support were available to teachers in a way which was absent in less successful schools. (Rutter et al., 1979, p. 184)

Every major research study on successful schools has noted the organizational phenomenon of collective action, agreed-on purpose, and belief in attainment (Pratzner, 1984, Rosenholtz, 1985). On the other hand, every major research study on ineffective schools has noted an absence of such purpose. Successful schools do not happen by accident: Supervision is the force that shapes the organization into a productive unit.

Clearly, one characteristic of successful schools is that each teacher has "a cause beyond oneself." Teachers do not view their work as simply what they carry out within their own four walls. In successful schools, teachers see themselves as part of the larger enterprise of complementing and working with each other to educate students. For successful schools, education is a collective rather than an individual enterprise.

Chapter 1 introduced three schools: Finnie Tyler High School, Germando Elementary School, and Progress Middle School. Neither Finnie Tyler High School nor Germando Elementary School was a successful school because both lacked "a cause beyond oneself." Teachers in one school were forced to do as they were told and therefore did not participate in formulating or working toward a common cause. In the other school, teachers could do whatever they liked and therefore did not participate in a common cause either. Unless the individual needs of staff members are linked with collective school goals, a school cannot be successful.

Successful schools are characterized by teachers who enjoy working with each other *as* they accomplish school tasks. In many schools, teachers enjoy being with each other, but the task dimension is missing. They laugh, they party, but they don't get anything done. In other schools, accomplishing tasks (writing curriculum, revising schedules, filling out forms, following the text) predominates over individual and social needs. People are busy, but their tension is evident in gossip, sidelong glances, and frowns. As a result, tasks are accomplished in a forced, hurried manner; the participants feel neither kinship with each other nor commitment to each other in carrying out the tasks. They may even resist carrying out the tasks because of the impersonal manner in which these tasks are chosen. Neither type of school is truly professional or effective. A successful school, like Progress Middle School, balances both dimensions so that people enjoy each other's company when they are accomplishing school goals.

What to Do with Successful Schools Research: Some Propositions

Based on research, certain propositions can be made concerning teachers' attitudes, confidence, awareness, stimulation, and thoughtfulness that can be promoted via supervision.

- Proposition 1: *Supervision can enhance teacher belief in a cause beyond oneself.* Teachers can see themselves not just as individuals separated by classroom walls, but as a body of people complementing and strengthening each other.
- Proposition 2: *Supervision can promote teachers' sense of efficacy.* Teachers can see themselves as being able to instruct students successfully, regardless of influences outside of school. Within the school they can learn to believe they do have control over management and instruction. They have power to reach students.
- Proposition 3: *Supervision can make teachers aware of how they complement each other in striving for common goals.* Teachers can observe each other at work, share materials, pick up techniques from each other, and learn how to support each other.

- Proposition 4: *Supervision can stimulate teachers to plan common purposes and actions.* Teachers can be given responsibilities to guide and assist others, to make decisions about schoolwide instruction, to plan professional development, to develop curriculum, and to engage in action research. Such involvement shows respect and trust in teachers and strengthens collective action.
- Proposition 5: *Supervision can challenge teachers to think abstractly about their work.* Teachers can be given feedback, questioned, and confronted to appraise, reflect, and adapt their current practices to future instruction. More varied practice and abstract thinking are the results.

In summary, supervision must be viewed as developmental if schools are to become more successful. Supervision must not only respond to current teacher performance but also encourage greater involvement, autonomous thinking, and collective action by teachers. The first order of business for a supervisor is to build the staff into a team. In order to improve school instruction, a supervisor has to work with staff to create a professional togetherness. They must share a common purpose for their instruction and they must have confidence that their collective action will make a difference in their students' lives.

Gaining knowledge of successful schools and effective classrooms is only the first step in improving schools. Using such knowledge in one's own school demands skill and practice. Skill and practice flow from knowledge. We have seen that the research on school success converges on the concept of a cause beyond oneself or a belief in collective action. To use that knowledge, a supervisor needs further understanding about teaching and the teaching profession to understand why such a cause beyond oneself does not occur naturally in schools.

Exercises

Academic

1. Write a personal reaction to this chapter's summary of the Coleman study, in which you support or criticize its major conclusions. Base your reaction on your own experience and/or observation of U.S. education.

2. The chapter summarizes the results of several studies of successful schools but also suggests that the majority of schools are not successful. Prepare a report expressing your agreement or disagreement.

3. Review three journal articles that deal with research on successful schools. Based on these readings and your reading of the text, compile a composite list of probable characteristics of a successful school.

4. Read single chapters dealing with the same topic from two books listed as references for Chapter 3. Write a paper comparing and contrasting the authors' conclusions concerning the chosen topic.

5. For each of the chapter's five propositions based on successful-schools research, write a description of a related supervisory activity that you believe could improve the ef-

fectiveness of teachers in a typical school setting. Write rationales to support the relationship between each proposition and the corresponding supervisory activity.

Field

1. The chapter asserts that effective supervision must provide for both completing tasks and meeting individual and social needs. Observe an administrator or supervisor who is able to balance task and human needs effectively. Write a report on your observations, including a description of the knowledge, skills, and procedures the supervisor draws on in meeting both organizational goals and teacher needs.

2. Present the chapter's five propositions based on successful-schools research to a group of educators. The group may include teachers, supervisors, or both. After presenting each proposition, ask for reactions from the educators, including their opinions as to whether each proposition is or can become a reality in their own educational setting. Record the interviews in writing or on audiotape.

3. Prepare a slide or transparency presentation on a summary of successful-schools research. Make your presentation to a group of educators. Ask for and record reactions to your presentation.

4. Visit a school that is perceived to be a successful school by both educators and community members. Seek and observe examples of effective leadership, communication, instruction, and other factors that researchers have found to be present in successful schools. Take photographs representative of the effective characteristics observed. Mount selected photographs on poster board, along with brief written descriptions of how the scene in each photograph relates to effective education. Display your photo essay to interested parties.

5. Conduct an interview with a supervisor or administrator in a business, industrial, government, or military setting, focusing on how he or she attempts to integrate organizational goals (task emphasis) with employees' individual and social needs (human emphasis). Write a summary of his or her attitudes, strategies, and methods as well as your opinion about whether they can be applied to a school setting.

Developmental

1. Maintain an ongoing review of prominent educational journals for reports on future successful-schools research. With each new research study, look for (a) findings not already indicated in the review of research in Chapter 3 and (b) any findings that tend to contradict the research cited in Chapter 3.

2. Monitor any major changes in leadership style, curriculum, professional development, or instruction within a local school system over the next few months. Examine such changes to determine which are at least partially based on recent research on successful schools.

3. Over the next few months, examine statements made by prominent educational, political, and civic leaders that include proposals for educational reform. To what extent do such proposals reflect what we have learned from research on successful schools?

References

Austin, G., & Reynolds, D. 1990. Managing for improved school effectiveness: An international survey. *School Organization 10*(2/3), 167–178.

Bennett, N., and Harris, A. (1997). *Hearing truth from Power? Organization theory, school effectiveness, and school improvement.* Paper presented at the Annual Meeting of the American Educational Research Association, Chicago, March.

Bollen, R. (1996). School effectiveness and school improvement: The intellectual and policy context. In D. Reynolds, R. Bollen, B. Creemers, D. Hopkins, L. Stoll, and N. Lagerweij, *Making good schools: Linking school effectiveness and school improvement.* New York: Routledge.

Chubb, J. E., and Moe, T. M. (1990). *Politics, markets, and America's schools.* Washington, DC: The Brookings Institute.

Coleman, J. S., Campbell, E. Q., Hobson, C. J., McPartland, J., Mood, A. M., Weinfield, F. D., and York, R. L. 1966. *Equality of educational opportunity.* Washington, DC: U.S. Government Printing Office.

Cook, B. G., Semmel, M. I., and Gerber, M. M. 1995. *Are recent reforms effective for all students?* Paper presented at the annual meeting of the American Educational Research Association, San Francisco, April. (ERIC ED 385 012)

Creemers, B. (1996). The school effectiveness knowledge base. In D. Reynolds, R. Bollen, B. Creemers, D. Hopkins, L. Stoll, and N. Lagerweij, *Making good schools: Linking school effectiveness and school improvement,* pp. 36–58. New York: Routledge

Cuban, L. (1998). How schools change reforms: Redefining reform success and failure. *Teachers College Record, 99*(3), 453–477.

Edmonds, R. 1979. Effective schools for the urban poor. *Educational Leadership 37*(1):15–24.

Glickman, C. D. 1987. *Concepts of change in school systems improving criterion-referenced test scores.* Paper presented at the annual meeting of the American Educational Research Association, Washington, DC.

Glickman, C. D. 1987. Good and/or effective schools: What do we want? *Kappan 68*(8): 622–624.

Glickman, C. D., and Pajak, E. F. 1986. *A study of school systems in Georgia which have improved criterion-referenced test scores in reading and mathematics from 1982 to 1985.* (ERIC ED 282 317)

Goodlad, J. I. 1984. *A place called school: Prospects for the future.* New York: McGraw-Hill.

Hallinger, P., and Murphy, J. 1987. *Social context on school effects.* Paper presented at the annual meeting of the American Educational Association, Washington, DC, April.

Hannaway, J., and Talbert, J. 1993. Bringing context into effective schools research: Urban-Suburban differences. *Educational Administration Quarterly 29*(2):164–186.

Hill, P. W. 1998. Shaking the foundations: Research driven school reform. *School Effectiveness and School Improvement, 9* (4), 419–436.

Hopkins, D., Ainscow, M., and West, M. 1994. *School improvement in an era of change.* New York: Teachers College Press.

Illich, I. D. 1972. *Deschooling society.* New York: Harrow Books.

James, William, as cited in Stone, R. 1986. A higher horror of the whiteness. *Harper's 273*(1639):54.

Jencks, C. 1972. *Inequality: A reassessment of the effect of family and schooling in America.* New York: Basic Books.

Joyce, B., Calhoun, E., and Hopkins, D. 1999. *The new structure of school improvement: Inquiring schools and achieving students.* Philadelphia: Open University Press.

Kozol, J. 1967. *Death at an early age.* Boston: Houghton Mifflin.

Levine, D. V. 1991. Creating effective schools: Findings and implications from research and practice. *Phi Delta Kappan 72,* 389–393.

Levine, D. V., and Lezotte, W. 1990. *Unusually effective schools: A review and analysis of research and practice.* Madison, WI: National Center for Effective Schools Research and Development.

Little, J. W. 1982. Norms of collegiality and experimentation: Workplace conditions of school success. *American Educational Research Journal 19*(3): 325–340.

Makedon, A. 1992. *Is Alice's world too middle class? Recommendations for effective schools research.* (ERIC ED 346 612)

Mortimore, P., Sammons, P., Stoll, L., Lewis, D., & Ecob, R. 1988. *School matters.* Berkley, CA: University of California Press.

Murphy, J. 1992. Effective schools: Legacy and future directions. In D. Reynolds, and P. Cuttance (Eds.), *School effectiveness: Research, policy, and practice* (pp. 164–170). London: Cassell.

National Commission on Education. 1983. An open letter to the American people. A nation at risk: The imperative for educational reform. *Education Week* 2(31):12.

Pajak, E. F., & Glickman, C. D. 1989. Dimensions of school district improvement. *Educational Leadership* 46(8), 61–64.

Peters, T. J., and Waterman, R. H. 1982. *In search of excellence*. New York: Harper and Row.

Pierce, L. V. (1991). *Effective schools for national origin language minority students*. Washington, DC: The Mid-Atlantic Equity Center.

Pratzner, F. C. 1984. Quality of school life: Foundations for improvement. *Educational Researcher* 13(3):20–25.

Purkey, S. C., and Smith, M. S. 1983. Effective schools: A review. *Elementary School Journal* 83, 427–452.

Reynolds, D., and Stoll, L. 1996. Merging school effectiveness and school improvement: The knowledge bases. In D. Reynolds, R. Bollen, B. Creemers, D. Hopkins, L. Stoll, and N. Lagerweij, *Making good schools: Linking school effectiveness and school improvement*, pp. 94–112. London and New York: Routledge.

Rosenholtz, S. J. 1985. Effective schools: Interpreting the evidence. *American Journal of Education* 93(3):352–388.

Rosenholtz, S. J. 1989. *Teachers' workplace: The social organization of schools*. New York: Longman.

Rutter, M., Maughan, B., Mortimore, P., Ouston, J., and Smith, A. 1979. *Fifteen thousand hours: Secondary schools and their effects on children*. Cambridge, MA: Harvard University Press.

Scribner, A. P. 1999. High performing Hispanic schools: An introduction. In P. Reyes, J. D. Scribner, and A. P. Scribner (Eds.), *Lessons from high performing Hispanic schools: Creating learning communities*. New York: Teachers College Press.

Silberman, C. E. 1971. *Crisis in the classroom: The remaking of American education*. New York: Random House.

Stedman, L. C. 1987. It's time we change the effective schools formula. *Kappan* 69(3):215–224.

Stone, R. 1986. A higher horror of the whiteness. *Harper's* 273(1639):49–54.

Stringfield, S., and Teddlie, C. 1987. *A time to summarize: Six years and three phases of the Louisiana School Effectiveness Study*. Paper presented at the annual meeting of the American Educational Research Association, Washington, DC, April.

Teddlie, C., and Stringfield, S. 1993. *Schools make a difference: Lessons learned from a 10-year study of school effects*. New York: Teachers College Press.

Wasley, P., Hampel, R., and Clark, R. 1997. The puzzle of whole-school change. *Phi Delta Kappan, 78*, 690–697.

Suggested Readings

Becker, M. 1992. *An effective schools primer*. Arlington, VA: American Association of School Administrators.

Garcia, E. 1994. *Understanding and meeting the challenge of student cultural diversity*. Boston: Houghton Mifflin.

Glickman, C. D. 1993. *Renewing America's schools. A guide for school-based action*. San Francisco: Jossey-Bass.

Hopkins, D., Ainscow, M., and West, M. 1994. *School improvement in an era of change*. New York: Teachers College Press.

Joyce, B., Calhoun, E., and Hopkins, D. 1999. *The new structure of school improvement: Inquiring schools and achieving schools*. Philadelphia: Open University Press.

Levine, D. V., and Lezotte, W. 1990. *Unusually effective schools: A review and analysis of research and practice*. Madison, WI: National Center for Effective Schools Research and Development.

Reyes, P., Scribner, J. D., and Scribner, A. P. (Eds.). 1999. *Lessons from high performing Hispanic schools: Creating learning communities*.

Reynolds, D., Bollen, R., Creemers, B., Hopkins, D., Stoll, L., and Lagerweij, N. 1996. *Making good schools: Linking school effectiveness and school improvement*. New York: Routledge.

Rosenholtz, S. J. 1989. *Teachers' workplace: The social organization of schools*. New York: Longman.

Teddlie, C., and Stringfield, S. 1993. *Schools make a difference: Lessons learned from a 10-year study of school effects*. New York: Teachers College Press.

Wasley, P., Hampel, R., and Clark, R. 1997. The puzzle of whole-school change. *Phi Delta Kappan, 78*, 690–697.

4

Adult and Teacher Development within the Context of the School

Clues for Supervisory Practice

This chapter will serve as a core for thinking and practicing supervision in a developmental framework. So far, we have defined "a cause beyond oneself" as a demarcation between the collective, thoughtful, autonomous, and effective staffs of successful schools and the isolated, unreflective, and powerless staffs of unsuccessful schools. Knowledge of how teachers can grow as competent adults is the guiding principle for supervisors in finding ways to return wisdom, power, and control to both the individuals and the collective staff in order for them to become true professionals. With the understanding of how teachers change, the supervisor can plan direct assistance, professional development, curriculum development, group development, and action research at an appropriate level to stimulate teacher growth and instructional improvement.

The research on adult development has been prolific (Belenky, Clinchy, Goldberger, and Tarule, 1986; Fiske and Chiriboga, 1990; Kegan, 1994; Loevinger, 1976; Levinson, 1977; Harvey, Hunt, and Schroeder, 1961; Neugarten, 1977; Whitbourne, 1986), and the research in teacher development is advancing (McNergney and Carrier, 1981; Sprinthall and Thies-Sprinthall, 1982; Oja, 1979; Burden, 1982; Burke, Christensen, Fessler, McDonnell, and Price, 1987; Levine, 1989). We have attempted to distill the knowledge of adult and teacher development that has direct applications for supervision and supervisors. Readers who desire more detail should refer to the references at the end of the chapter. The use of such readily available and potentially rich knowledge about human growth can be extremely valuable to those who work with adults. If schools are to be successful, supervision must respond to teachers as changing adults.

Adults as Learners

Instructional improvement takes place when teachers improve their decision making about students, learning content, and teaching. The process of improving teacher decision making is largely a process of adult learning. Thus, research and theory on adult learning is an important component of the knowledge base for instructional supervision. Two basic questions have driven much of the research on adult learning ability over the years: Does ability to learn diminish with age? Are there differences between the learning processes of adults and children? Since Thorndike (1928) first suggested that learning did not peak in youth and diminish steadily thereafter (a common belief of his day), learning theorists, psychologists, and educators have been trying to gain a better understanding of adult learning.

Fluid and Crystallized Intelligence

Lorge and his colleagues (1965) were the first to suggest that timed tests used to measure adult intelligence might be biased against older adults because of differences in their perceptual speed. Havighurst (1980, p. 6) later wrote, "Research studies of the relation of aging to learning during the past 20 years have found that there are two brands or categories of intelligence, one which increases during adulthood, while the other decreases." Horn and Cattell (1967), Long and Mirza (1980), and others have labeled these two categories of intelligence *fluid* and *crystallized*. Fluid intelligence depends on physiological and neurological capacities. This kind of intelligence peaks early, at about age 14 (Merriam and Caffarella, 1999), and explains why youth perform best on tasks requiring quick insight, short-term memorization, and complex interactions. Crystallized intelligence is more heavily influenced by education and experience. It is assessed by untimed measures calling for judgment, knowledge, and experience. This kind of intelligence seems to remain stable or show improvement as people age.

A number of researchers argue then that what is lost in fluid intelligence with aging is compensated for by crystallized intelligence. We think of the older person as getting wiser, even though he or she may experience memory lapses or need a little extra time to grasp a new task. Hence, older teachers are better able to rely on their learning assets when allowed to draw on experience than when asked to respond quickly to a novel situation. One implication for supervision is that experienced teachers are more likely to understand and utilize curricular and instructional innovations if the innovations can be linked to their past teaching experience and current expertise. Another is that beginning teachers can benefit from successful experienced teachers sharing with novices their experiences, accumulated knowledge, and insight about students and teaching.

Contemporary Theories of Intelligence

Contemporary theories of intelligence offer additional insights about the place of individual learning strengths, the role of experience in learning, and the importance of sociocultural context in what one defines as intelligent behavior. Howard Gardner's (1983) *theory of multiple intelligences* challenges the traditional conception of intelligence as a global overall ability. Bringing together earlier research on adults and children, Gardner posited that there are a number of different types of intelligence. Applying a consistent set of criteria, he initially identified seven possible types. Two of them, linguistic intelligence and logical-mathematical intelligence, have to do with the kinds of abilities in verbal communication and logical reasoning that have traditionally been measured by educators. The remaining five are musical intelligence, spatial intelligence, bodily kinesthetic intelligence, and two interdependent forms of personal intelligence—intrapersonal and interpersonal. Later, he added to the list an eighth type of intelligence—naturalistic. (Checkley, 1997)

Gardner proposed that thinking in terms of these multiple intelligences will help people in planning educational programs, as educators identify the intelligences of students and utilize this knowledge in selecting initial content to be taught and teaching methods. Gardner's ideas are also relevant to supervision: Supervisors can identify and utilize the learning strengths of individual teachers when assisting them with instructional improvement efforts. Supervisors also can assist teachers to expand gradually their repertoire of learning strategies.

Sternberg (1985, 1990) likewise has proposed a theory of intelligence that may be helpful in thinking about the cognition of teachers. His is called a *triarchic theory of intelligence* because it consists of three subtheories. The first subtheory is referred to as *componential;* it deals with cognitive processing. This part of the theory deals with what has traditionally been discussed in trying to understand intellectual ability. The second subtheory is *experiential,* which suggests that assessing intelligence requires consideration not only of the mental components but of the level of experience at which they are applied. Sternberg, intrigued by the differences between novices and experts, has suggested that experience brings both the ability to respond automatically to routine situations and to deal effectively with novel situations. Thus, novice teachers can be expected to require different types of supervision than those who are more experienced.

Although the first two subtheories deal with universal processes, Sternberg's third subtheory deals with *socially influenced abilities.* Individuals are said to cope with life's challenges by adapting to the environment, shaping the environment, or selecting a different environment—all the while being influenced by what is considered appropriate and intelligent behavior within one's cultural milieu. This last contextual subtheory becomes important when one looks at how teachers deal with challenging situations. Some obviously have greater capacities than others to adapt to or change the classroom and school environment. Through appropriate supervision, teachers can be assisted in broadening their array of adaptation and change strategies. It is this kind of practical intelligence that intrigues

Sternberg and other theorists who propose that not enough attention has focused on the demonstration of adult intelligence through the identification and solution of real-world problems.

Experiential Learning and Situated Cognition

At the heart of numerous conceptions of adult learning and education dating back to Dewey (1938) and Lindeman (1926) is the centrality of experience to learning. This concern with experience is reflected in Knowles's (1980) inclusion of the importance of adult experience as one of his original four assumptions about adult learning. It is also reflected in Kolb's inclusion of two phases focusing on experience (concrete experiences and active experimentations) as part of his four-phase model of the adult learning cycle (1984). Most recently, interest in the ties between adult learning and experience have been explored in examinations of learning in the workplace, which have found that much of the meaningful learning that occurs in that context is of the informal and incidental variety rather than the highly structured learning traditionally associated with workplace training (Kerka, 1998). Workplace environments that stimulate such learning are those which foster proactivity, critical reflection, and creativity (Marsick and Watkins, 1990). Smylie (1995) finds implications for school reform in such conceptions of adult learning, and identifies the characteristics of school learning environments that are conducive to teacher learning:

1. Teacher collaboration
2. Shared power and authority, in terms of relationships between teachers and administrators and among teachers
3. Egalitarianism among teachers emphasizing talents each has to bring over hierarchical status differences
4. Variation, challenge autonomy, and choice in teachers' work in the classroom and the district
5. Colloboratively developed goals and feedback mechanisms
6. Integration of work and learning
7. Accessibility of external sources of learning

The centrality of experience to learning takes on new dimensions when the emerging body of work on situated cognition is applied to consideration of adult learning. Many cite Brown, Collins and Duguid (1989) as a seminal work in proposing a theory of situated cognition. Essentially, they propose that education is misconceived to the degree that it emphasizes the acquisition of decontextualized, abstract knowledge. They insist that lasting knowledge emerges as learners engage in authentic activity embedded in specific situations. Learners, like apprentices, are said to learn by using the tools of their discipline or practice to solve real problems. Wilson (1993) extends the application of this theory specifically to adult learning and education, describing learning that is "fundamentally situated" as that which is social in nature, tool dependent (using the mechanisms provided by the setting, such as computers, maps, or measuring cups), and interactive with the setting. Linking situated cognition to Schon's (1983) work on acquisition of professional knowledge through "knowing-in-action," he suggests adults learn *in* experience as they act in situations and are acted upon by situations, rather than the traditional assumption that adults learn *from* experience.

Extending the parallel with craft apprenticeships, Brown, Collins, and Duguid (1989) and others emphasize the *cognitive apprenticeship* as a means for learners to acquire knowledge as participants in a community of practice. Wilson (1993) makes an analogy between the cognitive apprenticeship and Schon's (1983) reflective practicum. Lave and Wenger (1991) move away from the hierarchical notion of apprenticeship to recommend a strategy called *legitimate parallel participation,* in which novices become enculturated by interacting with other participants, skills, artifacts, symbols and ideas that are part of the culture. Each of these strategies offers a valuable approach for fostering professional development of teachers, particularly those who are new to the field or to a particular school culture. In line with situated cognition theory, teachers would most effectively acquire knowledge useful in a new situation by being directly immersed in real practice situations, with support from experienced colleagues whose methods might include modeling and coaching.

Theories of Adult Learning

The *theory of andragogy,* popularized in this country by Malcolm Knowles, has become one of the better-known theories of adult learning in recent years. Knowles (1980) proposed four basic assumptions of adult learning:

1. Adults have a psychological need to be self-directing.
2. Adults bring an expansive reservoir of experience that can and should be tapped in the learning situation.
3. Adults' readiness to learn is influenced by a need to solve real-life problems often related to adult developmental tasks.
4. Adults are performance centered in their orientation to learning—wanting to make immediate application of knowledge.

Later, Knowles added a fifth assumption—that adult learning is primarily intrinsically motivated (Knowles, 1984). The theory of andragogy no longer receives the uncritical acceptance that it once did, with questions increasingly raised about the extent to which these assumptions are exclusively true of adults (Tennant, 1986), the extent to which self-direction is an actual versus a desirable preference of adult learners (Brookfield, 1986), and the conditions under which andragogy may or may not apply (Pratt, 1988). Knowles himself, before his death in 1997, came to acknowledge that differences between adults and children as learners may be a matter of degree and situation rather than a rigid dichotomy. Nevertheless, the theory of andragogy is still accepted by many as a broad guide to thinking about adults' learning.

Another theory of adult learning that has received significant attention is Mezirow's *theory of perspective transformation* (1981, 1990). Drawing on the work of the philosopher Habermas, Mezirow emphasized the change in perspective that often accompanies adult learning. Transformative learning is said to most often follow some kind of disorienting dilemma—an event or series of events that alter the routine flow of life. Combined reflection and action, called *praxis* by Freire (1970), enable the adult to become aware of assumptions guiding his or her life and to act on this knowledge. Such a theory suggests that reflective and critical thinking must be encouraged as an important part of teacher learning as well as instructional improvement efforts.

Cranton (1994) recommends the educator should critically reflect on his or her own meaning perspective of being an educator. She also describes the processes by which the educator might accomplish this:

> The educator, in order to develop the meaning perspective of being an educator would: increase self awareness through consciousness-raising activities, make his or her assumptions about beliefs about practice explicit, engage in critical reflection on those assumptions and beliefs, engage in dialogue with others, and develop an informed theory of practice. (Cranton, 1994, p. 214)

The strategies Cranton suggests may be useful in this process are varied, including writing journals, visiting the classrooms of colleagues, conducting criteria analysis of incidents which epitomize their notions of success or failure in practice, experimenting with practice, eliciting feedback from learners, and consulting or engaging in dialogue with colleagues.

Stephen Brookfield (1986) has suggested six central principles of effective practice in facilitating adult learning. These principles appear to take into account the work of Mezirow as well as the assumptions of andragogy. These include the following:

1. Participation in learning is voluntary; intimidation or coercion have no place in motivating adult participation.
2. Effective practice is characterized by respect among participants for each other's self-worth.
3. Facilitation is collaborative, with learner and facilitators sharing responsibility for setting objectives and evaluating learning.
4. Praxis is at the heart of effective facilitation, with learners and facilitators involved in a continual cycle of collaborative activity and reflection on activity.
5. Facilitation aims to foster in adults a spirit of critical reflection. Educational encounters should assist adults to question many aspects of their personal, occupational, and political lives.
6. The aim of facilitation is the nurturing of self-directed, empowered adults who will function as proactive individuals.

Teachers as Adult Learners

Fullan (1991) pointed out that "educational change is a learning experience for the adults involved" (p. 66). Our knowledge of adult learning tells us that it is important to link learning about instructional innovations to teachers' past experiences, and to allow them ample time to integrate innovations gradually into their teaching repertoire. Yet, in recent years, teachers have been bombarded with a plethora of innovations as part of the educational reform movement. Fullan (1991) concluded that "many decisions about the kinds of educational innovations introduced in school districts are biased, poorly thought out, and unconnected to the stated purposes of education" (p. 8). This is no doubt why many innovations have failed. Other innovations potentially of significant value and technically sound have also failed. One reason for these failures may be that supervisors have not helped teachers to integrate the innovations with their past experiences or adapt the innovations to their current teaching practice. Moreover, teachers often simply are not provided sufficient time to learn about and adapt the innovation before a new innovation is given precedence by administrators and supervisors.

Sternberg's (1985, 1990) work on the experiential component of adult intelligence indicates that novice teachers need to be supervised differently than experienced teachers. One example of this need for differentiation is that many beginning teachers have more difficulty assessing and responding to novel teaching situations and problems than their experienced colleagues, and thus are in need of more intensive support. Both Sternberg's (1985, 1990) and Gardner's (1983) research on multiple intelligences take us beyond differences between novice and experienced teachers and point to the need for identifying and utilizing different learning strengths of teachers at all levels of experience.

The need to individualize teacher learning indicated by the literature on adult learning stands in sharp contrast to the actual treatment of teachers. Many supervisors treat teachers as if they were all the same, rather than individuals in various stages of adult growth. In most schools, teachers receive the same in-service workshops, the same observations, and the same assessments. It is as if teachers were stamped out of teacher training institutes as identical and thereafter have no further need to be viewed as individual learners. The research on adults shows the lack of wisdom of such assumptions (Mathis, 1987).

Sternberg's (1985, 1990) discussion of socially influenced abilities points to the need for teachers to engage in learning aimed at developing a variety of strategies for adapting to or changing their classroom and school environment. Both Mezirow (1981, 1990) and Brookfield's (1986) work on adult learning indicate that in order to learn and grow, teachers need to participate in a continuous cycle of collaborative activity and reflection on that activity, and need to develop the powers of critical thinking. Finally, the writings of Knowles (1980, 1984), Mezirow (1981, 1990), and Brookfield (1986) have all supported the notion of the supervisor facilitating teacher growth toward empowerment and self-direction.

Unfortunately, most schools do not foster collaborative action, reflection, critical thinking, or teacher empowerment. Rather, the hierarchical structure of most school systems—as well as the environmental problems of isolation, psychological dilemma, and lack of a shared technical culture discussed in Chapter 2—tend to work against the type of growth described in the adult learning literature.

Adult and Teacher Development

Literature on adult development can be seen as reflecting several distinct but related approaches. Just a few decades ago, the study of human development focused on children, and adulthood was either not a consideration or was thought to represent a period of stability. Theory and research on adult development for several decades emphasized development as an orderly progression. Because much of the work in this area was done by developmental psychologists, there was an emphasis on the change processes occurring in the individual with relatively little consideration to his or her interaction with the environment. The two approaches to adult development prominent for years were rooted in such a tradition.

Stage development theories represent one track of this research (Belenky et al., 1986; Gilligan, 1982; Kohlberg and Turiel, 1971; Loevinger, 1976; Perry, 1970; Riegel, 1973). This approach is concerned with adults' orderly progression toward increasing maturity and complexity, and tends to focus on systematic internal changes in thinking and orientation as individuals mature. Other researchers have focused on age-linked changes or *life cycle development* (Buhler, 1956; Gould, 1978; Levinson, Darrow, Klein, Levinson, and McKee, 1978). Like stage theorists, those looking at life cycle development tend to speak in terms of universal patterns of movement through the life course.

Alternative views of adult development also evolved, with less concern for a universal progression and greater interest in the interaction between the individual and the social environment. Neugarten (1977) became intrigued with how the social environment contributes to a sense of whether people are "on time" or "off time" relative to when we experience certain events in our lives. She also noted (Neugarten and Neugarten, 1987) how increasingly flexible social norms have blurred the lines—with expectant mothers of age 40 taking childbirth classes with expectant mothers of age 20. Many researchers in this tradition have focused on critical life events (Baltes and Baltes 1980; Brim and Ryff, 1980) or *transition* events (Fiske and Chiriboga, 1990) and the role that either preparation for or resources for coping with such events plays in one's growth and development. Other research (Juhasz, 1989; Merriam and Clark; 1991) seems to take a new look at *social roles,* stressing not the ages at which we take them on but rather the active role we take in balancing the degree of energy and commitment we give to different role domains (e.g., family, work, self-development, etc.) as we progress through life, and how involvement in one role domain impacts positively or negatively on other domains (Swanson, 1992). Finally, research utilizing each of the four perspectives on adult development presented here has indicated that adult development is significantly influenced by *gender.*

Subsequent sections of this chapter will discuss adult development according to these five subtopics: (1) stage development, (2) life cycle development, (3) transition events, (4) role development, and (5) the influence of gender on adult development.

Stage Theories of Adult and Teacher Development

We will begin discussion of adult development by focusing on developmental stage theories. Levine (1989) delineated the characteristics of stages:

> First and foremost is their structural nature. Each stage is a "structured whole," representing an underlying organization of thought or understanding. Stages are qualitatively different from one another. All emerge in sequence without variation; no stage can be skipped. Finally stages are "hierarchically integrated"; that is, progressive stages are increasingly complex and subsume earlier stages. Individuals always have access to the stages through which they have passed. Under ordinary circumstances or with proper supports, people will generally prefer to use the highest stages of which they are capable. (p. 86)

It may be helpful to look more closely at several specific stage theories.

Cognitive Development.   Piaget described four stages of cognitive development: sensorimotor, preoperational, concrete operations, and formal operations (Ginsburg and Opper, 1979). The first two stages are more relevant to childhood learning. The concrete operations and formal operations stages are relevant to adults. At the concrete operations stage, the individual can perform intellectual functions, such as reversibility, conservation, and ordering. The person at the formal operations stage has already progressed beyond reasoning only for the "here and now" and can project into and relate time and space. The formal operations stage is a higher stage than the concrete operations stage. A person at the formal operations stage uses hypothetical reasoning, understands complex symbols, and formulates abstract concepts.

Some researchers have found that formal thought is not demonstrated by all adults. Others question the extent to which cultural bias in the traditional Piagetian tasks plays a role in differential findings, particularly in non-Western cultures (Neimark, 1987). There has been considerable exploration of characteristic adult forms of thinking that go beyond Piaget's fourth stage to a postformal operations stage (Arlin, 1975; Kitchener, Lynch, Fischer, & Wood, 1993; Merriam and Caffarella, 1991; Riegel, 1973), with some positing alternative cognitive frameworks to describe adult thought (Perry, 1970, 1981). Terms like *dialectical thought* (Riegel, 1973; Kramer, 1983), *integrative thought* (Kramer, 1987), and *epistemic cognition* (Taranto, 1987) have been used to describe the highest stage of cognition observed in adults. A related strand of research has examined the meaning of wisdom (Clayton and Birren, 1980; Holliday and Chandler, 1986) often seen as the hallmark of advanced adult thinking. Taranto (1987) and Neimark (1987) pointed out that in real life, unlike in the typical Piagetian assessment tasks, adults must focus on ill-defined problems without definitive answers. Neimark contended that such thinking is best assessed by giving adults problems without clear-cut answers on which to make judgments. Such a methodology more closely resembles the kind of thinking teachers are required to do in the classroom and school. Figure 4–1 represents the adult cognitive developmental continuum.

Teachers' cognitive development was explored by Ammon and associates in a study of a two-year graduate teacher education program with an emphasis on Piagetian theory (Ammon, 1984). This emphasis was intended to teach the adult preservice and in-service teachers about child development as well as to promote the teachers' own development. As the teachers studied Piagetian and related developmental theory, their conceptions of students, learning, and teaching changed. They progressed from simplistic to more complex, interactive explanations of student behaviors, development, and learning. These teachers also moved from a conception of teaching as "showing and telling" to creating a learning environment designed to foster the students' learning and development. The teachers' views on learning shifted from passive reception to active construction. They also came to think of their roles differently, as facilitating learning rather than imparting knowledge.

Conceptual Development. One developmental framework that is closely related to cognitive development and that has been studied significantly with teachers is that of conceptual development. Hunt and others defined *conceptual level (CL)* "in terms of (1) increasing conceptual complexity, as indicated by discrimination, differentiation, and integration and (2) increasing interpersonal maturity, as indicated by self-definition and self-other relations" (Hunt, Butler, Noy, and Rosser, 1978). Hunt placed individuals on a continuum from most concrete (lowest CL) to most abstract (highest CL).

Persons of *low CL* evaluate things in a simple, concrete fashion. They tend to view issues in "black and white." Individuals of low CL have difficulty defining a problem they are experiencing and respond to the same problem in a habitual manner despite the fact that the repeated response is not solving the problem. They need to be shown how to solve the problem. Persons of *moderate CL* are becoming more abstract in their thinking. They can define the problem and generate a limited number of possible solutions but have difficulty formulating a comprehensive plan. They still need some assistance in solving a complex problem. Persons of *high CL* are abstract thinkers. They are independent, self-actualizing, resourceful, flexible, and possess a high capacity of integration. Figure 4–2 represents the conceptual development continuum.

High-concept teachers have been found to differ from low-concept teachers in terms of both teaching approach and teacher-generated classroom atmosphere. High-concept teachers rate higher on what are generally considered to be more positive characteristics (such as warmth, perceptiveness, empathy, flexibility, ingenuity, task effectiveness, smoothness, and consistency) and low-concept teachers

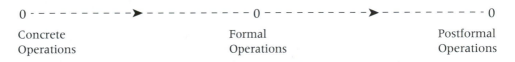

| Concrete Operations | Formal Operations | Postformal Operations |

FIGURE 4.1 ***Adult Cognitive Development Continuum***

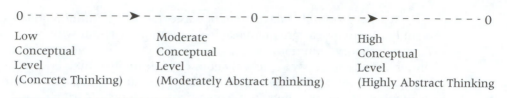

FIGURE 4.2   *Conceptual Development Continuum*

rate higher on more educationally negative characteristics (such as rule orientation, punitiveness, and anxiety) (Harvey, White, Prather, Alter and Hoffmeister, 1966; Heck and Davis, 1973). Harvey (1967) found high-concept teachers to have students with higher achievement, less nurturance, more cooperation, and more involvement in their work than low-concept teachers. Hunt and Joyce (1967) found correlations between teacher conceptual level and ability to use learners' needs as a basis for planning and evaluation. High-concept teachers used a greater range of learning environments and teaching methods. Murphy and Brown (1970) found that high-stage teachers could help students theorize and express, could ask precise questions, and could encourage exploration and group involvement significantly more effectively than low-stage teachers. Parkay (1979), in a study of inner-city high school teachers, found that high-concept teachers stimulated positive student attitudes and student achievement gains, and were less susceptible to professional stress. A study of 52 teachers by Calhoun (1985) found that teachers with high conceptual thought provided more corrective feedback to students, gave more praise, and were less negative and punitive. These teachers were more varied in their instructional strategies and were able to elicit more higher-order conceptual responses from their students than teachers of moderate and lower levels of conceptual thought. Thies-Sprinthall's study of teachers showed that as teachers acquired higher conceptual levels, their indirect teaching increased. Indirect teaching (the use of less lecture, more praise, and more acceptance of student ideas) has been positively associated with pupil achievement gain (Gage, 1978).

Moral Development.   Kohlberg and Armon (1984) identified three broad categories of morality: the preconventional level, the conventional level, and the postconventional level. They further delineated two stages of development within each of these levels, with the second stage more advanced and organized than the first. Across the three levels, reasoning shifts from a self-centered perspective to one that increasingly considers the perspectives and rights of others. The individual at Level I makes decisions from a self-centered orientation. At Level II, individuals "do the right thing" because that is what is expected according to social norms. Finally, at Level III, moral decisions serve to recognize the social contract and to uphold individual rights. Although conflicts between these principles and legal mandates are recognized as problematic in the lower stage of Level III, moral principles come to take precedence by the time an individual reaches the highest stage of moral development. Kohlberg sees the higher stages as superior, and he sees enhancing development as an appropriate aim for education. Figure 4–3 represents the moral development continuum.

It is important here to give mention to the work of Carol Gilligan (1979, 1982). Gilligan has compared conclusions from Kohlberg's model of moral development with conclusions from her own research with women discussing personal decisions. People at the top of Kohlberg's stages worry about interfering with others' rights, whereas those at the top of Gilligan's stages worry about errors of omission, such as not helping others when you could. At Gilligan's highest stage, morality is conceived in terms of relationships, and goodness is equated with helping others. Gilligan proposed that a different conception of development emerges from the study of women's lives:

> This conception of morality as fundamentally concerned with the capacity for understanding and care also develops through a structural progression of increasing differentiation and integration. This progression witnesses the shift from an egocentric through a societal to the universal moral perspective that Kohlberg described in his research on men, but it does so in different terms. The shift in women's judgement from an egocentric to a principled ethical understanding is articulated through their use of a distinct moral language, in which the terms "selfishness" and "responsibility" define the moral problem as one of care. Moral development then consists of the progressive reconstruction of this understanding toward a more adequate conception of care. (p. 442)

Several small-scale studies have investigated relationships between teachers' moral development and their understandings of teaching and learning. Lubomudrov (1982) found that teachers with lower scores on a test of moral reasoning viewed the teacher as the authority and paid little attention to student perspectives or intrinsic motivation. Teachers with higher moral development scores considered students' perspectives to be important, thought teachers should encourage students to express their feelings and perceived needs, and believed the teacher should foster cooperative student decision making. Johnston (1985) found that teachers scoring low on the same test of moral reasoning possessed a narrow conception of the on-task students (working quietly and individually on an assignment provided by the teacher). Teachers at Level II regarded a wider range of behavior and kinds of learning as on task and recognized that students who were quietly working on assignments were not necessarily learning. Teachers with the highest scores on moral reasoning considered students' perspectives and the complex, continuous nature of learning while resisting classifying students as on task or off task based solely on behavioral observation.

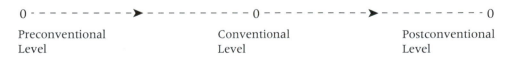

FIGURE 4.3 *Moral Development Continuum*

In a second study by Johnston (1989), teachers functioning at high levels of moral reasoning placed a higher value on individualized instruction, seeing it as a way to involve students in making decisions. They saw cooperative decision making as a way to incorporate students' needs and interests. Teachers at lower levels saw the curriculum as predetermined and their role as directive. To them, interests of groups rather than individuals were to be considered in selecting topics, and individualizing was viewed as a means to help individuals conform to expected group levels.

Ego Development.   Ego is both a process of striving for coherence and meaning in one's life, and a structure with its own internal logic (Levine, 1989). This is one of the few developmental theories derived from the study of women, but it has been applied subsequently to numerous samples of women and men. Loevinger (1976) has identified 10 stages of ego development that individuals can pass through. Orientations toward symbiotic, impulsive, and self-protective behaviors are manifest in the early stages. In these lower stages, a person depends on others for solutions to problems. In the middle stages of ego development, the individual exhibits conventional behaviors. At the higher stages, the adult becomes individualistic, autonomous, and integrated. The person at the highest stage of ego development is able to synthesize what seem to be unrelated or opposing concepts to individuals at lower stages (Witherell and Erickson, 1978). Adults at the beginning point on the continuum might be classified as *fearful.* Those at the midpoint on the continuum can be called *conforming.* Adults at the end of the continuum (those with the most mature egos) are referred to as autonomous. Figure 4–4 represents the ego development continuum.

Witherell and Erickson (1978) found in case studies of teachers that the teachers at higher levels of ego development were better able to analyze and explain teaching as a complex process, consider students' perspectives and emotional needs, and gather and use a variety of data in their teaching. Cummings and Murray (1989) found that teachers at different levels described different roles of a teacher, with those at lower levels of ego development focusing on the role of teacher as information disseminator and caregiver, and those at higher levels emphasizing the role of the teacher in helping students learn to learn. Based on their findings, they concluded that lower-level teachers may not have the resources to cope with the intricacies of the student-teacher relationships or deal with the complexity of the learning process. Levine (1989) suggested that higher levels of teacher ego development can be stimulated by providing experiences that require teachers to take the perspectives of different persons (including students) within the school. She recommended activities in which conflicts between school rules

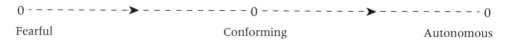

FIGURE 4.4   *Ego Development Continuum*

and individual rights are resolved and principles are formulated that recognize and reconcile the claims of both.

Levels of Consciousness. Robert Kegan (1994), a self-acknowledged neo-Piagetian, is a more recent entrant on the scene of adult developmental psychology. Concerned with how individuals come to see and interpret the world, he places little emphasis on the childhood stage he identifies as *magical* or *egocentric*. He pays greater attention to the adolescent and young adult stage that he refers to as *durable category;* the recognition that each person has a set of preferences and abilities that are enduring and that can be differentiated from other people and things. But it is those levels of consciousness he sees as associated with more mature adulthood in which he takes greatest interest.

As with the Piagetian shift from concrete to formal operations, the development of abstract thinking is a key characteristic of movement from the durable category level to to *cross-categorical consciousness.* The person functioning at the cross-categorical level is capable of thinking abstractly, reflecting on his or her own emotions, and being guided by beliefs and values which insure loyalty to the larger community. Only with the transition from cross-categorical to *systems consciousness,* however, does the individual move beyond defining himself or herself in terms of those duties, devotions, and values to become a truly independent and autonomous person. At this level we can look objectively at our own perspective, compare it with that of others, and work to reconcile differences. It is the systems level of consciousness which is said to be necessary to meet the various demands of modern adult life (parenting, partnering, working, continued learning), but Kegan contends many don't reach this stage until the their 30s or 40s, if at all. Finally, as is common with stage theories Kegan posits a level rarely achieved, *Trans-systems consciousness.* Dialectical thinking is associated with this level of consciousness, said to be rare before midlife.

Kegan also discusses the correspondence between adult levels of consciousness and adaptation to prevalent socio-cultural states. He postulates that those at the cross-categorical level are well prepared for the stability of traditional societies but may struggle with the demands of modern life, while those at the systems level are well-suited to the demands of modern life. The complexities and uncertainties of postmodern life, on the other hand, are thought to cause a challenge even to those adults, including most of us, who function at the systems level.

Kegan's model suggests our expectations may be high, both for ourselves and others. In the preface to his book "In Over Our Heads: the Mental Demands of Modern Life," he especially appeals to those who provide education, training, and supervision for other adults to be mindful of the mental demands we place on others. An example would be our expectation that teachers, even those recently graduated as traditional-age students, exhibit high levels of critical thinking and metacognitive skills, although he speculates these skills may not be fully evolved for many until their 30s and 40s. The emphasis Kegan places on continuing adult learning in the workplace as well as in other domains of adult life, along with his suggestion that teaching/coaching can stimulate developmental growth,

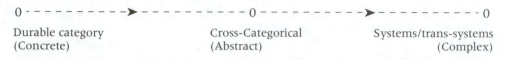

FIGURE 4.5   *Adult Consciousness Continuum*

makes this a promising model for future examination with practicing teachers. It also provides a framework that is consistent with the principles of developmental supervision. Figure 4.5 depicts the continuum of adult consciousness.

Stages of Concern.   In the 1960s and early 1970s, Frances Fuller (1969) conducted pioneer studies of teacher concerns. In analyzing both her own studies and six others, she found that the responses by hundreds of teachers at various stages of experience showed different concerns. Adams and others (Adams, Hutchinson, and Martray, 1980; Adams and Martray, 1981) have extended Fuller's initial work by additional investigations into stages of concern.

Teachers at the *self-adequacy* stage are focused on survival. They are concerned with doing well when a supervisor is present, getting favorable evaluations, and being accepted and respected by students and other teachers (Adams and Martray, 1981). Their primary concern is making it through the schoolday.

With survival and security assured, teachers think less of their own survival needs and begin to focus on *teaching tasks*. At this stage, teachers become more concerned with issues related to instructional and student discipline. They begin to think about altering or enriching the classroom schedule, the teaching materials, and their instructional methodology. Instructional concerns include the pressures of teaching, routinization and inflexibility of the teaching environment, student load, workload, and lack of academic freedom. Discipline concerns include class control, conflict between student and adult values and attitudes, and disruptive students (Adams and Martray, 1981). Concerns at this stage can be characterized as focused on the teaching environment and teaching responsibilities.

Superior teachers are at the highest stage of concern, referred to as the *teaching impact* stage. At this stage, teachers are most concerned with the impact on students' learning and students' well-being, even if it means departing from rules and norms. Academic concerns at this stage include diagnosing and meeting individual needs, sparking unmotivated students, and facilitating the intellectual and emotional development of students. The teacher with mature concerns also tends to be interested in the whole child, including interest in student health and nutrition, use of drugs by students, dropout prevention, and so on (Adams and Martray, 1981). The unfolding of teachers' concerns evolve on a continuum reflecting a shifting perspective, from "I" concerns to concerns for "my group" to concerns for "all students." Figure 4.6 represents the continuum of teacher concerns.

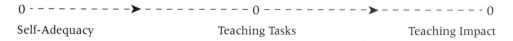

FIGURE 4.6   *Teacher Concerns Continuum*

Integrating Stage Development Theories.   Investigators of adult and teacher development have postulated that the various developmental characteristics are related (Oja and Pine, 1984; Sullivan, McCullough, and Stager, 1970). Although still somewhat speculative, these findings suggest that many teachers at a given level (low, moderate, or high) in one developmental characteristic may operate at the same general level in another developmental characteristic. The probable relationship of various developmental characteristics allows one to make tentative composite descriptions of teachers of generally low, moderate, and high levels of stage development. Figure 4.7 reviews the six adult/teacher development continuums.

The majority of teachers appear to be in relatively moderate to low stages of cognitive, conceptual, moral, and ego development—probably no different from the adult population at large (Oja and Pine, 1981; Rest, 1986; Wilkins, 1980). So what? What difference does it make that many teachers are not complex or autonomous? Perhaps one does not need higher-ordered thinking to teach. One could argue that if teaching is a simple enterprise with no need for decision making, then it would make little difference. In fact, if most teachers were autonomous and abstract, then trying to do a simple job would create great tension, resentment, and noncompliance. If teaching is a simple activity, schools need people who can reason simply. If teaching is complex and ever-changing, however, then higher levels of reasoning are necessary. A simple thinker in a dynamic and difficult enterprise would be subjected to overwhelming pressures.

Sociologists have documented the environmental demands posed by making thousands of decisions daily, by constant psychological pressure, and by expectations that the teacher must do the job alone—unwatched and unaided. A teacher daily faces up to 150 students of various backgrounds, abilities, and interests, some of whom succeed while others fail. Concrete, rigid thinking on the part of the teacher cannot possibly improve instruction. As Madeline Hunter (1986) has noted, "Teaching…is a relativistic situational profession where *there are no absolutes*" (italics in original). Researcher David Berliner (see Brandt 1986) has studied expert teachers and has reported, "We keep finding the behavior of these expert teachers unstable from day to day."

Teacher improvement can only come from abstract, multiinformational thought that can generate new responses toward new situations. Glassberg's (1979) review of research on teachers' stage development as related to instructional improvement concluded:

> In summary these studies suggest that high stage teachers tend to be adaptive in teaching style, flexible, and tolerant, and able to employ a wide range of teaching models…. effective teaching in almost any view is a most complex form of human behavior. Teachers at higher, more complex stages of human development appear as more effective in classrooms than their peers at lower stages.

The problem with the need for high-stage teachers is that, although the work by its nature demands autonomous and flexible thinking, teachers in most schools are not supported in ways to improve their thinking. The only alternative for a

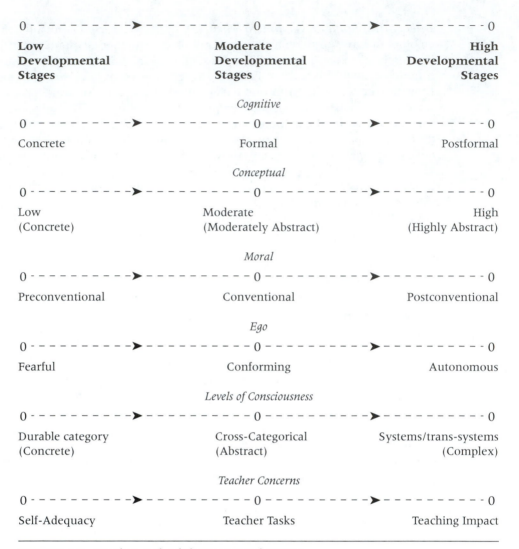

FIGURE 4.7 *Teacher and Adult Stage Development*

Source: Figures 4.1 through 4.5 and 4.7 are adapted from Stephen P. Gordon, *Assisting the Entry Year Teacher: A Leadership Resource.* Published 1990 by the Ohio Department of Education, Columbus, Ohio. Used with permission.

teacher in a complex environment who cannot adjust to multiple demands and is not being helped to acquire the abilities to think abstractly and autonomously is to *simplify and deaden the instructional environment.* Teachers make the environment less complex by disregarding differences among students and by establishing routines and instructional practices that remain the same day after day and year after year. Research on effective instruction (Berman and McLaughlin, 1978; O'Keefe and

Johnston, 1989; Porter and Brophy, 1988; Rutter et al., 1979) indicates that effective instruction is based on adaptation of curriculum and materials to local settings and particular learning goals. In other words, effective teachers think about what they are currently doing, assess the results of their practice, explore with each other new possibilities for teaching students, and are able to consider students' perspectives. Effective teaching has been misunderstood and misapplied as a set and sequence of certain teaching behaviors (review previous day's objectives, present objectives, explain, demonstrate, guided practice, check for understanding, etc.). This explanation of effectiveness is simply untrue, as can be seen in the prior references to Hunter (1986) and Berliner (quoted in Brandt, l986). Rather, successful teachers are thoughtful teachers (Porter and Brophy, 1988).

Evidence of the relationship between high-stage attainment of teacher development and effective instructional practice can be found in several research studies. The works of Thies-Sprinthall and Sprinthall (1987), Phillips and Glickman (1991), Oja and Pine (1981), and Parker (1983) are particularly important because they suggest that teachers, when provided with a stimulating and supportive environment, can reach higher stages of development, yet, other research indicates that most teachers do not reach those higher stages. Why, if optimal adult learning suggests a continued capability to learn, are teachers characterized by a lack of such cognitive growth?

One possible explanation is found in the nature of the work environment. Schooler (1989) found through a 10-year longitudinal study of 687 subjects that "occupational conditions that promote occupational self-direction or otherwise involved dealing with complex environments would increase intellectual flexibility, while conditions that limit occupational self-direction and environmental complexity would decrease intellectual flexibility" (p. 5). Indicators of environmental complexity (measured through detailed interviews about what people do when working with things, data, and people) included the degree of routinization on the job, the closeness of supervision, and the substantive complexity of work—the degree to which the work demands thought and independent judgment. Schooler concluded from this study, as well as others investigating working men and women, that jobs that limit self-direction actually decrease intellectual flexibility. Schooler's research is consistent with conclusions made by O'Keefe and Johnston (1989) after reviewing teacher stage development research: "Development is unlikely in environments that are repressive or restrictive. Dialogue, reflection, and challenge embedded in organizational and personal support systems are critical components of growth producing contests" (p. 24).

Sociologists have even suggested that, in some cases, problem-solving ability of teachers *decreases* over time. Phillip Jackson, in *Life in Classrooms* (1968), has noted the common pattern of nontechnical language and regulated responses among teachers. Judith Little, on the other hand, found that teachers in successful schools used precise, technical language in discussing instructional concerns (Little, 1982). Teachers in successful schools do continue to think and are challenged to extend the use of their mental abilities. If a supervisor could promote thinking among the school staff, school success might not be far behind. Thinking improves when people interact with each other, when they break routine by experimenting, when they observe others at work, and when they assess and revise their own actions. A cause beyond oneself becomes the norm, and the school becomes successful.

Teachers who are isolated in their classrooms, receive no systematic feedback, attend monthly faculty meetings only to listen to monologues of announcements, and spend a few minutes each day chatting idly in the lounge may be viewed as remarkable specimens of survival. Such teachers, however, are not contributors to a successful school.

Life Cycle Development, Teacher's Life Cycles, and the Teaching Career

The next area of adult development to be discussed is research on age-linked life cycle development. These theorists too have sought to define sequential and normative patterns of development. The pioneering theorists in this tradition tended to look at very broad age periods and the patterns or issues for resolution associated with them (Buhler, 1956; Erikson, 1950), whereas later theorists have tended to posit a greater number of specific age periods (Gould, 1978; Levinson et al., 1978).

The study by Daniel Levinson and his colleagues (1978) of 40 men aged from mid-30s to mid-40s is among the most frequently cited studies of life cycle development. This research described how individuals alternate through periods of stability and transition in a life structure whose critical components typically revolve on work and family. An occupational dream is said to be formed during young adulthood and nurtured, frequently with the assistance of the spouse and a mentor. Levinson's work is a coherent treatment of changes in a person's life but has limitations in that the subjects were all middle-class males from a limited set of occupations. A number of subsequent studies of women have substantiated the model in part, but differences have been found in the timing and quality of transitions and the ages associated with transitional periods among women (Roberts and Newton, 1987). Some of the variability among women is related to whether they have followed a more traditionally female orientation to family versus a more typically masculine orientation to career during early adulthood (Lieblich, 1986; Roberts and Newton, 1987).

Keeping in mind the variability in findings regarding women, Levinson's findings suggest some commonalities with other men and women in various occupations and might be particularly helpful in understanding the life transitions of teachers. The beginning years of adulthood are marked by active mastery of the outer world. As one approaches midlife, the issue of "making it" becomes important. One sees advancement to higher status and responsibility as important not only in itself but also as a sign of how high one might aspire. If promotion or advancement does not occur, the individual sees younger people move ahead while he or she remains on a plateau. With such an occurrence, the person can either accept the plateau, move to another organization within the same profession, or attempt to change careers. Becker (1971) has singled out a critical element in career success within the same organization and profession: Conforming to the social norms of the organization is imperative for career success. Advancing in a career is often tied to one's degree of assimilation to the conventions, standards, and rules of the organization. Levinson mentioned that a young adult has an advantage in an organization if he or she finds a mentor. A senior executive or other established person takes the young adult under his or her wing and cautions, advises, and protects. Through the mentor, the young adult learns how to behave for later success.

Young adulthood is often a time of feelings of omnipotence, when all one's dreams seem attainable. Middle adulthood is ushered in by a loss of such feelings of omnipotence, with the realization of one's limitations. It occasions a period of reexamination of self and a revision of plans. The mentor relationship becomes less important as the young adult continues to move toward his or her goals and the middle-aged mentor no longer appears so exalted or wise. On the one hand, the middle-aged adult becomes more autonomous in deciding his or her priorities; on the other hand, he or she confronts the limits to what he or she can ultimately hope to accomplish. This dilemma often results in so-called midlife crisis—a groping to find a consistent meaning to one's life. In older age, people accept their life and affiliations and focus on concluding important activities.

Occupational development of teachers appears to run counter to the needs of teachers as they progress through the adult life cycle. The work of Levinson (1977) and Neugarten (1977) has pointed to early adulthood as a period of bravado, romance, and the pursuit of dreams. The young adult aged 20 to 35 is on an exciting search for status, comfort, and happiness in work, family, and friends. The middle years, ages 35 to 55, provide some disillusionment, reflection, and reordering of priorities according to a reassessment of one's capabilities and opportunities. In teaching, however, the young adulthood period, which should be one of romance, quickly becomes one of disillusionment. The young person of age 24 or 25 who has entered teaching to pursue his or her dreams often finds after three years that work life is going nowhere. The job does not excite; the advancements do not exist; and the variety of work is nonexistent. The result can be intense boredom, leading to resignation—either *from* the job or *on* the job. What does it mean to education when a young teacher's natural inclination toward excitement and idealism is bound by a straitjacket of repetition?

Let's ask the next question. What happens when the natural inclination of the middle-aged teacher to reflect and reorder his or her teaching priorities confronts the same six periods of 30 students that he or she has faced for the past 20 years? One might expect a further despair of any impulse to change and to improve. Finally, what about the older teacher who is perceived by many as an anomaly, a relic who has remained in teaching because of inability to advance into administration or supervision. The acquisition of 30 years of experience coincides with the natural time for consolidating achievements and identifying one's remaining career objectives. Instead, there is only the same job—the same job as that of the new teacher down the hall, who might be the age of the older teacher's grandchild. Where is the sense of responsibility, generativity, and accomplishment in seniority? Old and new teachers are treated the same, accorded the same status, and expected to conform to the same routines.

Teaching appears to be a topsy-turvy occupation, running against the natural adult life cycle. Those who continue to make lasting improvement and enhance their students' educational lives should have our utmost respect. If not fortunate enough to be in a school that responds to and supports phases of the adult life cycle, the effective teacher truly transcends the system and educates in spite of, not because of, the school.

A small but growing body of literature focuses on the links between teacher development and issues related to the adult lifespan. Gehrke (1991) argued that we should more fully incorporate our understanding of adult development in developing programs for new teachers. This means both fostering the generative motivations of mature teachers and being sensitive to the fact that many young teachers are dealing with needs for intimacy.

Acknowledging what we know about adults as active agents in their own socialization, Gehrke's ideal school replaces the experience of isolation reported by many teachers with a "helping community." In this helping community, new teachers play an active role in selecting their own mentors, and natural helpers in the environment are encouraged to provide assistance as it is individually needed. Levine (1987) argued that profitable activities that capitalize on young teachers' enthusiasm might include opportunities to work on new teaching methods, to develop curricula, and to initiate projects. The key is nurturing their need for innovation and adventure and helping them establish and cultivate close collegial relationships that meet their needs for intimacy.

Midlife teachers who have spent their careers engaged in nurturing children may want to focus on nurturing other teachers or pursuing needs for personal growth and achievement at midlife. Levine (1987) encouraged placing midlife teachers in situations permitting "a combination of teaching and administrative responsibilities that expands an adult's authority and mobility without sacrificing his or her expertise with children" (p. 16). Work on decision-making committees and mentorship of younger colleagues can provide such an outlet. Krupp (1987) also pointed out that there may be gender differences in the kind of experiences needed, rooted in the frequently observed midlife shift on male-female polarities (women in traditional roles becoming more achievement oriented, men becoming more oriented toward relationships and nurturing).

Krupp (1987) argued that lack of career centrality and on-the-job retirement can be countered by bringing the older adults' interests into the school. For instance, older teachers' interests in computers, photography, and gardening can be brought into the curriculum or extracurricular programs for students. Levine (1987) also suggested that appropriate professional development for older adults may include workshops on financial planning, health care, and retirement. In this way, the shift toward greater concern with personal and family issues observed in many older adults (Krupp, 1987; Mathis, 1987) can be accommodated, and motivation for career role can be maintained.

Transition Events

A third approach to adult development focuses more explicitly on the kinds of events associated with life transitions. Some theorists resist accepting the study of what are variably called *life events, critical events,* or *marker events* as part of the rubric of adult development because such a focus does not attempt to describe a universal, orderly sequence of development. However, Fiske and Chiriboga (1990) noted that just as the assumption of adult stability has given way to models of adult development "as a progression of orderly transformations over time," more recent models emphasize the role of transition events in our lives.

Life events have been typologized in a variety of ways. One typology, offered by Willis and Baltes (1980), seems to relate directly to the salience of the event for the individual. They talk about *normative age-graded events*—events that occur in many people's lives and that are anticipated around certain ages (such as marriage, birth of first child, and widowhood), *normative history-graded events*—those that affect large numbers of people in a given age cohort simultaneously (such as World War II and the Depression), and *nonnormative events*—those personal events that are not anticipated as part of the life course even though they may occur for many (such as divorce, unemployment, and unexpected illness). Events can be positive or negative, anticipated or unanticipated. Although events associated with expected transitions in adult lives are often the impetus for adult growth (Aslanian and Brickell, 1981), it appears to be the unanticipated event, even if negative, that may provide the greatest opportunity for change and growth (Fiske and Chiriboga, 1990; Krupp, 1982).

Fiske and Chiriboga (1990) conducted an interdisciplinary study of 216 men and women sampled according to impending life transitions rather than age: (1) high school seniors entering adult life, (2) newlyweds potentially contemplating a first child, (3) parents about to experience the "empty nest," and (4) individuals likely to retire within the next few years. For those interested in the growth of adults in schools, the following conclusion from their study may be most noteworthy. "As we found in developing our stress typology, however, stressors need not always lead to pathology and decline and may in fact signal the beginning of a period of major growth. More important than the stressors may be the resources the person brings to the problem, the way he or she views the problem, and the social context" (p. 167).

Neugarten studied the timing of events such as childbearing, occupational advancement and peaking, children leaving home, retirement, personal illness, and death of a spouse or close friend. Many of these events are common to all or most adults; the time of their occurrence, according to Neugarten, influences how the person responds and continues with life. For example, the Blum and Meyer (1981) study of the recovery of adult men from severe heart attacks highlighted the difference in timing of critical events. Young men were bitter and hostile toward their heart attack and couldn't wait to resume their previous lives. Middle-aged men were reflective about the heart attack and seriously weighed whether they wanted to continue to live as they had before. They contemplated changes in family relations, job, and living environments. Older men were accepting and grateful that the heart attack had left them alive with the opportunity to finish some of their desired retirement plans. As one can see, the same event—a heart attack—resulted in quite different reactions, depending on the time and age of the adult.

Neugarten's interpretation of these differential responses relates to the experience of the events as "on time" versus "off time"—that is, occurring at an age considered socially appropriate or not. For example, becoming a widow at age 25 would be an off-time event, whereas getting married at that age would be considered an on-time event. Yet even in 1987, Neugarten and Neugarten acknowledged the increasing variability with regard to when certain events are experienced in society, blurring the social norms about what is "on time." Certainly the '90s have seen increasing variability in the timing of many common events.

Both personal transition events (marriage, birth of a child, divorce, death of a loved one) and professional transition events (entry into the profession, tenure, transferring schools, becoming a lead teacher or department chairperson) can have a significant impact on a teacher's career and teaching. Traditionally, personal and transitional events have been ignored and professional transitions have been given pro forma recognition by the school organization. Krupp (1987) has suggested that staff development programs providing an environment of trust and collegiality, as well as adult transition support networks within schools, can be an important means of assisting teachers as they prepare for anticipated change events, such as retirement, or cope with unanticipated changes, such as the sudden dependency of a parent. The support networks and professional development recommended by Krupp to assist teachers have been largely nonexistent in schools.

One exception in recent years has been the emergence of beginning teacher assistance programs, including the assignment of support teams and mentors to novice teachers. Hopefully, beginners' assistance programs will become the foundation on which career-long support for personal and professional transitions becomes available. Beyond formal support programs, schools need to become the type of collegial, caring, growth-oriented communities that sustain teachers in time of transition.

Role Development

The most recent direction in work on adult development has emphasized adult social roles, generally examining how adult lives are characterized by interacting roles related to work or career, family life, and personal development. Juhasz (1989) has developed a model of adult roles that incorporates each of three major roles: family, work, and self. These roles are depicted as intertwining, sometimes in synchrony, sometimes with different momentum and force. "This conceptualization of adult development processes accommodates a wide range of possible patterns and varied timing of life events relative to career options, family and relationship choices, and emphasis on self-development" (p. 301). This model emphasizes the active involvement of adults who take roles and choose which roles they will place emphasis on at given points in their lives, with self-esteem as the driving force "directing energies toward roles that will best enhance feelings of worth" (p. 307).

Merriam and Clark (1991, 1993) designed a questionnaire to study the relationship between life events in the domains of "work and love" (here broadly defined as in the instrumental and expressive components of life) and adult learning. In essence, people graphed their life patterns, using two separate lines to show the ups and downs in these two domains of life. Respondents were asked next to list major events occurring in the last 20 years of their adult life (age 18 or older) and to describe connected learning experiences. From their analysis of 405 respondents, they found evidence for three different models used to characterize linkages between work and family life: (1) segmentation—when there is little or no connection, (2) compensatory—where individuals seek in one area the satisfaction or activities that are lacking in the other, and (3) generalization—where attitudes formed in the work setting spill over into family life or vice versa.

More significant for our purposes was the predominance of work-related learning for both men and women and the evidence that more learning occurs when things are going well in both arenas (work and family life). However, learning that led to a real perspective transformation most often was associated with coping with the difficult times in either work (e.g., being fired) or family life (e.g., losing a parent). Since much of the most significant adult learning appears to be from life experience, the role of the supervisor may be critical in helping teachers to experience growth as an outcome of unsettling life experiences in the professional, personal, or family domains. Although the supervisor need not and should not assume the role of therapist, one implication of the social roles models of adult development is that a teacher's personal, family, and professional roles interact with and affect each other, and need to be addressed holistically by supervision.

School systems and supervisors traditionally have been concerned only with teachers' professional roles, ignoring their personal and family roles. The few efforts intended to address the relationship of the three domains have been criticized as being beyond the scope of supervision, an inappropriate use of school resources, and superfluous to the improvement of teaching and learning. Yet, the literature on adult role development tells us that we cannot compartmentalize the personal, family, and professional aspects of a teacher's life. Put succinctly, teachers' other adult roles have direct effect on their instruction. Supervision, however, has largely failed to provide teachers with support to help them understand the interaction of their various adult roles, cope with role conflict and resulting stress, or develop the proper balance and synergy among alternative roles.

The Role of Gender in Adult Development

Selected models of adult development have been included here to provide an overview of the literature on adult development for the reader. Yet, it is important to note that adult development literature in general, and several of the models presented here in particular, have been criticized for a tendency to make universal claims while being derived largely from the study of White, Western males. During the 80s and 90s a significant body of literature emerged examining the impact of gender on adult development. Much of this literature has looked specifically at women, in response to the initial claim that their lives and experiences were not accounted for in early development of adult development theory. Emerging theory and research have taken two forms, in some cases extending or adapting earlier work based primarily on men, and in other cases starting afresh with female or mixed gender samples. In the first strand is the work of Gilligan (1982), challenging Kohlberg's model of moral development (Kohlberg & Turiel, 1971). Her work suggested men and women base their moral decisions on different criteria, with women using an ethic of caring and men an ethic of justice. Similarly Joselson (1987) reexamined Erikson's stage theory of psychosocial development, postulating four potential outcomes of Erikson's identity stage for women. Primary among her findings was that maintaining a sense of connectedness and affiliation with others was crucial for women. Representing the second strand of research, based specifically on the original study of women's lives, is the work of Peck (1986). She theorized women's lives as consisting of three contiguous layers, including an outermost core of socio-historical context; a flexible, bi-directional "sphere of influence", consisting of the sum of multiple relationships; and, finally, a center core of self-definition. These spheres are presumed to be constantly interacting as women move through their lives. Caffarella and Olson (1993) summarized the research on women's development in terms of four themes: the centrality of relationships, the importance and interplay of social roles, the dominance of role discontinuities and change as the norm for women, and the diversity of experience across age cohorts. Given the predominance of women in the teaching workforce, it seems important that supervisors become familiar with those models of adult development that reveal the distinctive developmental concerns women may bring.

More recently, models of adult development based on both men's and women's lives have been critiqued for their universalizing character, tending to ignore or discount diversity among men and women, with individuals of each gender often exhibiting patterns described as typical of the opposite sex. For example, Anderson and Hayes (1996) found that men and women value achievement as well as relationships, derive self-esteem from similar sources, and struggle with ongoing issues of holding on (connection) and letting go (separation). The tendency of these models to ignore diversity related to race, class, and culture has also been criticized. Harris (1995) examined how men from different subcultures viewed each of 24 cultural messages about masculinity, and described differences related to class, race, sexual orientation, and community of origin (city, urban, rural). This literature may help understand why some men are more willing to break mainstream cultural norms that discourage their entry into the elementary education teaching force.

Both research on women's development and gender-related research moving beyond universal portrayals of either men or women have challenged our thinking about the degree to which any single theory of adult development can adequately describe all adult lives. Yet, these models can still provide a useful heuristic for thinking about the many ways in which adults continue to change throughout the course of their lives and the myriad forces which come to influence these changes. For those who seek to provide assistance to teachers, familiarity with this literature serves as a reminder of the tremendous degree of difference that exists among the adult learners who constitute the teaching force.

Review of Adult/Teacher Development Models

Table 4–1 presents a schematic review of the four conceptual frameworks for adult development. One thing all four approaches have in common is the supposition that adult lives are characterized by change and adaptation. For teachers, as with all adult learners, the one thing we can be certain of is that things will not remain the same; thus, individuals will need to cope with changes as they arise. Supervision provides the opportunity for ascertaining the levels, stages, and issues of adult development in schools and assisting the teacher's professional development in the context of these realities.

Developmental Theories of Motivation and Teacher Development

Teacher development can be seen in relation to human needs. Abraham Maslow developed a classical framework for understanding human motivation (Maslow, 1954). Maslow's premise was that there exists a hierarchy of needs that motivate humans to act, in the following order:

TABLE 4.1 *Conceptual Models of Adult Development*

Universal, Orderly, Sequential		Interactive, Socially Contexted	
Hierarchical Stages	*Life Cycle Phases*	*Transition Events*	*Role Development*
Cognitive	*Goal Phases*	*Critical Events*	*Family, Work, and Self*
Piaget, Perry, Belenky et al.	Buhler	Brim and Ryff	Juhasz
Moral	*Critical Issues*	*Stressful Events*	*Love, Work, and Learning*
Gilligan, Kohlberg	Erikson	Fiske et al.	Merriam and Clark
Conceptual	*Stability vs. Transition*	*On Time/Off Time*	
Hunt	Levinson	Neugarten	
Ego			
Loevinger			
Levels of Consciousness			
Kegan			
Concern			
Fuller			

- *Physiological needs:* The initial motivation for humans is to satisfy biological demands for food, oxygen, water, sleep, and exercise. Unless these needs are satisfied, a human is motivated by nothing else. For example, a person who is starving is not interested in security, money, or companionship; he or she will exert all his or her energy to find food. The same is true of any unmet physiological need.
- *Safety:* After physiological needs are satisfied, the individual is motivated to attend to the niceties of human life. He or she seeks a comfortable, regulated environment. Security, stability, dependency, and rules all eliminate anxiety and fear of the unknown. An individual is motivated to seek a shelter in a familiar location with a secure source of income.
- *Belonging and love:* After safety needs are satisfied and the individual has established a home in the broadest sense, he or she begins to seek involvement with others as a group member and as a partner. The person desires affectionate relationships with friends and acceptance as a member of a group—signified by affiliations in informal and formal clubs, associations, and teams. His or her identity becomes merged with other people in religious, social, civic, and/or informal groups.
- *Esteem:* Once needs for belonging and love have been satisfied, the individual's motivation changes from gaining acceptance within a group to becoming a contributing and leading member of the group. It is no longer adequate to be one of the gang; the person wants to be an admired and visible member. The individual takes a role of initiating actions, assuming leadership, and helping others so that they will see him or her as important. The attainment of status and prestige affirms his or her competence and value to the group.
- *Self-actualization:* The culminating human need comes after the acquisition of self-esteem and confidence in one's ability to be successful in the eyes of others. Motivation in the previous stage was based on being liked and admired by others. Now the motivation becomes to act and achieve according to one's own standards. The individual follows what he or she believes is best, regardless of what others might think. Being true to one's own inclinations becomes the mark of self-actualization or, as Maslow defined it, "What a man *can* be, he *must* be" (1954, p. 46). In strikingly similar terms, Belenky, Clinchy, Goldberger, and Tarule (1986, p. 137) defined woman's self-actualization as finding a voice of one's own.

Let's put the theory of human motivation into common language. An individual who is hungry is likely to be more concerned about his or her next meal than with shelter. A person who is no longer hungry begins to think about a roof to keep out the rain and four walls to ward off the cold. The person desires order and regulation in life. Once secure in his or her environment, the person cares about belonging and participating with others. After affiliating and becoming comfortable as a member of a group, he or she then desires to be regarded as an important member of the group. Finally, with confidence in the regard of others, the individual turns inward to what he or she wishes to become.

Human motivation is developmental. The needs of a lower stage must be satisfied before a person is motivated by needs of the next higher stage. The stages are hierarchical. Each person moves through them in the same sequence, from physiological needs to safety needs, to belonging and love needs, to esteem needs, to self-actualization needs. The rate of passage varies from individual to individual. Finally, retreat can occur when the individual's situation is dramatically altered. For example, a person might have acquired self-esteem in her present job, but when she is hired to fill a new position, she may suddenly be groping for safety, routine, and security in the work environment. Initially, she is concerned with how to get a parking permit, how to fill out voucher forms, and where to apply for medical insurance. The furthest thought from her mind is leading the group or being self-actualized. All she wants to know is where her territory is, what the rules are, and what she is expected to do.

This retreat and recapitulation of needs is exactly what happens with many beginning teachers. It is not necessarily that a beginning teacher has been in an egocentric self-survival stage all of his or her life. Any person thrown into a new environment, regardless of his or her previous functioning, will go through a transition period of floundering and feeling insecure before feeling safe and ready to contribute to the world outside the self.

Herzberg's 30 years of research on human motivation supports Maslow's hierarchy of needs (Herzberg, 1987). Herzberg, Mausner, and Snyderman (1959), in their study of engineers and accountants, were originally concerned with what business and service employees perceived as positive (or "satisfiers") and negative (or "dissatisfiers") about their jobs. To Herzberg's surprise, satisfiers and dissatisfiers were quite distinct from each other. Negative factors or dissatisfiers most often cited were:

- Organizational policy and administration
- Technical supervision
- Salary
- Working conditions
- Status
- Job security
- Effects on personal life
- Interpersonal relations

On the other hand, positive incidents most cited were:

- Work itself
- Achievement
- Possibility of growth
- Responsibility
- Advancement

Herzberg found that elimination of dissatisfiers did not improve an individual's performance. Dissatisfiers were maintenance or hygiene factors. In other words, if a person's major dissatisfaction with his job is poor working conditions (poor lighting or inadequate facilities), it will remain a source of irritation and might make him work less hard but, if corrected, will not make him work harder.

If the lighting is fixed, he will no longer be dissatisfied, but it will not increase his productivity. Rather, the individual will accept the correction as the way it should have been in the first place.

The positive factors that Herzberg called satisfiers did motivate individuals to work harder. When an employee found the work itself exciting, when she had a sense of achievement, when she saw future growth in her career, when she was given responsibility or advancement—then she improved performance. If a teacher is given increased responsibility for making decisions about materials to use in his classroom and is encouraged to modify his teaching lessons to add more topics or projects that he believes to be exciting and valuable, then he will tend to put more time and energy into changing and improving his performance. In other words, if a teacher is given increased responsibility to make decisions, he will work harder to see that he succeeds. Herzberg, therefore, cited satisfiers as the key motivators to improving work performance.

Since these original studies, there have been replications of Herzberg's research in other businesses (Herzberg, 1966; King, 1970; Hoy and Miskel, 1982) and in education (Sergiovanni, 1966; Schmidt, 1976). Studies that have used Herzberg's research methodology have found the same distinctions between negative (or hygiene) and positive (or motivating) factors. For example, a study by Sergiovanni (1966) consisted of interviews of teachers. He found the same loadings of factors as Herzberg except that work itself and advancement were less often cited by teachers as motivators. This was probably attributable to the nature of the teaching career, which offered little change in the work itself and almost no possibility of advancement (Lortie, 1975).

Cawelti (1976) and Drucker (1973) have pointed out the link between Maslow's theory of motivation and Herzberg's research on hygiene and motivators. We might view this relationship by placing Herzberg's factors side by side with Maslow's stages (see Figure 4–8).

Without forcing a perfect one-to-one correspondence, it is apparent that Herzberg's hygiene factors, which maintain performance, correspond to Maslow's lower-level needs—physiological, safety, and love and belonging. This interaction between hygiene and lower-level needs characterizes the teacher's working to find his or her niche. The individual is learning to perform in an acceptable manner that is officially sanctioned by his or her peers, technical supervisors (evaluators), and the formal organization.

Herzberg's motivation factors likewise correspond with Maslow's higher stages. This interaction between motivation and higher-level needs defines an area in which the teacher is "going beyond competence." The individual knows performance is acceptable and now strives for excellence. Notice the small overlapping area in Figure 4–7 (between "going beyond competence" and "finding one's niche") called "choice." This is the critical area in which a teacher can choose either to remain minimally competent or to grow in new ways. The choice becomes available when hygiene factors and lower-stage needs have been met and when there is encouragement to go beyond competence by providing a sense of achievement, responsibility, recognition, and advancement so that teachers can choose to improve their instruction.

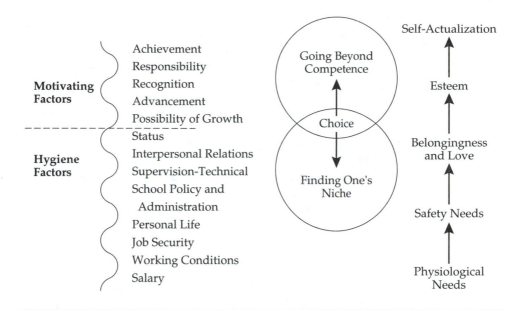

FIGURE 4.8 *Interacting Areas of Herzberg's Factors with Maslow's Stages*

Sources: F. Herzberg, B. Mausner, and B. Snyderman, *The Motivation to Work* (New York: Wiley, 1959); and A. H. Maslow, *Motivation and Personality* (New York: Harper & Row, 1954).

The motivational models of Maslow and Herzberg indicate the need for the functions of educational administration and supervision to combine to facilitate teacher development. The administrative function of a school should provide for Maslow's lower-level needs and Herzberg's hygiene factors that enable teachers to reach the plateau from which supervision for improvement of instruction can proceed. The supervisory function should provide for Maslow's higher stages and Herzberg's motivating factors.

Conventional schools—which foster hierarchy, dependency, isolation, and mistrust—fail to provide for lower *or* higher motivational factors. Congenial schools—which provide for friendly social interaction but not for professional dialogue, responsibility, and improvement—fail to provide the stimulation necessary for professional growth and self-actualization. Collegial schools provide the trust, support, professional interaction, choice, and challenge necessary to meet both lower- and higher-order human needs and to develop internal motivation based on a cause beyond oneself.

Development: Ebb and Flow

Cognitive researchers have shown that stages of thinking vary according to the domain or topic (Gardner, 1983; Case, 1986; Sternberg, 1988). The same can be said for motivation.

Perhaps a few examples will establish the point. Recently, an outstanding science teacher of advanced physics (a winner of state and national awards) was asked to teach an introductory biology class. Her level of thinking about physics was at a generative, flexible, and abstract stage, yet her thinking about general biology was, at least at the beginning of the year, at a concrete, imitative stage of needing to follow the teacher manual. Her motivation to succeed in both classes may have been equally high, but her operational level of thinking was quite different. The same can be seen in the case of a teacher who has a high level of abstract thinking about the subject matter he or she teaches and a lower level of abstraction about the method of teaching (or vice-versa).

Motivation has the same variation for an individual. Fred loves to teach art to his second-grade youngsters. He's constantly looking for ideas, finding materials, and expending energy to improve his art program. Yet when it comes to teaching mathematics, he puts in the required time, uses the worksheets, and muddles through the material. He never liked mathematics as a student and doesn't care to spend extra time on it. (The same variation can be seen in anyone's level of motivation when it comes to fixing a special meal versus cleaning the pots and pans afterwards.) Suffice it to say that teachers, like all humans, are not static in their levels of thinking and motivation about all endeavors.

Furthermore, development can regress, recycle, or become blocked. Because one has reached a high level of development in one arena does not mean that level of development is consolidated eternally. *Experience* is a relative term—a teacher (or supervisor) with 30 years of teaching (or supervising) can still be inexperienced in many ways. Change the expectations of the jobs and/or change the clientele served, and suddenly there is an inexperienced person trying to figure out how to survive. Likewise, a first-year teacher may, after only a few months, be experienced and able to reason according to concerns beyond his or her own survival.

Alterations to a person's personal or professional situation can usher in regression in levels of thinking and levels of motivation. A highly committed and thoughtful faculty, who had made their school an exciting and successful place, was jolted when negotiations between the teachers' union and the school board resulted in a bitter strike. The immediate result on the school was that teachers retreated within their four walls, carrying out the letter of their contract and removing themselves from involvement in school curriculum and instruction issues. Most teachers retreated to a self-survival stage.

Teacher or adult development is not monolithic, linear, or eternal. The research on developmental stages provides lenses for viewing teachers individually and collectively as to their current levels of thinking and motivation about instructional improvement. Through such lenses, we can explore possible interventions to assist teachers individually and collectively to move into higher stages of development.

Influences on Teacher Development

One theme of this book is that teacher development is crucial for deciding approaches and skills to help teachers become more abstract and altruistic. The ideal teacher is committed to the needs of all students and has the cognitive skills to improve his or her own instruction. In helping teachers grow, supervisors must consider characteristics of the teacher as a client. For example, one would not work with a highly abstract teacher in the same way as with a concrete and rigid teacher. Nor would one work the same way with a teacher who is highly motivated about one aspect of teaching and indifferent about another aspect. The approaches and skills used in direct assistance, professional development, curriculum development, group development, and action research will differ according to the level of motivation and level of thought of teachers. A supervisor must be able to choose those skills and techniques that will enable teachers to develop individually and collectively to create a cause beyond oneself. A commitment to that cause is essential for school success.

This chapter has been intentionally theoretical and research based. It provides the basis for choosing supervisory skills and strategies for working with individuals or groups of teachers. We can view teacher development against the background of adult learning, development, and motivation; influences on the work environment of the school; and characteristics of the teaching profession. The context of teacher development is illustrated in Figure 4–9. Imagine a large felt board representing the context of a teacher's life. At the center is the individual with his or her unique development embedded into the work environment of the school, which is in turn embedded into characteristics of the teaching profession. When viewing a teacher's growth (or lack of growth), we must consider both the characteristics of the individual and the influences of the work environment and the teaching profession.

For example, a teacher may be resistant because of previous negative experiences within the work environment of the school. Perhaps at one time the teacher was concerned with improving her class and used abstract thought to implement a new classroom design. Perhaps other teachers or a supervisor frowned on such experimentation and threatened the teacher with the loss of her job. This teacher, needing to keep the job for financial reasons, therefore gave up trying to change. She retreated from improvement because of adverse pressure. This teacher might now be resistant, but she still has the ability to improve. Improvement will not occur, however, until changes occur in her immediate work environment.

Another example might be a willing teacher who has found a satisfactory maintenance level of group instruction and can live comfortably with the school norms. The reasons he does not demonstrate further improvement might be traced to characteristics of the teaching profession. The teacher may see no future prospects for increased status, income, or responsibility. Without any prospects for career advancement, he may rationally decide to remain adequate but nothing more. The supervisor must develop ways to provide advancement, recognition, and/or status in this teacher's career in order to realize further growth.

The point is that characteristics of the individual teacher may not be fixed, but rather function as a part of the teacher's perceptions of the larger environment. Research on adults has demonstrated that teachers can become more motivated and more thoughtful about their work. Every person has the potential to improve: *Such potential might be blocked, slowed down, or even reversed, but it still exists.*

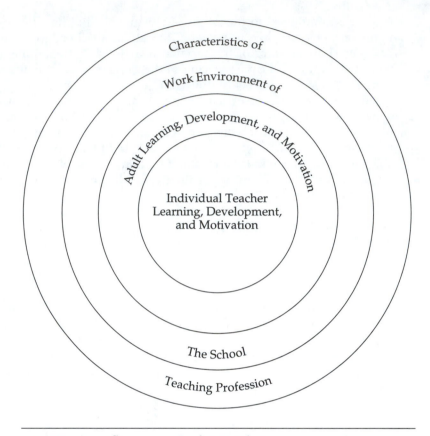

FIGURE 4.9 *Influences on Teacher Development*

The challenge for the supervisor is to treat teachers as individual adult learners to enable them to use their potential.

Propositions

This chapter has contrasted the research on adult learning, development, and motivation with actual teacher development. It has demonstrated that the work environment of most schools and traditional supervision tend to hinder rather than promote teacher growth. On the other hand, the text has shown that if teachers are provided with an appropriate environment and effective supervision, they can attain high levels of personal and professional development. Propositions that emerge from contrasting actual and optimal teacher development are as follows:

- Proposition 1: *Effective supervision responds to the principles of adult learning.* Teachers' learning should be related to their experiences, needs, and learning strengths; should include opportunities for collaborative action, reflection, and critical thinking; and should be directed toward teacher empowerment.

• Proposition 2: *Effective supervision responds to and fosters teachers' stage development.* Teachers function at different stages of cognitive, conceptual, moral, and ego development and at different stages of consciousness and concern. Teachers should not be treated as a homogeneous group. Rather, supervision should be matched to teachers' developmental stages. Supervision also should foster teacher growth toward higher stages of development.

• Proposition 3: *Effective supervision recognizes and supports different phases within teachers' life cycles.* Effective supervision responds to young teachers' excitement and idealism, helps middle-aged teachers cope with life reassessment and reprioritizing, and provides opportunities for older teachers to consolidate achievements and identify remaining career objectives.

• Proposition 4: *Effective supervision helps teachers to understand, navigate, and learn from life transition events.* Effective supervision provides special support and rewards for transitions from preservice to in-service teaching, probationary to tenured status, regular teaching duties to teacher leadership responsibilities, and employment to retirement.

• Proposition 5: *Effective supervision recognizes and accommodates teachers' various roles.* Effective supervision helps teachers to recognize the relationship of personal and family roles to their professional roles and to balance competing demands of all three roles.

• Proposition 6: *Effective administration and supervision foster teacher motivation.* Effective administration provides for Maslow's lower-level needs and Herzberg's hygiene factors. Effective supervision provides for Herzberg's motivating factors and Maslow's higher-stage needs, gradually increases teacher choice and decision making, and facilitates teachers' self-actualization.

These six propositions provide the general developmental *principles of action* that will serve as the core of supervisory thought and practice. The supervisory goal is to improve classroom and school instruction by enabling teachers to become more adaptive, more thoughtful, and more cohesive in their work. In the next chapter on prerequisite knowledge for developmental supervision, a supervisor's present platform of practice will be examined to determine its fit in the developmental framework.

Exercises

Academic

1. Review the theories of a major author on adult development, as found in the list of references that follows these exercises. Write a paper summarizing the author's theories and any research on which those theories are based.

2. Review the research of a prominent investigator of teacher development. Write a paper summarizing the major conclusions that researcher has drawn from his or her studies.

3. Review literature and/or research on adult learning. On the basis of your review, discuss in writing several generally accepted principles of adult learning. For each principle, infer and discuss implications for supervision.

4. Write an essay comparing Maslow's four highest human need categories to your own development within a work or social organization. Evaluate Maslow's theory of motivation in terms of whether it is relevant to your own needs, experiences, and growth in progressing from a novice to an experienced member of the selected organization.

5. Create a written list of six motivating (intrinsic) factors and six hygiene (extrinsic) factors related to teaching within a school setting. Categorize each of Herzberg's 12 factors according to one of Maslow's stages by placing an *A* (self-actualization), *E* (esteem), *B* (belonging), *S* (safety), or *P* (physiological) after each factor. Give a brief rationale for each Herzberg- and Maslow-related classification you decide on.

Field

1. Visit the classrooms of a teacher you perceive to be functioning at high stages of development and one you perceive to be at low stages of development. Write a report comparing the teachers in terms of teaching methods, interaction with students, classroom management, attention to individual student needs, and general teaching effectiveness. (Use fictitious names in your report.)

2. On the basis of observations of leader-teacher, teacher-teacher, and teacher-student interactions, faculty meeting activities, posted communications, and the like, infer a group of *social norms* that prevail at a selected school. Write a paper stating your perceptions of the school's social norms and your opinion of whether those norms are positive or negative influences on teachers' stage development.

3. Interview a veteran teacher who is nearing retirement. Ask the teacher to discuss the major transitions that have taken place during his or her career. Summarize the interview in writing.

4. Reflect on your own career and the major transitions that have taken place during your career. Choose an artifact that symbolizes each major transition. Prepare a display of your artifacts and an oral or written report explaining the relationship between your career transitions and these artifacts.

5. Ask a first-year teacher, a third-year teacher, and a teacher with at least 10 years of experience to list their concerns about teaching. Prepare a report comparing the various responses and drawing relevant conclusions.

Developmental

1. For the time that you will be reading the book, keep a diary of weekly decisions you have made. You might want to include the possible choices for each decision, the factors important in resolving your problems, and the success with which you carried out your decisions. Review your diary after six weeks or more. Do you see

any trends? What appear to be the most important considerations you use in making your decisions?

2. Begin a career scrapbook with the purpose of documenting your own professional development.

3. Begin an in-depth study of a major topic discussed in Chapter 4 (for example, adult learning, adult development, teacher development, the teaching career, or teacher motivation).

References

Adams, R. D., Hutchinson, S., and Martray, C. 1980. *A developmental study of teacher concerns across time.* Paper presented at the annual meeting of the American Educational Research Association, Boston, April.

Adams, R. D., and Martray, C. 1981. *Teacher development: A study of factors related to teacher concerns for pre, beginning, and experienced teachers.* Paper presented at the annual meeting of the American Educational Research Association, Los Angeles, April.

Ammon, P. 1984. Human development, teaching and teacher education. *Teacher Education Quarterly* 11(4):95–108.

Anderson, D. Y., and Hayes, C. L. 1996 *Gender, identity and self-esteem: A new look at adult development.* New York: Springer.

Arlin, P. K. 1975. Cognitive development in adulthood: A fifth stage. *Developmental Psychology* 11:602–606.

Aslanian, C. B., and Brickell, H. M. 1981. *Americans in transition.* New York: College Entrance Examination Board.

Baltes, P. B., and Baltes, M. 1980. Plasticity and variability in psychological aging: Methodological and theoretical issues. In C. Guerski (Ed.), *Aging and CNS.* Berlin: Schering.

Becker, H. S. 1971. Personal change in adult life. In H. S. Becker (Ed.), *Sociological work: Method and substance.* London: Allen Lane.

Belenky, M. F., Clinchy, B. M., Goldberger, N. R., and Tarule, J. M. 1986. *Women's ways of knowing. The development of self, voice, and mind.* New York: Basic Books.

Berman, P., and McLaughlin, M. W. 1978. *Federal programs supporting educational change, Vol. 8. Implementing and sustaining innovations.* Santa Monica, CA: Rand Corporation. (ERIC ED 159 289)

Blum, L. S., and Meyer, R. 1981. *Developmental implications of myocardial infarction for mid-life adults.* Paper presented at the annual meeting of the American Educational Research Association, Los Angeles, April.

Brandt, R. S. 1986. On the expert teacher: A conversation with David Berliner. *Educational Leadership 44*(2):4–9.

Brim, O. J., and Ryff, C. D. 1980. On the properties of life events. In P. B. Baltes and O. G. Brim (Eds.), *Lifespan development and behavior, Vol. 3.* New York: Academic Press.

Brookfield, S. 1986. *Understanding and facilitating adult learning.* San Francisco: Jossey-Bass.

Brown, J. S., Collins, A., and Duguid, P. 1989. Situated cognition and the culture of learning. *Educational Researcher, 18* (1): 32–42.

Bruner, J. S. 1960. *The process of education.* Cambridge, MA: Harvard University Press.

Burden, P. R. 1982. *Developmental supervision: Reducing teacher stress at different career stages.* Paper presented at the annual conference of the Association of Teacher Educators, Phoenix, February.

Burke, P. J., Christensen, J. C., Fessler, R., McDonnell, J. H., and Price, J. R. 1987. *The teacher career cycle: Model development and research report.* Paper presented to the annual meeting of the American Educational Research Association, Washington, DC, April.

Caffarella, R. S., and Olson, S. K. 1993. Psychosocial development of women: A critical review of the literature. *Adult Education Quarterly* 43(3):125–151.

Calhoun, E. F. 1985. *Relationship of teachers' conceptual level to the utilization of supervisory services and to a description of the classroom instructional improvement.* Paper presented at the annual meeting of the American Educational Research Association, Chicago, April.

Case, R. 1986. The new stage theories in intellectual development. In M. Perlmutter (Ed.), *Perspectives on intellectual development,* Vol. 19. Hillsdale, NJ: Lawrence Erlbaum.

Cawelti, G. 1976. "Selecting appropriate leadership styles for instructional improvement." Videotape. Alexandria, VA: Association for Supervision and Curriculum Development.

Checkley, K. 1997. The first seven.... and the eighth: A conversation with Howard Gardner. *Educational Leadership,* 55(1): 8–13.

Clayton, V., and Birren, J. 1980. The development of wisdom across the lifespan: A reexamination of an ancient topic. *Lifespan Development and Behavior 3:* 103–135.

Cranton, P. 1994. *Understanding and promoting transformative learning.* San Francisco: Jossey-Bass.

Cummings, A. L., and Murray, H. G. 1989. Ego development and its relation to teacher education. *Teaching and Teacher Education* 5(1): 21–32.

Dewey, J. 1938. *Experience and education.* New York: Collier.

Drucker, P. 1973. *Management.* New York: Harper and Row.

Erikson, E. H. 1963. *Childhood and society* (2nd ed.). New York: Norton.

Erikson, E. L. 1950. *Childhood and society.* New York: Norton.

Fiske, M., and Chiriboga, D. A. 1990. *Change and continuity in adult life.* San Francisco: Jossey-Bass.

Freire, P. 1970. *Pedagogy of the oppressed.* New York: Herder and Herder.

Fullan, M. G. 1991. *The new meaning of educational change* (2nd ed.). New York: Teachers College Press.

Fuller, F. F. 1969. Concerns of teachers: A developmental conceptualization. *American Educational Research Journal* 6(2):207–266.

Gage, N. L. 1978. *The scientific basis of the art of teaching.* New York: Teachers College Press.

Gardner, H. 1983. *Frames of mind: The theory of multiple intelligences.* New York: Basic Books.

Gehrke, N. J. 1979. Renewing teacher enthusiasm: A professional dilemma. *Theory into Practice* 18(3):188–193.

Gehrke, N. J. 1991. Seeing our way to better helping of beginning teachers. *Educational Forum* 55(3):233–242.

Gilligan, C. 1979. Woman's place in man's life cycle. *Harvard Educational Review* 49 (4): 431–446.

Gilligan, C. 1982. *In a different voice.* Cambridge, MA: Harvard University Press.

Ginsburg, H., and Opper, S. 1979. *Piaget's theory of intellectual development* (2nd ed.). Englewood Cliffs, NJ: Prentice Hall.

Glassburg, S. 1979. *Developing models of teacher development.* (ERIC ED 171 685)

Glickman, C. D. 1981. *Developmental supervision: Alternative approaches for helping teachers to improve instruction.* Alexandria, VA: Association for Supervision and Curriculum Development.

Glickman, C. D., and Tamashiro, R. T. 1982. A comparison of first year, fifth year, and former teachers on efficacy, ego development and problem solving. *Psychology in the Schools* 19(4):558–562.

Gonzalez Rodriguez, Y. E. & Sjostrom, Barbara R. 1998. Critical reflection for professional development: A comparative study of nontraditional adult and traditional student teachers. *Journal of Teacher Education, 49* (3), 177–186.

Gordon, S. P. 1990. *Assisting the entry-year teacher: A leadership resource.* Columbus: Ohio Department of Education.

Gould, R. L. 1978. *Transformations.* New York: Touchstone Books.

Harris, I. 1996. *Messages men hear: Constructing masculinities.* London: Taylor

Harvey, O. J. 1967. Conceptual systems and attitude change. In C. Sherif and M. Sherif (Eds.), *Attitude, ego involvement and change.* New York: Wiley.

Harvey, O. J., Hunt, D. E., and Schroeder, H. M. 1961. *Conceptual systems and personality organization.* New York: Wiley.

Harvey, O. J., White, B. J., Prather M., Alter, R., and Hoffmeister, J. 1966. Teachers' belief systems and preschool atmospheres. *Journal of Educational Psychology* 57:373–381.

Havighurst, R. J. 1980. Life-span developmental psychology and education. *Educational Researcher* 9(10):3–8.

Heck, E. J., and Davis, C. S. 1973. Differential expression of empathy in a counseling analog. *Journal of Counseling Psychology* 20:101–104.

Herzberg, F. 1966. *Work and the nature of man.* New York: World.

Herzberg, F. 1987. One more time. How do you motivate employees? *Harvard Business Review* 65(5):109–120.

Herzberg, F., Mausner, B., and Snyderman, B. 1959. *The motivation to work.* New York: Wiley.

Holliday, S. G., and Chandler, M. J. 1986. *Wisdom: Explorations in adult competence.* Basel: Karger.

Horn, J. L., and Cattell, R. B. 1967. Age differences in fluid and crystallized intelligence. *Acta Psychologica 26:* 107–129.

Hoy, W. K., and Miskel, C. G. 1982. *Educational administration theory, research and practice.* (2nd ed.). New York: Random House.

Hunt, D. E. 1966. A conceptual systems change model and its application to education. In O. J. Harvey (Ed.), *Experience, structure, and adaptability.* New York: Springer-Verlag, pp. 277–302.

Hunt, D. E., Butler, L. F., Noy, J. E., and Rosser, M. E. 1978. *Assessing conceptual level by the paragraph completion method.* Toronto: Ontario Institute for Studies in Education.

Hunt, D. E., and Joyce, B. R. 1967. Teacher trainee personality and initial teaching style. *American Educational Research Journal* 4(3):253–255.

Hunter, M. 1986. To be or not to be—Hunterized. *Tennessee Educational Leadership* 12:70.

Jackson, P. 1968. *Life in classrooms.* New York: Holt, Rinehart and Winston.

Johnston, M. 1985. How elementary teachers understand the concept of "on-task": A developmental critique. *The Journal of Classroom Interaction, 21,* 15–24.

Johnston, M. 1989. Moral reasoning and teachers' understanding of individualized instruction. *The Journal of Moral Education* 18(1):45–48.

Johnston, M., and Lubomudrov, C. 1987. Teachers' level of moral reasoning and their understanding of classroom rules and roles. *Elementary School Journal* 88, 65–78.

Juhasz, A. M. 1989. A role-based approach to adult development: The triple helix model. *International Journal of Aging and Human Development* 29(4):301–315.

Kegan, R. 1994. *In over our heads: The mental demands of modern life.* Cambridge, MA: Harvard University Press.

Kerka, S. 1998. *New perspectives on mentoring.* ERIC Digest No. 194. (ERIC ED 418249)

King, N. 1970. Clarification and evaluation of the two-factor theory of job satisfaction. *Psychological Bulletin 74:* 18–31.

Kitchener, K. S., Lynch, C. L., Fischer, K. W., and Woord, P. K. 1993. Developmental range of reflection judgement: The effect of contextual support and practice on developmental stage. *Developmental Psychology, 29* (5), 893–906.

Kitchener, K. 1983. Cognition, metacognition and epistemic cognition. Three models of cognitive processing. *Human Development 26:* 222–232.

Knowles, M. S. 1980. *The modern practice of adult education: From pedagogy to andragogy* (2nd ed.). Chicago: Association/Follett.

Knowles, M. S. 1984. *Andragogy in action: Applying modern principles of adult learning.* San Francisco: Jossey-Bass.

Kolb, D. A. 1984. *Experiential learning.* Englewood Cliffs, N J: Prentice Hall.

Kohlberg, L., and Armon, C. 1984. Three types of stage models used in the study of adult development. In M. Commons, F. A. Richards, and C. A. Armon (Eds.), *Beyond formal operations: late adolescent and adult cognitive development.* New York: Praeger.

Kohlberg, L., and Turiel, E. 1971. Moral development and moral education. In G. Lessor (Ed.), *Psychology and educational practice.* Chicago: Scott, Foresman.

Kramer, D. A. 1983. Post-formal operations? A need for further conceptualization. *Human Development* 26(2):91–105.

Kramer, D. A. 1987. *Improved learning in aging: Implications for education.* Paper presented at Information and Aging: Coalitions for the Future, New Brunswick, NJ, April. (ERIC ED 283 098)

Krupp, J. 1982. *The adult learner: A unique entity.* Manchester, CT: Adult Development and Learning.

Krupp, J. 1987. Understanding and motivating personnel in the second half of life. *Journal of Education* 169(1):20–47.

Lave, J., and Wenger, E. 1991. *Situated learning: Legitimate peripheral participation.* New York: Cambridge University Press.

Levine, S. L. 1987. Understanding life cycle issues: A resource for school leaders. *Journal of Education* 169(1):7–19.

Levine, S. L. 1989. *Promoting adult growth in schools.* Boston: Allyn and Bacon.

Levinson, D. J., et al. 1978. *The seasons in a man's life.* New York: Knopf.

Lieblich, A. 1986. Successful career women at midlife: Crises and transitions. *International Journal of Aging and Human Development* 23(4): 301–312.

Lindeman, E. 1926. *The meaning of adult education.* New York: New Republic.

Little, J. W. 1982. Norms of collegiality and experimentation: Workplace conditions of school success. *American Educational Research Journal* 19(3):325–340.

Loevinger, J. 1976. *Ego development.* San Francisco: Jossey-Bass.

Long, H. B., and Mizra, M. S., 1980. Some qualitative performance characteristics of adults at the formal operations stage. *Journal of Research and Development in Education* 13(3): 21–24.

Lorge, I., and others. 1965. *Adult learning.* Washington DC: Adult Education Association of the U.S.A.

Lortie, D. C. 1975. *Schoolteacher: A sociological study.* Chicago: University of Chicago Press.

Lubomudrov, C. 1982. Case studies of relationships among level of moral cognitive development, teachers' understandings of educational issues and teaching practices. *Dissertation Abstracts International 43 A*(4):1120.

Marsick, V. J., and Watkins, K. 1990. *Informal and incidental learning in the workplace.* New York: Routledge.

Maslow, A. H. 1954. *Motivation and personality.* New York: Harper and Row.

Mathis, C. 1987. Educational reform, the aging society and the teaching profession. *Journal of Education 169*(1):80–88.

McNeil, L. M. 1986. *Exit, voice and community: Magnet teachers' responses to standardization.* Presentation to the annual meeting of the American Educational Research Association, San Francisco, April.

McNergney, R. F., and Carrier, C. A. 1981. *Teacher development.* New York: Macmillan.

Merriam, S., and Caffarella, R. 1999. *Learning in adulthood* (2nd ed.). San Francisco: Jossey-Bass.

Merriam, S. B., and Clark, M. C. 1991. *Lifelines: Patterns of work, love and learning in adulthood.* San Francisco: Jossey-Bass.

Merriam, S. B., and Clark, M. C. 1993. Learning from experience: What makes it significant? *International Journal of Lifelong Education 12*(2):129–138.

Mezirow, J. D. 1981 A critical theory of adult learning and education. *Adult Education 32*(1): 3–24.

Mezirow, J. D., and associates. 1990. *Fostering critical reflection in adulthood. A guide to transformative and emancipatory learning.* San Francisco: Jossey-Bass.

Murphy, P., and Brown, M. 1970. Conceptual systems and teaching styles. *American Educational Research Journal 7:* 529–540.

Neimark, E. D. 1987. *Toward a cross-cultural examination of adult thought.* Paper presented at the Satellite Conference of the International Society of the Study of Behavior Development, Beijing, May. (ERIC ED 291 869)

Neugarten, B. L. 1977. Personality and aging. In J. E. Birren and K. W. Schaie (Eds.), *Handbook of the psychology of aging.* New York: Van Nostrand Reinhold.

Neugarten, B., and Neugarten, D. 1987. The changing meaning of age. *Psychology Today 21*(5): 29–33.

O'Keefe, P., and Johnston, M. 1989. Perspective taking and teacher effectiveness: A connected thread through three developmental literatures. *Journal of Teacher Education 40*(3):20–26.

Oja, S. N. 1979. *A cognitive-structural approach to adult ego, moral, and conceptual development through in-service education.* Paper presented at the annual meeting of the American Educational Research Association, San Francisco, April.

Oja, S. N. 1988. *A collaborative approach to leadership in supervision: Program assessment report. Part B of the final report.* ERIC ED 304 432

Oja, S. N., and Pine, G. J. 1981. *Toward a theory of staff development.* Paper presented at the annual meeting of the American Educational Research Association, Los Angeles, April.

Oja, S. N., and Pine, G. J. 1984. *Collaborative action research: A two-year study of teachers' stages of development and school contexts.* Durham, NH: University of New Hampshire.

Parkay, F. W. 1979. *Inner-city high school teachers: The relationship of personality traits and teaching style to environmental stress.* Paper presented to the Southwest Educational Research Association, Houston.

Parker, W. C. 1983. *The effect of guided reflection and role-taking on the interactive decision making of teachers.* Paper presented at the annual meeting of the American Educational Research Association, Montreal, April.

Peck, T. A. 1986. Women's self-definition in adulthood: From a different model? *Psychology of Women Quarterly, 10* (3), 274–284.

Perry, W. G. 1970. *Forms of intellectual and ethical development in the college years.* New York: Holt, Rinehart and Winston.

Perry, W. G. 1981. Cognitive and ethical growth: The making of meaning. In A. Chickering (Ed.), *The modern American college.* San Francisco: Jossey-Bass.

Phillips, M. D., and Glickman, C. D. 1991. Peer coaching: Developmental approach to enhance teacher thinking. *Journal of Staff Development 12*(2):20–25.

Piaget, J. 1955. *The language and thought of the child.* New York: World Publishing.

Porter, A. C., and Brophy, J. 1988. Synthesis of research on good teaching: Insights from the work of the Institute for Research on Teaching. *Educational Leadership 45*(7):78–85.

Pratt, D. D. 1988. Andragogy as a relational construct. *Adult Education Quarterly 38*(3): 160–172.

Rest, J. 1986. *Moral development: Advances in research and theory.* New York: Praeger.

Riegel, K. 1973. Dialectical operations: The final period of cognitive development. *Human Development 16:* 346–370.

Roberts, P., and Newton, P. M. 1987. Levinsonian studies of women's adult development. *Psychology and Aging 2:* 154–163.

Rutter, M., Maughan, B., Mortimore, P., Ouston, J. and Smith, A. 1979. *Fifteen thousand hours. Secondary schools and their effects on children.* Cambridge, MA: Harvard University Press.

Schlossberg, N. K. 1984. *Counseling adults in transition: Linking practice in theory.* New York: Springer.

Schmidt, G. L. 1976. Job satisfaction among secondary school administrators. *Education Administration Quarterly 12:* 68–85.

Schön, D. A. 1983. *The reflective practitioner: How professionals think in action.* New York: Basic Books.

Schooler, C. 1989. *A sociological perspective in intellectual development.* Paper presented at the Biennial meeting of the Society for Research in Child Development. (ERIC ED 308 932)

Sergiovanni, T. 1966. Factors which affect satisfaction and dissatisfaction of teachers. *Journal of Educational Administration 5:*66–82.

Smylie, M. A. 1995. Teacher learning in the workplace: Implications for school reform. In T. R. Guskey and M. Huberman (Eds.), *Professional development in education: New paradigms and practices.* New York: Teachers College Press.

Sprinthall, N. A., and Thies-Sprinthall, L. 1982. Career development of teachers: A cognitive developmental perspective. In H. Mitzel (Ed.), *Encyclopedia of educational research* (5th ed.) New York: Free Press.

Sternberg, R. J. 1985. *Beyond IQ: A triarchic theory of human intelligence.* New York: Cambridge.

Sternberg, R. J. 1988. *Triarchic mind: A new theory of human intelligence.* New York: Viking.

Sternberg, R. J. 1990. *Metaphors of mind: Conceptions of the nature of intelligence.* New York: Cambridge.

Sullivan, E. V., McCullough, G., and Stager, M. A. 1970. Developmental study of the relationship between conceptual, ego, and moral development. *Child Development 41:* 399–411.

Swanson, J. L. 1992. Vocational behavior, 1989–1991: Life-span career development and reciprocal interaction of work and nonwork. *Journal of Vocational Behavior 41:*101–161.

Taranto, M. 1987. *Wisdom and logic.* Paper presented at the annual symposium of the Jean Piaget Society, Philadelphia, May. (ERIC ED 282 099)

Tennant, M. 1986. An evaluation of Knowles' theory of adult learning. *International Journal of Lifelong Education 5*(2):113–122.

Thies-Sprinthall, L., and Sprinthall, N. A. 1987. Experienced teachers: Agents for revitalization and renewal as mentors and teacher educators. *Journal of Education 169*(1):65–79.

Thorndike, E. L., and others. 1928. *Adult learning.* New York: Macmillan.

Whitbourne, S. K. 1986. *Adult development* (2nd ed.). New York: Praeger.

Wilkins, R. A. 1980. If the moral reasoning of teachers is deficient, what hope for pupils. *Kappan 61*(8):548–549.

Willis, S. L., and Baltes, P. B. 1980. Intelligence in adulthood and aging: Contemporary issues. In L. W. Poon (Ed.), *Aging in the 1980s: Psychological issues.* Washington DC: American Psychological Association.

Wilson, A. L. 1993. The promise of situated cognition. In S. Merriam (Ed.) *An update on adult learning theory. New directions for adult and continuing education, no. 57.* San Francisco: Jossey-Bass.

Witherell, C. S., and Erickson, V. L. 1978. Teacher education as adult development. *Theory and Practice 17:*229–238.

Suggested Readings

Brown, J. S., Collins, A., and Duguid, P. 1989. Situated cognition and the culture of learning. *Educational Researcher 18*(1):32–42.

Cross, K. P. 1991. *Adults as learners.* San Francisco: Jossey-Bass.

Fessler, R. 1992. *The teacher career cycle: understanding and guiding the professional development of teachers.* Boston: Allyn and Bacon.

Hargreaves, A., and Fullan, M. D. (Eds.). 1992. *Understanding teacher development.* New York: Teachers College.

Levine, S. L. 1989. *Promoting adult growth in schools.* Boston: Allyn and Bacon.

Merriam, S. (Ed.) 1993. *An update on adult learning theory. New directions for adult and continuing education, no. 57.* San Francisco: Jossey-Bass.

Merriam, S., and Caffarella, R. 1999. *Learning in adulthood* (2nd ed.). San Francisco: Jossey-Bass.

Zehm, S. J., and Kottler, J. A. 1993. *On being a teacher.* Newbury Park, CA: Sage.

5

Reflections on Schools, Teaching, and SuperVision

As we seek ways to improve school and classroom instruction, we need to understand how present thinking, beliefs, and practices in the field of supervision interact with instruction and the assumptions about students and teachers as learners. This chapter will show how issues of school and teaching effectiveness are not clearly answered by research but instead must be resolved by human judgments about goals and purposes. Next, we will look at how supervisory beliefs are related to a particular educational philosophy or platform. An instrument will then be provided to help clarify each person's own supervisory belief, and we will examine how one's own supervisory belief fits along a control continuum. Finally, some propositions about supervisory belief and consequences for teacher development will be presented.

How do we reconcile the uncertainties of supervision, teaching, and instructional improvement? How do we know whether we are progressing in the desired direction? Unless we reflect on our own beliefs, there is little to steer us.

Sergiovanni and Starrat (1983) noted the importance of understanding one's own supervisory beliefs:

> What is needed is some firm footing in principle. Some have called our often unexpressed constellation of principles a platform. Just as a political party is supposed to base its decisions and actions on a party platform upon which it seeks election, so, too, supervisory personnel need a platform upon which, and in the light of which, they can carry on their work. With a clearly defined platform, they can begin to take a position relative to educational practices, looking beyond the surface behavior to probe for the real consequences of a variety of school practices. (pp. 226–227)

Knowing oneself as a supervisor is necessary before considering alternative practices and procedures. To move from a platform, we must first know where we are standing. Let's look at the human decisions that a supervisor must make about school improvement, teaching effectiveness, and one's purpose in working with teachers.

Effective Teaching Research: A Historical Perspective

Beginning in the 1970s, various studies, collectively known as *effective teaching research*, were carried out. These studies were the classroom equivalent of the effective schools research discussed in Chapter 3. They identified correlates between student performance on standardized achievement tests and teaching variables. One type of effectiveness research concerned the correlation between *teachers' attitudes and beliefs* and student achievement. These findings were summarized by Brophy and Evertson (1976):

1. Effective teachers have a sense of being in charge, a "can do" attitude. Although effective teachers face the same types of problems as ineffective teachers, they see them as challenges to be met, not suffering to be endured.
2. Effective teachers spend whatever time and effort is necessary to assure that all students learn. They give special attention, including reteaching and extra practice, to slower students.
3. Effective teachers have realistic, professional attitudes toward students. They possess neither romantic nor cynical views of their students. They see themselves as "diagnosticians and problem solvers," rather than as "mother-substitutes" or "disciplinarians" (Brophy and Evertson, 1976, p. 45).
4. Effective teachers expect their students to achieve. They believe that all students can learn essential knowledge and skills.

Another area of research examined the *classroom climate* created by the teacher. After reviewing the effectiveness research, Barnes (1981) identified two broad characteristics of a positive classroom climate: a work-oriented atmosphere and a warm, supportive environment. A work-oriented atmosphere is created by the teacher focusing on academics and explicitly communicating expected behaviors and attitudes to students. A warm, supportive environment is fostered by the teacher who provides specific praise when deserved, respects students' contributions, exhibits confidence and enthusiasm, engages in positive interactions with students, and maintains an orderly classroom with limits on social conversation.

In the area of *academic learning time*, researchers found that the more teacher and student class time spent on successful academic task performance, the higher was the level of student achievement (Denhan and Lieberman, 1980). Paschal, Weinstein, and Walberg (1984) synthesized 15 studies on *homework*. They concluded that assigned homework produces more learning than no homework, and that higher student achievement results when teachers return students' homework with comments or grades. In the area of *student diagnosis and evaluation*, Brophy and Evertson (1976) found that effective teachers relied less on frequent student testing than on techniques like observation of students, detailed note taking on student performance, and correcting daily student work.

The most widely disseminated results of the effective teaching research were findings concerning the *instructional process*. Researchers found strong positive correlations between higher scores on standardized achievement tests and "direct" or "explicit" instruction. Brophy (1979) summarized these findings: "Learning gains are more impressive in classrooms in which students receive a great deal of instruction from and have a great deal of interaction with the teacher, especially in public lessons and recitations that are briskly paced but conducted at a difficulty level that allows consistent success" (p. 747).

Based on his review of process-product research, Rosenshine (1983) identified a set of six instructional "functions":

1. Review, including checking of previous day's work and reteaching if necessary
2. Presentation of new content/skills
3. Initial student practice (and checking for understanding)
4. Feedback and correctives (and reteaching if necessary)
5. Student independent practice
6. Weekly and monthly reviews (p. 337)

Many interpreted Rosenshine's findings as confirming direct instruction as the one best instructional process, regardless of the students or content to be taught. Additionally, Rosenshine's six functions (or variations thereof) were extolled as the "essential elements" of any effective lesson. We will dispute these interpretations as our discussion of effective teaching continues.

Cautions Concerning Effective Teaching Research

Gary Griffin (1985) has cautioned educators against overreliance on the effective teaching research:

> Much research is correlational; the teaching behaviors associated with positive pupil outcomes were discovered in existing classroom settings. They were, if you will, naturally occurring phenomena in an untampered-with context. Few studies have been designed to determine if the same behaviors, when introduced experimentally into classrooms, result in the same pupil outcomes.... Also, much of the effective teaching research is situation specific, tied to certain grade levels with certain student populations in specific demographic and social contexts. Therefore, the results may not be generalizable to other situations. (p. 44)

Barak Rosenshine, the synthesizer of what has become commonly termed *effective instruction*, stated that the body of research on instruction that results in short-term basic-skills acquisition should be more aptly referred to as "teachers' effects" research.

> My main point is that it is difficult to apply some of the major findings which we have learned from the teaching of skills to lessons which teach content. Some of

these findings include checking for student understanding, providing for active student participation, providing for a high success rate, correcting errors, and providing for guided practice and independent practice. But such findings do not, and will not, transfer easily to the teaching of content, and we haven't faced this problem. (1986a, p. 14)

Furthermore, Rosenshine has written that explicit teaching is "less relevant for teaching compositions, writing of term papers, reading comprehension, analyzing literature, historical trends...discussion of social issues, or for teaching entangled concepts" (1986a, p. 60). He has openly expressed the opinion that teaching specific skills and factual knowledge, in which explicit direct instruction is appropriate, accounts for 40 percent of teaching at most. Other instructional goals account for the other 60 percent. To muddy the waters even further, there are some studies of elementary and secondary schools where teachers were trained and observed using "effective" teaching skills. It was found that their students had lower basic-skills achievement gains than students with teachers who had not been trained (Stalling, 1987; Gersten, Gall, Grace, Erickson, and Stieber, 1987). Therefore, it is inappropriate to view explicit, direct instruction as the model for effective teaching, valid for the majority of instruction in a classroom. Yet many school districts and states use this very misapplication of research in evaluating teachers against a template of "effective" instruction.

Jere Brophy, the noted pioneer of process-product research, stated the distinction succinctly. "In short, information about teachers' effects [in fostering students' achievement of academic knowledge and skills] is not the same as information about teachers' effectiveness" (1986, p. 2). Lest this explanation be seen as a polemic against explicit or direct instruction, remember that the critics of its overgeneralization and prescriptive applications are the researchers who conducted the actual studies and developed the instructional theory.

The Coast of Britain

Correct answers to questions about even physical matters are human decisions. Answers about social and educative matters are even more clearly human judgments (see Glickman 1987b). An example from geometry is illustrative. To the question, "How long is the coast of Britain?" the geometer Benoit Mandelbrot answered that the coast has no real length apart from human judgment (Hardison, 1986). If one uses a measurement scale of 100 miles to an inch to draw the British coastline, that coastline has large bays and capes. If one uses a scale of 10 miles to an inch, then new inlets and promontories appear. The coast becomes longer or shorter, depending on the scale used. Furthermore, what happens when measurement of the coast begins when the tide is coming in? Each incoming wave reduces the coast, and each outgoing wave lengthens the coast. Therefore, how does one find the length of the British coast? The question can be answered only by agreeing on the purpose of the measurement, the perspective and the unit of measurement to be used, and the particular time at which the measurement is to be made. The length of the coast is a mathematical fiction created so that humans can find a representation that will accomplish their purpose.

Effective and Good Schools: The Same?

In discussing questions about supervision, teaching, and school improvement, as in measuring the coast of Britain, there is no certainty about how to arrive at an answer. The issue of effective schools highlights the human values that drive school decisions and actions (Glickman, 1987a).

Many of the clarion calls for school reform cite the findings from research on effective teaching and effective schools as examples of how schools and classrooms should change. The reformers tell us that the goal of all schools should be effectiveness—as measured by such factors as students' scores on tests of basic skills, their attendance rates, and their performance on the Scholastic Aptitude Test (SAT). Furthermore, we ought to narrow the academic focus of the curriculum, test students more frequently, raise standards for promotion, and have teachers state specific, measurable objectives and follow a prescribed instructional approach that involves reviewing, explaining, demonstrating, guiding practice, checking for understanding, and summarizing. The findings of the recent research on effective teaching and effective schools are treated as scientific laws that apply to *all* teachers and *all* schools.

The findings of the research on effective teaching and effective schools are too often equated with what is desirable or good. By failing to distinguish between *effectiveness* and *goodness,* we avoid two central questions in education. The first question with which schools and school systems must deal is: What is good? Only after that question has been answered should we deal with the second question: How do we become effective? The current fascination with findings from the research on effectiveness has blinded schools and school systems to the more basic question of goodness.

Do higher SAT scores justify labeling a school "good" if the price for those higher scores has been an increase in the dropout rate? Are higher scores in reading and mathematics "good" if students gain them at the expense of time spent in studying science, social studies, art, or music? Is an average gain of eight points on reading test scores worth the increased allocation of time and resources to direct instruction in reading? Is that gain more desirable than maintaining current achievement levels in reading but devoting a greater proportion of class time to a whole-language approach that emphasizes creative writing or critical thinking? The research on effective schools and effective teaching does not answer these questions for us. The research is neutral: It does not choose our goals but simply tells us how to accomplish certain things (which may or may not be among our goals). Educators who care about the fate of all children must define *goodness* before they worry about *effectiveness;* as supervisors, we must first clarify our own definitions.

Changing Views: New Emphasis on Constructivist Teaching and Learning

In recent years the constructivist view has had increasing influence over teaching and learning in our nation's classrooms. Constructivism is an epistemology (a theory of the nature of knowledge) based on the work of a variety of philosophers, psychologists, and educators. Luminaries associated with constructivism include Immanuel Kant, Lev Vygotsky, John Dewey, Jean Piaget, Jerome Bruner, and Howard Gardner. Constructivism holds that people create new knowledge as a result of the interaction of their existing knowledge, beliefs, and values with new ideas, problems, or experiences. To the constructivist, knowledge is not universal, objective, or fixed, but is constructed or co-constructed by learners.

Although there are several different models of constructivism, these models can be classified into one of two broad categories. *Cognitive constructivism* is focused on the individual's intellectual development. It holds that learning is stimulated when the individual encounters an idea or experience that contradicts his or her present conception of reality. This discrepancy causes "cognitive conflict" and "disequilibrium" which stimulates the person to develop and assimilate new knowledge as a means of dealing with the discrepancy. The other broad category is social constructivism, which proposes that knowledge is not created by the individual but is constructed as a result of the individual's interaction with his or her social context. Furthermore, that interaction brings about changes to both the individual and the social context.

What are the practical implications of constructivism for instruction? Although constructivism does not contradict all of the teaching effectiveness research, it clearly conflicts with that part of the effectiveness research that supports direct teaching characterized by teacher presentation, student practice, and teacher correctives. Airasian and Walsh (1997) discuss what a constructivist approach means for teachers and students:

> In a constructivist approach, teachers will have to learn to guide, not tell; to create environments in which students can make their own meanings, not be handed them by the teacher; to accept diversity in constructions, not search for the one "right" answer; to modify prior notions of "right" and "wrong," not stick to rigid standards and criteria; to create a safe, free, responsive environment that encourages disclosure of student constructions, not a closed, judgmental system... (p. 148)

> ...Students will also have to learn new ways to perform. They will have to learn to think for themselves, not wait for the teacher to tell them what to think; to proceed with less focus and direction from the teacher, not to wait for explicit teacher directions; to express their own ideas clearly in their own words, not to answer restricted-response questions; to revisit and revise constructions; not to move immediately on to the next concept or idea. (p. 448)

Table 5.1 further illuminates the constructivist approach to teaching and learning by comparing traditional to constructivist classrooms.

Instructional Improvement and Effective Teaching

Let's continue this reflection on practice by taking an innocuous statement about supervision that virtually no one would take issue with: The goal of supervision is to improve instruction. It sounds nice, until we ask for a definition of what type of instruction we wish to improve. Do we wish to improve instruction for short-

TABLE 5.1 *Comparing Constructivist and Traditional Classrooms*

	Traditional Classroom	*Constructivist Classroom*
Educational Purpose	• Transmission of Knowledge	• Construction of Knowledge
Curriculum	• Content-centered • Rigid, sequential	• Problem-centered • Flexible, webbed
Instructional Focus	• Discreet pieces of information • Breadth	• Big ideas • Depth
Planning	• By teacher	• By teacher and students
Instructional Methods	• Lecture • Teacher questions with "correct" student responses • Student recitation • Student practice with teacher feedback • Independent student practice	• Open-ended discussion • Student-initiated questions • Problem solving • Inquiry, experimentation • Active learning • Cooperative learning • Self and group reflection on constructions
Assessment	• Distinct from learning • Intended to measure learning and grade students • Objective quizzes and tests • Designed externally or by teacher	• Integrated with learning • Co-planned by teacher and students • Seeks to understand student constructions • Authentic • Assessment of process and product equally important • Includes self, peer, and group assessment

term basic-skills acquisition or do we wish to improve instruction for cooperative learning, for critical thinking, for inductive reasoning, for intrinsic learning, for individualized learning? Do we agree with a single definition of desired instruction? Those who have researched and theorized about effective instruction have uniformly disclaimed any single definition (Council of Professors of Instructional Supervision, 1988). In the final analysis, what constitutes instructional improvement and effective teaching can be defined only within the context of particular instructional goals. This means that the search for a single set of instructional methods—effective for all learning content, students, and situations—is futile. A more productive course of action is to identify various instructional strategies that are effective in relation to corresponding instructional goals.

Joyce, Showers, and Rolheiser-Bennett (1987), in their review of research on various instructional models that have been experimentally tested in schools and classrooms, found high effect sizes (magnitude of the potential of the instructional model to affect student learning by analyzing the statistical significance and standard deviation of gains between experimental and control groups). The highlights of their findings were as follows:

- Cooperative learning approaches, representing social models of teaching, yield effect sizes from modest to high. The more complex the outcomes—higher-order thinking, problem solving, social skills and attitudes—the greater are the effects.
- Information-processing models, especially the use of advance organizers and mnemonics, yield modest to substantial effect sizes; and the effects are long-lasting.
- Synectics and nondirective teaching, exemplifying personal models of teaching, attain their model-relevant purposes and affect student achievement in such basic areas as recall of information.
- DISTAR, an example of the behavioral family of models, yields modest effect sizes in achievement and, further, influences aptitude to learn.
- When these models and strategies are combined, they have even greater potential for improving student learning. (p. 13)

Additionally, teachers' use of a combination of instructional models, including cooperative learning, inductive thinking, concept attainment, and mnemonics was accompanied by substantial increases in social studies and language achievement by formerly low performing students (Showers, 1990; Joyce and Calhoun, 1994).

Finally, let's return to the question: How do we define the instruction that supervision intends to improve? Should supervision emphasize one or two instructional models, should it emphasize all, should it emphasize a particular model first and then add others later? These are not easy questions. Regardless of what we decide as to the focus of supervision, as Mandelbrot has reminded us, we are still making a human judgment with competing consequences.

Our resolution is first to clarify what our goals as a school are (which will be reflected in the educational philosophy, curriculum, view of knowledge, and view of the learner) and clarify with individual teachers their particular classroom instructional goals. Next, the supervisor focuses on assisting teachers to make decisions as to the most appropriate instructional model to use for a particular learning goal and the most appropriate instructional models to emphasize in the context of the school's priorities. Then, as teachers become proficient in the use of a model of instruction, supervision assists them to identify further learning goals and the use of an increased repertoire of models (see Joyce and Weil 1986). With such a supervision emphasis, effective instruction is seen as the teacher's ability to use various ways of teaching according to a variety of learning goals and outcomes. As Porter and Brophy (1988) wrote,

> Effective teachers are clear about what they intend to accomplish through their instruction, and they keep these goals in mind both in designing the instruction and in communicating its purposes to the students....
>
> Effective teachers create learning situations in which their students are expected not just to learn facts and solve given problems but to organize information in new ways and formulate problems for themselves. Such learning situations include creative writing opportunities in language arts, problem-formulation activities in mathematics, and independent projects in science, social studies, and literature. Such learning situations are intrinsically more demanding for both teachers and students than expository instruction followed by drill-and-practice exercises, but they must be included along with these more familiar learning situations if instruction is to address higher-level cognitive objectives in addition to lower-level ones....
>
> Finally, effective teachers are thoughtful about their practice: They take time for reflection and self-evaluation, monitor their instruction to make sure that worthwhile content is being taught to all students, and accept responsibility for guiding student learning and behavior. (pp. 81–82)

To the mix of multiple learning goals and multiple instructional models, Ornstein (1990) adds the concept of *teaching style:*

> Teaching style is a truncated version of a personality and philosophical type. Everyone must develop his or her own style of teaching and feel comfortable in the classroom. In short, teachers must develop their own repertoire, relative to their own physical and mental characteristics and their students. Thus, there is no one ideal type but a multiple set of teacher types or styles. Teachers style is a matter of choice and comfort, and what works for one teacher with one set of students may not work for another. (p. 84)

Teaching styles, of course, can change and broaden over time, allowing for the expansion of a teacher's repertoire of instructional strategies. However, attempting to force teachers to immediately adopt strategies that strongly conflict with their current teaching style is inconsistent with both the principles of adult learning and the concept of the teacher as a professional. It is better to initially invite teachers to learn and try out new strategies which are consistent with their current style, and then facilitate teachers' continued development of teaching style and repertoire over time.

Instructional improvement can be defined as helping teachers acquire teaching strategies consistent with their general teaching styles that increase the capabilities of students to make wise decisions in varying contexts (with regard to peers, adults, academics, and life). Effective teaching consists therefore of those teaching decisions about actions, routines, and techniques that increase the decision-making capabilities of students.

Beliefs about Education

We've discussed how the definition of effective instruction depends on school and teacher instructional goals. Instructional goals, in turn, are ultimately based on beliefs concerning such things as the purpose of education, what should be taught, the nature of the learner, and the learning process. Whether or not they are conscious of it, teachers' and supervisors' educational philosophies have a significant impact on instruction and instructional improvement efforts. The following are summaries of educational platforms of three teachers with different beliefs about education.

> Joan Simpson believes that the purpose of education should be to transmit a prescribed body of basic knowledge, skills, and cultural values to students. To do this effectively, the teacher must exercise control over the classroom, lesson content, and students. Content should be broken first into discreet academic areas and then into small elements, and learning should take place in a series of small, sequential steps. All students should be expected to master the same content. Grades and other types of external motivation are necessary to assure student learning.

> Bill Washington believes that the purpose of education should be student growth, especially in inquiry and problem-solving skills. To promote such growth, the teacher conveys existing knowledge, but also encourages students to experiment in order to test old ideas and find solutions to new problems. Bill believes that since inquiry is most successful in a democratic environment, the teacher should share control of the learning environment with students. Because problem solving often takes place within a social context, students should learn social skills as well as academic content.

> Pat Rogers believes that each child is unique and that the primary purpose of education should be to meet students' individual needs. The teacher should foster the development of each student toward his or her fullest potential. This means addressing students as whole persons by fostering their physical, emotional, cognitive, moral, and social development. Such holistic education includes facilitating student self-inquiry. Pat believes that students should have as much control over their own learning environment as their maturity level permits. Teachers should base lessons on students' experience, concerns, and interests. Students should be allowed to participate in assessing their own learning.

The three educational platforms just described do indeed represent contrasting beliefs. Based on their educational beliefs, Joan Simpson, Bill Washington, and

Pat Rogers, no doubt, have quite different definitions of instructional improvement and effective teaching! You may view one of these educational platforms as quite similar to your own, you may agree with parts of each, or you may have an entirely different set of beliefs. In any case, it is important for you to clarify your own educational beliefs. By reflecting on the following questions, you can begin to build your educational platform:

1. What should be the purpose of education?
2. What should be the content of the school curriculum?
3. Who should control the learning environment?
4. What should be the relationship of teacher and students?
5. Under what conditions is student learning most successful?
6. What motivates students to do their best in school?
7. What is your definition of effective teaching?
8. What personal characteristics are possessed by a successful teacher?
9. How should the teacher assess student learning?
10. What is your definition of a good school?

Supervision Beliefs

Most supervisors, of course, are former teachers. As a result, their views about learning, the nature of the learner, knowledge, and the role of the teacher in the classroom influence their view of supervision. After all, supervision is in many respects analogous to teaching. Teachers wish to improve students' behavior, achievement, and attitudes. Supervisors similarly wish to improve teachers' behavior, achievement, and attitudes. The supervisory platforms of three supervisors are described next. As you read these platforms, note the relationship between the beliefs they contain and the teacher beliefs present in the three educational platforms discussed earlier in this chapter.

Bob Reynolds believes that the purpose of supervision is to monitor teachers to determine if their instruction includes the elements of effective instruction. If those elements are observed, the supervisor should provide positive reinforcement to assure that they continue to be included in the teacher's lessons. Bob believes that if a teacher is not using, or is incorrectly using, the elements of effective instruction, the supervisor has a responsibility to provide remedial assistance by explaining and demonstrating correct instructional behaviors, setting standards of improvement, and monitoring and reinforcing the teacher's improvement efforts. In short, the supervisor should have primary responsibility for instructional improvement decisions.

Jan White believes that the purpose of supervision is to engage teachers in mutual inquiry aimed at the improvement of instruction. The supervisor and teacher should share perceptions of instructional problems, exchange suggestions for solving those problems, and negotiate an improvement plan. The improvement plan becomes a hypothesis to be tested by the teacher with the supervisor's assistance. Thus, Jan believes that supervisors and teachers should share the responsibility for instructional improvement.

Shawn Moore believes that the purpose of supervision should be to foster teacher reflection and autonomy and to facilitate teacher-driven instructional improvement. The supervisor should be concerned with the teacher's self-concept and personal development as well as the teacher's instructional performance. It is critical for the supervisor to establish a relationship with the teacher characterized by openness, trust, and acceptance. Shawn believes that the supervisor should allow the teacher to identify instructional problems, improvement plans, and criteria for success. The supervisor can assist the teacher's self-directed improvement through active listening, clarifying, encouraging, and reflecting. Thus, the teacher should have primary responsibility for instructional improvement decisions, with the supervisor serving as an active facilitator.

These descriptions show that supervisory platforms can be as varied as educational platforms. When we compare the educational platforms of Joan Simpson, Bill Washington, and Pat Rogers with the supervisory platforms of Bob Reynolds, Jan White, and Shawn Moore, we can see that both types of platforms reveal basic beliefs about knowledge, human nature, and control. By answering the following questions, you can begin the process of clarifying your own beliefs about instructional supervision. We suggest that you write responses to the questions, save your responses, and reassess your supervisory platform after you have finished reading this text.

1. What is your definition of instructional supervision?
2. What should be the ultimate purpose of supervision?
3. Who should supervise? Who should be supervised?
4. What knowledge, skills, attitudes, and values are possessed by successful supervisors?
5. What are the most important needs of teachers?
6. What makes for positive relationships between supervisors and teachers?
7. What types of activities should be part of instructional supervision?
8. What should be changed about the current practice of instructional supervision?

Supervisory Platform as Related to Educational Philosophy

Many educators view discussions of educational philosophy as overly abstract and irrelevant to the real world of supervisors and teachers. Yet, a supervisor's actions in working with teachers are based on supervisory beliefs, which in turn reflect a broader educational philosophy. Many different philosophies exist. Some, such as idealism and realism, date back to ancient times. Others, such as pragmatism and behaviorism, have been developed within the last century. Even more recent has been the emergence of progressivism, reconstructionism, and existentialism. Philosophies are numerous and overlapping, and many have historical roots in each other. To unravel the major philosophical trends in education, one must decipher how philosophies differ from each other and then build overriding conceptual categories. Each conceptual category or superphilosophy is created by grouping various philosophies that have central agreement on the type and scope of education. In other words, there may be disagreement on the specific nature of knowledge, truth, and reality, yet they hang together as a general educational philosophy because they are in agreement on the purpose and treatment of education.[1]

With educational application in mind, divergent philosophies can be simplified and classified. Three major educational superphilosophies have direct relevance to supervision. These categories have been labeled, according to Johnson, Collins, Dupuis, and Johansen (1973), as essentialism, progressivism, and existentialism. We would like to substitute for progressivism the more general term *experimentalism*, as described by Van Cleve Morris (1961).

Essentialism

Essentialism as a philosophy is derived from idealism and realism. *Idealism*, which dates back to Plato, espouses a belief in absolutes: The world we live in is merely a reflection of reality. Reality, truth, and standards of morality exist beyond our common ways of knowing. Only by training the mind do we glimpse the ultimates. Yet training the mind is not sufficient in itself; it only brings the mind nearer to grasping reality. Divine revelation, insight, and faith are the necessary elements for ultimate knowledge of what exists. Therefore, idealism emphasizes truth and reality existing outside of people. It is absolute and unchanging. *Realism*, developed at the onset of the industrial age, places a similar emphasis on truth and reality being outside of people. Instead of humankind and the outer environment being separated from each other, realism maintains that humanity is part and parcel of that environment. The world is a preordained, mechanistic reality. All of existence operates according to scientific, cause-and-effect relations. It is as if existence is a clock that always runs according to mechanical principles governing levers, gauges, and gears. Humans have no existence apart from this clock; they are a part of the predetermined machine. Knowledge is learning how the machine works; truths are the scientific laws of regulation. Nothing exists outside the principles of nature. The purpose of education is to condition the mind to think in a natural, logical way. The mind should be trained to become consciously aware of the predetermined nature of the world.

Essentialism, created by William L. Bagley in 1938, encompassed the educational philosophies of idealism and realism. He took the ideas of knowledge being eternal and outside of humankind (idealism—absolutes; realism—natural laws) to form pedagogy. Essentialists emphasize that there is a body of timeless knowledge, both historical and contemporary, that is of value to the living.

Essentialism in terms of supervision emphasizes the supervisor as the person who teaches truths about teaching to teachers. Supervisors are those most knowledgeable about those absolute standards. Teachers are then handled mechanistically to systematize and feed content to students. As teachers digest these teaching truths, they move closer to being good teachers.

Experimentalism

As Western society became more industrialized, optimism and confidence in human ability to control nature emerged. The philosophy of *pragmatism* developed by Charles S. Pierce and William James emphasized what people can do to nature rather than what nature does to humankind. John Dewey, circa 1920, further expanded on the writings of James by putting the individual squarely in the context of society. Humans can both reform and be reformed by society. Dewey's philosophy is, of course, the well-known school of progressive thought. *Reconstructionism* is a further offshoot of both pragmatism and progressivism. Richard Pratte (1971) cited the pamphlet *Dare the Schools Build a New Social Order,* written by George S. Counts in 1932, as a guiding document for the then radical notion that schools and students were the reformers of society.

Experimentalism emerges from the philosophies of pragmatism, progressivism, and reconstructionism. They hold in common a historical break from the more traditional philosophies of realism and idealism. The essentialist idea that knowledge, truth, and morality exist as absolute and outside of humans was rejected. The emerging faith in the scientific method, the ability of humans to create their own laws, principles, and machines, and the fact that such man-made inventions would work for them demanded an accompanying philosophy. Experimentalism provided that philosophy.

Reality was what worked. If a person could form a hypothesis, test it, and find it to work, then it was regarded as tentatively true. On repeated experimentation with the same results, it became real. Yet experimentalists would never claim an absolute truth. The human environment was believed to be constantly changing, so that what one can do and prove today may not be probable tomorrow. A new situation and a different approach may alter yesterday's reality. Experimentalists point to the historical evidence of Newton's law of gravity as a past truth that has given way to Einstein's theory of relativity; they believe that in time a new theory will replace Einstein's.

Morality is also viewed in relation to what works for humanity and human society. *Morality* is that behavior that promotes one's working with the group to achieve greater ends. To be wise is to understand how the environment (of things and people) affects oneself and how one might affect it. Whether action is moral or not is determined by the degree of progress that has been achieved by the group. The use of trial and error in a laboratory setting is the key to evaluating the outcome of action. Therefore, experimentalists do not view knowledge as absolute or external to human capabilities. Rather, knowledge is a result of the inter-action between the scientific person and the environment.

The educational application of experimentalist thinking to supervision is well documented in the writing of Dewey. Teachers (as students) need to learn what are the truths of their time, but they should not rest content with that parcel of knowl-edge. Supervisors view schools as laboratories for working with teachers to test old hypotheses and to try new ones. Supervisors work democratically with teachers to achieve collective ends that will help everyone. Supervisors are not solely convey-ors of age-old wisdom; they are both the conveyors of the rudimentary knowledge of the time and the guiders of trial-and-error, exploratory learning.

Existentialism

Existentialism as a school of thought is derived from the rejection of the other philosophies encompassed in essentialism and experimentalism. As such, it is a large category for many diverse philosophers. They have in common a scorn for rational, empirical, and systematic thinking as the way of knowing reality. As pre-viously mentioned, the essentialists believe in rational thinking to help elevate the mind to uncover the absolutes of the universe. Experimentalists believe in ra-tional, scientific thinking to explore and frame the relevant knowledge of the times. However, the existentialists believe that this same rational thinking re-stricts humans from discovering existence and therefore keeps them ignorant.

This philosophy has roots in the writings of Sören Kierkegaard in the mid-nineteenth century. It has been popularized in drama and literature by such expo-nents as Albert Camus and Jean-Paul Sartre. The current popular cults of transcen-dental thinking, meditation, and introspection (knowing oneself) have a kinship with existentialism. The basic tenet of the philosophy is that the individual is the source of all reality. All that exists in the world is the meaning the individual puts on his or her own experiences. There is no absolute knowledge, no mechanical working of the universe, and no preordained logic. To believe in such inventions is merely the narrow, incorrect way humans interpret their own experiences.

Beyond the individual exists only chaos. The only reality that exists is one's own existence. Only by looking within oneself can one discern the truth of the out-side disorder. Humanity is paramount. Human dignity and worth are of greatest importance; they are the source and dispenser of all truth. With this realization, one acquires a profound respect for all human beings and their uniqueness. Human re-lations become very important, affirming individual worth and protecting the indi-vidual's right to discover his or her own truth. Morality is the process of knowing oneself and allowing others the freedom to do likewise. Faith, intuition, mysticism, imagery, and transcendental experiences are all acceptable ways of discovery. Humans are totally free, not shaped by others or restricted by the flux of the times. They hold within themselves the capacity to form their own destiny.

This philosophy of education, applied to supervision, means a full commit-ment to individual teacher choice. The supervisor provides an environment that enables the teacher to explore his or her own physical and mental capabilities. Teachers must learn for themselves. The supervisor does not dispense information

TABLE 5.2   *Comparing Three Super Philosophies*

	Essentialism	*Experimentalism*	*Existentialism*
View of Reality (knowledge, truth, morality)	Exists outside of humans, absolute, unchanging	Reality is what works; it is tentative, constantly changing	Individual is source of all reality; individual defines reality
How to Learn about Reality	Train the mind to think rationally	Interact with environment; experiment	Engage in self-discovery; create meaning
Application to Supervision	Supervisor is expert; mechanistically transmits instructional knowledge to teacher	Supervisor works democratically with teachers to test old hypotheses and try new ones	Supervisor facilitates teacher exploration and autonomous decision making

and shies away from intrusively guiding a teacher. Supervisors help when needed, protect the rights of others to self-discovery, and encounter the teacher as a person of full importance.

Table 5.2 compares the three superphilosophies.

Checking Your Own Educational Philosophy and Supervisory Beliefs

Two instruments are included here to test whether your supervisory beliefs have a relationship to your educational philosophy. The first, developed by Patricia D. Jersin and entitled "What Is Your Educational Philosophy?" is found in Appendix A. The second, developed by Glickman and Tamashiro (1981) and entitled "Determining One's Beliefs Regarding Teacher Supervision," helps you look at supervisor practices in school settings as reflective of three predominate systems. Those belief systems correspond to the philosophies of essentialism, experimentalism, and existentialism, and are labeled *directive* supervision, *collaborative* supervision, and *nondirective* supervision. Glickman and Tamashiro (1980) wrote:

> Directive Supervision is an approach based on the belief that teaching consists of technical skills with known standards and competencies for all teachers to be effective. The supervisor's role is to inform, direct, model, and assess those competencies.
>
> Collaborative Supervision is based on the belief that teaching is primarily problem solving, whereby two or more persons jointly pose hypotheses to a problem, experiment, and implement those teaching strategies that appear to be most relevant in their own surroundings. The supervisor's role is to guide the problem-solving process, be an active member of the interaction, and keep the teachers focused on their common problems.
>
> Non-Directive Supervision has as its premise that learning is primarily a private experience in which individuals must come up with their own solutions to improving the classroom experience for students. The supervisor's role is to listen, be nonjudgmental, and provide self-awareness and clarification experiences for teachers. (p. 76)

The inventory follows.

BOX 5.1 • *The Supervisory Beliefs Inventory*

This inventory is designed for supervisors to assess their own beliefs about teacher supervision and professional development. The inventory assumes that supervisors believe and act according to all three of the orientations of supervision, but that one usually dominates. The inventory is designed to be self-administered and self-scored. Supervisors are asked to choose one of two options. A scoring key follows.

Instructions: Circle either A or B for each item. You may not completely agree with either choice, but choose the one that is closest to how you feel.

1. A. Supervisors should give teachers a large degree of autonomy and initiative within broadly defined limits.
   B. Supervisors should give teachers directions about methods that will help them improve their teaching.
2. A. It is important for teachers to set their own goals and objectives for professional growth.
   B. It is important for supervisors to help teachers reconcile their personalities and teaching styles with the philosophy and direction of the school.
3. A. Teachers are likely to feel uncomfortable and anxious if the objectives on which they will be evaluated are not clearly defined by the supervisor.
   B. Evaluations of teachers are meaningless if teachers are not able to define with their supervisors the objectives for evaluation.
4. A. An open, trusting, warm, and personal relationship with teachers is the most important ingredient in supervising teachers.
   B. A supervisor who is too intimate with teachers risks being less effective and less respected than a supervisor who keeps a certain degree of professional distance from teachers.
5. A. My role during supervisory conferences is to make the interaction positive, to share realistic information, and to help teachers plan their own solutions to problems.
   B. The methods and strategies I use with teachers in a conference are aimed at our reaching agreement over the needs for future improvement.
6. In the initial phase of working with a teacher:
   A. I develop objectives with each teacher that will help accomplish school goals.
   B. I try to identify the talents and goals of individual teachers so they can work on their own improvement.
7. When several teachers have a similar class room problem, I prefer to:
   A. Have the teachers form an ad hoc group and help them work together to solve the problem.
   B. Help teachers on an individual basis find their strengths, abilities, and resources so that each one finds his or her own solution to the problem.
8. The most important clue that an in-service workshop is needed occurs when:
   A. The supervisor perceives that several teachers lack knowledge or skill in a specific area, which is resulting in low morale, undue stress, and less effective teaching.
   B. Several teachers perceive the need to strengthen their abilities in the same instructional area.
9. A. The supervisory staff should decide the objectives of an in-service workshop since they have a broad perspective on the teachers' abilities and the school's needs.
   B. Teachers and supervisory staff should reach consensus about the objectives of an in-service workshop before the workshop is held.
10. A. Teachers who feel they are growing personally will be more effective

BOX 5.1 • Continued

than teachers who are not experiencing personal growth.

B. The knowledge and ability of teaching strategies and methods that have been proven over the years should be taught and practiced by all teachers to be effective in their classrooms.

11. When I perceive that a teacher might be scolding a student unnecessarily:

A. I explain, during a conference with the teacher, why the scolding was excessive.

B. I ask the teacher about the incident, but do not interject my judgments.

12. A. One effective way to improve teacher performance is to formulate clear behavioral objectives and create meaningful incentives for achieving them.

B. Behavioral objectives are rewarding and helpful to some teachers but stifling to others; some teachers benefit from behavioral objectives in some situations but not in others.

13. During a preobservation conference:

A. I suggest to the teacher what I could observe, but I let the teacher make the final decision about the objectives and methods of observation.

B. The teacher and I mutually decide the objectives and methods of observation.

14. A. Improvement occurs very slowly if teachers are left on their own; but when a group of teachers work together on a specific problem, they learn rapidly and their morale remains high.

B. Group activities may be enjoyable, but I find that individual, open discussion with a teacher about a problem and its possible solutions leads to more sustained results.

15. When a professional development work shop is scheduled:

A. All teachers who participated in the decision to hold the workshop should be expected to attend it.

B. Teachers, regardless of their role in forming a workshop, should be able to decide if the workshop is relevant to their personal or professional growth and, if not, should not be expected to attend.

Scoring Key

Step 1. Circle your answer from Part II of the inventory in the following columns:

Column I	Column II	Column III
1B	1A	
	2B	2A
3A	3B	
4B		4A
	5B	5A
6A		6B
	7A	7B
8A		8B
9A	9B	
10B		10A
11A		11B
12A	12B	
	13B	13A
14B	14A	
	15A	15B

(continued)

BOX 5.1 • Continued

Step 2. Tally the number of circled items in each column and multiply by 6.7.

     2.1 Total response in column I _____ × 6.7 =_____
     2.2 Total response in column II _____ × 6.7 =_____
     2.3 Total response in column III_____ × 6.7 =_____

Step 3. Interpretation: The product you obtained in step 2.1 is an approximate percentage of how often you take a directive approach to supervision, rather than either of the other two approaches. The product you obtained in step 2.2 is an approximate percentage of how often you take a collaborative approach, and that in step 2.3 an approximate percentage of how often you take a nondirective approach.

Source: From Carl D. Glickman, *Developmental Supervision: Alternative Approaches for Helping Teachers Improve Instruction*, pp. 13–15. Reprinted by permission of the Association for Supervision and Curriculum Development, Alexandria, Va. Copyright © 1981 by the Association for Supervision and Curriculum Development. All rights reserved. This instrument has been field-tested six times with ninety supervisors and supervisor trainees. Response between the options indicated "good" item discrimination. The items were also critiqued by teachers, curriculum specialists, and college professors in education for theoretical consistency. Dr. Roy T. Tamashiro of Webster College, St. Louis, Missouri, developed this inventory with Carl D. Glickman.

What Does Your Belief Mean in Terms of Supervisor and Teacher Responsibility?

Beliefs about supervision and educational philosophy can be thought of in terms of decision-making responsibility (see Table 5.3). An essentialist philosophy is premised on the supervisor being the expert on instruction and therefore having major decision-making responsibility. A situation of high supervisor responsibility and low teacher responsibility is labeled *directive supervision.* An experimentalist philosophy is premised on the supervisor and teachers being equal partners in instructional improvement; equal supervisor and teacher responsibility is labeled *collaborative supervision.* Existentialist philosophy is premised on teachers discover-

TABLE 5.3 *Relationship of Philosophy, Control, and Supervisory Belief*

Educational Philosophy	*Decision-Making Responsibility*	*Supervisory Belief*
Essentialism	Supervisor high, teacher low	Directive
Experimentalism	Supervisor equal, teacher equal	Collaborative
Existentialism	Supervisor low, teacher high	Nondirective

ing their own capacities for instructional improvement. Low supervisor responsibility and high teacher responsibility is labeled *nondirective supervision*.

As we clarify our own educational philosophy and supervisory beliefs, we rarely find a pure ideological position. Therefore, Sergiovanni's idea of a supervisory platform becomes helpful. What combination of various philosophies and beliefs do we consider important? Perhaps our beliefs are mainly essentialist and directive yet contain parts of experimentalism and collaboration; or perhaps we have another combination of beliefs. A particular platform is not right or wrong; rather, it is an assessment of the bits and pieces we use to create the floor we stand on.

The Authors' Supervisory Platform

Earlier in this chapter we encouraged you to write your supervisory platform. We believe that readers of this book should have a clear idea of what *our* beliefs about supervision are.

Our own supervisory platform is based on the premise that human development is the aim of education. Therefore, supervision should be *eclectic* in practice, directed toward the goal of nondirective, existentialist supervision. Our goal as supervisors is eventually to return control to the teaching faculty to decide on collective, instructional improvements. Such an ideal cannot be achieved suddenly. Instead, the supervisor at times might use behaviors that come from an essentialist-directive belief structure as a point of entry, or might use behaviors that come from an experimentalist-collaborative belief structure as another point of entry. Regardless of the entry point, the supervisor should always strive to shift control to teachers. The supervisor may never allow total autonomy, but moving in that direction is worth the effort. The center of our platform is, therefore, collaborative experimentalism striving toward nondirective existentialism. Other key "planks" in our supervisory platform are listed here. We believe the following:

- All participants in instructional improvement efforts have knowledge to contribute to the supervisory process.
- Supervision should engage participants in reflective inquiry leading to professional growth and renewal.
- Successful supervision produces organizational growth through a synergy of individual and group efforts.
- Successful supervision fosters both common purpose and alternative means to contribute to that purpose; effective supervision recognizes teacher and student diversity.
- Successful supervision integrates various supervision functions into a comprehensive whole.
- Successful supervision is a long-term process; it balances the importance of completing the immediate task with the need to maintain positive long-term interpersonal relationships.

- Successful supervision is built on trust, openness, and mutual respect.
- Successful supervision creates an environment conducive to experimentation and risk taking.
- Successful supervision adapts to changing contexts and cultures within and outside of the school.
- Successful supervision fosters a critical examination of educators' beliefs about teaching and learning as well as movement toward congruence of beliefs and practice.
- Successful supervision requires a wide range of knowledge as well as technical and interpersonal skills.
- Successful supervision takes into consideration principles of adult learning and knowledge about adult and teacher development.

Summary, Conclusions, and Propositions

We have examined the relationship of educational philosophy to supervisory belief and practice. You were asked to define what is meant by good and effective schools and teaching effectiveness and then to determine your own supervisory platform. We revealed our platform of supervision as collaborative experimentalism striving toward nondirective existentialism within a developmental framework. We believe teachers will become collectively purposeful as they gain greater control over decisions for instructional improvement.

The following propositions about supervision that will enhance collective teacher actions are now possible:

- Proposition 1: *Supervisors should use a variety of practices that emanate from various philosophies and belief structures with developmental directionality in mind.* Directive, collaborative, and nondirective supervisory approaches are all valid as long as they aim to increase teacher self-control.
- Proposition 2: *As supervisors gradually increase teacher choice and control over instructional improvement, teachers will become more reflective and committed to improvement, and a sense of ethos or of a cause beyond oneself will emerge.*

Allowing for gradual choice will increase teacher abstraction and autonomy and lead to more altruistic, collective faculty action.

Exercises

Academic

1. Write your own educational platform. Your platform need not exclusively reflect any of the three major philosophies discussed in the chapter. Reflection on the open-ended questions on page 106 about your educational beliefs will help you to build the platform.

2. Write your own supervisory platform. Reflection on the open-ended questions on page 107 about your supervisory beliefs will help you to build the platform.

3. Design a chart comparing the three major philosophies discussed in the chapter in terms of what each philosophy assumes about:

   a. Human nature

   b. What constitutes reality

   c. The human relationship to the environment

   d. The human relationship to fellow humans

   Design a second chart comparing *implications* of the three philosophies in terms of:

   a. How people best learn

   b. The proper goal(s) of education

   c. The appropriate role of the teacher

   d. The appropriate role of the educational supervisor

4. Prepare a report in which you identify one of the three major philosophies discussed in the chapter (essentialism, experimentalism, existentialism) as the one most clearly reflected in U.S. education today. Provide a rationale for your choice.

5. Write a reaction to the authors' supervisory platform. Include your perceptions of problems that might be encountered by a supervisor attempting to make the authors' platform a reality within a public school setting.

Field

1. Ask five teachers from different school districts for single-paragraph descriptions of central office supervisors. Assuming each teacher has given an accurate description of at least one central office supervisor, classify each described supervisor according to his or her probable philosophy (experimentalist, essentialist, existentialist, or other). Summarize your study and conclusions in writing. (Supervisors and school districts should remain anonymous in the teacher descriptions; responding teachers should remain anonymous in your written summary.)

2. Ask five adults to list improvements that should be made in U.S. education. On the basis of the lists, attempt to relate each respondent to one of the major philosophies described in the chapter (essentialism, experimentalism, existentialism). Summarize your study and conclusions in writing.

3. Ask five teachers each to write one or two paragraphs on "What Makes an Effective Supervisor." On the basis of the teachers' responses, predict which supervisory approach each teacher would prefer during classroom supervision or staff development activities.

4. Ask five students to write one or two paragraphs on "What Makes a Good School?" Attempt to relate each student response to one of the three major philosophies described in the chapter (essentialism, experimentalism, existentialism). Write a report reviewing the students' responses and showing whether each response relates to one of the three philosophies, and if so, how.

5. Visit or recall the organization and climate of a selected school. On the basis of your observations or recollections, which of the three major philosophies described in the chapter (essentialism, experimentalism, existentialism) does the school's organization and climate most clearly reflect? Prepare a report discussing the school's organizational and climate characteristics and supporting your philosophical classification of the school.

Developmental

1. Begin an in-depth study of one of the philosophies described in Chapter 5. As you carry out the study, continue to relate your inquiry to education and educational supervision.

2. Plan to retake the Supervisory Beliefs Inventory after finishing this book in order to detect and interpret any changes in your attitude toward supervision.

3. Begin a review of the works of popular authors who present what they consider successful approaches to management, leadership, or interpersonal communication. For each author, consider whether his or her recommended approach or system most nearly resembles a directive, collaborative, nondirective, or eclectic approach. Make a personal evaluation of each author's proposals.

Endnote

1. The descriptions of philosophy in Chapter 5 are taken from C. D. Glickman and J. P. Esposito, *Leadership Guide for Elementary School Improvement:* *Procedures for Assessment and Change* (Boston: Allyn and Bacon, 1979), p. 20.

References

Airiasian, P. W., and Walsh, M. E. 1997. Constructivist cautions. *Phi Delta Kappan, 78*(6), 444–449.

Barnes, S. 1981. *Synthesis of selected research on teacher findings*. Austin, TX: Research and Development Center for Teacher Education.

Brophy, J. 1979. Teacher behavior and its effects. *Journal of Teacher Education 71*, 733–750.

Brophy, J. 1986. *Synthesizing the results of research linking teacher behavior to student achievement*. Paper presented at the annual meeting of the American Educational Research Association, San Francisco, April.

Brophy, J., and Evertson, C. 1976. *Learning from teaching: A developmental perspective*. Boston: Allyn and Bacon.

Council of Professors of Instructional Supervision 1988. *Resolution on effective teaching*. Annual meeting, San Antonio, November.

Denhan C., and Lieberman, A. (Eds.). 1980. *Time to learn*. Washington, DC: U.S. Department of Education.

Gersten, R., Gall, M., Grace, D., Erickson, D., and Stieber, S. 1987. *The differential effects of teacher behavior on high-ability and low-ability students in algebra classes*. Paper presented at annual meeting of the American Educational Research Association, Washington, DC, April.

Glickman, C. D. 1987a. Good and/or effective schools: What do we want? *Kappan 68*(8), 622–624.

Glickman, C. D. 1987b. Unlocking school reform: Uncertainty as a condition of professionalism. *Kappan 69*(2):120–122.

Glickman, C. D., and Tamashiro, R. T. 1980. Determining one's beliefs regarding teacher supervision. *Bulletin 64*(440):74–81.

Glickman, C. D., and Tamashiro, R. T. 1981. The supervisory beliefs inventory. In C. D. Glickman, *Developmental supervision: Alternative practices for helping teachers to improve instruction.* Alexandria, VA: Association for Supervision and Curriculum Development, pp. 12–16.

Griffin, G. A. 1985. Teacher induction: Research issues. *Journal of Teacher Education 36*(1), 42–46.

Hardison, O. B., Jr. 1986. A tree, a streamlined fish, and a self squared dragon: Science as a form of culture. *Georgia Review* (Summer):394–403.

Humphries, J. D. 1981. Factors affecting the impact of curriculum innovation on classroom practice. Unpublished Ph.D. dissertation, University of Georgia.

Johnson, J. A., Collins, H. W., Dupuis, V. L., and Johansen, J. H. 1973. *Foundations of American education.* Boston: Allyn and Bacon.

Joyce B., and Calhoun, E. 1994. Lessons in learning. *American School Board Journal, 81*(12):37–40.

Joyce, B., Showers, B., and Rolheiser-Bennett, C. 1987. Staff development and student learning: A synthesis of research on models of teaching. *Educational Leadership 45*(2):11–23.

Joyce, B., and Weil, M. 1986. *Models of teaching.* Englewood Cliffs, NJ: Prentice Hall.

McLaughlin, M. W., and Marsh, D. D. 1978. Staff development and school change. *Teacher College Record 80*(1):69–74.

Morris, V. C. 1961. *Philosophy and the American school.* Boston: Houghton Mifflin.

Ornstein, A. C. 1990. A look at teacher effectiveness research: Theory and practice. *NASSP Bulletin, 74*(528): 78–88.

Paschal, R. A., Weinstein, T., and Walberg, H. J. 1984. The effects of homework on learning: A quantitative synthesis. *Journal of Educational Research 78,* 97–104.

Porter, A. C., and Brophy, J. 1988. Synthesis of research on good teaching: Insights from the work of the Institute for Research on Teaching. *Educational Leadership 45*(8): 74–85.

Pratte, R. 1971. *Contemporary theories of education.* Scranton, PA: T. Y. Crowell.

Rosenshine, B. 1983. Teaching functions in instructional programs. *The Elementary School Journal 83,* 335–351.

Rosenshine, B. 1986a. *Unsolved issues in teaching content: A critique of a lesson on Federalist Paper No. 10.* Paper presented at the annual meeting of the American Educational Research Association, San Francisco, April.

Rosenshine, B. 1986b. A synthesis of research on explicit teaching. *Educational Leadership 43*(7): 60–69.

Sergiovanni, T. J., and Starrat R. J. 1983. *Supervision: Human perspectives* (3rd ed.) (pp. 226–227). New York: McGraw-Hill.

Showers, B. 1990. Aiming for superior classroom instruction for all children: A comprehensive staff development model. *Remedial and Special Education, 7*(3): 35–39.

Stalling, J. 1987. For whom and how long is the Hunter-based model appropriate? Response to Robbins and Wolfe. *Educational Leadership 44*(5): 62–63.

Vanezky, R. L. 1982. *Effective schools for reading instructions.* Address to the California (Calfee) Reading Project, Stanford University, January.

Suggested Readings

Borich, G. D. 1992. *Effective teaching methods.* New York: Macmillan.

Brandt, R. (Ed.). 1992. *Educational Leadership 49*(7). Theme issue on "Beyond 'Effective Teaching.'"

Brooks, J. G., and Brooks, M. G. 1993. *The case for Constructivist classrooms.* Alexandria, VA: Association for Supervision and Curriculum Development.

Joyce, B. R., and Weil, M. 1996. *Models of teaching* (5th ed.). Boston: Allyn and Bacon.

Kindsvatter, R. 1992. *Dynamics of effective teaching.* New York: Longman.

Oser, F. K., Dick, A., and Patry, J. (Eds.). 1992. *Effective and responsible teaching.* San Francisco: Jossey-Bass.

Power, E. J. 1996. *Educational philosophy: A history from the ancient world to modern America.* New York: Garland.

Waxman, H. C., and Walberg, H. J. 1991. *Effective teaching: Current research.* Berkeley: McCutchan.

Part II

Conclusion

Part II reviewed the prerequisite knowledge for supervision as the developmental function for effective schools. You have read about The Norm: Why Schools Are as They Are (Chapter 2); The Exception: What Schools Can Be (Chapter 3); Adult and Teacher Development within the Context of the School: Clues for Supervisory Practice (Chapter 4); and Reflections on Schools, Teaching and Supervision (Chapter 5). A number of propositions were constructed from each chapter to set the framework for supervision being viewed as a developmental function. Those propositions are placed together as general, guiding principles to review.

What Is

- Proposition 1: Supervision cannot rely on the existing work environment of schools to stimulate instructional improvement.
- Proposition 2: Supervisors cannot assume that teachers are reflective, autonomous, and responsible for their own development.
- Proposition 3: Supervisors will have to redefine their responsibilities—from controllers of teachers' instruction to involvers of teachers in decisions about school instruction.

What Can Be

- Proposition 1: Supervision can strengthen teachers' belief in a cause beyond oneself.
- Proposition 2: Supervision can promote teachers' sense of efficacy.
- Proposition 3: Supervision can make teachers aware of how they complement each other in striving for common goals.

- Proposition 4: Supervision can stimulate teachers to appraise, reflect, and adapt their instruction.
- Proposition 5: Supervision can challenge teachers toward more varied, abstract thought.

Implications of Contrasting Adult and Teacher Development

- Proposition 1: Effective supervision responds to the principles of adult learning. Teachers' learning should be related to their experiences, needs, and learning strengths; should include opportunities for collaborative action, reflection, and critical thinking; and should be directed toward teacher empowerment.
- Proposition 2: Effective supervision responds to and fosters teacher stage development. Teachers function at different stages of cognitive, conceptual, moral, and ego development and at different stages of consciousness and concern. Teachers should not be treated as a homogeneous group. Rather, supervision should be matched to teachers' developmental stages. Supervision also should foster teacher growth toward higher stages of development.
- Proposition 3: Effective supervision recognizes and supports different phases within teachers' life cycles. It responds to young teachers' excitement and idealism, helps middle-aged teachers cope with life reassessment and reprioritizing, and provides opportunities for older teachers to consolidate achievements and identify remaining career objectives.
- Proposition 4: Effective supervision helps teachers to understand, navigate, and learn from life transition events. It provides special support and rewards for transitions from preservice to in-service teaching, probationary to tenured status, regular teaching duties to teacher leadership responsibilities, and employment to retirement.
- Proposition 5: Effective supervision recognizes and accommodates teachers' various social roles. It helps teachers to recognize the relationship of personal and family roles to their professional roles and to balance competing demands of all three roles.
- Proposition 6: Effective administration and supervision foster teacher motivation. Effective administration provides for Maslow's lower-level needs and Herzberg's hygiene factors. Effective supervision provides for Herzberg's motivating factors and Maslow's higher-stage needs, gradually increases teacher choice and decision making, and facilitates teachers' self-actualization.

Supervisory Belief to Move from What Is to What Can Be

- Proposition 1: Supervisors should use a variety of practices that emanate from various philosophical and belief structures, with a developmental directionality in mind.
- Proposition 2: As supervisors gradually increase teacher choice and control over instructional improvement, teachers will become more reflective and committed to improvement, and a sense of ethos or cause beyond oneself will emerge.

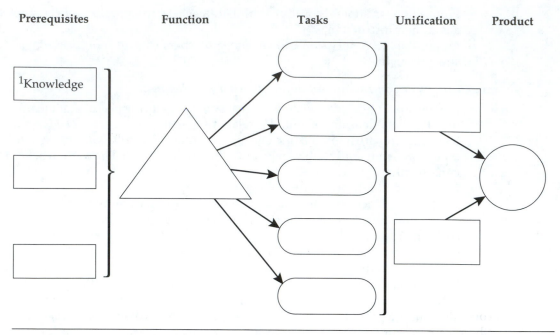

| Prerequisites | Function | Tasks | Unification | Product |

FIGURE II.I   *SuperVision for Successful Schools*

At the end of each of the book's remaining parts, you will be reminded of the organization of effective supervision as a developmental function. See Figure II.1, in which the knowledge prerequisite has been filled in but many geometric figures remain empty. The next section will deal with the prerequisite of interpersonal skills.

Interpersonal Skills

The organization of this book was outlined in Figure 1.1 in Chapter 1. The prerequisites for supervision as a developmental function are knowledge, interpersonal skills, and technical skills. Part II examined the critical knowledge base. Part III will describe interpersonal skills. Chapter 6 will introduce the supervisory behavior continuum, Chapter 7 will introduce the theory of developmental supervision, Chapter 8 will detail the use of directive control behaviors, Chapter 9 will detail the use of directive informational behaviors, Chapter 10 will detail the use of collaborative behaviors, Chapter 11 will detail the use of nondirective behaviors, and Chapter 12 will discuss in detail the theory and practice of developmental supervision.

Knowledge of what needs to be done for teacher growth and school success is the base of a triangle for supervisory action (see Figure III.1). Knowledge needs to be accompanied by interpersonal skills for communicating with teachers and technical skills for planning assessing, observing, and evaluating instructional improvement. We will now turn to the interpersonal skill dimension.

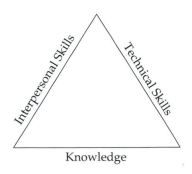

FIGURE III.1 *Prerequisite Dimensions for a Supervisor*

6

Supervisory Behavior Continuum

Know Thyself

This chapter looks at the range of interpersonal behaviors available to a supervisor who is working with individuals and groups of teachers. It will assess how supervisors typically behave with staff in school settings and then determine other behaviors that might be used skillfully and effectively. Later chapters will provide training in each of four clusters of interpersonal skills.

What are the categories of behaviors? After many years of collecting supervisors' observations in meetings with individuals and groups of teachers for purposes of making classroom or school decisions, broad categories of supervisory behaviors have been derived (Glickman, 1981; Wolfgang and Glickman, 1980). These categories encompass almost all observed supervisor behaviors that are deemed purposeful. A *purposeful* behavior is defined as one that contributes to the decision being made at the conference or meeting. The derived categories of supervisory behaviors are listening, clarifying, encouraging, reflecting, presenting, problem solving, negotiating, directing, standardizing, and reinforcing. Definitions of each category are as follows:

- *Listening:* The supervisor sits and looks at the speaker and nods his or her head to show understanding. Gutteral utterances ("uh-huh," "umm") also indicate listening.
- *Clarifying:* The supervisor asks questions and statements to clarify the speaker's point of view: "Do you mean that?" "Would you explain this further?" "I'm confused about this." "I lost you on...."
- *Encouraging:* The supervisor provides acknowledgment responses that help the speaker continue to explain his or her positions: "Yes, I'm following you." "Continue on." "Ah, I see what you're saying; tell me more."

FIGURE 6.1   *The Supervisory Behavior Continuum*

1	*2*	*3*	*4*	*5*
Listening	Clarifying	Encouraging	Reflecting	Presenting

T

s

Clusters of behaviors: Nondirective

Key: T = Maximum teacher responsibility   S = Maximum supervisor responsibility
       t = Minimum teacher responsibility   s = Minimum supervisor responsibility

- *Reflecting:* The supervisor summarizes and paraphrases the speaker's message for verification of accuracy: "I understand that you mean…." "So, the issue is…." "I hear you saying…."
- *Presenting:* The supervisor gives his or her own ideas about the issue being discussed: "This is how I see it." "What can be done is…." "I'd like us to consider…." "I believe that…."
- *Problem solving:* The supervisor takes the initiative, usually after a preliminary discussion of the issue or problem, in pressing all those involved to generate a list of possible solutions. This is usually done through statements such as: "Let's stop and each write down what can be done." "What ideas do we have to solve this problem?" "Let's think of all possible actions we can take."
- *Negotiating:* The supervisor moves the discussion from possible to probable solutions by discussing the consequences of each proposed action, exploring conflict or priorities, and narrowing down choices with questions such as: "Where do we agree?" "How can we change that action to be acceptable to all?" "Can we find a compromise that will give each of us part of what we want?"
- *Directing:* The supervisor tells the participant(s) either what the choices are: "As I see it, these are the alternatives: You could do A…, B…, or C…. Which of these make the most sense to you and which will you use?" *Or* the supervisor tells the participants what is to be done: I've decided that we will do…." "I want you to do…." "The policy will be…." "This is how it is going to be." "We will then proceed as follows."
- *Standardizing:* The supervisor sets the expected criteria and time for the decision to be implemented. Target objectives are set. Expectations are conveyed with words, such as: "By next Monday, we want to see…." "Report back to me on this change by…." "Have the first two activities carried out by…." "I want an improvement of 25 percent involvement by the next meeting." "We have agreed that all tasks will be done before the next observation."

FIGURE 6.1 *Continued*

6	7	8	9	10
Problem Solving	*Negotiating*	*Directing*	*Standardizing*	*Reinforcing*

				t
				s
Collaborative		Directive Informational	Directive Control	

• *Reinforcing:* The supervisor strengthens the directive and the criteria to be met by telling of possible consequences. Possible consequences can be positive, in the form of praise: "I know you can do it!" "I have confidence in your ability!" "I want to show others what you've done!" Consequences also can be negative: "If it's not done on time, we'll lose the support of…." "It must be understood that failure to get this done on time will result in…."

The foregoing categories of interpersonal supervisory behavior move participants toward a decision. Some supervisory behaviors place more responsibility on the teacher(s) to make the decision, others place more responsibility on the supervisor to make the decision, and still others indicate a shared responsibility for decision making. The categories of behaviors are listed in a sequence on the supervisory behavior continuum (Figure 6.1) to reflect the scale of control or power.

When a supervisor *listens* to the teacher, *clarifies* what the teacher says, *encourages* the teacher to speak more about the concern, and *reflects* by verifying the teacher's perceptions, then clearly it is the teacher who is in control. The supervisor's role is that of an active prober or sounding board for the teacher to make his or her own decision. The teacher has high control and the supervisor low control over the actual decision (big *T*, small *s*). This is seen as a *nondirective interpersonal approach*.

When a supervisor uses nondirective behaviors to understand the teacher's point of view but then participates in the discussion by *presenting* his or her own ideas, *problem solving* by asking all parties to propose possible actions, and then *negotiating* to find a common course of action satisfactory to teacher and supervisor, then the control over the decision is shared by all. This is viewed as a *collaborative interpersonal approach*.

When a supervisor *directs* the teacher in what the alternatives are from which the teacher might choose, and after the teacher selects, the supervisor *standardizes* the time and criteria of expected results, then the supervisor is the major source of information, providing the teacher with restricted choice (small *t*, big *S*). This is viewed as a *directive informational interpersonal approach*.

Finally, when a supervisor *directs* the teacher in what will be done, *standardizes* the time and criteria of expected results, and reinforces the consequences of action or inaction, then the supervisor has taken responsibility for the decision. (small *t*, big *S*). The supervisor is clearly determining the actions for the teacher to follow. These behaviors are called a *directive control interpersonal approach*.

Outcomes of Conference

Another way of clarifying the distinctions among supervisory approaches is by looking at the outcomes of the conference and determining who controls the final decision for instructional improvement.

Approach	Outcome
Nondirective	Teacher self-plan
Collaborative	Mutual plan
Directive informational	Supervisor-suggested plan
Directive control	Supervisor-assigned plan

In the nondirective approach, the supervisor facilitates the teacher's thinking in developing a self-plan. In the collaborative approach, both supervisor and teacher share information and possible practices as equals in arriving at a mutual plan. In the directive informational approach, the supervisor provides the focus and the parameters of possible actions, and the teacher is asked to choose within the supervisor's suggestions. In the directive control approach, the supervisor tells the teacher what is to be done. Nondirective provides maximum teacher choice; collaborative, mutual choice; directive informational, selected choice; and directive control, no choice in the outcome of the conference.

Valid Assessment of Self

After assessing our own approach to individuals and groups, we need to make sure that how we perceive ourselves is consistent with how others perceive us. For example, if we checked that we typically use a collaborative approach with individuals and a nondirective approach with groups, then we need further information to know whether that is true. If not, then later in this chapter we might recommend a continuation, refinement, or discontinuation with a cluster of behaviors that simply do not exist in anyone's mind but our own. As an example, let us give a personal instance of erroneous self-perception.

As a school principal in New Hampshire, one of the authors regarded himself as operating a successful school and being accessible to teachers. He could document success by external evidence—state and national recognition the school had received and complimentary letters from numerous visitors. He documented his accessibility through casual discussions with teachers in the lounge and by having an open-office policy for every staff member who wished to speak with him. In his third year as a principal at this particular school, the superintendent asked all principals in the school system to allow teachers to evaluate principal performance. One item on the evaluation form was "Ability to Listen to Others," followed by a numerical scale of responses from 1 ("rarely listens") to 7 ("almost always listens"). Before giving the form to teachers, the author filled out the same evaluation form according to his own perception of his performance. He confidently circled the number 7 on "ability to listen." Once the teachers' responses were collected and results were received, he was amazed to find that the lowest teacher rating on the entire survey was on that very item on which he had rated himself highest. To the author's chagrin, there was an obvious discrepancy between his own perception of performance and staff perceptions.

Johari Window

The Johari Window (Luft, 1970) provides a graphic way to look at what we know and do not know about our behavior (see Figure 6.2). Visualize a window with four windowpanes. In this scheme, there are four windowpanes of the self in which behaviors are either known or not known by self (the supervisor) and others (the teachers). In windowpane 1, there are behaviors that both supervisor and teachers know the supervisor uses. This is the *public self.* For example, the supervisor knows that when he or she is anxious, speech will become halting and hesitant; teachers are also aware of what such speech indicates.

In windowpane 2 is the *blind self*—behaviors the supervisor practices that are unknown to the self but are known to teachers. For example, as a school principal, one of the authors was displaying behaviors toward teachers that he thought were listening behaviors, but teachers saw the same behaviors as a failure to listen. Of

	Known to Supervisor	Not Known to Supervisor
Known to Teachers	1. Public self	2. Blind self
Not Known to Teachers	3. Private self	4. Unknown self

FIGURE 6.2 *Adaptation of Johari Window*

Source: Adapted from Joseph Luft, *Group Processes: An Introduction to Group Dynamics* (New York: National Press Books, 1970).

course, once one becomes aware of teachers' perceptions of those behaviors, the blind self becomes the public self.

In windowpane 3 is the *private self*—behaviors the supervisor has knowledge about but that teachers do not know. For instance, in new situations a supervisor might mask his or her unsureness by being extroverted in greeting others. Only the supervisor knows that this behavior is covering up insecurity, once the supervisor discloses this perception to others, the private self becomes public.

Finally, there is windowpane 4, the *unknown self.* There are actions a supervisor takes of which both supervisors and teachers are unaware. From time to time the supervisor might rapidly shift his legs while speaking behind a table. Neither supervisor or teachers are aware of this leg movement. Perhaps a supervisor becomes irritated while a certain teacher is speaking. The supervisor may not know why she is irritated or even that she feels this way, and the teacher may not know either. The unknown self is unconscious to all; it becomes private, blind, or public only by circumstances that create a new awareness.

What does the Johari Window have to do with supervision? We cannot become more effective as supervisors unless we know what we are doing. We may, at our discretion, decide to keep parts of ourselves private. (For example, we may not want teachers to know all the details of our life and personality.) Yet we need to understand that by remaining largely private and not sharing the experiences that bind us as humans, we are creating a distance when we work with teachers. We may prefer formality and distance and may be able to document that such privateness accomplishes certain results. On the other hand, we must also accept that our privateness will be reciprocal, and that staff may not easily discuss personal situations that may affect teaching performance. First, we must be aware of how private or public we are with our staff and determine if we desire teachers to be the same way with us. Second, as supervisors, we cannot afford to be blind to our own behaviors and the effect of those behaviors on others. We can improve only what we know; to believe only our own self-perceptions is to court disaster.

The author's perception of his listening behavior as a principal is a case in point. As long as he saw himself as a wonderful, accessible listener, it did not seem probable that teachers were not coming to him with instructional problems. However, he discovered that on two different occasions teachers had gone to the superintendent about instructional problems of which he was unaware. After the superintendent had told him that teachers were going over his head, he angrily confronted the teachers with their "unprofessional" behavior. It did not occur to the author that he might have been the one at fault. After the staff evaluations, he could no longer delude himself. Many teachers were not telling him their concerns because they did not believe that he would really listen. The author had to face the fact that the staff did not see him as accessible. He might have avoided collecting such information, continued with his euphoric self-perception, and then been devastated as the school fell apart.

We need to check the validity of our own perceptions. Try this: Photocopy the Supervisory Beliefs Inventory (Chapter 5). Allow a staff member who is trusted by the other teachers to distribute and collect the copies. Instructions to teachers should be that no names are to be written on the pages; only circles or checks need to be made on the response sheets. Confidentiality will increase the honesty of the responses. Teachers should know that only summarized results, prepared by the designated teacher, will be given to the supervisor. Therefore, a teacher's individual responses cannot be identified or used against him or her. The supervisor can see which of his or her supervisory beliefs and practices are public (consistent between his or her own perception and others') and which are blind (inconsistent between his or her own perception and others'). With such information, the supervisor can determine which are valid perceptions and which are invalid. With the invalid perceptions, we can attempt to move from the blind to the public self via a program of behavioral change.

Cognitive Dissonance

Invalidity of perceptions creates *cognitive dissonance,* according to a model of motivation by psychologist Leon Festinger (1957). The model is based on the premise that a person cannot live with contradictory psychological evidence—that is, thinking of himself or herself in one way while other sources of information indicate that he or she is different. When the author's perception of his listening abilities were contradicted by teacher perceptions, mental turmoil or cognitive dissonance was created. For example, if you believe that you are a collaborative supervisor and then you receive feedback from teachers that you are a directive supervisor, this will cause cognitive dissonance. We must wrestle with disparate perceptions and reconcile them. If not, the two differing sources of information will continue to bother us. This mental anguish strives to resolve the question of what is it that we really do. The resolution can come about in three alternative ways (Hyman, 1975).

First, we can dismiss the source of contrary evidence as biased and untrue. For example, the principal might rationalize, "I really am a good listener; teachers marked me low because they didn't like the way I scheduled bus duties." Or the supervisor might think he or she really is collaborative: "Teachers simply don't understand what collaboration is." By dismissing the other source of information as erroneous, we can continue to believe that we are what we originally thought. No further change is necessary.

Second, we can change our own self-perception to conform to the other source of information and can then live with the new perception of ourselves. We accept that they are right and we are wrong; thus, our perception will now be theirs. For example, "I really was wrong about my listening abilities, and I now reconcile myself to being a poor listener," or "The supervisor is really not collaborative but instead is, as the teachers say, directive." Accepting the other source of information makes dissonance vanish so that no further change is necessary.

Third, we can accept our original self-perception as how we wish to be perceived, use the other source of information as an indicator of how we are currently perceived, and then change our behaviors to be more similar to our wish. In other words, our perception was not accurate, but it still represents what we want to be. In our example, the author thought he was a good listener, but others said that he was not; so he attempted to change his listening behaviors in order to become a good listener. The supervisor thought he or she was collaborative but others said that he or she was directive; so he or she changed behavior to become more collaborative.

The third alternative to resolving cognitive dissonance creates behavioral change. Whenever we have an idea of how we desire to be matched against the reality of how others see us, there exist conditions for individual change. The acknowledged gap between what is and what should be becomes a powerful stimulus to change. We change our behaviors and gather feedback from others to determine whether others are forming new perceptions of us and more positive results are forthcoming.

Another way to stimulate cognitive dissonance and personal change is to collect objective data on our behaviors, then compare that data to our espoused supervisory platform or self-perceived behaviors. In a case study by Gordon and Brobeck (1995), a supervisor recorded conferences with teachers, then with the aid of a facilitator reviewed conference tapes in order to compare her actual supervisory behaviors with her espoused platform. The supervisor experienced three different types of cognitive dissonance while comparing conference interaction with different teachers to her platform.

Type 1 cognitive dissonance was experienced by the supervisor when her behaviors were inconsistent with her platform and had negative effects on her supervision. An example of this type of dissonance occurred when the supervisor, who espoused a nondirective platform, used directive behaviors with a teacher functioning at high levels of adult development and thereby inhibited the teacher's efforts to make instructional decisions. The supervisor resolved the dissonance by making a commitment to *change her behavior* in future conferences with the teacher by using a nondirective approach consistent with the supervisor's platform.

Type 2 cognitive dissonance was experienced by the supervisor when her behaviors were inconsistent with her platform but nonetheless had positive effects on the supervisory process. An instance of this type of dissonance occurred when the supervisor used directive behaviors which were incongruent with her nondirective platform, but found that her directive behaviors actually fostered teacher growth. Here, in addition to the dissonance between platform and actual behaviors, there was dissonance between the predicted negative results of violating one's platform and the actual results, which were positive. The supervisor resolved this dissonance by *modifying her platform,* adopting the belief that with some teachers in some situations directive or collaborative supervision might be more useful than nondirective supervision.

Finally, *type 3 cognitive dissonance was experienced by the supervisor when her behaviors were consistent with her platform but had negative effects on her supervision.* An example of this type of cognitive dissonance occurred when a teacher misinterpreted data the supervisor had collected during a classroom observation and the supervisor, holding true to her nondirective platform, did not correct the teacher's interpretation. The supervisor thus missed an opportunity to assist the teacher with an instructional problem the teacher was experiencing. The dissonance in this situation was between the predicted positive results of following one's platform and the actual results, which were negative. The supervisor resolved this dissonance by rejecting the part of her old platform that stated "nondirective supervision equals good supervision" and making a commitment to develop a repertoire of supervisory approaches (directive, nondirective, collaborative) and to match supervisory approach to teachers' developmental levels and specific instructional problems. The supervisor, therefore, resolved this third type of cognitive dissonance through a *combination of a modified platform and a commitment to behavioral change.*

Whether it is caused by becoming aware of others' perceptions of our supervision or by reflecting on objective information like tapes of us supervising teachers, cognitive dissonance by its very nature can be an unsettling experience. It is, however, an experience which can stimulate our own professional growth, with dividends for both teachers and students.

Summary, Conclusions, and Preview

This chapter outlined the supervisory behavior continuum and the clustering of interpersonal behaviors into nondirective, collaborative, directive informational, and directive control approaches. Several assessment instruments were provided. A discourse on the Johari Window and cognitive dissonance was given so that we might check the perceptions of our beliefs and behaviors by those who are recipients of our behaviors. To compare our own supervisory beliefs and self-perceived interpersonal behavior with teacher perceptions of our behavior or with objective data is believed to be important in refining and changing behaviors.

What information do we have from those we supervise to confirm or reject our perceptions? What if we find inconsistency in the ways we believe, the ways we work with individuals, and the ways we work with groups? In fact, in real life we may not be consistent in the ways we work with one individual as opposed to another individual, or with one group and another. Neither consistency nor inconsistency is being advocated here. A particular approach is not necessarily better than others. However, there is research evidence that the effectiveness of different supervisory behaviors and approaches is dependent on characteristics of individuals and groups of teachers.

We will next examine and practice the skills of each supervisory approach in terms of actual conferencing and meeting behaviors. Understanding how we behave as supervisors and then refining our present behaviors are the first steps toward acquiring new interpersonal behaviors.

Exercises

Academic

1. After reviewing the 10 categories of supervision defined in the chapter, list specific behaviors your supervisor has exhibited while supervising you. For each example, write a brief description of your feelings toward the supervisor while he or she was using the given behavior, as well as your behavioral response to the situation. What does a review of your feelings and responses tell you about the supervisory approach you most prefer? Least prefer?

2. The chapter proposes three possible ways of resolving the mental conflict brought about by cognitive dissonance. Prepare a report in which you cite examples of cognitive dissonance you have personally experienced and your reaction to each resulting dilemma. Based on your recollections, which of the three possible responses to cognitive dissonance has been your typical mode of resolution?

3. Label the left-hand column of a sheet of paper "Public Self" and the right-hand column "Private Self." Think of personality or other characteristics that you intentionally disguise in your work setting. For each characteristic, describe in a few words the image you consciously present to others (left-hand column) and the real you that your public behavior conceals (right-hand column).

4. Locate a research study on the effectiveness of one or more of the following supervisor approaches to supervisor-teacher conferences: (a) directive control, (b) directive informational, (c) collaborative, and (d) nondirective. Summarize the purpose, methods, results, and conclusions of the study in writing.

5. Chapter 6 relates an experience in which a discrepancy between a blind self and a public self led to communication problems with subordinates. Discuss in writing three other situations in which conflicts between a supervisor's blind self and public self might eventually lead to leadership problems.

Field

1. Arrange to visit a teacher's class and for a postobservation conference with that teacher. The postobservation conference should include an analysis of the teacher's instructional performance, the setting of instructional improvement goals, and planning a strategy for meeting those goals. Record the postobservation on audiotape. Refer to the categories of supervisor behavior in this book as you listen to the tape. Write a paper in which you state whether you used a primarily directive, collaborative, or nondirective approach during the postobservation conference. Cite examples of specific behaviors you exhibited during the postobservation conference. Compare those behaviors with your results on the Supervisory Beliefs Inventory.

2. Carry out the exercise suggested in the chapter. Prepare a written report on the results of the exercise and your reaction to those results.

3. Put yourself in the shoes of an individual you supervise or have supervised. (Even those not in formal supervisory roles have at one time or another been responsible for supervising others.) Write a description of your supervisory style; be careful to

describe your supervisory style as the other person would, not as you would. Compare this description of your supervisory style with your results on the Supervisory Beliefs Inventory.

4. Draw a two-frame cartoon for each of the following themes: (a) public self—private self, (b) my message—their perception, (c) cognitive dissonance. Base your cartoons on personal experiences or observations in a school setting. Write narratives explaining each cartoon.

Developmental

1. Begin to make mental notes on behaviors you use when supervising others. Look for patterns of behavior that can be related to an orientation toward supervision (directive, collaborative, nondirective, eclectic) of which you may not now be conscious.

2. Informally observe others in leadership roles. Do their behaviors tend to cluster toward a directive, collaborative, or nondirective approach?

3. Begin to examine discrepancies between your public self and your private self, and consider possible reasons for such discrepancies.

References

Festinger, L. 1957. *A theory of cognitive dissonance.* Stanford, CA: Stanford University Press.

Glickman, C. D. 1981. *Developmental supervision: Alternative practices for helping teachers improve instruction.* Alexandria, VA: Association for Supervision and Curriculum Development.

Gordon, S. P., and Brobeck, S. R. (1995). *Supervisor reflection on supervision: A new version of the post-conference analysis.* Paper presented at the annual meeting of the American Educational Research Association, San Francisco, April.

Hyman, R. T. 1975. *School administrator's handbook of teacher supervision and evaluation methods* (pp. 46–47). Englewood Cliffs, NJ: Prentice Hall.

Luft, J. 1970. *Group processes: An introduction to group dynamics.* New York: National Press Books.

Wolfgang, C. H., and Glickman, C. D. 1980. *Solving discipline problems: Alternative strategies for teachers.* Boston: Allyn and Bacon.

7

Developmental Supervision

An Introduction

This chapter provides an introduction to developmental supervision—a model that will be described in greater detail throughout the remainder of the text. We will begin by sharing four case studies of developmental supervision in action. As you read the four case studies, compare them in relation to the following:

1. The teacher's levels of development, expertise, and commitment to solving the problem
2. The nature of the problem
3. The interpersonal behaviors of the supervisor, including any shifts in supervisory behavior which take place

Case Study One

After receiving complaints about Gerald Watson's teaching methods from students, parents, and other teachers, principal Martha Cozero observed Gerald's science class on several occasions. Regardless of lesson content or student population, all of the observed lessons followed the same pattern. First, seat by seat and row by row, students would take turns reading paragraphs from the science text. Next, Gerald would pass out a worksheet for students to complete independently. If students finished their worksheets before the end of class, they were told to begin their homework assignment, which always consisted of written exercises from the textbook. During independent seatwork, Gerald usually sat at his desk reading sports magazines, looking up only to give an "evil-eye" to students who were talking to each other or out of their seats.

Martha was not surprised by Gerald's "instructional" routine. She *was* surprised that he made no attempt at more active teaching even during her classroom observations. Martha used the first of several conferences with Gerald to try to find out more about his attitudes toward teaching science. He admitted that he rarely graded or returned the written assignments that he required students to complete. Gerald stated that he neither understood nor used the hands-on science program that the middle school science team had agreed to adopt the previous year. He had not attended the science team's after-school meetings that led to the decision to adopt the program. He had taken personal days rather than attend the all-day workshops during which science teachers developed skills necessary to implement the program. Gerald told Martha that he was six years away from retirement and saw no reason to learn new skills or use new teaching methods.

After reflecting on her classroom observations and conference with Gerald, Martha designed an improvement plan that she presented to him during their next conference. During that conference, she told Gerald that his current instructional strategies and failure to learn about or implement the school's science program were detrimental to student learning and that his approach to teaching science was unacceptable. She stated that Gerald's improvement goals would be to engage in more active teaching and make use of instructional strategies consistent with the science curriculum's goals. Martha mandated the following steps on Geralds's part:

1. End excessive reliance on students taking turns reading aloud from the science text.
2. Reduce the use of worksheets as a primary instructional strategy.
3. Review written assignments completed by students, and provide students with feedback on their performance.
4. Review the school districts' written curriculum as well as teacher guides for the school's hands-on science program.
5. Visit other science teachers' classrooms to observe the science program in action.
6. Use more hands-on science activities consistent with the adopted science program.

The principal made it clear that the goals and activities she presented were not optional. Martha listened to Gerald's concerns and answered questions about the action plan. She promised to provide him with resources and materials necessary to implement the new science program. Martha scheduled a series of classroom observations that would allow her to monitor Gerald's progress with the plan and provide him with assistance and feedback on the new instructional strategies he would be trying out.

Gerald reluctantly began to implement the mandated improvement plan. Although progress was slow, his teaching methods did begin to change. Some of Gerald's attempts at hands-on learning worked well, others did not. Students were enjoying the hands-on activities and demonstrating levels of interest and learning that Gerald had not thought possible. Eventually, he admitted to Martha that missing the workshops on the new curriculum had been a mistake: There were many gaps in his knowledge of the new curriculum that his readings and observations had not filled.

Martha decided that Gerald needed formal training in how to implement the science program if he was going to continue to improve his teaching. She also decided that the effort and progress he had made warranted allowing Gerald some choice in how that training should be acquired. Martha offered Gerald three options for learning more about the program: attendance at two days of in-service education on the program offered by the program's publisher at a nearby intermediate unit, after-school workshops to be presented by the science supervisor at the district's other middle school, or individualized training by Jim Adams, the science coordinator at Gerald's middle school. Gerald had always liked Jim so he told Martha that he preferred to receive training from a colleague who was just down the hall and who he could call on if he had problems implementing the curriculum. Jim agreed to work with Gerald, and Martha and Jim designed a plan to provide Gerald with several hours of individualized training and intensive classroom coaching.

Case Study Two

Veteran teacher Bill Levin was assigned as beginning teacher Janice Smith's mentor. Janice had joined the middle school teaching staff eager to try out a variety of innovative teaching strategies she had been introduced to during her teacher preparation program. Now, just two months into her teaching career, Janice was considering leaving the profession at the Thanksgiving break. After a few observations of Janice's teaching, Bill was convinced that Janice had considerable potential as a teacher but that her classroom management problems might prevent her from reaching that potential. Although Janice had been exposed to brief discussions of student discipline problems in several of her teaching methods courses, she had never received systematic training in effective classroom management. Her lack of training and inexperience in dealing with middle school students was becoming increasingly apparent. On several visits to Janice's classroom, Bill observed considerable off-task behavior and numerous student disruptions. Rather than attempting to control the high noise level, Janice would first try to yell over the student conversations, then scream at disruptive students who had ignored her pleas to quiet down.

Janice knew she had classroom management problems but was not sure why the students behaved the way they did or what she could do to improve the situation. Based on his observations and discussions with Janice, Bill made the following suggestions to the novice teacher:

1. Establish a set of rules and procedures for classroom behavior and determine natural consequences for students who fail to follow those rules and procedures.
2. Share the rules and procedures with the students, explaining the rationale for each rule, procedure, and natural consequence.

3. Give the students the opportunity to practice each rule and procedure under simulated conditions, and provide them with feedback on their performance.
4. Consistently enforce all rules and procedures, providing positive feedback for student compliance and carrying through on natural consequences for noncompliance.

Bill offered to help Janice develop her rules and procedures, rehearse her presentation and explanation to students, and plan opportunities for students to practice new guidelines and receive feedback on their performance. Bill also suggested that Janice try out a number of nonverbal and verbal interventions to correct minor student misbehaviors before they reached a disruptive stage. He explained how in his own classroom he used nonverbal interventions such as eye contact, physical proximity, and touch control, as well as verbal interventions such as use of students' names, reminder of a rule or procedure, and explicit redirection. Bill invited Janice to visit his classroom and observe his classroom management techniques. He also offered to observe Janice's class as she implemented his suggested strategies and techniques, and to provide her with feedback based on the observations.

Janice agreed to try out Bill's recommendations. With considerable assistance from her mentor, she implemented the suggested strategies and techniques. After several weeks, most of the students in Janice's class had increased their amount of time on task considerably and student disruptions had decreased. Janice had made it through to Thanksgiving and was willing to give teaching another chance, at least until the end of the school year. She was still experiencing some problems with classroom management, particularly in the case of three students who regularly ignored the rules and procedures she had set up. These three students seemed to be unaffected by the natural consequences intended to discourage disruptive behavior. Janice informed Bill that the classroom management system, although generally effective, had failed with these three students.

Bill was pleased with the progress Janice had made but concerned about the students who seemed to be immune to his protégée's new classroom management strategies and techniques. He knew that even a few students could disrupt Janice's entire class if she was unable to help them change their behavior. The mentor offered two possibilities for dealing with the three disruptive students. One was for Janice to work individually with each of the problem students to develop a behavior contract. In the contract, teacher and student would negotiate specific behavioral improvement goals, a time period for meeting the goals, teacher and student actions, assessment of student progress, and rewards and consequences.

The second possibility suggested by Bill was that Janice keep daily logs of disruptive behaviors by each of the three students. The initial record keeping would last for a period of two weeks, with the students required to sign log entries each day. At the end of the two-week period, Janice could assign the three students individual improvement plans aimed at reducing the types of behaviors recorded in the logs. Once the plan was initiated, Janice could record both positive and disruptive student behaviors in the logs in order to document student progress toward improvement goals.

When Bill asked Janice to select one of the two options, she asked if it would be agreeable to use parts of both strategies by first logging student behaviors for two weeks and then negotiating a behavioral contract with each of the three students. Bill agreed that this would be an appropriate synthesis of the two strategies. He offered to assist Janice in reviewing the log entries and writing the three behavioral contracts—an offer that Janice readily accepted.

Case Study Three

Social studies teacher Mike Phillips had requested a conference with George Cantinni, his department chairperson. Mike was not satisfied with the quality of discussions in his current events class. George asked Mike to describe the type of class discussions he wanted to take place. Mike replied that he wanted to foster students' "higher-level" thinking and open dialogue concerning important social and political issues. When George asked Mike what was preventing such discussion, he replied that he probably hindered class discussions himself by asking too many simple recall questions rather than questions that would spark student interest and discussion. Another problem Mike discussed was that typically only a few students participated in class discussions, and he had done little to encourage those who did not participate to join in.

Based on Mike's description of the problem, George suggested that changes in the way Mike structured class discussions might be in order. He proposed that Mike and he take a few minutes to write down separately ideas for improvement. After both had reflected on and listed potential actions, George asked Mike to share his ideas. Mike's possible actions included asking students more open-ended questions, giving the entire class more time to think about a question before calling on one of the students to respond, and randomly calling on students in order to increase student participation. George responded that he agreed with the first two suggestions. He added that while randomly calling on students to respond was appropriate in some situations, he did not believe that it was a viable way to foster the open, reflective dialogue that Mike was hoping for.

George introduced additional possible actions by building on ideas already suggested by Mike. He suggested that Mike refer to the upper five categories of Bloom's taxonomy when planning discussion lessons, first to help determine the lesson's objectives and then to formulate relevant discussion questions. George reviewed Bloom's cognitive domain, which Mike vaguely recalled from his undergraduate years. To Mike's idea of giving the class time to think about questions before responding to them, George added the option of allowing students to discuss questions in small groups prior to whole-class discussion. Finally, George suggested that during whole-class discussions the class as well as individual students be provided adequate "wait time" to formulate their responses and that appropriate wait time also *follow* individual student responses.

Mike responded that he liked the idea of basing learning objectives and discussion questions on Bloom's taxonomy, but thought he might have trouble formulating the different types of questions. He asked George if he would be willing to help develop some questions for Mike's next few lessons. George agreed, and also offered to observe a few of Mike's lessons in order to record the number of questions asked within each category of Bloom's taxonomy. Mike replied that he would appreciate the feedback. Regarding George's suggestion of beginning discussions with small groups, Mike stated that for the time being he would prefer to lead whole-class discussions throughout his lessons. He said that he had a fairly good understanding of the different types of wait time, but would like to have some feedback on how many seconds he was allowing for each type of wait time. George agreed to collect data on Mike's wait time during the observations they had already agreed to. Mike and George also agreed that in addition to types of questions and wait time, George would track the number of students who participated in each class discussion.

After considerably more discussion, Mike and George had worked out an action plan for instructional improvement. The plan was written as follows:

Goal: to increase student participation in open discussion requiring student interpretation, application, analysis, synthesis, and evaluation.

Mike Phillips's Responsibilities:

1. Participate in the design of student learning objectives within each of Bloom's upper five categories of cognitive objectives (listed in goal statement).
2. Participate in the creation of open-ended discussion questions for each of the five types of learning objectives.
3. Allow at least five seconds after asking an open-ended question for a student to respond. Call on volunteers only.
4. Allow at least five seconds after calling on an individual student for the student to respond.
5. Wait at least five seconds after a student has responded to an open-ended question before continuing the discussion.

George Cantinni's Responsibilities:

1. Assist Mr. Phillips in designing student learning objectives based on the upper five categories of Bloom's taxonomy.
2. Assist in creating open-ended discussion questions corresponding to stated objectives.
3. Periodically observe Mr. Phillips's class discussions. Collect data on:
   a. Frequency of teacher questions inviting student responses requiring interpretation, application, analysis, synthesis, and evaluation
   b. Duration of wait time after teacher questions, after calling on students to answer questions, and after student responses
   c. Frequency of each student's participation in open-ended discussions

Criteria for Success:

1. In selected classes, open-ended questions will be asked and related discussions held at each of the five upper levels of Bloom's taxonomy.

2. When appropriate, at least five seconds of wait time will be provided after asking open-ended discussion questions, after calling on students to respond to questions, and after student responses.
3. Each student will make at least one contribution to each open-ended class discussion.

Working closely with George over a period of several weeks, Mike made steady progress toward his instructional improvement goal. Eventually, George suggested that Mike had developed sufficient skill at writing open-ended discussion questions that he no longer needed George's assistance during his lesson planning. Mike agreed, but asked George if he would review Mike's discussion questions for a few weeks and give him feedback on their quality. George and Mike also decided that in lieu of additional classroom observations by George, Mike would record his next few class discussions on audiotape. He would review his own performance by analyzing the tapes. George agreed to review the tape of any class discussion for which Mike requested expert feedback.

Case Study Four

Stella Simpson was assistant principal for instruction at Kennedy Elementary School. She had developed a professional development option for teachers wishing to participate in an individualized professional development program. Maria Sanchez had some tentative ideas for a program that would provide development opportunities for herself and others, and requested a meeting with Stella to discuss the plan.

During their meeting, Stella listened, reflected, clarified, and encouraged as Maria discussed a problem she saw emerging at the school. With the growing popularity of cooperative learning, a number of teachers had decided to try out cooperative strategies in their classrooms. Unfortunately, few of the teachers had received in-depth training in cooperative learning. Most had attended only a 60-minute awareness session provided at a recent districtwide in-service education day. Maria, who had received 30 hours of training in cooperative learning, was delighted that other teachers were taking an interest in cooperative learning. However, based on her classroom observations as part of the school's peer-coaching program, she was concerned that many teachers did not have a clear grasp of the basic elements of a cooperative learning lesson. Maria was concerned that if teachers did not develop sufficient expertise in cooperative learning, their use of it would be ineffective, and they would soon abandon it as an instructional strategy.

Stella paraphrased Maria's general concerns, then asked her to discuss specific problems teachers were having with cooperative learning. Maria replied that several teachers were attempting cooperative lessons without teaching students prerequisite social skills. She also stated that they were not building positive interdependence or individual accountability—two vital aspects of cooperative learning—into their lessons. Maria added that, based on her conversations with other teachers, these problems were not confined to teachers she had observed as a peer coach.

Stella agreed with Maria's observations. She had attended the same 30-hour training program as Maria, and her classroom observations verified Maria's concerns. Stella asked Maria for her perceptions of what could be done about the problem. As Maria presented her proposal, Stella continued to listen intently, sometimes paraphrasing Maria's statements, sometimes asking clarifying questions, other times encouraging Maria to elaborate. Maria proposed that she attend an advanced training program that would enable her to develop additional expertise in cooperative learning as well as skills necessary to deliver a training program to other teachers. After completing the advanced program, Maria would deliver a series of evening workshops providing 30 hours of basic training on cooperative learning to interested teachers. Maria also suggested that she provide classroom coaching to the teachers attending her workshops in order to assist them to transfer skills learned in the workshops to their classrooms.

Stella asked Maria if she had considered the difficulties she might encounter when attempting to provide instructional assistance to peers. Maria replied that she had considered the issue, but that since she would be working with volunteer teachers only, she did not see her peer status as a major problem. She reminded Stella that as a participant in the school's peer-coaching program she had successfully provided instructional assistance to many of the teachers who would attend the workshops. Also, she would not attempt to lead workshops for peers until she had received extensive leadership preparation.

Stella told Maria that if her plan was accepted, professional development funds could be used to pay for released time, the costs of Maria's leadership training, and the materials for the evening workshops that Maria would deliver. She told Maria that no funds were available to pay her for the considerable amount of personal time and energy Maria would have to spend to make the program a success. Stella asked Maria if she was willing to make the extensive commitment that her new leadership role would require. After receiving an affirmative response, Stella asked Maria to put together a detailed proposal, including goals, activities, needed resources, criteria for success, a time line, and a tentative budget.

Developmental Supervision

We stated in Chapter 5 that the ultimate aim of the supervisor should be reflective, autonomous teachers facilitated by nondirective supervision. However, the fact that many teachers are functioning at developmental levels or in situations in which self-direction is not feasible means that the supervisor often must initially use collaborative, directive informational, or, in rare cases, directive control behavior. Each of the four case studies represents a different entry point for supervision. In each case, the supervisor based his or her initial supervisory approach on the teacher's levels of development, expertise, and commitment and the nature of the situation.

The case studies provide examples of three phases of developmental supervision. In Phase 1, the supervisor diagnoses the teacher's developmental levels, expertise, commitment, and educational situation, and selects the interpersonal approach that creates the best supervisory match. In Phase 2, the supervisor uses the selected interpersonal approach to assist the teacher in instructional problem solving. In Phase 3 (illustrated in the first three case studies), the supervisor changes his or her interpersonal behavior in the direction of less supervisor control and more teacher control. Such a change in supervisory approach occurs only after the teacher has shown readiness to assume more decision-making responsibility.

In Case Study One, Martha Cozero determined that Gerald Watson was functioning at low levels of development, expertise, and commitment. She was convinced that Gerald's purposeless instructional routine was a serious impediment to student learning. Martha decided to use directive control behaviors in her initial supervisory approach. She identified the problem, presented Gerald with the instructional improvement goal, and directed him to carry out actions to reach the goal. Martha followed up by monitoring and providing feedback on Gerald's progress. Once Gerald had shown some improvement in teaching behaviors and motivation, Martha took a first step away from complete control, asking Gerald to choose one of three training formats.

In Case Study Two, novice Janice Smith's lack of classroom management and problem-solving skills created a different type of instructional problem. Janice initially had been highly motivated. She realized she had classroom management problems. What she needed was intensive assistance in identifying causes and solutions. After observing and conferencing with Janice, mentor Bill Levin decided to use directive informational behaviors during his initial assistance to Janice. Bill identified a goal for Janice of improved classroom management. He suggested a number of actions that she and he could take to move toward that goal. It was up to Janice to accept or reject Bill's suggestions. After Janice had made considerable progress under his mentorship, Bill encouraged her to choose from two alternative strategies for working with three students who displayed chronic discipline problems. Janice and Bill's negotiation and mutual agreement to integrate the two strategies represent movement toward a more collaborative relationship between novice and mentor.

In Case Study Three, Mike Phillips was able to define the problem he was experiencing and identify some causes, but he needed assistance in thinking through a plan to solve the problem. Chairperson George Cantinni decided to use a collaborative approach with Mike. After listening to Mike's perceptions, George shared his own point of view, then suggested that he and Mike both develop and exchange options for solving the problem. During the negotiation process, both Mike and George accepted, rejected, and proposed modifications to ideas presented by the other. Eventually, Mike and George reached mutual agreement on an action plan. George's suggestions several months later that Mike independently design his own discussion questions and tape and review his class discussions was an attempt to move away from collaborative and toward nondirective supervision. Their agreement that George would be available to review Mike's discussion questions and audiotapes indicated a transitional phase between collaborative and nondirective supervision.

In Case Study Four, teacher Maria Sanchez was clearly functioning at high levels of personal and professional development. Assistant principal Stella Simpson used nondirective interpersonal behaviors of listening, reflecting, clarifying, and encouraging as Maria discussed her concerns and proposal. Stella asked Maria to consider the consequences of her plan. Stella's request for a written proposal was made to encourage Maria to decide on details and standards and make a formal commitment to the plan.

Stella Simpson used noncontrolling interpersonal behaviors throughout Case Study Four, encouraging Maria Sanchez to assume full decision-making responsibility. Supervisors in the first three case studies used various levels of control, but *in each of the first three cases, the supervisor moved from more to less control and toward more decision-making responsiblity on the part of the teacher.* Developmental supervision thus is "developmental" in two ways. First, the entry-level supervisory approach is matched with the teacher's current developmental levels and the immediate situation. Second, supervisory behaviors are gradually modified to promote and accommodate long-range teacher development toward higher levels of reflection and problem solving ability.

We purposefully provided case studies that demonstrated a clear matching of teacher developmental levels with supervisory approach. In the real world, interactions are more complex and the idea that a supervisor clearly knows what approach a supervisee needs is suspect. The issue of who determines the approach for another and what should be the criteria for such choice will be explored after fuller explanations of each of the four approaches. For now, let us just suggest that observations and discussions between supervisor and supervisee are the main source of information when determining approach. A supervisee has as much right to be involved in the choice about the present and future approach as does the supervisor. This is not a unilateral decision. The supervisor, simply due to position of authority, does not automatically know what is best for someone else.

Summary and a Look Ahead

This chapter has provided a brief introduction to developmental supervision and case studies of supervisors using alternative supervisory approaches within a developmental frame.

Chapters 8 through 11 provide detailed discussions of the four supervisory approaches encompassed by developmental supervision. Chapter 12 includes in-depth discussions on the theory and application of developmental supervision.

8

Directive Control Behaviors

Supervisor: Have you been using the computers? I haven't seen any students at the desks.

Teacher: Well, I really don't think computers are such an important topic for seventh-grade mathematics. The students need training in basic geometry, not in how to play games with a computer.

Supervisor: As you know, part of the geometry curriculum is on a computer disk. It's not just fun and games. They could be learning geometry as they improve their technology skills.

Teacher: All this computer emphasis is ridiculous! It's another educational fad that's supposed to solve all our problems! I have enough trouble getting kids to learn what's in the book.

Supervisor: I understand your reservations about using the computer, but our school curriculum states that computers are to be used in seventh-grade mathematics. We're committed to doing so, particularly after spending so much money on the equipment and software.

Teacher: I think it's ridiculous.

Supervisor: That's beside the point. I want to see your kids using them.

Teacher: I'd rather not. Couldn't they teach computers in science class? After all, computers are science.

Supervisor: We're now using computers throughout the curriculum, including in science *and* in mathematics. I'd like to see at least one-third of your class begin the software program on plotting graphs by next Friday.

Teacher: Who's going to show them how to operate the program? I don't know how to.

Supervisor: Mrs. Techno, you were a participant in the computer class last summer. You know how to do it.

Teacher: I didn't understand the foggiest bit of it. Professor Wallenwood was a terrible teacher. He just paid attention to all those teachers who already had a computer background.

146

Supervisor: Well, I wasn't aware that you were unsure of how to use the computer in class. I'll call Fred Tirtial, director of media, to come into your class next week to demonstrate how to use the equipment. I'll see to it that he gets the program started in your class, and then you continue with it.

Teacher: Any help would be appreciated.

Supervisor: You keep me posted, and we'll shoot for at least one group of your students working on the graphing program by a week from Friday.

Directive Control Behaviors with Individuals

The foregoing scenario shows a supervisor using directive control behaviors to assist a teacher in improving instruction. The obvious question is that the teacher may respond to such directiveness with a firm refusal: "I am not going to meet with you or follow through with your plans." If the supervisor has a position of conferred authority over teachers, he or she can pull rank by restating the directive and telling the teacher to comply or suffer the consequences. If the supervisor does not have such authority—which, with the exception of school principals, is often the case—then he or she can direct only by convincing the teacher that the suggested plan is correct. Regardless of a line or staff relationship, the supervisor uses directive control behavior with teachers when there is an assumption that the supervisor has greater knowledge and expertise about the issue at hand. In other words, the belief behind directive control behaviors is that the supervisor knows better than the teacher what needs to be done to improve instruction.

It is evident in the scenario that the supervisor has taken over the teacher's problem. At first, the supervisor identified the problem by gathering information from his own observations and discussing this information with the teacher. Next, he told the teacher what to do and provided an explanation of why his suggestion would work. He concluded by reviewing the proposed action and reiterating his expectations for the teacher. The teacher was left with a concrete understanding of what she was expected to do. As we look at a typical sequence of behaviors along the supervisory behavior continuum (Figure 8.1), keep in mind that the sequence and frequency of behaviors will vary, especially in the beginning of the conference, but the directive control approach will end with the supervisor making the final decisions for the teacher. This chapter will accentuate directive behaviors that control teacher actions.

1. Presenting: *Identifying the problem.* The supervisor begins with a general idea of what the needs and difficulties are. Having used observations and gathered information from other sources, the supervisor tells the teacher what seems to be the problem: "I understand that there is a problem with...."
2. Clarifying: *Asking teacher for input into the problem.* The supervisor wants to gather direct information from the teacher about the problem prior to the solution stage. This is done by using the teacher in an advisory capacity, asking the teacher such questions as: "How do you see the problem?" "Why do you think these conditions exist?"

FIGURE 8.1   *The Supervisory Behavior Continuum: Directive Control Behaviors*

1	2	3	4	5
Listening	*Clarifying*	*Encouraging*	*Reflecting*	*Presenting*

T
s

1. Identifying the problem

2. Asking teacher for input into the problem

3. Understanding the teacher's point of view

6. Asking teacher for input into the expectations

Key: T = Maximum teacher responsibility   S = Maximum supervisor responsibility
      t = Minimum teacher responsibility   s = Minimum supervisor responsibility

3. Listening: *Understanding the teacher's point of view.* To gather maximum information in the shortest amount of time, the supervisor must attend carefully to what the teacher says. He or she listens both to the surface messages—"Computers are a waste of time"—and to underlying messages—"I don't know how to use them"—in formulating a complete problem.

4. Problem solving: *Mentally determining the best solution.* The supervisor processes the information and thinks, "What can be done?" After considering various possibilities, he or she selects the needed actions. The supervisor should be confident of indeed having a good, manageable solution to the problem before conveying it to the teacher.

FIGURE 8.1 *Continued*

6	7	8	9	10
Problem Solving	*Negotiating*	*Directing*	*Standardizing*	*Reinforcing*

t

S

4. Mentally determining best solution

5. Telling expectations for teacher

7. Detailing and modifying expectations

8. Repeating and following up on expectations

5. Directing: *Telling expectations to the teacher.* The supervisor tells the teacher in a matter-of-fact way what needs to be done: "I want to see you do the following…" The phrasing of the directive is important. Avoid timid, circular expectations: "Well, maybe you might consider doing…" "Don't you think it would be a good idea to…?" The supervisor is not asking or pleading with the teacher, but *telling.* On the other hand, directing does not mean being vindictive, overbearing, condescending, or insulting. Avoid personal slights or paternalistic references: "I don't know why you can't figure out what needs to be done." "Why can't you get it right in the first place?" "Now listen, honey, I'm going to help you by…." A supervisor should state actions as *I* statements, not as what others think. Tell the teacher what *I* want to happen, not what parents, other teachers, or the superintendent would want to see. A statement such as "If the superintendent saw this, he would tell you to do…" is hiding behind someone else's authority. The supervisor needs to make statements based on his or her own position, credibility, and authority.

6. Clarifying: *Asking the teacher for input into the expectations.* Possible difficulties with the supervisor's directive should be known before the teacher leaves the conference. For example, if circumstances exist that make teacher compliance with the directive impossible, it is better to adjust to those circumstances during the conference than to find out two weeks later why the plan failed. Therefore, after telling the teacher what is expected—"I want one-third of your students using the computers"—the supervisor needs to ask such questions as: "What do you need to carry out this plan?" "How can I help you carry out the plan?"

7. Standardizing: *Detailing and modifying expectations.* After considering the teacher's reactions to the directive, the supervisor solidifies the plan by building in the necessary assistance, resources, time lines, and criteria for expected success. The teacher is then told the revisions: "I can rearrange the visit time to…," "I will find those materials for you," "I will arrange for you to attend…," "I will change the time to three weeks."

8. Reinforcing: *Repeating and following up on expectations.* The supervisor reviews the entire plan and establishes times for checking on progress. The supervisor closes the meeting by making sure the teacher clearly understands the plan: "Do you understand what you're to do?" "Tell me what it is you're now going to do."

Directive Control Behaviors with Groups

Seven Physical Education Department members meet with their supervisor. The supervisor addresses them.

Supervisor: I've been noticing that our physical education classes have not been starting on time. They are to begin at 5 minutes past the hour and end at 15 minutes before the next hour. We're supposed to get in a full 40 minutes of physical education. Some classes are being dismissed early, some late, and the other teachers in the school are complaining. They say our sloppiness is causing other problems—students loitering in the halls, looking into class windows, and straggling in late. We need to begin and end on time. Why is this happening?

Fred Soccerman: Those regular classroom teachers are fine ones to talk! They send the kids to us at all times of the day.

Supervisor: Is that true of all of you? [The other members all nod their heads in agreement.] Are there other problems, Shirley?

Shirley Dancercise: I don't intend to dismiss my students early or late, but I don't think the clocks in the lunchroom are synchronized with the classroom clocks.

Supervisor: I'll check on that. Are there other reasons?

Fred Soccerman: The students get a full period in my class; I don't think this is a real issue.

Supervisor: Maybe not, but I'm going to emphasize that we all begin class at five past and dismiss at quarter of. In the meantime, I'll check with the custodians about seeing that the clocks are synchronized, and at the faculty meeting I'll mention our concerns about other teachers sending their students to you at the wrong time. Does everyone understand what I expect of you? Walt?

Walt Goalposter: I hope some of us are not intentionally letting the students out early. By gosh, we have enough to accomplish with the little time we have.

Supervisor: I'm not implying that we are shortening our instructional time. I'm simply stating that from now on we're going to have a full, consistent forty minutes of instruction for every teacher and every class. If need be, I'll be coming around to see that we are doing it.

Fred Soccerman: Let's not make this such a big deal. We'll get it done. Now can we talk about the new aerobic exercise elective that we're supposed to be planning?

Although the issue of starting time raised at the supervisor's meeting might appear to be of relative unimportance to staff members, it was important to the supervisor. Instead of letting the issue pass and risking further complications with other teachers, she decided to meet the issue head on. In the supervisor's role of leader, expert, and possessor of a larger view, she judged that the staff needed to know of her concern and that they would be expected to comply with her directive. At the same time, she was willing to listen to their reactions and to use their information to remedy the situation. It was clear from the outset that the supervisor was making the decision and that the staff was being used in an advisory, not a decision-making, capacity.

In group meetings, a supervisor uses directive control behaviors to give a clear message about what changes are expected. The supervisor states his or her understanding of the problem (*presenting*), asks group members if they have more to add (*clarifying*), listens to their input (*listening*), and then mentally reassesses the problem and possible solutions (*problem solving*). He or she proceeds to state what is to be done (*directing*), asks for input (*clarifying*), lays out the actual actions (*standardizing*), and monitors the expected performance (*reinforcing*).

A History of Overreliance on Control

Historically, control has been used by supervisors as a first rather than last resort. The tradition has been to rely on controlling behaviors with all teachers in all situations (Gordon, 1992). At times, this has been done by tying supervision to summative evaluation systems requiring certain teaching behaviors. At other times, social pressure has been applied to force teachers to conform to generic "research-based" teaching methods (the research cited during such efforts often has been misinterpreted and oversimplified). Even worse, some supervisors wishing to reduce teacher resistance have combined control and manipulation, hoping to convince teachers that they have participated in a decision when in fact the supervisor knew all along what the decision would be.

We strongly disagree with supervisors using directive control behaviors with all teachers and in all situations. We also oppose using directive control behaviors indefinitely. Finally, in all cases, we oppose control through *manipulation*. Although we admit that directive control is necessary with some teachers and groups in some situations, we believe that it should be used only when no other supervisory approach is feasible. When using a directive control approach with a teacher or group, the supervisor should be ready to move away from directive control toward noncontrolling behaviors as soon as possible.

Issues in Directive Control

Two of three major issues with using directive control behaviors have already been mentioned. One has to do with being forthright, the other with source of authority. The third issue is a consideration of time.

A supervisor who needs a teacher to do something has to tell the teacher exactly and honestly what it is. The precision and frankness of a message can be misconstrued or lost in a conference or meeting. Most of us find it difficult to look another person squarely in the eye and say, "I want you to do this." Instead, we often attempt to soften the message by equivocating. It is the difference between telling a person, "Maybe you could try to be more prompt in starting and ending your class" and telling him, "Starting tomorrow I want your class to begin at 8:05 A.M. and end at 8:45 A.M." "Be more prompt" is open to interpretation; "beginning tomorrow at 8:05" means just that. Being direct takes the ambiguity out of the expectations.

We will illustrate this with a personal example. An elementary supervisor would become angry at teachers for not doing what he expected of them, only to realize later that the teachers never understood what he meant. He learned a trick that helped him become clearer in giving such messages. He would write down word-for-word the critical statement he wanted to tell the teacher or group. He would keep the written statement in front of him during the conference or meeting. Thus, there was no guesswork involved in giving the message. After a meeting, he could look at the written statement and know whether he had delivered it or not.

To many, directive control connotes an adversary relationship. It conjures up an image of the pushy, authoritarian boss at work. This is a stereotyped connotation, however. Being directive basically involves letting the other person know (1) what the supervisor is convinced will improve the teacher's instruction *and* (2) that the supervisor is willing to assume complete responsibility for that decision. A teacher might welcome knowing the depth and clarity of the supervisor's expectations. It is better to be up front about the directive than to pretend that teachers have decision-making power over issues that in reality they do not control. Some supervisors avoid being directive controlling by going through the directive informational, collaborative, or nondirective behaviors of involving staff when they've already made the decision. One might be able to succeed with such manipulation temporarily, but once staff members become aware that their involvement was of no significance, they will be resistant to further involvement with the supervisor. With each issue, it is best to let teachers know the degree of their involvement, ranging from full involvement to none, rather than being nebulous. Anyone would prefer to work in a place where the game is *on,* not *under,* the table. Directive control should be viewed as being informative, decisive, and clear about what teachers have little control over. It also means listening and being willing to modify one's expectations according to reactions from teachers that point out the error of one's directives.

The other major issue raised by directive control behavior concerns power and authority. Unless a supervisor holds formal line authority over teachers, he or she cannot enforce directives. It is impossible to make the teacher do what he or she wants. Instead, a supervisor with a staff relationship can expect teachers to follow imposed plans only if they respect the supervisor and trust his or her judgment. The supervisor must demonstrate and convince the teachers of this superior expertise. If the supervisor has line authority over teachers, however, it is more difficult to separate teacher compliance due to respect for the supervisor from that due to a perceived threat to job security. The line supervisor might believe teachers are following orders because of his or her superior knowledge, but the teachers might actually believe the supervisor is an ignoramus. Because of such ambiguity, a line supervisor must be extremely careful when using directive control.

Directive control should be a measure of last resort when an immediate decision is needed. Other directive, nondirective, or collaborative approaches will normally ensure greater receptivity by teachers and greater likelihood of successful implementation of a decision, but decisions will take longer to make. Inevitably, when there are many people involved in a decision, discussion, conflict, and resolution will take more time than when only one person is deciding. However, not every instructional problem needs to be addressed at length; a supervisor using directiveness judiciously might actually save time for those decisions most important to staff. There are matters (such as scheduling or budgeting) in which teachers may not desire involvement. A supervisor who attempts to involve people in decisions they view as a waste of time is just as inept as one who does not involve people in decisions about which they care intensely. At times, a supervisor with such authority does better by being directive and making the decision.

The issue of time includes the need for directive control in response to emergencies. When the flow of school life is interrupted by irate parents, student defiance, malfunctioning heaters, or media investigations, the supervisor may have to be unilaterally decisive. He or she will simply not have time to meet with teachers before responding. For example, a middle school principal was called at home by a newspaper reporter who sought her reaction to a fire marshal's report about unsafe cardboard partitions in a classroom of her school. The principal, totally unaware of the marshal's visit, refused comment and called the fire marshal to confirm the report. The marshal told her that all cardboard in classrooms was to be removed by the following morning. Deciding not to fight the fire marshal's orders and thus to avoid further newspaper attention, the principal told each teacher arriving at school the next morning of the fire marshal's report and told them to have their rooms cleared of all cardboard partitions before ten o'clock. She also informed them that they would meet later that afternoon to discuss the fire marshal's ruling and determine whether they wanted to appeal it. For the moment, she had used her own judgment. Later, when there was time to review the matter, she and the staff decided collaboratively to meet with the marshal about a proposal to reinstall cardboard partitions covered with fire-resistant plastic. This example shows that at a time of emergency a supervisor, whether ultimately right or wrong, must be directive.

When to Use Directive Control Behaviors

Since directive behaviors raise issues of power, respect, expertise, and line and staff relationships, the following guidelines are given with caution. Directive control behaviors should be employed:

1. When teachers are functioning at very low development levels.
2. When teachers do not have awareness, knowledge, or inclination to act on an issue that a supervisor, who has organizational authority, thinks to be of critical importance to the students, the teachers, or the community, then the directive control approach should most likely be used.
3. When teachers will have no involvement and the supervisor will be involved in carrying out the decision. If the supervisor will be held totally accountable and the teachers will not, then the directive control approach should probably be used.
4. When the supervisor is committed to resolving the issue and the teachers are not. When decisions do not concern teachers, and they prefer the supervisor to make the decision, the directive control approach should most likely be used.
5. In an emergency, when the supervisor does not have time to meet with teachers, the directive control approach should be used.

To develop skills in the four supervisory approaches demands real-life practice. Item B2 in Appendix B provides a format for practicing directive control behaviors.

Moving from Directive Control toward Directive Informational Behaviors

In long-term supervisory situations and relationships, the supervisor should begin to shift from a directive control to a directive informational approach as soon as possible. Stabilizing an unstable situation or giving a teacher or group intensive support will tend to foster limited professional growth. Such growth is likely to continue only if the supervisor then begins to give the teacher or group limited opportunities to make decisions and assume some responsibility. One way to do this is to begin to allow the teacher or the group *"restricted choice."* For example, the supervisor might mandate an instructional improvement goal and then allow the teacher or group to choose from two or three clearly defined alternatives for meeting the goal. By doing this, the supervisor has begun movement toward directive informational supervision—an approach that is discussed in detail in the next chapter.

Summary

Directive control supervision is used to transmit supervisor expectations to teachers clearly. Supervisors in a line position *over* teachers can use directive controlling language and enforce via hierarchical control. Supervisors in a staff position can only hope for compliance based on trust and credibility with teachers. Directive control supervision consists of behaviors of presenting, clarifying, listening, problem solving, directing, standardizing, and reinforcing (with line authority). The direction of presenting, problem solving, and directing is mostly from supervisor to teacher. Directive control behaviors are useful in limited circumstances when teachers possess little expertise, involvement, or interest with respect to an instructional problem and time is short. In these circumstances, directive control is not an adversarial or capricious set of behaviors, but an honest approach with teachers to an emergency.

Exercises

Academic

1. Write an imaginary dialogue between a supervisor and a teacher during a conference in which the supervisor successfully uses a directive control approach. Be sure to include examples of each of the eight behaviors discussed in Chapter 8.

2. The chapter suggests that a sequence of eight directive control behaviors takes place during a directive conference. Think of a situation in which a successful directive control conference would start with the first suggested behavior (identifying the problem) and end with the eighth (repeating and following up on expectations), but have a different sequence of six intermediate behaviors. Describe the situation and modified sequence of directive behaviors in writing. Include a rationale for the suggested sequence.

3. Write an imaginary dialogue between a supervisor and a teacher in which the supervisor implements directive control procedures with mechanical precision but fails to be directive in an effective sense.

4. Write a paper comparing the directive control approach as described in this book with manipulative control that you have experienced or observed.

5. Assume you have recently attended a seminar at which a university professor argued against educational supervisors using the directive control approach with any teacher. The professor proposed that the supervisor should play the role of a helper, not attempt to control a teacher's behavior. The speaker argued that successful change cannot be brought about unless the teacher perceives the need for change and has had a part in deciding how to bring about the needed change. He concluded that a directive control supervisory approach will only alienate teachers and make supervisors unwelcome in many classrooms. You have been asked to reply to the professor's arguments at an upcoming seminar. Write a paper in which you present an argument for using directive control behaviors with some teachers and under some circumstances.

Field

1. Assume the role of a supervisor using a directive control approach by conducting a simulated postobservation conference with a teacher. Assume that the teacher is in clear violation of a policy and has refused to change his or her practice. Prepare a written report in which you (a) evaluate your success in displaying control behaviors, (b) summarize the problems discussed and decisions made during the conference, (c) give your perceptions of the teacher's responses to your directive control efforts, and (d) judge the conference in terms of overall success.

2. Observe an educational supervisor or other leader whom you know to possess a directive control orientation in dealing with individuals and/or groups. On the basis of your observations and/or an interview with the leader, write a paper describing both successes and failures the selected leader has experienced while using directive control behaviors. Include possible reasons why the directive leader has been more successful in some situations than in others.

3. Observe three teachers or staff members who clearly respond positively to directive control supervision. Write a paper examining personal and social characteristics of these individuals that may account for their positive response to a directive control approach.

4. Prepare a photo album entitled "Supervisory Direction for Instructional Improvement." Each photograph should be accompanied by a written explanation of how it relates to the album theme.

5. Videotape or audiotape a conference or professional development activity led by a supervisor who typically uses a directive control approach. As you review the tape, compare the recorded activities with the sequence of behaviors that, according to the chapter, exemplify the directive process. Prepare a report on your findings.

Developmental

1. Through interaction with various individuals in a variety of situations, begin to establish a set of personal guidelines that will indicate when the directive control approach is most appropriate for your own use in carrying out present or anticipated leadership functions.

2. Begin an in-depth study of assertiveness training (see the References and Suggested Readings). As you progress through your study, note how training in asser-

tiveness can be used by supervisors when they find themselves with teachers or in situations requiring a directive control approach.

3. Record a simulated or actual supervisor-teacher conference in which you, as supervisor, attempt to display directive control behaviors. Review the tape for analysis of your performance. Record another simulated or actual conference in four weeks. Review both tapes to discover any improvement in terms of successfully displaying behaviors the chapter describes as directive control.

References

Alberti, R. E., and Emmons, M. L. 1974. *Your perfect right: A guide to assertive behavior.* San Luis Obispo, CA: Impact.

Gordon, S. P. 1992. Paradigms, transitions, and the new supervision. *Journal of Curriculum and Supervision 8*(1): 62–76.

Lucio, W. H., and McNeil, J. D. 1979. *Supervision: A synthesis of thought and action* (3rd ed.). New York: McGraw-Hill.

Mager, R. F., and Pipe, P. 1970. *Analyzing performance problems or "You really oughta wanna."* Belmont, CA: Fearon.

Smith, M. 1975. *When I say no, I feel guilty.* New York: Dial Press
.

Suggested Readings

Bower, S. A. 1991. *Asserting yourself: A practical guide for positive change.* Reading, MA: Addison-Wesley.

Townend, A. 1991. *Developing assertiveness.* London: Routledge.

Wilson, K. 1993. *Assertion and its social context.* New York: Pergamon.

9

Directive Informational Behaviors

Supervisor: So, in conclusion, what I've observed is that 7 of your 26 students had little involvement in the discussion or question-and-answer period.

Teacher: Well, those seven who you are referring to show no interest in class. At least, if they are quiet, they don't interfere with the learning of others. However, I am surprised that they had such little involvement. I guess if they are quiet, I've just learned to tune them out.

Supervisor: I believe that a goal might be to involve those seven students actively in your future classes.

Teacher: I'd agree. None of my other classes are like this. If I only knew how to do that! When I call on them, they don't respond. When I give the class a controversial topic in U.S. history, most students jump right in, but Sheila, Aliendra, and the rest of them go blank, giggle, and seem not to care.

Supervisor: Well, based on my own experiences as a teacher and what I've seen others do with seemingly apathetic students, let me give you a list of possible actions. Think about them, and determine which of these are worth trying. First, you might establish individual contracts with each of those seven students, that they will be expected to participate at least twice in each class and can earn extra homework points for their participation. Second, you might move to the back and corners of the room during question-and-answer sessions. This is where most of these nonparticipating kids sit. In your lesson plans, make notes to call on each of these students at least once. Your physical presence close to them might help. Third, when you know that a topic to be introduced can be controversial, you might prep the students by using a cooperative learning format. Break the class into groups of three—put each of the nonparticipants with two active participants and ask each group to formulate a group position, with each member being responsible for reporting the position. Monitor the groups while they are working. At discussion times, occasionally call the nonparticipants to speak for the group. What do you think of these possibilities?

Teacher: Individual contracts for students aren't practical—other students would think I'm playing favorites. Moving around to the back and corners of the room is obvious, I could become more aware of doing that. The last idea of cooperative groups is one that I hadn't thought of with this class. I do that with my honors classes but never thought of using small groups here. I guess I assumed that it would be too confusing.

Supervisor: Which of these activities would you like to try?

Teacher: Moving to the back of the room, for sure! The cooperative learning, I'd like to try on a small scale to see how it would work. What do I need to do to prepare the groups to work together and how do I introduce the topic and task?

Directive Informational Behaviors with Individuals

The scenario, transcribed from a tape of an actual conference, shows a supervisor acting as the information source for the goal and activities of the improvement plan. The supervisor, through her observations, has determined a clear classroom goal for the teacher and directs the teacher to those activities she believes to have a high degree of probability in achieving the goal. Notice that, through each step of the conference, the supervisor remains the information source but always asks and considers teacher feedback. Furthermore, the supervisor provides a range of alternatives from which the teacher is asked to choose. The scenario concludes with the teacher's committing himself to using several activities. The supervisor then will detail with the teacher the what, when, and how of implementing the activities, set criteria for improvement, and reinforce the understanding of what is to be done. As we look at a sequence of directive informational behaviors (see Figure 9.1), keep in mind that the supervisor is constantly framing the direction and choices for the teacher.

1. Presenting: *Identifying the goal.* Based on the observation and previous experience she has with the teacher, the supervisor begins by reviewing her summarized observations and concluding with an interpretation that seven students being nonparticipants throughout a class period is problematic. Therefore, she sees an important goal as "involving all students."
2. Clarifying: *Asking the teacher for input into the goal.* The supervisor is careful not to move too quickly into a planning phase until she checks to see what the teacher thinks of her interpretation and goal. The teacher is surprised, agrees, and explains why these seven students have been neglected.
3. Listening: *Understanding the teacher's point of view.* The supervisor listens to determine if the teacher accepts the goal as an important one or if she needs to provide further explanation.
4. Problem solving: *Mentally determining possible actions.* The supervisor has given thought to some alternative actions that might be considered by the teacher. When the teacher explains the reasons for students being uninvolved and

FIGURE 9.1   *The Supervisory Behavior Continuum: Directive Informational Behaviors*

1	2	3	4	5
Listening	Clarifying	Encouraging	Reflecting	Presenting

T

s

				1. Identifying the goal
	2. Asking teacher for input into the goal			
3. Understanding the teacher's point of view				
6. Asking teacher for input into the expectations				
	8. Asking teacher to make a choice			

Key: T = Maximum teacher responsibility   S = Maximum supervisor responsibility
      t = Minimum teacher responsibility   s = Minimum supervisor responsibility

what has been done, the supervisor mentally prepares to lay out the alternative actions or suggestions.

5. Directing: *Telling alternatives for teachers to consider.* The supervisor carefully words the alternative actions as possibilities, based on her experience and knowledge, for the teacher to judge, consider, and respond.

6. Listening: *Asking the teacher for input into alternatives.* The supervisor asks the teacher to react to her suggestions. The teacher has the opportunity now to

FIGURE 9.1 *Continued*

6	7	8	9	10
Problem Solving	*Negotiating*	*Directing*	*Standardizing*	*Reinforcing*

t

S

4. Mentally
determining best
solution

           5. Telling
           expectations for
           teacher

           7. Framing the
           final choices

                      9. Determining
                      the actions to be
                      taken

                              10. Repeating and
                              following up on
                              plan

give the supervisor information to modify, eliminate, and revise before finalizing the choices.

7. Directing: *Framing the final choices.* In a straightforward manner, the supervisor lays out what the teacher could do: "So, in the final analysis, these are the actions you could take...."

8. Clarifying: *Asking the teacher to choose.* The supervisor asks the teacher to decide and clarify which activities or combinations he will use.

9. Standardizing: *Detailing the actions to be taken.* At this juncture, the supervisor assists the teacher in developing the specifics of the activities (i.e., introduce cooperative learning, set up threesomes, identify one controversial topic, try for 15 minutes next Tuesday, etc.) and the criteria for success (i.e., "Let's see, when I come in next Thursday, whether four of these seven students can be called upon and give prepared, on-target responses").

10. Reinforcing: *Repeating and following up on the plan.* The supervisor concludes the conference by restating the goal, the activities to be taken, the criteria for success, and the follow-up time for the next observation and/or conference.

Directive Informational Behaviors with Groups

The six grade-level chairpersons are meeting with the school's instructional lead teacher. The topic of discussion is a widespread concern with the placement of new students in classrooms during the school year. As a result of previous discussions, it has become apparent that some teachers believe it unwise simply to place new students in the classrooms with the fewest number of students, without accounting for the particular needs of students and teachers. The premise is that some teachers are better equipped to teach students with special needs (bilingual, gifted, learning disabled, withdrawn, etc.). Prior to this meeting, the instructional lead teacher has spoken with the principal, the assistant superintendent for instruction, and the director of pupil personnel. The topic is a pressing one, as there are five transfer students who will begin classes next Monday, four short days from now.

Supervisor: The issue is clear. How should we place transfer students in classrooms? In the past, I've done it strictly according to class enrollment. It doesn't have to continue that way. School board policy simply states that all classrooms are to be heterogeneously grouped.

Second-Grade Chair: Does this mean that as long as there isn't a disproportionate number of students with a particular level of ability in any one classroom, transfer students can be matched with the particular abilities of a teacher?

Supervisor: Yes and no. We have flexibility, but we can't make one classroom more of a place for all behavior-disordered students and another class for creative students.

Second-Grade Chair: I read you. We're on the same wavelength. But we do have flexibility within reasonable heterogeneity.

Supervisor: Yes. As I see it, we do have several options. We need to make a quick decision, because tomorrow there are five new students to place. We could do the following: (1) Leave placement as is—that is, let me continue to place new students according to classroom enrollment. (2) Let each grade chair determine the placement of each new student with the teachers in that grade. (3) Ask the individual teachers to identify the types of student that they can work well with and those that they don't work well with. That information could go either to me or to you, to make placements accordingly.

First-Grade Chair: I don't like that last idea. Some teachers would say that they don't work well with "rude" students. What's going to happen to them? Those teachers won't get any students who have records of misbehavior? Or if they do, they'll complain how someone went against their requests.

Third-Grade Chair: How about letting those grades who want to make their own placements do so, and for those who don't, you make them?

Supervisor: Nope, can't do that. I've talked with the principal and assistant superintendent. We need to be consistent in whatever we do. We can't have each grade level doing its own thing; we as a school must decide on a consistent procedure for placement of students. The choices, as I now see it, are (1) I do it according to numbers or (2) you do it according to your knowledge of individual teachers.

Third-Grade Chair: How about a combination of the two? You tentatively place according to classroom enrollment and then check with the grade-level chair to see if the receiving teacher is well equipped to work with the student. If not, between you and the grade level chair, another assignment can be made.

Supervisor: That's OK with me, just as long as all teachers are informed of the new procedures at tomorrow's meeting. We need to make sure that, if there is that disagreement that can't be resolved between me and the grade-level chair, someone will have the final say.

Fifth-Grade Chair: No sense in involving anyone else. You have the final say. Let's try this procedure out for the remainder of the year and see how the new placement works.

Supervisor: All right. Do we agree that beginning tomorrow, placement will be done in the following manner....?

The instructional lead teacher used a directive informational approach in having the group make a decision within a clearly articulated framework of supervisor alternatives. Each alternative initially proposed by the supervisor was acceptable to herself—she could live with any of them. After soliciting questions and discussions, she rejected some proposed alternatives as unacceptable, discarded one of her own as unacceptable to the group, and finalized the choices. At that point, she asked the group to choose from within the reconsidered and revised alternatives, and then detailed the specifics of the action (or combination of actions) to be implemented.

Comparing Directive Control and Directive Informational Statements

Students in supervision courses using this text often have difficulty distinguishing between directive control and directive informational behaviors, especially when practicing the different behaviors during role plays. This is not surprising, since there is often a thin line between controlling and informational language. And yet that thin line is a critical one. The precise language used by a supervisor using a directive approach can be the difference between a successful and unsuccessful supervisory conference or group meeting. The following examples will help you distinguish directive control from directive informational statements by a supervisor.

Directive Control (DC):   It is essential that you improve your classroom management during your first-period math class.

Directive Informational (DI):   I suggest the goal of improving your classroom management during your first-period math class.

DC: One of my expectations is that you attend the classroom management workshop being offered by the district.

DI: One alternative is for you to attend the classroom management workshop being offered by the district.

DC: You need to have a written lesson plan prepared for each class. Each plan must include the following elements…

DI: You could prepare more detailed lesson plans for this group. Each plan might include these additional elements…

DC: You must include a wider range of instructional strategies in your lessons.

DI: In my own teaching, I've found that using a wide range of instructional strategies improves student behavior and learning. You may wish to include a wider range of teaching strategies in your lessons.

DC: Do you have any questions concerning these new expectations?

DI: Do you have any questions concerning these possible actions?

DC: You will be required to make the changes we've discussed in accordance with this written timeline.

DI: Which of the alternatives that we have discussed do you wish to try out?

DC: I will be observing your class again in four weeks, and I expect to see the following changes…

DI: I would be willing to visit your class again in four weeks to observe your progress in implementing the changes you have selected.

To summarize, the supervisor using directive control behaviors is analogous to a judge or policeman giving directives which must be followed (although the analogy eventually breaks down because we know of no district where teachers go directly to jail for failing to follow a supervisor's suggestions for instructional improvement!). On the other hand, the supervisor using directive informational behaviors can be compared to a physician or attorney giving expert advice to a patient or client. The person receiving the advice does not have to follow it, but if they respect the expertise of the professional giving the advice they will probably conclude that it is in their best interest to act on the professional's suggestions. (If you begin to compare the salaries of physicians or attorneys with instructional supervisors, once again our analogy falls apart, but we've made our point!).

Issues in the Directive Informational Approach

Anyone who uses a directive informational approach needs to be aware of the degree of expertise that he or she has when delineating the choices available to others. Since the supervisor is placing himself or herself in the role of expert, the issues of confidence and credibility are crucial. The supervisor must be confident that he or she knows what practices will work in helping the teacher, because when the teacher chooses to use one or more of the supervisor's suggestions, the person ultimately responsible for the success or failure of the various practices will be the supervisor, not the teacher. After all, if I consider and select from your proposed actions, implement what you've suggested, and those actions don't work, I'm probably going to tell you the next time we meet, when we note that the goal is no closer to being achieved, "After all, I just did what you told me to do!"

The teacher is correct in holding the supervisor accountable for the results. Thus, the issue of credibility hovers above the directive informational approach. Not only must the supervisor be confident that his or her own knowledge and experience are superior to and different from those of the teacher, but the teacher must also believe that the supervisor possesses a source of wisdom that he or she does not have. When confidence and credibility in the supervisor's knowledge are shared by both parties, and the teacher is either unaware, inexperienced, or stumped about what changes can be made, then the directive informational approach can be a most valuable set of behaviors to use. When we begin on a path where we have not ventured before, there is much to be learned from a person who has explored that trail successfully many times in the past. This might be the reason why directive informational approaches are seen as most helpful to teachers when they are inexperienced, confused, unaware, or simply at a loss for what to do about a particular classroom or school goal.

Finally, with a directive informational approach, it is imperative to remember that the teacher exercises some control in choosing which practice(s) to use. (This is not the case when we look at the directive control approach.) You might ask, What if the teacher refuses to make a choice? If so, the issue of confidence and credibility has not been resolved, and the supervisor must make a judgment whether to change in midstream to another approach (collaborative or directive control), table the conference, or continue discussion further to convince the teacher of his or her wisdom.

When to Use Directive Informational Behaviors

Directive informational behaviors revolve on expertise, confidence, credibility, and limiting choice (Greiner, 1967). Therefore, they should be employed under the following circumstances:

1. When the teacher is functioning at fairly low developmental levels.
2. When the teacher does not possess the knowledge about an issue that the supervisor clearly possesses.
3. When the teacher feels confused, inexperienced, or is at a loss for what to do, and the supervisor knows of successful practices.
4. When the supervisor is willing to take responsibility for what the teacher chooses to try.
5. When the teacher believes that the supervisor is credible—a person who has the background and wisdom to know whereof he or she speaks.
6. When the time is short, the constraints are clear, and quick, concrete actions need to be taken.

Item B3 in Appendix B provides a format for practicing directive informational behaviors. Despite the similarities between directive control and directive informational behaviors, they do require different interpersonal skills. We recommend that after you have practiced both directive control and directive informational behaviors, some time be taken to reflect on and discuss the differences between the two approaches in action.

Moving from Directive Informational toward Collaborative Behaviors

In directive informational supervision, the teacher or group is given some choice but the supervisor still assumes *primary* decision-making responsibility. In the collaborative approach, the teacher and supervisor share decision-making responsibility equally. Movement from directive informational to collaborative is thus a matter of degree. The supervisor might begin that movement by suggesting an instructional improvement goal, asking the teacher or group to suggest one or two activities for moving toward the goal, and then suggesting a detailed action plan incorporating some of the teacher or group's proposed actions. Hopefully, the supervisor eventually will be able to enter a fully collaborative relationship with the teacher. This takes us to the topic of the next chapter—collaborative behaviors.

Summary

Directive informational supervision is used to direct teacher(s) to consider and choose from clearly delineated alternative actions. The supervisor is the major source of information, goal articulation, and suggested practices. However, the supervisor is careful to solicit teacher input as he or she revises and refines the choices; ultimately, the teacher is asked to make a judgment as to which practices or combinations are feasible and realistic. Such an approach is useful when the expertise, confidence, and credibility of the supervisor clearly outweigh the teacher's own information, experience, and capabilities.

Exercises

Academic

1. Write an imaginary dialogue between a supervisor and a teacher, during a conference in which the supervisor successfully uses a directive informational approach. Be sure to include examples of each of the 10 behaviors discussed in Chapter 9.

2. The chapter delineates six examples in which it is appropriate to use the directive informational approach. Write a description of a situation for each example. Can you think of any other circumstances, other than the six given, for which the directive informational approach would be appropriate? If so, include such an example in your answer.

3. Write an imaginary dialogue between a supervisor and a teacher during a conference in which the supervisor implements directive informational procedures with mechanical precision but fails to be successful for one or more reasons.

4. Explain what you would do if you as a supervisor worked with a teacher who always wanted you to use the directive informational approach with him or her. This experienced teacher is quite comfortable in the classroom and when asked can clearly articulate concerns or problems he or she has for his or her students and the school. Yet, unlike his or her peers, who prefer the collaborative or nondirective approach, this teacher favors being given a choice from your suggestions. Do you feel you should continue using the directive informational approach with this teacher? Write a summary of your position and give reasons for your decision.

5. Write a paper comparing and contrasting the directive control and directive informational supervisory approaches. Include advantages and disadvantages of each.

Field

1. Assume the role of a supervisor using a directive informational approach, by either using the simulated activity in item B3 of Appendix B or conducting an actual postobservation conference with a teacher. Prepare a written report in which you (a) evaluate your success in displaying directive informational behaviors, (b) summarize the problems discussed and decisions made during the conference, (c) give your perceptions of the teacher's responses to your directive efforts, and (d) judge the conference in terms of overall success.

2. Interview teachers who prefer the directive informational approach. Write a summary of your findings.

3. Record times you or a supervisor at your school has used the directive informational approach. Describe the situation being dealt with and the results. Overall, how successful have you or your supervisor been with this approach? Explain your answer.

4. Tape-record a faculty meeting during which the supervisor uses the directive informational approach. Analyze the tape to determine whether the meeting was successful. Make a chart with a space for each of the directive informational supervisory behaviors. As you listen to the tape, record each time a behavior is used and in what sequence. Does a correlation exist between the overall success of the

meeting and the frequency and sequence of the supervisory behaviors? Prepare a report of your findings.

5. Create a collage of pictures and/or words that shows when it is appropriate to use directive informational behaviors. Use the six examples given in this chapter to guide you. Provide a narrative explaining your collage.

Developmental

1. Tape-record a conference during which you, as the supervisor, attempt to use the directive informational approach. Review and analyze the tape. Note the sequence of behaviors. At a later date, record another conference during which you use the directive informational approach. Analyze the tape and note the sequence of behaviors. Was the sequence the same in both conferences? How did the sequences of behaviors affect the outcome?

2. Keep a log each time you use the directive informational approach. Record the problem discussed, the teacher(s) involved, and the decision made. After several months, study your log for any patterns. Do you use this approach with the same teachers? Are the problems similar? Consider the patterns, if any, to evaluate your behavior and effectiveness as a supervisor.

3. Begin a chart that delineates what you consider to be each teacher's expertise and experience level in your work situation. Ask four or five teachers to list those areas or topics about teaching in which they could use more information and specific suggestions. Do you find common areas where a directive informational group approach would be appropriate?

References

Grainer, L. E. 1967. Patterns of organizational change. *Harvard Business Review* 45:119–130.

See the "decisions from alternatives approach."

Suggested Readings

Acheson, K. A., and Gall, M. D. 1992. *Techniques in the clinical supervision of teachers* (3rd ed.). New York: Longman.

Pajak, E. 1993. Madeline Hunter's decision making. In *Approaches to clinical supervision* (pp. 183–208). Norwood, MA: Christopher-Gordon Publishers.

10

Collaborative Behaviors

Teacher: I refuse to have Steve sent out of my class.

Supervisor: Don't you think being hit by him and being bruised is the last straw?

Teacher: No, I don't. It's my body and I don't think Steve meant it. He was angry and didn't know what he was doing.

Supervisor: Listen, he's been in fights with other students since the first day of school, and the latest episode of striking could have resulted in serious damage. He has to come out.

Teacher: I know that you're thinking about my own welfare, but that kid is making progress. He's beginning to do some assignments and has been behaving better. The hitting incident was an accident. He's not bothering the other students too much.

Supervisor: I think you're wrong. Let's put him into a special classroom.

Teacher: No, he stays with me.

Supervisor: You know that whatever is done, we will both agree to do. You don't want him to leave and I think, for his own good, he should be given special attention. Steve is dangerous to you and the other students.

Teacher: I don't have anything against special attention. It's just that we've come so far and I hate to see him cut off from me and the class. He has a better chance to make it in our class than to begin all over in another class.

Supervisor: Then you would be receptive to having him receive special attention as long as he stays in your class?

Teacher: Yeah, I think so. I have no problem with a qualified person working with him in my classroom or even for a small part of the day outside of the classroom.

Supervisor: That seems reasonable, I think that we are getting somewhere....

Collaborative Behaviors with Individuals

The foregoing script, based on a real conference, highlights collaborative supervisory behaviors. The supervisor wishes to resolve a problem that is shared equally with the teacher. The supervisor encourages the teacher to present his or her own perceptions and ideas. Yet the supervisor also honestly gives his or her own views. The result is a frank exchange of ideas. Both participants know they will have to agree on any course of action. In fact, when the disagreement becomes obvious, the supervisor restates the disagreement and reassures the teacher that they will have to find a mutual solution. Disagreement is encouraged, not suppressed. As the conversation continues, some openings for possible agreements become apparent, and the supervisor steers the conversation toward those ends. Finally, they will either agree to an action or wind up stalemated. A stalemate will mean further negotiating, rethinking, and even the possible use of a third-party mediator or arbitrator.

Figure 10.1 shows a prototype of collaborative behaviors according to the supervisory behavior continuum. A conference between supervisor and teacher begins with an understanding of each other's identification of the problem and concludes with mutual agreement on the final plan. The reader should think of the supervisory behaviors as a piano keyboard, with the musician beginning by hitting the keys on the left, then playing the keys back and forth, and culminating by hitting the middle key—negotiating.

1. Clarifying: *Identifying the problem as seen by the teacher.* First, ask the teacher about the immediate problem or concern: "Please tell me what is bothering you." "Explain to me what you see as the greatest concern."
2. Listening: *Understanding the teacher's perception.* You (the supervisor) want to have as much information about the problem as possible before thinking about action. Therefore, when the teacher narrates his or her perceptions, the full range of nondirective behaviors should be used (eye contact, paraphrasing, asking probing questions, and being willing to allow the teacher to continue talking): "Tell me more." "Uh huh, I'm following you." "Do you mean…?"
3. Reflecting: *Verifying the teacher's perception.* When the teacher has completed his or her description of the problem, check for accuracy by summarizing the teacher's statements and asking if the summary is accurate: "I understand that you see the problem as…. Is this accurate?"
4. Presenting: *Providing the supervisor's point of view.* Until this point, we have seen an abbreviated nondirective conference. Instead of asking the teacher to begin thinking of his or her own possible actions, however, you now move in and become part of the decision-making process. Give your own point of view about the current difficulty and fill in any information about the situation of which the teacher might be unaware: "I see the situation in this way." "The problem, as I see it, is…." (To minimize influencing the teacher's position, it is better for you to give your perceptions only after the teacher has given his or hers.)

5. Clarifying: *Seeking the teacher's understanding of the supervisor's perception of the problem.* In the same way that you paraphrased the teacher's statement of the problem and asked for verification, you now ask the teacher to do likewise: "Could you repeat what you think I'm trying to say?" Once you feel confident that the teacher understands your views, problem solving can begin.

6. Problem solving: *Exchanging suggestions of options.* If you and the teacher are familiar with each other and have worked collaboratively before, you can simply ask for a list of suggestions: "Let's both think about what might be done to improve this situation." Then listen to each other's ideas. If the teacher is not familiar with you or with the collaborative process, however, he or she may feel apprehensive about suggesting an idea that is different from the supervisor's. It might be better to stop the conference for a few minutes and have both supervisor and teacher write down possible actions before speaking: "So that we don't influence each other on possible solutions, let's take the next few minutes and write down what actions might be taken and then read each other's list." Obviously, once actions are in writing, they will not change according to what the other person has written. You the supervisor, therefore, have promoted a spectrum of personal ideas that are ready to be shared and discussed.

7. Encouraging: *Accepting conflict.* To keep the conference from turning into a competitive struggle, you need to reassure the teacher that disagreement is acceptable and that there will be no winners or losers: "It appears that we have some different ideas on how to handle this situation. By disagreeing we will find the best solution. Remember our agreement—we both have to agree with the solution before it will take place." You must genuinely believe that conflict between two caring professionals is productive for finding the best solution.

8. Problem solving: *Finding an acceptable solution.* After sharing and discussing, ask if there are suggestions common to both—"Where do we agree?"—and if there are suggestions markedly different—"Where do we differ?" If you find agreement, then the conference proceeds. But if there is a vast difference in suggestions, then you can take four sequential actions. First, check to see whether the differences are as vast as they appear by having both yourself and the teacher explain thoroughly what is meant by your respective suggestions. Second, if the disagreement is still real, then find out how convinced each of you is that your suggestion be chosen: "How important is it to you that we do it your way?" If the importance of one person's suggestion is far greater than that of the other person's suggestion, then the question becomes whether one can give up his or her idea and live with the other's. Third, if grounds for agreement are not reached, you can consider a compromise: "How about if I give up this part of my suggestion and if you give up...." Or see if a totally new idea can be found: "Since we can't agree, let's drop our top choices for solutions and see if we can find another one." Fourth, if there is still no movement and a true stalemate remains, then you can either call for a period of time for both parties to reflect on the issue before meeting again—"Look, we're not getting anywhere. Let's sit on this

FIGURE 10.1 *The Supervisory Behavior Continuum: Collaborative Behaviors*

1	2	3	4	5
Listening	Clarifying	Encouraging	Reflecting	Presenting

T

s

                  1. Identifying the problem as seen by the teacher

2. Understanding the teacher's perception

                                                        3. Verifying teacher's perception

                                                                    4. Providing supervisor's point of view

                  5. Seeking teacher's understanding of supervisor's perception of problem

                                    7. Accepting conflict

                                      10. Agreeing to a final plan

Key: T = Maximum teacher responsibility   S = Maximum supervisor responsibility
      t = Minimum teacher responsibility   s = Minimum supervisor responsibility

matter and meet again tomorrow"—or ask for a third person to play the role of a mediator or arbitrator: "We can't agree; how about if we call someone that we both respect to help us resolve this?" "Since we can't agree, how about calling someone we both have confidence in to solve this for us?" A mediator or arbitrator is an extreme option for most conferences between a supervisor and a teacher and should remain a last resort. However, the teacher must know that the procedures of collaboration ensure that he or

FIGURE 10.1 *Continued*

6	7	8	9	10
Problem Solving	*Negotiating*	*Directing*	*Standardizing*	*Reinforcing*

t
—
S

6. Exchanging
suggestions of op-
tions

8. Finding an ac-
ceptable action

9. Agreeing on de-
tails of plan

she does not have to go along with a plan that he or she disagrees with.
There are other options available.

9. Standardizing: *Agreeing on details of plan.* Once agreement on an acceptable
   action has been reached, the supervisor needs to attend to the details of time
   and place. When will the plan be implemented? Where will it take place?
   Who will help? What resources are needed? These details need to be discussed and agreed to so there will be a clarity and precision to the final plan.

10. Negotiating: *Agreeing to a final plan.* The supervisor concludes the conference by checking that both parties agree to the action and details. The supervisor might do this verbally—"Could you repeat what you understand
the plan to be and then I'll repeat my understanding"—or in writing—"Let's
write this down together so that we are clear on what we've agreed to do."

Collaborative Behaviors with Groups

After meeting for the fourth time in the past month, most of the members of the
school science textbook adoption committee have reviewed all the new commercial textbook series and have made up their own minds about which one they
prefer. It is 5:30 on Wednesday afternoon, and the meeting is in its second hour.
The science supervisor, Roger Loren, is uneasy; he believes that some people have
not said what's on their minds. He asks, "Do we wish to discuss the science programs anymore before voting?" Of the 11 members, 10 shake their heads.

The supervisor, seeing that Phyllis Moonale has not joined with the others,
asks, "Phyllis, do you think we need more time before deciding?" Phyllis says quietly, "Yes, I do. From what I've been hearing from the other members, they already made up their minds to keep the old science program before we even
started. That old program is ridiculously out of date. Just because we might have
to change our lesson plans, bulletin board displays, and exam questions—that's
no reason to keep the same series. Let's think about the students! They're not
learning anything at all about recent science issues such as test tube babies or acid
rain. We can't ignore these real science topics for the convenience of keeping our
old lesson plans intact!"

The supervisor, after listening carefully, believes that what Phyllis has said is
right. The supervisor says, "I agree. We shouldn't keep the old textbook. There are
at least three others that would be an improvement over what we have now. I'd
go along with any of those three texts."

Fred Willopt, who has been an adamant spokesperson for the old textbook
series, speaks: "Come on, let's get on with it! We agreed that this was going to be
a group decision; if we couldn't agree unanimously then we would take a majority vote. It's not bad to keep an old program—we do right well by it! Phyllis, why
don't you teach those other radical topics all you want, but don't keep us from
doing what we want. You and Roger are in the minority. It's time to vote!"

The supervisor responds, "OK, Fred, you're right—we did agree that this
would be a group decision. I don't want that old series. Maybe others don't either.
We'll vote on it." Roger calls for a vote: "How many want to keep the old series?"
Ten hands go up. "How many want the new series?" Phyllis and Roger raise their
hands. Roger looks at Phyllis and can't help feeling disappointed. He says, "All
right, we keep the old series. I don't agree, but we'll go along with what the group
has decided. The meeting is over."

The supervisor has tried to convince the group to adopt his preference.
When it comes to the final decision, however, his vote has no more weight than

that of any other member. Furthermore, the group knows that the procedures for making the decision, explained at the first meeting, have been adhered to and that the final decision will be upheld.

A supervisor using a collaborative cluster of behaviors leads the members to a group decision. In the meeting described here, the collaborative supervisor did not exercise a veto when the decision was not turning out the way he preferred. The supervisor's responsibility is to ensure that the full range of ideas and feelings are discussed, including his or her own, before making the final decision. The example given was of a group meeting where collaborative supervision resulted in a decision by majority vote. Obviously, when collaboration is used in an individual conference with a single teacher, the final decision must be made by consensus. Both supervisor and teacher have equal say; if they disagree, no decision can be made. Further discussion about a compromise or alternative solution would be necessary to find a decision satisfactory to both persons. In a group meeting the same principle for resolving lack of consensus can be used with a majority vote. Collaborative supervisory behaviors, whether with an individual teacher or with a group of teachers, result in a mutually shared decision whereby the one-person, one-vote rule holds regardless of the status, title, or power of any individual.

The sequence of collaborative behaviors a supervisor uses in reaching a group decision are similar to those used in meeting with an individual. The main difference is that more time is needed for each member of the group to identify the problem and discuss everyone's suggestions. The supervisor needs to be sensitive to whether the meeting drags—for example, if the same issues are being discussed and positions are not being changed. The supervisor is both an advocate of his or her own position and an expediter of group movement toward a final decision. Let's quickly review collaborative supervisory behaviors in a group meeting.

The supervisor calls the meeting to order and, before discussion, *clarifies* the task and procedures for making the decision. He or she states that they are meeting on a certain issue (selecting next year's textbook) and that the procedures will be collaborative (one vote for each person, with the final decision being made either by consensus or by majority vote). Initiating the discussion, the supervisor asks each group member to *clarify* what he or she sees as the current needs in looking for a textbook. After soliciting group members' opinions, the supervisor *reflects* his or her understanding of what they have been saying, and then *presents* his or her own opinion. The supervisor's position is then clarified by asking the group to paraphrase his or her statements. The supervisor asks for questions. The next step is *problem solving*—asking the group to suggest possible actions to solve the identified problem. This is handled by allowing each individual to present his or her own suggestions. The supervisor might write down all suggestions coming from the group. The supervisor, as an equal member, offers any suggestions he or she may have. All group members are *encouraged* to offer their ideas, no matter how improbable or different from others'. When no more suggestions are forthcoming, the supervisor calls for the group to narrow down the list of possibilities to the two or three best ideas. If consensus about the best ideas is not apparent, the supervisor can ask members to rank all ideas and keep the three ideas with the highest scores. The group further whittles down the list to a single choice as the supervisor asks members to discuss the merits and demerits of each idea. Again, the supervisor leads the discussion by probing for agreements and negotiating between conflicting positions to find a common path. If agreement on a course of action is not emerging, the supervisor looks for ways to synthesize or compromise disparate ideas. Finally, if the choices of group members remain distant and there is no consensus, a majority vote can be taken. The winning idea is *standardized* by the group according to time, place, and persons to be involved in carrying out the plan. The supervisor must then *renegotiate* the final plan by consensus or majority vote on the final standardized and detailed plan.

Issues in Collaborative Supervision

Our work with collaboration has shown that it is a deceptively simple set of behaviors for supervisors to understand. The reason is that collaboration appears to be the democratic way of doing things. Most of us have been schooled in equality and democracy, and collaboration appears to be democracy in action. Therefore, it seems apparent that we should ask others for input and that decisions should be made by the majority. However, collaboration with an individual or a group involves more than democratic procedures. It is an attitude of acceptance and a practice of being equal. Therefore, it is not always the mechanical procedures of democracy that demonstrate whether or not collaboration is in use.

What appears to be nondemocratic might indeed be collaborative, and what appears to be democratic might not be collaborative. For example, two people can agree as equals that one is better qualified to make a particular decision; the less qualified person might ask the more qualified person to decide for both of them. Here, one person making the decision for both persons appears undemocratic, but it is collaborative.

On the other hand, two people can appear to make a collaborative decision, but if one person has discreetly let the other know of his or her power—for example, a personal acquaintanceship with the superintendent of schools—the less powerful person might profess agreement with the more powerful person even though inwardly he or she did not agree. On the surface, the agreement appears to be collaborative, but in reality one person has knuckled under to the power of the other. The purpose of collaboration is to solve problems through a meeting of minds of equals. True equality is the core of collaboration.

One difficulty in working collaboratively occurs when the teacher (or group) believes a supervisor is manipulating the decision when in fact he or she is not. The teacher appears to concur with the supervisor's ideas and suggestions not because of their merit but because the teacher believes the supervisor is really giving a directive. The underlying message the teacher perceives is: "This is my supervisor telling me what she thinks I should do. Even though she says we are making a joint decision, I know I had better do what she says." How does the supervisor know whether a teacher's agreement is sincere or mere compliance? The supervisor might confront the issue by asking the teacher whether he or she is agreeing or only pretending to agree with the supervisor's idea. Acknowledging that the supervisor suspects something is amiss brings the issue out into the open. A teacher who responds, "I don't believe you really are going to let me have equal say" can be dealt with more easily than is possible when a supervisor guesses at the teacher's hidden feelings.

Teachers who refuse to disclose their feelings probably have a history of being mistreated by supervisors. Until the supervisor can demonstrate consistently that he or she really means to be collaborative, no progress will be made. The teacher is not going to believe the supervisor is being collaborative until there is proof. True intent can be demonstrated by refusing to allow decisions to be made without teacher feedback. With nonresponsive and readily acquiescing teachers, a supervisor might say: "I don't know if you're agreeing with me because you like the idea or because of some power I hold over you. We won't carry out any action unless we both agree with that action. I want to be collaborative because I believe you have as much expertise on this matter as I do. Together we can make a better decision than separately. I'm uncertain why you are agreeing with me. Please tell me what you think."

A supervisor cannot find out what a teacher thinks without asking. As they continue to meet, the supervisor should begin by encouraging teachers to offer their own thoughts about the problem and suggestions for action. The supervisor should try to withhold any ideas of his or her own. Once the teacher's ideas are forthcoming, the supervisor can offer his or her ideas. When negotiating a final decision, the supervisor should let teachers take the lead. If teachers continue to be unresponsive or overly compliant with the supervisor after he or she has confronted the issue of perception and encouraged teacher initiative, then, after several unsuccessful attempts, the supervisor might consider another approach.

The collaborative group process appears to be predicated on the use of consensus or majority vote. However, a supervisor can work collaboratively with a group by using other decision-making procedures such as averaging, frequency ranking, the nominal method, the Delphi technique, or even minority or expert decision.

Collaboration is defined as working jointly with others in an intellectual endeavor (*American Heritage Dictionary,* 1982). The work is done jointly, but one person can participate more than another. The test of collaboration in supervision is whether the agreed-on decision to improve instruction was satisfactory to all participants. Therefore, although the degree of involvement may vary, the end results are equally determined. With such a definition, we are intentionally allowing for times when a supervisor, teacher, or individual member of a group might convince others of the value of his or her own ideas because of his or her persuasiveness, expertise, and credibility. If ideas are judged on the basis of their merits and not on the power of the individual, then collaboration is at work.

The issues of collaboration are complex. First, a supervisor must differentiate democratic procedure from collaboration. Second, he or she must differentiate between acquiescence to power and agreement with ideas. When acquiescence is suspected, the supervisor should bring the issue out into the open. Third, the supervisor needs to keep in mind that some teachers have a history of mistrusting supervisors and must be shown over a period of time that the supervisor truly intends to be collaborative.

It would be nice to say we can lay these issues to rest, but we cannot. Unless the supervisor remains conscious of the complexity of collaboration, he or she can mistakenly allow collaborative behaviors to become something other than they appear.

When to Use Collaborative Behaviors

There are circumstances in which a supervisor definitely should use collaborative behaviors. We will leave more detailed instructions for Chapter 12, but, for now, collaboration should be used:

1. When teachers are functioning at moderate or mixed developmental levels.
2. When the teacher(s) and supervisor have approximately the same degree of expertise on the issue. If the supervisor knows part of the problem and teachers know the other part, the collaborative approach should be used.
3. When the teacher(s) and supervisor will both be involved in carrying out the decision. If the teacher(s) and supervisor will be held accountable for showing results to someone else (say, parents or the superintendent), then the collaborative approach should be used.
4. When the teacher(s) and supervisor are both committed to solving the problem. If teachers want to be involved, and if leaving them out will lead to low morale and distrust, then the collaborative approach should be used.

Item B4 in Appendix B provides a format for skill practice in collaborative behaviors. Since the collaborative approach involves extensive teacher as well as supervisor input, you will probably find that your collaborative practice session is more complex and longer in duration than your directive simulations.

Moving from Collaborative toward Nondirective Behaviors

The developmental supervisor attempts gradually to move from collaborative toward nondirective interpersonal behaviors. As the teacher or group increases expertise, problem-solving capacity, and motivation, the supervisor hands over more and more decision-making responsibility. An example of a transitional phase between the collaborative and nondirective approach would be to use collaborative behaviors while assisting a teacher or group to decide on an instructional improvement goal, then shift to nondirective behaviors as the teacher or group decides on actions to reach the goal. Nondirective behaviors are discussed in the following chapter.

Collaboration and Cooperation

The supervisor using collaborative interpersonal behaviors jointly shares decision-making responsibility with the teacher or group. Collaborative supervision should not be confused with supervisor-teacher cooperation. To *cooperate* is "to work or act together toward a common purpose" (*American Heritage Dictionary,* 1982, p. 321). The supervisor should strive for cooperation with the teacher or group regardless of his or her supervisory approach. Supervisors and teachers can maintain positive professional relationships and work together toward the common purpose of instructional improvement whether the supervisor uses controlling directive, informational directive, collaborative, or nondirective behaviors, provided the supervisor selects and effectively implements the correct approach.

Summary

Collaborative supervision is premised on participation by equals in making instructional decisions. Its outcome is a mutual plan of action. Collaborative behaviors consist of clarifying, listening, reflecting, presenting, problem solving, negotiating, and standardizing. Collaboration is appropriate when teachers and supervisors have similar levels of expertise, involvement, and concern with a problem. The key consideration for a supervisor is the fact that collaboration is both an attitude and a repertoire of behaviors. Unless teachers have the attitude that they are equal, collaborative behaviors can be used to undermine true equality.

Exercises

Academic

1. Write an imaginary dialogue between a supervisor and a teacher during a conference in which the supervisor successfully makes use of a collaborative approach. Be sure to include examples of each of the 10 collaborative behaviors discussed in Chapter 10.

2. The chapter suggests that a sequence of 10 collaborative behaviors takes place during a collaborative conference. Think of a situation in which a successful collaborative conference would start with the first suggested behavior (identifying the problem as seen by the teacher) and end with the tenth (agreeing to final plan), but would have a *different sequence* of 8 intermediate behaviors. Describe the situation and modified sequence of collaborative behaviors in writing. Include a rationale for the suggested sequence.

3. Write an imaginary dialogue between a supervisor and a teacher in which the supervisor implements apparently collaborative procedures with mechanical precision but fails to be collaborative in an effective sense.

4. Prepare a report comparing the collaborative approach as described in this book with the version of collaboration espoused by an author cited in the References or Suggested Readings.

5. Listening, clarifying, presenting, problem solving, and standardizing are categories of behavior the chapter uses when describing the informational directive as well as the collaborative approach to supervision. Write a paper explaining how each of these five categories actually refers to different behaviors, depending on whether the informational directive or the collaborative approach is being used. For each of the seven behavior categories, give a specific behavior that might be displayed by an informational directive supervisor and a specific behavior that might be displayed by a collaborative supervisor.

Field

1. Assume the role of a supervisor using a collaborative approach by either using the simulation activity found in Appendix B (item B4) or conducting an actual postobservation conference with a teacher. Prepare a written report in which you (a) evaluate your success in displaying collaborative behaviors, (b) summarize the problems discussed and decisions made during the conference, (c) give your perceptions of the "teacher's" responses to your collaborative efforts, and (d) judge the conference in terms of overall success.

2. Participate in a group conference that results in a collaborative contract, with some type of instructional improvement as the anticipated result of contract fulfillment. Prepare a report on how the meeting was conducted, any problems that arose, and how the group reached decisions.

3. Observe an educational supervisor or other leader whom you know to have a collaborative orientation in dealing with individuals and/or groups. On the basis of your observations and/or an interview with the leader, prepare a report describing both successes and failures the selected leader has experienced while using collaborative behaviors. Include possible reasons that the collaborative leader was more successful in some situations than in others.

4. Prepare a photo album entitled "Collaboration for Instructional Improvement." Each photograph should be accompanied by a written explanation of how that entry relates to the album theme.

5. Videotape or audiotape a collaborative conference or professional development activity. As you review the tape, compare the recorded activities with the sequence of behaviors that, according to the chapter, exemplifies the collaborative decision-making process. Prepare a written report on your findings.

Developmental

1. Through interaction with various individuals in a variety of situations, begin to establish a set of personal guidelines that will indicate when the collaborative approach is most appropriate for your own use in carrying out present or anticipated leadership functions.

2. Initiate an in-depth study of Japanese-style management. As you proceed with your study, compare and contrast this style of management with the collaborative approach to supervision discussed in this chapter.

3. Record a simulated or actual supervisor-teacher conference in which you, as supervisor, attempt to display collaborative behaviors. Review the tape for analysis

of your performance. Over the next four weeks, attempt to practice collaborative leadership whenever appropriate opportunities arise. Record another simulated or actual supervisor-teacher conference, and determine what changes you have made.

References

American Heritage Dictionary. 1982. Boston: Houghton Mifflin.

Blumberg, A. 1980. *Supervisors and teachers: A private cold war* (2nd ed.). Berkeley, CA: McCutchan.

Cogan, M. 1973. *Clinical supervision.* Boston: Houghton Mifflin.

Gordon, T. 1977. *Leader Effectiveness Training, L. E. T.: The no-lose way to release the productive potential of people.* New York: Wyden Books.

Harris, T. 1967. *I'm OK—You're OK: Practical guide to transactional analysis.* New York: Harper & Row.

Wagner, A. 1981. *Transactional manager: How to solve people problems with transactional analysis.* Englewood Cliffs, NJ: Prentice Hall.

Wiles, K. 1967. *Supervision for better schools* (3rd ed.). Englewood Cliffs, NJ: Prentice Hall.

Suggested Readings

Pajak, E. 1993. Morris Cogan's clinical supervision. In *Approaches to clinical supervision* (pp. 73–98) Norwood, MA: Christopher-Gordon Publishers.

Schön, D. A. 1988. Coaching reflective teaching. In P. P. Grimmett and G. L. Erickson (Eds.), *Reflection in teacher education.* New York: Teachers College Press.

Sparks, D. 1990. Cognitive coaching: An interview with Robert Garmston. *Journal of Staff Development 11*(2):12–15.

11

Nondirective Behaviors

Teacher: (barging into supervisor's office) This damn place is a zoo! I can't stand it any longer. These kids are a bunch of ingrates! I've had it.

Supervisor: (looking at the teacher) Wow, you are angry! Tell me what's going on. Have a seat.

Teacher: (refusing to sit) I get no help around here from you or the administration. The students know that they can act any way they damn please and get away with it. I'm not going to put up with it anymore.

Supervisor: What have they been doing?

Teacher: Just now, I went back into the class after being called out for a message and they were jumping all over the place, running around, throwing papers, and being totally obnoxious. I can't leave them for a minute.

Supervisor: What did you do?

Teacher: What do you think? I screamed my bloody head off at them and after it all, Terence had the nerve to laugh at me.

Supervisor: Terence laughed at you?

Teacher: Yeah, that little snot! He always has the last word. He's so defiant it drives me mad!

Supervisor: Is he always like that?

Teacher: He sure is. Terence is my number one problem; if I could get him to behave and learn, the rest of the class would be no problem.

Supervisor: So the main problem is Terence. What do you do when he misbehaves?

Teacher: I've been sending him out of the room but that doesn't work. He couldn't care less about school and will only work when forced to. He really gets to me.

Supervisor: He's a lot to handle.

Teacher: He sure is! That kid is a bundle of jumping nerves. He doesn't pay any attention to what goes on in class.

Supervisor: He must really keep you hopping! Does Terence do anything right in class?

Teacher: Hardly! He's just not excited about anything in school. If he could live in a world of rock videos and football games, he'd be just fine.

Supervisor: (joking) Well, maybe we need a flashing movie room of video and football highlights to keep him entertained!

Teacher: (laughing and calming down) Oh, I don't know. He just drives me nuts. He's not a bad kid.

Supervisor: Could we capitalize on his interests to improve his classroom behavior?

Teacher: I need to sit down with him and talk to him one on one. I really want to find something in class that would interest him and keep him out of my hair.

Supervisor: What might that be?

Teacher: Students get to do special history projects in class. Maybe I could tie his love for music or sports into a history project, or maybe make a contract with him about his good behavior so that he could earn time to listen to music? Let me talk to him.

Supervisor: Sorry about your class today. It sounds to me as if Terence is the key and you have some ideas. Are there ways that I could help?

Nondirective Behaviors with Individuals

Nondirective supervision is based on the assumption that an individual teacher knows best what instructional changes need to be made and has the ability to think and act on his or her own. The decision belongs to the teacher. The role of the supervisor is to assist the teacher in the process of thinking through his or her actions.

As the foregoing hypothetical script shows, the supervisor behaves in ways that keep the teacher's thinking focused on observation, interpretation, problem identification, and problem solutions. Notice how in the example the nondirective approach allowed the teacher to move from an angry outburst about the entire class to an analytical focus on Terence's behavior. Rarely will a teacher move this rapidly from anger to reflection, but the pattern of the supervisor helping the teacher to come to his or her own conclusions is characteristic of a nondirective approach. The supervisor does not interject his or her own ideas into the discussion unless specifically asked. All verbalizations by the supervisor are intended as feedback or to extend the teacher's thinking; they do not influence the actual design.

Refer to the supervisory behavior continuum to understand how nondirective behaviors are used. Read carefully, because the misuse of listening, clarifying, encouraging, reflecting, problem-solving, and presenting behaviors can result in a decision that is not really the teacher's.

Figure 11.1 shows a typical pattern of supervisory interpersonal behaviors used in a nondirective conference. They begin with listening and end with asking the teacher to present his or her decision. The sequence of behaviors between

FIGURE 11.1   *The Supervisory Behavior Continuum: Nondirective Behaviors*

1	2	3	4	5
Listening	*Clarifying*	*Encouraging*	*Reflecting*	*Presenting*

T

s

1. Wait until the immediate message is finished

2. Verbalize inital problem—feeling and situation

3. Probe for underlying problem and/or additional information

4. Show willingness to listen further

5. Constantly paraphrase understanding of teacher's message

8. Ask teacher for commitment to a decision

10. Restate the teacher's plan

Key: T = Maximum teacher responsibility   S = Maximum supervisor responsibility
      t = Minimum teacher responsibility   s = Minimum supervisor responsibility

start and finish can vary, but the end should be the same—a noninfluenced teacher decision.

   1. Listening: *Wait until the teacher's initial statement is made.* Face and look at the teacher; concentrate on what is being said. Avoid thinking about how you see the problem or what you think should be done. It is not easy to restrain your mind from galloping ahead, but your job is to understand what the teacher initially has said.

FIGURE 11.1 *Continued*

6	7	8	9	10
Problem Solving	*Negotiating*	*Directing*	*Standardizing*	*Reinforcing*

t
S

6. Ask teacher to think of possible actions

7. Ask teacher to consider consequences of various actions

9. Ask teacher to set time and criteria for action

2. Reflecting: *Verbalize your understanding of the initial problem.* Include in your statement the teacher's feelings and perceived situation: "You're angry because students don't pay attention." Wait for an acknowledgment of accuracy from the teacher: "Yes, I am, but...." Do not offer your own opinion; your job is to capture what the teacher is saying.

3. Clarifying: *Probe for the underlying problem and/or additional information.* You now ask the teacher to look at the problem in some different ways and to consider new information that might be contributing to the problem. Clarifying is done to help the teacher further identify, not solve, the problem. Questions such as: "Do you mean that you are really fed up with school?" "Is it a particular student who is getting to you?" and "When has this happened before?" are appropriate information-seeking questions. Avoid questions that are really solutions in disguise. Such questions as: "Have you thought about taking up yoga to relax?" and "Maybe you could suspend that student for a few days, what do you think?" are inappropriate. Such leading or suggestive questions are attempts to influence the teacher's final decision.

4. Encouraging: *Show willingness to listen further as the teacher begins to identify the real problems.* Show that you will continue to assist and not leave the discussion incomplete. Statements such as: "I'm following what you're saying, continue on," "Run that by me again," and "I'm following you" are correct. Saying, "I like that idea," "Yes, that will work," "Ah, I agree with that," are, even unintentionally, influencing behaviors. A teacher, like any other person, cannot help but be influenced by the judgments a supervisor is making on what he or she says. Encouraging keeps the teacher thinking; praise, on the other hand, influences the final decision.

5. Reflecting: *Constantly paraphrase understanding of the teacher's message.* Throughout the discussion, check on the accuracy of what you understand the teacher to be saying. When the teacher adds more information to the perceived problem, or explains different sources of the problem, considers the possible actions, and finally makes a decision, the supervisor should paraphrase. First, whenever you are uncertain of what the teacher is saying, you should paraphrase with a statement such as: "I think you're saying..." or "I'm not sure but do you mean...." Then you can sit back and allow the teacher to affirm or reject your understanding. Second, when the teacher has come to a halt in thinking about the problem, the paraphrase should be used to jog the teacher's mind to reflect on what has already been said and what more needs to be done. For example, after a considerable pause in the teacher's talk, the supervisor might say, "Well, let me see if I can summarize what has been said so far..." or "So this is where you are—you're angry because...." Comprehensive summarizing allows the teacher to rest, mentally stand off from himself or herself, and think about what has been said. Usually, such paraphrasing will stimulate the teacher to interject, add, and continue. Reflecting should not become mechanical or artificial, with the supervisor paraphrasing every teacher statement. Instead, it should be used

judiciously when the supervisor is not completely clear about what has been said or when there is a long pause in the conversation. Incessant interjections of "I hear you saying…," without aid or purpose, make teachers skeptical about the supervisor's concern.

6. Problem solving: *Ask the teacher to think of possible actions.* After the teacher has finished identifying the problem and you are clear about his or her perception of the problem, your responsibility shifts to helping the teacher generate possible solutions. You can do this by asking straightforward questions: "What can you do about this?" "What else could be done?" "Think hard about actions that might help." "Let me see if you can come up with four to six possible solutions." It is helpful to allow the teacher to think for a minute or two about possible actions before verbalizing them. After actions have been proposed, you should reflect on the proposals, check on their accuracy, and probe for others. Regardless of whether the teacher proposes only a few or many possibilities, if further probing is not successful, then you should move the conference on.

7. Problem solving: *Ask the teacher to consider consequences of various actions.* The moment of truth is almost at hand. Your emphasis is on having the teacher move from possible to probable solutions. Taking each solution in order, ask: "What would happen if you did…?" "Would it work?" "What problems would be associated with it?" Finally, after having the teacher explore the advantages and disadvantages of each action, he or she should be asked to compare the various actions: "Which would work best?" "Why do you think so?" "How would that be better than the others?"

8. Presenting: *Ask the teacher for a commitment to a decision.* After you have explored possible actions and the teacher has compared their likelihood of success, you must emphasize that the teacher should select actions that are within his or her resources *(do-able),* can be implemented in a short period of time *(feasible),* and are concrete *(accountable).* A simple question—"Well, what will you do now that is likely to improve the situation?"—should cut quickly to the heart of the matter.

9. Standardizing: *Ask the teacher to set time and criteria for action.* The teacher is assisted in monitoring his or her own decision about future improvement by specifying the time period during which the action will be implemented, when various parts of the plan will be done, what resources are needed, and how the teacher will know the decision is working. A further series of supervisor questions to accomplish this purpose would be: "Now tell me what you are going to do." "What will be done first, next, last?" "What do you need in order to do it?" "How will you know it's working?" "When will it be done?" When the teacher can answer these questions, the conference is near completion.

10. Reflecting: *Restate the teacher's plan.* Before leaving, repeat the teacher's entire plan with "So you're going to do…." After the teacher verifies the restated plan, the session is over.

Nondirective Behaviors with Groups

As noted in the following scenario, whether the meeting is about bus schedules or textbook adoptions, the supervisory behaviors and sequence of steps are comparable to those of an individual conference.

Scenario: Nondirective Supervision

During fifth-period planning time, Supervisor Eldredge sits down with the sixth-grade middle school team of Mrs. Murdock, English teacher; Mr. Holtz, social studies teacher; Ms. Elright, mathematics teacher; and Mrs. Patrick, science teacher. The supervisor begins by asking, "Well, what's on your minds this week?" Mrs. Murdock replies, "I have a real problem with Mr. Handwright, the custodian. Twice in the last week, I've sent kids on errands and he has stopped them and started yelling at them for not being in the classroom."

Supervisor Eldredge listens until Mrs. Murdock finishes her account and then asks the team. "Has this occurred often with Mr. Handwright?" Mrs. Patrick replies, "Yes, it has. His voice just booms all over and he scares the kids to death." Mr. Holtz adds, "He's even yelled at students when they have been seated in my classroom. He talks through the open door and tells them not to scuff the floors or drop papers. I don't think it's right."

The supervisor responds, "Let me summarize. You are finding that Mr. Handwright is disciplining students in a loud and abusive way for things that they have not done or for things that are not his responsibility. You believe it is not the custodian's job to discipline?" Ms. Elright answers, "Yes, that's right! His job is to clean; our job is to discipline. He's putting his nose into things that are none of his business. He's upsetting our students and us."

Supervisor Eldredge now presses the team, "Ok, I understand the problem; now what do you think should be done?" "That's easy," says Mrs. Patrick. "Someone needs to tell him what is and what is not his job. The principal should do that." "I disagree," says Mr. Holtz. "I think that before we report him to the principal, we should talk with him. Maybe we are being remiss in cleaning up or we are doing some things that are bothering him."

Supervisor Eldredge listens to the discussion and asks Mrs. Patrick, "What do you think of Mr. Holtz's suggestion?" Mrs. Patrick replies to Mr. Holtz, "I don't object. Let's sit down with Mr. Handwright and straighten this out. Should we do it as a team or as individuals?" Ms. Elright says, "It would be less threatening if only one of us talked to him. John [Holtz], since you know him best, could you?" Mr. Holtz replies, "Sure I'll talk to him this afternoon."

The supervisor interjects: "You've agreed to talk to the custodian this afternoon, and John will be the representative. What should the topics be, and when will he report back?" Mr. Holtz answers, "I'm going to tell him that we don't want him to yell at students. If there's a problem, he's to come to the teacher and the teacher will handle discipline. I'm also going to see if there are ways that we can make his job easier. I'll give a progress report to all of you tomorrow morning...."

The supervisor would begin such a meeting by asking and *listening* to group members discuss their perceptions of the group issue. The supervisor would encourage all the members to express themselves and would constantly *clarify* and *reflect* on what they were saying. Once the problem had been discussed, the supervisor would ask the group to *problem solve* by asking each member to propose possible new actions. After compiling a list of possible actions generated by the group, he or she would ask members to discuss the consequences of each action on the list and would make sure that each proposed action was understood by the group. If not, the supervisor would ask for further clarification and then paraphrase the meaning so that the proposer of the action could verify accuracy. After the list of actions was understood, the supervisor would ask for a discussion of the merits of each proposed action and then ask for a comparison of actions most likely to succeed. After problem solving, the supervisor would ask if there was a consensus of action to be taken. If not, he or she would ask for further discussion and then ask the group to determine how to resolve the deadlock. The supervisor would not be part of the decision. After the decision was made, the supervisor would ask the group to detail the decision by *standardizing* the criteria. He or she would ask for a time line, specific activities each group member would take, resources needed by the group, and indications of success. If there was no clear consensus on details of standardizing the plan, the supervisor again would ask the group for further discussion.

Please note that the supervisor using nondirective behaviors is in the role of expediter of the group making its own decision. The supervisor does not offer his or her own ideas and does not influence the choices. The supervisor's role is to keep the group focused on steps for making its own decision.

Initiating Nondirective Supervision

At a workshop facilitated by one of the authors, the author decided to illustrate the nondirective approach with an unstructured simulated conference, with the author taking the role of a supervisor and a volunteer participant assuming the role of a teacher. The focus of the conference was a real-world problem that the volunteer, a mentor-teacher, was experiencing. After a successful simulation in which the author used nondirective behaviors to facilitate the teacher's reflection on the problem, consideration of alternative solutions, and an action plan for solving the problem, the author congratulated the volunteer on a simulation well done. The teacher responded, "I don't feel as if I did a very good job. I didn't know what you were trying to get me to say. Was my solution the one you were looking for?" The author explained that there was no preconceived solution to the problem, that the "supervisor" in the role play was not trying to elicit any particular responses from the teacher. The teacher, who had been selected by his district as a mentor of other teachers because of his outstanding teaching and leadership, explained that he simply did not know how to respond to nondirective supervision because in his many years of teaching he had never been exposed to a nondirective approach.

The above story illustrates the point that supervisors seldom use nondirective behaviors with teachers (indeed, the supervisory approach most often used is directive; Gordon, 1989). Moreover, supervisors sometimes create the illusion of using nondirective behaviors when in fact they are manipulating a supervisory conference or group meeting toward a predetermined decision. When this happens often enough, teachers realize that the supervisor is attempting to manipulate them. Without any experience with authentic nondirective supervision, then, it's no wonder that teachers are leery of the supervisor who is trying to use that approach with them for the first time.

What's the solution when a teacher is perfectly capable of solving his or her own instructional problems but who, because of past experience, is likely to become confused or suspicious of the supervisor's first use of nondirective supervision? One technique is to simply explain to the teacher or group what nondirective supervision is, what specific behaviors are involved, and why the supervisor believes the teacher or group can benefit from the nondirective approach. Even when the supervisor has provided a rationale for nondirective supervision, some teachers may still be reluctant to identify problems, consider actions, commit to decisions, or establish criteria for success. When this happens, the supervisor should not automatically assume that the nondirective approach is inappropriate for the teacher or group. Rather the supervisor should continue to build trust and rapport through active listening, probe for problems and related information, and encourage the teacher or group to describe situations and feelings. Eventually, the teacher or group should reach a stage of trust and self-confidence that will enable them to consider alternatives and generate an improvement plan. Supervisor commitment to teacher self-direction, along with the use of appropriate interpersonal behaviors, will ultimately lead to teacher-driven instructional improvement.

Nondirective, Not Laissez Faire, Supervision

Some educators have criticized nondirective supervision by arguing that supervisors who use nondirective behaviors are abdicating their responsiblity to assist teachers to improve their instructional peformance. This is a valid argument against laissez faire supervision, which advocates minimal supervisor involvement in the instructional improvement process. However, under our definition of nondirective supervision, the supervisor is actively involved in instructional improvement, clarifying, encouraging, reflecting, and facilitating teacher decision making at each stage of the improvement process. Also, in developmental supervision the nondirective approach is used only with those teachers who are operating at high levels of abstraction, motivation, and expertise. The developmental supervisor uses one of the other three supervisory approaches with teachers who are not ready to assume full decision-making responsibility.

Issues with Nondirective Supervision

Based on numerous skill-training sessions conducted with school leaders on employing nondirective behaviors, some common issues and practical questions have arisen:

1. Can a supervisor really remain nonjudgmental and not influence the teacher's or group's decision?
2. What happens if the teacher or group desires the supervisor's input?
3. What does a supervisor do with a teacher or group that is reluctant or not capable of generating solutions?
6. How exact or variable is the sequence of nondirective behaviors?
7. In what circumstances should nondirective behaviors be used?

Whether a supervisor can really remain nonjudgmental is a legitimate concern. Even when one is consciously avoiding praise, not interjecting one's own ideas, and not offering solutions in the guise of questions, some influencing probably will take place. Studies by Mears, Shannon, and Pepinsky (1979) analyzing the tapes of counseling sessions conducted by the most renowned expert on nondirectiveness, psychologist Carl Rogers, revealed a definite pattern to his interrupting the patient and to which statements he selected to paraphrase. It is apparent that any interaction between humans is bound to be influential. Frequency of eye contact, timing of questions, facial expressions, and ways of paraphrasing can always be interpreted by a teacher as approving or disapproving. There is no way to avoid influencing through unconscious supervisory responses. The best one can do is to minimize those behaviors that knowingly influence. One should not knowingly offer ideas, praise, or directions that will influence the teacher's decision.

What if the teacher or group asks for the supervisor's suggestions? The answer to this question centers on timing. If the suggestions are asked for and given in the initial stages of a conference or meeting before the teacher or group has been required to think through the issue, then such feedback will structure the stream of subsequent thought and heavily influence the decision. If the suggestions are given after the teacher or group has already narrowed its own choices of actions, however, a supervisor's answer will not be as influential. Ideally, it is better to refrain completely from giving one's own ideas. If asked, the supervisor might respond, "I'm sorry, but I don't want to answer that. Instead, I want you to think through what can be done. Only you know your own situation. Therefore, what *I* think is not as important as what *you* think." If the teacher or group will not make a decision without knowing the supervisor's ideas, then he or she might as well give up being nondirective and move into a more collaborative mode.

Being nondirective with an individual or group that is reluctant or not capable of generating solutions is tricky. Reluctance and capability are not necessarily inversely related. If the teacher is reluctant but capable, the worst possible response would be for the supervisor to take over decision making for the teacher.

Such a move might reinforce the teacher's reluctance to speak his or her own mind. Reluctance usually stems from a disbelief that one will be listened to or allowed to act on one's own initiative. The supervisor must be patient, give constant encouragement, and be persistent. Patience is shown by listening and waiting, encouragement by accepting what the teacher says, and persistence by not allowing the teacher to rest without making a decision. A supervisor can be persistent by asking questions, by taking breaks from the conference, and by giving the teacher time for further reflections.

Capability is a different matter. What if a teacher or group is incapable of making a decision? If they continually insist they do not know what the problem is or have no ideas about what could be done, and if every supervisory prompt is met by vacant stares and shrugs of shoulders, then patience, encouragement, and persistence on the part of the supervisor will create further frustration and perhaps antagonism. If they simply don't know, no matter how nondirective the supervisor is, no decisions will be forthcoming. Obviously, if lack of capability is the source of nonresponsiveness, then the nondirective approach is an unwise choice of supervisory behaviors.

Finally, there is the question of sequence of nondirective behaviors. How precise is the order? The description of nondirective behaviors presented a prototype of 10 steps within the supervisory behavior continuum (Figure 11.1). The behaviors are: (1) listening-waiting, (2) reflecting-verbalizing, (3) clarifying-probing, (4) encouraging-willing, (5) reflecting-paraphrasing, (6) problem solving—asking for possible actions, (7) problem solving—asking for probable consequences, (8) presenting—asking for a commitment, (9) standardizing—asking for criteria, and (10) reflecting—restating the plan. Again, one might visualize these steps as analogous to playing the left-hand side of a piano keyboard. The supervisor-pianist begins the musical score with the furthest left-hand note (listening-waiting) and will end the score at note 10 (reflecting-restating). During the score (conference or meeting) the adept player will strike the notes (behaviors) back and forth between 1 and 10 pounding on some notes, lightly touching on others, returning, and swelling the underlying tone of the teacher or group voice. The score ends on note 10—reflecting and restating the teacher's or group's decision. The behaviors are not a prescription of fixed steps but rather a directionality of movements with a definite beginning and end.

When to Use Nondirective Behaviors

When and with whom should nondirective behaviors be used? A supervisor should consider using a nondirective approach:

1. When the teacher or group is functioning at high developmental levels.
2. When the teacher or group possesses most of the knowledge and expertise about the issue and the supervisor's knowledge and expertise are minimal: "If you don't know anything about it and they do, let them solve it."

3. When the teacher or group has full responsibility for carrying out the decision and the supervisor has little involvement: "If they are going to be accountable for it and you aren't, let them solve it."
4. When the teacher or group is committed to solving the problem but the problem doesn't matter to the supervisor: "If they want to act and you couldn't care less, let them decide."

The criteria of (1) developmental level, (2) expertise, (3) responsibility, and (4) commitment appear to be straightforward. Chapter 12 will show the greater complexity of these criteria and the critical role of supervisor judgment. For now, let us add that there are special circumstances in which initial use of nondirective behaviors are appropriate even if the above criteria are not met. Regardless of teacher developmental level, expertise, responsibility, or commitment, when a teacher or group has become extremely emotional over a problem, rational problem solving using any of the four supervisory approaches may be unproductive. What may be more beneficial in such situations is the initial use of the nondirective behaviors of listening, clarifying, encouraging, and reflecting as the teacher or group describes the problem and expresses the anger, frustration, fear, resentment or other feelings the problem has generated. Once the teacher or group has had the opportunity to vent emotions in the presence of an empathetic listener, the supervisor can then shift to a problem-solving mode, using the criteria of developmental level, expertise, responsibility, and commitment to select the appropriate supervisory approach for the problem-solving phase of the conference or meeting.

Nondirective Supervision, Teacher Collaboration

Although nondirective supervision can be a valuable means of assisting individual teacher development, we see its greatest potential in the supervisor facilitating expert teachers collaborating with each other for classroom and schoolwide instructional improvement. An example of nondirective supervision of teacher collaboration at the classroom level would be the supervisor facilitating a teacher-driven peer-coaching program. An example of nondirective supervision for schoolwide instructional improvement would be the supervisor assisting a group of teachers as the group plans, implements, and evaluates a series of integrated instructional units cutting across several content areas. The ultimate goal of developmental supervision is for the supervisor to be facilitating a self-actualized teaching staff engaged in collaborative and continuous instructional improvement.

Item B5 in Appendix B allows you to practice nondirective behaviors. Practice in nondirective supervision is especially important, since research indicates that it is the most difficult supervisory approach to implement (Gordon, 1990). After you have practiced all four supervisory approaches under simulated conditions, another idea is to try out the various supervisory approaches in work and personal situations. A note of caution is in order if you decide to practice the different approaches in real life situations: Be careful with whom you try out directive control behaviors. Used with certain colleagues, friends, and spouses, directive control can be dangerous to your health!

Summary

Supervisors can use nondirective behaviors in helping teachers determine their own plans. Such supervisory behaviors consist of listening, reflecting, clarifying, encouraging, and problem solving. When individuals and groups of teachers are functioning at high developmental levels and possess greater expertise, commitment, and responsibility for a particular decision than the supervisor does, then a nondirective approach is appropriate. Important considerations for a supervisor when using nondirectiveness are attempting to be nonjudgmental, hesitating in response to teachers' wishes for more supervisor input, and adjusting one's behavior when teachers demonstrate reluctance to generate solutions. The purpose of nondirective supervision is to provide an active sounding board for thoughtful professionals.

Exercises

Academic

1. Write an imaginary dialogue between a supervisor and a teacher during a conference in which the supervisor successfully uses a nondirective approach. Be sure to include examples of each of the 10 nondirective behaviors discussed in Chapter 11.

2. The chapter explains a sequence of 10 nondirective behaviors that take place during a nondirective conference. Think of a situation in which a successful nondirective conference would start with the first suggested behavior (listening-waiting) and end with the tenth (reflecting-restating the plan), but would have a *different sequence* of 8 intermediate behaviors. Describe the situation and modified sequence of nondirective behaviors in writing. Include a rationale for the suggested sequence.

3. Write an imaginary dialogue between a supervisor and a teacher in which the supervisor implements nondirective procedures with mechanical precision but still fails to be truly nondirective.

4. Write a paper comparing the nondirective approach as described in this book with the version of nondirective assistance espoused by an author cited in the References or Suggested Readings.

5. Assume you have just listened to a talk by a school administrator in which he or she argued against the use of nondirective behaviors by educational supervisors with *any* teacher. The thrust of the administrator's argument was that such an approach is essentially *laissez faire* and allows complete deference to teacher decisions, even when such decisions are clearly in error and are likely to result in harm to the teacher's instructional performance or to the students. The administrator further

argued that for a supervisor to withhold his or her observations, perceptions, and suggestions, unless they are requested by the teacher, is counterproductive to the supervisory process. You have been asked to prepare a reply to the administrator to be presented at an upcoming seminar. Write a paper in which you argue for the use of nondirective behavior with certain teachers. Address the administrator's objections in your paper.

Field

1. Use a nondirective approach by either using the activity found in Item B5 of Appendix B or conducting an actual postobservation conference with a teacher. Prepare a written report in which you (a) evaluate your success in displaying nondirective behaviors, (b) summarize the problems discussed and decisions made during the conference, (c) give your perceptions of the "teacher's" responses to your nondirective efforts, and (d) judge the conference in terms of overall success.

2. Observe an educational supervisor or other leader whom you know to possess a nondirective orientation. Based on your observations and interview with the leader, write a paper describing both successes and failures that he or she has experienced while using nondirective behaviors. Include possible reasons for the nondirective leader's greater success in some situations than in others.

3. Observe three teachers or staff members who clearly respond positively to nondirective supervision. Prepare a report examining personal and social characteristics of these individuals that may account for their positive response to a nondirective approach.

4. Prepare a picture album entitled "Self-Direction for Instructional Improvement." Each picture should be accompanied by a written explanation of how that entry relates to the album theme.

5. Videotape or audiotape a conference or professional development activity in which the supervisor is using a nondirective approach. As you review the tape, compare the recorded activities with the sequence of behaviors that, according to the authors, exemplifies the nondirective approach of a supervisor during a decision-making process. Prepare a report on your findings.

Developmental

1. Trough interaction with various individuals in a variety of situations, begin to establish a set of personal guidelines that will indicate when the nondirective approach is most appropriate in carrying out present or anticipated leadership functions.

2. Begin an in-depth study of the writings of a prominent humanistic educator or psychologist. Relate that author's ideas to the concepts of nondirective supervision discussed in this chapter.

3. Record a simulated or actual supervisor-teacher conference in which you, as supervisor, attempt to display nondirective behaviors. Review the tape for analysis of your performance. Over the next four weeks, practice nondirective leadership whenever appropriate opportunities arise. Record another simulated or actual conference in four weeks. Review both tapes to discover any improvement in terms of successfully displaying nondirective behaviors.

References

Carkhuff, R. R. 1969. *Helping and human relations: A primer for lay and professional helpers, Vol. 2: Practice and research.* New York: Holt, Rinehart and Winston.

Combs, A., Avila, D. L., and Purkey, W. H. 1979. *Helping relationships: Basic concepts for the helping professions* (2nd ed.). Boston: Allyn and Bacon.

Gazda, G. M., Asbury, R. R., Balzer, F. J., Childers, W. C., and Walters, R. P. 1977. *Human relations development: A manual for educators* (2nd ed.). Boston: Allyn and Bacon.

Gordon, S. P. 1989. *The theory of developmental supervision: An investigation of the critical aspects.* Doctoral Dissertation, University of Georgia, Athens.

Gordon, S. P. 1990. Developmental supervision: An exploratory study of a promising model. *Journal of Curriculum and Supervision* 5:293–307.

Mears, N. M., Shannon, J. W, and Pepinsky, H. B. 1979. Comparison of the stylistic complexity of the language of counselor and client across three theoretical orientations. *Journal of Counseling Psychology* 26(3):181–189.

Mosher, R. L., and Purpel, D. E. 1972. *Supervision: The reluctant profession.* Boston: Houghton Mifflin.

Rogers, C. R. 1951. *Client-centered therapy: Its current practice, implications, and theory.* Boston: Houghton Mifflin.

Suggested Readings

Gitlin, A., and Price, K. 1992. Teacher empowerment and the development of voice. In C. D. Glickman (Ed.), *Supervision in transition.* Alexandria, VA: Association for Supervision and Curriculum Development.

Pajak, E. 1993. *Approaches to clinical supervision.* Norwood, MA: Christopher-Gordon Publishers. See the following: (1) Robert Goldhammer's Clinical Supervision (pp. 25–50), (2) Ralph Mosher and David Purpel's Ego Counseling Model (pp. 51–72), (3) Arthur Blumberg's Interpersonnel Intervention (pp. 103–126), and (4) Noreen Garman's "Reflective Heart" of Clinical Supervision (pp. 296–298).

Retallick, J. A. 1990. *Clinical supervision and the structure of communication.* Paper presented at the Annual Meeting of the American Educational Research Association, Boston, April.

Symth, W. J. 1990. *Problemizing teaching through a "critical" approach to clinical supervision.* Paper presented at the Annual Meeting of the American Educational Research Association, Boston, April.

12

Developmental Supervision
Theory and Practice

Thus far in Part III we have introduced the supervisory behavior continuum, provided an overview of developmental supervision, and explained each of the four supervisory approaches (directive control, directive informational, collaborative, and nondirective). This chapter provides an in-depth discussion of developmental supervision as an integrated model. The first part of the chapter presents the underlying rationale for developmental supervision. The second part explains how the model can be applied in practice.

Rationale for Developmental Supervision

One aspect of developmental supervision is the match of initial supervisory approach with the teacher's or group's developmental levels, expertise, and commitment. In Chapter 4, we described characteristics of teachers functioning at various stages of adult and career development. Teachers functioning at generally low developmental levels were described as performing at the concrete operations stage of cognitive development, low conceptual levels, the preconventional level of moral reasoning, the fearful stage of ego development, the durable category level of consciousness, and the self-adequacy stage of concern. Teachers or groups of low developmental levels, expertise, and commitment seem well matched to directive supervision. They have difficulty defining problems, have few ways of responding to problems, and are unlikely to accept decision-making responsibility. They clearly are in need of the structure and intensive assistance provided by directive supervision. For most teachers in need of direction, an informational directive approach is appropriate. For teachers functioning at extremely low levels of development, expertise, and commitment, and with serious instructional problems, a controlling directive approach might be necessary.

Teachers of generally moderate developmental levels were described as functioning at the formal operations stage of cognitive development, moderate conceptual levels, the conventional level of moral reasoning, the conforming stage of ego development, the cross-categorical level of consciousness, and the teaching tasks stage of concern. Teachers or groups at moderate developmental levels, expertise, and commitment are usually best served by a collaborative supervisory approach. They can generate some possible solutions to an instructional problem, but still need some assistance in examining all options and developing a comprehensive plan for instructional improvement. The brainstorming inherent in collaborative supervision allows the teacher or group to share perceptions and offer some possible alternatives for future action, but also receive the benefit of supervisor perceptions and proposals. Negotiated action plans made during collaborative supervision allow teachers to meet needs of emerging independence while receiving the moderate guidance needed to assure that the plan will lead to instructional improvement.

Teachers functioning at generally high developmental levels were described in Chapter 4 as being at the postformal operations stage of cognitive development, high conceptual levels, the postconventional level of moral reasoning, the autonomous stage of ego development, the systems or trans-systems level of consciousness, and the teaching impact stage of concern. Teachers or groups functioning at generally high developmental levels, expertise, and commitment are ready for the self-direction fostered by the nondirective supervisory approach. They are autonomous, explorative, and creative. They can think of a problem from many perspectives, generate a variety of alternative actions, think through each step of an action plan, and follow the plan through to completion.

The Problem of Variability

The fact that the criteria for selecting a supervisory approach may fluctuate means that choosing the best approach can become more complicated than the broad guidelines just discussed might suggest. The following possibilities must be kept in mind:

1. Individual or group levels of development, expertise, and commitment may vary. For example, a teacher might be functioning at high levels of consciousness as well as cognitive, conceptual, and moral development but at only moderate levels of ego development, concern, and commitment. In addition, a group might include teachers of low, moderate, and high developmental levels. Some general guidelines are to use a controlling directive approach if most characteristics of an individual or group indicate an extremely low decision-making capacity, informational directive supervision if most attributes point to a fairly low capacity, a collaborative approach if most characteristics indicate a moderate capacity, and nondirective supervision if most attributes point to a high capacity for decision making. When

working with an individual or group with widely fluctuating characteristics, a collaborative approach would probably be most effective.

2. Characteristics of teachers and groups might change in certain situations. For example, a teacher who has successfully taught general science to middle school students for 10 years might regress to lower levels of development, expertise, or commitment after being transferred to a senior high school to teach chemistry and physics. Similarly, a faculty at a former junior high school might regress to lower levels of group development, expertise, or commitment after the campus has been converted to a middle school. In short, the developmental supervisor sometimes must change supervisory behaviors in order to adapt to a change in the teacher or group's situation.

Teachers' Preferences for Supervisory Approach

Because most teachers probably function at moderate or mixed levels of development, expertise, and commitment, the collaborative approach should be the most successful entry approach with most individuals and groups of experienced teachers. Research on teachers' preferences for supervisory approach is consistent with this hypothesis. When a stratified sample of 210 K–12 teachers were asked for their preferred supervisory approach, 63 (30 percent) preferred a supervisor to work with them nondirectively; 141 (67 percent) preferred a supervisor to work with them collaboratively, and only 6 (3 percent) preferred a supervisor to work with them directively (Ginkel, 1983). Blumberg also surveyed experienced teachers about supervisory behaviors they perceived to be most positive. As with the Ginkel study, experienced teachers split primarily into two groups. One group perceived collaborative supervisory behaviors—listening to the teacher as well as presenting the supervisor's own views—as most positive. The other group saw nondirective supervisory behaviors—primarily listening, reflecting, and asking the teacher—as most positive. Experienced teachers generally did not view forms of directive behaviors as positive (Blumberg and Weber, 1968; Blumberg, 1980).

Student or neophyte teachers prefer a different range of supervisory approaches. Various studies of preservice teachers have been conducted by Zonca (1973), Vudovich (1976), Copeland and Atkinson (1978), Copeland (1980), and Lorch (1981). The findings were consistent in that most preservice teachers preferred a directive informational supervisory approach. Most of them wanted a supervisor to tell them precisely what changes they could be expected to make to improve instruction. However, Humphrey (1983), in a study of entry-level teachers, found most of them to prefer a collaborative approach.

Three tentative conclusions can be drawn from these studies of experienced and preservice teachers:

1. Experienced teachers vary in their preference of supervisory behaviors between nondirective and collaborative. Between the two, collaborative supervisory behaviors are preferred by the majority of teachers.

2. Directive forms of supervisory behaviors are preferred by only a small minority of experienced teachers.
3. Neophyte teachers (student and beginning teachers) initially prefer a directive informational approach or collaborative approach by their supervisors.

The research on teachers' preferences for supervisory approach, although informative, must be viewed with caution. It is possible that the approach some teachers say they prefer might not be most beneficial to them in a particular situation. This caution may be especially appropriate when working with teachers functioning at low levels of development, expertise, and commitment who prefer a collaborative or nondirective approach.

Research on adult and teacher development and teachers' supervisory preferences can suggest guidelines for determining the best supervisory approach. The tremendous variability of teacher characteristics, however, means that the supervisor must choose his or her approach on a case-by-case basis, relying on the knowledge base on teacher characteristics, recent observations of and interactions with the teacher or group, and analysis of the current situation.

One way to describe developmental supervision is to say that it provides teachers with as much initial choice as they are ready to assume, then fosters teachers' decision-making capacity and expanded choice over time. But why be so concerned with teacher choice? Why not simply train teachers in effective teaching methods, monitor classroom instruction, reinforce successful teaching, and remediate (or eliminate) ineffective teachers? In short, why not simply do one's best to control teachers and instruction for the sake of students and society, who, after all, are the real clients of the schools? This question will be answered through the following discussions of motivation, choice, and controlling versus informational environments.

deCharms and Deci on Motivation

What does current research say about human motivation? There have been scores of studies on the undermining effect of control versus individual choice (Morgan, 1984). The research led by deCharms (1968, 1976) and Deci (1975, 1982) not only validates the work of Maslow and Herzberg (discussed in Chapter 4) but also adds to the understanding of why the interacting area of "choice" is the critical determinant in teacher improvement.

deCharms conducted studies with findings that contradicted motivation theories based on external stimulus. The most prevalent practices in industry and schools are based on the premise that individuals will change and increase their production if reinforced by rewards, bribes, or coercion (Ouchi, 1981). Extrinsic-motivation theory posits that one motivates others by either positive means—praising, rewarding, and providing salary incentives—or negative means—threatening job security, withholding pay, or criticizing. Such motivation is based on behavioral, stimulus-response psychology identified with B. F. Skinner (1971), which maintains that humans are conditioned by external forces. Pure behaviorists consistently advocate positive reinforcement and believe that the use of negative reinforcement is ineffective. Yet practitioners of behavioral psychology in most organizations do not make such distinctions and readily mix rewards with punishments. deCharms's research upset the behavioral applecart in finding that the most basic of behavioral propositions—positive rewarding of appropriate behavior—has undesirable after-effects. deCharms's experiments showed that groups of students and teachers who were not rewarded performed *better* on tasks than did groups who were positively rewarded (deCharms 1968, Chapter 10).

Deci (1975, 1982) has amplified deCharms's studies and has looked closely at the consequences of individual freedom of choice as contrasted with reinforcing an individual to act according to someone else's dictates. Deci and associates have conducted sets of controlled laboratory experiments wherein comparable groups of adults were placed in rooms with an assortment of puzzle activities. Members of one group were told to perform a certain activity and that they would be paid for completing that activity. The other group was told they could choose from any of the activities and could work as long as they pleased. No reinforcement was provided to the second group. The first study found that the rewarded subjects spent less time with the assigned activity and were less satisfied with doing the activity than were the subjects who had free choice. In the second study, the same groups of subjects returned to the activity room and were told to work as they pleased. The previously rewarded group showed decreased attention and performance. The rewarded group avoided the activity they had been paid to do previously, whereas the free-choice group tended to return to the activity they had worked on before. The attitude and commitment of the previously unrewarded group was significantly higher than that of the rewarded group. Thus Deci, like deCharms before him, concluded that there are indirect and undesirable consequences of using external reinforcement to motivate humans.

The Issue of Choice

Deci, as a laboratory researcher, is convinced—and as a field-based educators we concur—that reinforcement or extrinsic motivation is not the way to promote professional and personal growth. External reinforcement is necessary in an organization as a way of satisfying Maslow's low-stage needs—physiological, safety, and the sense of belonging—and the hygiene factors of salary, work conditions and job security, to maintain minimal competence. Once the person is minimally competent, external reinforcements, even positive ones, are not growth inducing.

Any type of organization must control employee behaviors within broad limits. Control means that some person representing the governance of the organization has the job of getting employees to comply with those limits. With compliance inevitably comes some form of resistance. Although a person will do what he or she is told to do if the reward or sanction is great enough, the controller knows there will be an indirect consequence of resistance. If resistance were not inevitable, there would be no reason to control. The employee will perform but also might resent the controller, do the task grudgingly, or even do the opposite of what the controller wants when the controller is not present.

A study by Brown (1975) found that teachers, when ordered by a supervisor to perform in a prescribed manner, often did the opposite of the orders. This type of resistance can be seen when teachers are told to use certain textbooks they do not like as part of school policy. They will bring out the books when the controller (principal or superintendent) is there. When the controller is not there, however, they will use the books halfheartedly (as a part of their lesson) or not at all (to keep the door open or for short students to sit on). An experienced school administrator or teacher is well aware that control leads to immediate compliance and subsequent resistance.

Many issues that arise with teachers in schools are issues of control. As part of the school organization, teachers simply must behave in certain ways. As the controls are articulated clearly, a teacher becomes familiar with the norms and minimum expectations of the organization. *However, let's not confuse controlling behavior with improving instruction.* Ultimately the individual teacher always has a choice, even when the choice is "Do what I say or get out!" Yet the narrowing of choice is not motivating; rather, it is the expansion of choice or the opportunity to decide that motivates a teacher to go beyond competence.

Controlling versus *Informational Environments*

Deci distinguished between working with people in controlling environments and informational environments. *Controlling* environments, as already mentioned, restrict individual choice, gain compliance, and create resistance. *Informational* environments expand individual choice, promote autonomy, and encourage commitment to improvement. An informational environment is one in which the individual considers alternative sources of feedback on his or her performance, thinks through consequences of his or her actions, and freely chooses according to his or her own interests and curiosity. The premise of an informational environment is that humans are innately curious and desire to follow their own inclinations. deCharms has called this drive to be powerful, independent, and active the quality of being an "origin." Persons who have been conditioned by a controlling environment to feel powerless, dependent, and passive deCharms has called "pawns." When the professional environment matches the individual's need to be an initiator, then—and only then—does enduring improvement occur.

Pajak and Seyfarth (1983) clarified the distinction between controlling and informational environments by referring to supervisory language. According to them, it is the difference between a supervisor working with a teacher in a "must" manner as opposed to working with a teacher in a "can" manner. Words such as *must, should, ought to,* and *need to* connote supervisor control and lack of teacher choice. Words such as *can, could, consider,* and *might* connote supervisor information and teacher choice. Anyone in a formal supervisory position might consider using the *must* context only when control is the paramount issue and using the *can* context when information and improvement are of greatest importance. Studies have shown that teachers are extremely sensitive to the differences between controlling and informational language used by a supervisor (Pajak and Glickman, 1984, 1989). Woe to the person who mistakenly uses *must* to mean *can,* or *consider* to mean *should.* People have trouble enough communicating true intent to others without compounding the problem by unwittingly using control words when they mean to use informational ones or vice versa.

Finally, this discussion of human motivation in a supervisory context brings us back to the use of the delineated interpersonal approaches—directive control, directive informational, collaborative, and nondirective. For a supervisor working with individual teachers and group members, two environments must be considered when using various approaches. These two environments are depicted in Table 12.1.

In an informational environment, the supervisor allows the teacher to make his or her own choice. Yet the supervisor varies the source and amount of information depending on the teacher's expertise and competence in problem solving. The directive, informational approach (cell A), in which the supervisor tells the teacher what can be done to improve instruction ("I think student attention would be greater if you had smaller groups"), is predicated on the supervisor's knowledge of possibilities and the teacher's lack of such knowledge. The collaborative informational approach (cell B) is premised on both supervisor and teacher having helpful information ("This is what you think can be done....This is what I think...."). The nondirective informational approach (cell C) is premised on the teacher's expertise and the supervisor's facilitation of teacher knowledge ("How do you see your classroom?"). When we move into controlling environments, we are responding to beginning and/or insecure teachers' needs for safety, structure, and security. If the supervisor does possess formal authority, he or she can use the directive controlling approach (cell D) in emergency or survival situations ("You *must* stop using corporal punishment, it is against school policy"). The collaborative, controlling approach (cell E) and the nondirective, controlling approach (cell F) have no place in schools. To use collaborative skills to manipulate teachers to

TABLE 12.1 *Supervisory Environment and Approach*

Environments	Approaches		
	Directive	*Collaborative*	*Nondirective*
Informational	[A]Supervisor's information for teacher to consider	[B]Sharing information for both to consider	[C]Actively listening to teacher's information
Controlling	[D]Supervisor telling teacher what to do	[E]Guise of involvement: Make teacher believe he/she shared in decision	[F]Manipulating teacher to think he/she is making own decision

do what the supervisor had wanted all along or to use nondirective skills to subtly reinforce compliance with a supervisor's demand is dishonest and unethical. Besides the questionable ethics of such behavior, once the game is known the supervisor will reap the undesirable consequence of resistance from teachers.

A supervisor should use directive control in situations of potential harm to students and in cases of incompetence of a teacher. After all, directive control is really an evaluation approach for achieving compliance from an employee. The supervisor should use directive information, collaborative information, and nondirective information in his or her everyday work.

SuperVision for Teacher Development

The long-term goal of developmental supervision is teacher development toward a point at which teachers, facilitated by supervisors, can assume full responsibility for instructional improvement. In addition to the motivational factors already discussed, there are several other reasons why we believe that teacher development should be a critical function of supervision. First, as described in Chapter 4, teachers functioning at higher developmental levels tend to use a wide variety of instructional behaviors associated with successful teaching. Second, teachers who have themselves reached high stages of cognitive, conceptual, moral, and ego development are more likely to foster their own students' growth in those areas. In a democratic society, it is vital that students learn to think reflectively, function at high stages of moral reasoning, and be autonomous decision makers. Finally, teachers at higher levels of adult development, expertise, and commitment are more likely to embrace "a cause beyond oneself" and participate in collective action toward schoolwide instructional improvement—a critical element found in the effective schools research. This section has focused on the *why* of developmental supervision. The remainder of the chapter is concerned with *how* developmental supervision can be applied in the real world of schools and teachers.

Applying Developmental Supervison

Chapter 7 introduced the three phases of developmental supervision. To review, they are (1) choosing the best entry-level supervisory approach, (2) applying the chosen approach, and (3) fostering teacher development while gradually increasing teacher choice and decision making responsibility. Our discussion of applying developmental supervision addresses each of these three phases.

Phase 1: Choosing the Best Approach

There are two primary ways to assess a teacher's developmental levels, expertise, and commitment, all of which should be considered when choosing the supervisory approach to be used. One way is to observe the teacher teaching or working with other teachers. Another way is to discuss with the teacher his or her ideas about students, teaching, and instructional improvement. Below are excerpts from actual observation reports on behaviors of teachers diagnosed at various development levels (Gordon, 1989). First, let's review excerpts from reports on teachers who supervisors perceived to be in need of directive informational supervision:

- I found her rigid and uptight in her relationships with the students.
- He was inconsistent in applying rules of behavior. His directions for the lesson were unclear and confusing. As a result, the students became disruptive. Some students even became hostile, while others started telling him what to do. He gave up on an activity in social studies because he said the class was too noisy. Actually they were confused over the poor directions.
- In watching her in her classroom…half of the time was spent correcting, redirecting. "Sit in your seats…," "How many times do I have to tell you to raise your hand?"
- He found out that games worked…his lectures, and workbooks, and games, and that was about it.

Below are excerpts from observation reports on teachers for whom supervisors chose a collaborative approach:

- In committee work, I have found him dependable and willing to cooperate but not an initiator of ideas.
- I've worked with this teacher for several years…. I've observed her growth…. She is becoming more independent and is willing to try some new ideas and methods.
- (The teacher) possesses several (instructional) strategies but has difficulty adopting strategies and individualizing (instruction).

Finally, some observations of teachers matched with a nondirective approach follow:

- She develops her own units of instruction with minimum guidance. She is able to start with an idea for an instructional unit and then pool available resources. If a resource is not availible, she often makes it herself. She is very artistic and has a wealth of good ideas.
- He uses a variety of teaching methods.
- She is sensitive to her students' needs and is even thinking beyond (this year) to next year. They will be going to a new school, and her concerns now are to make the students more responsible, self-sufficient, etc., so they'll function (successfully) at the new school.
- Students are treated like individuals, and creativity and expression of feelings encouraged.
- This teacher sees the child in a holistic way: a growing, developing human being whose learning style is multifaceted and whose learning occurs in all

areas—cognitive, social, emotional, and physical. She gears instruction not only to groups of learners but also to individuals.

- He has served as president of a statewide educational association. He has written several books and journal articles for teachers and parents, conducts workshops, and is very active in local organizations dedicated to the improvement of teaching.

The best way to determine teacher characteristics and supervisory approach is to combine observations of teachers in action with supervisor-teacher discussion. To assess teacher characteristics, the supervisor can use discussions with the teacher to find answers to the following questions:

1. Is the teacher aware of improvements that can be made in the classroom? Can the teacher identify those needs?
2. Has the teacher considered possible causes of the instructional needs? Does the teacher gather information from multiple sources about the instructional needs?
3. Can the teacher generate several possible solutions? How carefully does the teacher weigh the merits of each solution? Does the teacher consider what he or she can do to reach the goal without looking unrealistically for outside help?
4. Can the teacher be decisive in choosing a course of action? Does the teacher commit himself or herself to an implementation procedure?
5. Does the teacher do what he or she says?

Teacher responses to questions like these can provide clues to the appropriate supervisory approach.

The following quotes are excerpts from supervisor reports on discussions with teachers. The first set of excerpts describe teachers for whom supervisors selected a directive informational approach:

- At the end of the lesson I observed he said, "I need help. Please tell me what to do."
- A student below grade level was transferred to her class. She wanted me to list appropriate materials to use with this child and asked me to come to her school and demonstrate appropriate techniques with this child. I did this, and I think she felt more relaxed about the situation, although she still seeks and receives much guidance in working with this child.
- He has (said) to me that "at this age, lecturing seems to be the only way to get ideas and materials across to students."
- In conferences, when I ask for goals or what types of things would she like to work on, she doesn't know. She says, "I just don't know."

Following are supervisor's reports on conferences with teachers who supervisors matched with a collaborative approach:

- He has come to me on many occasions asking me how to handle things and has been able, at the same time, to give me some of his ideas.
- In seeking assistance in her classroom she is seldom without ideas or suggestions. However, she does not feel totally secure in trying out new ideas without first discussing them with the principal or me.
- This teacher is open to ideas but does not like to be told what to do...he is starting to make some decisions on his own.

Last, some supervisor descriptions of conference behaviors of teachers matched with nondirective supervision follow:

- She often comes to me to talk about the things that she has going on in her classroom, not because she wants me to help make a decision, but because she simply wants to sound out what she plans to do.
- This teacher's performance at our meetings is impressive. He comes prepared and is really capable of handling the meetings himself....He always manages to work out any problems himself.

Some cautions need to be made here concerning the organizational relationship between the individual providing supervision and the teacher or group receiving supervision. Generally, directive control supervision should be used only by supervisors in line relationships with teachers (supervisors who have been given formal authority by the school district over teachers they are supervising). Informational directive supervision should be used only by those who are acknowledged by the organization to have special expertise. Examples of individuals with acknowledged expertise include supervisors in line or staff relationships with teachers, lead teachers, mentors of beginning teachers, and so on. Collaborative and nondirective behaviors can be used by supervisors in line or staff relationships, teachers designated as instructional leaders, and teachers in reciprocal helping relationships, such as peer coaches. Table 12.2 provides a review of supervisory approaches normally appropriate for use by those carrying out some common supervisory roles. The task of the person in a particular supervisory role is to choose the best approach from those appropriate for his or her role.

TABLE 12.2 *Supervisory Roles and Approaches*

	Approaches Appropriate for Particular Supervisory Roles			
Supervisory Roles	*Directive Control*	*Directive Informational*	*Collaborative*	*Nondirective*
Line Supervisor	X	X	X	X
Staff Supervisor		X	X	X
Lead Teacher		X	X	X
Designated Mentor		X	X	X
Peer Coach			X	X

Phase 2: Applying the Chosen Approach

Previous chapters provided scenarios of supervisors using each of the four supervisory approaches. But can a supervisor shift from one approach to another when working with teachers and groups at different developmental levels? Stated differently, can the same supervisor effectively use directive informational, directive control, collaborative, and nondirective behaviors? The question of *supervisor flexibility* was addressed by Gordon (1989, 1990) during a study in which he trained supervisors in developmental supervision, then asked each supervisor to work with separate teacher triads. The supervisors attempted informational directive supervision with one teacher, collaborative supervision with a second teacher, and nondirective supervision with a third teacher (supervisors based their decisions on supervisory approach on earlier observations of and conferences with teachers). When supervisors attempted the different approaches, their conferences with teachers were audiotaped. The taped conferences were analyzed to determine if attempted approaches were effectively used. The investigator found that 93 percent of the supervisors were able to implement informational directive supervision, 100 percent were able to engage in collaborative supervision, and 70 percent were able to use nondirective supervision. An implication of this study is that supervisors being trained to use developmental supervision must receive their most intensive training in nondirective supervision, which seems to be the most difficult approach for many to use.

In Gordon's study, the preponderance of teachers and supervisors involved in each of the three types of supervision reported that the supervisory approach (informational directive, collaborative, or nondirective), *when effectively implemented,* was the appropriate approach for the individual teacher and had assisted the teacher to improve his or her instruction. Teachers experiencing each type of supervision made substantial progress toward instructional improvement objectives identified during supervisor-teacher conferences. However, teachers matched with nondirective supervision made the *most* progress toward improvement objectives, and teachers matched with collaborative supervision made more progress than those matched with directive informational supervision. These results support the argument that the supervisor-teacher relationship should move toward less supervisor control as the teacher becomes capable of assuming more decision-making responsibility.

Rigorously controlled, experimental, school-based studies on matching supervisory approaches to developmental characteristics of teachers have not been performed. Although we can make a substantial case for why certain supervisory approaches are more appropriate for certain teachers, we have not proved it empirically. No one has taken a random sample of teachers, divided them into five groups, trained supervisors in each of the four approaches and applied a directive control approach to one group, a directive informational approach to another, a collaborative approach to a third group, a nondirective approach to the fourth group, and no treatment to the fifth group, and then compared class performance changes across all five groups. Although studies have been completed that do show positive correlations between teachers' stages of development and supervisory approaches (Gordon, 1990; Rossicone, 1985; and Akinniyi, 1987), it is unlikely that a fully controlled, experimental study within a school or school system will ever be possible.

What if a supervisor in the early stages of working with a teacher or group—even after preliminary observation and discussion—is not sure which supervisory approach to use? A good rule of thumb in such cases is to *prepare to use a collaborative approach, but be ready to shift to a nondirective or directive approach if necessary.* When preparing to use a collaborative approach a supervisor determines possible improvement goals, actions, and criteria to be considered and potentially integrated with goals, actions, and criteria suggested by the teacher or group. However, if during the early phases of the conference or meeting it becomes apparent that the teacher or group will be able to identify an appropriate goal and action plan on their own, then the supervisor can forget about his or her possible suggestions and shift to nondirective behaviors as a means of facilitating self-directed teacher planning. If, on the other hand, the teacher or group is unable to identify an obvious problem, any of its underlying causes, or any possible solutions, the supervisor can shift to a directive mode, mandating (directive control) or suggesting (directive informational) a goal, actions, and improvement criteria.

One type of *supervisor flexibility* is the ability to plan and implement different supervisory approaches with different teachers and groups. The ultimate supervisor flexibility, however, is the ability to "shift supervisory gears," so to speak, and effectively use an approach not originally planned because of new discoveries about teachers or the situation at hand. Like successful teachers, successful supervisors must be able to think on their feet, and flex accordingly.

Phase 3:   Fostering Teacher Development

Simply matching the best supervisory approach to the teacher or group's current developmental levels can promote some degree of teacher development. For example, Siens and Ebmeier (1996) found that teachers assisted by supervisors trained to tailor their conference approaches to teachers' levels of motivation, analytical skill, and knowledge experienced significantly more growth on a measure of reflective thinking than did a control group of teachers receiving only the regular supervision provided at their schools. Previous chapters in this text have discussed facilitating teacher development by gradually decreasing supervisor control and increasing teacher control over the decision-making process. There are additional strategies that supervisors can use to stimulate teacher development. One method is to introduce teachers to new information about students and learning, innovative teaching strategies, and novel ways to frame and solve problems. Initially, new ways of thinking and acting that teachers are invited to explore should be linked to their existing knowledge, experience, and values. Gradually, teachers can be exposed to a broader spectrum of theory and practice.

Another method is to assign teachers to decision-making teams or learning groups in which most of the other members are functioning at slightly higher developmental levels. Significant, ongoing professional interaction with teachers of somewhat higher development will tend to pull the teacher of lower development toward the group's functioning level. Unfortunately, the reverse is also true. Teachers of higher developmental levels assigned to groups in which the majority of teachers are functioning at lower developmental levels tend to be "pulled down" to the group's level.

Lois Thies-Sprinthall (1984) has identified five conditions necessary to promote psychological/cognitive growth:

1. Role-taking experiences
2. Careful and continuous guided reflection
3. Balance...between real experience and discussion/reflection
4. Both personal support and challenge
5. Continuity (programs should be at least six months in length with meetings at regular intervals). (p. 54)

Thies-Sprinthall (1984) included all of the five conditions in a course for supervising teachers that also provided more structure and guidance for teachers of low conceptual levels (CL) and less structure, more theory, and research projects for teachers of moderate and high conceptual levels. The course included the following expectations:

1. Learn and apply the theory of psychological development as a basis for understanding associate teacher's (i.e., student teacher's) current conceptual level.
2. Practice supervisory conferences with differentiated supervisory methods depending on associate teacher's CL.
3. Practice levels of active listening and responsive teaching.
4. Implement a variety of direct and indirect teaching methods.
5. Use a variety of observation instruments to rate colleagues' teaching behaviors.
6. Complete a file of materials to be used as a resource guide by an associate teacher.
7. Complete a guide for differentiated supervison (of an associate teacher). (pp. 56–57)

Thies-Sprinthall found that teachers who attended the program experienced substantial gains on tests of conceptual level, principled judgment, and communication skills.

Phillips and Glickman (1991) studied a peer-coaching program that incorporated Thies-Sprinthall's five conditions for psychological/cognitive growth. The participants were 22 teachers who attended four professional development sessions in which they learned observation, problem solving, and collaborative and nondirective interpersonal skills. The workshops included lectures, demonstrations, practice observations, conference role-playing, outside readings, and opportunities for discussion and reflection. A coaching cycle consisted of a pre-conference, classroom observation, postobservation conference, and follow-up session. Coaching partners engaged in four coaching cycles. Each teacher assumed the role of coach in two of the cycles and was coached by his or her partner in the other two cycles. The instructor and participants engaged in group debriefing sessions after each coaching cycle. Phillips and Glickman measured participants' conceptual levels before and after the program, and found that a significant increase in teachers' conceptual levels had occurred by the end of the program.

Research on attempts to foster teacher development is still in its early stages. Small-scale studies such as those reported by Thies-Springhall and Phillips and Glickman, however, indicate that stimulation of teacher growth toward higher developmental levels is possible.

Not Algorithms, But Guideposts for Decisions

Eventually, we must discuss, question, and ask each other (in a supervisor-supervisee relationship) which supervisory approach has been most helpful in the past, which will be most helpful in the present, and which approach we should be striving for in the future. With the exception of emergency situations, this is the responsibility of both parties.

Life in the school world is ragged and complex. This chapter offers a great deal of information to ponder about available behaviors, human motivation, types of environments, and characteristics of individuals and groups. There are no algorithms to provide exactly correct responses to human behavior. Such formulas as "if individual exhibits characteristics A, B, and C, then supervisor Y should do D, F, and G" do not and should not exist. Such algorithms are useful only in mechanically and technically controlled systems (such as computer operations, assembly production, or chemical alterations). Algorithms work in technical but not human endeavors, and it would be misleading to suggest that such supervision formulas are available. Instead, what is available is information about ourselves and others that can serve as guideposts to suggest what *might* be of use. Such developmental guideposts can help reduce some of the infinite complexity of the school world so that supervision can be a purposeful and thoughtful function for improving instruction.

Summary

This chapter explored the theory and practice of developmental supervision in detail. We discussed the rationale for matching various supervisory approaches with different teacher characteristics, as well as the problem of variability of those characteristics. We cited research showing that most entry-level teachers appear to prefer directive informational to collaborative approaches, whereas a large majority of experienced teachers prefer the collaborative and nondirective approaches. This preference was explained according to developmental theory. Human motivation, according to Maslow, Herzberg, deCharms, and Deci, explains why information environments that provide choice for teachers are more likely to sustain instructional improvements than are control environments that limit choice. We also argued that the long-term goal of supervision should be to foster teacher growth toward higher levels of development, expertise, and commitment.

In the second part of the chapter, we discussed the application of developmental supervision. We suggested observations of and discussions with teachers as ways to assess teacher characteristics, and shared supervisor descriptions of teachers matched with directive, collaborative, and nondirective supervision. We reported research on supervisors' efforts to use a variety of supervisory approaches and the effects of different approaches on teachers. We discussed two long-term programs designed to stimulate teacher development. Finally, we proposed that the supervisor needs to use his or her own decision-making abilities to determine the most appropriate interpersonal approaches to use with his or her staff.

Exercises

Academic

1. Prepare written composite profiles of (a) a teacher who would benefit most from nondirective supervision, (b) a teacher who would benefit most from collaborative supervision, (c) a teacher who would benefit most from directive informational supervision, and (d) a teacher who would benefit most from directive control supervision.

2. Write scenarios in which the same teacher or group requires different supervisory approaches in two different situations. Explain in your paper how the supervisor changes his or her interpersonal approach from the first to the second scenario.

3. Write a paper in which you discuss two or more alternative theories of motivation, and relate those theories to supervision and teachers. Use at least three outside references in your paper.

4. Describe a situation in which a supervisor would be required to use directive control, and explain what specific behaviors you as a supervisor would exhibit in that situation. Describe a second set of circumstances in which directive information would be more appropriate, and explain specific behaviors you would display if you were the supervisor in that second situation.

5. Design a program for stimulating teachers' cognitive, conceptual, moral reasoning, and/or ego development over a nine-month period.

Field

1. Ask five teachers each to write a paragraph or two on the topic "What Motivates Me to Improve My Teaching." Write a paper comparing the teachers' responses with the research findings of deCharms and Deci.

2. Observe and hold separate discussions about students, teaching, supervision, and instructional improvement with five different teachers. Write a paper describing each teacher's characteristics and identifying which of the four supervisory approaches discussed in this text would be most appropriate for each teacher.

3. Examine a professional development program at a school or school district where you work or with which you are familar. Write a paper summarizing the program and discussing the presence or absence of each of Thies-Sprinthall's five conditions necessary to promote psychological/cognitive growth.

4. Examine developmental characteristics of an individual for whom you have supervisory responsibility. Use the supervisory approach (nondirective, collaborative, directive informational) that you perceive as the best match for the selected individual. Summarize and evaluate your matched supervision.

5. Examine developmental characteristics of a group for which you have supervisory responsibility. Use the supervisory approach (nondirective, collaborative, or directive informational) that you perceive as the best match for the group. Summarize and evaluate your matched supervision.

Developmental

1. Begin an in-depth investigation of one of the following:

   a. Achievement motivation

   b. Organizational management

   c. Creative problem solving

   d. Job satisfaction

2. Continue to observe differing characteristics of beginning teachers, experienced teachers, and superior teachers. Hypothesize how supervision might be modified to accommodate such differences.

3. Begin to analyze ways in which your needs, concerns, and motivations change in relation to varying situations and changing circumstances.

References

Akinniyi, G. O. 1987. Perceptions and preferences of principals' and teachers' supervisory behavior. Unpublished doctoral dissertation, University of Wisconsin.

Blumberg, A. 1980. *Supervisors and teachers: A private cold war* (2nd ed.). Berkeley, CA: McCutchan.

Blumberg, A., and Weber, W. A. 1968. Teacher morale as a function of perceived supervisor behavioral style. *Journal of Educational Research* 62:109–113.

Brown, A. F. 1975. Teaching under stress. In B. M. Harris, *Supervisory behavior in education* (2nd ed.) (p. 218). Englewood Cliffs, NJ: Prentice Hall.

Cawelti, G. 1976."Selecting appropriate leadership styles for instructional improvement." Videotape. Alexandria, VA: Association for Supervision and Curriculum Development.

Clark, C. M., and Joyce, B. R. 1976. *Teacher decision making and teacher effectiveness.* Paper presented at the annual meeting of the American Educational Research Association, San Francisco.

Clinton, B. C., Glickman, C. D., and Payne, D. A. 1982. Identifying supervision problems: A guide to better solutions. *Illinois School Research and Development* 9(1).

Copeland, W. D. 1980. Affective dispositions of teachers in training toward examples of supervisory behavior. *Journal of Educational Research* 74:37–42.

Copeland, W. D., and Atkinson, D. R. 1978. Student teachers' perceptions of directive and non-directive supervision. *Journal of Educational Research* 71:123–127.

deCharms, R. 1968. *Personal causation.* New York: Academic Press.

de Charms, R. 1976. *Enhancing motivation: Change in the classroom.* New York: Irvington.

Deci, E. L. 1975. *Intrinsic motivation.* New York: Plenum.

Deci, E. L. 1982. *Motivation.* Paper presented to the annual meeting of the Midwest Association of Teachers of Educational Psychology, Dayton, OH, October 30.

Drucker, P. 1973. *Management.* New York: Harper and Row.

Gates, P. E., Blanchard, K. H., and Hersey, P. 1976. Diagnosing educational leadership problems. *Educational Leadership 33*(February):348–354.

Ginkel, K. 1983. *Overview of study that investigated the relationship of teachers' conceptual levels and preferences for supervisory approach.* Paper presented at the annual meeting of the American Educational Research Association, Montreal, April.

Gordon, S. P. 1989. The theory of developmental supervison: An investigation of the critical aspects. Unpublished Ed.D. dissertation, University of Georgia.

Gordon, S. P. 1990. Developmental supervision: An exploratory study of a promising model. *Journal of Curriculum and Supervision 5*:293–307.

Humphrey, G. L. 1983. The relationship between orientations to supervision and the developmental levels of commitment and abstract thinking of entry-year teachers. Doctoral dissertation, University of Tulsa. *Dissertation Abstracts International 44*:1644A.

Hunt, D. E., and Sullivan, E. V. 1974. *Between psychology and education.* Hinsdale, IL: Dryden Press.

Kohlberg, L. 1969. Stage and sequence: The cognitive developmental approach to socialization. In D. Goslin (Ed.), *Handbook of socialization theory and research.* Chicago: Rand McNally.

Levine, D. V. 1991. Creating effective schools: Findings and implications from research and practice. *Phi Delta Kappan 72*(5):389–393.

Lorch, N. 1981. Teaching assistant training: The effects of directive and non-directive supervision. Unpublished Ed.D. dissertation, University of California, Santa Barbara.

Morgan, M. 1984. Reward-induced decrements and increments in intrinsic motivation. *Review of Educational Research 54*(1):5–30.

Ouchi, W. G. 1981. *Theory Z: How American business can meet the Japanese challenge.* Reading, MA: Addison-Wesley.

Pajak, E. F., and Glickman, C. D. 1984. *Teachers' perceptions of supervisory communication: Control versus information.* Paper presented at the annual meeting of the American Educational Research Association, New Orleans, April.

Pajak, E. F., and Glickman, C. D. 1989. Informational and controlling language in simulated supervisory conferences. *American Educational Research Journal 26*(1).

Pajak, E. F., and Seyfarth, J. J. 1983. Authentic supervision reconciles the irreconcilables. *Educational Leadership 40*(8):20–23.

Piaget, J. 1965. *The moral judgements of the child.* New York: Free Press-Macmillan.

Phillips, M. D., and Glickman, C. D. 1991. Peer coaching: Developmental approach to enhancing teacher thinking. *Journal of Staff Development, 12*(2):20–25.

Porter, A. C., and Brophy, J. 1988. Synthesis of research on good teaching: Insights from the work of the Institute for Research on Teaching. *Educational Leadership 45*(8):74–85.

Riley, J. F. 1980. Creative problem solving and cognitive monitoring as instructional variables for teaching training in classroom problem solving. Unpublished Ed.D. dissertation, University of Georgia.

Rossicone, G. N. 1985. The relationship of selected teacher background versus preferences for supervisory style and teacher perceptions of supervisory style of supervisors. Doctoral dissertation, St. John's University. *Dissertation Abstracts International 46*:321A.

Siens, C. M., and Ebmeier, H. 1996. Developmental supervision and the reflective thinking of teachers. *Journal of Curriculum and Supervision 11*(4):299–319.

Skinner, B. F. 1971. *Beyond freedom and dignity.* New York: Knopf.

Suzuki, S. 1970. *Zen mind, beginner's mind.* New York: Weather Hill.

Thies-Sprinthall, L. 1984. Promoting the developmental growth of supervising teachers: Theory, research programs, and implications. *Journal of Teacher Education 35*(3): 53–60.

Vudovich, D. 1976. *The effects of four specific supervision procedures on the development of self-evaluation skills in pre-service teachers.* Paper presented at the annual meeting of the American Educational Research Association. (ERIC ED 146–224)

Zonca, P. H. 1973. A case study exploring the effects on an intern teacher of the condition of openness in a clinical supervisory relationship. Unpublished Ph.D. dissertation, University of Pittsburgh, 1973. *Dissertation Abstracts International 33*:658–659A.

Suggested Readings

Boggiano, A. K., and Pittman, T. (Eds.). 1992. *Achievement and motivation.* Cambridge: Cambridge University Press.

Ford, M. E. 1992. *Motivating humans.* Newbury Park, CA: Sage.

Gordon, S. P. 1990. Developmental supervision: An exploratory study of a promising model. *Journal of Curriculum and Supervision* 5:293–307.

Phillips, M. D., and Glickman, C. D. 1991. Peer coaching: Developmental approach to enhancing teacher thinking. *Journal of Staff Development 12*(2): 20–25.

Conclusion

Critical vocabulary words in Part III included *supervisor behaviors; nondirective, collaborative, directive informational, and directive control approaches; skill practice;* issues of *control* versus *information; motivation* and *choice;* and *human variation, development,*and *complexity*. The purpose of Part III was to equip the supervisor with the interpersonal skills and behaviors needed to assist individuals and groups of teachers to develop their own thinking capacities. The question behind Part III

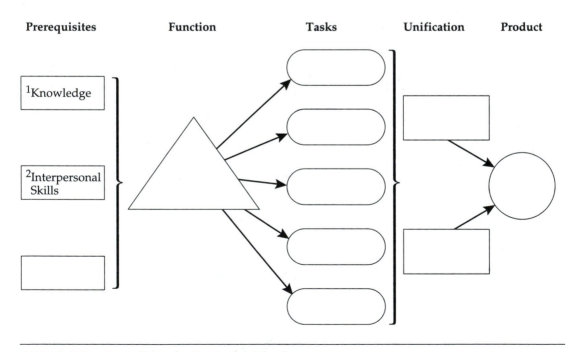

| Prerequisites | Function | Tasks | Unification | Product |

FIGURE III.2 *SuperVision for Successful Schools*

was not how a supervisor motivates teachers to improve instruction, but rather how the supervisor provides choice to teachers to motivate themselves. The matching of interpersonal behaviors and approaches to teachers' developmental levels is one skill base for doing this. Having gained knowledge and interpersonal skills, you can now turn to the third dimension of supervision as a developmental function: the technical skill dimension.

Figure III.2 shows us where we've been and where we are going. We have concluded our discussion of the second dimension of interpersonal skills. One more prerequisite dimension remains before we apply the function of supervision to the five task areas.

Technical Skills

The supervisor who knows about characteristics of successful schools, the norms that mediate against success, and the ways teacher development contrasts with optimal adult development can begin to formulate a supervisory belief system that becomes a reality when interpersonal and technical skills of supervision are applied in practice.

The previous section matched directive, collaborative, and nondirective interpersonal skills in working with developmental levels of individuals and groups of teachers. Part IV deals with the technical supervisory skills needed in working with teachers to assess, plan, observe, research, and evaluate. Understanding schools and relating well to teachers are necessary components, but technical skills are equally important for accomplishing the tasks of supervision.

13

Assessing and Planning Skills

A popular term used in the organizational literature is *envisioning* (Bennis, Benne, and Chin, 1985). In discussing successful schools in Chapters 1 and 3 of this book, we mentioned the importance of collective instructional goals that give power and purpose to individuals working in the same educational setting. The school engages in "the moral equivalent of war," teachers and administrators are involved in "a cause beyond oneself," and the function of supervision is to assist all educators in the school to make better instructional decisions about ways to improve student learning. Such thinking about the role of supervision and instructional leadership in bringing about a collective vision of what can be is a necessary first step. To create and implement that vision, those in supervision roles need technical skills of assessing and planning.

Assessing and planning skills are useful to a supervisor in setting goals and activities for himself or herself as well as for others. The chapter begins with personal organization of time—assessing one's current use of professional time and then planning and managing the use of future time. It goes on to focus on techniques for organizational planning for the improvement of instruction. Whether the changes to be made are in curriculum development, professional development, or direct assistance to teachers, a supervisor's forethought about the sequencing and organization of the program can increase the chances of successful implementation.

Assessing and planning are two sides of the same coin. *Assessing* involves determining where you and your staff have been and where you and your staff currently are. *Planning* includes deciding where you want to go and choosing the path you and your staff hope to traverse in order to reach that destination. Until you are certain of the origination and destination of your travel, a map is useless. Once you are certain, a route can be created.

Personal Plans

One of the authors visited a school system to meet with several first-year principals. The purpose of the consultation was for the new principals to talk to the consultant privately about their beginning experiences and to discuss possible changes that might improve their situations.

One principal stated that she was averaging three hours a day observing and participating in classrooms. Her major concern was with the amount of waiting time students were experiencing. Most of her teachers had divided their heterogeneous classrooms into numerous small groups. The principal wondered whether, if certain classes were grouped homogeneously to begin with, there might be fewer groups and less waiting time. The principal and consultant discussed the possible consequences of such a major change and whether less radical changes within the existing instructional program might be better. She left the session with a plan to discuss with the faculty the issue of waiting time and student grouping at the next school meeting.

The second beginning principal said that his major problem was getting out of his office to visit teachers. He wanted to be with his staff but found that paperwork, phone calls, and student discipline referrals kept him trapped in the office. He could find barely an hour a day to talk with staff and visit classrooms. Furthermore, the one-hour time outside the office was often interrupted by the school secretary calling him back with urgent business. The consultant and principal discussed why he was trapped in his office and what changes might be made.

After hearing about the second principal's situation, the consultant realized that the second principal had no more constraints on his time than did the first principal, who was averaging three hours a day visiting classrooms. Both had schools of comparable size in the same neighborhood. They worked for the same superintendent and had identical job responsibilities. Yet one principal was functioning as a supervisor attending to instructional improvement, while the other one was functioning only minimally in the realm of supervision. It seemed that the real difference between the two principals was not their intentions to function as supervisors but their ability to assess and plan professional time to correspond with professional intentions. Let's look at the use of professional time.

Assessing Time

To organize future time, one must assess one's current use of time. This can be done by keeping a daily log for 5 to 10 consecutive school days. Those supervisors who keep detailed appointment books might need only to return to their books at midday and at the end of the day to add notations on what actually transpired. Those who do not operate with such planned schedules can keep a daily log to be filled out at midday and at the end of the day. The log should be simple and should require only a few minutes to fill out. It might look like this:

Monday

8:00–8:50	Walked halls, visited teachers and custodians
8:50–9:20	Conference with parent
9:20–9:35	Phone call from textbook salesperson
9:35–10:30	Emergency—covered for sick teacher
10:30–12:00	Worked on class schedules—made 3 phone calls, received 5 phone calls
12:00–12:30	Ate in cafeteria with teachers
12:30–12:35	Wrote morning log
12:35–12:55	Met with textbook salesperson
12:55–1:30	Classroom visitation of Mr. Tadich
1:30–2:30	Meeting at superintendent's office
2:30–3:00	Helped supervise school dismissal
3:00–3:15	Talked with parents
3:15–4:00	Faculty meeting
4:00–4:15	Talked with teachers informally
4:15–4:50	Answered mail
4:50–5:00	Wrote afternoon log

After at least 5 days (preferably 10), the supervisor can analyze his or her current use of time by subsuming daily events in the log under large categories of time consumption. Figure 13.1 shows a sample categorical scheme.

Before transferring the daily log entries onto the time consumption chart, the supervisor should look at his or her job description and determine how his or her time *should* be spent according to job priorities. Which categories of supervisory involvement ought to receive the most attention? The supervisor can indicate approximate percentages according to this ideal use of time. After making a list of ideal time use, he or she can then write in actual time on the consumption charts, add up total time for each category, and then find the actual percentage of time being consumed for each category. He or she then has a comparison between preferred and actual consumption of time. The comparison might look like this:

Preferred Time	*Actual Time*
Paperwork—10%	25%
Phone calls—5%	6%
Private conferences—25%	25%
Students—5%	10%
Parents—3%	5%
Faculty—10%	5%
Auxiliary—3%	1%
Central office—1%	1%
Others—3%	3%
Group meetings—25%	28%
Students—2%	5%

	Preferred Time	*Actual Time*
	Parents—5%	2%
	Faculty—15%	7%
	Auxiliary—1%	6%
	Central office—1%	8%
	Others—1%	0%
	Classroom visits—25%	10%
	School hall and ground visits—5%	2%
	Private time for thinking—3%	1%
	Miscellaneous visits—2%	3%

FIGURE 13.1 Supervisor Time Consumption Chart

	Monday	*Tuesday*	*Wednesday*	*Thursday*	*Friday*	*Total*	*%*
Paperwork							
Phone calls							
Private conference							
Students							
Parents & community							
Faculty							
Auxiliary personnel							
Central office							
Others							
Group meetings							
Students							
Parents & community							
Faculty							
Auxiliary personnel							
Central office							
Others							
Classroom visits							
School hall and ground visits							
Private time for thinking							
Miscellaneous: emergencies							

This comparison of time was that of the second principal, who complained about the inability to get out of his office. The comparison showed that he was indeed spending much more time in the office (10 percent preferred, 25 percent actual) and much less time on classroom visits (25 percent preferred, 10 percent actual). Further discrepancies were noted in considerably more time spent in private conferences with students (5 percent preferred, 10 percent actual) and group meetings with central office (1 percent preferred, 8 percent actual).

Changing Time Allocations: Planning

With this information on preferred and actual time use in front of the supervisor, he or she can decide what changes realistically can be made to attain the goal of increasing visitation time with teachers. The supervisor can consider a range of options to increase teacher visitation time. Some possibilities might be:

Paperwork: Delegate more clerical work to secretary, aides, or assistants. Schedule paperwork for uninterrupted hours after school.

Private conferences: Spend less time disciplining students by setting more stringent procedures for teacher referrals of students to office.

Group meetings: See if central office meetings could be shortened or scheduled after school hours.

Classroom visits: Increase classroom visits from one to two periods a day. Set up backup system with secretary to cover all but real emergencies when in the classroom. Schedule visits for a set time each day.

Naturally, this supervisor cannot hope to achieve exact congruence between preferred and actual time use, but he can come closer to his preference. Some time constraints, such as the time of central office meetings, probably are not under the principal's control. There are other factors over which he does have direct control: when he will meet parents, accept phone calls, do paperwork, and accept student referrals. The key to future planning of time use is to accept the limitations that exist and work on those time periods that can be altered.

The first part of a plan to make actual use of time closer to preferred time use is to answer the question: What is the objective? A sample response might be: To double classroom visitation time. The second part of the plan is to answer the question: What actions need to be taken? A sample response might be: (a) Schedule set times each day for two classroom observations, (b) schedule uninterrupted paperwork in two two-hour blocks of time after school. The third part of the plan is to answer the question: When will these activities be done? Sample responses might be: (a) Classroom visits from 9 to 11 A.M. Monday and Wednesday and 1:00 to 2:30 P.M. Tuesday and Thursday, (b) paperwork scheduled for Monday and Friday 3:00 to 5:00 P.M. The fourth part of the plan is to answer the question: What resources will be needed to implement the activities? Sample responses might be: (a) Explain to secretary the need to protect uninterrupted times, (b) discuss with faculty the change and rationale behind my new schedule and arrange classroom visitation schedule. The fifth and final part of the plan is to answer the question: How will the success of the goal be evaluated? A sample response might be: Check whether the new schedule was followed and, after two weeks, review daily log to see if time in classrooms has doubled.

A supervisor could engage in more elaborate planning techniques by developing a flowchart (see Figure 13.2). Although flowcharts look impressive, they are not necessary for simple plans. When looking at more complex planning, however, keep flowcharts in mind. As long as we can answer the five questions dealing with (1) objective, (2) activities, (3) time deadlines, (4) resources, and (5) evaluation, then implementation can proceed. If we cannot answer any of the five questions,

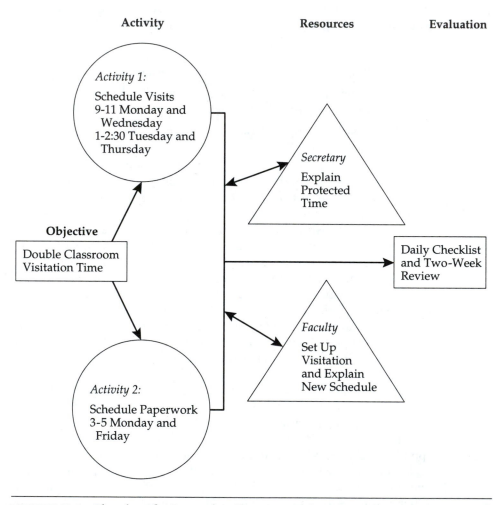

FIGURE 13.2 *Flowchart for Increasing Classroom Visits*

the plan is incomplete. For example, if we know our objective but don't know what activities, resources, or evaluation to use, then we are unsure of what to do. However, if we know our objective, activities, and resources but don't know how to evaluate our success, we will be acting without any knowledge of results.

As we move from assessment and planning of personal change to assessment and planning of faculty improvement, the elements to be considered become more complex and planning becomes more detailed. Other techniques for planning may be necessary. Let's use a "wild" analogy. When a naturalist is tracking a single large elephant, she can basically track the beast by herself. But when the naturalist's task expands to tracking three herds of 45 elephants each, then she needs other people, more equipment (radios, binoculars, cameras, jeeps, and helicopters), and an awareness of multiple potential obstacles (ill staff workers, malfunctioning equipment, rough terrain). This analogy can be extended only so far, as supervisors are not naturalists, nor are teaching faculties herds of elephants, but the point is that the larger the organizational effort, the more carefully one needs to account for the sequence and the relationships of activities, resources, and evaluation to overall objectives.

Assessing and Planning within the Organization

The five steps of assessing and planning are the same for both personal and organizational plans. Only the complexity and specificity differ. We might think of assessing and planning as a recipe (Bruce and Grimsley, 1979). A plan for direct assistance, professional development, curriculum development, or group development has the same elements as a cooking recipe. *We decide our objective:* "to bake a sweet potato soufflé" (thanks to Ms. Donna Bell for providing this culinary example). Knowing our family's previous history of food preferences, we are confident that if we cook the soufflé correctly, they will enjoy it and we will be held in positive regard for at least 10 minutes. Next, *we determine the activities and when they will take place.*

> *Activity 1:* Mash 6 cups of cooked sweet potatoes.
>
> *Activity 2:* Beat into the mashed potatoes: 4 eggs, 1 cup butter, 2 cups sugar, 1 cup milk, 1 teaspoon vanilla.
>
> *Activity 3:* Spread out in unbuttered pan.
>
> *Activity 4:* Mix in a separate bowl: 1 cup brown sugar, 2/3 cup flour, 1 cup butter, 1 cup chopped pecans.
>
> *Activity 5:* Spread this mix (Activity 4) evenly over the potatoes (Activity 3).
>
> *Activity 6:* Bake at 350° for 1 hour.

With the activities and times determined, *we need to identify resources.* Equipment resources are an oven, measuring cups, measuring spoons, a large bowl, a pan, a mixing fork, and a spreading knife. Food resources are potatoes, eggs, butter, sugar, vanilla, brown sugar, flour, pecans, and milk.

Finally, *we will evaluate the success* of our cooking endeavor by the following criteria: Everyone in our family will eat the sweet potato soufflé. At least two of the three members will ask for seconds. All of them will tell us we're wonderful cooks, and they will volunteer to wash the dishes.

If the supervisor tries acting as a gourmet of instructional cookery and planning recipes for success, all staff members will delight in the soufflé of instructional improvement. The food analogy has run its course (by now, you are probably heading for the refrigerator), and we can turn to assessing and planning within the school context. For purposes of illustration, let's take an example of an elementary reading supervisor who is responsible for developing revised curriculum guides in reading.

Ways of Assessing Need

The first question for the reading supervisor is: What do we hope to accomplish with a new curriculum guide? To answer this question, we need to collect information about the past and present state of reading instruction. The supervisor can use multiple ways of assessing need: (1) eyes and ears, (2) official records, (3) third-party review, (4) written open-ended survey, (5) check and ranking list surveys, (6) the Delphi technique, and (7) nominal group technique.

Eyes and Ears

Talk to teachers, administrators, aides, and anyone else who works directly with the task under consideration. In this case, the supervisor would want to ask teachers and aides individually and in small groups what they believe are the strengths and weaknesses of the curriculum guide. How is it being used? Is it helpful, and in what ways? Where does it break down? When is it not useful?

Official Records

Look at any documents that indicate the current use and effect of the task under consideration. In this case, what do reading achievement test scores show? How about diagnostic reading tests? Are students mastering reading skills, or are there certain areas (comprehension, fluency, vocabulary) that are consistently out of line with others? What about the curriculum guide itself? When was it last revised? What recent knowledge about writing curriculum guides, instructional approaches to reading, and reading topics are not reflected in the current curriculum?

Third-Party Review

Having a neutral outside person review the task area can be helpful. The supervisor might contact a university or central office consultant, a graduate doctoral student, or some other person with expertise to do an investigation and write a report. The third-party person should be given a clear description of the task (to look at the strengths and weaknesses of the reading curriculum guides), and care should be taken not to bias the third-party person's judgment. The report can then serve as an additional source of objective knowledge, not tied to any special interest in the forthcoming project.

Written Open-Ended Survey

To document and add to the information already received through eyes and ears and official records, a written survey can be administered. Send out a brief questionnaire that asks teachers, aides, administrators, and parents what they think about the current reading curriculum. Keep the survey brief, and word the questions simply, without education jargon. Again, an example of a survey is found in Figure 13.3.

Check and Ranking List

After gathering ideas of the strengths and weaknesses of the task at hand from many sources, the supervisor can ask staff to rank the ideas. The supervisor can then compile a group frequency and numerical priority for each idea previously

---

FIGURE 13.3   *Survey of Reading Curriculum*

Explanation: As you may know, this year we are determining changes to be made in our reading curriculum. Would you please take a few minutes to respond to the following questions. Please be frank! We will use the information to rewrite our curriculum guides.

Question 1. What do you think about the current reading curriculum?

Question 2. What are the strengths of the current reading curriculum?

Question 3. What are the weaknesses of the current reading curriculum?

Question 4. What changes do you believe would improve the reading curriculum?

---

mentioned. For example, if—through eyes and ears, official documents, and open-ended surveys—the supervisor has collected a list of ideas about perceived weaknesses of the current reading program, he or she then could disseminate the list back to teachers, aides, and others. The disseminated form might be as shown in Figure 13.4. The supervisor can meet with the staff and show the frequency of numbers assigned to each idea and the average score for each item. Those items receiving frequent low scores and/or with the lowest average scores would be the first to focus on when discussing curriculum revisions. The ranking list can be further refined by having the participants do two separate rankings—first, to see how all the ideas rank, and second, to rerank a shortened list of prioritized ideas.

Delphi Technique

Another written way to prioritize needs is the Delphi technique, developed by the Rand Corporation (Hostrop, 1975; Weaver, 1971). The technique, originally intended to forecast future trends, is often used for needs assessment. It is a combination of open-ended survey and ranking. The supervisor sends around a problem statement to staff: "We are looking at revisions in the reading curriculum. Write down what you believe needs to be done." The supervisor retrieves the written comments, reproduces everyone's comments, and returns all the comments to the participants. They read the comments and then individually write a synthesis of the various ideas. The supervisor then collects everyone's syntheses and makes a new list of all synthesized ideas. The new list goes back to the participants for ranking. The supervisor collects and computes average and fre-

---

FIGURE 13.4 *Ranking Ideas for Improving Reading Curriculum*

Directions: The following are the ideas for possible changes that you have suggested. Please prioritize this list by placing the number 1 next to the idea needing the greatest attention, number 2 next to the item needing the next most attention, and so on, until all items are ranked.

_____   Format of the guides.

_____   Readability of the guides.

_____   Activities to go with curriculum objectives.

_____   Objectives and units dealing with reading newspapers.

_____   Objectives and units dealing with reading in other subject areas.

_____   More phonic and word recognition objectives.

_____   Cross-reference units with materials in the classrooms.

_____   Cross-reference objects with fourth-grade competency based reading test.

---

quency of ratings and then returns the tallies to participants to rerank. This procedure continues until clear priorities emerge.

Nominal Group Technique

The nominal group technique, made popular by Delbecq, Van de Ven, and Gustafson (1975), is an effective way to involve all individuals within large groups of stakeholders in needs assessment and goal setting. The process is outlined here in eight steps:

1. The large group is divided into small groups. Each small group is assigned a facilitator to explain and coordinate the process.
2. Each individual within a small group silently generates and writes perceived needs.
3. In round-robin manner, participants orally share with their small group one perceived need at a time. The facilitator records each idea on a flip chart. At this point, there is no discussion—only listing of perceived needs.
4. Small-group discussions of each perceived need are led by the facilitators. The purpose of the discussion is clarification of the perceived needs, not debate on their validity.
5. Individuals within each small group rewrite and rate all of the perceived needs that were listed in step 3. This step usually takes the form of participants assigning each perceived need a numerical value. For example, the facilitator might instruct group members to rate each need from 1 to 5, with an item assigned a value of 1 considered to be unimportant and an item rated a 5 perceived to be an extremely important need.
6. Each small-group facilitator collects all group members' ratings and calculates a mean for each perceived need. The facilitator rewrites the perceived needs in rank order by mean and shares the results with the small group.
7. Each small group submits its list of ranked needs (without the means) for large-group consideration. By preagreement, each small group might submit only its top-ranked needs (perhaps its top five needs) to the large group.
8. A lead facilitator then takes the large group through steps 4 through 6. In the large-group version of step 4, any participant can ask for clarification of any perceived need, with the appropriate small-group facilitator providing the requested clarification. In the whole-group version of step 5, each participant rates all perceived needs presented to the large group. The product of the large-group version of step 6 is a list of organizational needs in rank order.

Analyzing Organizational Needs

Some organizational needs are easily understood and addressed by supervisors and teachers. Others are more complicated. They require analysis to determine their underlying causes before a plan can be formulated. For decades, W. Edwards Deming argued for the use of data displays to examine factors that may contribute to organizational needs and problems. In this section we'll discuss a few types of charts suggested by Deming and his colleagues. We'll do this by applying each chart to a school situation. The words of Mary Walton (1986) should allay any anxiety concerning the use of such charts that the reader without expertise in complex data analysis might be experiencing:

> Some of the most useful statistical tools are neither difficult nor complicated to master. The level of mathematics necessary is no more than a seventh or eighth grader might learn. Several of the basic tools are merely ways of organizing and visually displaying data. In most cases, employees can collect the data and do much of the interpretation, and they are happy to do so because it gives them more responsibility. (p. 94)

Cause and Effect Diagrams

Figure 13.5 is an example of a cause and effect diagram, often referred to as a *fishbone diagram.* In our example, a newly formed staff-development committee has received feedback from teachers throughout the district that recent staff-development programs have been ineffective. Based on a series of interviews with representative groups of teachers, the committee constructed the cause and effect diagram in Figure 13.5.

Four general causes were identified for the ineffective professional development: (1) poor planning, (2) low-quality staff-development sessions, (3) inadequate support for the program, and (4) unsatisfactory program evaluation. Contributing causes within the poor planning category included failure to involve teachers in the planning process, the fact that the professional development plan was not based on teacher needs, and the absence of alternatives for staff from different grade levels, content areas, and specialty areas.

The poor quality of the staff-development sessions was ascribed to the fact that too many teachers were present, each session was a one-shot workshop unrelated to the other workshops in the program, and the workshop presentations were of poor quality. The workshops were perceived to be substandard because the outside presenters did not have a good understanding of the school culture or the purposes of the program, and their presentations were too abstract to evoke teacher interest.

Problems with support included a lack of funds to purchase instructional materials necessary to implement ideas introduced in the workshops and a failure to provide support for teachers attempting to transfer workshop concepts to the classroom. Finally, the committee found that the district's evaluation of the program had been inadequate. The evaluation forms used by the district were the same ones used for all staff-development workshops; they were not relevant to the specific content of the workshops being assessed. Additionally, the wording of the evaluation questions was so general that teachers were not sure what the questions were asking. Since no formal analysis of evaluation data took place, no information on program outcomes was available and no program revisions were made. The "anatomy of a failure" depicted in Figure 13.5 is not the most pleasant project the planning committee could have undertaken. Yet, the completed diagram was a valuable tool in planning future professional-development programs.

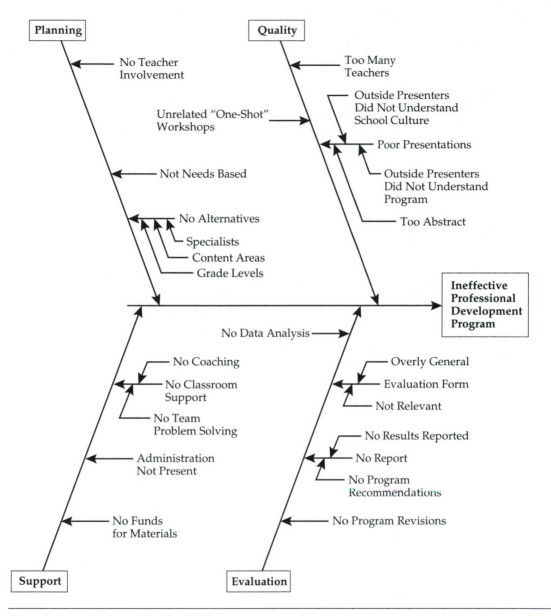

FIGURE 13.5 *Cause and Effect Diagram*

Flowcharts

A flowchart can be used to review a process when either the process or conflicting perceptions of the process are resulting in unmet needs. When different parties involved in a process draw their own flowcharts, the charts often are dissimilar. Figure 13.6 shows a flowchart tracking what happens from the time a student is

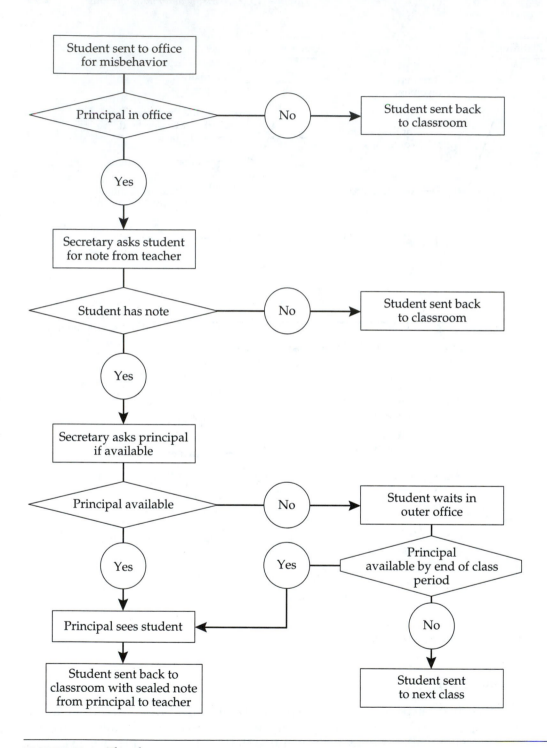

FIGURE 13.6   *Flowchart*

sent to the office for misbehavior until the student returns to class. This chart was drawn by the principal's secretary. Flowcharts of the same process drawn by the principal, the teacher, and the student might be very different from the secretary's and each other!

Pareto Charts

A Pareto chart illustrates in descending frequency of size those factors that cause a need or problem. Displaying the relative impact of causal factors gives planners information to help them set priorities and allocate resources. Figure 13.7 illustrates a Pareto chart with bars showing the percentage of students dropping out of a senior high school for each of several reasons. Above the bars, a cumulative

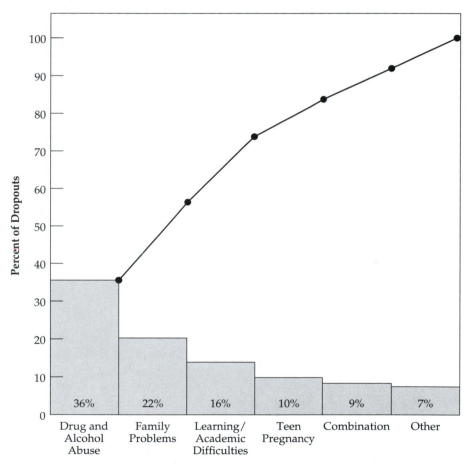

FIGURE 13.7 *Pareto Chart*

percentage line runs across the chart. This data would be valuable to a planning team designing a dropout prevention program.

Scatter Diagrams

Scatter diagrams can reveal the relationship between two variables. A group of elementary teachers were concerned about the low level of student on-task behavior. Before collaborating on an action plan to increase on-task behavior, they decided to investigate relationships of various teaching methods and mean percentage of students on task. Figures 13.8 and 13.9 illustrate two of several scatter diagrams they constructed based on classroom observation data. In Figure 13.8, the wide dispersion of points in scatter diagram A means that there was no strong correlation across 16 classes between percentage of time spent on teacher lecturing and student on-task behavior. Scatter diagram B in Figure 13.9 displays data on a different group of lessons. The clustering of points from the midleft to upper

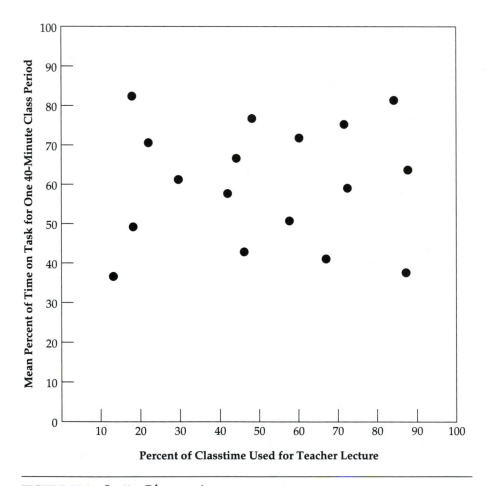

FIGURE 13.8 *Scatter Diagram A*

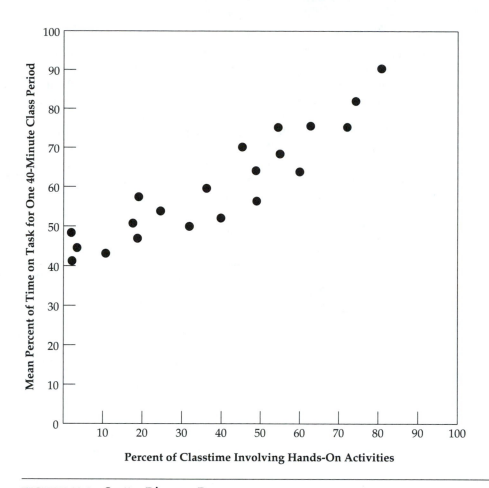

FIGURE 13.9   *Scatter Diagram B*

right areas of the diagram indicates a positive correlation between hands-on learning activities and time on task.

The first step in meeting an organizational need is to identify the underlying causes of that need. Cause and effect diagrams, flowcharts, Pareto charts, and scatter diagrams can be valuable tools for identifying causes and indicating specific problems that must be addressed in order to met identified needs.

Planning

After assessing and prioritizing needs and identifying causes, planning proceeds. Techniques of planning discussed in this section include impact analysis charts, management by objectives (MBO), Gantt charts, and program evaluation and review technique (PERT).

Impact Analysis Charts

Impact analysis charts are usually constructed early in the planning process. Their purpose is to assist planners in projecting who and what a potential program or change will affect and what the effects might be. In Figure 13.10, triangles represent people and things a revised reading curriculum would impact. Predicted effects are symbolized by rectangles. Impact analysis charts can become far more complex than the example in Figure 13.10 (the more ambitious the goals, the more extensive the chart). Building and discussing impact analysis charts can help planners to create a "conceptual map" of areas they want to address during the planning process. They can also help planners to include objectives, activities, and evaluation procedures in their formal plan that they might otherwise neglect.

Management by Objectives (MBO)

Most teachers are familiar with classroom performance objectives used in lesson planning. Management by objectives basically involves setting performance objec-

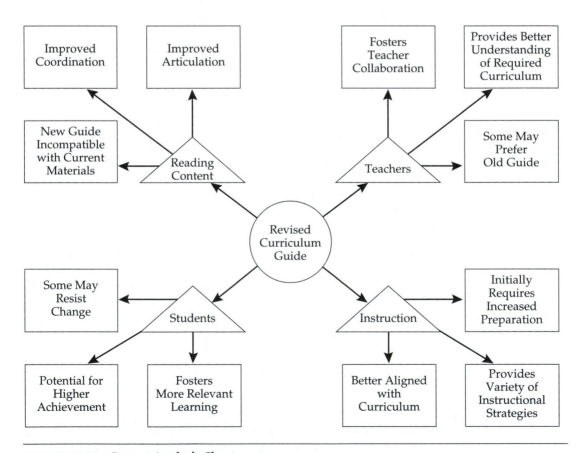

FIGURE 13.10   *Impact Analysis Chart*

tives for organizational planning (Knezevich, 1972). Management objectives make explicit how the goal is to be accomplished. The objective has four elements:

1. What will be performed?
2. When will it be performed?
3. Who will do it?
4. What will be the criteria of success?

Our example of reading curriculum revisions might contain an overall goal: "The reading faculty will update and revise curriculum guides to better meet the instructional needs of students." The goal provides general intent but does not offer the specifics of how it is to be accomplished. After conducting a needs assessment, the reading faculty might have decided on the following management objective: "By October 15, 1998, all reading teachers will be able to write daily lesson plans that incorporate objectives and activities of the new written curriculum guides."

Notice how the management objective has all four elements: what is to be done ("will be able to write daily lesson plans that incorporate objectives and activities of the new curriculum guides"); when it will be performed ("by October 15, 1998"); who is to do it ("reading teachers"); what are to be the criteria of success ("*all* reading teachers"). To reach this management objective, management activities are specified, such as the following:

1. A representative teacher from each grade level will read the reading curriculum guides, write notations on changes to be made, and submit the changes to the curriculum council on October 1.
2. By December 1, the curriculum council will review five different formats for writing curriculum guides and approve a single format to be used for all grade levels.
3. The resource center director and staff will read the current guides and recommend a procedure for cross-referencing curriculum units with library and media materials to the council by February 1.
4. By April 1, the director of competency-based education and the council will decide on procedures of cross-referencing the sixth-grade competency reading exam with all lessons contained in the curriculum guides.
5. A reading consultant and four teachers will be selected by the council to do the actual rewriting and reformatting of the curriculum guides in order to have the final guides completed by August 1.
6. On August 28, the consultant, the four curriculum writing teachers, and the council will conduct a half-day in-service session for all reading teachers on the use of the new curriculum guides.

A comprehensive MBO system will have an identification of resources for each management activity. Figure 13.11 is an example of writing a complete management activity, including procedures and resources.

FIGURE 13.11   *Revisions of Curriculum Guides*

I. Management objective:

By October 15, 1998, all reading teachers will be able to show on their written daily lesson plans the use of the new curriculum guides.

Management activity

A. A representative teacher from each grade level will read their reading curriculum guides, write notations on changes to be made, and submit the changes to the curriculum council on October 1.

Procedures

1. _____ Explain task at first faculty meeting.

2. _____ Ask grade departments to elect representatives.

3. _____ Devise questions for representative teachers to use in their notations.

4. _____ Meet with representatives and review work to be done.

5. _____ Check on progress of individuals.

6. _____ Convene council meeting on October 1.

Resources: Meeting room, stipend of $100.00 for each teacher = $400.00 total, two copies of each curriculum guide, written questions mimeographed.

MBO provides a clear description of the system for implementing a goal. It demands that the supervisor think of the necessary steps and time lines for successful completion of the overall task. Time lines can be shown graphically by using a technique called a Gantt chart.

Gantt Charts

A Gantt chart is simply a graph that portrays the beginning and completion dates of each activity involved in completing the overall task (Bishop, 1976). As shown in Figure 13.12, the activities for revising the curriculum guides are placed on the left-hand side of the chart. The beginning and ending time for each activity is shown by a black solid line across the time line. The supervisor can refer to the chart at any time to check on the progress of the project and be reminded of what groups and what subtasks should be receiving his or her attention.

Program Evaluation and Review Technique (PERT)

PERT is another planning technique used for large projects that depend on the coordination of many individuals, groups, and subtasks. It shows the interrelationships of activities needed in a large project. It is usually found in conjunction with

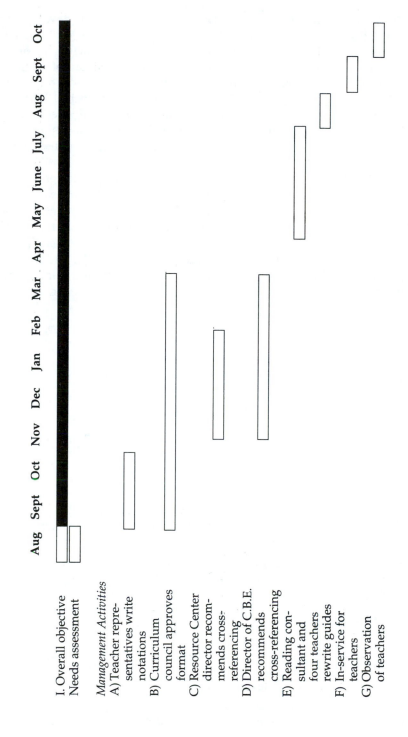

FIGURE 13.12 *Gantt Chart Task: Revising Curriculum Guides*

an MBO system and a Gantt chart. The PERT flowchart was developed by the organizers of the Polaris Fleet Ballistic Missile Program in 1958. It enabled federal managers to coordinate the work of hundreds of subcontractors in completing the construction of the ballistic missile program two years ahead of original expectations. Since then, it has been adapted to planning in education settings (Case, 1969; Cook, 1966; Anderson, 1975; Bishop, 1976; Knezevich, 1984).

The supervisor thinks of all the events and activities needed to complete the task. Then he or she puts those events and activities into a sequence with durations of time. The sequence and duration of events and activities are then flowcharted (see Figure 13.13).

The circled numbers represent important points (meetings, selections, and reports) on the way to completing the task. The critical path is the straight line. (1) → (3) → (7) → (9) → (10) → (11) → (12) → (13). The circles outside the critical path are activities at work simultaneously with other activities. They must also be carried out in order for the critical decision points to be completed. Circles stand for events such as reports submitted, decisions made, and documents produced. Arrows represent activities such as individual and committee work in progress. The numbers above the arrows (30) are the time (in days) needed to complete the activity.

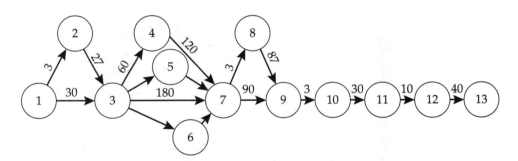

1. Needs assessment of faculty, students, parents, and consultants.
2. Select grade-level representatives to write notations on currrent guides.
3. Curriculum council meeting to assign task of formatting the guides.
4. Curriculum council proposes format.
5. Director of competency-based education proposes format.
6. Resource center director proposes format.
7. Curriculum council formalizes format.
8. Select four teachers with consultant to rewrite guides.
9. Curriculum council reviews and approves new guides.
10. Curriculum council plans in-service.
11. In-service held.
12. Council chooses, observes, and meets with teachers to explain rationale and logistics for observations.
13. Observation of teachers' lesson planning.

FIGURE 13.13   *PERT: Revising Curriculum Guides*

A PERT chart provides for close monitoring of a project and a clear description of how events and activities fit together. It also displays to persons involved with the project how their own work fits into the overall scheme.

Models Combining Assessment and Planning

Thus far we have considered assessment and planning as separate entities. Two models that combine these functions are the PDSA cycle and strategic planning. Both models attempt to address the dynamic, unpredictable nature of complex organizations. In recent years these two models, originally developed for business and industry, have been applied to education.

PDSA Cycle

W. Edward Deming's popular "14 points for managers," "seven deadly sins," and data-based approach to quality control (see Walton, 1986) have had enormous impact in Japan and North America. Educators have jumped on the total quality management (TQM) bandwagon, adapting the ideas of Deming and others associated with TQM to teaching and school leadership (see Bonstingl, 1992a, 1992b; Brandt, 1992). Full discussions of Deming's management method and TQM are beyond the scope of this chapter. However, one process with its origins in the total quality movement is especially relevant to our discussion of assessment and planning. That process is the PDSA cycle (alternative versions of the process are referred to as the *Shewhart, Deming,* or *PDCA cycle*).

The PDSA cycle consists of *planning, doing, studying,* and *acting.* The cyclical relationship of these four stages is illustrated in Figure 13.14. In the *planning* stage, assessment and planning take place. In the *doing* stage, the plan is implemented, usually on a small scale. In the *studying* stage, data are collected on the implementation process and its effects. In the *acting* stage, the data are analyzed and conclusions about strengths and weaknesses of the plan and its implementa-

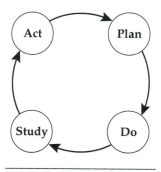

FIGURE 13.14   *PDSA Cycle*

tion are drawn. A new cycle then begins with the formulation of a revised plan. The PDSA cycle is the heart and soul of "continuous quality improvement."

Strategic Planning

Strategic planning assumes that a plan's implementation and results will be affected by the organization's internal and external environments, and that it is impossible to completely predict and control the future in our rapidly changing world. There are many versions of strategic planning (see, for example, Dyson, 1990; Kaufman, 1991) as well as applications to education (Cook, 1990; Kaufman, 1992). A nine-step strategic planning process is presented below:

1. *Identify common beliefs.* This first stage of strategic planning becomes the foundation of everything that follows. Cook (1990) discusses the statement of beliefs:

   It is a formal expression of the organization's fundamental values: its ethical code, its overriding convictions, its inviolate commitments. Essentially, it describes the moral character of the organization. That means that the statement of beliefs of an organization must represent a composite, a distillation, of the personal values of those who make up the organization. (p. 89)

2. *Identify the organization's vision.* The organization's vision is its scenario of what *should be* in the future. For a school district or school, this includes such things as the abilities and attitudes graduates should possess. A vision statement should focus on intended outcomes, not processes. One common visioning strategy the authors have found successful is to ask planners what characteristics they would like their next kindergarten class to possess when those students graduate from high school.

3. *Identify the organization's mission.* A mission statement is a summary (usually one sentence in length) of the organization's purpose. The mission is based on the organization's beliefs and vision. It becomes the focus of all remaining phases of the strategic planning process.

4. *Formulate policies.* In relationship to strategic planning, policies are ground rules that will apply to the remaining phases of the planning process, the content of the strategic plan, and its implementation. An example of a strategic policy is "All action plans will be based on the best interest of the school district's students." Another example is "No new curricula or instructional programs will be established without the agreement of at least three-fourths of the teachers who will have responsibility for implementing the new curriculum or program." Strategic policies become the boundaries within which future planning and change take place.

5. *Conduct external analysis.* This phase consists of analysis of demographic, economic, political, social, and technological factors in the external environ-

ment. Current conditions and predicted futures concerning each of these five factors are analyzed. The purpose of external analysis is to identify external *threats* to the organization's mission as well as *opportunities* for external assistance or collaboration in carrying out the mission. Threats or opportunities within each of the five factors are identified.

6. *Conduct internal analysis.* The internal analysis consists of examination of such factors as school governance, culture, leadership, staff expertise and commitment, curriculum and instruction, student characteristics, and student achievement. As with external analysis, both current conditions and future predictions within each factor are examined. The purpose of internal analysis is to determine the organization's *strengths* and *weaknesses,* especially in respect to its mission.

7. *State objectives.* The objectives are tied directly to the organization's mission. In other words, if all of the organization's objectives are met, then in all probability the mission will be achieved. Like the vision statement, the objectives focus on outcomes, not processes. Strategic objectives should be student centered, few in number, specific, measurable, and clearly stated.

8. *Develop and analyze alternative strategies.* At this point in the strategic planning process, action teams can be formed for each objective. After reviewing decisions made during the first seven phases of the process, action teams develop and analyze alternative strategies for reaching their assigned objective. Alternative strategies are then compared. One type of comparison is carried out by testing each strategy for consistency with the organization's beliefs, vision, mission, and policies. Another type of comparison involves considering the feasibility of each strategy in light of external threats and opportunities as well as internal strengths and weaknesses. A third way to compare strategies is to create scenarios of each strategy being implemented, projecting the strategic effects on the organization and its mission.

9. *Design action plans.* Based on the analysis from phase 8, action teams choose the strategies most likely to achieve the objectives, and sequence those strategies into action plans. The action plans involve time lines for implementation as well as provisions for monitoring progress and outcomes. Since the effects of any plan are not completely predictable, strategic action plans have built-in contingencies—back-up plans enabling adaptation to changing external or internal conditions. During implementation of action plans, periodic reviews are carried out to determine if alternative strategies are needed.

Strategic plans can be comprehensive district or school-based plans (macroplans) or specific programs (microplans). In school-based strategic planning, care must be taken to assure that the school and district's beliefs, visions, missions, and policies (phases 1–4) are consistent. Specific program planning begins with a review of the organization's existing beliefs, vision, mission, and policy, with actual program planning beginning in phase 5.

Planning: To What Extent?

Keep in mind that a plan is intended to help you and your staff get where you want to go. It is a *means,* not an end in itself. Planning should not get in the way of doing. The extent of planning should depend on how much detail is needed. Frymier (1980) warned of the dangers of overplanning. Planning can be seductive; drawing circles and wording one's objectives can camouflage inactivity. Most supervisory tasks in schools do not need extensive management objectives, flowcharts, graphs, or cost analysis. Providing immediate help only requires a supervisor to pause, think about what needs to be done, and then step out of the office and do it.

Extensive planning is helpful when the proposed change will take place over a considerable amount of time (half a year or more) and will involve many individuals and groups. Extensive planning helps people remember the stages of a project. It is also helpful when many groups or individuals have overlapping or concurrent responsibilities; plans can help the supervisor know whom to contact and when. Finally, extensive planning is essential when funding is contingent on such details. It is no coincidence that public school supervisors began writing plans with management objectives, time lines, and flowcharts in the late 1960s, when federal funding became more available to schools. The federal government required such specifications as part of any proposal. Now most school superintendents, school boards, and state directors expect to see similar planning devices whenever a major instructional change is contemplated.

A final word about planning: Remember that plans are not ironclad or unchangeable from beginning to end. As organizational theorists remind us, schools are not linear and rational places that move logically from one step to the next (Clark, Lotto, and Astuto, 1984). Plans with nicely graphed charts, arrows, and circles are, at most, a guide to the much more complex world of real life. People become ill, snow days cancel critical meetings, and new initiatives and deadlines unexpectedly come tumbling down to interfere with anticipated plans. Plans provide a direction to success; when circumstances make a preplanned activity or event unnecessary or problematic, the supervisor and staff should be flexible enough to make substitutions and alterations. The final aim is to reach the goal, not to implement a predetermined plan.

Summary

This chapter has explained the complementary nature of assessment and planning for realizing a vision about instructional improvement. It began with examining ways to assess and plan supervisory time. The next topic was assessing and planning organizational change. Assessment techniques discussed were: eyes and ears, official records, third-party review, written open-ended surveys, check and ranking lists, the Delphi technique, and the nominal group technique. Ways of determining the underlying causes of needs discussed were: cause and effect diagrams, flowcharts, Pareto charts, and scatter diagrams. Planning techniques discussed were: management by objectives (MBO), Gantt charts, program evaluation and review techniques (PERT), the PSDA cycle, and strategic planning. The last section discussed when to use extensive written and formalized plans. Assessing and planning skills are generic; they help us to organize our own professional life as well as organize instructional improvement programs that involve many people. Assessing and planning enable us to take stock of present conditions, analyze consequences, and choose events, activities, and resources.

Exercises

Academic

1. Prepare a written summary of the major suggestions of one writer on time management. Discuss how the suggestions can be applied to educational supervision.

2. Describe and compare two program assessment processes successfully used in a public school system and not discussed in this book.

3. Locate outside literature on the Deming management method (such discussions may be included in the literature under the topics "Total Quality Improvement," "Total Quality Control" or "Total Quality Management"). Write a paper reviewing Deming's ideas and discussing how they could be or have been applied to educational assessment and planning. Include at least three outside references in your paper.

4. Write a paper comparing and contrasting any two of the following:
   a. Management by objectives (MBO)
   b. Program evaluation and review techniques (PERT)
   c. The PDSA cycle (sometimes referred to as the Deming, Shewhart, or PDCA cycle)
   d. Strategic planning

   Include in your paper at least two references on both models.

5. Write a paper describing how one of the planning models listed in academic exercise 4 has been successfully applied to an educational setting.

Field

1. After using the methods suggested in this chapter for assessing your work time (daily log, time consumption chart, comparison of preferred priorities to actual time spent), write out a personal plan for making actual use of time closer to preferred use. Be sure each of the five questions in a personal improvement plan is answered. Implement your plan over a period of two weeks. At the end of the implementation period, prepare a written evaluation of your plan.

2. Write out a personal work improvement objective. Prepare a flowchart as an aid for reaching your objective. Carry out the activities outlined in your flowchart; then evaluate whether your objective has been met. Write a report analyzing your

improvement plan and its implementation. Include a discussion of the utility of the flowchart as part of your improvement effort.

3. Use at least one of the six ways of assessing need within an organization (eyes and ears, official records, third-party review, written open-ended survey, Delphi technique, nominal group technique) to determine needs within an educational program. Write a report on your assessment. Include a discussion of the assessment process and the needs that were discovered.

4. Participate in a group in which an educational improvement plan is created, using at least one of the following planning techniques: (a) management by objectives (MBO); (b) Gantt charts; (c) flowcharting; (d) program evaluation and review techniques (PERT); (e) the PDSA cycle; (f) strategic planning. Prepare a written report on the experience.

5. Interview a leader in business, industry, government, or the military who has had extensive experience with one of the planning techniques listed in the previous exercise. Prepare a report on your interview, including a description of how the technique is used in the interviewee's field and a discussion of how it might be modified for use in an educational setting.

Developmental

1. Use a Gantt chart to plan a long-range personal project. Carry the project through to completion.

2. Volunteer for participation in an educational planning process.

3. Begin an in-depth exploration of what prominent authors in educational supervision have to say about educational assessment and planning.

References

Anderson, S. 1975. *Encyclopedia of educational evaluation.* San Francisco: Jossey-Bass, pp. 290–293.

Bennis, W. G., Benne, K. D., and Chin, P. 1985. *The planning of change.* New York: Holt, Rinehart and Winston.

Bishop, L. J. 1976. *Staff development and instructional development: Plans and procedures.* Boston: Allyn and Bacon.

Bostingl, J. J. 1992a. The total quality classroom. *Educational Leadership* 49(6):67.

Bostingl, J. J. 1992b. *Schools of quality: An introduction to total quality management in education.* Alexandria, VA: Association for Supervision and Curriculum Development.

Brandt, R. (Ed.). 1992. *Educational Leadership 50.* Theme issue on "Improving School Quality."

Bruce, R. E., and Grimsley, E. E. 1979. Course supplementary reading—Introduction to super vision. Unpublished manuscript, University of Georgia.

Case, C. M. 1969. The application of PERT to large-scale educational and evaluation studies. *Educational Technology* 9:79–83.

Clark, D., Lotto, L., and Astuto, T. 1984. Effective schools and school improvement: A comparative analysis of two lines of inquiry. *Educational Administration Quarterly* 20:41–68.

Cook, D. L. 1966. PERT: *Applications in education.* Cooperative Research Monograph No. 17. Washington, DC: U.S. Government Printing Office.

Cook W. J. 1990. *Bill Cook's strategic planning for America's schools* (rev. ed.). Arlington, VA: American Association of School Administrators.

Delbecq, A. L., Van de Ven, A. H., & Gustafson, D. H. 1975. *Group techniques for program planning.* Glenview, IL: Scott, Foresman.

Deming, W. E. 1986. *Out of the crisis*. Cambridge, MA: Massachusetts Institute of Technology.

Dyson, R. G. 1990. *Strategic planning: Models and analytical techniques*. Chichester, England: John Wiley and Sons.

Frymier, J. 1980. *Practical principles of educational leadership*. Annual Johnnye E. Cox lecture of the Georgia Association of Curriculum and Instructional Supervision, Athens, September.

Hostrop, R. W. 1975. *Managing education for results* (2nd ed.). Homewood, CA: ETC Publications.

Kaufman, R. 1991. *Strategic planning: An organizational guide*. Glenview, IL: Scott, Foresman.

Kaufman, R. 1992. *Mapping educational success: Strategic thinking and planning for school administrators*. Newbury Park, CA: Corwin.

Knezevich, S. J. 1972. MBO—Its meaning and application to educational administration. *Education 93*:12–21.

Knezevich, S. J. 1984. *Administration of public education*. New York: Harper and Row.

Schmoker, M. J., and Wilson, R. B. 1993. *Total quality education: Profiles of schools that demonstrate the power of Deming's management principles*. Bloomington, IN: Phi Delta Kappa.

Walton, M. 1986. *The Deming management method*. New York: Putnam.

Weaver, W. T. 1971. The Delphi forecasting method. *Kappan 52*:267.

Suggested Readings

Bonstingl, J. J. 1992. *Schools of quality*. Alexandria, VA: Association for Supervision and Curriculum Development.

Cook, W. J. 1990. *Bill Cook's strategic planning for America's schools*. Arlington, VA: American Association of School Administrators.

Holcomb, E. L. 1996. *Asking the right questions: Tools and techniques for teamwork*. Thousand Oaks, CA: Sage.

Kaufman, R. 1991. *Strategic planning plus*. Glenview, IL: Scott, Foresman.

Kaufman, R. 1995. *Mapping educational success*. Thousand Oaks, CA: Corwin.

Kaufman, R., and Zahn, D. 1993. *Quality management plus: The continuous improvement of education*. Newbury Park, CA: Corwin.

Schmoker, M. J., and Wilson, R. B. 1993. *Total quality education: Profiles of schools that demonstrate the power of Deming's management principals*. Bloomington, IN: Phi Delta Kappa.

14

Observing Skills

Observation seems simple. Anyone with normal vision appears to be observing every moment his or her eyes are open. Why, then, are there so many books, approaches, and debates about the types and uses of observation for instructional improvement (Acheson and Gall, 1992; Beegle and Brandt, 1973; Simon and Boyer, 1967; Jones and Sherman, 1980; Eisner, 1985)? *Observation* is actually the act of (1) noting and then (2) judging. The issue of observation in educational settings has focused on questions of instruments and the basis for inferences. These are some of the issues:

1. Is there a need for an externally structured instrument to measure what is happening in a classroom, or can a supervisor instead use subjective, anecdotal methods of observation?
2. What is the basis for inferring that observed instructional practices such as student behaviors or teacher actions are good or bad?
3. Does inference need to be derived from a numerical accounting of classroom events, or can a supervisor judge effective practices from a feel for the classroom?

These are complicated questions. The purpose of this chapter is to answer them by arriving at general agreement on observation procedures, describing the various methods of observation that can be used by supervisors, and then providing criteria for choosing appropriate observation forms.

Consider the classroom shown in Figure 14.1. If you were an observer of this classroom, what would you say is happening? Of course, one illustration is not enough basis for an observation, but pretend you are seeing this episode for an entire class period. Could you say that the students have behavior problems, discipline is lax, the teacher is not responding to the students' interests, or the teacher is lecturing too much?

If your observations are similar to those listed here, then you have fallen into the *interpretation trap,* which is the downfall of most attempts to help people

FIGURE 14.1 *Classroom Picture*

improve their performance. How would you respond if your evaluator—say, the superintendent of schools—observed you conducting a faculty meeting and later told you that teachers lack respect for you? Your response probably would be a combination of defensiveness ("It isn't so"), confusion ("What do you mean?"), and quiet hostility ("Who are you to say that to me?"). The superintendent has inadvertently turned you against him or her, and compliance on your part will be grudging at best.

Observation is a two-part process—first *describing* what has been seen and then *interpreting* what it means. The mind almost simultaneously processes a visual image, integrates that image with previously stored images related to satisfactory and unsatisfactory experiences, and ascribes a value or meaning to that image. If a student yawns, our mind signals "boredom." If a teacher yells at students, our mind registers "losing control." A judgment derives from an image or a description of events. We must be aware of splitting that almost simultaneous process, of separating description from interpretation. When we lose the description of the event and retain only the interpretation, we create communication difficulties and obstacles to improvement.

Let's return to the superintendent's interpretation that "teachers lack respect." How much different would your response have been if the description behind the interpretation had been shared with you: "I saw that 6 of the 15 teachers arrived late to your faculty meeting." You could agree that, indeed, 6 members did arrive late; however, you might disagree with the interpretation of lack of respect as arbitrary. You could not only accept that 6 members had been late but also do something about it. You cannot do anything about lack of respect because you don't know what needs to be changed. On the other hand, you can correct lateness and eventually improve the superintendent's interpretation of the teachers' respect. Sharing the description of events is the forerunner of professional improvement. Interpretation leads to resistance. When both parties can agree on what events occurred, they are more likely to agree on what needs to be changed.

Remember that if the goal of supervision is to enhance teachers' thought and commitment about improving classroom (and school) practice, observations should be used as a base of information to create an instructional dialogue between supervisor and teacher. Using description first when talking to a teacher about his or her classroom creates an instructional dialogue. Providing interpretations and evaluative statements first ushers in defensiveness, combativeness, or resentment in the teacher and stifles discussion (see Glickman and Jones, 1986).

Differentiating description from interpretation in observation is so crucial for instructional improvement that we need to refer back to our original illustration of the classroom (Figure 14.1). Look at the picture again and tell what you now see going on. You might say that there are three students looking away from the teacher and talking to each other while the teacher stands in front of the room calling on a student in the front row. Can we agree that this is happening? Probably so, and thus we can *later* judge the rightness or wrongness of the event in regard to student learning. The teacher can more readily change the events of three students talking to each other and two others looking away than he or she can change being "a poor classroom manager."

Formative Observation Instruments Are Not Summative Evaluation Instruments

A formative observation instrument used to describe what is occurring in a classroom (consistent with what teacher and supervisor agreed to focus on and later discuss) is a means for professional growth and instructional improvement. Therefore, the use of a formative observation instrument is conditioned on prior agreement about what is most worthy of learning by that teacher in that classroom—whether the interest is derived from a desire to know more about himself or herself as a teacher, attempting a particular instructional model, experimenting with a new practice or strategy, or struggling with a problem or weakness. A summative evaluation instrument, on the other hand, is an externally imposed, uniformly applied measure, intended to judge all teachers on similar criteria to determine their worthiness, merit, and competence as employees within the same organization. Summative evaluation instruments are intended to summarize and judge competence. Formative observation instruments are intended to provide information to teachers on what they and their supervisors have agreed to as important; competence is not the issue. Therefore, summative evaluation instruments tend to be checklists, rating scales, or narratives of worth about the teacher's competence, whereas formative observation instruments are descriptive findings that move to interpretations for further goals and professional learning. Formative observation instruments are chosen for use between teacher and supervisor. Summative evaluation instruments are dictated to teacher and evaluator. Although summative evaluation instruments have their rightful place in schools, they should not be confused with formative observation instruments. Distinctions between summative and formative evaluation are discussed in detail in Chapter 15.

Ways of Describing

In describing, the goal is to eliminate any confusion about what is happening. A good check is to use a person off the street as corroborator. One can feel confident about one's description of what is happening in a classroom if a sidewalk passerby could be pulled into the classroom and (no matter what his or her credentials) would in fact see what the observer is seeing. If the passerby would have to make any professional judgment—about, say, the rapidity of presentation, the responsiveness to learning style, or the permissiveness of discipline—then it would no longer be a description. If the passerby could describe such happenings as the frequency of teacher-student talk, interruptions, the arrangement of the room, the physical space used by the teacher, and what teacher and students are saying, then the person-off-the-street check has been passed, and you may remove the passerby from your mind. (Please do not physically pull people from the street into the classroom—the neighborhood school concept can be taken only so far.)

There are many ways to record descriptions. At the end of this chapter, there are multiple references to various observation methods and instruments. An observation instrument is a tool for organizing and recording different categories of classroom life. It can be as simple as a single category or as complex as a matrix of dozens of possible coded combinations. For example, an instrument can be used to count the displays on a classroom wall or to record the hundreds of students' and teachers' verbal and nonverbal interactions.

We have formed a strong bias concerning observation instruments as a result of our working with hundreds of administrators, supervisors, and teachers. Observation instruments developed for research purposes are usually too time consuming and cumbersome to be used by practitioners. We do not mean to attack instruments such as those developed by Bales (1951), Flanders (1970), or Medley and Mizel (1963). These instruments have contributed immensely to research on effective teaching and have directed practitioners toward instructional practices that need to be emphasized. However, the instruments have been used by trained (usually paid) data collectors and are not as easily used by a single supervisor with 30 or more faculty members to observe. We believe there are ways to adapt the more complicated instruments so that they can be used to provide valid descriptions for the nonresearch purpose of describing classroom events to a teacher. A listing and explanation of many adapted ways of observing will follow.

We will first look at quantitative observations, including categorical instruments, performance indicator instruments, visual diagramming, and space utilization. The second section will deal with qualitative observations, including verbatim, detached, open-ended narrative, participant observation, focused questionnaire observation, and educational criticism. Finally, we will discuss tailored observations—quantitative or qualitative observations designed to gather data on specific teacher concerns.

Quantitative Observations

Quantitative observations are ways of measuring classroom events, behaviors, and objects. Definitions and categories must be precise. Eventually, the observations can be used for statistical operations.

Categorical Frequency Instrument

A categorical instrument is a form that defines certain events or behaviors that can be checked off at frequency intervals and then counted. There is nothing mysterious about it. Almost any aspect of classroom life can be isolated and counted. For example, teacher behaviors can be divided into verbal and nonverbal categories. Each category can then be subdivided into countable subcategories. Verbal behaviors could be information giving, questioning, answering, praising, direction giving and scolding. An instrument might look like Figure 14.2.

The observer, after clearly defining each subcategory, would listen to each teacher verbalization and move down the sheet for each different statement made. One check exists for each horizontal line. Most instruments that record teacher verbal behavior also record student verbal behavior, so that verbal interactions between teacher and student and student and student can be analyzed.

Figure 14.3 is a categorical instrument that measures the frequency of different types of questions asked by the teacher. The seven categories of teacher questions are based on Bloom's taxonomy (the taxonomy is explained in Chapter 19). By dividing the number of questions in each category by the total number of

	Information Giving	Questioning	Answering	Praising	Direction Giving	Scolding
1.	X	X	X			
2.	X	X	X			
3.	X					
4.	X					
5.			X			
6.			X			
7.	X					
8.	X					
9.						
10.						
11.	X					
12.	X					
13.	X					
14.	X					
15.						
16.						

FIGURE 14.2 *Teacher Verbal Behaviors*

Question Category	Tally	Total	Percent
Evaluation		0	0
Synthesis	/	1	5
Analysis	/	1	5
Application	//	2	10
Interpretation	///	3	15
Translation	////	4	20
Memory	︥﹨﹨ ////	9	45
Total of Questions Asked = 20			

FIGURE 14.3 *Teacher Questions*

questions asked by the teacher during the lesson, the observer can calculate the percent of total questions each category represents.

Other classroom topics can be observed with categorical instruments. For example, one can focus on on-task and off-task behavior. To complete the instrument in Figure 14.4, the observer begins a sweep of the classroom every 5 minutes. During each sweep, the observer focuses on each student for approximately 20 seconds, then records that student's behavior. During a 40-minute lesson, 8

Student	Time When Sweep Began							
	9:00	9:05	9:10	9:15	9:20	9:25	9:30	9:35
Andrew	A	C	D	E	E	A	B	B
Shawn G.	A	A	D	E	E	A	C	B
Maria	A	A	D	E	E	C	B	B
Sam	I	F	F	E	F	A	B	C
Barbara	H	F	D	E	E	F	F	B
Angie	C	G	G	C	E	G	G	G
Jeff	A	A	C	E	E	A	B	B
Jessica	F	F	D	E	E	A	B	E
Shawn L.	A	A	D	E	H	H	B	B
Chris	F	F	D	E	E	A	B	C
Michele	A	A	D	E	H	H	B	B
Mark	**A**	I	I	F	I	I	I	F
Melissa	C	A	D	E	E	C	H	B
John	J	A	J	I	J	J	J	J
Rolanda	A	C	D	E	E	A	B	F

Key

A = on task, listening / watching   F = off task, passive
B = on task, writing   G = off task, doing work
C = on task, speaking   for another class
D = on task, reading   H = off task, listening to others
E = on task, hands-on activity   I = off task, disturbing others
                                                       J = off task, playing

FIGURE 14.4   Student On-Task and Off-Task Behavior

sweeps can be made. The instrument allows the observer to record specific on-task and off-task behaviors listed in the key at the bottom of the chart.

Performance Indicator Instruments

A performance indicator instrument records whether or not actions listed on the observation instrument have been observed. With some instruments, a third option—"not applicable" (N/A)—is included. Performance indicator instruments may also include space for the observer to add supplemental notes concerning the presence or absence of the action. Figure 14.5 is a performance indicator instru-

FIGURE 14.5 *Hunter Model Performance Indicators*

Elements	Response	Comments
Anticipatory set	Yes___ No___ N/A___	_____ _____ _____
Statement of objective and purpose	Yes___ No___ N/A___	_____ _____ _____
Input	Yes___ No___ N/A___	_____ _____ _____
Modeling	Yes___ No___ N/A___	_____ _____ _____
Checking for understanding	Yes___ No___ N/A___	_____ _____ _____
Guided practice	Yes___ No___ N/A___	_____ _____ _____
Independent practice	Yes___ No___ N/A___	_____ _____ _____

ment used to record the presence or absence of the elements in Madeline Hunter's lesson design model, a model well suited for direct instruction. Figure 14.6 is an instrument to assess whether or not each of the basic elements of a cooperative learning lesson are present.

Remember that performance indicators used for observation purposes should not imply an absolute standard. The fact that a teacher does not perform all of the activities listed on the observation instrument may or may not be a cause of concern. Only after the supervisor and teacher have discussed the circumstances surrounding the teacher's instructional procedures can they be properly interpreted.

Visual Diagramming

Visual diagramming is another way to portray what is occurring in a classroom. Videotaping a classroom captures the closest representative picture of actual oc-

FIGURE 14.6   *Cooperative Learning Performance Indicators*

Elements	Response	Comments
Explanation of academic and social objectives	Yes___ No___ N/A___	_____ _____ _____
Teaching of necessary social skills	Yes___ No___ N/A___	_____ _____ _____
Face-to-face interaction	Yes___ No___ N/A___	_____ _____ _____
Positive interdependence	Yes___ No___ N/A___	_____ _____ _____
Individual accountability	Yes___ No___ N/A___	_____ _____ _____
Group processing	Yes___ No___ N/A___	_____ _____ _____

currences. Without videotapes, however, there are other ways to portray observations, such as verbal interactions among teachers and students and how a teacher uses space. After diagramming the occurrence, the supervisor and the teacher can view the picture and then analyze the events.

Classroom verbal interactions can be charted by drawing arrows symbolizing verbal statements between members in a classroom (see Figure 14.7). The observer can use six separate sheets of this diagram and fill out one sheet for each

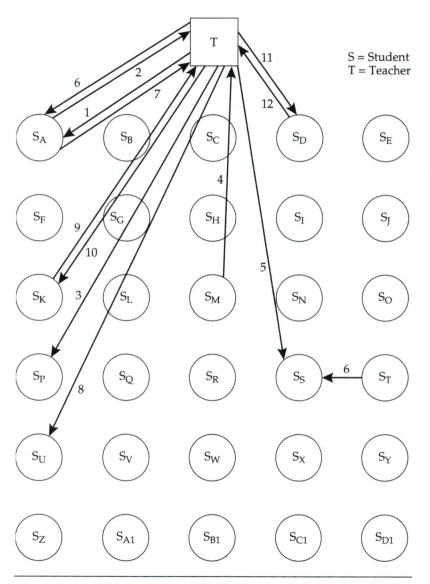

FIGURE 14.7 *Diagram of Verbal Interaction, 9:10–9:15*

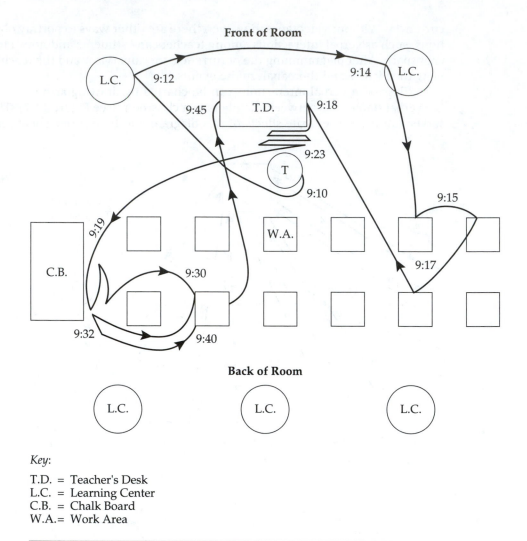

FIGURE 14.8   *Teacher Space Utilization*

time sample of five minutes spaced throughout the hour. Each arrow drawn on the diagram would indicate a full statement directed to another person. The arrows are numbered in the sequence of statements. After diagramming, the observer would then have information on the frequency of individual student interaction, the amount of interaction with different areas of the room, which students triggered interactions among others, and which students were excluded. For illustration purposes, if the diagram was a sample consistent with the other five samples of the classroom period, the observer would be able to state some of the following conclusions:

1. Interaction is mainly directed toward the left aisle and front row.
2. There is almost no attention to the last two rows in the back of the room or the two rows on the right.
3. Of 14 interactions, 12 included the teacher and 2 were between students.

Such diagramming is easier to follow with small groups and when students are not moving around the classroom. Class activities such as teacher lecturing interspersed with questions and answers or classroom discussions would be instructional sessions appropriate for diagramming. Another type of diagramming is flowcharting teacher space utilization, which follows the teacher's movement throughout the classroom. A sketch of the physical classroom is done first; then the observer follows the teacher by using arrows on the sketch (see Figure 14.8).

Figure 14.8 on the previous page illustrates a period of reading instruction. The arrow follows the teacher with each movement and is labeled with the time on the clock. After a class period, the observer and the teacher can see where the teacher has been and for how long. Such information might help make a teacher aware of the relationship of his or her space utilization to concerns of classroom management and instruction. For example, in Figure 14.8 there is much physical presence in the front and on the left side of the classroom, with no presence at the rear learning centers or the middle work area.

Quantitative and Qualitative Instruments

Structured forms used to record categorical frequencies, physical indicators, performance indicators, and visual diagrams all measure classroom occurrences. Categorical forms can measure the amount of verbal, nonverbal, on-task, or off-task behaviors of teachers and students. One can derive percentages, ratios, and means of total and type of behaviors (total teacher talk, ratio of teacher to student talk, breakdown of amount of teacher questions, directions, answers, and so on). The performance-indicator instruments are a measure of occurrence (yes/no), or frequency of occurrence. For example, a performance indicator entitled "Feedback on Tests" can be measured by teacher-written comments. Therefore, the observer looks for teacher-written comments on tests and possibly at the number of tests. Diagramming events in classrooms is another way to count occurrences, lengths of occurrences, and placement of occurrences. For example, the observer can record how much time a teacher spends in different areas of the classroom and the frequency with which the teacher repeats certain walking patterns. All these instruments are quantitative in that they isolate occurrences in the classroom, provide a measurement standard for compiling the frequency of occurrences, and lend themselves to further statistical treatment. Structured instruments enable the observer to know precisely what he or she is looking for prior to entering the classroom.

There are alternative means of observing based on not knowing exactly what is to be recorded. These are called qualitative or descriptive forms of observation.

The observer goes into the classroom with a general focus, or no focus at all, and records events as they occur. The events are not made to fit into a specific category, nor are they measured. Only after the recording of events does the observer re-arrange his or her observations into themes. Such recording of observations defies the use of an instrument (an instrument is technically a measurement device). In-stead, qualitative observations record the complexity of classroom life. Suppose two supervisors go into the same classroom. Supervisor A fills out a quantitative instru-ment on interaction; supervisor B qualitatively describes classroom life. They both observe the teacher asking: "Why did Britain go to war in Argentina? Doesn't anyone know? What a bunch of dummies." Supervisor A listens and places two check marks in the teacher question box and another check in the teacher state-ment box. Supervisor B writes: "Ms. Egghart smiles and asks if anyone knows why Britain went to war. With no response, she asks if anyone understands the ques-tion. She looks up, rolls her eyes, throws up her hands and says 'What a bunch of dummies.' The students smile and laugh. She laughs with them."

The quantitative observation reveals the *amount* and ratios of teacher ques-tions and statements; the qualitative instrument reveals the *nature* of teacher questions, statements, and relations. Both observations are correct. However, one observation reduces the amount of information into fixed categories; the other builds a range of description to be compiled later into common, emerging themes.

Qualitative Observations

There are several types of qualitative observations. We will look at verbatim, de-tached open-ended narrative, participant observation, focused questionnaire ob-servation, and educational criticism. These observations can be used by a supervisor to provide a broad and complex recording of classroom life.

Verbatim

The observer taking verbatim notes (sometimes called scripts) records all verbal interaction taking place in the classroom. Verbatim notes allow the observer and teacher to identify patterns of interpersonal behavior during a lesson. Verbatim also provides specific examples of teacher-student or student-teacher interac-tions. For more efficient recording, the observer may abbreviate words and leave out words that add no meaning to the transcript. Despite these time-savers, ver-batim can be an arduous process requiring the observer to spend every moment taking notes, with no time for attention to anything else going on during the les-son. One alternative to verbatim is *selected verbatim,* in which the observer records only those interactions that relate to a particular focus agreed to by the observer and teacher prior to the observation. Figure 14.9 provides an excerpt from selec-tive verbatim notes focused on teacher responses to students who initially gave incorrect or partially correct answers to teacher questions.

```
C = Chris D.                                        10:20
T = Teacher

T.  C, what are 3 branches of Fed. Govt.?
C.  President, House, Senate
T.  What branch Fed. Govt. is pres. head of?
C.  Ah, I don't know
T.  The president is Chief _____.
C.  Executive! Executive branch!
T.  The House and Senate are both part of what branch?
C.  Legislative
T.  Legislative branch, but both mean same thing. That's 2 branches,
    exec. and leg. What is the third branch?
C.  The Courts.
T.  What branch is made of Sup. Ct and other fed. cts.
C.  Judicial
T.  Right!
```

FIGURE 14.9 *Excerpt from Selective Verbatim Notes*

Originally published in S. Gordon (1990). *Assisting the entry-year teacher: A leadership resource.* Columbus, OH: Ohio Department of Education.

Detached Open-Ended Narrative

Detached open-ended narrative occurs when the supervisor steps into a classroom and records every person, event, or thing that attracts his or her attention. At the start, the pages are empty, without questions, indicators, or categories. The heading might simply say:

Open-Ended Narrative

Observation Teacher: _____ Time: _____ Observer: _____

The recorder then has the task of writing, writing, and more writing. A sample of such an observation might read:

Students begin arriving at 10:13; the teacher is at his desk correcting papers. The bell rings at 10:15 to begin third period. Students keep arriving. Mr. X gets up from his desk to begin class at 10:25. In the meantime, students have put away their school bags and are awaiting instruction, except three girls in the back corner who are talking, combing their hair, and spreading the contents of their pocketbooks on their desks. Five minutes after Mr. X begins, he talks to them and they put away combs and pocketbooks. Mr. X describes the activities for the day but then cannot find his prepared handouts. After two minutes of looking, he finds the papers in his desk drawer.

The intercom comes on at 10:30 with two announcements by the principal. Mr. X gives the assignments, and the class begins to read at 10:33. Two students are reprimanded for talking, and occasional student talk can be heard as Mr. X moves around and reviews yesterday's homework with students. He talks with 12 students before asking for class attention at 10:45. He then lectures on the classification of insects. The overhead projection on the board is difficult for students in the back to read. One student asks if he can darken the lights....

With practice, the observer can write in shorthand to keep up with the flow of events. It is impossible to record all that could possibly be seen and heard in a classroom. The observer must constantly scan the entire classroom and decide what is significant.

Participant Open-Ended Observation

Participant open-ended observation occurs when the supervisor becomes a functioning part of the classroom (Spradley, 1980). He or she assists in the instruction, helps students with questions, uses classroom materials, and talks with the teacher and students. Being involved in the classroom gives the supervisor an inside-out view of the classroom different from that of the detached observer who tries to be invisible and keep away from students and teachers. Obviously, events cannot be written down as they occur if the supervisor is engaged in talking, moving, and assisting. Instead, he or she must write between pauses in the action. The observation form can be carried on a clipboard so that notes can be taken on the run.

The participant observer takes sketchy notes (catch phrases and words) during classroom time so that afterward he or she can write in greater detail. These quick notes serve to remind the observer of the situation that will be described more fully after the observation period is over. The following is an example of such short notes.

Teacher X directs students into study groups.

John B. does not understand the assignment. I work with him on organizing the theme of a play.

Sally T. and Ramona B. are wandering around. I ask them if they need help; they say no and leave the room (ask teacher about this).

Sondra and her group are ready to role-play their theme. I listen as they read through their parts.

Steven's group is stuck; he doesn't know how to find materials on historic buildings. I suggest calling the town historic society.

Susan is not participating at all—looking at *Teen Magazine*. The rest of the group just leaves her alone. (I wonder why?)

The filmstrip shown has everyone's attention.

Teacher B dismisses the class. I overhear a student say, "This class goes so quickly. I wish other classes were as much fun."

These are some notes from a 50-minute classroom period. Much more happened in the classroom than is noted, but the observer picks up insights from his or her involvement. The supervisor can later fill in details—the two girls leaving the classroom, the specifics of John's confusion about the theme, Susan's absorption in *Teen Magazine*, and so on.

Focused Questionnaire Observation

Qualitative observation can be done in a more focused manner by having general topics to use in recording events. An observer seeks information about specific questions.

Particular instructional models and learning goals can be used in a focused questionnaire. For example, if a teacher were attempting to use a teacher-centered, direct instruction model to teach short-term, specific skills or facts in a lesson, the following questions to focus the observer on recording relevant descriptions might be appropriate (Rosenshine, 1986).

What Does the Teacher Do to

1. Review the previous learnings that are prerequisites for the lesson?
2. Present new materials (statement of goals, examples, modeling, checking for understanding)?
3. Provide guided practice (questions, feedback, success rate, closure before independent practice)?
4. Feedback for correct answers and incorrect answers (clues, reteaching) and specific praise?
5. Provide independent practice (overview, initial steps, practice, automatic response, routines for slower students)?
6. Conduct weekly and monthly reviews?

If a teacher were attempting to use a student-centered approach aimed at increasing critical and creative thinking about a current world concern, the observer might be able to focus descriptions according to the following questions (Marzano, Brandt, Hughes, Jones, Presseisen, Rankin, and Suhor, 1988).

What Does the Teacher Do to Assist Students to Acquire Core Thinking Skills for

1. *Focusing:* Defining problems and setting goals?
2. *Information gathering:* Observing to obtain information and formulate questions to seek new information?
3. *Remembering:* Storing and retrieving information?
4. *Organizing:* Comparing, classifying, observing, and representing?
5. *Analyzing:* Identifying attributes and components, relationships and patterns, main ideas, and errors?
6. *Generating:* Inferring, predicting, and elaborating?
7. *Integrating:* Summarizing and restructuring?
8. *Evaluating:* Assessing the reasonableness and quality of ideas?

A focused questionnaire can revolve on a particular instructional model, such as direct instruction, cooperative learning, jurisprudence, advanced organizers, or indirect learning. It can be as narrow as looking at one or two questions within a particular model or be as extensive as to include numerous questions about a model, or be generic in posing questions that would cross different teaching practices.

In order to answer the questions, the observer writes pertinent evidence. For example, Harris (1975, pp. 364–376) has developed a detached observation questionnaire that has as its topics: (1) classroom, (2) teacher, (3) pupil, and (4) lesson. Figure 14.10 shows sample questions taken from each category.

An observer enters the classroom with questions in hand and looks for the answers. Some questions lend themselves to detached observations; others demand participant observations. For example, the question "What shows that the teacher has a warm, friendly relationship with pupils?" could be answered by participant observation, such as: "Overheard three students saying how nice Ms. Y is. Noticed how Ms. Y put her hand on the shoulders of five different students when speaking to them." The question "How is the classroom made attractive?" could be

FIGURE 14.10 *Focused Questionnaire*

Topic 1: Classroom
How is the classroom made attractive?

Topic 2: Teacher
What shows that the teacher has a warm, friendly relationship with the pupils?

Topic 3: Pupil
What indicates that pupils know what they are doing and why they are doing it?

Topic 4: Lesson
How do classroom and homework assignments indicate that consideration is given to, and use made of, resources of the community and real-life situations of pupils?

---

answered by detached observation: "Classroom freshly painted, bulletin boards have recent work. Student art work is framed and evenly spaced." It is the task of the observer to respond to these questions with descriptions of the evidence.

Educational Criticism

Elliott Eisner (1985) has developed an approach to observation that merges detached and participant observation with description and interpretation. Observers are trained to look at the classroom as an art critic might look at a painting. Just as a person would have to accumulate the experience of viewing numerous paintings and become knowledgeable in the history and variations of particular art forms to be a critic, so must an educator become familiar with many types of classrooms and forms of instruction to be an education critic.

Eisner has stated classroom observations can be done via the same procedures of criticism. He calls the needed educational expertise "connoisseurship." Just as a wine connoisseur can look at the color, viscosity, smell, and taste of a wine to form specific judgments about its overall quality, so can an educational connoisseur make judgments about the specifics of classroom events and the overall quality of classroom life.

Eisner argued that supervisors can develop educational connoisseurship by finding what the classroom *means* to the participants. The education critic attempts to take the perspective of students and teachers in viewing the influence of the classroom environment, events, and interactions and then makes the hidden meaning of the classroom known to the participants to see whether they agree. Teachers and students may be so involved in the classroom that they are unaware of the meaning of what they do. The participant observer attempts to describe and interpret events through their eyes.

The following are excerpts from observations and interpretations of a college composition class made by Sugie Goen,* one of Eisner's students. In the first excerpt, Goen provides a vivid description of "Life in Room 132:"

> A few minutes after six, the teacher Helen Deakin, enters the room—streams in is more like it. Her movements are liquid, from the way her loose fitting clothing flows around her as she moves into the room, to the way she repeatedly gathers full handfuls of long thick hair that, in one sweeping gesture, she lifts from her forehead, releasing great locks that spill languidly down her back. She flows into the room slowly, in no apparent hurry even though it is now several minutes past six o'clock. Her students are in no apparent hurry either. Right at six o'clock, the scheduled start time for class to begin, only six of the seventeen students are present. Students continue to arrive until half past the hour, an arrival pattern that I was to witness during each of my visits. This is clearly a class where no one rushes. Life in Room 132 doesn't gush, torrent or swell. It flows; it spreads out thickly and slowly; maybe even, I would soon suspect, deliberately.

*Excerpts are from "School Choice and the Teaching of First-Year Composition: The Story of Room 132," Sugie Goen, Stanford University. Reprinted with permission.

While students are arriving, Helen stands in front of the class, gazing out at the students sitting at the even rows of tables. "Do you want to sit this way? Or in a circle like before?" No rhetorical question here, for she stands patiently still, waiting for a response. When none comes, she poses the question again, and again she waits. Now, I know that I too have posed a similar question to my students. But, when I do so, I am using the tried-and-true teacher strategy of giving a directive camouflaged as a question. And my students know it, too, because they tend to immediately move their chairs into a circle. Not so with these students; they think over the question; some shrug their shoulders, and by tacit consent, they decide to remain seated in horizontal rows. They seem to know that Helen's question conveys an authentic offer of choice to be determined by the students' actual preferences.

The next excerpt from Goen's narrative illustrates the interpretive dimension of educational criticism:

Helen dares to design a course that explores the contours of choice and one that wonders aloud how selection determines what can and cannot be known. And, the question of choice in Room 132 is not mere intellectual calisthenics. At every turn, Helen provides opportunities for her students to practice choosing: how to arrange their seats, what writing prompt to use, from what vantage point to view their classmate's clothing, to what time class should adjourn.

Yet, choice comes with a lot of baggage. For instance, Helen deliberately allows much more time for the flow of classroom management than I could ever imagine being comfortable with. And though she comments more than once about "the luxury of time" afforded by the three hour and twenty minute class sessions, the time required to decide the seating arrangement, or to discuss and vote on whether to proceed with or without a scheduled break, eats up enormous chunks of class time. And at times, I get the distinct impression that students are frustrated by all the choices, for instance, when Thanh blurts out "who cares" when faced with yet another decision. Furthermore, I could not help but notice that only a few students make the vast majority of decisions. Of the seventeen students, I estimate that nearly half rarely speak at all. Moreover, in matters of classroom management, the "policymakers" tend to be the same three of four men (with the exception of Keesha, by far the most vocal student, either male or female). In short, practicing student choice is enormously time consuming and I wonder if such choice is possible, or even desirable, in the fifty or ninety minute class formats of the regular academic school year. Moreover, it strikes me as necessarily labor intensive to properly monitor participation in decision making to safeguard against this "tyranny" of the vocal minority.

Of more concern to me, however, are the tensions that manifest around the idea of language choice. A number of students express discomfort with the idea of deliberately choosing language to convey a point of view. Miguel, in particular, voices his concern that to deliberate over word choice in order to persuade for a particular point of view renders writing biased when it is supposed to be "objective." Even in a writing assignment that asks them to examine the particular language choices of newspaper journalists, Miguel worries about how he can "write an unbiased paper about an article that is biased?" Besides, another student adds "if you have no opinion about affirmative action before, when you read all the articles you will form an opinion by the time you finish, so how can you be objective?" And yet another student chimes in that examining these articles is like looking for strategies writers use "to get something over on you."

It both interests me and concerns me that by focusing attention on the choices that writers use to express a point of view, the students in Room 132 may be deciding that choice is a negative thing, that it somehow suggests bias, prejudice, and manipulation at the cost of objectivity, whatever that is. But then again, their experiences in the world outside of school may be inadvertently reinforced each night in Room 132. After all, the students who command a facile use of language are more able (or willing) to vie for their position in class decision making. Perhaps the feelings of Miguel and others suggest that they occasionally feel manipulated by their more verbally powerful classmates. Perhaps they feel that something has been "gotten over on them." Perhaps too, they cling tenaciously to notions of objectivity as the promise of a world where everyone is equal, where no single perspective can persuade over another, where bias and prejudice don't exist at all. For these students, maybe college is supposed to be just such an "objective" place. Viewed this way, what does it mean for these students to be encouraged to choose when the playing field isn't level? Are we inviting them to play in a game where only the fittest survive?

Notice how language is expository, nontechnical, and elaborated. The writing is intended to capture the tone or feel of the class so that the observation can be used to verify the particulars and the general aspects of classroom life. Education critics record their information by playing both roles of distant and participant observer—distant observer by being apart from the classroom and participant observer by listening to students and teachers talk with each other to uncover further insights into the participants' perceptions of the classroom.

At first glance, an education critic would seem to differ little from the observer mentioned in the beginning of this chapter. That observer failed to distinguish between interpretation and description and instead wrote what he or she liked or disliked ("the classroom is a mess"). However, the education critic knows the difference. The critic has carefully recorded descriptions intermingled with interpretations derived from the participants' perspective. The education critic has caught the atmosphere (which later would be given to the teacher to verify); the nondiscriminating evaluator is left with only his or her own judgments of events.

Tailored Observation Systems

Supervisors often observe lessons to collect data on unique instructional concerns or improvement efforts. If no observation system exists that is capable of gathering the desired data, the supervisor can design a tailored observation system. Tailored observation systems can be quantitative, qualitative, or a combination of both. Figure 14.11 is a system designed to collect four specific types of data. The teacher in this example requested that the observer collect data on (1) how often the teacher called on each student; (2) whether each student's response was correct or incorrect; (3) whether the teacher drew out correct student responses through encouragement or prompting, especially after a student's initial response was incorrect; and (4) how often the teacher provided positive feedback to students making correct responses. In Figure 14.11, codes symbolize both student re-

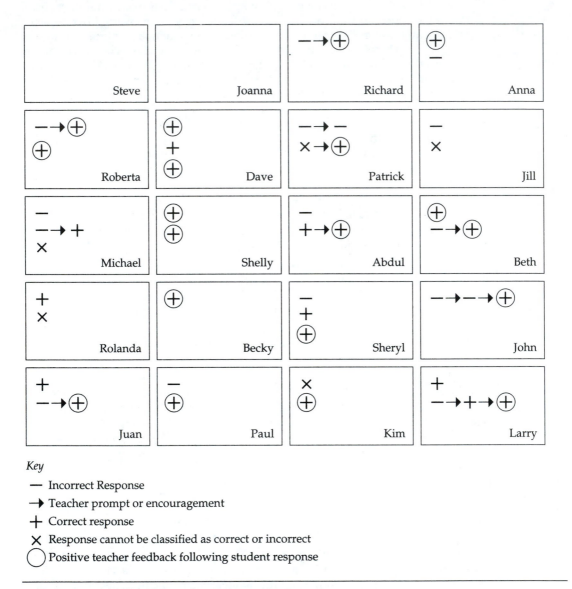

Key

— Incorrect Response

→ Teacher prompt or encouragement

+ Correct response

✕ Response cannot be classified as correct or incorrect

◯ Positive teacher feedback following student response

FIGURE 14.11   *Tailored Question-Response Instrument*

sponses (—, +, x) to teacher questions, and teacher reactions (→, o) to student responses. Several codes on the same line indicate verbal behaviors that were part of the same series of interactions. Codes on different lines indicate separate series of interactions.

In another example, teacher Simmons was concerned about the conduct of one of his students and asked the supervisor to collect data on the student's behaviors, Simmons's responses, and the effects of those responses on the student. Figure 14.12 is the observation chart completed by the supervisor. Arrows point to immediate responses of the teacher to selected student behaviors and immediate responses of the student to relevant teacher behaviors. Some of the most meaningful and helpful classroom observation data we have viewed has been collected with instruments designed by supervisors and teachers focused on specific teacher concerns.

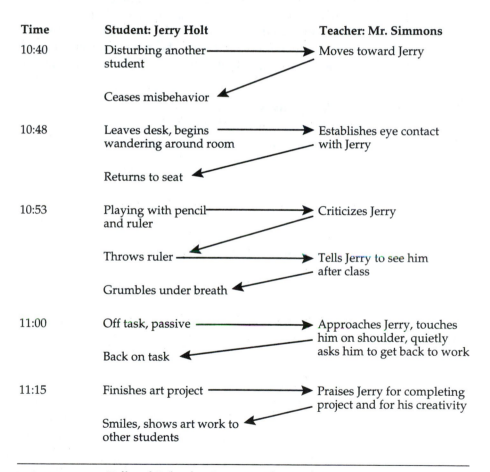

Time	Student: Jerry Holt	Teacher: Mr. Simmons
10:40	Disturbing another student	Moves toward Jerry
	Ceases misbehavior	
10:48	Leaves desk, begins wandering around room	Establishes eye contact with Jerry
	Returns to seat	
10:53	Playing with pencil and ruler	Criticizes Jerry
	Throws ruler	Tells Jerry to see him after class
	Grumbles under breath	
11:00	Off task, passive	Approaches Jerry, touches him on shoulder, quietly asks him to get back to work
	Back on task	
11:15	Finishes art project	Praises Jerry for completing project and for his creativity
	Smiles, shows art work to other students	

FIGURE 14.12   *Tailored Behavior-Response Observation*

Types and Purposes of Observation

Figure 14.13 illustrates the types of observation available to a supervisor. The purpose of the observation should determine the type, method, and role of observation. The categorical-frequency observation is a quantitative method used by a detached observer for the purpose of counting, totaling, and statistically analyzing behaviors. The performance-indicator observation is quantitatively used by a detached observer to record evidence of human behavior. Visual diagramming is a quantitative observation used by a detached observer for the purpose of depicting verbal interaction. Human space utilization observation is a quantitative measure used by a detached observer for the purpose of depicting the length and pattern of physical movement. Verbatim is a qualitative method in which the observer records all verbal interaction. The detached open-ended narrative is a qualitative observation used by a detached observer for recording events as they unfold. Participant open-ended observation is a qualitative technique used to record how people and events unfold to one involved in the classroom. The focused questionnaire is another qualitative method that can be used by a detached or participant observer for the purpose of gathering evidence according to general questions

FIGURE 14.13 Observation Alternatives

| Type | Method | | Role of Observer | | Purpose |
	Quantitive	Qualitative	Detached	Participant	
Categorical frequency	x		x		Count behaviors
Performance indicator	x		x		Evident or not
Visual diagramming	x		x		Picture verbal interaction
Space utilization	x		x		Picture movement
Verbatim		x			Script of verbal interaction
Detached open-ended narrative		x	x		Attention to unfolding event
Participant open-ended observation		x		x	Inside-out view
Focused questionnaire		x	x or	x	Focus on particular events
Educational criticism		x	x or	x	Meaning to participants
Tailored	x or	x	x or	x	Address unique concerns

about classroom topics. Educational criticism is a qualitative observation conducted by a combination of detached and participant observation for the purpose of capturing the meaning of classroom life from the teacher's and students' perspective.

Finally, tailored observation systems cut across the different categories previously discussed. They are designed by the supervisor (or supervisor and teacher) to collect data on specific teacher concerns when there is no existing observation system for collecting such data. They may be quantitative or qualitative and may be used by a detached or participant observer.

Further Cautions When Using Observations

To reiterate, the purpose of observation should determine the type, method, and role used. No one type of observation is superior to all others; rather, some types of observations are better for serving certain purposes. If the goal of an observation is to determine the frequency of praise, then educational criticism or open-ended narrative would be inappropriate when categorical frequencies would accomplish the goal. If the purpose of an observation is to determine those activities with greatest student interest, then a categorical- or performance-indicator instrument would be of little value, and a focused questionnaire would be more useful. There is a tendency for educators to view a new method of observation as a panacea to use at every opportunity. This has been the case with categorical-frequency instruments. Training programs, workshops, and courses have prepared thousands of supervisors with skills in defining and checking off categories. Hordes of prepared supervisors have run back into classrooms ticking off behaviors. In some cases, it was important for future instructional improvement to know the ratio of teacher statements, questions, and directions given. In other classrooms, interaction frequencies and ratios were never a concern to begin with, and the observation was meaningless. The new techniques of educational criticism should not be used indiscriminately by every supervisor in every classroom simply because they are new. Instead, they should be used only when the supervisor and teacher share a concern about the meaning of the classroom to participants. An instrument should not become a focus for all observation because of its availability or newness. It should be used only if it matches a priority concern of teachers and supervisors.

Summary

There are many ways to observe classrooms. The choice of a particular type of observation depends on the purpose and focus of the observation. Observation enables a supervisor to put a mirror of the classroom up to the teacher, who can then attend to matters previously unknown. Several studies (Brophy and Good, 1974, pp. 297–328) have shown that teachers often change instructional behaviors on their own after their classrooms have been described to them by an observer. The mirror can often be the stimulus for change. The observer must be careful in using interpretations, because such value judgments can actually cloud the mirror and prevent the teacher from seeing his or her own image. At all times, the observer needs to distinguish description from interpretation when recording and explaining events to the teacher.

Exercises

Academic

1. Write a paper contrasting observation systems used purely for assisting teachers to improve their instruction with summative teacher evaluation systems. Cite at least three outside references in your paper.

2. Locate three formative observation instruments in the literature on instructional supervision. Describe the instruments and discuss the specific purpose and procedures for the use of each.

3. Write a paper comparing and contrasting quantitative classroom observation with qualitative classroom observation. Cite relevant works found in the references for Chapter 14 in your writing.

4. Write a paper summarizing Eisner's ideas on educational connoisseurship.

5. Write an essay giving your position on each of the three issues presented at the beginning of this chapter. Support your position with citations from relevant readings listed in the references for Chapter 14.

Field

1. Use a categorical-frequency instrument. Arrange to observe a class and try out the instrument.

2. Use a performance-indicator instrument. Use the instrument during a classroom observation.

3. Write a detached open-ended narrative during a visit to a classroom.

4. Visit a classroom. Write a description of the classroom, learning activities, and teacher-student interactions from the teacher's perspective. Next, write descriptions of the classroom, learning activities, and teacher-supervisor interactions from the students' perspective.

5. Review an instrument used by supervisors in a selected school district during classroom observations. Prepare a written evaluation of the instrument. Include your opinion on whether the instrument fulfills its stated purpose.

Developmental

1. Continue to differentiate between *descriptions* and *interpretations* of observed events by listening to others discuss observations they have made and by reviewing your own comments regarding your observations.

2. Continue to review systems and instruments designed for use as tools for quantitative observations. Attempt to match different systems and instruments with different observation purposes and goals.

3. Through continued readings and practice in classroom observation, especially in listening to teachers and students, begin to develop the skills of Eisner's educational critic.

References

Acheson, K. A., and Gall, M. D. 1992. *Techniques in the clinical supervision of teachers. Preservice and inservice applications* (3rd ed.). White Plains, NY: Longman.

Bales, R. 1951. *Interaction process analysis.* Reading, MA: Addison-Wesley.

Beegle, C., and Brandt, R. M. (Eds.). 1973. *Observational methods in the classroom.* Washington, DC: Association for Supervision and Curriculum Development.

Brophy, J. E., and Good, T. L. 1974. *Teacher-student relationships: Causes and consequences.* New York: Holt, Rinehart and Winston.

Eisner, E. W. 1985. *The educational imagination: On the design and evaluation of school programs,* 2nd ed. New York: Macmillan.

Eisner, E. W. 1986. *A secretary in the classroom.* Paper presented to the American Educational Research Association, San Francisco, April.

Flanders, N. A. 1970. *Analyzing teacher behavior.* Reading, MA: Addison-Wesley.

Glickman, C. D., and Jones, J. W. 1986. Research in supervision: Creating the dialogue. *Educational Leadership* 44(3):83.

Harris, B. M. 1975. *Supervisory behavior in education,* 2nd ed. Englewood Cliffs, NJ: Prentice Hall.

Hyman, R. T. 1975. *School administrator's handbook of teacher supervision and evaluation methods.* Englewood Cliffs, NJ: Prentice Hall.

Jones, K., and Sherman, A. 1980. Two approaches to evaluation. *Educational Leadership* 37:553–557.

Marzano, R. J., Brandt, R., Hughes, C. S., Jones, B. F., Presseisen, B. Z., Rankin, S. C., and Suhor, C. 1988. *Dimensions of thinking: A framework for curriculum and instruction.* Alexandria, VA: Association for Supervision and Curriculum Development.

Medley, D. M., and Mizel, H. E. 1963. Measuring classroom behavior by systematic observation. In N. L. Gage (Ed.), *Handbook of research on teaching.* Skokie, IL: Rand McNally.

Rosenshine, B. V. 1986. Synthesis of research on explicit teaching. *Educational Leadership* 43(7): 60–69.

Simon, A., and Boyer, E. C. 1967. *Mirrors of behavior: An anthology of classroom observation instruments.* 6 vols. Philadelphia: Research for Better Schools.

Spradley, J. P. 1980. *Participant observation.* New York: Holt, Rinehart and Winston.

Suggested Readings

Acheson, A. A., and Gall, M. D. 1992. *Techniques in the clinical supervision of teachers* (3rd ed.). New York: Longman.

Goldhammer, R., Anderson, R. H., and Krajewski, R., J. 1993. *Clinical supervision: Special methods for the supervision of teachers* (3rd ed.). Fort Worth: Harcourt Brace Jovanovich.

15

Research and Evaluation Skills

Perhaps no area in education has gone through such a dramatic expansion in knowledge, techniques, and attention than the field of educational research and evaluation. What once seemed the province of experts, consultants, and "university types" doing laboratory experiments has now become a part of day-to-day operations in schools. The national accountability and testing movement has certainly been a contributing cause. More important has been the role of the literature on effective and successful schools, which has made clear that decisions about instructional changes should be made from a base of comprehensive and credible data about students and that those affected most directly by instructional change (i.e., teachers) should be involved in defining, implementing, and interpreting the research and evaluation agenda.

For example, in a study of 15 exemplary elementary and middle schools in three school districts that had improved instruction in reading and mathematics over a three-year period, a common characteristic of these schools was found to be the deliberate collection of information about student progress and the use of that information to decide on schoolwide actions for changing curriculum, lesson planning, professional development, and individual assistance to teachers. The schools continuously collected and used data about student achievement to determine whether positive changes had resulted and what further revisions in practice needed to be implemented.

> What was notable in all schools and central offices in the three systems was a constant dialogue about instruction. There was time built into the normal work days and there were people who saw their responsibility as engaging teachers in talk about...their students' progress. Teachers were involved in planning and implementing actions. (Glickman and Pajak, 1987, p. 48)

Similarly, Gottfriedson (1986) found that two features prominently mentioned in connection with effective schools were

- A system for monitoring performance and achievement, and use of data to assess progress.
- Collaborative planning and collegial relations, a bias for action. (p. 11)

In schools and districts that do improve instruction, evaluation and research are not perfunctory paper assignments done by a particular person or division to fulfill district or state requirements. Rather, evaluation and research are seen as the basis for determining professional actions as to the what and the how of improving learning for students. Knowledgeable decision making about instruction comes from intense and critical study of the consequences of the common work of teachers: teaching. Including teachers in determining the criteria, procedures, and use of evaluative data in schools is not simply a nice thing to do—*it is essential to do.* If teachers are to extend their own thinking and commitment about collective instruction, they have to be part of the research and evaluation process. Without their involvement, policy makers have denied teachers the intellectual engagement of viewing teaching as a collective activity—"a cause beyond oneself."

Such engagement, in itself, enhances thinking and decisions about individual practice. In a high school in the Southeast, during the year when teachers and administrators in the school began to collect data on profiles of high school dropouts, the dropout rate decreased by more than 12 percent (Glickman, 1989). This was *before* the school had determined what interventions to make. One teacher said, "It simply never occurred to me, until we researched and evaluated our school, that we had a problem with dropouts. I and most of my peers have certainly changed our attitudes towards average students. The dropout rate is coming down right now because of our awareness. I can't wait until next year when we implement new programs!"

Alternative Approaches to Research and Evaluation

Research on and evaluation of instructional programs is based on methodology derived from one of two broad approaches to research, or in some cases a combination of both approaches. These two approaches are *quantitative* and *qualitative*. The difference between quantitative and qualitative research goes way beyond the fact that quantitative results are reported numerically and qualitative results are reported through narrative. The two approaches are based on different conceptions of reality, the purpose of research, the researcher's role, the role of values in research, the relationship between researcher and subject, and appropriate research methodology. Let's begin this discussion by outlining the major differences between these two alternatives

Quantitative and Qualitative Research Compared

A number of scholars have compared quantitative and qualitative research in relation to critical research issues (Bogdan and Biklen, 1992; Borg and Gall, 1989; Fang, 1995; Hathaway, 1995; Lincoln and Guba, 1985; Shank, 1994). The assumptions of quantitative and qualitative researchers regarding seven such issues are discussed below.

What Is the Nature of Reality and Knowledge?   Quantitative research is based on the assumption that there is a single, external reality. Knowledge consists of objective measurements of phenomena which are part of that reality. Complex phenomena can be broken down into simple variables that can be studied independently. Eventually, the study of component variables leads to an overall understanding of a phenomenon, which in turn can lead to prediction and control of the phenomenon.

Qualitative research is based on the assumption that the world consists of multiple realities that are constructed by individuals or groups. Knowledge comes with understanding of an individual's or group's assumptions, relationships, intentions, actions, perceptions, and feelings within a given context. A phenomenon can only be studied holistically. Since each phenomenon is unique, prediction and control of future phenomena are unlikely.

What Are the Goals of Research?   The goals of quantitative research are to identify relationships between variables, explain causes, predict and control phenomena, and develop knowledge that is *generalizable* to other contexts. The goals of qualitative research are to describe phenomena from the perspective of participants, discover multiple realities, and develop a holistic understanding of individual phenomena within particular contexts. This is done through a continuous cycle of intense observation and in-depth description, formation of working hypotheses, more observation and description, and so on.

What Is the Researcher's Role?   In quantitative research the researcher assumes the role of the detached observer. The purpose of detachment is to avoid bias. This detachment extends to the researcher's relationship with the *subjects* of the study. The researcher is to have as little interaction with the subjects as possible. Quantitative research methods are designed to minimize the effects of any unavoidable interaction between the researcher and the study or subjects.

Qualitative research assumes that the researcher and the study will interact and affect each other. In fact, the qualitative researcher intentionally becomes deeply involved with the phenomenon being studied. The researcher attempts to develop empathy, trust, and even friendship with the study's *participants*. The researcher documents interactions with the study and its participants, and critically examines his or her effects on the research and results.

What Is the Importance of Context in Research?   Context is the setting or framework within which the phenomenon being studied exists. The quantitative view is that a phenomenon can be studied independently of its context. Indeed, quantitative research attempts to develop context-free generalizations. Qualitative research assumes that a phenomenon is greatly influenced by its particular context. The whole is greater than the sum of its parts. This is why a qualitative study places so much emphasis on describing context, and usually will not attempt to generalize results to other contexts.

What Place Do Values Have in Research?   Both quantitative and qualitative research admit that values can affect research. Quantitative research responds to the values issue by attempting to make the research as value free as possible through the use of objective research methods. Qualitative research is based on the assumption that the researcher, participants, context, and research methodology all possess values that will inevitably influence the study, and so it is best to describe those values and their effects as part of the study.

What Is the Relationship of Cause and Effect?   Quantitative research assumes that every *effect* can be explained by a preceding *cause* or combination of causes. It attempts to identify cause-effect relationships. Qualitative research assumes that variables which are part of a phenomenon are mutually and simultaneously affecting each other. Thus it is impossible to separate causes from effects.

How Should Research Studies Be Designed?   Shank (1994) compares the quantitative approach to manufacturing: A blueprint for the study is created, then quality control ensures that production takes place according to the blueprint. A hypothesis is stated. A research design, such as correlational, experimental, or quasi-experimental, is chosen. Formal data collection instruments such as inventories, questionnaires, or tests are selected or developed. Subjects are identified and grouped according to precise procedures (random selection, stratified samples, experimental and control groups, and so on). Only after all of the above have been completed does data collection begin; and after data collection is complete, data analysis begins. Analysis involves the use of statistical techniques intended to reduce bias and error, control for extraneous variables, determine whether or not the hypothesis is correct, and indicate to what extent results can be generalized.

Shank (1994) compares qualitative research to *hunting and gathering*—the qualitative researcher is not trying to test a predetermined hypothesis, but is searching for evidence and understanding of processes and relations. The qualitative research design is broad, emergent, and flexible. The research sample is small and hand picked to meet the purpose of the study. Data collection methods include long-term observation, participation, open-ended interviews, gathering of documents and artifacts, videotaping, and photography, to name a few. The most important data collection instrument is the *researcher.* Data analysis consists of: reviewing; inductive coding; comparing; integrating; and constructing themes, concepts, hypotheses, and models. Data collection and data analysis are cyclical and interactive; initial data collection and data analysis may lead to the formulation of a working hypothesis which then calls for a new round of data collection and analysis. The aim of this continuously evolving research design is to develop a body of in-depth knowledge concerning the particular phenomena being studied.

Table 15.1 summarizes our comparison of quantitative and qualitative research.

TABLE 15.1   *Comparison of Quantitative and Qualitative Research*

Research/ Issue	Quantitative Research	Qualitative Research
Nature of Reality and Knowledge	A single, external reality; Knowledge consists of objective measures	Multiple realities; Knowledge comes with understanding of these realities
Goals of Research	Explain causes; Predict and control; Develop generalizable knowledge	Describe phenomena; Discover multiple realities; Holistic understanding
Researcher's Role	Detached observer	Interact and become involved with phenomenon being studied
Importance of Context	Phenomenon can and should be studied separate from context	Phenomenon is greatly influenced by its context; they must be studied together
Values in Research	Make research objective (value free)	Describe values and their inevitable effects
Cause and Effect	Each effect has preceding cause; Identify cause-effect relationships	Variables mutually and simultaneously affect each other
Research Design	Correlational, experimental or quasi-experimental; formal instruments; precise procedures; statistical techniques; Determine if predetermined hypothesis is correct, if results are generalizable	Broad, emergent, and flexible; long term observation, participation; Data collection and analysis are cyclical and interactive; Formulate working hypothesis, developing in-depth knowledge of particular phenomena

Can Quantitative and Qualitative Methods Be Used in the Same Study?

Is it desirable or even possible to effectively use both quantitative and qualitative methods in the same research or evaluation study? There are a number of positions on this issue taken by different experts. One position, taken by some quantitative and some qualitative proponents, is that the approach they embrace is not only incompatible with the other approach, but is so superior to it that the approach they favor should be the only one used in any serious study. A second group of experts agrees with the first group's contention that quantitative and qualitative research are incompatible, but does not endorse one approach as superior to the other. This group takes the position that quantitative research is the more appropriate methodology for some studies, but that qualitative research is more appropriate for others.

A third group of experts believes that quantitative and qualitative research are compatible and that the best studies combine the two approaches. This view may seem curious in light of the comparison of quantitative and qualitative research provided above. But proponents of mixing the two approaches point out that each approach can generate types of information that the other cannot, that only quantitative and qualitative perspectives used together can form a complete picture of the phenomenon being studied, and that the results of one method can help to explain and validate the results of the other (Piontek, 1992).

As the reader of previous chapters in this text may have already predicted, the authors adhere to a fourth, eclectic view concerning the quantitative-qualitative debate. First, we do not agree that quantitative and qualitative research are in all cases incompatible, or that either approach is inherently superior to the other. Based on our own experience as researchers and evaluators, we believe that:

- For *some* studies, using quantitative methods is the best approach.
- For *some* studies, using qualitative methods is the best approach.
- For *many* studies, a combination of quantitative and qualitative methods is the best approach.

The following criteria are recommended for determining whether a quantitative, qualitative, or combined approach is the most appropriate methodology for a research or evaluation study:

1. The context of the study (school history, demographics, culture, climate, and so on)
2. The goals of the study
3. The values and skills of the person or group conducting the study
4. The resources available for the study
5. The values of those who will participate in the study (principals, teachers, students, parents), as well as the time and effort participants are able and willing to contribute (Qualitative studies often require more participant time and effort than quantitative studies.)
6. The values and needs of the audience to whom the study will be reported

In the remainder of this chapter we'll examine individual program evaluation and evaluation of the overall instructional program. The following pages will provide examples of how quantitative and qualitative methods can be applied to each of these types of evaluation.

Judgments

How do we know our instructional programs are successful? Should we continue with the same curriculum, instructional methods, scheduling, and grouping practices, or should changes be made? Evaluating is the act of making such a judgment. How do we decide whether something is good or bad? Frequently, we make judgments with statements such as, "What a great reading program," "What a lousy classroom," or "What wonderful students." How do we really know if something is great, lousy, or wonderful? Wolfe (1969) has offered a tongue-in-cheek classification of five typical methods by which we make such judgments:

Cosmetic method: You examine the program, and if it looks good it is good. Does everybody look busy? The key is attractive and full bulletin boards covered with projects emanating from the project.

Cardiac method: No matter what the data say, you know in your heart that the program was a success. This is similar to the use in medical research of sub-clinical findings.

Colloquial method: After a brief meeting, preferably at a local watering hole, a group of project staff members conclude that success was achieved. No one can refute a group decision.

Curricular method: A successful program is one that can be installed with the least disruption of the ongoing school program. Programs that are truly different are to be eschewed at all costs.

Computational method: If you have to have data, analyze it to death. Whatever the nature of the statistics, use the most sophisticated multivariate regression discontinuity procedures known to humans.

Wolfe's humor aside, let's look at reasonable, valid ways of evaluating. In the turbulence of instructional change, it is useful to know whether the new practice is going to be any better than the old. If not, then we may be investing large amounts of energy without a justifiable increase in instructional benefits to students. As discussed in Chapter 13 (assessing and planning), if we are to make a commitment to instructional change, we must also make a commitment to evaluating that instructional change. If not, then we truly do not know what we are doing.

Evaluating Specific Instructional Programs

How does one make a judgment of worth? When assessing specific instructional programs, there are six components of a comprehensive program evaluation:

1. *Evaluation of needs assessment:* The most basic question that program evaluators can ask is: Was there a need for the program? At first glance, this might seem like an unnecessary evaluation component. Why would a school expend resources to adopt a program unless there is clear evidence of need? Yet, after studying innovations in urban secondary schools, Nelson and Sieber (1976) concluded that schools often adopted innovations because of good salesmanship, the innovation's transportability, or the publicity value of the innovation rather than a desire for educational reform. Also, Berman and McLaughlin (1976) found that schools often adopted innovations in order to receive external funding rather than to respond to locally identified needs. Many new programs, of course, are adopted as a result of genuine needs assessments. In these cases, the needs assessment process (data gathering, data analysis, conclusion drawing) should be reviewed to determine if the assessment was valid—if it identified actual educational needs.

2. *Evaluation of program design:* In Chapter 13 we saw that program planning can take a variety of different forms. For educational programs, some type of coherent, written plan should be made. A second component of program evaluation is to review the written plan. Evaluations should determine whether program goals and objectives are consistent with the needs the program was created to meet (if the goals and objectives are met, will the needs be met?) and whether program activities are consistent with program goals and objectives (if the activities are effectively carried out, will the objectives and goals be met?). Finally, evaluators need to determine if adequate human and material resources have been committed to the program.

3. *Evaluation of readiness:* No matter how critical a need or how logical a plan, programs often fail because some stakeholders (principals, teachers, students, parents, other community members) are not prepared to support implementation. For instance, a sex education program that has been extremely successful in other school districts might be a complete failure in a conservative district if stakeholders are not provided with extensive information about the program and opportunities to have their concerns addressed. Likewise, a peer-coaching program, by itself, is not likely to be successful in a school with a history of teachers exhibiting distrust and animosity toward each other. Extensive communication and trust-building activities would have to precede the peer-coaching program. To carry out this component, evaluators determine if stakeholders were ready for the program, and, if not, whether effective readiness activities were carried out prior to program implementation.

4. *Implementation evaluation:* Key questions evaluators need to answer in this component are: Was the program implemented as planned? If not, why not? and if not, how did the program's implementation differ from the original plan? Three phases of implementation need to be examined: (1) program initiation, (2) program continuation over time, and (3) program integration with the school culture. Implementation evaluation is important because many programs have "failed" because they were never actually implemented as intended, or because initial implementation was followed by a gradual loss of program fidelity. One aspect of implementation that evaluators are wise to examine is the level of administrative support for the program. (In our own work as program evaluators, we have found that a key aspect of effective implementation is continued, coordinated support by central office administrators, supervisors, and principals.)

5. *Evaluation of outcomes:* There are two types of outcomes or products that evaluators can measure. *Intended outcomes* are the program goals and objectives. *Unintended outcomes* are unforeseen results of the program. Unintended outcomes can be positive or negative. We will take a detailed look at measuring program outcomes later in this chapter.

6. *Cost-benefit analysis:* In cost-benefit analysis, evaluators compare the costs of the program (human and material resources expended, unintended negative outcomes) to its benefits (intended and unintended positive outcomes). This component, used infrequently in educational program evaluations, takes us beyond whether or not program goals were met, to judgments about the relative worth of the program.

The authors' observation and review of program evaluations in education have caused us to conclude that most schools do not engage in comprehensive evaluations involving these six components. Rather, typical evaluations tend to include only component 5: evaluation of outcomes. The number of components included in an evaluation will depend on the school's resources, the size of the program to be evaluated, and the purpose of the evaluation. However, a study including all six components will provide those with program decision responsibilities (school committees, curriculum councils, superintendents, school boards, state and federal agencies) the most thorough and informative evaluation results.

Key Decisions in the Program Evaluation Process

Regardless of how many of the six components are included in a program evaluation, a number of key decisions must be made. We will examine each of these decisions.

What Is the Purpose of the Evaluation?

There are two broad purposes of educational evaluation. *Formative evaluation* is intended to improve a program. It is carried out while the program is in progress and can be ongoing throughout the life of the program. *Summative evaluation* results in a definitive judgment about the value of a program. It is carried out after a program has been in existence for a period of time. A summative evaluation is usually the basis for a decision about whether the program will continue, undergo major revisions, or be terminated. Formative and summative program evaluations are not always mutually exclusive. For instance, data gathered for formative evaluations might be reanalyzed later as part of a summative evaluation.

Who Will Evaluate?

Whether the supervisor, a team of faculty members, central office personnel, or private consultants should have major control over evaluation depends on the particular school's resources and the purpose of the evaluation. However, it is critical that teachers be involved in evaluation of instructional programs and the overall instructional effectiveness of their schools and district. All stakeholders (those affected by the decisions from the evaluation) should be not only subjects of study but co-investigators of the study as well. As Greene (1986) has noted, there exists a "consensus on the need for stakeholder participation" (p. 1), and such participation is defined as "shared decision making, rather than just advising or providing input" (p. 9).

For example, Crosby (1982) suggested that teachers—the primary stakeholders in professional development programs—take part in the evaluation of such programs by participating in:

- Clarifying the program's goals and determining indicators of success...
- Developing a design for the evaluation study
- Developing methods of measurement...
- Responding to interviews and other evaluation instruments...
- Reporting on the evaluation study (pp. 152–155)

In short, Crosby proposed that teachers participate in decision making throughout all phases of the evaluation.

What Questions Need to Be Answered?

Specific questions can be formulated for each of the six components of a comprehensive evaluation discussed earlier in this chapter. Evaluation questions will depend on the nature of the program and what members of the evaluation's audience wish to learn about the program. Let's say that a new social studies curriculum is to be evaluated. An *implementation* question might be: To what extent has the new curriculum been implemented at the classroom level? An *outcomes* question might be: What changes in students' knowledge, skills, and attitudes have resulted from the new curriculum? Once the evaluation questions have been formulated, they become the basis for the remainder of the evaluation.

What and How Will Data Be Gathered?

Data sources are persons, places, things, events, or processes from which data needed to answer evaluation questions can be gathered. Examples of data sources are students, teachers, principals, parents, teaching episodes, student products, and school records. *Data-gathering methods* are ways to collect data from sources. Examples include testing, observations, content analysis, case studies, review of records, administration of rating scales and surveys, and interviewing. Our bias is toward using multiple sources of data and multiple data collection methods for each evaluation question. Later in this chapter, we will provide examples of program and school evaluations using multiple sources and methods.

How Will the Data Be Analyzed?

Data analysis is largely determined by the evaluation questions and types of data. Decisions to be made include how to organize, summarize, and display data, and how to reach conclusions based on the data. Central office, university, or private experts may be necessary to assist with complex quantitative or qualitative analysis. Stakeholders, however, can make valuable contributions to data analysis, especially by reviewing results and suggesting explanations, implications, and conclusions.

How Will the Evaluation Be Reported?

After collecting and analyzing the results of tests, observations, surveys, interviews, and testimonials, how should the evaluation be reported? The answer is largely determined by the audience. Most school board members and superintendents will not read a 200-page technical report on the raw data, statistical treatments, and evaluation methodologies. They are interested in the results and conclusions. The technical report should be available to decision makers as a reference to the summarized paper. Any reader of the condensed paper who is confused or desires more information about certain parts of the paper can check the complete technical report.

On the other hand, if the audience for the evaluation report consists of people with sophisticated evaluation skills, a complete technical report would be in order. In a study of violations of evaluation standards (Newman and Brown, 1987, p. 9), among the most frequent violations were "those concerning the evaluator's lack of knowledge of the audience."

Regardless of the audience, there are certain types of information included in most evaluation reports (again, these components will vary in length and technical sophistication depending on the audience). Typical evaluation reports include discussions of

1. The purpose of the evaluation
2. A description of the program being evaluated
3. Evaluation questions or objectives
4. Methodology: data sources, data gathering methods, and data analysis methods
5. Results and conclusions, including strengths and weaknesses of the program
6. Recommendations for the future

Evidence of Program Outcomes

One of the six components of a comprehensive evaluation introduced earlier in this chapter is evaluation of outcomes. In this section, we will focus on what constitutes evidence of the outcomes of a project, grade level, department, school, or district. The criteria and guidelines for the Joint Dissemination Review Panel (1986) of the United States Department of Education, which is commissioned to examine evidence from schools that claim to be effective in attaining goals, describes several models of evidence:

Model One: Achievement/Changes in Knowledge and Skills of Students

Types of Evidence
- Tests of all types (norm referenced, criterion referenced, locally developed)
- Direct ratings of performance/products of performance (e.g., holistic or analytical ratings of writing samples)
- Structured observations of skill demonstrations
- Content analyses of students' projects or products

Model Two: Improvements in Teachers' Attitudes and Behaviors

Types of Evidence
- Assessment of attitudes in the form of rating scales, surveys, and interviews
- Structured observations of changes in teaching behaviors
- Records of teachers' use of instructional time (e.g., planning books, logs)
- Self-reports of instructional time use and instructional methods
- Case studies of changes in teaching behaviors/classroom climate

Model Three: Improvements in Students' Attitudes and Behaviors

Types of Evidence
- School records review (e.g., attendance, courses, grades, promotion and retention, vandalism)
- Health records review
- Attitude assessments
- Case studies of individual students, classes, or schools
- Structured interviews with teachers, parents, and students
- Structured interviews with community service agencies, police, etc.
- Records of disciplinary action
- Postgraduate follow-up to next school level, college, or career choice
- Participant and/or expert testimonials

Selected evidence from these models can be used to research and evaluate a particular instructional project with a selected population within a school (i.e., computer literacy for special education students in elementary school or a new approach to teaching humanities to bilingual students in middle school) or can be used to research and evaluate grade-level, departmental, school, or district instruction.

Multiple Sources and Methods

Now that we've taken a close-up look at evaluating outcomes, let's extend the idea of using multiple data sources and multiple data-gathering methods to a comprehensive evaluation of a science program that has been in place for two years. In the first evaluation component, *evaluation of needs assessment,* data sources might be school records of student achievement in science prior to the new program, teachers who used the old science program, and data from the needs assessment administered to science teachers prior to the school's decision to adopt the new program. Data-gathering methods could include interviews of teachers and review of student achievement and needs assessment data.

For the second component, *evaluation of program design,* data sources might be the new science curriculum (goals, objectives, activities, resources and materials, assessment) and the original needs assessment (for comparison with the curriculum). Data would be collected during comparison of these two sources.

The third component, *evaluation of readiness,* could include as sources the science supervisor, teachers, and records of professional-development activities intended to prepare teachers to implement the new program. Data-gathering methods might be interviews, rating scales asking the supervisor and teachers to rate teacher readiness for the new program, and document review.

In the fourth component, *evaluation of implementation,* we would determine whether the new science curriculum was being used as intended. Data sources could be teachers, science lessons, and reports on material utilization. Corresponding data-gathering methods might be teacher self-reports and surveys, classroom observations, and document review.

For the fifth component, *evaluation of outcomes,* data sources could be test scores, grades, exhibits, awards, extracurricular science activities, students, teachers, and parents. Data-collection methods might include review of school records and student products, classroom observations, interviews, and surveys.

Finally, the sixth component, *cost-benefit analysis,* would involve reviewing the data from component 5 as well as the human and material resources expended on the program, and listing program costs and benefits for review by decision makers.

In the same manner, when we are to assess the overall success of an entire school, we would wish to use multiple sources of data. Besides the usual criterion-referenced and norm-referenced achievement test scores, grades, promotion and retention rates, attendance, enrollment, and discipline referrals, we might desire to assess the school climate and attitudes, perceptions, and behaviors of teachers and students in a school by means of a learning and attitude inventory such as *The Effective School Battery* (Gottfriedson, 1985), the Organizational Climate Description Inventory (Hoy and Clover, 1986), or the National Study of School Evaluation (1987). Many schools are looking at student achievement through a wider lens than standardized competencies tests by collecting portfolios of students' works, exhibits, and projects (Wolf, 1988) and measuring the problem solving and creative and critical thinking of students (Shepard, 1989; Shipman, 1983; Watson and Glaser, 1980; Torrance, 1974). In some school districts, teachers and supervisors develop their own achievement tests to measure what they believe important for their students to learn (Rose, 1987). This practice is quite common in other countries, such as Australia, where panels of teachers make up yearly subject-area examinations and there is virtually no reliance on nationally normed or criterion-referenced, standardized tests (MacCrostie and Hough, 1987).

Epstein (1988) counseled that evidence and design for research and evaluation needs to be conducted in a realistic manner, within the limited scope, financial resources, and human time of a school. She urged that schools first look to existing data—such as student progress reports, achievement scores, exhibits, and attendance—before looking for additional data. Likewise, Gable (1986), in reviewing guiding principles for program evaluation, stated, "Data collection for evaluation will, to the extent possible, make primary use of existing data sources. The history of local school district practices in effectively using existing information for evaluation is poor" (p. 5). Epstein concluded by reminding us of the purpose of evaluation: "Research and evaluation are not magical processes. Good evaluations make intuitive sense—they ask meaningful questions and answer them in logical ways. What questions do you ask yourselves when you wonder how well your program is doing? Those are the questions you should be answering" (p. 12).

Overall Instructional Program Evaluation

Evaluating a school's overall instructional program is different from evaluating specific programs. In this section we'll outline an evaluation model that we have used when serving as consultants to schools wishing to evaluate the quality of their instruction with an eye toward comprehensive, school-wide instructional improvement. We always recommend extensive participation by the school community in planning the evaluation, developing data collection methods, analyzing data, and drawing conclusions about current quality and needed change.

Phase One: Selecting Areas to Be Examined

The evaluation process begins with a meeting with the school's administration and an evaluation steering committee representing key stakeholders from the school community. At that meeting we recommend the following broad areas for evaluation, based on the rationale that each of these areas is significantly related to the success of the school's overall instructional program:

1. Community characteristics
2. School culture and climate
3. School governance
4. Student characteristics
5. Teacher characteristics
6. Parent characteristics
7. Instructional supervision
8. Curriculum and curriculum development process

9. Classroom teaching practices
10. Student assessment methods
11. Student achievement
12. Professional development programs
13. Parent and community involvement programs
14. Relationships with other schools, central office, and external organizations

Of course it's up to the school district or school to decide which areas to evaluate, and the steering committee may wish to delete or add evaluation areas. However, most steering committees agree that a comprehensive evaluation needs to examine all of the above areas. At this initial meeting we also propose the remainder of the evaluation process outlined here, with the understanding that the actual evaluation plan will result from a collaborative effort of the consultants and steering committee with input from all of those who will be affected by the evaluation.

Phase Two: Identifying Specific Evaluation Questions

The second phase of the process begins with a large group session attended by administrators, teachers, other staff members, parents, and other community members. After a general session to review the areas to be examined in the evaluation, the group splits up into small planning teams. The number of planning teams is equal to the number of areas to be examined. To the extent possible, each of the stakeholder groups listed above is represented within each planning team. Each team is assigned one of the areas for evaluation decided on in phase one and the task of recommending specific evaluation questions for their area. For example, the *community characteristics* planning team agrees on a set of evaluation questions about the community that it believes should be answered by the evaluation, the *school culture and climate* team proposes a set of evaluation questions concerning their assigned area, and so on. A *community characteristics* evaluation question might be "To what extent are community resources used to enhance teaching and learning in our school"? A *school culture and climate* question might be "Is our school culture consistent with the research on cultures found in successful schools?"

After all planning teams agree on proposed evaluation questions for their broad area, each team presents and explains its recommendations to a general session. Suggestions for deleting, adding, or revising questions are made by general session participants, then considered by the appropriate teams. After each planning team has had the opportunity to revise proposed questions, each team presents its final recommendations to another general session. At this final general session, the entire body of participants votes on whether to include each proposed evaluation question in the evaluation. After the large group session is completed, the consultants and steering committee rewrite the evaluation questions for each area, so that the questions can be presented in a common format. Although the language of a question may be revised, the basic content of the question must remain as it was approved at the general session.

Phase Three: Designing the Evaluation

Phase three consists of consultants, the steering committee, and planning teams collaborating to design the evaluation proper. Teams propose sources (persons, places, things, events, processes) from which data necessary to answer each of their evaluation questions can be gathered, as well as data-gathering methods (testing, observations, content analysis, case studies, record review, rating scales, surveys, interviews, and so on). For reasons of coordination and efficiency, however, it is the evaluation steering committee that makes the final decisions on data sources and data-gathering methods.

After identifying sources and methods, it is time to select or design data gathering instruments such as tests, classroom observation systems, written surveys, interview guides, and so on. Planning teams make suggestions for specific test items, survey and interview questions, classroom behaviors to be observed, and so on, then the consultants and steering committee construct the instruments. With the wide variety of areas to be assessed, efficiency becomes critical. For example, let's assume that six planning teams each propose several teacher survey questions aimed at gathering data for their assigned areas and research questions. Rather than constructing six different surveys, the consultants and evaluation committee might design a single survey divided into six sections, with the questions within each section designed to gather data sought by a different evaluation team. Figure 15.1 provides a matrix for planning an evaluation of a school's overall instructional program. The grid is used to develop an overview of data sources and data-gathering methods relative to each area to be assessed.

Phase Four: Gathering and Analyzing Data

Teachers, supervisors, and consultants can all assist in gathering data needed to answer evaluation questions. For example, teachers can interview or survey students, gather representative student work, or videotape sample lessons. Supervisors can conduct classroom observations, interview or survey parents, or gather schoolwide student-achievement data. Consultants can provide technical assistance, interview or survey teachers, or conduct qualitative case studies. The best matches of personnel with data gathering assignments will depend on the nature of the data to be collected and the skills and interests of participants, and thus will vary from school to school. In any evaluation, however, it is essential to clearly define (1) who will be responsible for collecting each type of data, and (2) the data gathering procedures they will follow. Teachers and other staff who will collect data may need staff development to acquire necessary data gathering skills.

Teachers can also work with supervisors and consultants to analyze evaluation data. Although it may be necessary for consultants to perform more complex statistical or qualitative analysis, teachers can engage in a variety of data analysis activities. They can assist in organizing, reviewing, comparing, and interpreting most types of data, and can participate in data-based decisions concerning needed improvements in the school's instructional program.

FIGURE 15.1 Planning Grid for Evaluating Overall Instructional Program

Areas to Be Assessed	Data Sources and Data-Gathering Methods																															
	Students				Teachers				School Leadership				Parents				Community				Central Office				Written Curriculum				School Records			
	R	O	S	I	R	O	S	I	R	O	S	I	R	O	S	I	R	O	S	I	R	O	S	I	R	O	S	I	R	O	S	I
Community Characteristics																																
School Culture & Climate																																
School Governance																																
Student Characteristics																																
Teacher Characteristics																																
Parent Characteristics																																
Instructional Supervision																																
Curriculum																																
Classroom Teaching																																
Student Assessment																																
Student Achievement																																
Professional Development																																
Parent-Community Involvement																																
External Relations																																

Key: R = Review of existing data (demographic data, student achievement data, etc.)
O = Observation or videotaping
S = Written survey, rating scale, etc.
I = Interview

Checks (✓) are placed in appropriate cells to indicate the relationship of areas to be assessed, data sources, and data gathering methods.

Data gathering and data analysis need not be treated as discreet activities. Analysis of data gathered early in the evaluation process may indicate the need to collect additional data in order to adequately answer an evaluation question. Data gathering and analysis thus can be viewed as an interactive cycle rather than a linear process. The data gathering and analysis process is coordinated by the consultants and steering committee. Figure 15.2 contains an example of a chart which can be used to coordinate gathering and analysis of data for each evaluation question.

Phase Five: Preparing and Presenting the Evaluation Report

Due to the variety of areas addressed in an evaluation of the overall instructional program, this type of evaluation report will be more extensive than an evaluation report on a specific program. The report should address not only each area that was assessed, but also *relationships* between those areas. For example, if most teachers report that the school culture (one area assessed) affects their classroom teaching (another area), observed effects should be discussed in the report. Conclusions made in the report should be based on data gathered during the study and collaborative interpretation of that data.

Recommendations for improving the school's overall instructional program should be directly related to the study's results and conclusions. Some recommendations for improvement will be for specific areas (school governance, curriculum, classroom teaching, and so on), but others will be comprehensive, involving suggested changes that will impact several or all of the areas that have been assessed. Since implementation of all recommendations may not be feasible, they should be rank ordered. Like reports on specific programs discussed earlier, the depth and length of the report on an evaluation of the overall instructional program should be tailored to the intended audience, with different audiences receiving different types of reports. Finally, just as we have argued that teachers and other stakeholders should be involved in planning and carrying out the evaluation, we also recommend that representatives of these various groups participate in scheduled presentations of results to the central office, school board, and community groups.

Other Considerations for Program Evaluation

Certain considerations arise for a supervisor regardless of the type of evaluation to be employed.

Statistical versus Educational Significance

The discussion of quantitative research of special school projects should include the distinction between statistical significance and educational significance. An uninformed consumer of educational research can be impressed by statistics and

FIGURE 15.2 Chart for Planning Data Gathering and Analysis

Evaluation Question	Coordinator	Evaluation Team Members	Data Sources	Data Gathering Methods	Data Analysis Methods	Evaluation Timeline	Resources Needed
1)							
2)							
3)							
4)							
5)							
6)							

lose sight of educational significance. *Statistical significance* is the mathematical analysis of scores that gives a confidence level about the truth of the results. *Educational significance* includes the overall benefits of using a particular treatment program. For example, if we study the results of a professional development program for social studies teachers and find that student attitude gains from the experimental teachers were significant at the .01 level over student attitude gains from the control group, does this mean that all social studies teachers should undergo the program? Maybe, but maybe not. Besides the obvious need to see whether there were other student gains—in achievement, attendance, or work completed—we also need to consider the *magnitude* of the gain against its *cost*. If we had tested attitudes of 100 students in both experimental and control groups and found that on a nine-point scale the experimental students increased from a pretest average score of 5.0 to a posttest score of 6.5, and the control students increased from a pretest average of 5 to a posttest score of 6.1, the 0.4 difference might be statistically significant at the .01 level. The instructional supervisor would have to consider whether a 0.4 difference on a nine-point attitudinal scale is worth the program cost, including teacher time, expense for consultants, administrative work, and so on. Decisions about educational significance can be aided greatly by knowledge of statistical significance, but human judgment must be used to weigh the overall benefits.

What about Achievement Tests and New Forms of Assessment?

The use of achievement tests as a single indicator of academic achievement of program or school effort is misleading and can give schools inaccurate results, leading to inaccurate evaluation. Educators can improve test scores without making real changes in curriculum and instruction, by such ploys as withholding the test from students expected to perform poorly, relabeling students at a lower grade level on test-taking days, teaching test items, and guiding students to the correct answers (see Prell and Prell, 1986). As a result of such manipulations, test scores can be high and totally invalid. Furthermore, even without manipulations, gains or losses in achievement scores can be erroneously interpreted. For example, schools evaluate the success of their basic-skills programs by comparing the previous year's standardized test scores with the current year's scores. Unfortunately, only a comparison of alternative forms of the same test will yield valid results. Likewise, schools might use the same publisher's test in early fall and late spring and find large but inaccurate gains because the scores in late spring were normed to the fall population of test takers. Another common error in using achievement tests for evaluation is the lack of pre- and posttest scores for *each* student. Often, the average pretest scores of a group of students will be compared to the average posttest scores of the same group, even though the group at the end of the year is seldom the same group as at the beginning. Some students will have moved away, been suspended, or been reassigned; new students will have replaced them. Only the scores of those students who participated in the project both at the beginning and at the end can be used for program evaluation.

A further problem with achievement tests is using the score on the selection test for a program as the pretest and then using an alternative form of the same test as the posttest. This is a common problem with federally funded and state-funded compensatory programs in schools. If a remedial reading program or a gifted education program uses an alternative form of the original screening test as a posttest, the results will be hopelessly skewed because of what is called *regression toward the mean*. If we test all students on an achievement test and then retest the lowest and highest scorers on the following day, the low scorers will test significantly higher and the high scorers will test significantly lower. This is true because of the test, not the students. Therefore, using a form of the test used to screen high or low students as a posttest for program evaluation will show gains or losses that have nothing to do with the program. The easiest way to prevent this problem is to use a different test, not a different form of the screening test, for pre- and posttest evaluation. (A supervisor who plans to use achievement tests for program evaluation should read the excellent and inexpensive federal publication entitled *A Practical Guide to Measuring Project Impact on Student Achievement*, No. 1, U.S. Office of Education, Washington, DC.)

A growing number of states have mandated *high-stakes achievement tests*—standardized tests used to evaluate student achievement, accompanied by performance-based sanctions and rewards. Such tests can be used to determine whether students are promoted or graduate as well as the effectiveness of teachers, schools, and districts. Newspapers invariably compare the test scores of schools within the community, and scores can affect the amount of state funding received by schools. Not surprisingly, tremendous pressure to improve test scores is felt by administrators, supervisors, and teachers.

Corbett and Wilson (1991) argue that policy makers misuse testing in three ways:

1. They inappropriately use student test scores as guides for correcting complex systems.
2. By using uniform measures, they ignore differences among schools.
3. The tests create local conditions which make the reforms intended by the policy makers impossible.

Madaus (1988) also criticizes high-stakes testing:

The long-term negative effects on curriculum, teaching, and learning of using measurement as the engine, or primary motivating power of the educational process, outweigh those positive benefits attributed to it. The tests can become the furious master of the educational process, not the compliant servant they should be. Measurement-driven instruction invariably leads to cramming; narrows the curriculum; concentrates attention on those skills most amenable to the multiple-choice format; constrains the creativity and spontaneity of teachers and students; and finally demeans the professional judgment of teachers. (pp. 84–85)

Research tends to support critics of high-stakes testing.* Darling-Hammond and Wise (1985) interviewed teachers from three large districts, each in a different mid-Atlantic state. They reported that standardized tests caused narrowed curriculum, teaching to the tests, and a reduction in regular testing. Corbett and Wilson (1989) identified effects of a mid-Atlantic state's testing program, including teaching to the test, disruption of teachers' work lives, decreased reliance on teachers' professional judgment, and increased concern about legal liability.

Gilman and Reynolds (1991) reported that side effects of a midwestern states' mandated test included the state's indirect control of curriculum and instruction, cheating by administrators and teachers, unhealthy competition between schools, negative effects on school-community relations, negative psychological and physical effects on students, and loss of school time. Brown (1993) interviewed administrators and teachers in a southern, midwestern, and eastern state on their perceptions of high-stakes tests in those states. These educators mistrusted the state legislature and education agency, were confused about the tests' purposes, challenged the tests' effectiveness, believed test results were overemphasized, and considered the tests to be inappropriate measures of accountability.

Ivory (1993) found a wide gap between minority groups and White Non-Hispanics on scores of a southwestern state's high-stakes test, with the latter group scoring higher. Ivory suggested that this disparity in test scores might be due to differential preparation of different ethnic groups, or to test cultural bias. Holman (1994) found that Latino students from a district in the same southwestern state passed a Spanish version of the state's test at the beginning of the third grade but failed the English version of the test taken at the end of the fourth grade. Holman (1995a, 1995b, 1996) also carried out a series of studies in which she found that students of higher economic status and non-Hispanic White students scored higher on the test than students of lower economic status and minority students.

Finally, Gordon and Reese (1997) surveyed and interviewed teachers in a southwestern state on the effects of high-stakes testing on students, teachers, and schools. They found that most teachers were required to relate their daily lesson plans to the test, and taught to the test through "drill and kill" teaching methods. These teachers reported that high-ability students were bored with sitting through drill on test objectives that they had already learned, and at-risk students became demoralized by test failure and assignment to remedial classes designed to raise their test scores. Teachers reported less emphasis in areas of the curriculum not measured by the state test, including a de-emphasis on teaching higher-level thinking skills. Teachers in the study agreed that the state test was not a valid indicator of school success.

Considering all of the negative effects of high-stakes testing, is there an alternative method of measuring student learning and school success? The answer is yes! At the student level, performance-based assessments of what students can

*This discussion of research on high-stakes testing summarizes a review found in Gordon and Reece (1997).

actually do in real situations can be documented through the review and rating of student projects, presentations, and portfolios containing samples of student work collected over a period of time. At the school level, overall instructional program evaluations based on comprehensive models like the one proposed in this chapter can include but go well beyond the use of standardized achievement test results to measure school success and identify areas for schoolwide improvement.

Bernhardt (1994) recommends the use of *school portfolios* to document school effectiveness and improvement goals. Her recommendations for entries in the student achievement section of a school portfolio include the following:

- A description of the student population
- Essential intended student learning
- A description of instructional and student assessment strategies
- A variety of measures of student learning over time, including disaggregated standardized achievement test results, rubrics that rate student performances, student exhibition scores, and ratings on continuous student improvement continuums
- Student learning needs
- Descriptions of strategies to meet learning needs
- Evaluation of the implementation and effects of strategies
- Improvement goals

Perhaps the most far-reaching change in education over the last decade has been an expanded conception of assessment. Hopefully, states will discard standardized achievement tests as the sole measure of school effectiveness, and adopt a variety of authentic assessment measures. In the future we expect a great proliferation at the local school, district, state, and national levels on assessments that move beyond the traditional multiple-choice, paper-and-pencil, one-right-answer format (Spray, 1993).

What Is the Supervisor's Role in Program Evaluation?

A supervisor cannot be personally involved in every evaluation but should be responsible for seeing that evaluation of special projects and of the overall instructional programs is ongoing. The supervisor—whether school principal, department head, lead or master teacher, district director, or assistant superintendent—should constantly remind himself or herself of the standards for evaluation of educational programs (Stufflebeam, 1981).

1. *Utility:* Ensure that an evaluation will serve the practical information needs of the audiences.
2. *Feasibility:* Ensure that an evaluation will be realistic, prudent, diplomatic, and frugal.

3. *Propriety:* Ensure that an evaluation will be conducted legally, ethically, and with due regard for the welfare of those involved in the evaluation, as well as those affected by its results.

4. *Accuracy:* Ensure the conveyance of technically adequate information.

With these standards in mind, there are two questions that serve as the core to a purposeful school (Hamilton, 1980):

1. Is what we are doing working?

2. How does it work?

Answers to those questions can be gathered through informal means such as surveys, interviews, and group discussions, or through the more formal means of observations, questionnaires, and tests. Only as we remind ourselves of these questions and seek answers can actions be taken that improve instruction. Chapter 20 will show how such asking and answering can be an integral supervisory task of everyday school life.

Teacher Evaluation

Although teacher evaluation involves some of the same skills as program evaluation (e.g., data gathering, data analysis), it is essentially a separate process requiring different strategies and techniques. In this section we will compare summative and formative teacher evaluation, propose that these two types of evaluation be carried out separately, discuss self-evaluation, and consider team evaluation.

Comparing Summative and Formative Teacher Evaluation

Summative and Formative are two broad categories of teacher evaluation. **Summative Teacher Evaluation** is an administrative function intended to meet the organizational need for teacher accountability. It involves decisions about the level of a teacher's performance. Summative evaluation always seeks to determine if the teacher has met minimum expectations. If the teacher has not met his or her professional responsibilities, the summative process documents inadequate performance for the purpose of remediation and, if necessary, termination. Sometimes summative evaluation also gathers data to determine if a teacher is eligible for rewards provided by the district for outstanding performance.

Summative evaluation is based on policies which mandate its purpose, frequency, and procedures. Teacher performance is usually documented on an evaluation form. On the form, an administrator completes check lists, rating scales, or narratives indicating the extent to which the teacher has met performance criteria. Evaluation forms usually are standard (same criteria for all teachers) and global (general enough to apply to teachers with different responsibilities). Evaluation forms judge teachers on the quality of their instruction, including such areas as classroom climate, planning, the teaching act, and classroom management (Shinkfield & Stufflebeam, 1995). But evaluation criteria usually include non-instructional areas as well, such as compliance with school regulations, cooperation with colleagues, completion of extra-curricular assignments, and so on.

Evaluation instruments must be valid (accurate) and reliable (consistent). Valid instruments are those that include all criteria considered essential for effective performance, exclude criteria considered extraneous to effective performance, and weight relevant criteria in proportion to their importance (Haefele, 1993). Reliable instruments include low inference (as nearly objective as possible) rather than high inference (requiring a high level of evaluator subjectivity) indicators. For example, *"teacher clarity"* is an example of a high inference indicator, and *"uses examples when explaining"* is an example of a low inference indicator (Haefele 1993, p. 25). Reliability also requires that administrators be properly trained in the use of the evaluation instrument, so that they become aware of rating errors to avoid and develop a high level of inter-evaluator reliability (agreement with experts and other administrators in their ratings of the same teacher).

In addition to validity and reliability of individual evaluations, experts suggest that evaluations be done several different times during the evaluation period rather than relying on a one-shot visit to a teacher's classroom. Also recommended are a pre-evaluation conference in which the administrator and teacher discuss the evaluation process, and a post-evaluation conference in which the administrator reviews the results of the evaluation. Finally, legal and ethical considerations require that when a teacher's performance has been judged to be inadequate, the teacher be notified of deficiencies, given an opportunity to respond, provided a remediation plan and support for implementing the plan, and be re-evaluated (Sutton, 1989).

Formative teacher evaluation is a supervisory function intended to assist and support teachers in professional growth and the improvement of teaching. It is focused on the needs of teachers rather than on the organization's need for accountability. Unlike summative evaluation, which usually considers teacher behavior inside and outside the classroom, formative evaluation is focused only on teaching and learning. While summative evaluation is concerned with a summary of performance over a specific time period, formative evaluation is ongoing and concerned with continuous improvement. Rather than relying on standardized evaluation instruments that gather data on all essential performance criteria, formative evaluation is usually based on *systematic observation*, which is limited to a single aspect of classroom process (e.g., questioning techniques, student participation, classroom movement, and so on). Thus, the observation systems described in Chapter 14 are well suited for formative evaluation.

McGreal (1989) recommends that, in addition to classroom observation data, classroom artifacts be analyzed to evaluate teaching. Artifacts include such things as assignments, experiments, practice activities, projects, quizzes, and tests. Although artifacts could be used as summative evaluation data, their variety and idiosyncrasy mean that comparing many of them to standardized criteria is difficult if not impossible. Artifacts are more useful for formative evaluation. Analysis of artifacts can help supervisors and teachers identify specific areas for instructional improvement as well as plan and monitor improvement efforts. Analysis of systematic observation data and artifacts together increases the value of formative evaluation.

Because it is not concerned with standardized, global criteria, formative evaluation can concentrate on particular contexts and needs of individual teachers. Since its purpose is helping teachers, not judging them, formative evaluation is not concerned with legal issues like due process. Rather, it is concerned with building trust and rapport, developing a collegial relationship between evaluator and teacher, and addressing teacher needs and concerns. Although some have recommended that students, peers, and parents participate in summative evaluation, administrators and teachers have resisted such involvement. However, student, peer, and parent feedback is much more likely to be offered and accepted if done as part of formative evaluation, purely for the purpose of helping the teacher to improve his or her instruction.

Table 15.2 summarizes our comparison of summative and formative teacher evaluation.

Why Summative and Formative Evaluation Should be Separate

Most school districts have a single evaluation system, and maintain that their system meets both summative and formative needs. However, when schools attempt to carry out summative and formative evaluation simultaneously, they tend to place primary emphasis on summative goals, and formative evaluation is reduced to secondary status (Stiggins and Bridgeford, 1984). *"Too often school districts espouse a strong growth-oriented position but the evaluation system constructed does not reflect that stance"* (McGreal, 1989, p. 38).

Evaluation systems that purport to combine summative and formative evaluation while relying on rating scales alone are particularly suspect. *"A school system that relies solely on periodic evaluations of teacher performance through rating scales may capture data suited for in-system summative purposes but will be handicapped in pursuing formative/developmental objectives..."* (Allison, 1981, p. 15; emphasis in original). One reason for this is that summative rating scales are designed to be standardized, global, legally defensible, efficiently completed and processed, and include many non-instructional criteria. This means not only that the ratings have little value for formative evaluation, but also that the richest, most meaningful data for formative assessment is precluded (Allison, 1981; Stiggins and Bridgeford, 1984).

It is widely recognized that summative evaluation, while necessary to make employment decisions, does not lead to instructional improvement for most teachers (Stiggins and Bridgeford, 1984). In fact, summative evaluation can actually discourage improvement by promoting *"negative feelings about evaluation*

TABLE 15.2 *Comparison of Summative and Formative Teacher Evaluation*

	Summative	Formative
Function	Administrative	Supervisory
Purpose	Accountability; Judgment on teacher performance; Employment decisions	Assistance; Professional development; Improvement of teaching
Scope	Instruction, Compliance with regulations, Extracurricular responsibilities, Personal qualities	Instruction
Focus	Evaluation form	Any classroom data (observation, artifacts, etc.) relevant to the teacher's instructional concerns and needs
Duration	Set period (usually one academic year)	Ongoing (aimed at continuous improvement)
Concerns	Standardization, validity, reliability, due process	Building trust, rapport, collegiality; Understanding context; Understanding and addressing teacher concerns and needs
Evaluator	Usually an administrator; Final decision by administrator	Administrator, supervisor, self, peers, students, sometimes parents

which, in turn, lead to a lack of participation and a lower likelihood of teachers being willing to alter classroom behavior" (McGreal, 1982, p. 303). Successful formative evaluation depends on trust and open communication between the teacher and evaluator. Yet summative evaluation is potentially punitive (Sutton, 1989). The possibility of a bad performance rating is always lurking in the background. It's no wonder that the two types of evaluation don't mix!

We're not arguing that summative evaluation should be eliminated in favor of formative evaluation. Both types of evaluation are necessary. Like Popham (1988), we maintain that since they have entirely different purposes, they need to be kept separate. With McGreal (1982), we argue that the likelihood that either type of evaluation system will succeed is greater if both systems are internally consistent, which can only be accomplished by the two systems being kept separate. If separated, can the two systems co-exist? Yes, but only if the purpose of each is clearly defined, they are perceived by teachers as distinct, and the integrity of each is protected (Allison, 1981).

How to Separate Summative and Formative Evaluation

One way to separate the two types of evaluation is to use different evaluators. For example, first year teachers (who clearly need to have both types of evaluation) could have their summative evaluation carried out by an administrator and formative evaluation by an experienced teacher assigned as their mentor. Experienced teachers could receive summative evaluation from the principal and formative evaluation from an assistant principal for instruction, lead teacher, or peer coach. There are many different combinations of summative and formative evaluators. The important thing is to make clear to everyone who is responsible of each type of evaluation, and to have each evaluator carry out their assessment separately from the other.

Another way to separate summative and formative evaluation relates to the time period when each is carried out. For example, all summative evaluations could be carried out in the fall of each school year, leaving the remainder of the year for formative assessment. When this strategy is used, the same person or persons can perform both types of evaluation. This strategy does not work as well if formative evaluation is carried out in the fall and summative evaluation takes place throughout the rest of the year. This is because the teacher involved in formative evaluation during the fall realizes that summative evaluation is looming on the horizon. That knowledge may affect the willingness of the teacher to engage in open and honest communication about his or her need for instructional improvement. Better to get the summative evaluation out of the way early in the year, give the teacher his or her "seal of approval," and then allow the teacher and supervisor to engage in non-judgmental assessment for the remainder of the school year. A long-term variation of the "separate time periods" strategy is to conduct summative evaluation throughout the first year of a multi-year cycle, and then focus on formative evaluation for the next two to three years, returning to a summative year at the beginning of the next three to four year cycle. Should serious problems with a teacher's performance develop during a formative assessment year, that teacher could be shifted back to a summative evaluation-remediation track until the problem is resolved.

A third way of separating summative and formative evaluation has been suggested by Thomas McGreal (1983). Under McGreal's model, a clear and visible set of minimum performance expectations would be developed, including administrative, personal, and instructional expectations. Teacher performance regarding these minimal expectations would be continuously, informally monitored, but no special procedures or evaluation instruments would be established. If a problem occurred with a teacher's performance, the administrator would remind the teacher of minimum expectations. If the problem continued to occur, the administrator would issue to the teacher a written notice of the teacher's deficiency, with a copy placed in the teacher's file. If serious violations continued even after the formal notice, the administrator would recommend more serious administrative action. Beyond the contingencies outlined above, there would be no standard summative evaluation process or annual write-up. This would take care of summative evaluation. Most of the time and energy spent on evaluation would be for formative assessment, including goal setting, a focus on teaching, systematic classroom observation, and collecting and analyzing additional classroom data. This additional data could include peer, parent, student, and self-evaluation, as well as student performance and classroom artifacts (McGreal, 1983).

Which strategy for separating summative and formative evaluation is the best for a district or school will depend on the level of administrative and supervisory expertise, the size of the staff, teacher preference, and available resources. The important thing is that they be kept separate. Doing so will mean that both summative and formative evaluation are carried out more effectively.

Self-Evaluation

Self-evaluation can be an important part of the formative evaluation process for teachers functioning at moderate or high levels of development, expertise, and commitment. Self-assessment can take a variety of forms, including any of the following:

- Visits to the classrooms of several expert teachers for the purpose of comparing expert teaching to one's own teaching, and identifying self-improvement goals based on such comparison
- Videotaping one's own teaching across several lessons, then analyzing teaching performance while reviewing the videotape
- Designing or selecting and analyzing results of surveys or questionnaires administered to students or parents
- Interviewing supervisors, peers, students, or parents about effective teaching and learning or about one's own instructional performance
- Keeping a journal of teaching experiences, problems, and successes, accompanied by critical reflection for the purpose of instructional improvement
- A comprehensive review of student achievement on traditional tests as well as student projects, presentations, portfolios, social behavior, and so on
- The development of a teaching portfolio for the purpose of self-reflection and analysis. Danielson (1996) recommends a variety of items for possible inclusion in a portfolio, including unit and lesson plans, knowledge of students and resources, videotapes of teaching, examples of student work, written reflections on lessons taught, and logs on professional service, growth, and research. Langer (Teaching for Performance, 1996) argues for a more focused approach, in which the teacher's portfolio documents a process in which the teacher defines a problem, sets an improvement goal, designs a plan to reach the goal, implements the plan, collects data on professional growth, and reflects upon results. Both Danielson's broad approach and Langer's focused approach go beyond the documentation of

teaching accomplishments (the purpose of portfolios used in summative teacher evaluation) by providing teachers with opportunities for self-assessment as the basis for instructional improvement.

It's important to note that self-evaluation of teaching need not be done in isolation. Videotapes, survey or interview results, journals, student achievement data, and teacher portfolios can be analyzed and discussed collaboratively with a supervisor or peers, and in some cases with students or parents. The process is called self-evaluation because the teacher assumes full responsibility for decision making regarding planning and implementing the evaluation as well as the instructional improvement plan which results. Once the teacher has completed the self-evaluation, she or he may select from a number of vehicles for meeting instructional improvement goals. The teacher might request clinical supervision from a formally designated supervisor, become part of a peer coaching program (see Chapter 16), or begin an individualized professional development program (see Chapter 18).

Team Evaluation

McGreal (Brandt, 1996) has called for a new generation of formative evaluation models focused on teams of teachers evaluating their teaching and developing group instructional improvement plans consistent with school goals. In team evaluation, the supervisor assumes the role of facilitator and meets with the team periodically (Brandt, 1996). This movement toward team evaluation and team-based instructional improvement is consistent with research findings that successful schools are characterized by collegiality and collaboration centered on discussion, critique, and improvement of teaching.

Summary

Educational program evaluation has been influenced heavily by educational research design. The attention to school performance has stimulated multiple data sources, research designs, and compositions of evaluation teams. A consensus on the need for involving stakeholders in program evaluation has occurred. We must be cautious in selecting instruments that measure what we truly wish to find out about a program. Various types of educational evaluations are used for specific programs and for the overall instructional program. It is not sufficient to know intuitively that a program is good or bad. Rather, decisions about revising, improving, or discarding need to be made with multiple sources of information. The school as a collective enterprise must center its work on questions of educational value and use answers to those questions as guidance for instructional change. Finally, summative and formative teacher evaluation are both necessary but need to be separate. Formative evaluation is more likely to lead to the improvement of instruction.

Exercises

Academic

1. Locate one qualitative study and one quantitative study in educational research. Write a summary of each study. Include in each summary a description of the study's purpose, participants, methodology, results, and conclusions.

2. Locate and summarize evaluations (not descriptions) of three instructional programs. Include in each summary a description of the evaluation participants, methodology, results, and conclusions. Discuss your perceptions of the quality of each evaluation.

3. Locate and review a program evaluation model not discussed in Chapter 15. Write a description and critique of the model.

4. Compare and contrast quantitative research with qualitative research. Refer to at least four outside sources in the paper.

5. A traditional debate in supervision is whether summative and formative teacher evaluation should be integrated within the same evaluation system or kept separate. Find authors (other than the authors of this book) on both sides of this issue. Write a paper summarizing the arguments of the authors.

Field

1. Interview the individual in a school district who is ultimately responsible for evaluating specific and overall instructional programs about procedures for carrying out such evaluations. Write a report summarizing the interview and evaluating the school district program's specific and overall instructional evaluation methods.

2. Interview a person who has served on a self-study team as part of a school evaluation. Include questions on the interviewee's role and function as a team member, self-study methods used by the team, team conclusions and recommendations, changes ultimately made as a result of the self-study, and the interviewee's reactions to his or her participation. Prepare a report on the interview.

3. Develop a written plan for evaluating a specific instructional program with which you are familiar (for example, a K–6 math program, a senior high school Spanish program, or a remedial reading program).

4. Interview a supervisor to determine his or her views on three universal concerns about program evaluation addressed in the chapter: Who should evaluate? How should an evaluation be reported? What is the supervisor's role in evaluation? Prepare a written or verbal report on the interview.

5. Interview a school administrator who has primary responsibility for both summative and formative evaluation of teachers. Ascertain whether the administrator attempts to separate these two functions, and if so, how he or she attempts to maintain such separation. Question the administration on the advantages and disadvantages of such dual responsibility. Prepare a report on your interview.

Developmental

1. Begin to analyze judgments made by educational leaders and others regarding instructional programs to determine which decisions are based on comprehensive

evaluation and which are based on cosmetic, cardiac, colloquial, curricular, or computational methods.

2. Begin an in-depth investigation of alternative models for instructional program evaluation.

3. If the opportunity presents itself, volunteer for membership on a school self-study team or a visiting school evaluation team.

References

Allison, D. J. 1981. *Process evaluation: Some summarizing and integrating notes on the organizational implications of this form of teacher evaluation.* (ERIC ED 235 580)

Berman, P., and McLaughlin, M. 1976. Implementation of educational innovation. *Educational Forum 40*(31):345–370.

Bogdan, R. C., and Biklen, S. K. 1992. *Qualitative research for education: An introduction to theory and methods* (2nd ed.). Boston: Allyn and Bacon.

Borg, W. R., and Gall, M. D. 1989. *Educational research: An introduction* (5th ed.). New York: Longman.

Brandt, R. 1996. On a new direction for teacher evaluation: A conversation with Tom McGreal. *Educational Leadership 53*(6): 30–33.

Brown, D. F. 1993. *The political influence of state testing reform through the eyes of principals and teachers.* Paper presented at the Annual Meeting of the American Educational Research Association, Atlanta, GA, April.

Corbett, H. D., and Wilson, B. L. 1989. *Statewide testing and local improvement: An oxymoron?* Philadelphia: Research for Better Schools.

Corbett, H. D., and Wilson, B. L. 1991. Testing, reform, and rebellion. Norwood, NJ: Ablex.

Crosby, J. 1982. Participation in evaluation as staff development. *Journal of Staff Development 3*(1):147–155.

Danielson, C. 1996. *Enhancing professional practice: A framework for teaching.* Alexandria, VA: Association for Supervision and Curriculum Development.

Eisner, E. W. 1983. Anastasia might still be alive, but the monarchy is dead. *Educational Researcher 12*(5):23–24.

Epstein, A. S. 1988. A no frills approach to program evaluation. *High Scope Resources 7*(1):1–12.

Fang, Z. 1995. On paradigm shift in reading/literacy research. *Research Psychology 16:* 215–260.

Gable, R. K. 1986. *State and local collaborative efforts toward participatory evaluation: Connecticut's priority school district program.* Paper presented at the annual meeting of the American Educational Research Association, San Francisco, April.

Gilman, D. A., and Reynolds, L. L. 1991. The side effects of statewide testing. *Contemporary Education 62*(4):273–278.

Glickman, C. D. 1989. *The story of Ogelthorpe County High School: Five years of shared decision making.* Athens, GA: Monographs in Education.

Glickman, C. D., and Pajak, E. F. 1987. *Concepts of change in school systems improving criterion referenced test scores.* Presentation to the American Educational Research Association, Washington, DC, April.

Gordon, S. P., and Reese, M. 1997. High-stakes testing: Worth the price? *Journal of School Leadership 7:* 345–368.

Gottfriedson, G. D. 1985. *The Effective School Battery: User's manual.* Odessa, FL: Psychological Assessment Resources.

Gottfriedson, G. D. 1986. *Using the Effective School Battery in school improvement and effective schools programs.* Presentation to the annual meeting of the American Educational Research Association, San Francisco, April.

Greene, J. C. 1986. *Participatory evaluation and the evaluation of social programs: Lessons learned from the field.* Paper presented to the annual meeting of the American Educational Research Association, San Francisco, April.

Haefele, D. L. 1993. Evaluating teachers: A call for change. *Journal of Personnel Evaluation in Education, 7*(1): 21–31.

Hall, G. E., and Hord, S. M. 1987. *Change in schools: Facilitating the process.* Albany: State University of New York Press.

Hamilton, S. F. 1980. Evaluating your own program. *Educational Leadership 37*(6):545–551.

Darling-Hammond, L., and Wise, A. E. 1985. Beyond standardization: State standards and school improvement. *The Elementary School Journal* 85(3):315–336.

Hathaway, R. S. 1995. Assumptions underlying quantitative and qualitative research: Implications for institutional research. *Research in higher education, 36*(5): 535–562.

Holman, L. J. 1996. An examination of predictors of prior criterion-referenced test status, ethnicity, and socioeconomic status for at-risk students on the exit level administration of a high-stakes, criterion-referenced test. Paper presented at the Annual Meeting of the American Educational Research Association, New York, April.

Holman, L. J. 1995a. Impact of ethnicity, class, and gender on achievement of border area students on high-stakes examination. Paper presented at the Annual Meeting of the American Educational Research Association, San Francisco, April.

Holman, L. J. 1995b. An examination of predictors of prior criterion-referenced test status, ethnicity, and socioeconomic status for the at-risk student on a criterion-referenced, high stakes test. Paper presented at the Rocky Mountain Educational Research Association Conference, Albuquerque, October.

Holman, L. J. 1994. An examination of potential dissonance between state mandated testing programs and certain philosophies underlying second language acquisition. Paper presented at Arizona Educational Research Association/Rocky Mountain Educational Research Association Annual Fall Conference, Tempe, AZ.

Hoy, W. K., and Clover, S. I. 1986. Elementary school climate. *Educational Administration Quarterly* 22(1):93–110.

Ivory, G. 1993. Investigating ethnic bias in the mathematics portion of the exit-level Texas assessment of academic skills. Paper presented at the Annual Texas Testing Conference, Austin, TX, March. (ERIC Document Reproduction Service No. ED 362 574)

Joint Dissemination Review Panel. 1986. *Criteria and guidelines for the JDRP.* Washington, DC: United States Department of Education.

Lincoln, Y. S., and Guba, E. G. 1985. *Naturalistic inquiry.* Beverly Hills: Sage.

MacCrostie, J., and Hough, M. 1987. Personal conversations with Australian educators, November.

Madaus, G. F. 1988. The influences of testing on the curriculum. In L. N. Tanner (Ed.), *Critical issues in curriculum: Eighty-seventh yearbook of the National Society for the Study of Education,* (pp. 83–121). Chicago: University of Chicago Press.

McGreal, T. L. 1982. Effective teacher evaluation systems. *Educational Leadership, 39*(4): 303–305.

McGreal, T. L. 1983. *Successful teacher evaluation.* Alexandria, VA: Association for Supervision and Curriculum Development.

McGreal, T. L. 1989. Necessary ingredients for successful instructional improvement initiatives. *Journal of Staff Development, 10*(1): 35–41.

National Study of School Evaluation. 1987. *School evaluation stimulation.* Falls Church, VA: Author.

Nelson, M., and Sieber, S. 1976. Innovations in urban secondary schools. *School Review 84:* 213–231.

Newman, D. C., and Brown, R. D. 1987. *Violations of evaluation standards: Frequency and seriousness of occurrence.* Paper presented at the annual meeting of the American Educational Research Association, Washington, DC, April.

Patton, M. Q. 1980. *Qualitative evaluation methods.* Beverly Hills, CA: Sage.

Piontek, M. E. 1992. *Synthesized approaches: Expanding the perspectives and impact of qualitative and quantitative evaluation.* Paper presented at the annual meeting of the American Evaluation Association, Seattle, November.

Popham, J. 1988. The dysfunctional marriage of formative and summative evaluation. *Journal of Personnel Evaluation in Education, 1:* 269–273.

Popham, W. J. 1975. *Educational evaluation.* Englewood Cliffs, NJ: Prentice Hall.

A practical guide to measuring project impact on student achievement. Number 1 in a series of monographs on evaluation in education. Under contract OEC-0 = 73–6662, U.S. Office of Education, Washington, DC.

Prell, J. M., and Prell, P. A. 1986. Improving test scores—teaching test-wiseness: A review of the literature. *Research Bulletin,* CEDR, Phi Delta Kappa, No. 5., November.

Rose, J. S. 1987. *Better curriculum, instruction, and evaluation.* Paper presented at the annual meet ing of the American Educational Research Association, Washington, DC, April.

Shank, G. 1994. Shaping research in educational psychology. *Contemporary educational Psychology 19:*340–359.

Shepard, L. A. 1989. Why we need better assessments. *Educational Leadership* 46(9):4–9.

Shipman, V. 1983. *New Jersey Test of Reasoning Skills.* Upper Montclair, NJ: IAPC Test Division, Montclair State College.

Spray, M. 1993. State assessment programs: Images of state reform. *R and D Preview 8*(6):4–5.

Stufflebeam, D. 1981. *Standards for evaluations of educational programs, projects, and materials.* New York: McGraw-Hill.

Sutton, J. H. 1989. *Evaluation: A prime for teachers.* (ERIC ED 310 146)

Teaching for performance: New assessments help reshape classroom practice (1996, December). *Education Update 38*(8): 1, 6.

Torrance, E. P. 1974. *Torrance tests of creative thinking: Directions manual and scoring guide.* Lexington, MA: Ginn.

Watson, G., and Glaser, E. M. 1980. *Watson-Glaser critical thinking appraisal.* San Antonio: Psychological Corp.

Wise, A., 1988. *Restructuring schools.* Presentation to the Annual Georgia Leadership Institute, Athens, GA, June.

Wolf, D. P. 1988. Opening up assessment. *Educational Leadership 45*(4):24–29.

Wolfe, R. 1969. A model for curriculum evaluation. *Psychology in the Schools 6*:107–108.

Suggested Readings

Borg, W., and Gall, M. D. 1989. *Educational research: An introduction* (5th ed.). White Plains, NY: Longman.

Costa, A. L., and Kallick, B. 1995. *Assessment in the learning organization: Shifting the paradigm.* Alexandria, VA: Association for Supervision and Curriculum Development.

Danielson, C. 1996. *Enhancing professional practice: A framework for teaching.* Alexandria, VA: Association for Supervision and Curriculum Development.

Duke, D. L. (Ed.). 1995. *Teacher evaluation policy: From accountability to professional development.* Albany, NY: State University of New York Press.

Eisner, E. W., and Peshkin, A. 1990. *Qualitative inquiry in education.* New York: Teachers College.

Gredler, M. E. 1996. *School-based evaluation: A dialogue for school improvement.* Oxford, UK: Elsevier Science.

Kremer-Hayon, L. 1993. *Teacher self-evaluation: Teachers in their own mirror.* Boston: Kluwer.

McColskey, W., and Egelson, P. 1993. *Designing teacher evaluation systems that support professional growth.* Greensboro, NC: Southeastern Regional Vision for Education, School of Education, University of North Carolina at Greensboro. (ERIC ED 367 662)

McGreal, T. L. 1983. *Successful teacher evaluation.* Alexandria, VA: Association for Supervision and Curriculum Development.

Nevo, D. 1995. *School-based evaluation: A dialogue for school improvement.* Oxford, UK: Elsevier Science.

Patton, M. Q. 1990. *Qualitative evaluation and research methods.* Newbury Park, CA: Sage.

Shrinkfield, A. J., and Stufflebeam, D. 1995. *Teacher evaluation: Guide to effective practice.* Boston: Kluwer Academic Publishers.

Spray, M. 1993. State assessment programs. Images of state reform. *R and D Preview 8*(6): 4–5.

Stufflebeam, D. L. 1991. *The personnel evaluation standards: How to assess systems for evaluating educators.* Newbury Park, CA: Sage.

Part IV

Conclusion

Part IV was devoted to the technical skills the supervisor needs in assessing, planning, observing, researching, and evaluating. Let's highlight some of these skills. Chapter 13 looked at organizing personal plans; managing time; flowcharting; conducting needs assessments; cause and effect diagrams; Pareto charts; scatter diagrams; management by objectives; Gantt charts; program evaluation and review techniques; the PDSA cycle; and strategic planning. Chapter 14 dealt with description and interpretation; quantitative uses of categorical frequencies, performance

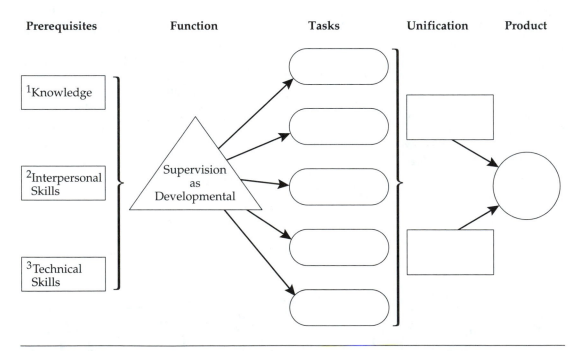

FIGURE IV.1 *SuperVision for Successful Schools*

indicators, and visual diagramming; qualitative uses of verbatim, narrative partici-pant involvement, focused questionnaires, and educational criticism; and tailored observation systems used to collect quantitative or qualitative data. Chapter 15 discussed research and evaluation skills, including quantitative and qualitative re-search, evaluation components and decisions, sources of data and methods of gathering data, evaluating the overall instructional program, achievement tests, new forms of assessment, and teacher evaluation.

The technical skills of Part IV have concluded the prerequisites needed by a supervisor in implementing the supervision function (see Figure IV.1). With knowledge about schools, teachers, and self, with interpersonal skills matched to developmental characteristics of teachers, and with technical skills in assessing, planning, observing, researching, and evaluating, the supervisor can function knowingly and skillfully in the realm of instructional improvement and can carry out the five developmental tasks of supervision.

Part V

Tasks of SuperVision

If one has responsibility for the improvement of instruction, what does one do? We've accounted for what the supervisor needs to possess in terms of knowledge, interpersonal skills, and technical skills. What are the tasks of supervision that can bring about improved instruction? They are direct assistance to teachers, group development, professional development, curriculum development, and action research. How does instruction improve?

> *Direct assistance:* The supervisor can provide or facilitate one-to-one feedback with teachers to improve instruction.
>
> *Group development:* The supervisor can provide for instructional problem-solving meetings among teachers to improve instruction.
>
> *Professional development:* The supervisor can provide learning opportunities with teachers to improve instruction.
>
> *Curriculum development:* The supervisor can provide for changes in teaching content and instructional materials to improve instruction.
>
> *Action research:* The supervisor can provide teachers with ways to evaluate their own teaching to improve instruction.

Each of these tasks is directly related to improved instruction. A supervisor needs to take responsibility for these tasks if a school is to become increasingly effective. Part V will detail how these tasks can be performed so that teachers take individual and collective responsibility for instructional improvement.

16

Direct Assistance to Teachers

Direct assistance to help teachers improve instruction can come from different sources. This book has contended that someone needs to take responsibility for the supervisory function of direct assistance to ensure that teachers receive feedback, are not left alone, and are involved as part of a collective staff. Research by Dornbush and Scott (1975) and Natriello (1982) has shown that teachers who receive the most classroom feedback are also most satisfied with teaching. Other research studies have shown that teachers in need of assistance tend to seek out first fellow teachers and second supervisory or administrative personnel (Lortie, 1975, pp. 75–77). Direct assistance to teachers is one of the crucial elements of a successful school (Little, 1982; Rosenholtz, 1985). Keeping the frequency and source of direct assistance in mind, we will look at an established structure for assisting teachers and then at some alternative ways of implementing the structure.

Clinical Supervision

Although there are multiple ways of observing, the model for conducting observations with teachers is relatively standard and accepted, and has a respectable research base (Sullivan; 1980; Adams and Glickman, 1984; Pavan, 1985; Nolan, Hawkes, and Francis, 1993). In fact, over 90 percent of school administrators in a southern and a midwestern state have cited their knowledge of the use of this structure with teachers (Bruce and Hoehn, 1980). The model, commonly referred to as *clinical supervision,* is derived from the pioneering work of Morris Cogan with supervisors of intern teachers at Harvard University. Cogan's *Clinical Supervision* (1973) and Robert Goldhammer's book, also entitled *Clinical Supervision*(1969), are publications resulting from this pioneer work. Since then, numerous refinements and alterations of clinical supervision have been made (Goldhammer, Anderson, and Krajewski, 1993; Acheson and Gall, 1992; Costa and Garmston, 1985; Anderson and Snyder, 1993; Pajak, 1993). Those desiring an in-depth study of the research and development of clinical supervision can find references at the end of this chapter.

Clinical supervision is both a concept and a structure. Goldhammer, Anderson, and Krajewski (1993) reviewed nine characteristics of clinical supervision as a concept:

1. It is a technology for improving instruction.
2. It is a deliberate intervention into the instructional process.
3. It is goal-oriented, combining the school needs with the personal growth needs of those who work within the school.
4. It assumes a professional working relationship between teacher(s) and supervisor(s).
5. It requires a high degree of mutual trust, as reflected in understanding, support, and commitment to growth.
6. It is systematic, although it requires a flexible and continuously changing methodology.
7. It creates a productive (i.e., healthy) tension for bridging the gap between the real and the ideal.
8. It assumes that the supervisor knows a great deal about the analysis of instruction and learning and also about productive human interaction.
9. It requires both pre-service training (for supervisors), especially in observation techniques, and continuous in-service reflection on effective approaches. (pp. 52–53) (parenthetical explanation provided)

The structure of clinical supervision can be simplified into five sequential steps:

1. Preconference with teacher
2. Observation of classroom
3. Analyzing and interpreting observation and determining conference approach
4. Postconference with teacher
5. Critique of previous four steps

Step 1. At the *preconference*, the supervisor sits with the teacher and determines (1) the reason and purpose for the observation, (2) the focus of the observation, (3) the method and form of observation to be used, (4) the time of observation, and (5) the time for postconference. These determinations are made before the actual observation, so that both supervisor and teacher are clear about what will transpire. The purpose of the observation, as mentioned in Chapter 14, should provide the criteria for making the remaining decisions on focus, method, and time of observation.

Step 2. The next step, *observation*, is the time to follow through with the understandings of the preconference. The observer might use any one observation or combinations of observations. Methods include categorical frequencies, performance indicators, visual diagramming, space utilization, verbatim, detached open-ended narratives, participant observation, focused questionnaire, educational criticism, and tailored observation systems. The observer should keep in mind the difference between *descriptions* of events and *interpretations*. Interpretation should follow description.

Step 3. The *analysis* and *interpretations* of the observation and determination of approach are now possible. The supervisor leaves the classroom with his or her observations and seeks solitude in an office or corner. He or she lays out the recorded pages of observations and studies the information. The task might be counting up frequencies, looking for recurring patterns, isolating a major occurrence, or discovering which performance indicators were present and which were not. Regardless of the instrument, questionnaire, or open-ended form used, the supervisor must make sense out of a large mass of information. Then the supervisor can make interpretations based on the analysis of the description. Figure 16.1 is a form that can be used to organize this task.

A case study might help to clarify this worksheet. Supervisor A has completed a verbal interaction instrument for students and teacher. She reviews the 10 sheets, tallies the columns, and writes in the worksheet under analysis:

1. The teacher asked 27 questions and received 42 answers.
2. Out of 276 total verbal moves, 6 were student to student; the other 270 were teacher to student or student to teacher.
3. …

The supervisor, knowing that the purpose of the lesson was to encourage student involvement, now makes interpretations on the worksheet *corresponding* to the analysis:

1. The teacher encouraged students to answer questions.
2. There was little interaction among students.
3. …

FIGURE 16.1 *Worksheet for Analysis and Interpretation of Data*

A. Analysis: Write the major findings of your observation. Write down only what has been taken directly from your observation.

1.

2.

3.

4.

5.

B. Interpretations: Write below what you believe is desirable or not desirable about the major findings.

1.

2.

3.

4.

5.

Note the relationship between analysis 1 and interpretation 1. There is clear documentation of evidence leading to the supervisor's judgment.

Let's examine one more case, this time of supervisor B doing a participant observation. The supervisor reads through his brief classroom notes, picks out the most significant events, and writes under "Analysis":

1. James, Tyrone, Felix, and Sondra asked me about the assignment they were supposed to be doing.
2. Kirk and Felipe were talking with each other about sports the three times I overheard them.
3. ...

From this analysis, the supervisor makes the following interpretation:

1. The teacher was not clearly communicating the directions to some students.
2. At least a couple of students were not interested in the classwork.
3. ...

Although one could argue with the supervisor's interpretation, it is readily apparent how it was logically derived from the recorded descriptions.

The last determination for the supervisor to make in step 3 of the clinical structure is to choose what interpersonal approach to use with the teacher in the postconference. The directive control, directive informational, collaborative, and nondirective approaches to supervision were explained in Chapters 8, 9, 10, and 11, respectively. Should the supervisor use a directive approach by presenting his or her observations and interpretations, asking for teacher input, setting a goal, and either telling the teacher what actions to take (directive control) or providing teachers with alternative actions to choose from (directive informational)? Should the supervisor be collaborative by sharing the observation, allowing the teacher to present his or her own interpretations, and negotiating a mutual contract for future improvement? Should the supervisor be nondirective by explaining his or her observations and encouraging the teacher to analyze, interpret, and make his or her own plan? The supervisor must consider the individual teacher's level of development, expertise, and commitment as explained in Chapter 12. When working with a teacher who is best matched with a collaborative or nondirective approach and who has experience with clinical supervision, some supervisors provide the teacher with the observation data prior to the postconference. This allows the teacher to review the data in advance and bring his or her preliminary interpretations to the postconference.

Step 4.   With the completed observation form, completed analysis, and interpretation form, and with the chosen interpersonal approach, the supervisor is ready to meet with the teacher in a *postconference*. The postconference is held to discuss the analysis of the observation and, finally, to produce a plan for instructional improvement.

The first order of business is to let the teacher in on the observation—to reflect back to the teacher what was seen. Then the supervisor can follow the chosen approach—directive controlling, directive informational, collaborative, or nondirective. The responsibility for developing a future plan may reside with the supervisor, be equally shared, or belong to the teacher. The conference ends with a plan for further improvement. Figure 16.2 can be used to develop such a plan.

The *objective* is a statement of what the teacher will attain for the next observation: "I will improve student-to-student interaction by 50 percent in group discussions." *Activities* are listed preparation points to accomplish the objective: "(1) Practice pausing at least three seconds before answering a student response. (2) Practice using open-ended questions. (3) Set up ongoing mini-debates." *Resources* are the materials and/or people needed to do the activities: "(1) Read a book on *Leading Discussion Groups*. (2) Attend a workshop on 'Involving Students.' (3) Observe Mr. Filler when he holds a science discussion." *Date* and *time* specify when the teacher will be ready to display his or her improvement. Such a plan—whether designed by the teacher, the supervisor, or both—should be clearly understood by both parties before they leave the postconference.

Step 5. The *critique* of the previous four steps is a time for reviewing whether the format and procedures from preconference through postconference were satisfactory and whether revisions might be needed before repeating the sequence. The

FIGURE 16.2 *Plan for Instructional Improvement*

Postconference Date _____   Observed Teacher _____

Time _____   Peer Supervisor _____

Objective to be worked on:

Activities to be undertaken to achieve objectives:

Resources needed:

Time and date for next preconference:

critique might be held at the end of the postconference or in a separate conference after a few days. It need not be a formal session but can be a brief discussion, consisting of questions such as: What was valuable in what we have been doing? What was of little value? What changes could be suggested? The critique has both symbolic and functional value. It indicates that the supervisor is involved in an improvement effort in the same way as the supervisee. Furthermore, the feedback from the teacher gives the supervisor a chance to decide on what practices to continue, revise, or change when working with the teacher in the future.

The five steps are now complete, and a tangible plan of future action is in the hands of the teacher. The supervisor is prepared to review the plan in the next preconference and reestablish focus and method of observation.

Comparing Clinical Supervision with Teacher Evaluation

In Chapter 15 we discovered the differences between summative and formative evaluation. Clinical supervision is consistent with formative evaluation; it provides non-judgmental assistance aimed at improving the teacher's instruction. Indeed it has been equated by some with formative evaluation. Clinical supervision actually includes but goes beyond formative evaluation by helping the teacher to design and implement an action plan to meet instructional improvement goals.

Clinical supervision is *not* consistent with summative evaluation; it is not intended to gather data to make judgments about whether teachers are meeting performance criteria for continued employment. Some school districts have confused the two processes by calling their summative evaluation cycle clinical supervision. At one level this is understandable. Both clinical supervision and summative evaluation can take place within similar structures, including a preconference, classroom visit, and postconference. To understand the difference between the two concepts we must look beyond the structure to the purpose and principles of clinical supervision, which clearly are not consistent with summative evaluation. The two processes need to be separate, for the same reasons that summative and formative evaluation should be separate (see Chapter 15).

Integrating Clinical Supervision and Developmental Supervision

As discovered in Part III, developmental supervision calls for the supervisor to match one of four interpersonal approaches—directive control, directive informational, collaborative, or nondirective—with teachers' developmental levels, expertise, and commitment. Are all four of these interpersonal approaches consistent with clinical supervision? The answer to this question depends to some extent on the model of clinical supervision being considered. Goldhammer's (1969) text on clinical supervision emphasizes a nondirective interpersonal approach. Cogan's (1973) clinical cycle reflects a collaborative orientation. Hunter's (1980, 1983, 1984, 1986) clinical model supports a directive approach. Our own view is that directive informational, collaborative, and nondirective supervisory approaches are all consistent with the clinical model.

Using a directive informational approach, the supervisor can suggest and explain two or three alternative observation foci and data collection methods in the preconference, and ask the teacher to select from the options provided. In the postconference, the supervisor can help the teacher to interpret observation data, and ask the teacher to choose from a limited range of possible improvement objectives, activities, and follow-ups. The supervisor and teacher engaged in a collaborative preconference can consider observation alternatives and select a mutually agreeable observation focus and data collection method. In the collaborative postconference, the supervisor and teacher can share decision making responsibility as they build an action plan for instructional improvement. The supervisor using nondirective behaviors in a preconference can ask the teacher to choose the focus of the observation, and facilitate the teacher as he or she chooses or creates an observation system that the supervisor would feel comfortable using. In the postconference, the supervisor would clarify, encourage, and reflect as the teacher designed his or her own improvement plan.

Although directive control behaviors are necessary in rare situations, we do not consider those behaviors to be consistent with the purpose and principles of clinical supervision. Directive control should be used only in short-term, crisis situations, not as part of a normal clinical cycle.

Peer Coaching

The number of teachers that a supervisor has will influence the frequency of clinical observations conducted by the supervisor. An English department head who teaches five periods a day and has 15 staff members will have a difficult time conducting full clinical cycles with every teacher during the school year. A principal of a large school, without assistants to take on administrative and disciplinary responsibilities, will find it an overwhelming task to meet and observe each teacher frequently. From experience, we know the frustration of starting a preconference only to be interrupted by an irate parent, a breakdown of the plumbing system, or two misbehaving students. A supervisor cannot provide direct assistance to teachers unless he or she establishes priority, energy, and time for doing so. Other nonsupervisory matters will have to be ignored, delegated to others, or simply put off. Most often, direct assistance to teachers receives the lowest priority. This sad state of affairs is shown by the evidence that the overwhelming majority of school teachers receive little or no direct assistance (Natriello, 1982; Ellett and Garland, 1986). Most teachers state that supervisors do not visit them for the purpose of providing help. In most cases, when a supervisor or administrator is in the classroom, he or she is there to pass on school information or to pick up attendance records.

If a supervisor is convinced of the critical need to provide direct assistance to teachers and cannot do it alone, the question is: Who else can do it? This is where the technical skill of planning becomes important. The supervisor has to determine the amount of time available for direct assistance, how many teachers can be seen in that time, and which teachers should be given special attention. In a pilot study of principals providing an intensive two cycles of direct supervision to teachers, it was found that the upper limit was nine to eleven teachers. Beyond that number, administrative and other instructional services began to suffer (Gwinnett County Pilot Teacher Evaluation Framework, 1987). Then the supervisor needs to determine how else assistance for all teachers can be provided on a regular basis. Authorities on clinical supervision believe the cycle should be conducted a minimum of twice a year with each teacher (see Snyder, Johnson, and MacPhail-Wilcox, 1982).

Since teachers naturally turn to each other for help more often than to a supervisor, and since supervision is concerned primarily with improving instruction rather than with summative evaluation (renewal of contracts), teachers helping teachers has become a formalized and well-received way of assuring direct assistance to every staff member. With the advent of extended responsibilities for career-ladder teachers, mentor teachers, master teachers, grade-level chairpersons, team leaders, and department heads, the time and resources for peer assistance have increased (see the theme issues of *Educational Leadership* 1987a, 1987b; and *Journal of Staff Development,* 1987). Keedy (1987) recommends that principals and supervisors provide instructional leadership through the coordination of instructional specialists like those listed above, rather than by attempting on their own to provide direct assistance to all teachers in the school. If teachers become proficient in observation skills and the format of clinical supervision, the supervisor can take on the role of clarifier, trainer, scheduler, and troubleshooter—clarifier by determining the purpose; trainer by preparing the teachers for the task; scheduler by forming teams or trios of teachers who take responsibility for preconferencing, observing, and postconferencing with each other; and troubleshooter by consulting with teams of teachers who are experiencing difficulties and with individual teachers who need more specialized attention. The use of teachers helping teachers through clinical supervision has been labeled *peer supervision* or *colleagueship* (Alfonso and Goldsberry, 1982). Joyce and Showers (1982) introduced the term *coaching* to characterize practice and feedback following staff development sessions. The terms *peer supervision* and *peer coaching* have now become indistinguishable in the literature. Research has shown positive results with peer assistance (Roper, Deal, and Dornbush, 1976; Goldsberry, 1980; Joyce and Showers, 1982, 1988; Mohlman, 1982; Coe, 1985; Sparkes and Bruder, 1987; Gordon, 1990, 1993a, 1993b; Gordon, Badiali, and Nolan, 1992; Hillkirk and Nolan, 1991; Gordon, Nolan, and Forlenza, 1994). If direct assistance is a worthy task for instructional improvement but a supervisor cannot provide it on a regular basis, the choice is either to have teachers provide help to each other or simply not to offer the help.

Obviously, the way to begin such a program is not to call a staff meeting and announce, "Since I can't see each of you as much as I would like, why don't you start to visit each other? Go to it!" Without planning and resources, disaster is inevitable. To be successful, peer coaching needs components addressing purpose, preparation, scheduling, and troubleshooting. Let's take each in turn.

Purpose

Before beginning a peer-coaching program, clarity of purpose and goals are necessary (Garmston, 1987). First, is it really a question of peer assistance (reciprocal interactions of equals) or is it a matter of hierarchical, one-way assistance (a better trained or more experienced teacher helping less well-trained or less experienced teachers)? Mentoring programs to help novices are fine, and master teacher programs to help struggling teachers are worthy, but they are not peer programs. Second, in a peer program, who is to be the recipient of assistance? Should a teacher who is the observer take from the observation some ideas to use, or should the teacher who is the observed take from the observation some actions to use? Third, will the observations and feedback focus on common instructional skills that each teacher is attempting to learn and implement, or will the observations and feedback focus on the teacher's own idiosyncratic concern with his or her teaching? Fourth, should the observations and feedback focus on the teacher's teaching or on individual students' behaviors? Fifth, is the goal of coaching to be greater awareness and more reflective decision making, or is it to implement particular teaching skills? Ultimately, how does the coaching goal fit into the larger school goal of improving instruction for students?

These are not idle questions. A peer-coaching program void of articulated definition and purpose has no rudder for steering and selecting the training, scheduling, and troubleshooting essential for success. Instead, it becomes another fad, exciting in that it's on the "cutting edge" of school change, but lacking substance in terms of what is to be accomplished. If there is a lack of direction in peer-coaching programs, well-intentioned teachers will have a vague sense of having done something pleasant but little sense of accomplishment (see Little, Galagaran, and O'Neal, 1984). Therefore, the first step is to meet with teachers to discuss how a proposed peer-coaching program would fit into a school's or district's instructional goals and then to decide on the specific purposes of the program. For example, if the purpose is simply to acquaint teachers with each other's teaching strategies less preparation is needed than if the purpose is to provide teachers with feedback on their teaching and assist them to develop action plans for instructional improvement. The next subsection provides some training guidelines for proceeding with a peer-coaching program that is focused on the purpose of reflective decision making.

Preparation

Before implementation, preparation of teachers would include training on (1) understanding the purpose and procedures of peer coaching, (2) conducting a preconference for determining the focus of observations, (3) conducting and analyzing an observation to distinguish between observing and interpreting classroom events, and (4) conducting two postconferences with different approaches for developing action plans—one using a nondirective approach, the other using a collaborative approach.

A standard form for writing instructional improvement plans in the postconference should be reviewed. The form should be simple and easy to fill out. Each peer member should understand that a completed plan is the object of the first four clinical steps and the basis for beginning the next round of supervision. For purposes of training, you may use the forms found in this chapter and in Chapter 14.

Training sessions of about six hours should provide the minimum knowledge and skills to begin peer coaching. Chapter 18 (Professional Development) will provide more detail on the sequencing of training to ensure some degree of transference from the training to initial implementation. After peers have gained some familiarity with the process through demonstrations, modeling, and practice in the workshop setting, they will be anxious but ready to begin a coaching cycle. For the initial attempts, perfection is not expected, of course. After the first cycle of implementation, a follow-up meeting should be held to discuss what has occurred and what revisions need to be made before beginning the second cycle. It is often convenient to review the past cycle and conduct the preconference for the next cycle during the same meeting. This gives participants a sense of sharing and learning from each other, enables the trainer to answer questions, allows for observation schedules to be arranged, and eliminates the need to meet another time to hold the preconference. From this point on, follow-up meetings concluding and beginning further cycles can be held every two to three weeks until the agreed-upon number of peer cycles have been finished. For the first year, it is recommended that at least four cycles be conducted—two times being the coach and two times being coached.

Toward the end of the year, a culminating meeting should be held to summarize the advantages and disadvantages of using peer coaching and to make a recommendation on whether to continue the program for the following year.

Let's emphasize that the program should be based on *agreement* and *volunteerism*. If an entire staff is willing to be involved, that's fine, but if only three teachers are willing, it is still a beginning and a previously unavailable source of help for those three teachers.

Scheduling

A teacher will have a more difficult time becoming enthusiastic about a project if it means increasing the amount of personal time and energy expended beyond an already full day. Because peer coaching will require additional time, the program should be voluntary, at least in the beginning. Greater participation of teachers is likely if the supervisor can schedule time for peer coaching during the schoolday. For example, placing teachers together in teams that share the same planning or lunch periods would allow for pre- and postconferences during the schoolday. Hiring a few substitutes for two days, twice a year, would allow teachers to be relieved of class duties so that they can observe their peers. One substitute could relieve six classroom teachers for one period at a time. Relief could also be found by having the titled supervisor (we mean you!) occasionally substitute for a teacher for one class period. This would enable the teacher to observe and would also give the supervisor a glimpse into the operating world of the classroom. Another way of freeing time for peer observations is for teachers to release each other by periodically scheduling a film, lecture, or some other large-group instruction so that two classes can be taught by one teacher. Whatever the actual schedule used to release teachers for peer coaching, preplanning by supervisor and teachers is needed to ensure that teachers can participate without extreme personal sacrifice. Research on lasting classroom change has shown that scheduling released time for teachers during the school day is critical (Humphries, 1981).

Another issue is arranging teams of teachers. As in most issues in education, there are no hard and fast rules. Generally, teachers should be grouped with each other so that they are comfortable together but not necessarily at identical levels of experience and/or competence. It may be useful to put experienced teachers with new ones, superior teachers with adequate ones, or adequate teachers with struggling ones.

Cognitive psychologists have demonstrated that an individual's thinking becomes more abstract and varied when he or she interacts with persons at higher levels of mental organization (Kohlberg, 1969). Such matching enables a person to consider ideas he or she would not have thought of; the novelty of the ideas spurs the person to rethink problems. If the groupings are too disparate—a concrete thinker with a highly abstract thinker, or a struggling teacher with a self-assured teacher—then little of such sparking of ideas will occur. There must be some degree of understanding and comfort to begin with. Hence, it is undesirable to match people who think alike but also undesirable to match those who think too differently. The goal is to match people who are different but still can respect and communicate easily with each other.

Cognitive matching will work if there are enthusiastic participants who are willing to be matched. A supervisor working with staff who are skeptical about using peer coaching in the first place might be better served by forgetting cognitive matching and instead allowing self-selection of teams. Each teacher could present anonymously a list of teachers he or she would like to work with. The supervisor could then match up preferences. The choice is between an ideal way to match people based on cognitive growth and a practical way to match them based on people's need for security with a new program. The practical match might be best when starting the program; after peer coaching becomes a familiar ongoing activity, the supervisor could rearrange teams toward greater cognitive matching.

Troubleshooting

The third component of establishing a peer-coaching program is the close monitoring of peer progress. The supervisor should be available to peer teams as a resource person. For example, what happens when the preconference concludes with an agreement to observe a teacher's verbal interaction in the classroom, and the peer coach is at a loss about where to find such an observation instrument? The training program should answer such questions, but orientation meetings cannot cover all possible needs. The supervisor must therefore monitor the needs of peer teams and be able to step in to help.

An elaborate monitoring device is not necessary. The supervisor might simply wander around the halls and check with peer coaches every few weeks. At periodic faculty meetings, he or she might ask peer coaches to write a note on their team progress. The supervisor should be sure that books, films, tapes, instruments on clinical supervision, and methods/instruments for observations are catalogued and available to teachers in the professional library.

Now that the supervisor can attend to *purpose, training, scheduling,* and *troubleshooting,* a peer-coaching supervision program can be implemented. The initial implementation of such a program undoubtedly will create more work for the supervisor. However, the initial work is less than would be necessary for providing clinical supervision to every teacher two or three times a year. If it is important enough to supervisor and staff, the time spent at the start in preparing for the program will pay off with ongoing instructional improvement of teachers.

Other Forms of Direct Assistance

Clinical supervision and peer coaching are currently two of the most popular forms of direct assistance in schools, but a variety of other forms are available. A few additional examples of direct assistance follow:

• *Demonstration teaching:* The supervisor or expert peer can be a guest teacher, demonstrating a new teaching model or method for the teacher requesting assistance. Alternatively, the teacher seeking to learn new skills can visit an expert peer's classroom for a demonstration lesson. A demonstration teaching cycle can include a preconference in which the demonstrator previews the lesson, and a postconference in which the demonstrator and observer analyze the completed lesson and discuss how the model or methods can be adapted to the observer's teaching.

• *Co-teaching:* The supervisor or expert peer and the teacher seeking assistance together can plan, teach, and evaluate a lesson. Co-teaching establishes trust and rapport, and fosters the collegiality, dialogue, and mutual reflection that foster teacher growth.

• *Assisting with resources and materials:* An unglamorous but vital supervisory activity is providing, explaining, and demonstrating instructional resources and materials. All of us in education are aware of teachers who make little or no use of particular instructional resources and materials (from manipulatives to computers) because of a lack of awareness or expertise. Many teachers would benefit greatly from the effective use of such resources and materials, but they need individualized assistance for technical mastery and adaptation to teaching content and students.

• *Assistance with student asssessment:*   There is a clear trend within the educational reform movement toward alternative forms of student assessment, especially authentic assessment (Barone, 1991; Krechevsky, 1991; Paulson, Paulson, and Meyer, 1991; Brandt, 1992; Herman, Aschbacher, and Winters, 1992; Schnitzer, 1993). In the coming years, teachers will likely need considerable direct assistance from supervisors in developing criteria and skills for assessing such things as student portfolios, "real-world" performances, and integrative projects. No doubt, authentic assessment techniques will be introduced to teachers through group in-service sessions. However, adapting new assessment techniques to particular content areas, grade levels, and individual students will, we believe, require individualized assistance.

• *Problem solving:*   Teachers experience a variety of professional problems that can be solved in one-to-one conferences and without classroom observation. Once a relationship of openness, trust, and rapport has been established, a supervisor can assist a teacher through a problem-solving process involving (1) identification of the problem, (2) generation and weighing of alternative actions, (3) selection of the most appropriate actions, and (4) planning follow-up to assess the results of chosen actions.

As with clinical supervision, other forms of direct assistance require the supervisor to select the appropriate supervisory approach. The supervisor selects from directive control, directive informational, collaborative, or nondirective interpersonal behaviors.

Establishing Procedures for Direct Assistance

It is 10:30 A.M., and Ms. Golan, the reading supervisor, is on her way to present the recommended reading budget for next year to the principal. Principal Malone told her last week that the recommendations were to be in today by 11 A.M. if he was to have them for his luncheon meeting with the superintendent. Ms. Golan has worked on the budget day and night for the last three days and finally has it finished. She needs to explain some of the budget items to Principal Malone personally. Suddenly, someone catches her by the arm and gently spins her around. It's Phillip Arostook, the remedial reading teacher, who says, "Boy, am I glad you're here. I have a meeting with Mr. and Mrs. Cougar at noon. They want my head. They claim I've been neglecting their son William, and that he's not learning anything. They want him out of my class. How do I handle this? I need your help!"

This incident is typical of the numerous unplanned occasions on which one is called to provide direct assistance. Clinical supervision is focused on long-term, carefully planned instructional improvement. There is still the matter of immediate needs, however. It is just as important for teachers to have someone to confer with in handling the short-term issues that arise each day. What would you do (or what have you done) in Ms. Golan's place? Ms. Golan could handle the situation by (1) telling Phillip she'll be back to see him in half an hour; (2) telling Phillip she is pressed for time and can speak to him only for a few minutes on her way to the principal's office; (3) telling Phillip she's sorry but she has no time and he'll have to handle it on his own; or (4) sending the budget with a note to the principal via a student, forgetting about explaining the budget, and then calmly sitting down with Phillip. Ms. Golan (and Phillip) would have been better off if there were an established procedure for handling frequent needs for human assistance. The procedure should be premised on *accessibility, arranged time,* and *delegation.*

Human help must be physically available and *accessible.* On a daily basis, the supervisor should visit in the lounge or in classrooms with teachers before school, during breaks, and after school. Of course, the supervisor cannot hold lengthy conversations with every teacher daily and also have time for much of anything else. Therefore, the supervisor might consider brief check-ins with teachers—taking the time to pause and speak with a certain number of teachers each day to ensure that by the end of the week every teacher has had the opportunity to bring up classroom concerns. Often, such a brief exchange will alert the supervisor to a teacher's concern that should be followed up with a scheduled conference.

The supervisor's schedule should also have *arranged weekly times* set aside for such conferences. The supervisor might plan a particular afternoon every week to follow up on teacher concerns. Teachers know that the supervisor will be in the lounge or office every Thursday afternoon to listen and help. Finally, the supervisor should consider *delegation.* The supervisor can use these Thursday afternoon times to provide personal help, can refer the concern to a specialist such as the school counselor or reading teacher, or can use the time for teachers to share instructional concerns and help each other. For example, some schools set aside every other Thursday for voluntary after-school meetings, in which teachers share discipline problems and plan concrete ways to help each other (see Glickman and Esposito, 1979). More about specific procedures and structures for efficient meetings can be found in Chapter 17 on group development.

Let's return to the case of Ms. Golan and Phillip Arostook. If Ms. Golan had planned for accessibility, scheduled time, and delegation, the crisis situation could have been prevented, with both the budget report and Phillip's need for counseling being satisfied. She would have known from checking in with Phillip that he was having difficulties with William. With a scheduled time for conferences, they could have reviewed the matter and scheduled a meeting with the parents.

The hectic life of schools—even when accessibility, arranged time, and delegation are planned—will still create unusual dilemmas for the supervisor (as anyone involved in education well knows). Planning for direct assistance will reduce the number of such dilemmas if teachers know they will be able to speak to their supervisors weekly to discuss serious problems and find resources to meet their needs. Such supervisory attention to ongoing concerns creates a climate of confidence and purpose rather than one of confusion and frantic reaction to unexpected crises.

Developmental Considerations in Direct Assistance

When thinking about ways to improve direct assistance to staff, it is once again critical to involve people who are affected by the decision in making the decision. A study group composed of teachers, building administrators, and central office staff (with a majority of teachers) is one approach to dealing with the issue of direct assistance. Teachers' union representatives should be active members of the study group, because proposed changes will often involve issues subject to collective bargaining. Proposed changes should usually be piloted first with a few schools, grades, or departments and evaluated and revised before full-scale implementation.

The same factors must be considered if particular direct-assistance interventions are to be tried in an individual school. Perhaps a school study group can be established; maybe a few teachers are willing to try peer coaching, or a high school department head wants to try his or her skills in working with a few teachers. The idea is to pilot, revise, and expand.

The word *development* implies that school units will be in different stages of readiness, commitment, and abstraction with regard to improving direct assistance to teachers. In one school it may be the principal and two teachers who are willing to spend observation time in direct assistance and formative feedback, to see if this new way (as distinct from summative evaluation) is worth pursuing. In another school a majority of teachers might want to arrange for informal conferences about teaching on the first Thursday of each month.

A few years ago, one of the authors explained to a district study group the need to move slowly in implementing a full-scale direct-assistance supervision program. The 15 school representatives asked him why. They were excited, ready to go, and didn't want to lose momentum. They were ready to move, and who was the author to say no? The point is a simple one. Educators ask themselves the question: How can we improve direct assistance to teachers in our school? Remember that organizations as well as individuals are at different levels of development. The answer to the question may be to begin on a small or a large scale, but the important thing is to answer the question rather than avoiding it. We cannot ignore demonstrated benefits of implementing direct-assistance supervision programs in public schools. Such programs have resulted in improved teacher reflection and higher-order thought, more collegiality, openness, and communication, greater teacher retention, less anxiety and burnout, greater teacher autonomy and efficacy, improved attitudes, improved teaching behaviors, and better student achievement and attitudes (Glickman and Bey, 1990). We must think seriously about whether we can afford to dismiss direct assistance to teachers and continue to use summative evaluation as the prime reason for observing and talking with teachers.

Summary

Regardless of how or where the responsibilities reside, no school or school system can hope to improve instruction if direct assistance is not provided to teachers. To leave classroom teachers alone and unobserved in their classrooms, without professional consultation and without school resources tailored to their unique needs, is a statement (intended or not) that teaching is unimportant. The message to teachers is that what is important is keeping your class quiet, your doors shut, and your problems to yourself. Assuredly, this is not the message we want to give.

A different message can be given by arranging for observation, feedback, and discussion of classroom improvement. Within the structure of clinical supervision, peer coaching is a recognizable structure for assistance that teachers can use to help each other. Furthermore, supervisors can be accessible, facilitate self- and group evaluation, arrange contact times, and refer specialists to teachers. Direct assistance, separated from summative evaluation, will help teachers confide, improve, and move with each other toward collective action.

Exercises

Academic

1. Locate three research studies on clinical supervision. Write a summary of each study, including purpose, participants, methodology, results, and conclusions.

2. Write a paper (a) giving advantages and disadvantages of having clinical supervision done by a formally designated supervisor and (b) giving advantages and disadvantages of having clinical supervision performed by other teachers (peer coaching). Refer to at least three outside sources in your paper.

3. Locate three research studies on peer coaching. Write a summary of each study, including purpose, participants, methodology, results, and conclusions.

4. Assume you are a supervisor who has been asked by the superintendent to begin a peer-coaching program in one of the district's medium-sized schools. Prepare a written plan for introducing peer-coaching to all the school's teachers, training a volunteer group of teachers in the clinical process, selecting teams (matching teachers), scheduling an initial round of clinical cycles, and monitoring the peer-coaching program.

Field

1. Interview a supervisor who follows the clinical model in supervision of teachers on the practical advantages and disadvantages of clinical supervision. Prepare a report on your interview.

2. Arrange to supervise a teacher using the clinical model (preconference, observation, analysis and interpretation, postconference, critique). Record the preconference, postconference, and critique on audiotape, and write a summary of the clinical cycle.

3. Conduct a group interview with a team of teachers involved in peer coaching on the specifics of the program, problems encountered, and perceived value of peer coaching for instructional improvement. Prepare a report on the interview.

4. Prepare a survey instrument to be completed by teachers that (a) defines direct assistance, (b) asks teachers to list the types of direct assistance they desire from supervisors, and (c) asks teachers to list the types of direct assistance they desire from other teachers. Distribute the survey to at least ten teachers, and request that they respond anonymously, in writing, to the two survey questions. Collect the surveys and process and analyze response data. Prepare a report on which types of direct assistance the respondents desire from supervisors and from fellow teachers.

Developmental

1. Begin an in-depth study of the development of clinical supervision by comparing three major works in clinical supervision, such as Goldhammer (1969); Cogan (1973); and Goldhammer, Anderson, and Krajewski (1993).

2. Begin an in-depth study of peer coaching.

3. As you continue your readings on the tasks of supervision, note the interrelationship of direct assistance with the other tasks of supervision and how previously discussed knowledge and skills of supervisors are common prerequisites for each task.

References

Acheson, A. A., and Gall, M. D. 1992. *Techniques in the clinical supervision of teachers* (3rd ed.). New York: Longman.

Adams, A., and Glickman, C. D. 1984. Does clinical supervision work? A review of research. *Tennessee Educational Leadership 11*(11):38–40.

Alfonso, R. J., and Goldsberry, L. F. 1982. Colleagueship in supervising. In T. J. Sergiovanni (Ed.), *Supervision of teaching.* Alexandria, VA: Association for Supervision and Curriculum Development.

Anderson, R. H., and Snyder, K. J. (Eds.). 1993. *Clinical supervision: Coaching for higher performance.* Lancaster, PA: Technomic Publishing.

Barone, T. 1991. Assessment as theater: Staging an exposition. *Educational Leadership 48*(5): 57–59.

Brandt, R. (Ed.). 1992. *Educational Leadership 49*(8). Theme issue on Performance Assessment.

Bruce, R. E., and Hoehn, L. 1980. *Supervisory practice in Georgia and Ohio.* Paper presented at the annual meeting of the Council of Professors of Instructional Supervision, Hollywood, FL, December.

Coe, E. E. 1985. Towards collegial inquiry: A case study in clinical supervision. (ERIC Document ED 281 847)

Cogan, M. 1973. *Clinical supervision.* Boston: Houghton Mifflin.

Costa, A. L., and Garmston, R. 1985. Supervision for intelligent teaching. *Educational Leadership 42*(5):70–80.

Dornbush, S. M., and Scott, W. R. 1975. *Evaluation and the exercise of authority.* San Francisco: Jossey-Bass.

Educational Leadership. 1987a. Theme issue: Staff Development through Coaching *44*(5).

Educational Leadership. 1987b. Theme issue: Collegial learning *45*(3).

Educational Leadership. 1987c. Theme issue: Progress in Evaluating Teaching *44*(7).

Egelson, P. 1994. *Teacher evaluation plans that support professional growth.* Paper presented at The Third Annual National Evaluation Institute, Gatlinburg, TN, July. (ERIC ED 026 286)

Garmston, R. J. 1987. How administrators support peer coaching. *Educational Leadership 44*(5):71–78.

Glatthorn, A. 1984. *Differentiated supervision.* Alexandria, VA: Association for Supervision and Curriculum Development.

Glickman, C. D., and Bey, T. M. 1990. Research on supervision in teacher education. In R. Houston (Ed.), *Handbook of research on teacher education.* New York: Macmillan.

Glickman, C. D., and Esposito, J. P. 1979. *Leadership guide for elementary school improvement.* Boston: Allyn and Bacon, pp. 233–250.

Goldhammer, R. 1969. *Clinical supervision: Special methods for the supervision of teachers.* New York: Holt, Rinehart and Winston.

Goldhammer, R., Anderson, R. H. and Krajewski, R. J. 1993. *Clinical supervision: Special methods for the supervision of teachers* (3rd ed.). Fort Worth: Harcourt Brace Jovanovich.

Goldsberry, L. F. 1980. Colleague consultation: Teacher collaboration using a clinical supervision model. Unpublished Ed.D. dissertation, University of Illinois, Urbana-Champaign.

Gordon, S. P. 1990. *Teacher directed peer clinical supervision: Participants' reactions and suggestions.* Paper presented at the annual meeting of the American Educational Research Association, Boston, April.

Gordon, S. P. 1993a. *Leadership cadre, phase II: Teachers as leaders and learners.* Paper presented at the annual meeting of the American Educational Research Association, Atlanta, April.

Gordon, S. P. 1993b. *The instructional leadership triad: University professors, school administrators, and teacher-leaders.* Paper presented at the annual convention of the University Council for Educational Administration, Houston, October.

Gordon, S. P., Badiali, B. J., and Nolan, J. F. 1992. *Teacher administrator leadership cadre, phase one: Preparing instructional leaders.* Paper presented at the annual meeting of the American Educational Research Association, San Francisco, April.

Gordon, S. P., Nolan, J. F., and Forlenza, V. (in press). Peer coaching: A cross-site comparison. *Journal of Personnel Evaluation in Education.*

Gwinnett County pilot teacher evaluation framework. 1987. Unpublished manuscript, Lawrenceville, GA.

Harris, B. M. 1975. *Supervisory behavior in education* (2nd ed.). Englewood Cliffs, NJ: Prentice Hall.

Hazard, W. R. 1993. *Legal aspects of teacher evaluation.* Paper presented at the Annual Convention of the National Organization on Legal Problems in Education, Philadelphia, November. (ERIC ED 377 182)

Herman, J. L., Aschbacher, P. R., & Winters, L. 1992. *A practical guide to alternative assessment.* Alexandria, VA: Association for Supervision and Curriculum Development.

Hillkirk, R. K., & Nolan, J. F. 1991. A focus on the culture of teaching: Instructional leadership through shared ownership, inquiry, and reflective coaching. *Journal of Staff Development 12*(4): 42–47.

Humphries, J. D. 1981. Factors affecting the impact of curriculum innovations on classroom practice: Project complexity, characteristics of local leadership and supervisory strategies. Unpublished Ed.D. dissertation, University of Georgia.

Hunter, M. 1980. Six types of supervisory conferences. *Educational Leadership, 37:* 408–412.

Hunter, M. 1983. Script-taping: An essential supervisory tool. *Educational Leadership, 41*(3): 3.

Hunter, M. 1984. Knowing, teaching, and supervising. In P. L. Hosford (Ed.), *Using what we know about teaching.* Alexandria, VA: Association for Supervision and Curriculum Development.

Hunter, M. 1986. Let's eliminate the preobservation conference. *Educational Leadership, 43*(6), 69–70.

Journal of Staff Development. 1987. Theme issue: Peer Coaching, *8*(1).

Joyce, B., and Showers, B. 1982. The coaching of teaching. *Educational Leadership 40*(1):4–10.

Joyce, B., and Showers, B. 1988. *Student achievement through staff development.* New York: Longman.

Keedy, J. L. 1987. Principals as instructional leaders: A realistic definition. *ERS Spectrum: Journal of School Research and Information, 5*(1), 3–7.

Kohlberg, L. 1969. Stage and sequence: The cognitive-development approach to socialization. In D. Goslin (Ed.), *Handbook of socialization theory and research.* Chicago: Rand-McNally.

Krechevsky, M. 1991. Project spectrum: An innovative assessment alternative. *Educational Leadership 48*(5): 43–48.

Little, J. W. 1982. Norms of collegiality and experimentation: Work place conditions of school success. *American Educational Research Journal 19*(3):325–340.

Little, J. W., Galagaran, P., and O'Neal, R. 1984. Professional development roles and relationships: Principles and skills of "advising." (Contract 400-83-003.) San Francisco: Far West Laboratory for Educational Research and Development.

Lortie, D. C. 1975. *School teacher: A sociological study.* Chicago: University of Chicago Press.

McColskey, W., and Egelson, P. 1993. *Designing teacher evaluation systems that support professional growth.* Greensboro, NC: Southeastern Regional Vision for Education, School of Education, University of North Carolina at Greensboro. (ERIC ED 367 662)

McGreal, T. L. 1982. Effective teacher evaluation systems. *Educational Leadership 39*(4):303–305.

Mohlman, G. G. 1982. *Assessing the impact of three inservice teacher training models.* Paper presented at the annual meeting of the American Educational Research Association, New York, March.

Natriello, G. 1982. *The impact of the evaluation of teaching on teacher effect and effectiveness.* Paper presented at the annual meeting of American Educational Research Association, New York, March.

Nolan, J., Hawkes, B., and Francis, P. 1993. Case studies: Windows into Clinical Supervision. *Educational Leadership 51*(2): 52–56.

Oliva, P. F. 1976. *Supervision for today's schools.* New York: Harper & Row.

Pajak, E. 1993. *Approaches to clinical supervision: Alternatives for improving instruction.* Norwood, MA: Christopher-Gordon.

Paulson, F. L., Paulson, P. R., and Meyer, C. A. 1991. What makes a portfolio a portfolio? *Educational Leadership 48*(5): 60–63.

Pavan, B. N. 1985. *Clinical supervision: Research in schools utilizing comparative measures.* Paper presented at the annual meeting of the American Educational Research Association, Chicago, April.

Popham, W. J. 1988. The dysfunctional marriage of formative and summative teacher evaluation. *Journal of Personnel Evaluation in Education 1*:269–273.

Roper, S. S., Deal, T. E., and Dornbush, S. 1976. Collegial evaluation of classroom teaching: Does it work? *Educational Research Quarterly* (Spring):56–66.

Rosenholtz, S. J. 1985. Effective schools: Interpreting the evidence. *American Journal of Education 93*:352–388.

Schnitzer, S. 1993. Designing an authentic assessment. *Educational Leadership 50*(7): 32–35.

Snyder, K. J., Johnson, W. L., and MacPhail-Wilcox, B. 1982. *The implementation of clinical supervision.* Paper presented at the annual meeting of the Southwest Educational Research Association, Austin, TX, February.

Sparkes, G. M., and Bruder, S. 1987. *How school-based peer coaching improves collegiality and experimentation.* Paper presented at the annual meeting of the American Educational Research Association, Washington, DC, April.

Sullivan, C. G. 1980. *Clinical supervision: A state of the art review.* Alexandria, VA: Association for Supervison and Curriculum Development.

Suggested Readings

Acheson, A. A., and Gall, M. P. 1992. *Techniques in the clinical supervision of teachers* (3rd ed.). New York: Longman.

Anderson, R. H., and Snyder, K. J. 1993. *Clinical supervision: Coaching for higher performance.* Lancaster, PA: Technomic.

Coe, P. E. 1990. *Toward collegial inquiry: Is there more to clinical supervision than the improvement of practice?* Paper presented at the annual meeting of the American Education Research Association, Boston, April.

Goldhammer, R., Anderson, R. H., and Krajewski, R. J. 1993. *Clinical supervision: Special methods for the supervision of teachers* (3rd ed.). Fort Worth: Harcourt Brace Jovanovich.

Pajak, E. 1993. *Approaches to clinical supervision.* Norwood, MA: Christopher Gordon.

Willerman, M., McNeely, S. L., and Koffman, E. C. 1991. *Teachers helping teachers.* New York: Praeger.

17

Group Development

Learning the skills of working with groups to solve instructional problems is a critical task of supervision. Just as cooperative learning with students has been found to produce significant gains in academic and social outcomes (Slavin, 1987), so have collegial adult groups been shown to produce higher adult achievement and performance than individualistic or competitive learning (Johnson and Johnson, 1987b). This chapter covers knowledge, skills, and procedures for developing productive instructional improvement groups: using group observations, changing group leadership styles, dealing with dysfunctional members, resolving conflict, preparing for meetings, and facilitating large-group involvement.

Professional people who are brought together to deal with pressing mutual problems have the right to expect results. Meetings that drag on, with seemingly endless and unfocused discussion, are morale breakers. Participants become reluctant, apathetic, and sometimes hostile toward future meetings. They might even suspect that the group leader is deliberately leading them astray, so that the group's inability to decide can be used as an excuse for the leader to do whatever he or she wishes. Regardless of whether the leader is actually trying to create confusion or truly desires a group decision, the lack of clear results erodes unity and common purpose. We already know how important unity, common purpose, and involvement are in developing a cause beyond oneself related to school success.

Groups that work productively, efficiently, and harmoniously generally have a skillful leader. Unfortunately, since being part of a group is such an everyday occurrence in professional, personal, and social life, we seldom stop to think about what makes some groups work well and others fail. It is unrealistic for the leader of a new group to expect the group to proceed naturally in a professional manner. A leader needs to be conscious of the elements of a successful group, select clear procedures for group decision making, be able to deal with dysfunctional behavior, use conflict to generate helpful information, and determine appropriate leadership style.

Dimensions of an Effective Group

There are two dimensions of an effective professional group (Bales, 1953): the task dimension and the person dimension. The *task* dimension represents the content and purpose of the group meeting. The task is what is to be accomplished by the end of the meetings. Typical tasks of professional groups might be deciding on a new textbook, writing a new instructional schedule, coordinating a particular curriculum, or preparing a professional development plan. An effective group, obviously, accomplishes what it sets out to do. The *person* dimension of an effective group comprises the interpersonal process and the satisfaction participants derive from working with each other. Concern and sensitivity to participants' feelings create a climate of desiring to meet with each other from week to week to accomplish and implement the group task.

Let's explain these two dimensions in a different way. Specific task behaviors are clarifying the group's purpose, keeping discussions focused, setting time limits, and appraising group progress toward the goal. A leader who says, "We're getting off the track; let's get back to discussing textbooks," is exhibiting a task behavior. Specific person behaviors seen in a group include recognizing people for their contributions, smiling, injecting humor, and listening attentively. A leader who says, "Fred, I'm following what you've been saying; it's a point worth considering," would be demonstrating a person behavior. Imagine a group that exhibits only task behaviors. The meeting would be formal, cold, and tense. People would not receive feedback, would not be encouraged, and probably would swallow hard before addressing the unsmiling, staring faces. Such a group would accomplish its task quickly, with little mutual support. The decision would be quick because participants would wish to remove themselves from the tense environment as soon as possible. The formality of the sessions would prevent in-depth discussions of feelings, attitudes, and differences of opinion. Decisions would be made on the basis of incomplete information and commitment from group members. The implementation of the decision would be problematic at best.

Next, imagine a group that exhibits only person behaviors. There would be much personal chatter, humorous story telling, and frequent back slapping and touching. People would be smiling and laughing. The image of a raucous cocktail party might characterize a group with all person behaviors and no task behaviors, and the morning-after hangover is also analogous to the sense of accomplishment after a meeting devoid of task behaviors. People would enjoy each other's company for its own sake; everyone would have a wonderful time, but little would be done.

Little's study of six urban, desegregated schools (three elementary and three secondary schools) provides evidence that the two schools identified as "high success" on teacher involvement in schoolwide projects held meetings that encompassed both personal and task behaviors. Little (1982) described the successful schools in this way:

> Teachers engage in frequent, continuous, and increasingly concrete and precise talk about teaching practice.... By such talk, teachers build up a shared language

adequate to the complexity of teaching, capable of distinguishing one practice and its virtues from another, and capable of integrating large bodies of practice into distinct and sensible perspectives on the business of teaching. (p. 331)

As Little has shown, successful schools have collegial, industrious meetings. Teachers involve themselves with each other in professional dialogue to accomplish better schoolwide instruction. In summary, productive groups have meetings that emphasize both task and person dimensions. It falls to the group leader to ensure that both dimensions are present.

Group Member Roles

First, the leader needs to determine what behaviors are indicative of roles already in existence. Are some members displaying task roles and/or person roles? What roles are ongoing? Are certain roles lacking? Remember that both task and person roles are functional to group performance. Another set of roles and behaviors, called *dysfunctional*, distract a group from task and person relations. Dysfunctional roles, unlike functional roles, are a concern when present. After listing and briefly describing the most common functional member roles, we will examine dysfunctional roles.

Task Roles

The following descriptions are adapted from those listed by Benne and Sheats (1948):

Initiator-contributor: Proposes original ideas or changed ways of regarding group problem, goal, or procedure. Launches discussion, moves group into new areas of discussion.

Information seeker: Asks for clarification in terms of factual adequacy. Seeks expert information and relevant facts.

Opinion seeker: Asks for clarification of values pertinent to the group undertaking or to proposed suggestions. Checks on others' attitudes and feelings toward particular issues.

Information giver: Provides factual, authoritative information or gives own experience relevant to the issue.

Opinion giver: Verbalizes his or her own values and opinions on the group problem; emphasizes what the group should do.

Elaborator: Picks up on others' suggestions and amplifies with examples, pertinent facts, and probable consequences.

Coordinator: Shows the link between ideas and suggestions, attempts to pull diverse proposals together.

Orienter: Clarifies the group's position, gives a state-of-the-scene review. Summarizes what has been discussed, points out where discussion has departed from the goal, and reminds the group of their ultimate goal.

Evaluator-critic: Evaluates the proposals of the group against a criteria of effectiveness. Assesses whether proposals are "reasonable," "manageable," "based on facts," and derived through fair procedures.

Energizer: Focuses the group to move toward decisions. Challenges and prods group into further action.

Procedural technician: Facilitates group discussion by taking care of logistics. Sees that the group has the necessary materials for the task (paper, pencils, chalk, and so on).

Recorder: Writes down the group's suggestions and decisions. Keeps an ongoing record of what transpires in the group.

A group needs these member roles to keep moving toward accomplishing its task. A leader can use these descriptions to figure out what roles are missing. Additional roles might need to be assigned to group members or incorporated by the leader. For example, if a group has many opinion givers but no information givers, then decisions would be made on the basis of feelings, without regard to actual experience or knowledge. A leader would need to consider ways to add more information giving. Perhaps he or she could assign people to gather more knowledge or ask outside experts for assistance. Likewise, if a group has many opinion givers and information givers but lacks orienters and coordinators, the members may be talking past each other. There would be a lack of direction and a lack of synthesis of the relationships among members' ideas. The leader would need to plan ways to coordinate discussions. As a final example, a group might contain most of the task roles except for a procedural technician or recorder. Such a group probably would converse easily but would bog down on recalling what has been said. The leader who knows what roles are needed can ask for a volunteer to be a recorder and summarizer. Knowledge of task roles and behaviors enables a leader to assess what roles are evident and what further roles need to be assigned. The leader might take on some of the missing roles, assign them to others, or add particular persons to a group.

Person Roles

The knowledge of person roles and behaviors provides a guide to the group leader. Consider the following descriptions:

Encourager: Affirms, supports, and accepts the contribution of other members. Shows warmth and a positive attitude toward others.

Harmonizer: Conciliates differences between individuals. Looks for ways to reduce tension between members through nonthreatening explanations and humor.

Compromiser: Offers to change his or her proposals for the good of the group. Willing to yield position or to acknowledge own errors by meeting other opposing ideas halfway.

Gatekeeper or expediter: Regulates flow of communication by seeing that all members have a chance to talk. Encourages quiet persons to speak and puts limits on those who dominate the conversation. Proposes new regulations for discussions when participation becomes unbalanced.

Standard setter: ego ideal: Appeals to group's pride by not letting group members give up when trouble occurs. Exudes confidence that the group is a good one and can make sound decisions.

Observer and commentator: Monitors the working of the group. Records who speaks to whom, where and when most roadblocks occur, and the frequency and length of individual members' participation. Provides feedback when the group wishes to evaluate its procedures and processes.

Follower: Is willing to accept the decisions of the group and follow them even though he or she has not been active or influential in those decisions. Serves as a listener to group discussion.

The seven person roles provide human satisfaction and group cohesiveness. People feel positive about meeting and talking with each other and comfortable enough to express their ideas. As a result, meetings are seen as pleasant times to continue the group's work. When person roles are missing, a group may face severe difficulties in making acceptable and committed decisions. Without person behaviors and roles, only the strongest, most assured, and vocal members will speak. Decisions might be made that more timid persons strongly reject but the group may not know that such strong disapproval exists. Again, it is the group leader's responsibility to see if people roles are evident. If roles are missing, then he or she can confront the group with their absence, pick up the role(s) himself or herself, quietly suggest particular roles to existing members, or add to the group other individuals who more naturally play such roles. *Both task and person roles, when not already in existence, need to be added.*

Dysfunctional Roles

Dysfunctional roles and behaviors are those that are conspicuous in their presence. Such roles and behaviors disrupt the progress towards a group goal and weaken group cohesiveness. Consider the following:

Aggressor: Personally attacks the worth of other members. Belittles and deflates the status, wisdom, and motivation of others. Examples of such verbal attacks are: "That's the most ridiculous thing I've ever heard," "You must be crazy to suggest...."

Blocker: Sees all opinions and suggestions by group members as negative. Opposes any decision being made and stubbornly refuses to propose alternatives. Examples of such blocking statements are: "That's a terrible idea," "I don't want to do that," "It's futile to do anything."

Recognition-seeker: Uses the group setting to receive personal attention. Examples of such behaviors are dropping books, scattering papers, coughing incessantly, pretending to be asleep, raising hand and then forgetting what one would have said.

Self-confessor: Uses the group to ventilate personal feelings not related to the group's tasks. Talks about personal problems or feelings of inadequacy whenever he or she can see ways to slip such confessions into the group discussion. Examples of self-confessing statements are: "This discussion reminds me of when I was a little child and the weight problem I had," or when the group is talking about differences of opinion, "You should hear my son and me fight; I don't know what to do about him."

Playboy or playgirl: lack of interest and involvement by using the group setting to have a merry time. Distracts other members from the group's purpose. Tells private jokes, passes notes, makes faces at others, plays cards, and so on.

Dominator: Asserts superiority in controlling group discussion and dictates what certain members should do. Claims to know more about the issue under discussion and have better solutions than anyone else. Has elaborate answers to almost every question and monopolizes the discussion.

Help-seeker: Tries to gain group's sympathy by expressing feelings of inadequacy or personal confusion. Uses such self-derogation as reason for not contributing: "This is all too confusing for me," "I can't make a decision on my own," "Why ask me? I can't help."

Special-interest pleader: Has no opinion or suggestions of his or her own but instead speaks for what others would say or do. Cloaks own bias by using an outside group: "We couldn't do that. Do you know what the school board would think?" "If those parents down in the local restaurant ever heard that we were going to change...."

Dysfunctional roles are fairly self-evident in a group. The leader's responsibility is to reduce or eliminate such dysfunctional roles before they severely harm the morale and efficiency of the group. He or she might try to understand the dysfunctional member's reason for acting as an aggressor, playboy, special interest pleader, and so on, and then might either confront the person privately or provide changes within the group to satisfy the unmet needs that are leading to the dysfunctional behavior. Methods for dealing with dysfunctional behaviors will be discussed shortly, but first let's focus on leadership styles matched with maturity levels of groups.

Changing Group Leadership Style

If a group lacks either task or person behaviors, the leader can choose a style that will fill the void. A group that exhibits much initiative, information, and competitiveness (high task) as well as hostility, aggression, and bitterness (low person) could benefit from a leadership style that is encouraging, praising, harmonizing, and humorous (high person). A group that exhibits much positive camaraderie (high person) but is being uninterested, apathetic, or uninformed (low task) could benefit from a leadership style that presses for information, sets goals, and enforces procedures (high task).

The work of Hersey and Blanchard (1969, 1988) on what they call the "life-cycle theory of leadership," also known as *situational leadership,* is a comprehensive theory of leadership style in response to group characteristics. Hersey and Blanchard identified four styles of leadership based on the relative emphasis on task and relationship (person) behavior:

Style 1 (S1):   High task, low relationship. This is an autocratic style, whereby the leader tells the group members what is to be done, when, and by whom. The leader makes decisions for the group. This style is similar to directive supervision, discussed in Chapters 8 and 9. One word that describes this style is *telling.* The leader determines both the process and the content of decision making.

Style 2 (S2):   High task, high relationship. This is a democratic style whereby the leader actively participates with the group both as a facilitator of the decision-making process and an equal member contributing his or her own ideas, opinions, and information. This style is similar to collaborative supervision, explained in Chapter 10. One word that describes this influencing style is *selling.* The leader attempts to influence both the processes and the content of decision making by being a persuasive equal.

Style 3 (S3):   High relationship, low task. This is an encouraging and socializing style whereby the leader promotes cohesion, open expression, and positive feelings among the members but does not influence or interfere with the actual decision. (The leader's role is one of clarification, encouragement, and reflection.) The style is similar to nondirective supervision, described in Chapter 11. Note that the leader participates by helping members express their ideas, opinions, and needs but does not participate in the sense of offering his or her own ideas, opinions, and needs. The leader participates in the process but not in the content of decision making.

Style 4 (S4):   Low relationship, low task. This is a hands-off or laissez-faire style whereby the leader turns the task over to the group and does not participate in any manner. The leader tells the group what the task is and then physically or mentally removes himself or herself from any further involvement. One word that describes this style is *delegating.* The leader is involved in neither the process nor the content of decision making.

Hersey and Blanchard (1988) stated that effective leadership is based on matching leadership style to the readiness of the group. The readiness of a group depends on the particular task; the same group could be of high readiness for one task and low readiness for another. Readiness can be assessed according to the characteristics of ability and willingness.

Ability is the knowledge, skills, and experience to achieve without the need for outside assistance.

Willingness is the degree of motivation, confidence, and interest in accomplishing certain tasks.

The leader can assess the readiness of individuals and a group according to these levels (Hersey and Blanchard 1988, pp. 176–177).

* *Readiness Level One (Rl)*
  Unable and unwilling
  Unable and insecure

* *Readiness Level Two (R2)*
  Unable but willing
  Unable but confident

* *Readiness Level Three (R3)*
  Able but unwilling
  Able but insecure

* *Readiness Level Four (R4)*
  Able and willing
  Able and confident

Situational leadership matches leadership style to the readiness level of the group (see Figure 17.1 on matching and directionality of a developing group). An R1 group is best matched with a *telling* autocratic style (Sl). An R2 group is best matched with a *selling*, democratic style (S2). An R3 group is best matched with a *participating*, encouraging style (S3). An R4 group is best matched with a *delegating*, laissez-faire style (S4).

Hersey and Blanchard's theory was originally called *life-cycle leadership* but is now more commonly referred to as *situational leadership*. This is an unfortunate change in terminology, because *life cycle* connotes development or growth in both leader and group behaviors, an implication that is missing from the term *situational*. Groups are complex human entities that respond to the gradual shifting of a group leader's external control in the same manner that an individual teacher will respond to gradual shifting of supervisory control. In other words, an R1 (low readiness) group with an S1 (telling and autocratic) leadership style will not develop until the leader gradually allows them to gain greater internal control. An unmotivated group might work most efficiently with S1 leadership at first. As the group gains experience, as members become acquainted with each other, and as

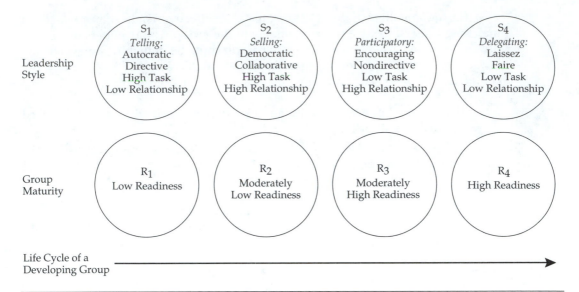

FIGURE 17.1 *Matching and Directionality of a Developing Group*

the group acquires expertise, the leader should be alert to those signals of increasing readiness and provide for greater group involvement by shifting to an S2 leadership style. It is conceivable that a group working on a long project might complete the entire life cycle by beginning with S1 (telling) leadership and concluding with S4 (delegating) leadership. A group leader might work toward eliminating his or her control over the group. The ultimate goal should be for a group to provide its own task and person behaviors and not be dependent on formal leadership.

Dealing with Dysfunctional Members

The fact that a group is made up of individuals with varying temperaments and motivations is important when thinking about ways to work with groups. Dealing with individuals, particularly those who display dysfunctional behaviors, is an additional responsibility of a group leader.

If the leader has observed the group at work and has determined that his or her own leader behaviors are appropriate for most members of the group, yet there continue to be a few dysfunctional members, then individual treatment might be in order. The procedure for treating a dysfunctional member is (1) observe the member, (2) try to understand why the member is acting unproductively, (3) communicate with the member about the behavior, (4) establish some rules for future behavior, and (5) redirect the unfavorable behavior (Corey and Corey, 1982; Kemp, 1970). Each step of this procedure will be amplified.

1. *Observe the member:*   When and with whom does the dysfunctional behavior occur? What does the group member do, and how do others respond? For example, a dominator might start monopolizing the conversation as soon as he or she walks into the meeting. Other people might be interested in the dominator's talk for the first few minutes of the meeting but become increasingly annoyed as the dominator continues. They might roll their eyes, yawn, fidget, or make comments to each other.

2. *Try to understand the member:*   Why does the member persist with dysfunctional behavior? Does he or she know the behavior is unproductive? Is the behavior being used to mask some underlying emotion? For example, a playboy might be insecure about his own worth and pretend not to care rather than exposing inner thoughts to the scrutiny of the group.

3. *Communicate with the member:*   What can you communicate about the group member's behavior and the situation? Describe the situation and the behavior to the member without denigration. Instead of saying, "You're being an aggressive son of a gun," say, "I've noticed that you speak loudly and angrily to Sara. At the last meeting, you told her to keep her mouth shut." Tell the dysfunctional member the effect of the behavior on you as group leader: "When you tell Sara to shut up and tell Bob that he's stupid, it starts an argument that takes time away from the meeting. I can't complete the agenda on time when those arguments take place" (see Gordon, 1980).

4. *Establish some rules for future behaviors:*   Either ask the member to suggest some rules that he or she can abide by in the future, or tell the member your future rules, or establish them jointly. Regardless of which tactic is chosen, the leader should think of rules that would minimize further disruptions to the group. For example, the leader might say to a self-confessor, "The next time you have a personal problem, come speak to me privately about it," or to a dominator, "I'm going to enforce a two-minute limit on every member's participation," or to a blocker, "If you don't think we're on the right course, tell us your objection once and only once."

5. *Redirect the unfavorable behavior:*   Pick up on the group member's dysfunctional behavior, and try to make it functional. A dominator can be assigned the role of recorder, summarizer, or time keeper. A playboy can be given an opening time for sharing a funny story to relax the group before starting official business. An aggressor can be asked to play devil's advocate and argue the position of an adversary.

The five steps outlined here will help the meeting leader understand and deal with individual dysfunctional behavior. The steps are predicated on the leader confronting the dysfunctional member in private. Dysfunctional behaviors that occur infrequently and in isolated situations might simply be ignored. The leader can respond to infrequent misbehaviors or make light of them: "Sara, I guess you really got wound up today; perhaps we might hear from someone else now." Only incessant behaviors that distract the entire group need to be dealt with via direct confrontation. Confrontation is not easy but is necessary at times for the sake of the group. Role play 17.1 provides for a demonstration of how to deal with a dysfunctional group member.

Resolving Conflict

The key to a productive group is the way ongoing conflict is resolved. Conflicts are particular disagreements that occur between two or more members at a particular time. *Conflict is not necessarily dysfunctional.* In fact, research has shown that

ROLE PLAY 17.1 • *Dealing with a Dysfunctional Group Member*

Context. The purpose of this role play is for a subgroup of four to provide a demonstration to the remainder of the group on how to effectively deal with a dysfunctional group member. Participants will need approximately 20 minutes of preparation time away from the rest of the group. In the role play, a "supervisor" and three "teachers" are members of a committee meeting to discuss a schoolwide instructional issue. In their preparation for the role play, the role players may choose the school level (elementary, middle, or high school), the issue to be discussed, and any other details of the fictional situation that they need to agree on to perform an effective role play. The group is assigned or chooses a dysfunctional role that one member of the group will assume during the role play. The role play is presented in three scenes.

Scene 1 (10 minutes). The supervisor and three teachers begin the meeting. Throughout the scene, one of the teachers assumes a dysfunctional role that is clearly impeding the rest of the group's efforts to resolve the issue. The supervisor observes the teacher's dysfunctional behaviors. This scene ends with a break in the meeting, with the issue unresolved. During the break the other two teachers leave to get a cup of coffee, and the supervisor and teacher are left alone.

Scene 2 (10 minutes). In a private discussion with the dysfunctional teacher during the break, the supervisor uses techniques suggested under this chapter's heading "Dealing with Dysfunctional Group Members" to address the teacher's behaviors. The specific discussion will depend on the dysfunctional role that the teacher has been playing. The discussion culminates with an agreed upon plan for minimizing future disruptions.

Scene 3 (10 minutes). The other teachers return and the meeting resumes. Due to the agreements worked out during the break and the supervisor's support during the second part of the group meeting, the teacher's dysfunctional behaviors are greatly reduced. The group is able to resolve the issue under discussion.

Whole Group Processing (10 minutes). The entire group discusses what the dysfunctional role was, specific behaviors that indicated the dysfunctional role, and effects of the dysfunctional role on the group in Scene One. Next, the group discusses the techniques used by the supervisor in Scenes Two and Three to deal with the dysfunctional role, and the effects of those techniques on the teacher and group.

successful groups exhibit much conflict (Johnson and Johnson, 1987a). As Roger Johnson stated, "A critical moment of truth in a…group is when two teachers disagree strongly with each other and argue…" (Brandt, 1987). A group can make wise decisions only when there is a wealth of information and ideas to consider. Information and ideas are generated through conflict. To suppress conflict is to limit the group's decision-making capacity. Therefore, the leader should encourage conflict, not stifle it. Of course, conflict, if not handled correctly, can degenerate into adversarial and harmful relations. It is not conflict that is bad; it is the way the leader deals with it that determines its value.

Conflict occurs when there is a disagreement over ideas. The leader should keep the disagreement focused on the ideas rather than on the personalities of the members. The following procedure for handling conflict serves as a ready reference for the group leader:

1. Ask each member to state his or her conflicting position.
2. Ask each member to restate the other's position.
3. Ask each member if conflict still exists.
4. Ask for underlying value positions: Why do they still stick to their positions?
5. Ask other members of the group if there is a third position that synthesizes, compromises, or transcends the conflict. If not, reclarify the various positions. Acknowledge that there exists no apparent reconciliation, and move the discussion to other matters.

The following is an application of conflict-resolution procedures to a high school meeting:

> The supervisor from the central office has called a meeting of the English high school department heads to discuss possible changes in the tenth-grade English curriculum. The topic of composition writing comes up, and two department heads begin to argue. Mrs. Strick of Toofarback High School says, "We need to require three formal compositions each semester from each tenth grader. Each composition should be graded according to spelling, punctuation, and format. I'm sick and tired of seeing kids coming into the eleventh grade without being able to put a sentence together!"
>
> Mr. Ease of Space High School objects: "Are you serious? Six technical compositions a year should just about kill any remaining interest that tenth graders have in writing. That is a ridiculous idea!"

The language supervisor, Mr. Cool, is now aware of a conflict and wants to capitalize on these varying points of view in providing information to the group. At the same time, he is aware of emotional intensity in this conflict (words such as "sick and tired" and "ridiculous") and wishes to soften the emotion and promote the ideas. So he uses step 1 and asks the two members to state their conflicting positions.

> "Mrs. Strick and Mr. Ease, you both have definite ideas about the requirements of technical compositions. We are interested in fully understanding what you think. Would you each take a few minutes and further explain your positions?"

After Mrs. Strick and Mr. Ease have stated their positions, the supervisor moves to step 2 by asking each member to restate the other's position.

> "Now that you have stated your position, I want to make sure that you fully understand each other. Mrs. Strick, would you please paraphrase Mr. Ease's position, and Mr. Ease, would you repeat Mrs. Strick's position." Mrs. Strick says, "Mr. Ease thinks that technical writing assignments are a waste of time and students lose interest." Mr. Ease replies, "No, I didn't say they are a waste of time; but if such assignments are frequent, students learn to hate English class." Mr. Ease then restates Mrs. Strick's position: "You're saying that tenth graders need skills in the basics of writing. Required compositions would ensure proper spelling, grammar, and format." Mrs. Strick replies, "Yes, that's what I'm saying."

Now that both positions have been made and paraphrased, Supervisor Cool goes to step 3 and asks if conflict still exists.

> He asks Mrs. Strick and Mr. Ease: "Are you both still far apart about composition requirements for tenth-grade English?" Mrs. Strick nods, but Mr. Ease says, "Well, not as far apart as at the beginning. I'm not against some technical writing requirements. It's the number, three for each semester, that hangs me up. I could accept one per semester." Mrs. Strick replies, "Well, I can't. If they are going to write correctly, they must do it frequently. Three compositions a semester is just the minimum!"

Mr. Cool, knowing that Mrs. Strick is adamant about her position, goes to step 4, asking for the underlying value:

> Mr. Cool asks Mrs. Strick: "Could you explain why technical composition writing is important to you?" Mrs. Strick says, "Kids today don't get any basics in writing. Everything is creativity, expression, write it like you speak it in the streets! I was taught standards of good manners and proper English. If these kids are to succeed in later life, they have to know how to write according to accepted business and professional standards. I'm not being hardnosed for my own sake. It's them I'm concerned about!" Mr. Cool turns to Mr. Ease and says, "What about you? Why do you disagree?" Mr. Ease replies, "I don't completely disagree, but I'm against making tenth-grade English class a technical writing drill. Writing should be a vehicle for expression and students should love, not dread, it. They should be able to write personal thoughts, juggle words and formats, and not worry about every comma and dotted *i*. Let them play with words before pushing standards at them. I don't write letters with one-and-a-half-inch margins to my friends or in my diary—why should kids have to? Sure, there is a need for them to learn to write formally, but not at the expense of hating to write!"
>
> Mr. Cool restates the conflict to the group: "We have an obvious disagreement between Mrs. Strick and Mr. Ease. Mrs. Strick believes there should be at least three technical compositions per semester in the tenth grade. Mr. Ease believes there should be less emphasis on technical writing and more on expressive writing."

Supervisor Cool goes to step 5: *Asking other members of the group if there is a third position that can be taken.* Some members might side with one over the other, suggest a compromise (one technical composition in the first semester, two in the second semester), or offer a new alternative (let's require a three-week minicourse of technical writing and let each school decide the type of work and assignments). If the conflict between Mrs. Strick and Mr. Ease does not resolve itself, the supervisor acknowledges that the conflict remains: "We understand the difference of opinion that you both have, and we can't find a ready solution." Then he moves to other matters: "Eventually the committee will have to decide or vote on what to do about required assignments. For now, we'll leave this particular issue and discuss the tenth-grade testing program."

Conflict cannot and should not be avoided. Conflict, if encouraged and supported, will enable a group to make better decisions. It is the group leader's handling of conflict that makes the difference. The group should have the feeling that it is all right to disagree and that anyone who does disagree will be able to make his or her full position known. Role play 17.2 provides for demonstrations of the right way and the wrong way to deal with conflict within a group.

ROLE PLAY 17.2 • *Resolving Conflict*

Context. The purpose of this role play is for a subgroup of five to provide a demonstration to the remainder of the group on how to effectively resolve conflict within a group. Participants will need approximately 20 minutes of preparation time away from the rest of the group. In the role play, a "supervisor" and four "teachers" are members of a committee meeting to discuss a schoolwide instructional issue. In their preparation for the role play, the role players may choose the school level, the issue to be discussed, and any other details of the fictional situation that they need to agree on to perform an effective role play. The group is assigned or chooses a conflict to be played out between two members of the group during the meeting. The role play is presented in two scenes.

Scene 1: Wrong Way (10 minutes). Soon after the beginning of the meeting, a conflict breaks out between two of the "teachers." The supervisor and the other teachers in the group deal with the conflict poorly, and the meeting deteriorates rapidly. The meeting breaks up with neither the interpersonal conflict nor the original issue resolved.

Scene 2: Right Way (10 minutes). This scene involves the same group, the same setting, and the same issue. The same conflict breaks out between the same two teachers. This time, however, the supervisor and teachers in the group use procedures discussed under this Chapter's topic "Resolving Conflict" to facilitate a resolution of the conflict and the original issue by the end of the meeting.

Whole Group Processing (10 minutes). The entire group discusses the nature of the conflict, the failed efforts to resolve it, and effects of the conflict on the group in Scene One. Also discussed are the techniques used to resolve the conflict, and the effects of the conflict resolution process in Scene Two.

Preparing for Group Meetings

A group can proceed more easily with its task if the leader has made certain preparations. Shelton and Bauer (1994) suggest that pre-meeting planning should involve decisions about whether a meeting is necessary, who should attend the meeting, setting, agenda, and preparation. Figure 17.2 includes specific questions that Shelton and Bauer recommend planners consider when preparing for a meeting. Some especially important aspects of preparing for a meeting include planning an agenda, establishing ground rules, and writing guided discussion questions.

Agendas

A group has to be clear on its task and purpose. Why are they meeting? What are they to accomplish? Is there to be a product? An agenda distributed several days

FIGURE 17.2   *Shelton and Bauer's Pre-Meeting Planner*

Should We Meet?
1. Can a memo be used instead of holding a meeting?
2. Is there a goal for the meeting?

Who Should Attend the Meeting?
3. Who needs to come to the meeting?
4. Will there be less than 15 participants?

The Setting
5. Where will the meeting be held?
6. Is the site convenient to participants?
7. Will a circular table arrangement be used?
8. Is the room temperature comfortable?
9. Have refreshments been arranged?

The Agenda
10. Have all participants been asked for agenda input?
11. Are the "For Information" items stated in sentence format?
12. Are the "For Discussion" items stated in question format?
14. Has the draft agenda been proofed?
15. Has the agenda been distributed, with at least 2 days lead time?

The Preparation
16. Have possible "troublesome items" been thought through?
17. If problem solving is a goal of the meeting, has the problem been adequately explained to meeting participants?
18. Has someone been asked to take minutes?
19. Has a follow-up on the previous evaluations been done?
20. Have evaluation forms (Blips) been distributed?

Source: Maria M. Shelton and Laurie K. Bauer, *Secrets of Highly Effective Meetings*, p. 43. Copyright © 1994 by Corwin Press. Reprinted by Permission of Sage Publications, Inc.

before the actual meeting will inform members of the reasons for the meeting and what will be accomplished. The agenda need not be elaborate. See Figure 17.3 as a sample agenda. Notice how the agenda includes a brief explanation and a breakdown of items. Time limits for each item provide members with a sense of priorities as well as the assurance that the leader plans to end on time. Keeping to starting and ending times displays respect for group members' personal schedules.

Establishing Ground Rules

Participants will need to know not only agenda items like the meeting's purpose, place, time, and topics, but also behaviors that are expected of them at the meeting. Ground rules can be established in advance concerning any of the following:

- Type of participation expected (Sharing of information, professional dialogue, choosing from established alternatives, brainstorming, problem solving, conflict resolution, and so on)
- Roles to be assigned (coordinator, time keeper, information giver, recorder, etc.)
- Interpersonal expectations (everyone contributes, use active listening, criticize ideas but not people, consider each person's views, use agreed upon conflict management strategies, and so on)
- Decision-making method (decision by averaging individuals' opinions, majority vote, consensus, etc.)
- Type of follow-up expected (assigned tasks, continued dialogue, classroom implementation, follow-up meeting, and so on)

FIGURE 17.3 *Sample Agenda*

To:	All physical education teachers
From:	Morris Bailey, athletic director
Subject:	Agenda for the meeting of February 23 in Room 253, 3:30–5:00

Next Thursday will be the last meeting before voting on the revisions of our student progress forms. Remember, bring any progress forms you have collected from other school systems. Sally and Bruce are to report on the forms provided by the State Department. At the conclusion of the meeting, we are to make specific recommendations of changes.

Agenda

I.	Review purpose of meeting	3:30–3:40
II.	Report from Sally and Bruce on State Department forms	3:40–4:00
III.	Report on other school system forms	4:00–4:20
IV.	Discussion of possible revisions	4:20–4:40
V.	Recommendations	4:40–5:00

See you Thursday. Please be on time!

Guided Discussion

When meeting with a small group to discuss an issue, it is helpful to have in mind the type of questions to ask. Typically, questions to be asked will shift during a meeting. At the beginning of the meeting, the leader usually spends time clarifying the topic for discussion. During the meeting, the leader uses open-ended questions that allow for seeking, elaborating, and coordinating of ideas, opinions, and information. At the conclusion of the meeting, the leader asks questions that summarize what has been accomplished and what remains to be done.

Some discussion questions that might help as a reference are presented in Figure 17.4. Prior to a meeting, the leader might review the questions in Figure 17.4 and write down specific questions concerning the topic to have in front of him or her. When the discussion stalls, the leader can look at his or her notes and ask one of the preselected questions. A discussion guide helps the leader ensure that the topic will be thoroughly examined.

Procedures for Large-Group Involvement

With small groups of up to 10 members, all members have a chance to participate actively throughout the decision-making process (Hare, 1976, pp. 230–231). When the number of group members is large, however, it becomes difficult for everyone to participate actively. For example, what does a curriculum director do when there is an important curriculum decision to make involving over 100 teachers? What does a school principal do when there is an important rescheduling decision to make that involves a faculty of 70 persons? From 75 to 100 teachers sitting in a cafeteria to discuss an issue would be an exercise in folly. At best, only a few brave souls would speak up, and the leader would have no sense of what others thought. If the leader truly wants the involvement of all members in making a decision, then tightly planned procedures are necessary. With all the procedures about to be described, faculty should clearly understand the decision-making method to be used for the final decision (majority vote, consensus, frequencies, and so on).

Three different procedures will be explained. An example involving a staff of 75 teachers brought together for the purpose of deciding on how to allocate the use of six new microcomputers in the high school resource center will be used. All three methods are based on breaking the entire group into subgroups of seven to twelve and having a representative committee of one member from each subgroup. Please refer to Figure 17.5 as the three procedures are explained.

Procedure A, postrepresentational, begins with step 1. The leader convenes the entire group and explains the task and procedures to be used and the method of decision making. Step 2 is assigning the 75 faculty members to seven subgroups of 10 to 11 members each. The leader should have decided on assignments of subgroups according to logical criteria (grade level, content field, or years of teaching experience). Grouping can be made horizontally (teachers of the same grade, content field, or teaching experience) or vertically (teachers from different grade

FIGURE 17.4 *Questions for Use in Leadership Discussion*

Questions Designed to Open Up Discussion

1. What do you think about the problem as stated?
2. What has been your experience in dealing with this problem?
3. Would anyone care to offer suggestions on facts we need to better our understanding of the problem?

Questions Designed to Broaden Participation

1. Now that we have heard from a number of our members, would others who have not spoken like to add their ideas?
2. How do the ideas presented so far sound to those of you who have been thinking about them?
3. What other phases of the problem should be explored?

Questions Designed to Limit Participation

1. To the overactive participant: We appreciate your contributions. However, it might be well to hear from some of the others. Would some of you who have not spoken care to add your ideas to those already expressed?
2. You have made several good statements, and I am wondering if someone else might like to make some remarks?
3. Since all our group members have not yet had an opportunity to speak, I wonder if you would hold your comments until a little later?

Questions Designed to Focus Discussion

1. Where are we now in relation to our goal for this discussion?
2. Would you like to have me review my understanding of the things we have said and the progress we have made in this direction?
3. Your comment is interesting, but I wonder if it is germane to the chief problem that is before us.

Questions Designed to Help the Group Move Along

1. I wonder if we have spent enough time on this phase of the problem. Should we move to another aspect of it?
2. Have we gone into this part of the problem far enough so that we might now shift our attention and consider this additional area?
3. In view of the time we have set for ourselves, would it be appropriate to look at the next question before us?

Questions Designed to Help the Group Evaluate Itself

1. I wonder if any of you have a feeling that we are blocked on this particular question? Why are we tending to slow down?
2. Should we take a look at our original objective for this discussion and see where we are in relation to it?
3. Now that we are nearing the conclusion of our meeting, would anyone like to offer suggestions on how we might improve our next meeting?

(continued)

FIGURE 17.4   *(Continued)*

Questions Designed to Help the Group Reach a Decision

1. Am I right in sensing agreement at these points? (Leader then gives brief summary.)
2. Since we seem to be tending to move in the direction of a decision, should we consider what it will mean for our group if we decide the matter this way?
3. What have we accomplished in our discussion up to this point?

Questions Designed to Lend Continuity to the Discussion

1. Since we had time for partial consideration of the problem at the last meeting, would someone care to review what we covered then?
2. Since we cannot reach a decision at this meeting, what are some of the points we should take up at the next one?
3. Would someone care to suggest points on which we need further preparation before we convene again?

Source: Produced in group development course at the University of Georgia.

levels, content fields, or years of teaching experience). The subgroups are assigned to discuss the topic, make recommendations, and select a representative both to report the group's position and to be a member of the representative committee. After the subgroup meeting, the representatives report orally on their subgroup's position to the entire faculty. After each subgroup has reported, the entire faculty recesses. In step 3, the representative committee, consisting of the seven representative members, meet on their own to recommend or decide the use of the microcomputers. In step 4, the entire faculty reconvenes to hear the representative committee's recommendation or decision. Again, the leader should have made clear at the beginning whether the representative group would come to the faculty with a recommendation or a decision. If it was to be a recommendation, the entire faculty would vote on the proposal; if it was to be a decision, the entire faculty would listen to the decision.

The advantages of the postrepresentative procedure is that a decision can be made after only a few meetings. The disadvantage is that subgroup members might feel that hidden influences are affecting the representative committee. Since most faculty members (in the example, 68 out of 75) are omitted from the representative committee meeting, speculation might abound about what transpires in the representative group. However, since each faculty member helped to choose the representatives, trust in their work should prevail.

Procedure B, open representation, is similar to procedure A except that an open chair or open forum is added to the representative committee. This procedure provides an opportunity for every faculty member to have input throughout the decision-making process. Step 1 is an explanation to the entire faculty of the task. Step 2 involves subgroup meetings with the election of a representative and a

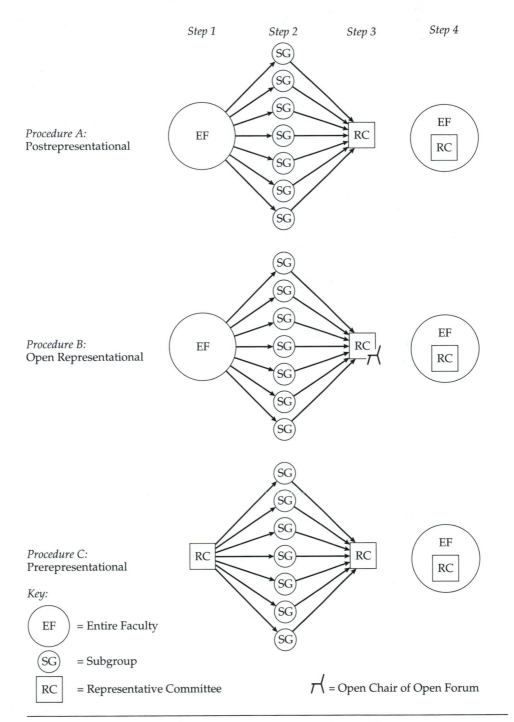

FIGURE 17.5   *Three Procedures for Large-Group Decision Making*

report of the subgroup's position to all faculty. Step 3 is a meeting of the representative committee with an invitation for any other faculty member to attend and participate. The representative committee deliberates in an open meeting. Times are built into the meeting for the use of an open chair or open forum where outside faculty might make comments. The open chair is at the table of the representative committee. An outside member can take the seat and speak for a certain length of time (usually two minutes), and then must relinquish the seat. Outside members are limited to a certain number of appearances. An open forum is similar except that an outside member does not physically have to move to a chair. He or she can raise his or her hand and speak when called on. Certain times at the beginning, middle, and closing of the meeting are established for outside-member participation. The representative committee can then consider outside-member contributions throughout their deliberations. In step 4, the representative committee makes its recommendation or decision to the entire group.

The advantage of open representation is the elimination of suspicion. All members, whether representatives or not, can be involved. A faculty member cannot rationally complain that he or she was excluded from the process. The open chair or forum invites participation but does not require it. Those faculty members who are indifferent about the decision, trust the representative group, or have other priorities are under no pressure to attend. On the other hand, those faculty members who care intensely or are distrustful have an opportunity to participate. For these various reasons, it is important to schedule the representative group meetings at a time that is convenient for all faculty members. (Releasing seven representatives from teaching duties for an 11:00 A.M. meeting and calling it an open meeting is not good enough.) The disadvantage of open representation is duration. Allowing input from other members throughout the process will slow down the proceedings of the representative groups. The leader might consider the tradeoff. Is it more important to have some involvement for a quicker decision or greater involvement for a slower decision?

Procedure C, prerepresentational, is the quickest of all but is predicated on the greatest amount of trust between faculty and leader. It begins with a selected representative group, *before* the entire faculty convenes. In step 1, the leader selects a seven-member committee that he or she believes best represents the entire faculty. The representative committee meets on its own to develop tentative recommendations to the entire faculty. In step 2, the representative committee reports its tentative recommendations to the entire faculty for the purpose of gathering reactions. Reactions are gathered by each member of the representative committee sitting with a subgroup of faculty. The subgroups, having just heard the representative committee's report, can now tell the representative member what they think. The representative member takes careful notes and at the conclusion of the subgroup meeting summarizes the reactions and tells the subgroup that he or she will personally give those reactions to the representative committee at their next meeting. In step 3, the representative committee reconvenes privately, listens to the report of each subgroup's reactions, and then decides whether to revise, change, or keep the original recommendation. In step 4, the representative committee gives its recommendation (to be voted on) or decision (to be implemented) to the entire faculty.

The critical element in procedure C is the leader's selection of the representative committee. The leader might be open to the criticism that the representative committee was selected on the basis of allegiance to the leader's own views and that the process was therefore manipulated. However, if faculty trust the leader's motives and understand the criteria for selection of the committee, the procedure should be effective.

The three procedures are alternative ways to have large-group involvement on important decisions. The task has to be important, of concern, and affect each person in order to justify such involvement. If the task is not important, if persons are indifferent and the effect will be minimal, the leader should not subject the faculty to such procedures. Decisions of lesser importance should be made in less involving ways. As a rule of thumb, decisions no one cares about should be made by the leader, decisions that already have been made by superordinates should simply be reported, and decisions that concern and affect some and not others should be made by those concerned and affected. The use of any of these large-group procedures should be reserved for only the most crucial decisions of broad impact.

Summary

This chapter examined the knowledge and skills needed to help professional groups develop. Particular emphasis was put on the supervisor's role in terms of behaving, confronting dysfunctional members, resolving conflict, and preparing for meetings.

The theme of looking at professional groups in a developmental manner should be familiar by now. As a group works together, the leader needs to practice skills that enable the group to become more cohesive, responsible, and autonomous. Eventually the leader would hope to lessen his or her own control and influence so that the group becomes a wise and autonomous body.

Exercises

Academic

1. Assume you are the leader of a group that is very person-oriented but is routinely failing to attend to tasks for which it is responsible. Assume further that you have determined that the roles of initiator-contributor, coordinator, orienter, and energizer are missing and that their absence is largely responsible for the group's failure to attend to assigned tasks. Write a paper explaining what steps you can take to make sure these task roles become present.

2. Assume you are the leader of a group that is generally functioning well but contains a blocker and a recognition seeker, each of whom is reducing the effectiveness of the group. Write a paper discussing plans for dealing individually with each of these group members to eliminate or reduce their dysfunctional behaviors.

3. Summarize three small-group research studies. Include a discussion of the purpose, participants, methodology, results, and conclusions of each study. Analyze the findings in terms of whether they are congruent with information presented in this chapter.

4. Assume you have been charged with leadership of a meeting at which a department/team of nine teachers will decide on a new textbook series to be used by those teachers. (You may decide the subject area and grade or age levels for which the text is to be used.) Prepare a written plan for leading the group meeting. Include a general format, an agenda, your plan for opening the meeting, and a discussion guide with preselected questions.

5. Assume you have been assigned to organize a meeting of 130 teachers who are to decide on a proposal to adopt a building-wide system of discipline. Write a paper discussing the procedure and specific strategies you will use in facilitating a group decision on the proposal.

Field

1. Record and analyze an audiotape of yourself leading a group decision-making process. Determine any leadership deficiencies you exhibited during the discussion. Was there a lack of preplanning for the meeting? Was your leadership lacking in facilitation of task or person behaviors? Did you fail to deal effectively with a dysfunctional member? Did you fail to handle conflict properly? Based on your analysis, prepare a self-improvement plan to be followed in a second group session. If possible, analyze an audiotape of a second meeting to see if you improved your leadership in the selected areas.

2. Assign task, personal, and dysfunctional roles to various members of a simulated group decision-making meeting. After the simulation, allow each member of the group to express personal reactions to the behaviors of the various role-players. Hold a group discussion on how each member affected the group's effectiveness.

3. Hold a one-to-one meeting with a dysfunctional group member of a real group that you lead. The conference should aim to improve that individual's in-group behavior. Write a summary of the conference and its results.

4. Prepare for and lead a real-life small-group meeting. Prepare a written evaluation of your small-group leadership.

5. Prepare for and lead a large-group decision-making process, using one of the procedures for large-group involvement discussed in this chapter. Write a report on the success of the process.

Developmental

1. Using knowledge and skills you have acquired in group development, continue to facilitate long-range development of a group of which you are a leader or member.

2. Begin an in-depth study of one of the following areas:

   a. Small-group research

   b. Group counseling skills

   c. Leadership style

   d. Organizational management

   e. Group discussion/interaction

3. Begin a file of group development activities. Each group activity can be summarized on an index card and classified according to categories that are useful for you.

References

Bales, R. F. 1953. The equilibrium problem in small groups. In T. Parsons, R. F. Bales, and E. A. Shils (Eds.), *Working papers in the theory of action* (pp. 111–161). Glencoe, IL: Free Press.

Benne, D. D., and Sheats, P. 1948. Functional roles of group members. *Journal of Social Issues* 4(2):41–49.

Brandt, R. 1987. On cooperation in schools: A conversation with David and Roger Johnson. *Educational Leadership* 45(3):14–19.

Corey, G., and Corey, M. 1982. *Groups: Process and practice*. Monterey, CA: Brooks/Cole.

Gordon, T. 1980. *Leadership effectiveness training—L.E.T.* New York: Bantam Books.

Hare, A. P. 1976. *Handbook of small group research* (2nd ed.). New York: Free Press.

Hare, A. P. 1982. *Creativity in small groups*. Beverly Hills, CA: Sage.

Hersey, P., and Blanchard, K. H. 1969. Life-cycle theory of leadership. *Training and Development Journal* 23(5):26–34.

Hersey, P., and Blanchard, K. H. 1988. *Management of organizational behavior: Utilizing human resources* (5th ed.). Englewood Cliffs, NJ: Prentice Hall.

Johnson, D. W., and Johnson, R. T. 1987a. *Joining together: Group theory and group skills* (3rd ed.). Englewood Cliffs, NJ: Prentice Hall.

Johnson, D. W., and Johnson, R. T. 1987b. Research shows the benefits of adult cooperation. *Educational Leadership* 45(3):27–30.

Kemp, C. G. 1970. *Perspectives on the group process: A foundation for counseling with groups* (2nd ed.). Boston: Houghton Mifflin.

Little, J. W. 1982. Norms of collegiality and experimentation: Workplace conditions of school success. *American Educational Research Journal* 19(3):325–340.

Shelton, M. M., and Bauer, L. K. 1994. *Secrets of highly effective meetings*. Thousand Oaks, CA: Corwin Press.

Slavin, R. E. 1987. Cooperative learning and the cooperative schools. *Educational Leadership* 45(3):7–13.

Suggested Readings

Chivers, J. 1995. *Team building with teachers*. London: Kogan Page.

Folger, J. P., Poole, M. S., and Stutman, R. K. 1993. *Working through conflict*. New York: HarperCollins.

Harrington-Mackin, D. 1994. *The team building tool kit: Tips, tactics, and rules for effective workplace teams*. New York: AMACOM.

Katzenback, J. R., and Smith, D. K. 1994. *The wisdom of teams: Creating the high-performance organization*. New York: HarperCollins.

Kayser, T. A. 1990. *Mining group gold*. El Segundo, CA: Serif.

Maeroff, G. I. 1993. *Team building for school change*. New York: Teachers College Press.

Moran, L., Musselwhite, E., and Zenger, J. H. 1996. *Keeping teams on track: What to do when the going gets rough*. Chicago: Irwin.

Morley, C. L. 1994. *How to get the most out of meetings*. Alexandria, VA: Association for Supervision and Curriculum Development.

Orsburn, J. D., Moran, L., Musselwhite, E., and Zenger, J. H. 1990. *Self-Directed work teams: The new American challenge.* Chicago: Irwin.

Parker, G. M. 1994. *Cross-functional teams: Working with allies, enemies and other strangers.* San Francisco: Jossey-Bass.

Phillips, G. M. (Ed.). 1990. *Teaching how to work in groups.* Norwood, NJ: Ablex.

Prior, D. W., Thompson, J. W., and Miller, M. J. 1991. Teaching decision making using situational leadership. *Journal of Creative Behavior* 25(1):34–42.

Shelton, M. M., and Bauer, L. K. 1994. *Secrets of highly effective meetings.* Thousand Oaks, CA: Sage.

Tjosvold, D. 1993. *Learning to manage conflict.* New York: Lexington.

Zenger, J. H., Musselwhite, E., Hurson, K., and Perrin, C. 1994. *Leading teams: Mastering the new role.* Burr Ridge, IL: Irwin.

18

Professional Development

Bob Jeffries, director of professional development, calls six school principals into his office to plan for the upcoming in-service day. He begins by explaining that the in-service program will start with a morning session, attended by the entire school system faculty, in the high school auditorium. The afternoon will consist of individual school activities, with the principal being responsible for whatever transpires. Mr. Jeffries asks the principals, "What might we do for the morning session?" One principal suggests that at this time of year teachers could use an emotional lift, and that an inspirational speaker would be good. Another principal adds that she had heard a Dr. Zweibach give a great talk entitled "The Thrill of Teaching" at a national principals' conference last summer. She thinks he would be a terrific speaker. Bob Jeffries likes these suggestions and tells the principals he will call Dr. Zweibach and make arrangements for his appearance.

On the in-service day, 238 teachers file into the auditorium and fill all but the first eight rows of seats. Mr. Jeffries makes a few introductory remarks about how fortunate "we" are to have Dr. Zweibach with "us" and then turns the session over to Dr. Zweibach. A rumpled, middle-aged university professor walks to the microphone and launches into his talk on the thrill of teaching. Within 10 minutes, signs of restlessness, boredom, and bitterness are evident throughout the audience. It seems that 12 of the teachers are sitting through a talk they had heard Dr. Zweibach deliver verbatim two years earlier at a teacher convention; 15 others are thinking about the classroom work they could be doing to prepare for next semester and wondering, "Why in the world are we sitting through this talk?" Another 22 teachers have become impatient with Dr. Zweibach's continual reference to the academic high school settings where he found teaching thrills. Their own work settings are vocational, special education, and elementary; they can't relate what he is saying about high schools to their world. Eventually, some teachers begin to correct papers, read, or knit; a few appear to fall asleep. On the other hand, nearly half the members of the audience remain attentive and give Dr. Zweibach a rousing ovation when he concludes. The other half appear relieved that the talk is finally over and they can return to their own schools. Upon leaving the auditorium, one can overhear such remarks as "What a great talk!" and "Why do we have to put up with all this staff-development crap?"

This depiction of an in-service day is typical of many school systems. Some teachers find it valuable, but many do not. Staff development has been referred to as "the slum of American education, neglected and of little effect" (Wood and Thompson, 1980). Professional development is often viewed by supervisors, administrators, and teachers as a number of days contracted for in the school calendar that simply need to be endured. Three crucial questions will shape this chapter: (1) Why is professional development needed? (2) How should it be planned and conducted? (3) Are teachers to be the objects or the agents of professional development? A supervisor with responsibility for professional development cannot hope to make every activity interesting and valuable to every teacher, but he or she can expect professional development to be, overall, of value and interest to most if not all staff members. The ultimate outcome should be improved instruction for students.

Why the Need for Professional Development?

Over 85 percent of a total school budget is used to pay employee salaries. Education is a human enterprise. The essence of successful instruction and good schools comes from the thoughts and actions of the professionals in the schools. So, if one is to look for a place to improve the quality of education in a school, a sensible place to look is the continuous education of educators—that is, professional development. Some of the options that school districts can provide for professional development are contracted in-service days, optional in-service sessions for recertification credits, early-morning or after-school times for workshop mini-sessions, college courses, faculty meetings, teacher centers, visits to other schools, attendance at local, state, and national conferences, travel for cultural enrichment, and readings and video- and audiocassettes (Speak and Hirsh, 1988). Virtually any experience that enlarges a teacher's knowledge, appreciation, skills, and understandings of his or her work falls under the domain of professional development.

When one of the authors gave a presentation to a Michigan school board to explain the need to allocate more money for professional development, he used an analogy to the automobiles made in Detroit. When a customer purchases a new car costing upwards of $30,000, he or she brings it in every 5,000 miles for preventive maintenance and fine-tuning. The customer continues to put additional money into the car to prolong its life and performance. Simply to run the car into the ground would be a dumb way to protect such an investment! In education, the school board is the customer, who purchases more than a new car with its $30,000 initial investment—it purchases a living and breathing professional! Without resources for maintaining, fine-tuning, and reinvigorating the investment, the district will run teachers into the ground. This is far more consequential than a neglected car. The district will lose teachers, physically and/or mentally. The real losers will be the students of these teachers.

Professional development has gathered increased attention in both research and resource allocation across the nation. States have dramatically increased their expenditures for professional development in local districts and schools since the series of national reports issued in the mid-1980s. The National Staff Development Council has become the fastest-growing educational organization in the United States. Until 1957, only about 50 studies had been conducted on professional development in schools (Showers, Joyce, and Bennett, 1987). Now several times that number of studies are being conducted every year.

Too often teachers receive little of substance from professional-development programs (Guskey, 1986). In a study of the attitudes and beliefs of 150 highly competent teachers, Karst (1987) found that "they found their avenues of growth outside of the normal in-service and professional development routines" (p. 26) and that these teachers continued to grow despite the lack of meaningful school-derived learning experiences. "It was amazing how silently resistant most of them felt about [school and district] philosophy that included no serious organizational plans for dealing with their professional aspirations and development" (p. 28). For teachers who are not so resilient, self-directed, and efficacious, "These are the conditions that create teachers who quit teaching...become dead souls, without vision, without ideals, without hope that things will get better" (p. 28).

Since professional development should be a responsibility of those who supervise, the research and application discussed here will focus on the use of successful professional development to improve instruction. According to a study of teachers and administrators in New York state (Tetenbaum and Mulkeen, 1987, p. 11), the primary criticisms of professional development programs are that the activities are "one-shot deals" and that there is "no integration with a comprehensive plan to achieve school goals." Let's see how these criticisms can be avoided.

Characteristics of Successful Professional Development Programs

A considerable knowledge base exists on successful professional development. One line of research has focused on skill development programs.

Lawrence (1974) examined 97 studies and evaluation reports, primarily on skill development programs. He concluded that the following were characteristics of effective programs:

1. Involvement of administrators and supervisors in planning and delivering the program
2. Differential training experiences for different teachers
3. Placement of the teacher in an active role (generating materials, ideas, and behaviors)
4. Emphasis on demonstrations, supervised trials and feedback, teacher sharing, and mutual assistance

5. Linkage of activities to the general professional development program
6. Teacher choice of goals and activities
7. Teacher self-initiated and self-directed training activities

Berman and McLaughlin (1978) synthesized findings of a four-year Rand Corporation study on the effects of educational innovations funded by the federal government. They found that effective projects in school districts were characterized by mutual adaptation of project and staff. Elements that fostered mutual adaptation included the following:

1. Concrete, teacher-specific, and extended training
2. Classroom assistance from project or district staff
3. Teacher observations of similar projects in other classrooms, schools, or districts
4. Regular project meetings that focused on practical problems
5. Teacher participation in project decisions
6. Local materials developed
7. Principal participation in training (p. 9)

Joyce and Showers (1980, 1983, 1988) have shown that skill development programs that use presentation, demonstration, and practice as well as classroom feedback and coaching are more successful than programs that do not use feedback and coaching. In other words, teachers acquire and use new skills more readily when there is follow-up into their own classrooms. Stallings (1980) has shown that small-group problem-solving workshops in which six to seven teachers share and experiment show greater results than workshops with large groups.

Mohlman has compared three different skill development models (Mohlman, 1982; Mohlman-Sparks, 1986). The first contained presentation, demonstration, practice, and feedback; the second contained presentation, demonstration, practice, and feedback followed by peer observation; and the third contained presentation, demonstration, practice, feedback, and trainer coaching. She found that participants acquired more classroom skills with the second model of peer observation. The trainer-coaching model ranked second in skill acquisition, and the model that did not have peer observation or expert coaching ranked last.

The Mohlman, Kierstead, and Gundlach model (1982), used with the California Department of Education, incorporates various elements of effective skill development. It includes:

1. Small-group workshops spaced three weeks apart
2. Peer observations
3. Postobservation analysis and conferencing focused on skills introduced in workshops
4. Classroom experimentation and modification of implemented skills

Modern professional development has a variety of purposes beyond skill training, including facilitation of teachers' self efficacy, cognitive development, and career development, as well as teacher collegiality and the improvement of school culture. The broadening of professional development has been accompanied by an expanding body of literature on effective development programs, including original research and reviews of research and best practice (Loucks-Horsley, et al., 1987; Orlich, 1989; Wood and Thompson, 1993; Guskey, 1994; Corcoran, 1995; U.S. Department of Education, 1996; Hawley and Valli, 1996; Joyce, Calhoun, and Hopkins, 1999). Although these reports do not agree on all factors, there are a number of common characteristics:

1. Involvement of participants in planning, implementing, and evaluating programs
2. Programs that are based on school-wide goals, but that integrate individual and group goals with school goals
3. Long range planning and development
4. Programs that incorporate research and best practice on school improvement and instructional improvement
5. Administrative support, including provision of time and other resources as well as involvement in program planning and delivery
6. Adherence to the principles of adult learning (see Chapter 4)
7. Attention to the research on change, including the need to address individual concerns throughout the change process (see Chapter 21)
8. Follow-up and support for transfer of learning to the school or classroom
9. Ongoing assessment and feedback
10. Continuous professional development that becomes part of the school culture

As you review the characteristics listed above, think of a professional development program that you are familiar with. How many of the ten characteristics are present in that program?

Individual Teacher-Based Professional Development

There are many ways to determine topic priorities for professional development programs. Chapter 13 detailed the techniques of eyes and ears, official records, third party review, written open-ended surveys, check and ranking lists, the Delphi technique, and the nominal group technique. Any of these techniques would give a planning committee an idea of topics desired by participants. For example, the director of professional development might survey the teaching personnel of the school system for individual priorities and might find that *discipline* appears as the top-priority topic for both elementary and secondary teachers. This does not mean, however, that the planning committee can be assured that if they find an expert on discipline to work with staff throughout the school year, they will have a successful program. When teachers check off a topic such as discipline as their top priority, *those individual checks mean different things to different people.* An eleventh-grade teacher who checks discipline thinks, "I want to learn how to handle those big, tough, obnoxious students who keep making me back down." Another eleventh-grade teacher checks the discipline box thinking, "I want to learn how to conduct class discussions so students will listen more attentively to each other." A seventh-grade teacher checks the discipline box thinking, "I want to encourage self-discipline and have students take on more responsibility for their homework, studying for tests, and asking for help." A professional development program on discipline that does not account for what individual teachers mean will be a hit-or-miss affair. The content of a general session on discipline will, by chance, fit the needs of some and miss those of others. A consultant who is an expert on teaching assertive behavior will be of real benefit to the eleventh-grade teacher who is being intimidated by students; the same consultant would be of some benefit to the eleventh-grade teacher who wants to conduct classroom discussions but of little benefit to the seventh-grade teacher who desires students to develop self-discipline. To be relevant, professional development needs to be planned not only according to prioritized topics but also according to the individual meanings ascribed to the topics.

Gene Hall and his associates have made substantial contributions to the planning of professional development programs based on individual meaning to participants (Hall and Hord, 1987). They found that teachers have different levels of interest, commitment, and needs when it comes to instructional changes. As in our example on discipline, they found that an innovation such as individualized instruction, mastery learning, or team teaching has different meanings to individuals and that teachers are concerned with different aspects of the proposed topics.

How does one find out what a teacher means by his or her priority for inservice? As Hall and associates found, the best way to find out is simply to ask. If discipline emerges as a school system's number-one priority for professional development, a follow-up form might be sent to teachers. A simple open-ended form has been developed by Newlove and Hall (1976):

WHEN YOU THINK ABOUT DISCIPLINE, WHAT ARE YOU CONCERNED ABOUT? Do not say what you think others are concerned about, but only what concerns you now. Please write in complete sentences, and please be frank.

From reading the responses, the planning committee can group the concerns into different categories. Some may be concerned with assertiveness, some with leading discussion groups, some with giving students more self-responsibility, and some with schoolwide rules. Common concerns could be handled through large-group instruction; more individualized concerns could be handled by various choices of small-group workshops.

Alternative Professional Development Formats

We are rapidly moving away from the era when professional development usually means either a 60-minute speech by an outside consultant or a "one-shot" workshop. A variety of new formats for professional development have emerged over the last several years. Some examples follow:

- *Mentoring programs:* An experienced teacher is assigned to a novice for the purpose of providing individualized, ongoing professional support.
- *Skill development programs:* This consists of several workshops over a period of months, and classroom coaching between workshops to assist teachers to transfer new skills to their daily teaching.
- *Teacher centers:* Teachers can meet at a central location to engage in professional dialogue, develop skills, plan innovations, and gather or create instructional materials.
- *Teacher institutes:* Teachers participate in intensive learning experiences on single, complex topics over a period of consecutive days or weeks.
- *Collegial support groups:* Teachers within the same school engage in group inquiry, address common problems, jointly implement instructional innovations, and provide mutual support.
- *Networks:* Teachers from different schools share information, concerns, and accomplishments and engage in common learning through computer links, newsletters, fax machines, and occasional seminars and conferences.
- *Teacher leadership:* Teachers participate in leadership preparation programs and assist other teachers by assuming one or more leadership roles (workshop presenter, cooperating teacher, mentor, expert coach, instructional team leader, curriculum developer). The teacher-leader not only assists other teachers but also experiences professional growth as a result of being involved in leadership activities.
- *Teacher as writer:* This increasingly popular format has teachers reflect on and write about their students, teaching, and professional growth. Such writing can be in the form of private journals, essays, or reaction papers to share with colleagues, or formal articles for publication in educational journals
- *Individually planned professional development:* Teachers set individual goals and objectives, plan and carry out activities, and assess results.
- *Partnerships:* Partnerships between schools and universities or businesses, in which both partners are considered equal, have mutual rights and responsibilities, make contributions, and receive benefits. Such partnerships could involve one or more of the previously described formats.

There can be considerable overlap between various professional development formats (not to mention between professional development and the other four tasks of supervision!). Our own experience as staff developers and researchers has led us to conclude that many of the most successful professional development programs combine multiple formats. Next, we will describe several professional development programs, each including a combination of formats.

Examples of Effective Professional Development Programs

We will describe six professional development models, including two comprehensive programs, a lead-teacher center, a self-directed program, a teacher induction program, and site-based staff development. Each of the examples is either an actual program or a composite based on several actual programs.

Comprehensive Professional Development Programs

The *St. Mary's Achievement Related Teaching program (SMART)* was based on a written needs assessment of all district teachers conducted by the district's professional development planning committee, comprised of a majority of teachers. During the first year of the program, a group of 18 volunteer instructional leaders (14 teachers, 3 building administrators, and 1 central office supervisor) chosen by the committee participated in professional development leadership preparation. The leadership preparation was conducted by a team of professors from a nearby university that had entered into a formal partnership with the district. Leadership preparation addressed the following areas:

  I. Generic Instructional Skills
    A. Classroom Management
    B. Lesson Design
    C. Student Assessment
    D. Teacher Expectations
    E. Questioning Skills
    F. Student Motivation
 II. Instructional Models
    A. Concept Attainment
    B. Compare and Contrast
    C. Cooperative Learning
    D. Concept Mapping
III. Coaching and Leadership
    A. An Overview of Peer Coaching
    B. Systematic Observation of Instruction
    C. Conferencing Skills
    D. Professional Relationships
    E. Matching Coaching to Teacher Concerns

Leadership training consisted of 12 workshops over the course of a year. Between workshops, doctoral students from the university visited the school district and provided coaching to the staff developers as they implemented new instructional strategies and models in actual classroom lessons. This expert coaching was intended to (1) assist the staff developers to master strategies and models they would be conducting workshops on the following year and (2) allow the staff developers to observe effective coaches in action.

During subsequent years, the staff developers became workshop presenters as small groups of regular teachers (groups of approximately 15) were cycled through the instructional strategies and models components of the program. Just as they had been coached by doctoral students in their leadership preparation, the district's staff developers provided coaching between workshops to assist new participants to transfer skills to their classrooms. While participation in the program was voluntary, participants were required to attend all workshops and participate in a specified number of coaching cyles.

A different type of comprehensive professional development program was conducted by **North Allegheny School District.** Like Saint Mary's, North Allegheny's program involved a university partnership, administrators and teachers as professional-development leaders, workshops, and coaching. Unlike Saint Mary's, North Allegheny carried out a variety of programs from which teachers chose the one in which they wished to participate. During the first year of the university-school partnership, the district's professional development planning committee (with a majority of teachers) collaborated in a needs assessment, including both a written survey and focus group interviews with teachers from the elementary, middle, intermediate, and senior high school levels. Data analysis indicated the need for a variety of programs on instructional strategies and technology.

During the second year of the partnership, university professors conducted a leadership preparation program for over 30 teachers, supervisors, and administrators who volunteered to be professional development leaders. All participants attended a set of core workshops covering topics such as peer coaching, systematic observation of instruction, and conferencing skills. Specialized workshops on topics such as cooperative learning, assisting the student who has special needs, and instructional technology were attended only by the small professional development teams that would be responsible for conducting workshops on those topics. The leaders coached each other between workshops in order to master instructional skills and practice peer coaching. During the summer after leadership preparation, small professional development teams planned a variety of staff development programs for the following school year.

Beginning with the third year of the program, the district's teachers were invited to attend 1 of 10 professional development programs provided by the leadership teams, including programs on instructional strategies and instructional technology:

    I. Programs on Instructional Strategies
       A. Communication Arts
       B. Creating a Needs-Satisfying Environment
       C. Teaching Higher-Level Thinking Skills

       D. Cooperative Learning

       E. Meeting Diverse Learning Needs

  II. Programs on Instructional Technology

       A. Introduction to Macintosh Computers

       B. Word Processing for Macintosh Computers

       C. Graphics on Macintosh Computers

       D. Multimedia/Hypercard

       E. Interactive Video/Telecommunications

Each program included a series of workshops and individualized assistance between workshops. Individualized assistance was provided on four levels:

1. Workshop participants' observations of professional development leaders demonstrating skills during actual classroom lessons
2. Expert coaching of workshop participants in their classrooms by professional development leaders
3. Co-coaching, with a professional development leader and a workshop participant coaching a second workshop participant in his or her classroom
4. Peer coaching between workshop participants, in each other's classrooms

The university's role during the third year of the program was limited to assisting the school district with formative program evaluation. After the third year, the school-university partnership ended, and the district assumed full responsibility for implementing and evaluating subsequent program cycles for new groups of teachers.

Although different in scope, both of the comprehensive professional development programs described here included several of the staff development formats discussed in the previous section, including school-university partnerships, teacher leadership, skill development programs, and peer coaching.

The ACT Lead-Teacher Center

The ACT Lead-Teacher Center is one of nine such centers supported by grants from the Pennsylvania Department of Education. The purpose of the centers is to prepare teachers to assume leadership roles in their districts for instructional and school improvement. Basic principles of the centers are the following:

- Lead teachers are volunteers.
- Lead teachers are chosen by peers.
- Lead teachers have collegial, nonevaluative roles.
- A team orientation is promoted (including supervisors and administrators as team members).
- Lead teachers continue to teach.

Specific roles that lead-teacher centers prepare teachers for include:

- Mentors
- Facilitators

- Resource persons
- Peer coaches
- Classroom researchers
- Community education coordinators
- School renewal team members

The ACT Lead-Teacher Center has focused on establishing teacher networks, curriculum projects, grants for teacher research, partnerships with universities, distance education, and "trainer of trainer" skill development. Some sample ACT program topics include the following:

- Grant Writing
- Elementary Writing
- Performance-Based Education and Authentic Assessment
- Leading Work Teams
- Multicultural Education and Learning Styles
- Hands-on Science Electricity Project
- Whole Language Frameworks
- Strategic Planning

Each year, teachers served by the ACT Center and other lead-teacher centers gather for a statewide conference to share regional activities and innovations. Additionally, the lead-teacher centers sponsor a publication entitled *The Pennsylvania Journal of Teacher Education*. The journal consists of articles "by teachers for teachers," and allows teachers to share "ideas, experiences, reflections, and action research" (Lead Teacher Centers of Pennsylvania, no date).

The ACT-Lead Teacher Center is another example of multiple professional development formats. Included within the umbrella teacher-center format are skill development workshops, teacher institutes, networks, teacher leadership, teacher as writer, individualized professional development, and partnership formats.

Individually Planned Professional Development

An individually planned professional development program at Holidaysburg Area School District (Wilshire, 1991) consisted of five phases:

1. *Invitation:* Interested teachers were invited to a meeting to discuss the program. After an overview of the program was provided, teachers who wished to participate completed biographical data sheets. The biographical information was used to match the volunteer teachers to facilitators from a nearby university. The role of the facilitators was to aid professional planning.
2. *Assessment:* Facilitators audiotaped individual interviews with participating teachers. Interview questions were designed to determine individual teachers' needs, interests, and preferred professional development formats. Facilitators reviewed interview transcripts and generated potential professional

development projects or learning activities in which individual teachers might be interested.

3. *Validation-Negation:* In a second meeting with individual teachers, facilitators shared interview data and data-based professional development options. Teachers could select from options presented by their facilitators, propose their own options, or decide to reflect further on various options. Eventually, teachers, assisted by facilitators, developed their own written professional-development plans, including goals, objectives, activities, assessment, and needed resources and materials.

4. *Disclosure:* During a group meeting of facilitators and participants, the teachers shared their individual plans with each other. Collaboration was encouraged when two or more plans were similar.

5. *Implementation:* After a meeting with a district administrator to approve the individual plans, implementation began. Teachers had two years to complete their self-directed programs. Facilitators remained available to assist the participants as they carried out their plans. Participants were required to provide the district with products developed during their self-directed programs, which became resources for the district and its teachers.

Individual plans in the Holidaysburg program included developing new curricula, learning and using new instructional strategies, engaging in interdisciplinary team teaching, and collecting information about successful educational practices to share with school personnel. The Holidaysburg model and other individually planned programs open the door for individual teachers to become involved in any of the staff development formats discussed earlier in this chapter, including *group* staff development to help them to reach their individual goals.

A Beginning Teacher Assistance Program

Buckeye School District's efforts to support beginning teachers began with the design of a beginning teacher assistance program by a planning committee made up of administrators, supervisors, and teachers. A key component of the program is a pool of experienced mentor teachers. Volunteer mentors are selected by a screening committee. Selection criteria include years of experience in the school system, effective teaching performance, interpersonal skills, past commitment to the profession, flexibility, and willingness to spend time helping beginning teachers. The selected teachers take part in an intensive mentor-preparation program, including the following elements:

- Introduction to the knowledge base on problems of beginning teachers, beginning teacher assistance programs, and mentoring
- Overview of the district's beginning teacher assistance program
- Research on effective classroom management

- Research on effective teaching
- Principles of adult learning
- Adult and teacher development
- Goal setting and action planning
- The coaching of teaching, including conferencing skills and observation skills
- Action research

A number of variables are considered when assigning mentors to beginning teachers, including grade level and content area, classroom location, and philosophical and personal compatibility of mentor and beginner. An attempt is made to make an overall "best match" of mentor and beginner.

Prior to the beginning of the school year, a special orientation for beginners is attended by novices and their mentors. During this orientation, new teachers are walked through key information about the community, district policies and procedures, and the curriculum they will be responsible for teaching. Later in the orientation, they are given tours of their schools and meet with building administrators and instructional leaders. Their mentors review building policies and procedures and provide them with a profile of the school, its staff, students, and parents.

The orientation is only the beginning of assistance for the beginning teacher in Buckeye School District. Ongoing support is provided throughout the school year. For each beginner, a support team is formed, consisting of a building administrator, department chairperson or instructional team leader, and mentor. The team meets on a regular basis. Continuous assistance is based on written needs assessments and discussions with support teams. Workshops are provided for beginners on such topics as classroom management, effective teaching, and working with parents. Mentors visit beginners' classrooms on a regular basis to provide nonevaluative assistance, including expert coaching following the five-step model presented in Chapter 16. Beginners visit the classrooms of mentors and other effective teachers to observe best practice. Mentors are available on a daily basis to provide beginners with psychological support, information, and instructional assistance.

Mentors too are given support by the district in the form of follow-up workshops, support seminars, tuition reimbursement for relevant university coursework, released time, and stipends. Their contributions to beginners and the district are recognized during faculty meetings, in district publications, and at an annual recognition dinner.

Buckeye School District's support program includes a partnership with a nearby university. Professors from the university collaborated with Buckeye School District in the design of its support program. The same professors assist with mentor preparation and offer course credit for mentors willing to do outside work beyond the mentor workshops. Finally, the professors assist in the delivery of several of the workshops for beginning teachers. To summarize, although mentoring is the heart and soul of Buckeye School District's beginning teacher assistance program, other formats—such as skill development programs, collegial support groups, and partnerships—are part of the overall program.

Site-Based Initiatives

There are numerous recent examples of staff development planned and implemented by school councils and school task forces as part of site-based initiatives to address the educational priorities of the particular school. Faculty and parents assess their current instructional programs, establish learning goals for students, and then decide whether the expertise to conduct staff development programs lies within or outside the school. The various school renewal networks—such as the League of Professional Schools, the Coalition of Essential Schools, the Accelerated Schools, and the Comer Schools—have many powerful examples of decentralized, staff development plans derived by faculty interested in learning new methods of instruction (such as models of teaching, cooperative learning, conflict mediation, service learning, Socratic discussions, interdisciplinary curriculum, higher-order thinking, nongraded schedules, team teaching, and technology integration). The schools plan their own retreats, staff development days, and summer institutes. The results of many of these efforts have been major improvements in student achievement and attitudes, higher attendance, and lower incidents of discipline and vandalism (see Levin, 1994; Glickman, 1992; and Gursky, 1990).

Ponticell (1995) provides a description of a site-based professional development program in an inner city Chicago high school. The aim of the program was instructional improvement based on collegial learning and support. The program was supported by a $12,000 grant from a nearby university and facilitated by a professor from the university. The program began with a professional retreat where teachers engaged in reflective dialogue about teaching and began to build collaborative relationships.

Following the retreat, the teachers began to read and discuss research on effective teaching and professional development alternatives. Next, the teachers developed a cycle of monthly professional development activities including the following phases:

1. Teachers identified an instructional concern, read current research addressing that concern, selected ideas that made sense, developed a strategy for classroom implementation, and created a checklist of planned teacher behaviors.
2. Teachers videotaped themselves implementing improvement strategies, analyzed their own videotapes, and compared their actual behaviors to the checklist of anticipated behaviors.
3. Peer coaching, focused on the month's strategy, with a coaching cycle consisting of a preconference, observation, and postconference.
4. End-of-month group meetings in which teachers met to share video clips, discussed what aspects of the month's strategy had worked and not worked, reflected on what they had learned, and determined the topic of study for the following month.

Based on pre- and postinventories, direct observation, analysis of audiotapes of group discussions, and interviews with participants, Ponticell (1995) found that the site-based program had increased collegiality, improved self-analysis of teaching, enabled teachers to learn new ways of collaboratively observing and discussing each other's teaching, and fostered learning and experimenting with new teaching strategies.

In this section, we have presented examples of how various formats can be combined to build staff development programs. In the next section, we will discuss stages of staff development that apply to any long-term staff development program.

Stages of Professional Development

Professional development typically involves three stages of learning: (1) orienta- tion, (2) integration, and (3) refinement. To illustrate these three stages, we will relate them to staff development on the cooperative learning instructional model.

In the ***orientation stage,*** benefits, responsibilities, and personal concerns about involvement in the staff development are addressed. Next, participants engage in learning necessary for initial "real-world" application. In our coopera- tive learning example, orientation topics might include the following:[1]

- Differences between cooperative, competitive, and individual learning
- Differences between cooperative learning and traditional group work
- Research on cooperative learning
- Basic elements of cooperative learning (teaching social skills, positive inter- dependence, face-to-face interaction, individual accountability, group processing)
- Forming cooperative groups
- Standard cooperative learning structures (think-pair-share, jigsaw, student teams achievement divisions ([STAD], teams-games-tournaments [TGT], group investigation, and so on)
- Planning cooperative lessons

Failure to take teachers beyond the orientation stage is one reason why many staff development programs are ineffective: Teachers are given rudimentary knowledge or skills and then are left to fend for themselves.

In the ***integration stage,*** teachers are assisted as they apply previous learn- ing in their classrooms and schools. One aspect of integration is learning to adapt general learning to specific situations. In the cooperative learning example, this would mean learning to alter cooperative teaching strategies to make them ap- propriate for different learning content and students. A related aspect of integra- tion is regular and effective use of the new learning. This would mean, for example, the teacher develops enough competence and confidence in cooperative learning methods to make them part of his or her standard repertoire of instruc- tional strategies.

In the ***refinement stage,*** teachers move from basic competence to expertness through continuous experimentation and reflection. In the refinement stage of staff development on cooperative learning, teachers would become expert at a wide range of cooperative learning strategies and at mixing and matching those strategies for optimal student learning. Teachers in the refinement stage synthesize different types of previous learning in order to create new learning. In our cooperative learning example, a teacher at this stage might combine aspects of two or more standard cooperative learning structures to create a more complex structure. For another example, a teacher at the refinement stage might synthesize whole language and cooperative learning strategies to create an entirely new teaching strategy. Perhaps the best thing that a supervisor can do when teachers have reached this stage is to sign them up as teacher-staff developers!

Matching Professional Development to Teacher Characteristics

The goals and formats of professional development programs obviously are important factors in selecting specific professional development activities. For instance, for a program with the goal of increasing teacher interaction and collaboration through a collegial support format, a 90-minute lecture on the elements of effective instruction would *not* be an appropriate activity! Keeping in mind the need for consistency between goals, formats, and activities, there are a number of factors that can help tailor specific activities to teachers' levels of personal development, expertise, and commitment and stages of staff development. These factors are experience impact, degree of structure, sequence, and pace.

Experience Impact

Harris (1989) has listed 28 specific activities, each of which could be used within a variety of staff development formats. He has calculated an "experience impact" score for each activity. Experience impact is the degree to which the individual participant will be totally involved on each dimension of senses, interactions, experience control, focus, activeness, originality, and reality. Harris defined these seven factors as follows:

1. *Senses involved:* Extent of involvement of the various senses called upon.
2. *Interactions multiple:* Extent to which communication flow is two-way or three-way or multichanneled.
3. *Controlled experience:* Extent to which character of the experience is under control—has structure.
4. *Focus:* Extent to which the experience is given a focus, has unity, internal consistency.
5. *Activeness:* Extent to which the experience calls for active use of inputs.
6. *Originality:* Extent to which inputs are original in content, form, or relationships.
7. *Reality:* Extent to which realities rather than abstractions are utilized as frames of reference. (p. 79)

The experience impact score is derived by totaling the scores (1 = low, 3 = high) for each dimension of the activity. The total score is an estimate of the impact on the individual. Although Harris's (1989) experience impact scale is theoretically derived and not empirically tested, it has much common-sense appeal when deciding on activities.

In Table 18.1, we have listed Harris's activities in order of experience impact scores, with scores in parentheses after each activity. Table 18.1 also relates Harris's activities to the stages of professional development. Checks indicate activities that we recommend as options for the various stages.

TABLE 18.1 *Activities, Experience Impact, and Stages of Professional Development*

Activity and Experience Impact Score	Stages of Professional Development		
	Orientation	*Integration*	*Refinement*
Lecturing (7)	X		
Tape, radio, record listening (7)	X		
Panel presenting (8)	X		
Interviewing, informative (9)	X		
Visualizing (9)	X	X	X
Discussing, leaderless (10)	X	X	X
Film, television, filmstrip viewing (10)	X		
Discussing, leader facilitated (11)	X	X	X
Demonstrating (12)	X	X	
Material equipment, viewing (12)	X	X	X
Mediating (12)	X	X	
Writing or drawing (12)	X	X	X
Brainstorming (13)		X	X
Observing, systematically in classroom (13)		X	X
Social interaction (13)	X	X	X
Buzz session (14)	X	X	X
Reading (14)	X	X	X
Interviewing, problem solving (15)		X	X
Analyzing and calculating (16)		X	X
Group therapy (16)		X	X
Role playing, spontaneous (16)	X	X	X
Testing (16)		X	
Videotaping or photographing (16)		X	X
Interviewing, therapeutic (17)		X	X
Microteaching (18)		X	X
Role playing, structured (18)	X	X	X
Guided practice (19)		X	X
Firsthand experience (21)		X	X

Source: Activities and experience impact scores adapted from B. M. Harris, *Inservice Education for Staff Development*, 1989, Allyn and Bacon. Adapted by permission of Ben M. Harris, © copyright, 1989. All rights reserved. Checks suggesting appropriate activities for each stage provided by the authors of this text.

For teachers functioning at lower levels of development, expertise, and commitment and in the orientation stage of professional development, the bulk of activities should be low impact, with some activities of moderate impact, and an occasional high-impact activity. Teachers of moderate to high or mixed levels of development, expertise, and commitment and in the integration and refinement stages of professional development can engage primarily in moderate- to high-impact activities. We need to keep in mind that teachers initially functioning at lower levels of development, expertise, and commitment can experience growth in these characteristics, enabling them to profit from higher-impact activities as they move through the stages of professional development.

Degree of Structure

The degree of structure can help to adapt staff development activities for teachers with different characteristics and in different stages of professional development. To illustrate, let's discuss a few different ways to structure the activity of teacher writing. Teachers functioning at low levels of development, expertise, and commitment and in the orientation stage could be asked to complete the highly structured task of providing written responses to a set of specific questions on their concerns, questions, and expectations about a new model of teaching. Teachers functioning at moderate or mixed levels of development, expertise, and commitment and in the integration stage could be asked to write journal entries about their implementation of the new model under the broad topics of (1) descriptions of classroom applications, (2) assessment of classroom applications, and (3) plans for improving future classroom applications. Such open-ended writing within broad guidelines would constitute a moderate degree of structure. Finally, teachers of high levels of development, expertise, and commitment and in the refinement stage of professional development could be invited to submit short articles about their implementation of the new model to the school district's newsletter or a professional journal. This invitation to choose one's own topic and approach to writing involves a low degree of structure.

As teachers experience growth toward higher levels of development, expertise, and commitment, the degree of structure provided in professional development activities can be gradually reduced.

Sequence

Specific activities can be adapted to different teacher characteristics and stages of professional development through appropriate sequencing. One approach is to proceed gradually from lower to higher experience impact. It is especially important to use low-impact activities to initiate professional development for teachers of low levels of development, expertise, and commitment. Another approach is to alternate between lower- and higher-experience impact. For example, lower-impact activities might be used to allow teachers to process learning from a preceding higher-impact activity or to "recharge" for a subsequent higher-impact activity.

Whichever approach is chosen, sequencing according to experience impact should be balanced with (1) the need to move from simple to complex learning and (2) the need to sequence activities in a manner that allows teachers to engage in a continuous cycle of action and reflection.

This discussion indicates that sequencing professional development activities is a complicated task. Let's look at how we can select and sequence activities of different experience impacts while planning professional development for three hypothetical situations involving various groups of teachers concerned with discipline.

Situation 1.   Group 1 consists mostly of teachers who readily use punishment for most student infractions. They are unaware of and reluctant to use other approaches to discipline. Their concern is with how to get students to "shape up." Behavior problems are viewed as student problems, not problems for which the teacher might share responsibility.

We can identify this group as in the orientation stage of professional development with low levels of development, expertise, and commitment. They appear to need professional development that will focus both on demonstration of new approaches and on discussion of the personal benefits of using new approaches.

The criteria for choosing activities are that they should provide specific, demonstrated skills but be nonthreatening and of low-experience impact. Planners of professional development consider the list of experience impact activities (Table 18.1). They might choose to begin with these five activities:

1. *Panel presenting:* A group of representative teachers will discuss their current difficulties with discipline, what they have tried, and what they would like to do in the future. This is a low-impact, cognitive, large-group activity that involves the visual and audio senses.
2. *Discussing, leader-facilitated:* The next activity will have small groups of teachers discuss their own attitudes, problems, and thinking about new approaches to discipline. This small-group activity is of modest experience impact; involves audio, visual, and oral senses; and will provide a chance for teachers to assess their own beliefs.
3. *Lecturing:* An expert on discipline will present discipline approaches that have been found to be efficient in reducing teacher time for handling troublesome students. This low-experience, audio, cognitive, and large-group activity provides a concrete understanding for the teachers of the benefits and use of specific skills.
4. *Demonstration:* An activity in which an expert shows the teachers how to use the skills explained in the previous lecture. The expert might actually work with a group of students in front of the teachers, or show a videotape of such work, or use teachers to play the roles of students. This activity is of low-experience impact, involves the visual and auditory senses, is a cognitive activity, and can be done with a medium-sized group.

5. *Role-playing, structured:* Teachers will now be asked to try out the demonstrated skills in a nonthreatening, gamelike situation. Teachers are assigned roles and asked to use the new skills. This activity uses all the senses, helps a teacher gain confidence in being able to use the practiced skills later in a real classroom setting, is best done in small groups, and provides for cognitive learning.

Situation 2.   Group 2 comprises mostly teachers who have been dissatisfied with their current classroom discipline practices and have been attempting in a random fashion to do things differently. They read articles on discipline in popular teacher magazines and are aware of some of the new practices. They are experiencing difficulties in selecting and integrating new practices (a time-out area, new classroom rules, a conflict resolution system) into their instruction. Many of the new practices have been started haltingly but stopped when unforeseen problems arose. The teachers want to improve discipline, are willing to continue to work on improvement, but desire help in organizing and streamlining their actions.

We can identify this group as being at moderate levels of development, expertise, and commitment, and in the integration stage of professional development. They can define their discipline problems, have a sense of changes that might be made, but are uncertain about making these changes on their own.

Activities should provide classroom practice, direct observation, coaching by an expert, peer observation, and peer coaching. The focus of professional development would be on applying skills in the ongoing classroom. The experience impact should be relatively high, using all senses, and should involve each teacher with practice in his or her own classroom. The sequence of activities might be as follows:

1. *Demonstrating:* This relatively low-experience impact activity, conducted by an expert or by teachers themselves, serves as a review of the various discipline practices that might be used. Discipline practices that have been used by teachers in the group could be demonstrated to the entire group. Thus, the in-service begins on a cognitive, informational basis.

2. *Role-playing:* This higher-impact activity will consist of individual teachers selecting one or two of the previously demonstrated skills and practicing those skills in a workshop setting. An example might be a role-playing triad. One teacher might be a disruptive student in class, a second teacher would practice a skill of dealing with the disruptive student, and a third teacher would be an observer giving feedback to the teacher after the scenario was concluded. The actors would then switch roles until each teacher had a chance to practice and receive feedback.

3. *Firsthand experience:* The teachers will then try out the new skill over a period of time in their classrooms and keep a report of their progress. This real experience then serves as the basis for future guided practice and observation.

4. *Guided practice:* This activity will incorporate the use of another person (perhaps a supervisor) in reviewing the teacher's firsthand progress with the

skill and reviewing what the teacher will attempt to practice during a short classroom observation. The teacher will demonstrate the skill prior to the session, and the supervisor will suggest corrections. The teacher will then demonstrate the same skills during the classroom observation. This activity is of high impact, involves all the senses, and is reality based.

5. *Discussion, leader-facilitated:* The teachers will step away from the classroom with an activity that provides a chance to discuss in small groups the future work needed to consolidate their new practices into the ongoing classroom routine. They might explain their needs, receive suggestions from other teachers, and arrange to observe each other. The activity leader helps each individual teacher to organize classroom practice and arranges for peer classroom visits.

6. *Systematic observation in classroom:* This technical, moderate-impact activity will prepare teachers to observe each other. They will learn how to focus on the specific classroom practices they have learned as a result of in-service. They will be given observation forms and use these forms on trial tapes. This activity is of moderate experience impact, is both cognitive and affective in nature, and is best done in small groups.

7. *Guided practice:* This highly involving activity will repeat itself. This time teachers will guide and observe each other's practice rather than having the formal supervisor do so. Teachers will have the opportunity to learn how others are using the in-service skills and be able to provide feedback to each other. This activity is of high experience impact, involving all the senses.

At this point, integration of new practice should be well established, and the group should be ready for the refinement stage.

Situation 3.   Group 3 consists of teachers who are highly proficient with respect to discipline. They are confident in their ability to handle classroom disruption but believe that discipline could be even more productive if teachers used complementary discipline approaches from classroom to classroom. They realize that from time to time even the best teacher will confront a situation with an individual student or small group of students that will strain his or her tolerance. They are concerned with ways to help each other when stressful discipline situations occur, and they are concerned with adopting mutual practices to improve discipline throughout the school.

This is a group of teachers functioning at high levels of development, expertise, and commitment, and in the refinement stage of professional development. They view discipline in highly abstract ways by considering multiple options for dealing with disruptive students. They have a history of being decisive and thorough in implementing new procedures.

The activities chosen should be ones that help teachers reflect on current individual practice and think about ways to complement each other. The first activities might be cognitive, collaborative, and of low-experience impact. The next phase might be implementation activities, which are of high-experience impact.

Implementation might be followed by collaborative activities to revise and refine team practices. Let's follow a sample sequence of activities on discipline that should build individual discipline skills into consistent team skills.

1. *Analyzing and calculating:* Teachers will individually express how teaming efforts could help their own classrooms. Teachers will fill out a form and then read what they have written to the entire group. This activity, of moderate-experience impact, allows for each person's thoughts to be considered by the entire group before they discuss the merits and drawbacks of ideas.

2. *Discussion, leaderless:* Teachers will work in small groups to discuss common ways to support each other in the area of discipline. They might be grouped according to grade level, department, or adjoining classrooms. Some solutions a small group could decide on might include a system of signals to call on other teachers to leave their classrooms to help when a particular teacher finds himself or herself facing an emergency, or a reinforcement system for certain students that would be consistent from classroom to classroom. This cognitive, low-impact activity serves as preparation for the implementation phase.

3. *Role-playing, structured:* The team will practice among themselves the new practices to be used. For example, a consistent reinforcement system might be practiced by having teachers role-play, responding to different disruptive behaviors, and then determining whether teachers have applied consistent rewards and sanctions. This activity is close to reality. It is of higher-experience impact than the previous two activities and is basically cognitive.

4. *Firsthand experience:* This activity will usher in the experimentation phase, and teachers will keep notes on the progress of the plan. They are now individually responsible for their own parts in the team plan. The activity is of the highest-experience impact, involving all senses, with both cognitive and affective involvement.

5. *Buzz session:* The individuals will return to an activity that enables them to reflect on the firsthand experience and discuss their progress reports. They reveal happenings, actions, and feelings about the plan. This low-impact activity allows teachers to be empathetic and reflective about each other's progress and involvement. This session is a time for generating feelings and thoughts without judging individual progress.

6. *Discussion, leaderless:* This activity kicks off the cycle of refining and changing team practices. Team members have learned from the firsthand experience and have shared in the buzz session what they perceive to be happening. In this activity, they agree as a team on changes to be made before going on to the next phase of role-playing and firsthand experience.

Keep in mind that these situations and plans are "snapshots" of groups of teachers at particular times. As we noted in our initial discussion of experience impact, as teachers move toward higher levels of development, expertise, and commitment, staff development activities should be adjusted from lower to higher impact.

Pace

A model calling for simply matching activities appropriate for different stages of professional development (orientation, integration, and refinement, respectively) with levels of teachers' development, expertise, and commitment (low, moderate or mixed, and high, respectively) is inadequate for many situations. For one example, even teachers with high levels of development, expertise, and commitment will revert to the orientation stage regarding wholly new learning content. For another example, if teachers of low levels of development, expertise, and commitment never go beyond the orientation stage, they will never integrate learning into their daily teaching.

Modifying the experience impact, structure, and sequence of staff development activities can help teachers with different characteristics move through the stages of professional development. Another strategy is to adjust the pace at which teachers with different characteristics progress through orientation, integration, and refinement stages. Teachers functioning at low levels of development, expertise, and commitment need to move quite gradually through each stage, with intensive professional development beginning with the orientation stage and continuing throughout the program. These teachers may never reach the refinement stage, but need eventually to move to the integration stage for meaningful learning to occur. Teachers of moderate or mixed levels of development, expertise, and commitment can move quickly through the orientation stage then at a slower pace through the integration and refinement stages. Intensive professional development for these teachers begins with the integration stage and continues through the refinement stage. Teachers of high levels of development, expertise, and commitment can move at a brisk pace through the orientation and integration stages, and at a slower pace through the refinement stage. Intensive professional development for these teachers takes place in the refinement stage. Figure 18.1 illustrates the suggested pace of professional development as well as when intensive development can be provided for teachers of various levels of development, expertise, and commitment.

The caution we gave during our discussions of experience impact, degree of structure, and sequence of staff development activities holds true for the pace of staff development: If the staff development program itself causes increases in teachers' development, expertise, and commitment, the pace of activities should be increased accordingly.

Of course, most school faculties, departments, and grade levels are not composed of teachers at identical levels of development, expertise, and commitment. One alternative for dealing with this reality is a professional development plan that meets the needs of the majority of the faculty and allows individual options for those with different needs. A second option would be a differentiated approach, with different groups of teachers participating in alternative programs. A

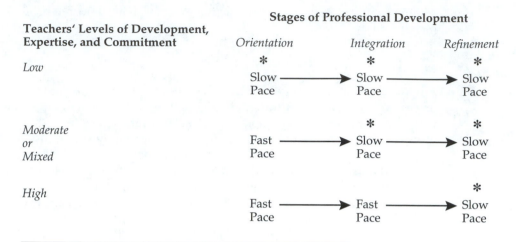

FIGURE 18.1 *Stages and Pace of Professional Development*

* = Intensive professional development during these stages.

third option would be an individualized program with a faculty sharing component, like the Holidaysburg program discussed earlier in this chapter. The school's professional development goals, faculty size and characteristics, and resources should all be considered when deciding which option to choose. Regardless of the option chosen, professional development aimed at promoting interaction among knowledgeable professionals can help achieve a schoolwide commitment to "a cause beyond oneself," which is a key characteristic of successful schools.

The Nuts and Bolts

Professional development does not always need to take place in group sessions, but groups remain a major component of the majority of staff development formats and programs. The best planning for a group session is useless if the supervisor forgets the nuts and bolts. What value is an excellent speaker who lectures in a room where the acoustics garble every word? What good is a fast-paced microteaching demonstration if it conflicts with other teacher meetings so that few can attend? What good is an exciting role-playing activity whose participants have had no chance to eat, unwind, or use the restroom during the previous two hours? If one is going to the trouble to plan professional development, then one should go the extra step to ensure an environment that enables participants to be responsive and comfortable. Here are six important considerations:

1. *Prepare speakers by telling them exactly what they are expected to do.* If a speaker is invited to conduct an activity, make sure he or she understands the assignment. Speakers will do whatever they normally do unless someone tells them otherwise. Most speakers have their own topics, their own rehearsed presentations, and their own formats. If a speaker is expected to demonstrate a particular skill (for example, asking higher-order questions) or to include role-playing (scripts of classroom discussions), *tell him or her so.* Speaker and participants are both in an embarrassing situation when the speaker, through no fault of either party, is not doing what the participants have been led to expect.

2. *Check the facility beforehand for seating arrangements, media, and acoustics.* Make sure the facility is appropriate to the activity. For example, small-group discussions in an auditorium give teachers stiff necks and a stiffer attitude toward the next in-service. See that all equipment is operating correctly. Check microphones, cassettes, and overheads. Move around the room to see if displays on screen or walls can be viewed clearly by everyone. Have at hand spare bulbs and replacement equipment in case of an equipment failure.

3. *Provide refreshments and transition time at the beginning.* Tell participants where the restrooms are. Provide drinks and snacks. Informally greet the participants at the door and tell them when the session will begin. When formally beginning, inform participants when other breaks are scheduled.

4. *Check the comfort of the room.* Beforehand, check whether the room will maintain a comfortable temperature. Find out if the heating or cooling system is turned off at the time of the meeting and, if so, arrange to have the system operating. Estimate the temperature of the room when it is full. A room that feels comfortable when only a few people are present can become oppressively hot when full to capacity.

5. *Have materials run off and a plan for easy dissemination to participants.* Prior to the session, check with the leader of the activity to make sure all desired materials will be prepared. Also before the session, figure out a distribution system for materials. Often it is sufficient to place a table next to the entrance with collected materials and make one person responsible for telling entrants to pick up the materials.

6. *Have evaluation forms for participants to fill out after the session.* Asking participants to evaluate the session allows existing problems to be corrected before the next session. A simple form to be filled out anonymously by participants can be seen in Figure 18.2.

Teachers as Objects or Agents in Professional Development

A superintendent remarked that he had been at a national conference and attended a presentation on "Elements of Effective Instruction." He decided that this was exactly what the teachers needed. As a result, the district was off and running with a three-year commitment to training all principals and teachers in

FIGURE 18.2 *Professional Development Evaluation*

We would like your feedback to plan future professional development sessions. Please circle the number closest to your feelings and provide comments in the space provided on the form. If you need more space, feel free to use the back of the sheet. As you leave, please drop this form in the box on the back table.

Professional Development Topic _____

Date _____

	Poor	Satisfactory	Good	Excellent
1. The session today was	1	2	3	4

Comments

_____

_____

_____

2. The organization of the session was	1	2	3	4

Comments

_____

_____

_____

3. The meeting room was	1	2	3	4

Comments

_____

_____

4. The materials were	1	2	3	4

Comments

_____

_____

Suggestions for future meetings:

_____

_____

"elements." Highly paid national consultants were brought in; personnel were identified for advanced training and traveled during the summer to faraway sites; and virtually all contracted in-service time and school supervision was devoted to "elements." It was not long before a new evaluation instrument was established to check that every teacher was using the training in effective instruction in the same prescribed manner. Over the three years, expenditures by the school district exceeded $300,000, not including the cost of human time. What have been the results? No appreciable gain in student achievement, considerable grumbling by a core of "malcontent" teachers, enthusiasm by the chosen core of teachers who received special training and compensation, and a firm claim by the superintendent that "we now have focused long-term professional development on scientifically derived principles, and our teaching is more effective."

In recent years, education has been bombarded by packaged programs on "effective teaching," "effective schools," "effective supervision," and "effective discipline." All claim to be derived from research and to have documented success, and all use the components and sequence of transfer of training that have been sorely lacking in traditional professional development programs. The programs provide for explanation, demonstration, modeling, role-playing, practice, and coaching. They are not one-shot programs—they are focused and they are classroom based. The only problem is that the people who think these programs are worth the cost and effort are the same people who have a personal investment and commitment to use them (see Garman and Hazley, 1988; DiBernardo and Stiles, 1988). If the programs are not as successful as predicted, the decision makers do not blame the program but rather the lack of enough training to ensure that teachers "do it right" (Lambert, 1988). Schools, districts, and states that have committed themselves to such programs come to the ludicrous conclusion that they need more training, more money, and greater enforcement to see that all teachers will finally learn to teach as prescribed more frequently and correctly. This is an incredible rationalization by policy makers that their initial decision was right, regardless of the effect that the program is having on teachers.

This rationale underscores the point that was made about adult development and motivation earlier in the book. Motivation is premised on two dimensions: one is choice and the other is responsibility to make knowledgeable decisions about one's work. That's why the superintendent wants so badly to see this program on "effective elements" work. The superintendent had the choice and took responsibility for making the decision. The selected core of teachers also want to see this program work, because they were given choice and responsibility in making decisions on how to train others. Yet most teachers and principals were not given any choice or responsibility in these decisions about the needs of their students and themselves. Instead, they were treated as objects rather than as agents of professional development, without due regard for their capacity to make wise decisions in the interest of students and teaching. Without choice or responsibility to make knowledgeable decisions about their work, they have little motivation or commitment to somebody else's program.

To use knowledge about sequencing training for transfer of learning, without an awareness of the need truly to involve teachers as decision makers in professional development, will leave us where we currently are. We will be more sophisticated in teaching teachers how to follow someone else's program, but we will find little commitment on the part of teachers or little stimulation to increase teachers' own collective and critical capacities to make lasting changes.

Summary

For professional development to be meaningful to teachers and to lead to teacher renewal and instructional improvement, it must operate at two levels. First, teachers as individuals should have a variety of learning opportunities to support their pursuit of their own personal and professional career goals. Second, teachers as part of a school and district organization should together define, learn, and implement skills, knowledge, and programs that achieve common goals of the organization. Professional development must be geared to teachers' needs and concerns. Research on successful professional development programs has shown an emphasis on involvement, long-term planning, problem-solving meetings, released time, experimentation and risk-taking, administrative support, small-group activities, peer feedback, demonstration and trials, coaching, and leader participation in activities. Consideration for individual and group characteristics can help make professional development more relevant to the participant. Teachers move through three stages of professional development: orientation, integration, and refinement. Teachers also vary in levels of development, expertise, and commitment. The experience impact of professional development activities can be used to choose activities for particular groups. The degree of structure, sequence, and pace of staff development can also be adjusted for different groups. Nuts-and-bolts considerations—informing speakers, checking facilities, and providing refreshments, materials, and evaluation—can increase the comfort and attentiveness of teachers. It is time to change the perception that professional development is a waste of teachers' time to the perception of professional development as time well spent. Viewing teachers as the agents rather than the objects of professional development will be the impetus for such change.

Exercises

Academic

1. Write a paper defining and discussing the concept of mentoring teachers. Include descriptions of successful mentoring found in the professional literature.

2. A small group of senior high teachers has requested a professional development program on making better use of open-ended questions during class discussions. The teachers are at moderate levels of development, expertise, and commitment, and at the integration stage. Outline a plan for a professional development program for these teachers on the requested topic.

3. A small group of elementary teachers from the same school district has requested a professional development program on strategies for more effective team teaching. All these teachers have had considerable experience in team teaching, but they wish to improve their skills in this area. The teachers are at high levels of development, expertise, and commitment, and in the refinement stage of professional development. Outline a plan for a professional development program on team teaching for these teachers.

4. A general needs assessment, administered districtwide, has revealed that the number-one perceived need of teachers in the district is for increased communication skills. Prepare a plan for assessing *specific* needs of various groups of teachers within this general topic, and for including teachers in planning a professional development program that will meet their group and individual needs.

5. Write a paper summarizing three recent research studies on professional development not discussed in this chapter. Include the purpose, participants, methodology, results, and conclusions of each study. Analyze the findings in terms of whether they are congruent with research findings cited in this chapter.

Field

1. Evaluate the needs assessment process a school district employs in planning professional development programs. As part of your evaluation, interview teachers to determine whether decisions on professional development activities reflect actual teacher needs. Include recommendations for improvement of the needs assessment process.

2. Attend a professional development session for teachers. Evaluate the session in terms of (a) the extent to which the session reflects the major research findings on effective professional development, (b) whether varying levels of teacher development, expertise, and commitment are taken into consideration, (c) organization, (d) facilities, and (e) materials. Note informal reactions of teachers attending the session. Include suggestions for improving future professional development sessions.

3. Interview five teachers concerning a professional development program that is being proposed or introduced in their school. On the basis of interviews, attempt to classify each teacher according to his or her stage of professional development (orientation, integration, or refinement).

4. Interview an individual who has considerable experience at planning professional development sessions on the practical aspects of preparing for such sessions. Ask him or her to relate past experiences that illustrate potential problems to avoid, eventualities to consider, and areas in which special preparation is necessary. Prepare a report on your interview.

5. Interview the individual in charge of professional development on a school system's long-range professional development program. (Be sure the school system *has* a long-range professional development program before arranging the interview!) Prepare a report describing and evaluating the program.

Developmental

1. As you attend professional development activities over a period of time, observe the experience impact of different activities on various groups of teachers (the effects of high- and low-impact activities on teachers of various levels of development, expertise, and commitment).

2. Develop a file of ideas for professional development activities. Research on successful professional development programs can serve as a planning source. Activities can be developed for individuals and groups at various levels of development,

expertise, and commitment, and various stages of professional development (orientation, integration, refinement). Experience impact can be considered when designing activities for teachers with different characteristics.

3. Volunteer to help plan and implement professional development activities in your school or school system. Try to incorporate the research on effective professional development into the plans.

Endnote

1. Outlining a complete professional-development program on cooperative learning is beyond the scope of this text. Some critical topics are listed to provide examples of the types of learning in each stage of professional development. Sources of cooperative learning professional development topics are Johnson, Johnson, and Holubec (1991) and Kagan (1992).

References

Berman, P., and McLaughlin, M. W. 1978. *Federal programs supporting educational change, Vol. 8. Implementing and sustaining innovations.* Santa Monica, CA: Rand Corp. (ERIC ED 159 289)

Corcoran, T. B. 1995. *Helping teachers teach well: Transforming professional development.* CPRE Policy Briefs, RB-16-June. New Brunswick, NV: Rutgers University, Consortium for Policy Research in Education.

DiBernardo, G., and Stiles, D. 1988. The Madeline Hunter and Lee Canter teacher improvement packages: What every school needs? *Democratic Schools 3*(2):1–9.

ERIC. 1980. ERIC Research Action Brief—Clearinghouse on Educational Management, No. 10. Eugene, OR: University of Oregon. (ERIC ED 021 256)

Garman, N. B., and Hazley, H. M. 1988. Teachers ask: Is there life after Madeline Hunter? *Kappan 69*(9):669–672.

Glickman, C. D. 1992. The essence of school renewal. *Educational Leadership 50* (1):87–97.

Gursky, D. 1990. A plan that works. *Teacher* (June/July):46–54.

Guskey, T. R. 1986. Staff development and the process of teacher change. *Educational Research 15*(5):5–12.

Guskey, T. R. 1994. *Professional development in education: In search of the optimal mix.* Paper presented at the annual meeting of the American Educational Research Association, New Orleans, April. (ERIC 369 181)

Hall, G. H., and Hord, S. M. 1987. *Change in schools: Facilitating the process.* Albany: State University of New York Press.

Harris, B. M. 1975. *Supervisory behavior in education* (2nd ed.). Englewood Cliffs, NJ: Prentice Hall.

Harris, B. M. 1980. *Improving staff performance through in-service education.* Boston: Allyn and Bacon.

Harris, B. M. 1989. *In-service education for staff development.* Boston: Allyn and Bacon.

Hawley, W. D., and Valli, L. 1996. *The essentials of effective professional development: A new consensus.* Paper presented at the AERA Invitational Conference on Teacher Development and School Reform, Washington, D.C.

Johnson, D. W., Johnson, R. T., and Holubec, E. J. 1991. *Cooperation in the classroom.* Edina, MN: Interaction Book Company.

Joyce, B., Calhoun, E., and Hopkins, D. 1999. *The new structure of school improvement: Inquiring schools and achieving students.* Philadelphia: Open University Press.

Joyce, B. R., and Showers, B. 1980. Improving in-service training: The message of research. *Educational Leadership 37*:379–385.

Joyce, B. R., and Showers, B. 1983. *Power in staff development through research on training.* Alexandria, VA: Association for Supervision and Curriculum Development.

Joyce, B. R., and Showers, B. 1988. *Student achievement through staff development.* New York: Longman.

Kagan, S. 1992. *Cooperative learning.* San Juan Capistrano: Kagan Cooperative Learning.

Karst, R. R. 1987. *New policy implications for in-service and professional development programs for the public schools.* Presentation to the annual meeting of the American Educational Research Association, Washington, DC, April.

Lambert, L. 1988. Staff development redesigned. *Kappa* 69(9):665–668.

Lawrence, G. 1974. *Patterns of effective in-service education: A state of the art summary of research on materials and procedures for changing teacher behaviors in in-service education.* Tallahassee: Florida State Department of Education. ERIC ED 176 424.

Lead Teacher Centers of Pennsylvania. No date. *Pennsylvania lead teachers: Enhancing the teaching profession.* Harrisburg: Pennsylvania Department of Education.

Levin, H. M. 1994. Learning from accelerated schools. In S. H. Block, S. T. Evertson, and T. R. Guskey (Eds.), *Selecting and integrating school improvement programs.* New York: Scholastic Books.

Loucks-Horsley, S., Harding, C. K., Arbuckle, M. A., Murray, L. B., Dubea, C., and Williams, M. K. 1987. *Continuing to learn: A guidebook for teacher development.* Andover, ME: The Regional Laboratory for Educational Improvement of the Northeast and Islands.

McLaughlin, M. W., and Marsh, D. D. 1978. Staff development and school change. *Teachers College Record* 80(1):69–94.

Mohlman, G. G. 1982. *Assessing the impact of three inservice teacher training models.* Paper presented at the annual meeting of the American Educational Research Association, New York.

Mohlman-Sparks, G. 1986. The effectiveness of alternative training activities in changing teaching practices. *American Educational Research Journal* 23(2):217–225.

Mohlman, G. G., Kierstead, J., and Gundlach, M. 1982. A research-based in-service model for secondary teachers. *Educational Leadership* 40(1):16–19.

Newlove, B. W., and Hall, G. E. 1976. *A manual for assessing open-ended statements of concern about an innovation.* Austin: Research and Development Center for Teacher Education, University of Texas.

Oja, S. N. 1981. *Adapting research findings in psychological education: A case study.* Presentation at the annual meeting of the American Association of Colleges for Teacher Education, Detroit, February.

Orlich, D. C. 1989. *Staff development: Enhancing human potential.* Boston: Allyn and Bacon.

Ponticell, J. A. 1995. Promoting teacher professionalism through collegiality. *Journal of Staff Development* 16(3):13–18.

Rubin, L. (Ed.). 1978. *The in-service education of teachers.* Boston: Allyn and Bacon.

Speak, L., and Hirsh, S. 1988. A rationale for released-time staff development in the Richardson Independent School District. *The Developer* (March):1–4.

Stallings, J. 1980. Allocated academic learning time revisited or Beyond time on task. *Educational Researcher* 9(11):11–16.

Tetenbaum, T. J., and Mulkeen, T. A. 1987. *Prelude to school improvement: Understanding perceptions of staff development.* Presentation to the annual meeting of the American Educational Research Association, Washington, DC, April.

Thies-Sprinthall, L. 1981. Promoting the conceptual and principled thinking level of the supervising teacher. Unpublished research funded by St. Cloud State University, 1978 and 1979. Reported in *Educating for teacher growth: A cognitive developmental perspective.* Paper presented at the annual meeting of the American Educational Research Association, Los Angeles, April.

U.S. Department of Education. 1996. National Center for Education Statistics. *Measures of inservice professional development: Suggested items for the 1998–1999 Schools and Staffing Survey.* Working Paper No. 96-25, Washington, DC: Author.

Wilsey, C., and Killion, J. 1982. Making staff development programs work. *Educational Leadership* 40(1):36–38, 43.

Wilshire, D. K. 1991. Teachers in transition: An exploratory study of self-selected change and educational planning in professional development. Unpublished doctoral dissertation, Pennsylvania State University.

Wood, F. W., and Thompson, S. R. 1980. Guidelines for better staff development. *Educational Leadership* 37(5):374–378.

Wood, F. W., and Thompson, S. R. 1993. Assumptions about staff development based on research and best practice. *Journal of Staff Development* 14(4):52–57.

Suggested Readings

American Federation of Teachers. (1995). *Principles for professional development: AFT's guidelines for creating professional development programs that make a difference.* Washington, DC: Author.

Bell, L., and Day, C. 1991. *Managing the professional development of teachers.* Philadelphia: Open University.

Burke, P., Heideman, R., and Heideman, C. (Eds.). 1990. *Programming for staff development.* London: Falmer.

Caldwell, S. D. (Ed.). 1989. *Staff development: A handbook of effective practices.* Oxford, OH: National Staff Development Council.

DeBolt, G. P. 1992. *Teacher induction and mentoring.* Albany: State University of New York.

Gordon, S. P. 1991. *How to help beginning teachers succeed.* Alexandria, VA: Association for Supervision and Curriculum Development.

Grimmett, P. P., and Neufeld, U. (Eds.). 1994. *Teacher development and the struggle for authenticity.* New York: Teachers College Press.

Guskey, T. R., and Huberman, M. (Eds.). 1995. *Professional development in education: New paradigms and practices.* New York: Teachers College Press.

Joyce, B. (Ed.). 1990. *Changing school culture through staff development.* Alexandria, VA: Association for Supervision and Curriculum and Development.

Levine, S. L. 1989. *Promoting adult growth in schools.* Boston: Allyn and Bacon.

National Staff Development Council & National Association of Elementary School Principals. 1995. *Standards for staff development: Elementary school edition.* Oxford, OH: Authors.

National Staff Development Council. 1994. *Standards for staff development: Middle level edition.* Oxford, OH: Authors.

National Staff Development Council and National Association of Secondary Schools Principals. 1995. *Standards for staff development: High school edition.* Oxford, OH: Authors.

Orlich, D. C. 1989. *Staff development: Enhancing human potential.* Boston: Allyn and Bacon.

Pink, W. T., and Hyde, A. H. 1992. *Effective staff development for school change.* Norwood, NJ: Ablex.

Sparks, D., and Hirsh, S. 1997. *A new vision for the staff development.* Alexandria, VA: Association for Supervision and Curriculum Development (and Oxford, OH: National Staff Development Council).

19

Curriculum Development

"Teaching is a moral activity that implies thoughts about ends, means, and their consequences" (Zeuli and Buchmann, 1987). Moral activity is explicitly expressed in a school's curriculum. To be an effective school is of little matter unless the personnel within an organization first have defined what is meant by a good school—what should students learn in order to be well educated? The institutional job then becomes one of effectively achieving that definition of goodness. As Sergiovanni (1987) remarked, "It's not important to do things right, unless we are doing the right things!" Curriculum is the moral deliberation on what is "right" for students to be taught.

Hirsch, in *Cultural Literacy: What Every American Needs to Know* (1987), attacked American education as abandoning the essential literature, ideas, and facts of the national culture. Bloom, in *The Closing of the American Mind* (1987), likewise indicted schools for abandoning the core programs of traditional liberal arts education. In *What Do Our 17-Year-Olds Know?* (1987), educators Ravitch and Finn wrote that a large proportion of high school students don't know such basic facts as in what half-century the Civil War took place. Hirsch, Bloom, Ravitch, and Finn believe it is both necessary and right to reduce the school curriculum to a focus on predetermined, essential knowledge.

Yet the National Assessment of Educational Progress (NAEP), in its report card on high school students' knowledge of literature and U.S. history, suggests that students' inadequate knowledge may be because "the typical course relies heavily on a textbook…students regularly are expected to memorize important information, and are tested frequently…class time is spent listening to the teacher lecture" (Applebee, Langer, and Mullis, 1987). Indeed, what is taught and how it is taught according to the NAEP study of literature and history is no different from what Goodlad found in his national study of schooling. Goodlad (1984) found that nearly 90 percent of teaching across all subjects and grade levels is up-front teaching—lecturing, with students passively listening except for an occasional opportunity to answer questions. On one side, academic essentialists argue that the problem with curriculum is that too much stress is placed on process skills (problem solving, inquiry, and critical thinking) to the detriment of straight, old-fashioned teaching of content and basic skills. Social activists and experimentalists such as Goodlad reply that such teaching is what already exists and is to blame for inadequate student comprehension. Their argument is that there should be less facts and memorization and more active problem solving and conceptual understanding.

A study of the elementary mathematics curriculum by Porter (1987) brings out related curriculum issues of coverage and balance.

> We found that 70 to 75% of mathematics instruction was spent teaching skills, essentially how to add, subtract, multiply, and divide, and occasionally how to read a graph. (p. 7)
>
> Our findings of heavy emphasis on skill development and slight attention to concepts and applications is consistent with the United States' relatively poor standing among other nations on mathematics problem solving. In some ways the U.S. curriculum is even more out of balance than the above suggests. (pp. 9–10)
>
> As troublesome as the lack of emphasis given to problem solving and conceptual understanding, a very large percentage of the topics taught receive only brief, perhaps cursory coverage. (p. 11)

Sizer (1984) reasoned that schools are too concerned with teaching all subjects superficially. Instead, schools should teach fewer subjects, topics, and skills more thoroughly—"teach less, better" rather than "teach more, quicker." Others argued that curriculum should expose students to a vast array of educational experiences. Howard Gardner, a noted cognitive psychologist, stated (in Brandt 1988b) that his research on human intelligence indicates that elementary and middle schools should not be concerned with subjects; instead, curriculum should focus on long-term core projects that integrate rather than separate learning of language, mathematics, science, reading, art, and physical education.

How does one make sense of these topsy-turvy controversies about curriculum? How can so many esteemed experts have so many contradictory ideas? It comes down to a matter of educational philosophy (as discussed in Chapter 5). Curriculum experts are humans too! They possess the same ideological, philosophical, and political biases as the rest of us. They may argue more eloquently and have better support for their claims than we do, but at the bottom of their discourse are philosophical premises and assumptions about education no different from ours. Ultimately, decisions about a good school, appropriate curriculum, and needs of students should be made by those closest to students. After considering the available experts, research, readings, and articulated conflicts, people in the schools, districts, and local communities should ultimately decide what is worthy to teach. However, by default, pressure, and abdication, curriculum decisions have generally been made by those farthest from the classroom action.

Sources of Curriculum Development

Curricula can be developed at many levels—by outside specialists, school district specialists, school curriculum teams, and teachers alone. At the national level, commercial materials such as textbooks, learning kits, and audiovisual materials are developed mainly by outside specialists. The common practice of textbook publishers is to hire subject-matter experts from universities or private agencies to write their materials. There might be a public school representative on the advisory or consulting board for a curriculum textbook, and occasionally teachers are used to field-test the materials before they are mass-produced. Curriculum is supported at the federal level, but for the most part this is true only in legislated areas such as education for the disabled, bilingual education, and vocational education. At the state level, departments of education have become increasingly active in curriculum development. Many states have legislated statewide competency tests for student promotion and graduation and have developed curriculum guides for local schools to ensure the teaching of those competencies. (For example, in the state of Georgia, there now exist mandated and state-developed minimum curricula in every subject area for grades K–12.) At the local level, many school systems have written their own curriculum guides for coordinating instruction across grade levels. This is done either by having curriculum specialists at the district level write the guides themselves or by having such specialists work with representative teams of teachers (perhaps with community and student representation). Rarely do local schools turn curriculum development over entirely to teachers.

We can think about sources of curriculum development according to Figure 19.1 (see Oliva, 1992). Much curriculum is developed at the state, federal, and commercial levels. Commercial companies are by far the greatest producers of curricula. In other words, most curricula are produced far away from the local teacher and the local schools.

Teacher-Proof Curriculum

Imagine we have just heard about a phenomenal new chemistry curriculum that has been field-tested in 27 school systems throughout the United States and has resulted in a 100 percent student success rate. The curriculum has been created by some of the most distinguished chemists and educators in the country. All students in grades 10, 11, and 12 who have been taught by the new curriculum have scored in the upper 10 percent of a nationally normed chemistry achievement test. Furthermore, their attitudes toward chemistry are far superior to those of comparable high school students who have been taught by other chemistry curricula.

To verify this success story, we travel to some of the school sites, review the curriculum materials, and look over test results. We find that it's true, and we decide that the curriculum should be used immediately in our schools. We will need to purchase the materials and hire a consultant to show teachers how to use the curriculum. We believe we will have immediate success.

The truth is that if we proceed as planned, we will probably not achieve much success with this curriculum. Teachers will use it half-heartedly and keep returning to their old lecture notes and traditional instructional activities. Within a few years, most of the new materials will be lost or abandoned; 10 years from now, stacks of the new curriculum materials might be gathering dust in the school attic.

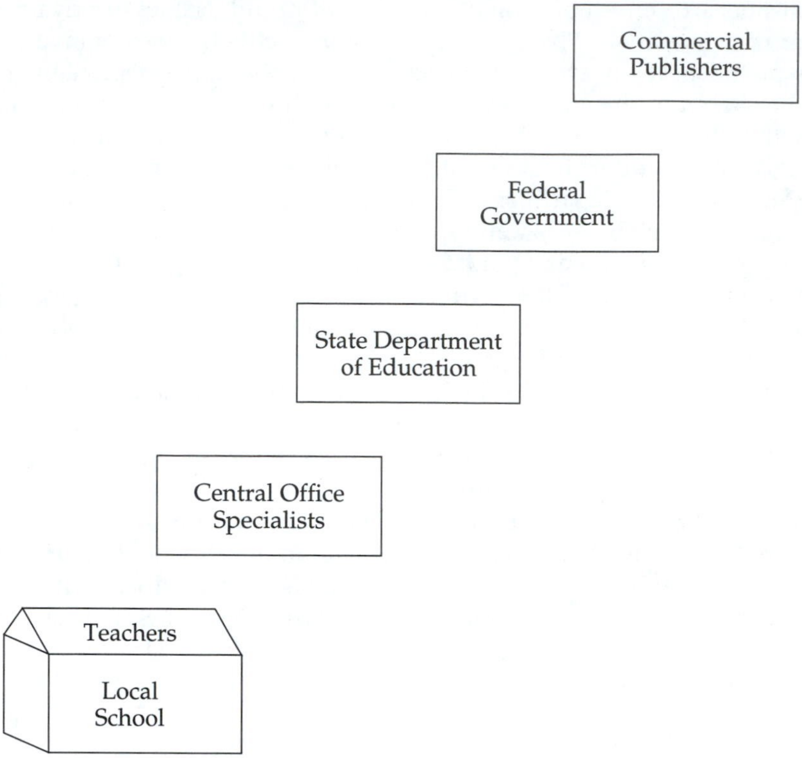

FIGURE 19.1   *Illustration of Sources of Curriculum Development*

From the late 1950s to the early 1970s, the National Science Foundation allocated millions of dollars for the development of such new curricula. University scholars were hired to develop materials to improve instruction in elementary and secondary science and mathematics. The U.S. Office of Education similarly spent large sums of money to hire subject specialists to develop curricula in English and social studies. The curricula were carefully constructed, field-tested, revised, and tested again—only to be resisted, misused, and abandoned when implemented in public schools.

Some of the best curricula developed, such as "Man: A Course of Study" (MACOS) and the Physical Science Study Committee's physics course (PSSC) showed overwhelming student success during the pilot phase, yet they are hardly used now. A series of reports on the results of 20 years of federally supported curriculum development concluded that nearly all such curricula have been bypassed by schools (see Ponder, 1979; Yager and Stodghill, 1979; Gibney and Karns, 1979). Why is this so? Doll (1989) explained "It seems likely that an important reason many of the massive curriculum projects...proved so disappointing is that they did not take into account the differing situations in which the projects were expected to take root."

One lesson to be learned by supervisors is that it makes no difference how good a curriculum is if teachers will not use it. To think of any curriculum as being teacher-proof—the label used for those federally supported curricula—was a mistake. *Teacher-proof* implies that the curriculum is so complete and detailed that it is immune to teacher practice and belief. Since then, we've learned a multimillion-dollar lesson: Curricula cannot be teacher-proof as long as schools are loosely coupled organizations (Weick, 1976).

A *loosely coupled* organization is one in which there is an absence of continual monitoring of the work force. A *tightly coupled* organization, on the other hand, is characterized by managers closely monitoring the work force. Schools are loosely coupled because teachers are surrounded by four walls; only infrequently does anyone with managerial control see what they do. Educators know among themselves (but keep the fact from the public) that *basically teachers do whatever they want to do*. Therefore, in a loosely coupled organization, unless a teacher really desires to implement a curriculum, he or she won't. No one is going to stand over a teacher six hours a day, 180 days a year to see that the curriculum is being implemented. On those rare occasions when a person in authority does stand over a teacher, the teacher can usually give the person what he or she is expecting and then return to the usual method once the authority is gone. Therefore, any notion of a curriculum being teacher-proof simply flies in the face of reality. For a curriculum to be implemented by teachers, they have to be involved in choosing, adapting, and developing it. It must serve the needs of teachers, and they must want to use it.

Sir Alex Clegg wrote disparagingly of such so-called teacher-proof materials:

> I have no time whatever for any system which recruits highpowered thinkers to contour and foist a curriculum on the schools. This cannot work unless we believe that the teacher of the future is to be a low-grade technician working under someone else's instructions rather than a professional making his own diagnoses and prescribing his own treatments. (cited in Tanner and Tanner, 1980, p. 629)

Denver Superintendent Jesse H. Newlon knew about curriculum and loosely coupled organizations as far back as 1922, when he originated the Denver plan, which gave curriculum development and implementation to committees of teachers. Tanner and Tanner wrote of Newlon as a person of

> deep and abiding faith in the teacher as a professional. Because of this confidence and because he believed that the study of curriculum problems was the best possible kind of inservice training, Newlon put teachers at the heart of the curriculum-making process. (Tanner and Tanner, 1980, p. 341)

The eight-year study completed in 1942 confirmed Newlon's idea of the teacher at the heart of curriculum. In this historic study, thirty private and public secondary schools were selected on the basis of having a nontraditional, noncollege-preparatory curriculum. Instead, the curriculum was unique to each high school and was developed by the high school faculty. The students who graduated from these 30 schools were matched with students who graduated from high schools having a traditional, college preparatory curriculum with little faculty involvement in curriculum development.

Both groups of students were followed through college. It was concluded from the study that graduates of the innovative, teacher-involved schools had higher grade-point averages, received more academic honors, and were found to be more precise, systematic, objective, and intellectually curious than were those who graduated from the traditional schools that did not involve teachers in curriculum development (Aiken, 1942). It was clear that schools operating with teacher involvement in curriculum development provided a better education than did schools operating without such involvement.

Some 33 years later, the Rand Corporation found that lasting and successful curriculum implementation projects were characterized by "mutual adaptation." The Rand researchers found that when teachers were involved in selecting, revising, and changing an externally prescribed curriculum, the curriculum took hold and lasted (Berman and McLaughlin, 1978).

It is clear that in order for schools to be successful, teachers need to be involved in curriculum development. The issues that remain are:

1. What should be the purpose of the curriculum?
2. What should be the content of the curriculum?
3. How should the curriculum be organized?
4. In what format should the curriculum be written?
5. At what level of curriculum development should teachers be involved?

Forthcoming sections will discuss each of these issues.

What Should Be the Purpose of the Curriculum?

Alternative beliefs about the purpose of the curriculum are described by Miller and Seller (1985) as orientations to curriculum. They describe three "metaorientations" or positions:

- In the *transmission position* the function of education is to transmit facts, skills, and values to students. Specifically, this orientation stresses mastery of traditional school subjects through traditional teaching methodologies. (pp. 5 and 6) (emphasis supplied)
- In the *transaction position* the individual is seen as rational and capable of intelligent problem solving. Education is viewed as a dialogue between the student and the curriculum in which the student reconstructs knowledge through the dialogue process. The central elements in the transaction position are an emphasis on curriculum strategies that promote problem solving…application of problem solving skills within social contexts in general and within the context of the democratic process…and development of cognitive skills within the academic disciplines. (pp. 6 and 7) (emphasis supplied)

- The *transformation position* focuses on personal and social change. It encompasses...teaching students skills that promote personal and social transformation...(and) a vision of social change as movement toward harmony with the environment rather than an effort to exert control over it. (p. 8) (emphasis supplied)

If Miller and Seller's three orientations to curriculum sound vaguely familiar, it may be due to your review of educational philosophies in Chapter 5. The transmission curriculum orientation is related to the educational philosophy of essentialism. The transactional curriculum orientation is based largely on the philosophy of experimentalism. Finally, aspects of the transformation orientation are related to the philosophy of existentialism. In Chapter 5, we found that our educational beliefs help to shape our definition of effective teaching and instructional improvement. Similarly, curriculum orientations drive the curriculum-development process and affect curriculum purpose, content, organization, and format. Therefore, it is important that early in the curriculum design process the curriculum-development team examines alternative curriculum orientations and clarifies its own orientation. The most basic decision the team needs to make (with input from all stakeholders) is whether the purpose of the curriculum will be to transmit, transact, transform, or accomplish some combination thereof.

What Should Be the Content of the Curriculum?

Curriculum, for purposes of this book, is the *what* of instruction—what is intentionally taught to students in a district, school, or classroom. The elements of curriculum are sequence and continuity, scope, and balance (Doll, 1989). *Sequence* is the ordering of learning experiences, and *continuity* is the length or duration of such experiences. *Scope* is the range of learning experiences to be offered. *Balance* is the degree and amount of topics, subjects, and learning experiences that adequately prepare students. A curriculum is developed by deciding: (1) What should students learn? (2) What is the order of content for the student to follow? (3) How is the learning to be evaluated? (See Firth and Newfield, 1984; Glatthorn, 1987; Brandt, 1988a.)

Decisions about curriculum content are influenced by priorities of state and federal governments, values of professional educators and local community, knowledge of student development, current economics, and future societal conditions. Underlying all decisions about curriculum content are curriculum orientations (transmission, transaction, or transformation), which ultimately are derived from educational philosophies (essentialism, experimentalism, or existentialism).

Benjamin Bloom's taxonomy of learning might serve as a guide for determining types of learning within or across content areas (Table 19.1). His lower-level learnings—(1) memory and (2) translation—are based on students recalling and demonstrating known answers. Curriculum objectives calling for memory and translation tend to dominate a curriculum with the purpose of transmission.

TABLE 19.1   Bloom's Taxonomy

Category Name	Description
1. Memory	Student recalls or recognizes information.
2. Translation	Student changes information into a different symbolic form or language.
3. Interpretation	Student discovers relationships among facts, generalizations, definitions, values, and skills.
4. Application	Student solves a life problem that requires the identification of the issue and the selection and use of appropriate generalizations and skills.
5. Analysis	Student solves a problem in the light of conscious knowledge of the parts and forms of thinking.
6. Synthesis	Student solves a problem that requires original creative thinking.
7. Evaluation	Student makes a judgment of good or bad, right or wrong, according to standards designated by student.

Source: G. Manson and A. A. Clegg, Jr., "Classroom Questions: Keys to Children's Thinking?" *Peabody Journal of Education 47*, No. 5 (March 1970): 304-305. Reprinted by permission of Peabody Journal of Education.

Bloom's intermediate levels of learning—(3) interpretation, (4) application, and (5) analysis—are based on students using logic to discover relationships, solve problems, and reflect on their own thought process. Curriculum objectives at the interpretation, application, and analysis levels are emphasized in a curriculum with the purpose of transaction. Finally, Bloom's higher levels of learning—(6) synthesis and (7) evaluation—are based on combining various knowledge, facts, skills, and logic to make unique personal judgments. Curriculum objectives at the synthesis and evaluation levels are prevalent in a curriculum with the purpose of transformation. By examining a written curriculum, then, we can ascertain whether its purpose (and the curriculum developers' underlying orientation) is transmission, transaction, or transformation.

How Should the Curriculum Be Organized?

Three broad approaches to organizing curriculum content are discipline based, interdisciplinary, and transdisciplinary. A *discipline-based curriculum* is described by Jacobs (1989):

> The discipline-based content design option focuses on a strict interpretation of the disciplines with separate subjects in separate time blocks during the school day. No

attempt for integration is made, in fact, it is avoided. Traditional approaches to subjects such as language arts, mathematics, science, social studies, music, art, and physical education are the usual fare. In secondary programs, these general academic and arts areas break down into more specific fields, such as algebra under mathematics or American history under social studies. There are some variations of block scheduling and the way the week or cycle is programmed. Nevertheless, knowledge is presented in separate fields without a deliberate attempt to show the relationships among them. (p. 14)

Because of its emphasis on breaking learning down into discreet segments of traditional content to be learned in specified blocks of time, the discipline-based approach is best suited to a curriculum with the purpose of transmission. This approach clearly has been the dominant curriculum organization pattern in the United States.

In an *interdisciplinary curriculum*, common themes connect traditional content areas. For instance, different aspects of an instructional unit on transportation might be taught in science, math, social studies, language arts, art, music, and physical education. Or, a set of common concepts or skills (for example, technology or problem-solving skills) might connect different subject areas throughout the year. Figure 19.2 illustrates an interdisciplinary curriculum. A curriculum organization of this type requires extensive team planning. Since the interdisciplinary approach encourages students to discover relationships and make applications across existing content areas, it is most appropriate for a curriculum with the purpose of transactional learning.

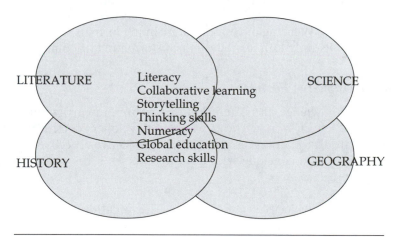

FIGURE 19.2 *Illustration of an Interdisciplinary Curriculum*

Source: From Drake, S. M., Bebbington, V., Laksman, S., Mackie, P., Maynes, N., & Wayne, L. (1992). *Developing an Integrated Curriculum Using the Story Model,* p. 4. Ontario: The Ontario Institute for Studies in Education Press. Reprinted with permission of University of Toronto Press.

In a *transdisciplinary curriculum,* traditional disciplines do not exist. The entire curriculum is organized around common themes, skills, or problems. Daily learning activities are built around the topic being studied rather than conforming to academic disciplines or class schedules. For example, while studying the concept of commerce, students could spend all of their school time developing, managing, and analyzing their own in-school "marketplace." Students might study selected content from economics, math, sociology, communication, politics, ethics, history, and other academic disciplines, but only as such content became relevant to the commercial community they were developing. Transdisciplinary curricula usually begin with very broad intended learning outcomes. The integration into the curriculum of contemporary problems from the real world and students' interests and concerns become part of an ongoing curriculum development process. This type of curriculum organization can be successful only if teachers are willing to totally reconceptualize their concept of the school curriculum. A transdisciplinary curriculum organization requires students to synthesize knowledge and skills from various content areas and encourages student creativity and self-direction. Such an organizational pattern is most consistent with a curriculum with the purpose of transforming teaching and learning.

In What Format Should the Curriculum Be Written?

This section will discuss various formats used in writing curriculum. Behavioral objective, webbing, conceptual mapping, and results-only formats will be described. Like the content and organization of curriculum, the format it is written in reflects a curriculum orientation. Behavioral-objective formats reflect a transmission orientation. Webbing or conceptual mapping formats reflect a transaction orientation. Results-only formats reflect a transformation orientation.

Behavioral-Objective Format

Predetermined knowledge, facts, and skills are written in curriculum guides in a linear cause-and-effect format. The curriculum developers determine what is to be learned, state the learning as a behavioral objective, specify the teaching/learning activities, and conclude with a posttest to see if the objective has been achieved. The progression is

Objective   Activity   Evaluation

Figure 19.3 is an example of a behavioral-objective guide written for a fifth-grade social studies class. Curriculum developers break their unit into the most important facts or skills that cover the subject. They write behavioral objectives for each fact or skill. Each behavioral objective is the basis for a sequence of activities and evaluation. The teacher who uses such a curriculum guide is expected to

FIGURE 19.3 *Behavioral-Objective Format*

Behavioral objective: At the end of the week, students will recall and spell the original 13 colonies at a 100 percent level of mastery.

Activities:
1. Lecture on 13 colonies.
2. Students fill in map of 13 colonies.
3. Students read pp. 113–118 of text and do assignments on p. 119 as homework.
4. Call on students at random to spell the various colonies.

Evaluation: Ask students to recall the names and spell correctly each of the 13 original colonies on a sheet of paper.

follow the sequence of activities and administer the evaluation. Recycling activities might be included in the guide for those students who do not pass the evaluation. Each behavioral-objective plan is tightly sequenced so that one objective is mastered before a student moves to the next (for example, after identifying and spelling the original 13 American colonies, the next objective might be identifying and spelling those states that came into the Union from 1776 to 1810).

Most school curricula that have been written in the last two decades follow a behavioral-objective format. It is particularly easy to use in subjects such as mathematics and physical sciences, where skills are obvious and facts are clear. (2 plus 2 is always 4, for example, but is war always justifiable?) So prevalent has been the behavioral-objective format in curriculum writing in the last few years that many educators know of no other way to write curricula.

Webbing

Curriculum can be written in a format that shows relationships of activities around a central theme. William Kilpatrick popularized this type of curriculum in writing about the work unit (Kilpatrick, 1925). Instead of predetermining the knowledge or skills, the curriculum developer determines the major theme, related themes, and then possible student activities.

The webbing format can be conceived of in this way:

2. Related theme
3. Activities
4. Possible outcomes

2. Related theme
3. Activities
4. Possible outcomes

1. SUBJECT THEME

2. Related theme
3. Activities
4. Possible outcomes

2. Related theme
3. Activities
4. Possible outcomes

After the activities have been written, the curriculum developers write possible learning outcomes: "Students will be able to identify four major environmental issues," "Students will be able to argue and give evidence for both the pro and con sides of each issue," "Students will take a personal stance on each issue." In planning activities, developers consider multimodes of learning via reading, writing, listening, and constructing, and then integrate many fields of knowledge around a central theme. Notice how the theme of environmental issues integrates activities in sociology, mathematics, economics, history, journalism, physics, and biology. Included in the guide are the resources needed to conduct the activities. In our example, resources might include tape recorders, newspapers, books, and community volunteers.

A webbing curriculum guide would contain a blueprint of the web followed by sections for each related theme with activities, possible outcomes, and resources needed (see Figure 19.4). Notice that the webbed curriculum includes possible outcomes and allows for the possibility of others. In a behavioral-objective curriculum, activities are controlled toward predetermined ends. In a webbed curriculum, activities lead to possible and unanticipated learning.

Conceptual Mapping Format

Posner and Rudnitsky (1982) developed a curriculum format, called *conceptual mapping,* which is an interesting integration of webbing and behavioral objectives. It includes the following:

1. Rationale for the course including the overall educational goals.
2. List of intended learning outcomes for the course, categorized according to type of learning.
3. Conceptual maps depicting the relationship among the important ideas to be learned in the course.
4. Instructional plan describing a) what each unit is about, b) what learning outcomes each unit is intended to accomplish and c) what general teaching strategies could be used in each unit to accomplish the intended learning outcomes.
5. Evaluation plan describing behavioral indicators for each high-priority intended learning outcome (main effects), together with a list of some unintended, undesirable learning outcomes (side effects) to be on the lookout for. (Posner and Rudnitsky, 1982, p. 8)

Conceptual mapping combines webbing and behavioral-objective formats. It provides the teacher with specific directions for accomplishing predetermined skills, as well as general strategies for teaching concepts.

Results-Only Format

A results-only format for curriculum provides teachers with the widest latitude for using materials, activities, and methods. Such a curriculum specifies the goals

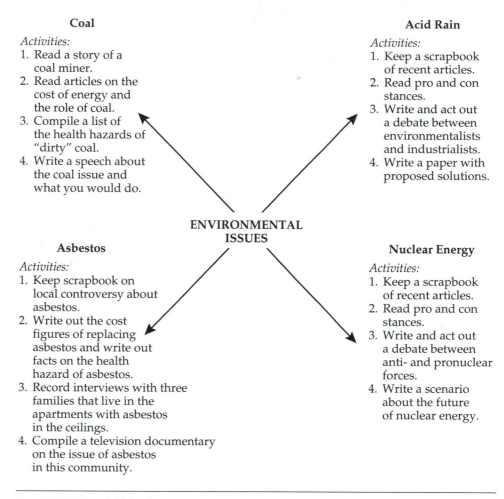

Coal

Activities:
1. Read a story of a coal miner.
2. Read articles on the cost of energy and the role of coal.
3. Compile a list of the health hazards of "dirty" coal.
4. Write a speech about the coal issue and what you would do.

Acid Rain

Activities:
1. Keep a scrapbook of recent articles.
2. Read pro and con stances.
3. Write and act out a debate between environmentalists and industrialists.
4. Write a paper with proposed solutions.

ENVIRONMENTAL ISSUES

Asbestos

Activities:
1. Keep scrapbook on local controversy about asbestos.
2. Write out the cost figures of replacing asbestos and write out facts on the health hazard of asbestos.
3. Record interviews with three families that live in the apartments with asbestos in the ceilings.
4. Compile a television documentary on the issue of asbestos in this community.

Nuclear Energy

Activities:
1. Keep a scrapbook of recent articles.
2. Read pro and con stances.
3. Write and act out a debate between anti- and pronuclear forces.
4. Write a scenario about the future of nuclear energy.

FIGURE 19.4 *Webbing Format*

and general learning about a subject, theme unit, or course. The guide might include ways to evaluate the learning. For example, a results-only guide in elementary reading might specify the following skills to be learned:

Comprehension
1. Develops powers of observation
2. Classifies by name, color, shape, size, positions, use
3. Anticipates endings to stories
4. Discriminates between fact and fantasy
5. Understands who, what, when, where, how, and why phrases
6. Recalls a story sequence
7. Reads to find the main ideas of a story

8. Reads to draw a conclusion

9. Compares and contrasts stories

It is then left to the teacher to determine when and how to teach these skills. The teacher is held accountable only for the results, not for the procedures used.

Curriculum Format as Reflective of Choice Given to Teachers

The less specificity and detail a curriculum has, the greater the choice given to teachers to vary instruction according to the situation. Figure 19.5 illustrates the enlargement of teacher choice by curriculum.

Picture being in a curriculum cone where, at the behavioral-objective bottom, a teacher can barely budge. As the teacher moves toward the webbing and conceptual-mapping area, he or she finds room to move hands, feet, elbows, and knees. At the results-only end of the cone, the teacher can extend fully. If the teacher is allowed to step out of the curriculum cone, there are no limits on where and how he or she can move. Behavioral-objective formats predetermine the *what* and *how* of teaching as much as possible in a loosely coupled organization. Webbing and conceptual-mapping formats focuses on themes and relationships of possible activities for teachers but give them a choice of actual activities, duration of activities, and evaluation methods. A results-only format focuses on generalized learning and gives teachers the latitude to proceed as they wish.

It would appear relatively easy to match teacher stages of development to curriculum formats. It is not so easy, however; further examination of type and degree of involvement in curriculum development is necessary.

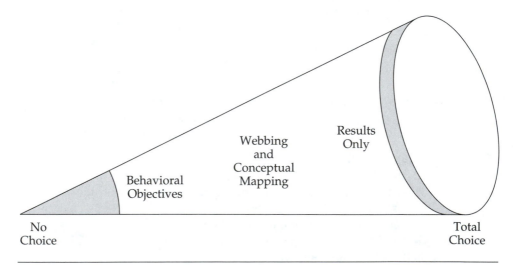

FIGURE 19.5 *Curriculum Format as a Reflection of Teacher-Choice: The Curriculum Cone*

If a school has decided to use a behavioral-objective format, that does not necessarily mean that classroom teachers have little choice about how to teach. Perhaps the teachers have chosen to use that format; perhaps they wrote the curriculum themselves. Also, an elaborately detailed behavioral-objective curriculum could be presented to teachers as a reference guide to use as they wish. Simply knowing the format of the curriculum would not tell us how much choice was given to teachers. Although behavioral curricula usually are used as prescriptive teaching and can be equated with limiting choice, this is not always so. Therefore, before completing the picture of curriculum and teacher choice, it is necessary to consider how curricula are developed, interpreted, and implemented.

Relationship of Curriculum Purpose, Content, Organization, and Format

In previous sections we have proposed logical links between curriculum purpose, content, organization, and format. To review, a curriculum with the purpose of transmission is logically matched with memory and translation learning content, discipline-based curriculum organization, and behavioral-objective format. A curriculum with the purpose of transaction is well matched with interpretation, application, and analysis learning content; interdisciplinary curriculum organization; and webbing or conceptual-mapping format. A curriculum with the purpose of transformation is consistent with synthesis and evaluation learning content, a transdisciplinary curriculum organization, and a results-only format. Table 19.2 illustrates logical relationships of curriculum purpose, content, organization, and format.

The "natural matches" we've outlined, of course, don't occur in all curricula. For instance, not all webbing and conceptual-mapping formats are found within interdisciplinary curricula. The webbing format in Figure 19.4, for example, could be part of a science course within a discipline-based curriculum. For another instance, a results-only curriculum format could focus on learning content at the lower and intermediate as well as the higher levels of Bloom's taxonomy, or could be part of a discipline-based or interdisciplinary rather than a

TABLE 19.2 *Logical Relationships of Curriculum Purpose, Content, Organization, and Format*

Curriculum Purpose:	Transmission	Transaction	Transformation
Curriculum Content:	Memory Translation	Interpretation Application Analysis	Synthesis Evaluation
Curriculum Organization:	Discipline Based	Interdisciplinary	Transdisciplinary
Curriculum Format:	Behavioral Objective	Webbing Conceptual Mapping	Results Only

transdisciplinary curriculum. In general, however, our own review of K–12 curricula indicate that the logical matches in Table 19.2 tend to hold true in most schools.

Levels of Teacher Involvement in Curriculum Development

Tanner and Tanner (1980) wrote of teachers and local schools functioning in curriculum development at one of three levels: (1) imitative maintenance, (2) mediative, or (3) generative. Teachers at level 1 are concerned with maintaining and following the existing curriculum. Teachers at level 2 look at development as refining the existing curriculum. Teachers at level 3 are concerned with improving and changing the curriculum according to the most current knowledge about learning and societal conditions. Tanner and Tanner explained these three levels according to Table 19.3.

Level I: Imitative Maintenance
Teachers operating at Level I rely on textbooks, workbooks, and routine activities, subject by subject. Skills are treated as dead ends rather than as means of generating further learning. Readymade materials are used without critical evaluation, resulting in a multiplicity of isolated skill-development activities. (The already segmental curriculum is further fragmented.) The imagination of the teacher does not go beyond maintaining the status quo. This teacher would like to think that he or she has less freedom than he or she may actually have for curriculum improvement. In the secondary school, concern for curriculum development is largely confined to each departmental domain.

When change is made, it is made on the adoption level, without adaptation to local needs. As shown in Table 19.3 curriculum development at this level is plugging in the package to the existing situation without attention to the resulting interactions. Teachers at this level tend to be left alone to struggle with innovations that are handed to them from above. Schools are turned inward, with the principal as the sole resource for classroom assistance.

Level II: Mediative
Teachers at Level II are aware of the need to integrate curriculum content and deal with emergent conditions. (Societal problems such as the energy crisis and children's questions about things that interest and concern them are examples of emergent conditions.) Although teachers at this level may have an aggregate conception of curriculum, implementation does not go beyond the occasional correlation of certain subjects. The focus of curriculum remains segmental; theory remains divorced from practice; curriculum improvement remains at the level of refining existing practice.

Yet teachers at the second level of curriculum development do not blindly plug in an innovation or curriculum package to the existing situation. The neces-

TABLE 19.3 *Levels of Teacher Involvement in Curriculum Development*

Level	Locus	Tasks and Activities	Principal Resources
Level I: Imitative maintenance	Microcurriculum Established conditions Segmental treatment	Rudimentary Routine Adoptive Maintenance of established practice	Textbook, workbook, syllabi (subject by subject), segmental adoption of curriculum packages, popular educational literature School principal
Level II: Mediative	Microcurriculum Established conditions Segmental treatment Awareness of emergent conditions aggregate treatment macrocurriculum	Interpretive Adaptive Refinement of established practice	Textbook, courses of study (subject by subject with occasional correlation of subjects), multimedia, adaptation of segmental curriculum packages, professional literature on approved practice Pupils, teacher colleagues, helping teacher, supervisor, curriculum coordinator, parents, community resources, school principal, inservice courses
Level III: Generative	Macrocurriculum Emergent conditions Aggregate treatment	Interpretive Adaptive Evaluative problem-diagnosis problem-solving Improvement of established practice Search for improved practice	Textbook, courses of study (across subjects and grade levels), alternative modes of curriculum design, professional literature on research and approved practice, multimedia, projects Pupils, teacher colleagues, helping teacher, supervisor, curriculum coordinator, parents, community resources, school principal, in-service courses, outside consultants, experimental programs, professional conferences and workshops

Source: Daniel Tanner and Laurel N. Tanner, *Curriculum Development: Theory into Practice,* 2nd ed., p. 637. Copyright © 1980 by Macmillan Publishing Co., Inc., New York. Reprinted by permission.

sary adaptations, accommodations, and adjustments are made [see Table 19.3] of and capitalize on a range of resources for curriculum improvement, including pupils, parents, and peers; and they utilize resources beyond the local school. Teachers are consumers of professional literature on approved practices and tap the resources of the university through in-service courses. The mediative level is a level of awareness and accommodation. Teachers are attracted to, and can articulate, new ideas but their efforts to improve the curriculum fall short of the necessary reconstruction for substantive problem solving.

Level III: Creative-Generative

As shown in [Table 19.3] teachers at Level III take an aggregate approach to curriculum development. Ideally, the curriculum is examined in its entirety by the teacher and the whole school staff, and questions of priority and relationship are asked. While individual teachers can and should be at the generative-creative level, a macrocurricular approach requires cooperative planning for vertical and horizontal articulation.

Granted that teachers as individuals usually cannot create new schoolwide curricula, an individual teacher can establish continuities and relationships in his or her own teaching and with other teachers. Teachers at Level III use generalizations and problems as centers of curriculum organization. They stress the broad concepts that specialized subjects share in common, and they use and develop courses of study that cross subject fields. These are aggregate treatments.

Teachers at the third level of curriculum development think about what they are doing and try to find more effective ways of working. They are able to diagnose their problems and formulate hypotheses for solutions. They experiment in their classrooms and communicate their insights to other teachers.

Teachers at this level are consumers of research and seek greater responsibility for curriculum decisions at the school and classroom levels. They exercise independent judgment in selecting curriculum materials and adapt them to local needs. They regard themselves as professionals and, as such, are continually involved in the problems of making decisions regarding learning experiences. To this end, their antennae are turned outward to a wide range of resources. (Daniel Tanner and Laurel N. Tanner, *Curriculum Development: Theory into Practice*, 2nd ed., pp. 636, 638–639. Copyright © 1980 by Macmillan Publishing Co., Inc., New York. Reprinted by permission.)

Integrating Curriculum Format with Developers and Levels of Development

To integrate what has been said about curriculum format, developers, and development, refer to Figure 19.6. When the developers are either outside the school system or from the district level and the curriculum is in a tightly prescribed format, development will be primarily *imitative,* characterized by teachers following the course of study. When the developers are intermediate teams of teachers led by district specialists and the curriculum is written with objectives and suggested activities, development will be primarily *mediative,* characterized by teachers revising and adapting the course of study to their immediate situation. When curriculum developers are teams of teachers using specialists as resource persons or individual teachers with a results-only curriculum format that identifies what students should learn and leaves activities to the teacher, then development is *generative,* characterized by on-going creativity.

Of course, there are other variations of these combinations. For example, the developers might be an inside team of teachers assisted by a central office curriculum specialist, and they might develop a tightly presented curriculum. There-

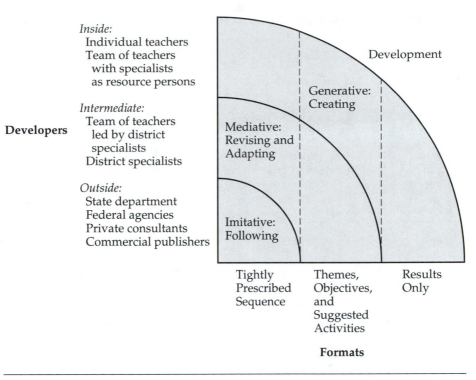

FIGURE 19.6 *Integrating Curriculum Format with Developers and Levels of Development*

fore, the development would be at a generative level, with the implementation at an imitative level.

Matching Curriculum Development with Teacher Development

A progression of curriculum development matched with teacher development might look like Table 19.4. The supervisor might think of his or her staff in terms of the commitment, thinking, and expertise they currently bring to curriculum and then determine whether the current curriculum is appropriately matched with the teachers' level of curriculum functioning. If the present curriculum is inappropriate to teachers' development, readjustments to the curriculum would be in order.

A staff that has a low level of curriculum functioning—as displayed by little commitment to change, little ability to suggest possible changes, and little curriculum expertise—would be appropriately matched with an outside-developed,

TABLE 19.4   *Progression of Curriculum Matched with Characteristics of Staff*

Staff Characteristics	Low	Moderate	High
Commitment to curriculum change	Low commitment to change	Would like to make change	Eager to make change
Level of thinking about curriculum	Low ability to think about possible changes	Can think of some possible changes	Has many suggestions
Expertise in curriculum procedures	Low expertise in how to proceed	Does not know how to write curriculum	Knows how to proceed
Curriculum Characteristics			
Developers	Outside developers	Outside developed but substantially revised by team of teachers led by specialists	Internally developed by team of teachers with specialists as resource
Format	Behavioral-objective, highly structured	Eclectic format using behavior objectives, webbing, and/or conceptual map	Results-only, with suggested activities
Development	Imitative, with allowance for minor revisions	To be mutually adapted	To be discussed and changed continually

behavioral-objective, and imitative curriculum. They should be allowed to make minor revisions in adapting the curriculum to their classrooms. On the other hand, a staff that has a moderate level of curriculum functioning (as displayed by a desire to change, ability to think of possible changes, but a lack of expertise in writing curriculum) would be appropriately matched with a curriculum originally developed by outside experts but substantially revised by an internal team of teachers led by a curriculum specialist. The format of the curriculum might be eclectic in its use of behavioral objectives, webbing, and conceptual maps. Throughout the development and implementation, teachers should have problem-solving meetings for purposes of curriculum adaptation. Finally, a staff that is at a high level of curriculum functioning (as displayed by initiating and suggesting ways to change and knowing how to proceed in creating curriculum) would be appropriately matched with an internally developed curriculum. The format should emphasize "results only" with *suggested* activities, and should be continuously open to revision.

The supervisor should keep in mind the question: How does one increase teacher control over curriculum making? If a staff has been appropriately matched—for example, low-functioning staff with an imitative curriculum—and successful implementation is occurring, then the supervisor should plan for the next cycle of curriculum development to give teachers additional responsibilities by serving on decision-making teams under the leadership of a curriculum specialist. This would lead to more mutually adaptive curriculum and at the same time continue to stimulate and increase teacher commitment, development, and expertise.

The supervisor wishing to facilitate changes in curriculum purpose, content, organization, and format must remember that successful change will be based on teachers changing their conceptions of curriculum and their level of involvement in curriculum development. Change in teachers *and* curriculum is more likely to be successful if done in an incremental manner. For example, rather than announcing that the school will be moving from a discipline-based to interdisciplinary curriculum organization, the supervisor could initially encourage small teams of teachers functioning at moderate to high levels of development, expertise, and commitment to plan and teach a few interdisciplinary units of instruction throughout the school year. In another school already operating at an interdisciplinary level, movement toward a transdisciplinary curriculum could begin with a group of teachers operating at high levels of development, expertise, and commitment forming a "broad field." A *broad field* results from the fusion of two or more separate disciplines. Courses or subjects (rather than departments) with titles like "humanities," "social science," and "natural science" usually reflect a broad-field approach. The formation of one or more broad fields involving a subset of faculty and curricula would not represent a fully transdisciplinary curriculum, but would be a major step in that direction.

Let's consider two more examples, this time in the area of curriculum formatting. A conceptual-mapping curriculum would be an appropriate format for a group of teachers at moderate to high levels of development, expertise, and commitment who are ready to move away from a purely behavioral-objective format. This is because conceptual mapping would allow the teachers to link a new format (webbing) to a format with which they were already familiar (behavioral objectives). In a different school with teachers of relatively high levels of development, expertise, and commitment who wish to move to a results-only format, it might be wise to include *suggested* (but not required) thematic webs, activities, and materials so that teachers can gradually make the transition to the highest levels of curriculum decision-making responsibility.

Large-scale teacher-driven changes in curriculum content, organization, and format will not take place unless teachers change their curriculum orientations or beliefs about the purpose of curriculum. Yet, teachers are not likely to change their orientations unless their levels of understanding of and involvement in curriculum development gradually increase. Supervisor openness and trust building, staff development in curriculum design, and time, support, and rewards for teacher involvement can all foster teacher *and* curriculum development. Throughout the curriculum-development process, the supervisor must remember that if he or she has a curriculum orientation or favors a curriculum content, organization, or format different from teachers, he or she is not necessarily right and the teachers wrong. Government mandates, the community, the school's mission and culture, parents, teachers, and students must all be considered when deciding which direction curriculum development should take and at what rate it should proceed.

The supervisor also might think about using curriculum matching when working with individual teachers for improving classroom instruction. Some teachers of low levels of development, expertise, and commitment would benefit, at least initially, from a highly prescriptive curriculum. Other teachers with moderate or mixed levels of development, expertise, and commitment would benefit from the use of an eclectic curriculum that offered choices of two or more texts or guides. The highly developed, committed, and expert teacher would benefit from having the freedom to choose and create his or her own plans.

Curriculum Development as a Vehicle for Enhancing Collective Thinking about Instruction

It is a shame that most educators view curriculum as something given, which they must follow. Books about curriculum development are widely neglected. Coursework in educational leadership programs gives curriculum short attention (at best, one required course). The criteria for assessing school leaders' performance largely ignores curriculum work as an important aspect of leadership responsibilities. Instead, assessment criteria emphasize "the monitoring of teachers using the district curriculum."

Why is it that curriculum is no longer a province for school inquiry and action, but rather a matter of complying with external mandates? The reason is that in the era of legislated learning, teachers and school leaders are seen as incapable of knowing what their students should be taught.

State Mandated Curriculum

In many states, legislatures are now mandating the curriculum to be taught in all public PK-12 schools. The purpose of the mandated curriculum is to transmit knowledge and skills deemed essential by the state legislature or educational bureaucracy. The required curriculum is often presented as a laundry list of required objectives in each subject area (or at least each "basic" subject area) at each grade level. Objectives tend to be within the lower categories of Bloom's taxonomy, at the memory or translation level. There are seldom any connections made between the objectives in different content areas. Even the objectives within a given content area are usually discreet from one another. In short, in terms of purpose, content, organization, and format, state mandated curriculum tends to be at the lowest level of curriculum development. It is therefore very difficult for teachers in states with mandated curricula to function beyond the imitative maintenance level of involvement in curriculum development.

One argument often made by state officials discussing this reality is that teachers don't need to have a say in the curriculum because they can use their professional expertise and creativity when they plan how to teach the curriculum in their classrooms. These policy makers fail to understand that *the curriculum, if rigidly enforced, has a significant impact on how teachers teach.* For example, teachers working under a highly prescribed curriculum with long lists of required objectives will approach instruction quite differently than teachers with a webbed curriculum that they have designed themselves. In short, *what* get's taught (curriculum) has a strong impact on *how* it gets taught (instruction).

High Stakes Tests and the Curriculum

One way states have attempted to control curriculum in schools is through the use of high stakes tests (discussed in detail in Chapter 15). When aligned with the state-mandated curriculum, state test scores are used as a measure of whether teachers are effectively implementing the curriculum. In states without a mandated curriculum but with high stakes tests, the test itself becomes the curriculum. In these states the original notion of alignment (start with the curriculum and align instruction and assessment with the curriculum) is turned on its head, with local schools aligning their curricula with the state test.

> A standardized test would set the educational objectives for the teacher. Curriculum alignment would insure that the teacher would cover the material to be tested. The teacher would prepare plans and write reports to inform supervisors in the bureaucracy that the material was being covered. Evaluators would observe and inspect to make sure that teachers were using the proper methods. And, finally, the external test would demonstrate whether the teacher had properly executed his or her duties. (Wise, 1988, p. 330)

We don't want to imply that learning standards and assessment are by their very nature bad. Standards and assessment that have been constructed with wide participation and are thoughtful and reasonable for students to achieve can be a way to address class, race, and gender inequities of expectations, resources, and targeted assistance. The issue here is one of who should define such standards, what should be multiple ways of assessing such learning, what should be the consequences for students, teachers, and schools, and as importantly, what flexibility, freedom, and authority should be given to classrooms and schools to be accountable? After all, it is hard to be accountable for what one has no control over (Elmore and Rothman, 1999; Darling-Hammond, 1997; Glickman, 1999).

In states with highly narrow and prescriptive standards and assessments based on a single conception of required, essential knowledge, teachers, leaders, and school council members who believe differently about what is most important for students to be able to know and do are left with limited options. They can (1) rebel against the external tests, (2) accept and help students to do well on the tests in an engaging manner, or (3) develop their own inquiry and performance based assessments that incorporate the external knowledge and skills to be tested (See Glickman, 1999, 2000; Darling-Hammond, 1997; Kohn, 1999).

The tragedy of curriculum being simply a response to state tests is the loss of a powerful vehicle for creating a broader instructional dialogue in a school or district, which could enhance teachers' individual and collective thinking about the questions what is worth teaching, how shall we teach, and how shall we assess? Most teachers—when trusted, when given time and money, and when given the assistance, choice, and responsibility to develop curricula—will make extraordinarily sound decisions about what students should be taught. Often, their decisions will be far superior to those made in central offices, state departments, or commercial publishing firms (McEvoy, 1986; McNeil, 1988).

Teachers who are involved in making decisions about school curriculum go through changes in their own thinking about teaching. To discuss, debate, and finally come to an agreement with peers about what is important for students to know is an intellectually challenging experience. Curriculum development is a less intimidating task for a group than the other supervision tasks (direct assistance, professional development, group development, and action research). After all, the question here is not *how* we teach but *what* we should teach (what the goals, objectives, themes, and materials for our students should be).

Summary

Teachers will implement curriculum successfully if they have been involved in its development and can adapt it to their specific classroom and school situation. The failure of the teacher-proof curriculum movement should remind us that imposing curriculum from outside is useless. Instead, the questions for supervisors to consider have to do with type and degree of curriculum development. The supervisor can pick from six arenas. The first arena includes sources of development, ranging from teachers to district-level personnel, state and federal experts, and commercial writers. The second arena involves the purpose of the curriculum, based on one of three curriculum orientations: transmission, transaction, or transformation. The third arena consists of the content emphasis of curriculum: the lower, middle, or higher levels of Bloom's taxonomy. The fourth arena involves curriculum organization, including discipline-based, interdisciplinary, and transdisciplinary curricula. The fifth arena is curriculum format, including behavioral-objective, webbing, conceptual-mapping, and results-only formats. Finally, the sixth arena consists of levels of teacher involvement, including imitative-maintenance, mediative, and creative-generative levels. The supervisor and teachers should work together to select curriculum purpose, content, organization, and format that (1) is most appropriate for the students and (2) increases teachers' choice and commitment to curriculum implementation. Curriculum, when treated as a task for school action, is a powerful, relatively nonthreatening intervention for enhancing collective thought and action about instruction.

Exercises

Academic

1. Review a report on the results of federally supported curriculum development. Prepare a written summary and discussion of the highlights of the chosen report.

2. Prepare a written summary and discussion of one of the following:
   a. Teacher-proof curriculum
   b. The Eight-Year Study
   c. The Rand Corporation study

3. Summarize the recommendations of two curriculum textbook authors for providing each of the following in a school curriculum:

   a. Sequence and continuity

   b. Scope

   c. Balance

4. Create one or two sample pages of curriculum guides that reflect each of the following formats for curriculum development:

   a. Behavioral-objective format

   b. Webbing format

   c. Results-only format

5. Summarize, analyze, and evaluate the concept of an interdisciplinary curriculum.

Field

1. Examine the curriculum guide of a school with which you are *not* familiar. What orientation to curriculum is reflected by the curriculum guide? What national, regional, and local priorities are reflected? What examples of knowledge of student development, current economics, and predicted future societal conditions can be derived from the guide? What format was used in developing the curriculum? What categories from Bloom's taxonomy are evident in the curriculum objectives? What parental, central office, teacher, and student influences are recognizable? What commercial publishing influences can be discerned? Does the guide reflect an imitative-maintenance, mediative, or generative level of curriculum development? Was the guide most likely developed by outside developers with minimal revision, by outside developers with substantial revision, by a team of teachers led by a specialist, or internally by a team of teachers with specialists as resource people?

   Write a paper answering each question and provide examples from the guide to support your answers.

2. Examine the living curriculum of a school (what is actually taught) to determine how the development of that curriculum has been significantly affected by one of the following:

   a. The federal government

   b. The state department of education

   c. The local community

   d. Parents of students attending the school

   e. Central office personnel

   f. Teachers

   g. Students

   Write a paper discussing the effects of the chosen entity on the development of the school's living curriculum.

3. Examine a so-called canned curriculum, including the teacher's guide, teacher-proof texts and/or materials, programmed methods of measuring student progress, and all other major components of the program. Prepare a report describing and

evaluating the selected curriculum. If your report is a verbal one, display and discuss physical components of the curriculum as part of your presentation.

4. Interview a teacher to determine to what extent the school's curriculum guide determines what he or she teaches. Probe for other influences on what is taught (for example, what the teacher was taught when he or she was a student, the text being used, other teachers, administrators, nationally normed achievement tests, and so on). Prepare a report summarizing and analyzing the interview.

5. Observe a working meeting of a curriculum development or curriculum review committee. What is the prevailing educational philosophy of the group? What influences (government, community, parental, administrative, commercial publishers) are influencing the group's decision making? What are some characteristics of individual members of the group (levels of commitment, development, expertise)? Is the curriculum development taking place at an imitative, mediative, or generative level? What curriculum-development format (behavioral-objective, webbing, conceptual mapping, or results-only) is in evidence? Prepare a report on your observation, including answers to each of these questions. Support your answers with descriptions of behaviors or artifacts observed at the meeting.

Developmental

1. Volunteer for membership on a curriculum development or review committee.

2. Examine the writings of authors on educational supervision to compare their positions on the role and function of the supervisor in curriculum development.

3. Over a period of time, compare a school's written curriculum with its living curriculum (what is actually taught from day to day). How much congruence is there between the formal curriculum and what is actually taught?

References

Aiken, W. M. 1942. *The story of the eight-year study.* New York: Harper.

Applebee, A. N., Langer, S. A., and Mullis, V. S. 1987. *Literature and U.S. History: The instructional experience and factual knowledge of high school juniors. The nation's report card.* Princeton, NJ: Educational Testing Service.

Berman, P., and McLaughlin, M. W. 1978. *Federal programs supporting educational change, Vol. 8. Implementing and sustaining innovations.* Santa Monica, CA: Rand Corp. (ERIC ED 159 289)

Bloom, A. 1987. *The closing of the American mind.* New York: Simon and Schuster.

Brandt, R. S. (Ed.). 1988a. Content of the curriculum, 1988. In *ASCD Yearbook.* Alexandria, VA: Association for Supervision and Curriculum Development.

Brandt, R. S. 1988b. On assessment in the arts: A conversation with Howard Gardner. *Educational Leadership* 45(4):30–34.

Brubaker, D. L. 1982. *Curriculum planning: The dynamics of theory and practice.* Glenview, IL: Scott, Foresman.

Cornbleth, C. 1981. Curriculum materials can make a difference. *Educational Leadership* 38(7):567–568.

Cremin, L. A. 1976. *Public education.* New York: Basic Books.

Darling-Hammond, L. 1997. *The right to learn: A blueprint for creating schools that work.* San Francisco: Jossey-Bass Publishers.

Doll, R. C. 1989. *Curriculum improvement: Decision making and process* (6th ed.). Boston: Allyn and Bacon.

Drake, S. M., Bebbington, J., Laksman, S., Mackie, P., Marnes, N., and Wayne, L. 1992. *Developing an integrated curriculum using the story model.* Toronto: The Ontario Institute for Studies in Education.

Driscoll, M. 1988. Transforming the "under achieving" math curriculum. *ASCD Curriculum Update* (January), p. 6.

Eisner, E. W., and Vallance, E. 1974. *Conflicting conceptions of curriculum*. Berkeley, CA: McCutchan.

Elmore, R. F., and Rothman, R. (Eds.). 1999. *Testing, teaching, and learning; A guide for states and school districts*. Washington, D.C.: National Academy Press.

Firth, G. R., and Newfield, J. W. 1984. Curriculum development and selection. In J. M. Cooper (Ed.), *Developing skills for instructional supervision*. New York: Longman.

Gibney, T., and Kams, E. 1979. Mathematics education, 1955–1975: A summary of the NSF findings. *Educational Leadership* 36(5):356–359.

Glatthorn, A. A. 1987. *Curriculum renewal*. Alexandria, VA: Association for Supervision and Curriculum Development.

Glickman, C. D. 1999. *School based authority and responsibility*. Unpublished invited report to the Georgia Governor's Education Reform Study Commission. Atlanta, GA: The Office of the Governor of Georgia.

Glickman, C. D. 2000. *Holding sacred ground: Standards, choices, and substenance*. Distinguished lecture to the Annual Conference of the Association for Supervision and Curriculum Development. New Orleans, March.

Goodlad, J. 1984. *A place called school*. New York: McGraw-Hill.

Hirsch, E. D., Jr. 1987. *Cultural literacy: What every American needs to know*. Boston: Houghton Mifflin.

Jackson, P. W. 1969. Technology and the teacher. In Committee for Economic Development, *The school and the challenge of innovation*. New York: McGraw-Hill.

Jacobs, H. H. 1989. *Interdisciplinary curriculum: Design and implementation*. Alexandria, VA: Association for Supervision and Curriculum Development.

Kilpatrick, W. H. 1925. *Foundations of method*. New York: Macmillan.

Kirst, M., and Walker, D. 1971. An analysis of curriculum policy-making. *Review of Educational Research 41*(5):479–509.

Kohn, A. 1999. *The schools our children deserve*. Boston: Houghton Mifflin Co.

McEvoy, B. 1986. *"Against our better judgements."* Three teachers' enactment of mandated curriculum. Paper presented at the annual meeting of the American Educational Research Association, San Francisco.

McNeil, L. N. 1988. Contradictions of control, Part 2. Teachers, students and curriculum. *Kappan* 69(6):432–438.

Miller, J. P., and Seller, W. 1985. *Curriculum: Perspectives and practice*. New York: Longman.

Oliva, P. F. 1992. *Developing the curriculum* (3rd ed.). New York: HarperCollins.

Ponder, G. 1979. The more things change...the status of social studies. *Educational Leadership* 36(7):515–518.

Porter, A. 1987. *A curriculum out of balance: The case of elementary school mathematics*. Paper presented to the annual meeting of the American Education Research Association, Washington, DC, April.

Posner, G. J., and Rudnitsky, A. N. 1982. *Course design: A guide to curriculum development for teachers* (2nd ed.). New York: Longman.

Ravitch, D., and Finn, L. E., Jr. 1987. *What do our 17-year-olds know? A report of the First National Assessment of History and Literature*. New York: Harper and Row.

Rutter, M., Maughan, B., Mortimore, P., Ouston, J., and Smith, A. 1979. *Fifteen thousand hours: Secondary schools and their effects on children*. Cambridge, MA: Harvard University Press.

Saylor, J. G., Alexander, W. M., and Lewis, A. 1981. *Curriculum planning for better teaching and learning* (4th ed.). New York: Holt, Rinehart and Winston.

Sergiovanni, T. 1987. *Introduction to the Breckinridge Conference on Restructuring Schools*. San Antonio, August.

Sizer, T. R. 1984. *Horace's compromise: The dilemma of the American high school*. Boston: Houghton Mifflin.

Tanner, D., and Tanner, L. W. 1980. *Curriculum development: Theory into practice* (2nd ed.). New York: Macmillan.

Weick, K. E. 1976. Educational organizations as loosely coupled systems. *Administrative Science Quarterly 21*:1–19.

Wise, A. 1988. Legislated learning revisited. *Kappan* 69(5):328–333.

Yager, R. E., and Stodghill, R. 1979. School sciences in an age of science. *Educational Leadership* 36(6):439–445.

Zeuli, J. S., and Buchmann, M. 1987. *Implementation of teacher thinking research as curriculum deliberation*. Presentation to the annual meeting of the American Educational Research Association, Washington, DC, April.

Suggested Readings

Connelly, F. M., and Clandinin, D. J. 1988. *Teachers as curriculum planners.* New York: Teachers College Press.

Darling-Hammond, L. 1997. *The right to learn: A blueprint for creating schools that work.* San Francisco: Jossey-Bass Publishers.

Drake, S. M., Bebbington, J., Laksman, S., Machie, P., Maynes, N., and Wayne, L. 1992. *Developing an integrated curriculum using the story model.* Toronto: The Ontario Institute for Studies in Education.

Elmore, R. F., and Rothman, R. (Eds.). 1999. *Testing, teaching, and learning; A guide for states and school districts.* Washington, DC: National Academy Press.

Hass, G., and Parkay, F. W. 1993. *Curriculum planning: A new approach* (6th ed.). Boston: Allyn and Bacon.

Jacobs, H. H. (Ed.). 1989. *Interdisciplinary curriculum: Design and implementation.* Alexandria, VA: Association for Supervision and Curriculum Development.

Kohn, A. 1999. *The schools our children deserve.* Boston: Houghton Mifflin Co.

Kovalik, S., and Olsen, K. 1994. *ITT: The model integrated thematic instruction* (3rd ed.). Kent, WA: Books for Educators.

Oliva, P. F. 1992. *Developing the curriculum* (3rd ed.). New York: HarperCollins.

20

Action Research

The School as the Center of Inquiry

> *Why should our schools not be staffed, gradually if you will, by scholar-teachers in command of the conceptual tools and methods of inquiry requisite to investigating the learning process as it operates in their own classrooms? Why should our schools not nurture the continuing wisdom and power of such scholar-teachers? (Schaefer, 1967, p. 5)*

Thus were the questions raised by James Schaefer over three decades ago in *The School as the Center of Inquiry.* Those questions have been posed from time to time, and different eras of school reform have either responded or chosen to ignore them. The progressive era from the 1920s to the early 1940s and the open education era from the mid-1960s to the early 1970s were times of responsiveness. Since then, the potential of teachers and supervisors as investigators of school improvement has largely been ignored. A noted exception has been the Institute for Research on Teaching at Michigan State University which incorporated practicing teachers as scholars in research. At that time, "the idea of teachers as researchers of practice was foreign and novel. Skeptics outnumbered the enthusiasts. Now the reverse is true" (Gross, 1986). Consistent with the renewed attention to school practitioners as researchers of instruction has been the inauguration and growth of North American journals edited, written, and published by practitioners (*Teacher as Researcher* and *Democratic Schools,* both established in 1986).

Furthermore, numerous coalitions, networks, and programs of schools and districts have committed to the concept of teachers and administrators as site-based scholars in the investigation of instructional improvement. This flurry of activity is derived from a concept of inquiry that is often referred to as *action research.* In this chapter, action research as the integrating task for instructional improvement will be examined. A brief history will be given, examples of individual teachers and schools will be explained, and a procedure for making decisions about schoolwide action research will be illustrated.

Action Research: The Concept

The famous social scientist, Kurt Lewin, devoted his career to studying democracy and the relationships of individuals within groups. His contributions ushered in the school of gestalt psychology, group dynamics, and the concept of action research. He argued that social research should be based on the actions groups take to improve their conditions. Social research should not focus on controlled experiments, removed from real conditions. As people plan changes and engage in real activities, fact finding should determine whether success is being achieved and whether further planning and action are necessary (Lewin, 1948, p. 206).

Stephen Corey applied Lewin's concept of action research to education. He argued that traditional research is done mainly by researchers outside the public school and has little influence on school practice. Corey wrote:

> Learning that changes behavior substantially is most likely to result when a person himself tries to improve a situation that makes a difference to him…when he defines the problem, hypothesizes actions that may help him cope with it, engages in these actions, studies the consequences, and generalizes from them, he will more frequently internalize the experience than when all this is done for him by somebody else, and he reads about it…. The value of action research…is determined primarily by the extent to which findings lead to improvement in the practices of the people engaged in the research. (1953, p. 9)

Thus, action research in education is study conducted by colleagues in a school setting of the results of their activities to improve instruction. Although an individual teacher can conduct action research, in most cases it is best done as a cooperative endeavor by faculty attempting to improve on a common instructional concern.

As Richard Sagor (1993) wrote, "By turning to *collaborative* action research… we can renew our commitment to thoughtful teaching and also begin developing an active community of professionals" (p. 10). Action research implies that the practitioners are the researchers. The objectivity and rigor of research methodology can be questioned by classical researchers, but the benefits of the process for students and teachers seem to outweigh the loss of experimental purity.

In addressing the power of teacher-led research, Hubbard and Power (1993, p. xiii) wrote: "Teachers throughout the world are developing professionally by becoming teacher-researchers, a wonderful new breed of artists-in-residence. Using our own classrooms as laboratories and our students as collaborators, we are changing the way we work with students as we look at our classrooms systematically through research."

How Is Action Research Conducted?

There is little mystery to the process of action research, whether conducted individually, as a small group, or in an entire school. Calhoun (1992) identified five basic phases of action research. First, there is a problem-identification phase—the staff identifies a schoolwide area of interest focused on teaching and learning.

Second, there is a planning phase, where it is decided what data will be collected, how and how often it will be collected, and what resources will be needed. Third is an organization phase, where it is decided how the data can best be organized and presented in order to provide the staff with a clear and concise picture of the findings. Fourth is an evaluation phase of analyzing and interpreting the data in light of the stated goals and objectives. Fifth is an action phase of revising and modifying goals, objectives, and activities based on the analysis and interpretation of results.

If these five phases sound suspiciously similar to the development of action plans with individual teachers in Chapter 16 (direct assistance), you have won the first round of the supervision concentration game. The aim of direct assistance to teachers is to promote increased thought, choice, and responsibility in individual teachers, and this can be done through cycles of classroom action research. The supervisor's role is to determine what type of assistance the individual teacher needs (directive informational, collaborative, or nondirective), depending on the developmental levels of the teacher with respect to the particular topic. Figure 20.1 depicts Calhoun's five phases of action research.

A Developmental Approach to Action Research

The developmental model we have discussed throughout this text can be applied to action research. Of the four supervisory approaches discussed in Part III, the

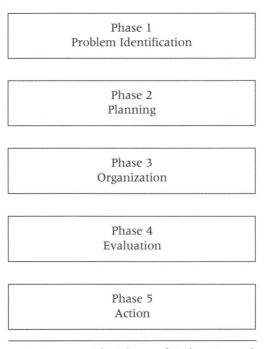

Phase 1
Problem Identification

Phase 2
Planning

Phase 3
Organization

Phase 4
Evaluation

Phase 5
Action

FIGURE 20.1 *Five Phases of Action Research*

directive informational, collaborative, and nondirective approaches are appropriate for supervising action research. Since teacher action research involves teachers making their own decisions about inquiry and instructional improvement, controlling directive supervision is inappropriate for such research.

Teachers of *very* low levels of development, expertise, and commitment are probably not ready to engage in action research. They will need to receive intensive direct assistance and staff development to help them develop the minimal decision-making capacity and motivation necessary for successful action research. They might be asked to read and discuss articles about action research, shadow a teacher or group engaged in research, or attend a workshop to develop action research skills. For teachers of *fairly* low levels of development, expertise, and commitment, the supervisor can use directive informational supervision while suggesting alternative goals, data-collection and analysis methods, and action plans, and then asking teachers to choose from the alternatives. Since this type of action research involves limited teacher decision making, the supervisor will wish to move toward collaborative action research as soon as teachers are ready to assume more decision-making responsibility.

The supervisor can engage in collaborative action research with teachers of moderate or mixed levels of development, expertise, and commitment. In this approach, the supervisor engages in joint decision making with teachers during the goal identification, action planning, implementation, evaluation, and revision phases of action research. Even collaborative action research is a transitional form of teacher inquiry. The ultimate goal is for teachers to reach levels of development, expertise, and commitment that allow teacher-driven research, in which the supervisor uses nondirective supervision to facilitate teacher decision making during each of the five phases of action research. Houser (1990) described full-fledged "teacher-researchers": "They initiate every aspect of the research project. They are responsible for formulating the questions, selecting the (research) tools, and collecting, analyzing, and interpreting the data" (p. 58).

Decisions about Action Research

Collective action research can integrate direct assistance, group development, professional development, and curriculum development. Prior to the beginning of action research, the supervisor chooses an appropriate entry strategy for working with an action research team. The choice of interpersonal approach is shown in Table 20.1.

First, the team conducts a needs assessment of faculty and collects baseline data to determine common goals for improvement of instruction. Techniques for conducting a needs assessment can be chosen from the following list:

- Eyes and ears
- Official records
- Third-party review

TABLE 20.1   *Choosing an Interpersonal Approach*

Interpersonal Behaviors	Decision
Nondirective: listening reflecting clarifying encouraging	High teacher/low supervisor
Collaborative: presenting problem solving negotiating	Equal teacher/equal supervisor
Directive informational: presenting problem solving directing alternatives	Low teacher/high supervisor

Characteristics of Teachers	
levels of development expertise commitment	

- Written open-ended survey
- Check and ranking lists
- Delphi technique
- Nominal group
- Cause and effect diagrams
- Flowcharts
- Pareto charts
- Scatter diagrams

Explanations of each assessment technique can be found in Chapter 13.

Second, the team brainstorms activities that will cut across supervision tasks. The team can respond to these four questions corresponding to supervisory tasks:

1. What type and frequency of direct assistance must be provided to teachers to reach our instructional goals?
2. What meetings and discussions need to be arranged as part of group development for faculty to share and reach our instructional goals?
3. What professional development opportunities, such as lectures, workshops, demonstrations, courses, and visits, need to be provided for faculty to reach our instructional goals?

   4. What is the necessary curriculum development, in terms of course content, curriculum guides, lesson plans, and instructional materials, to reach our instructional goals.

These tasks of supervision are explained in Chapters 16, 17, 18, and 19.

   Third, the team makes a plan relating activities to goals. Techniques for writing plans are as follows:

- Impact analysis chart
- Listing of activities with items and person(s) responsible
- Simple flowchart
- Management by objectives (MBO)
- Gantt chart
- Program evaluation and review techniques (PERT)

A description of each planning device can be found in Chapter 13.

   Fourth, the team determines ways to observe the progress of the action plan as it is implemented in classrooms. Observations can be made with the use of the following instruments:

- Categorical frequency
- Performance indicator
- Visual diagramming
- Space utilization
- Verbatim
- Detached open-ended narrative
- Participant open-ended observation
- Focused questionnaire
- Educational criticism
- Tailored observation systems

Use of these instruments is explained in Chapter 14.

   Fifth, the team chooses a research and evaluation design that will enable them to analyze data, determine whether objectives have been met, and decide what further actions need to be taken. The design can be quantitative, qualitative, or a combination of both. Components of a comprehensive evaluation are:

- Evaluation of needs assessment
- Evaluation of program design
- Evaluation of readiness
- Implementation evaluation
- Evaluation of outcomes
- Cost-benefit analysis

To understand the uses of each design and the components of a comprehensive evaluation, refer to Chapter 15.

Action Research: Vehicle for a Cause beyond Oneself

Action research is used in many schools under various names, ranging from "organizational development committees," to "leadership councils," to "quality circle groups." Regardless of the name, action research is a wonderful vehicle for bringing together individual teachers' needs with organizational goals to achieve a cause beyond oneself.

Previously, each task of supervision (direct assistance, group development, professional development, and curriculum development) was discussed separately. In reality, any effort to improve instruction must relate each task to the others. It is time to soften the boundaries between the tasks and show how action research can be the vehicle for their integration.

Action research is focused on the need to improve instruction, as perceived by the faculty. As instructional improvements are identified, faculty and supervisor plan related activities to be implemented in each of the tasks of supervision (see Figure 20.2).

Think of action research as a huge meteor falling into the middle of the supervision ocean. As it hits, it causes a rippling of water that activates the four seas of direct assistance, professional development, curriculum development, and

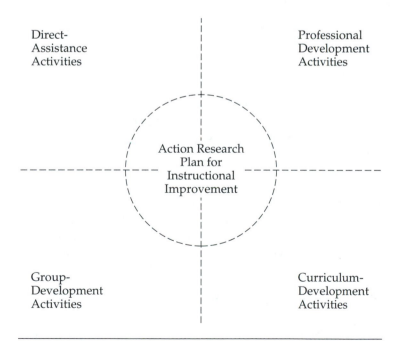

FIGURE 20.2 *Action Research as the Core of Related Supervisory Activities*

group development. The rippling of water continues to increase in force until a giant wave gathers and crashes onto all instructional shores, sweeping away the old sand of past instructional failures and replacing it with the new sand of instructional improvement. Stepping away from the beach, let's look at some examples of action research related to supervisory activities.

Examples of Action Research

Box 20.1 is an excellent example of action research in an individual classroom conducted by teachers (Joossens and Tierney, 1987). There are virtually no limits to instructional topics for action research. The basic question to be answered is: Are students better off as a result of instructional changes?

Action research at the school level can be seen in various cases. Using the *Effective School Battery* (Gottfredson, 1985), five middle/junior and high schools in Maryland choose to measure themselves on scales of teacher reports of safety, morale, planning and action, smooth administration, pro-integration attitudes, and job satisfaction, as well as student reports of safety, respect for students, fairness of rules, clarity of rules, attachment to school, and belief in rules (Hollifield, 1986). They use the scores of the survey assessment with other data about students and parents to set goals, objectives, and action plans for the year, and then reassessment is conducted to determine whether improvement has occurred. Some of the participants' reactions were recorded by Hollifield (1986): "First time in the 23 years that I've been here that I've seen anything like this.... It helps you see your school as an outsider might see it" (p. 4). A participant from one school said that after the initial shock of seeing the results of teachers' attitudes towards students, "We were no longer surprised. We had a lot [of teachers] who believed strongly that if the kids don't want to learn, then the heck with them" (p. 7). A participant from a third school remarked, "The results were eye opening.... We thought we were better than the results indicated.... We thought students had better feelings about the school" (p. 13).

The fifth school was a high school with a 99 percent African American population, 85 percent on free lunch, and only 15 percent who went on to further education. The school staff was surprised to find that many more students had aspirations to pursue higher education. In one year's time the school made progress toward meeting each of the six standards it had set. Student attendance rose from 45 percent to above 90 percent; teacher attendance increased from 89 percent to 96 percent; math scores increased by 11 percent; reading by 5 percent; and parent ratings and student ratings of school increased above the school's target (p. 18). Hollifield noted that the ultimate measure of improved school climate in a high school might be the serendipitous finding that the doors were put back in the rest rooms!

In Newark, New Jersey (Azumi, 1987), teams from each school consisting of three teachers, one administrator, and one parent were established in 1985. Each team served as catalyst for schoolwide change. The teams eventually expanded in

BOX 20.1 • *Classroom Research Using the Graphic Organizer in English*

Need

To aid student motivation in the last quarter of the year. To increase student ability to read books above the reading level with some independence. To develop a positive attitude toward reading.

Experimental Classes

32 students were designated in the eleventh grade regular level English classes. For the most part, they were not college bound and had expressed little interest in reading stories or novels. Their average DRP score was 72, but 10 of the students had a DRP score below 60. The literature textbook is designated by the College Board as being 61 DRP.

Action Plan

A generic plan of an interactive lesson was followed by the Reading Resource Specialist and the participating English teacher to execute the study of novels and short stories during the fourth quarter. The most important step was the first—creating the graphic organizer. Conferences were held between RRS and teacher to identify the key concepts and vocabulary and then make a structured overview which could be shared with the students at the outset of the lesson. The emphasis was to be placed on student-centered, interactive lessons with little emphasis on handouts.

Data Collection

Five methods of Data Collection were agreed upon between the teacher and RRS. First, the third quarter grades were to be compared to the fourth quarter grades. Second, the students were to take the Mikulecky Behavioural Reading Attitude Measure to determine the attitude toward reading in general. The teacher was reluctant to agree to this because she had found in the past that the nearer the end of school came, the more the students tended to resist reading of any kind. Third, DRP scores from the pre- and posttests would be compared. Fourth, videotaping would be done to determine through observation the level of student interaction. And fifth, comments and observations of students would be noted.

Implementation of the Strategy

The RRS and the English teacher worked together closely in implementing the 6 generic steps of an interactive lesson. The teacher was aware that her traditional approach to classroom management would change with more emphasis on interaction between student, teacher, and text. The novel that was studied during this period was *The Pearl*. The Structured Overview was left on the board from the outset, and the students all took notes as they brainstormed and discussed the concepts and vocabulary and generated study questions. Videotapes were made of the lessons using the steps.

Evaluation

At the end of the 10 weeks the students again took the two tests to determine if any growth had been made. Using an assignment of 5 points for each positive response on the Mikulecky Behavioural Reading Attitude Measure, the students improved from 61 to 66. The DRP test results averaged 72 in pretesting and 76 in posttesting (instructional level), which is an average year's growth.

Students were taped going through Steps I, II, and III. Their interaction with the teacher is clearly visible and the implementation of the strategies is easy to follow.

Most important, however, was that the grades of fourth quarter were better than third quarter. The students' average for third was 75 and for fourth the average was 81. To improve during fourth quarter is a difficult goal, and the students were pleased.

(continued)

BOX 20.1 • Continued

Students made comments about the increased interaction and preparation for reading: "I really wanted to read the book so that I could learn how Kino was like I am about greed."

"I understood the book and stories we read because we had plenty of time to discuss what we already knew about the big idea (concept)."

"Copying down what we come up with is a lot better than copying down what the teacher says or draws on the board for us."

"I like to think my ideas are important. That is what I like best about Miss Tierney's new way of teaching."

Conclusion

The strategies used in implementing the 10-week study proved very successful for the students and met the needs identified. A drawback was found that more time is spent by the teacher in organizing the lesson. However, less time is actually spent getting the students to understand the concepts because they are involved in the process of learning!

The teacher was delighted that the students reacted positively to being more directly involved in the lessons. When she first started the interactive lessons, she found that the students wanted to quit doing the brainstorming and vocabulary

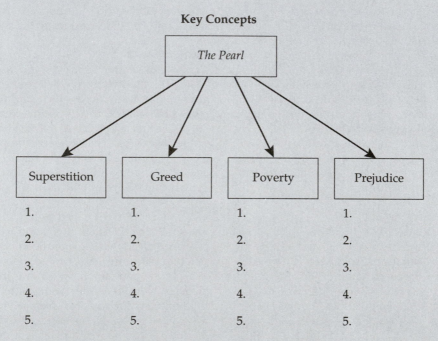

Key Concepts

The Pearl

Superstition	Greed	Poverty	Prejudice
1.	1.	1.	1.
2.	2.	2.	2.
3.	3.	3.	3.
4.	4.	4.	4.
5.	5.	5.	5.

Source: Joossens and Tierney, Classroom research using the graphic organizer in English, in *Teacher as Researcher*, Vol. 2, No. 2 (June 1987), pp. 4–5. Reprinted with permission of the publisher.

BOX 20.1 • Continued

discussions and categorizing so that they could READ THE BOOK! It concerned her at first, but then she realized that the students had never asked to be alone to start reading anything on their own.

The Attitude Inventory revealed that even unmotivated students can become more excited about reading.

The videotapes have been shown during several presentations and are used in Apopka High School's Interdisciplinary Workshops to show other teachers how the strategies they are learning can be applied to a sequential unit.

The 6-step Interactive Lesson has been adapted by many of the Apopka High School teachers and many are learning to use the graphic organizer. It is proving valuable to have a success story to share.

Apopka's Steps for an Interactive, Student-Centered Lesson

1. Teacher-Made Graphic Organizer
   - Key Concepts
   - Key Vocabulary
   - Structured Overview
2. Brainstorming/Predicting
3. Categorizing Words
4. Student-Generated Questions for Study Guide
5. Synthesized Information
   - Lecture/Notetaking
   - Text
   - Small/Large-Group Discussion
   - Student-Generated Structured Overviews
6. Review

composition and numbers. They conducted needs assessments, devised action plans, and assessed their progress. A study of all 54 elementary schools after a two-year implementation period found that most of the schools indicated improvement in at least one area (p. 13). Azumi cautioned that two years may be too short a time to be sure of the effects of school improvement and that study of these schools over three to five years would provide more conclusive results.

Parkay (1986) wrote about the dramatic improvement in two inner-city Miami elementary schools involved in a model for school improvement based on organizational development and problem solving. The model is based on the work of Joyce, Hersh, and McKibbin (1983).

1. A shared understanding of what school improvement means.
2. Emphasis on developing the total school so that it becomes more effective instead of meeting specific research-based criteria for effectiveness.
3. The expectation of a commitment to improvement and growth by school and district staff, with the school as the unit of change and the classroom as the unit of influence.
4. Participatory processes for assessment, problem solving, decision making, and evaluation according to the criteria of effective schools.
5. An organizational structure that includes clear leadership, a team approach, and school-wide responsibilities with clearly defined roles for all staff members.

6. Training for roles and responsibilities that includes theory, modeling, practice, structured feedback, and support through coaching or on-site follow-up.
7. Ownership of and continuous sharing of the results of the ongoing school improvement process.

The results of both school improvement projects (one entitled Project Pride and the other Champions of Excellence) were remarkable. "After nearly two years of school improvement work, both schools reported increased student achievement, attendance, and involvement. In addition, teachers demonstrated a strong commitment to professional growth, and many reported a renewed zest for teaching" (Parkay, 1986, p. 10). Furthermore, one of these schools was selected as one of the top ten schools in the county.

For each of you, there are examples closer to home in which individual teachers, department and grade-level teams, and schools have come together to assess, plan, act, and reassess their effects on behalf of students. Cases can be found that are as ordinary as a school improving discipline and cooperative behavior of students, or as extraordinary as creating an entirely new school curriculum. For example, a local elementary school in Georgia had been committed to mastery learning and had experienced considerable student success. However, teachers expressed concern about the lack of consistent classroom and school rules and enforcement procedures. The principal agreed to form a representative committee composed of seven teachers. The action research committee met and, with input from the entire faculty and administration, developed a set of common expectations for students and enforcement procedures for classroom teachers, specialists, lunchroom monitors, bus drivers, and principals. At the same time, inservice activities aimed at improving teacher management methods were arranged. Teachers altered the curriculum by teaching students the new rules and procedures. They met as a group on an ongoing basis to brainstorm and problem solve further improvements. Supervisors and peers observed each other and provided feedback on progress. The committee collected information on teachers' perceptions of improved student behavior, decreases in referrals to the principal's office, amount of time for classroom instruction, and improved student achievement. The committee conducted a simple pre- and posttest evaluation four weeks and then three months after the new procedures had been implemented. The results showed major improvement. The committee decided to keep the new policies in effect and to continue monitoring progress.

As a further example, long-term action research was conducted over several years by the faculty of the Annehurst (Ohio) school. A leadership committee of teachers worked with their school principal and several university consultants to improve schoolwide instruction over a period of three and a half years. The objectives of the action project were to individualize instruction, to provide multilevel and varied materials suitable for each student, and to implement team teaching (Mills, 1981). The product of the project has been the creation by the faculty of a widely acclaimed curriculum, the Annehurst Curriculum Classification System (Frymier, 1977). The evaluation of student progress since implementation of the action plan had shown a major increase in student achievement for over six years (Cornbleth, 1981).

The attention given to effective and successful schools has been a stimulant to action research in schools. Brookover's studies of improving schools (Brookover et al., 1979), Edmond's studies of effective schools (1979), the study by Rutter and colleagues of effective high schools (1979), Little's study of successful schools (1982), Berman and McLaughlin's study of successful program implementation (1978), the Phi Delta Kappa Commission on Schools with Good Discipline (Wayson et al., 1982), and Rosenholtz's (1985) and Parkey and Smith's (1983) review of the effective-schools literature have all reported the collective participation of faculty in planning action research as a characteristic of successful schools.

Lezotte (1986) stated that the school effectiveness research has given impetus to school improvement programs as a form of action research. School improvement should include *a focus on teaching and learning, evidence, and analysis of evidence.* The strategic unit of change should be the individual school, with collaboration among principal, teachers, central office personnel, and parents.

Action Research Leagues

A development coinciding with the growing popularity of action research has been the formation of school-university alliances or *leagues* in which university experts assist school-based action research teams. University assistance may take the form of training teachers in action research skills, on-site consultations, or the facilitation of meetings at which schools within the league share action plans and results. One outgrowth of these leagues has been the gathering by participating universities of a variety of data on what happens when action research takes place in schools. Two successful action research leagues are the League of Education Action Researchers in the Northwest (Project Learn) and the League of Professional Schools.

Project Learn involves Washington State University and several dozen schools (Sagor, 1991). It's purpose is to facilitate school improvement through action research. School teams receive training on the basic steps of action research, write and implement action plans, receive assistance from experienced researchers, attend follow-up workshops, and share their first year's research. A continuing support network and advanced training is available for school teams continuing to conduct action research after their first year in the league. Sagor (1991) reported that successful teams within the league chose important projects, received external support, and possessed drive, commitment, and "chemistry." Teams that failed chose projects perceived as unimportant, lacked external support, and were divisive and leaderless.

The League of Professional Schools, formed by the Program for School Improvement (PSI) at the University of Georgia (Glickman, 1992), includes over 100 schools. Schools that join the league are provided with training on shared decision making and action research, share school initiatives, are linked to an information retrieval system, and receive a network newsletter, consultation, and on-site visits by an expert facilitator (Calhoun and Allen, 1994). League schools have conducted action research in such areas as student learning goals, instructional innovations, curriculum development, inclusion, scheduling, student motivation, school communication, the school environment, and developing core school values (Calhoun and Allen, 1994). Based on their study of a variety of action research projects carried out by schools within the league, Calhoun and Allen (1994) present the following recommendations for supporting schoolwide action research.

1. Seek and work with policy-makers to ensure time for collaborative work.
2. Use an inquiry mode for learning to conduct school-wide action research; one does not have to be "ready" or all-knowing to begin the journey.
3. Develop and tend to a core group to lead the effort.
4. Include students in the action research process.
5. Keep the focus on student learning.
6. Seek technical assistance, if needed, and provide staff development for innovations. (p. 22)

A prerequisite for membership in the League of Professional Schools is a commitment to shared governance, our next topic for discussion.

Shared Governance for Action Research

A shortcoming of earlier studies of school improvement and action research has been the lack of descriptions of how individual schools or districts went about the process of change (Fullan, 1985, p. 398). Achieving "a cause beyond oneself" in pursuing collaborative and collective instructional goals for students sounds admirable, but how does a supervisor initiate and sustain such efforts? What follows is one explanation, using case studies from the public schools that are part of the League of Professional Schools (Glickman, 1992). The model of shared governance and schoolwide instructional change has been adapted and used in elementary, middle, and secondary schools in Georgia, South Carolina, Vermont, Michigan, and the United States Department of Defense Dependent Schools in Europe.

Premises

Three declarative premises underlie shared governance. Those premises are:

1. Every professional in the school who so desires can be involved in making decisions about schoolwide instructional improvements.
2. Any professional in the school who does not desire to is not obligated to be involved in making decisions about schoolwide instructional improvements.

3. Once a decision is made about schoolwide instructional improvements, all staff must implement the decision.

Thus, an individual can choose to be or not to be part of the decision-making process. However, once decisions are made, all individuals must implement the agreed-upon actions. Operationalizing these premises allows a school to move forward with people who are interested in participating, without forcing any individual who is not interested into a corner. Afterwards, an individual who did not wish to participate in making decisions has no grounds for complaint about decisions about schoolwide instructional actions. Perhaps when the next issue, concern, or topic is brought up for schoolwide action, nonparticipants who have been disgruntled with previous decisions will have a renewed interest in participating.

Principles

The principles in operating shared governance for instructional improvement are:

1. *One person, one vote.* Each representative has the same rights, responsibilities, and equal vote as any other representative. Each teacher who sits on the representative schoolwide council has the same vote as the school principal or any other administrator or formal supervisor. This means, in practical terms, that an individual administrator or supervisor cannot get his or her own way with decisions about instructional improvement, just as a single teacher representative cannot get his or her own way. Decisions are made by the group, so expertise, influence, and credibility are more important than power and authority.

2. *Limit decisions to schoolwide instruction within the control and sphere of responsibility of the school.* Action research and shared governance involves the core of a school's existence: curriculum and instruction, or teaching and learning. Areas for decision making should be schoolwide and instructional. Issues of day-to-day administration, contracts, school board policies, other schools, and personnel are not the concerns of shared governance for schoolwide action research. The scope of concerns for deliberations, decisions, and actions is always grounded in the question: What should *we* be doing *here* with *our* school to improve learning for *our* students?

This is not to dismiss the influence on student learning of external policies and operations, nor is it to suggest that changes to improve conditions for students should not be pursued at levels beyond the school. It is simply to suggest that unless a school has a clear, streamlined mechanism for keeping the focus on creating a dialogue about instruction within the school, shared governance will often dissipate into a depository of complaints about noninstructional concerns. Time and energy spent on complaining or proposing what other schools, parents, central office, and school board should do (which the individual school has no legal or direct control over) take time and energy away from instructional changes that *can* be made. (Talking about others can be an excuse for not talking about ourselves.)

3. *Authentic feedback necessitates small groups.* To call a faculty meeting with a large staff for the intended purpose of an open, freewheeling discussion of ideas, opinions, and positions is at best misguided, if not outright manipulative. Large meetings result in input from the most confident, the loudest, and the most powerful persons—who are not necessarily the wisest, most insightful, or most interested persons. A true forum for intellectual discourse is a small group (ideally, 7 to 11 members); so, shared governance in large schools must operate in small groups.

Operational Model

The work of Schmuck, Runkel, Arends, and Arends (1977) has provided the basis for an operational model for shared governance, action research, and school improvement that uses the premises of individual choice of involvement and implementation by all and the principles of one-person, one-vote; focus on teaching; and small groups. The model discussed here is a compilation of various models used by schools in the League of Professional Schools (see Glickman, 1992; Allen and Glickman, 1992). Many schools use comparable models of operation and have their own specific versions. The goal is not to advocate a particular model of shared governance, but rather to achieve the premises and principles of shared governance and action research, leading to a purposeful, collective, and thoughtful school—a school that is the center of inquiry.

The Formal Groups.   Shared governance in this model involves three groups (see Figure 20.3). *The executive council* is a 7- to 11-member body, consisting of a

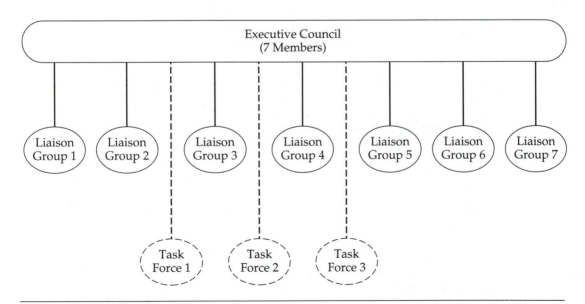

FIGURE 20.3 *Action Research as the Core of Related Supervisory Activities*

majority of teachers with administrators. Parent and student representatives can serve as well. (For more details about representation of other groups, see Glickman, 1993.) Teachers could be democratically chosen from liaison groups (described in the following paragraph) or from among grade-level heads, team leaders, department heads, and union representatives. They could be elected at large from the faculty, or some combination of election and appointment could be used. They hold a term of at least three years and move off the council at staggered times. Teachers serve as chairperson and co-chairperson of the executive council. The principal is a member of the committee with the same rights and responsibilities as any other member. The executive council's responsibility is solely for acting on and monitoring schoolwide instructional improvement recommendations. *The council does not make recommendations;* it is an approving board. Recommendations must come from task force groups within the school. The executive council does not involve itself in administrative matters, community relations, school board policies, personnel matters, or issues that are departmental in nature. It acts on instructional improvement recommendations that the faculty has the legal power to carry out. This differentiation between instructional and administrative responsibilities helps avoid problems that can arise from delving into matters beyond the school's own control.

Liaison groups are formal groups set up as communication links between the faculty and executive council concerning needs, reactions, opinions, and ideas about schoolwide instruction. Liaison groups are an important unit for considering the faculty's ideas and opinions about assessing instructional goals and responding to proposed recommendations. For example, in the case of a school with 50 teachers, there could be seven liaison groups consisting of approximately 7 faculty members each. An alphabetized list of all faculty names is gathered and each person is assigned a number from 1 to 7. All 1s go to liaison group 1, all 2s go to liaison group 2, and so forth. This assignment procedure ensures that members in each liaison group come from various departments and grade levels. Each liaison group is a microcosm of the entire school. Each group elects a representative to the council. The executive council member can (a) call the liaison group together from time to time for a brief meeting to review a specific recommendation under executive council consideration, (b) gather written opinions about a particular proposal, or (c) simply drop by and talk to the various liaison group members.

Task forces are the last groups shown in Figure 20.2. These ad hoc task groups of volunteers are formed after the executive council has solicited feedback from all the liaison groups about perceived schoolwide instructional needs and reviewed any existing data on schoolwide instruction. The executive council then targets priority instructional areas for the next one to three years. Schoolwide priorities might be such matters as increasing instructional time, coordinating curriculum, improving student attitudes, teaching higher-order thinking, increasing student success rates, improving school discipline, improving school and classroom climate, improving the quality of feedback to students, or improving test scores.

Once the needs for improvement have been selected by the executive council, ad hoc task force groups are formed by recruiting volunteers who have an interest in and a commitment to the particular topic. At least one executive council member serves on each task force, but this person normally does not serve as chair of the task force. The task force volunteers meet, review their task, select their own chairperson, schedule meetings, and set a time line for making a final recommendation for schoolwide action to the executive council. Depending on the topic, one task force might meet three times over three weeks to make a recommendation, whereas another task force might meet every other week for five months before making a recommendation.

Decision-Making Procedures.   When the task force is ready to make a recommendation, it makes its report in three parts: (1) goals and objectives, (2) action plan (What will be done, by whom, and when?), (3) evaluation action research (How will the success of actions be known?) The executive council discusses the recommendations and either makes an immediate decision to approve (most councils use a consensus vote to approve a first-time recommendation) or, without the required vote, tables the recommendation until the next meeting. During the interim, the executive council members can discuss the recommendation and check with their respective liaison groups to gather input from the entire faculty. At the next meeting, a second vote can be taken. (Most councils use a two-thirds vote to approve a tabled recommendation.) By the second vote, the council will have a good sense of total faculty receptivity and the chances of successful implementation. Some issues are deemed so important by the council that the final decision is made by going back to the entire faculty, parents, and students.

Implementation.   After a decision has been made, the executive council (with the task force) announces the approved plan to the school. The task force then disbands, and the executive council implements the plan. It becomes the responsibility of the executive council (including the principal) to enforce the schoolwide decisions and to oversee action research that monitors and evaluates the results.

Personal Examples of School-Based Action Research Plans

To provide some insight into the developmental nature of organizations (their receptivity and focus of concern with instructional improvement) and the use of action research to integrate the other tasks of supervision—direct assistance, group development, professional development, and curriculum development—let us highlight two schools from the League of Professional Schools that one of the authors has been associated with over an extended period of time.

When educators at Norton Elementary School, a K–5 school of nearly 900 students, began their efforts in shared governance and action research, their first two years were spent creating democratic processes, building trust, and learning new roles. Action research activities in these early years were sporadic, with no central focus, and there was no common understanding of the value of a shared governance process. As teachers began to see the value of being involved in collegial work outside of their individual classrooms, they began to look for ways to facilitate such collegiality. During the second year, the faculty concluded that until someone was explicitly responsible for action research in the school, it would continue to be a hit-or-miss effort. At this point, a lead teacher who had been involved in action research took on the needed leadership role. The educators also learned that if teachers were going to be actively involved in schoolwide issues, they needed time during the school day to do so. Alternatives were considered for freeing teachers so that they would not have to do all the work on their own time.

During the third year, teachers led the way in planning, implementing, evaluating, and fine-tuning their own professional development program. Their action research focused on the extent that ideas and teaching techniques covered in their professional development program were being put to use in classrooms. They developed questionnaires for each of the three areas of teaching practices addressed in their professional development activities (student-centered instructional techniques, performance-based assessment, and use of technology equipment). The questionnaires were given in August, during the school's preplanning days, and again in March of the same school year. Results showed that a vast majority of the teachers were implementing the information and techniques covered in *their* professional development program. Their professional development was having a positive impact on students! This information was exhilarating to everyone, especially those who had been heavily involved in the planning and delivery of the professional development. The data gave them something to point to with pride. This shared sense of accomplishment pulled people together. It indicated they were on the right track and that their efforts were making a difference. Additionally, the information helped them decide what adjustments were needed for the next year's efforts in these areas. Action research is helping the school create a collegial, instructionally focused climate. Decisions are now based on formal processes that seek input and information from all the staff rather than the informally held perceptions of a selected few.

When Duluth High School, a 9–12 school of approximately 1,400 students, first joined the League, many of the teachers were skeptical. Was this going to be a new way of doing business or was it going to go away like so many educational trends? A brave few hesitantly started using informal, play-it-by-ear processes to focus on several heart-felt concerns dealing with issues like smoking areas in the school and the use of the public address system. Although they understood that eventually they would want to focus on curricular and instructional issues, they felt they had some administrative housekeeping to take care of first. While addressing these issues, these leaders and many of the skeptics began to realize the power of collective, democractic decisions and a schoolwide dialogue open to all staff members. As people learned to work together and the new procedures demonstrated their effectiveness, they moved to formalize them through a governance charter.

In Duluth's second year, through their shared governance processes, a general concern bubbled up to the leadership team that many students were not experiencing the kind of success that the staff expected of them. A task force was appointed and it set about collecting data to help define these concerns. Grade distributions, attendance records, and disciplinary records were aggregated by grades. What emerged was a clear pattern: Students in ninth grade were struggling far more than students in the other three grades. Based on this information, the staff collectively set about creating an interdisciplinary ninth-grade transition program.

One year later, they are very encouraged. The percentage of ninth-graders receiving As and Bs increased while the percentage receiving Ds and Fs declined. Students with histories of chronic absences were improving their attendance and the number of ninth-grade students being suspended was dropping dramatically. A schoolwide dialogue created by a collegial decision-making process and the use of action research helped Duluth High School define a problem, create a program to address the problem, and then monitor the program's effects. In their third year, with shared governance and action research processes becoming institutionalized, the staff was routinely addressing curricular and instructional issues with a growing sense of optimism about their new way of doing business.

These are two good schools, striving to be better. The work of such schools (in rural, urban, and suburban settings) has resulted in national recognition and documented improvements in (1) student achievement, attendance, attitudes towards learning, promotion and graduation rates, student discipline, and scholarship opportunities; (2) parent involvement and satisfaction with schools; and (3) faculty satisfaction, better communication, and improved school climate.

There are many such schools throughout the country. Some are part of other school networks, such as the Coalition of Essential Schools, the Accelerated Schools, and the Comer Schools. Some are working alone. You might work in one and know of other bolder examples of change and action research. Why is it that such elementary, middle, and senior high schools—which, according to most research on schools, should be stagnant and recalcitrant to change—are not? Many of these good schools are situated in fiscally poor communities and lack the advantages of dealing with the children of highly educated parents. These teachers should be "stressed out," "burnt out," and full of "despair" and "helplessness." But they are not. In fact, they willingly increase work for themselves, and each roadblock or failure in helping students succeed makes them want to work harder. Why do they do this? The pay is not great, the facilities not luxurious, the community not gushing in recognition or praise. One of these principals remarked, "If I ever asked teachers to do what they are requiring themselves to do, I'd be lynched." So why do they work harder and smarter? Because it's their school, their students, their goals, and their decisions—nobody else's! These good schools are not utopias. Nor are they maverick organizations, without limitations and responsibilities to regulatory agencies. They are different because those who have responsibilities for supervision of instruction have squarely placed the practice of inquiry and decision making about instruction as central to the work of teachers.

Conclusion: Focus, Structure, and Time for Development

Supervision provides a focus, structure, and time for teachers to be engaged in dialogue, debate, research, decisions, and actions about instruction. Without focus, teachers will not discuss teaching, because it has not been an accepted norm for discussion in most schools. Without structure, there are no clear apparatus, procedures, and rules for how decisions are made and implemented. Without time, there is no functional or symbolic expression that teachers have the capacity to make collective and wise instructional decisions on behalf of students. Although examples have been given at the school level, the same applications of shared governance and action research (with curriculum and instruction) can be made at the district level.

As Carlson and Matthes (1987) stated, a major pitfall in school improvement is "ignoring the effects of different organization life stages on cultural issues." Edelfelt (1983) and Sohns (1984) have noted that organizations, like individuals, are at different stages of development, proceed at different rates, and are vulnerable to external forces. The 15 years of site-based governance of schools in Salt Lake City (McLeese and Malen, 1987) provide an excellent example of how faculty committees have grown from advisory to decision making; from concerns that were teacher-centered and of a physical and maintenance nature to concerns that have become student-centered and of a curricular and instructional nature. The developmental progression is not linear, and it's fragile, but action research is predicated on shared governance as the essence of professional work. The local unit must determine where the point of entry should be, where the initial focus should be, and how those in supervision should work with teachers to increase collective choice, thought, and action. The overall goal, however, remains the same: the school as the center of inquiry.

Exercises

Academic

1. Assume you have been assigned the task of speaking in favor of a proposal to provide funding for action research at the next school board meeting. Write your speech, telling how you and your staff will carry out such research and what the benefits will be. To attempt to convince the school board, include in your speech references to sources other than this book.

2. Describe two action research projects that have been reported in the literature and not discussed in this book.

3. Select an objective for instructional improvement that can be adapted to action research. Based on that objective, prepare a written plan for an action research project. Make sure that procedures for conducting action research listed in this chapter are addressed in your plan.

4. Briefly describe an action research project that might be carried out by a small group of teachers facilitated by a supervisor. Next, describe the knowledge and skills the supervisor would need in order to lead the group successfully in the action research. Rely on previous chapters of this book for your answer.

5. Create a model for evaluating action research projects. Components of the model should provide for evaluation of needs assessment, objectives, planning and sequencing of activities, implementation of activities, measurement techniques, and data analysis. Each component should be accompanied by critical questions to be asked concerning the appropriate phase of the action research project.

Field

1. Plan and carry out a short-term, individual action research project. Report on the action research, its results, your conclusions, and your recommendations.

2. Observe, evaluate, and report on an action research project currently being carried out in a school setting. Include a discussion of whether all four of the other tasks of supervision have been integrated in the action research.

3. Describe an instructional improvement recently introduced in a school with which you are familiar. Suggest how the innovation could have been tried out as action research before being fully implemented. Your suggested plan should meet all the requirements (necessary procedures, integrated supervision tasks) for authentic action research.

4. Determine an instructional improvement that would benefit a school with which you are familiar. Suggest how each of the following four tasks of supervision would be carried out as a part of an action research project intended to meet the instructional improvement objective:

    a. What direct assistance would have to be provided to facilitate the instructional improvement?

    b. What types of group development would faculty need?

    c. What professional development activities would be necessary?

    d. What curriculum development would be necessary?

5. Interview faculty and supervisors of a clearly successful school to determine whether action research is carried out in that school. If so, do faculty members participate collectively in planning for action research? What is the mechanism for such participation (curriculum council, research committees, circle groups)? What are some examples of action research that have been carried out?

    If the selected school does not conduct action research, are teachers allowed opportunities for professional interaction, discussion of ideas for instructional improvement, and reflective and collective thinking? If so, how are such opportunities provided? Prepare a report on your interviews.

Developmental

1. Volunteer to supervise or participate in a long-range group action research project within an educational setting.

2. Take advantage of future opportunities to hold discussions with those involved in school action research. Such discussions can help you generate your own ideas for action research projects and effective supervision of action research.

3. Continue to explore the literature and research on action research. Begin a file of articles appropriate for sharing with educators interested in action research.

References

Allen, L., and Glickman, C. D. 1992. School improvement: The elusive faces of shared governance. *NASSP Bulletin* 76(542):80–87.

Azumi, J. E. 1987. *Effective schools characteristics, school improvement and school outcomes: What are the relationships?* Paper presented to the annual meeting of the American Educational Research Association, Washington, DC, April.

Berman, P., and McLaughlin, M. W. 1978. *Federal programs supporting educational change, Vol. 8: Implementing and sustaining innovations.* Santa Monica, CA: Rand Corp. (ED 159-289)

Brookover, W., Beady, C., Flood, P., Schweiter, J., and Wisenbaker, J. 1979. *School social systems and students' achievement: Schools can make a difference.* New York: Praeger.

Calhoun, E. F. 1992. *A status report on action research in the League of Professional Schools.* Paper presented at the annual meeting of the American Educational Research Association, San Francisco, April.

Calhoun, E. F., and Allen, L. 1994. *Results of schoolwide action research in the league of professional schools.* Paper presented at the annual meeting of the American Educational Research Association, New Orleans, April.

Carlson, R. V., and Matthes, W. A. 1987. *"Good" rural schools: An organizational-cultural perspective.* Paper presented at the annual meeting of the American Educational Research Association, Washington, DC, April.

Corey, S. M. 1953. *Action research to improve school practices.* New York: Teachers College, Columbia University.

Cornbleth, C. 1981. Curriculum materials can make a difference. *Educational Leadership* 38(7):567–568.

Edelfelt, R. A. 1983. In-service education: Moving from professional development to school improvement. *Urban Educator* (Winter).

Edmond, R. 1979. Effective schools for the urban poor. *Educational Leadership* 37(1):15–24.

Frymier, J. R. 1977. *Annehurst curriculum classification systems: A practical way to improve instruction.* West Lafayette, IN: Kappa Delta Pi.

Fullan, M. 1985. Change processes and strategies at the local level. *Elementary School Journal* 85(3):391–421.

Glickman, C. D. 1989. *Shared governance at Ogelthorpe County High School.* Athens, GA: Monographs in Education.

Glickman, C. D. 1992. The essence of school renewal: The prose has begun. *Educational Leadership* 50(1): 24–27.

Glickman, C. D. 1993. *Renewing America's schools. A guide for school-based action.* San Francisco: Jossey-Bass.

Glickman, C. D., and Wright, L. V. 1986. Decision making in schools. In P. R. Burden (Ed.), *Establishing career ladders in teaching: A guide for policy makers* (pp. 111–129). Springfield, IL: Charles C. Thomas.

Gottfredson, C. 1985. *Effective school battery: User's manual.* Odessa, FL: Psychological Assessment Resources.

Gross, S. (Ed.). 1986. Teacher collaboration: New partnership to attack old problems. *Communication Quarterly* 9(1):1–4. (Institute for Research on Teaching).

Hollifield, J. H. 1986. *How schools react to assessment data.* Presentation to the annual meeting of the American Educational Research Association, San Francisco, April.

Houser, N. O. 1990. Teacher-researcher: The synthesis of roles for teacher empowerment. *Action in Teacher Education* 12(2):55–60.

Hubbard, R. S., and Power, B. M. 1993. *The art of classroom inquiry: A handbook for teacher-researchers.* Portsmouth, NH: Heinemann.

Joossens and Tierney. 1987. Classroom research using the graphic organizer in English. *Teacher as Researcher* 2(2):4–5.

Joyce, B., Hersh, R., and McKibben, M. 1983. *The structure of school improvement.* New York: Longman, 1983.

Lewin, K. 1948. *Resolving social conflicts.* New York: Harper and Brothers.

Lezotte, L. W. 1986. *School effectiveness, reflections, and future directions.* Presentation to the annual meeting of the American Educational Research Association, San Francisco, April.

Little, J. W. 1982. Norms of collegiality and experimentation: Workplace conditions of school success. *American Educational Research Journal 19*(3):325–340.

McLeese, P., and Malen, B. 1987. *Site based governance: The Salt Lake City experience 1970–1985.* Paper presented to the annual meeting of the American Educational Research Association, Washington, DC, April.

Mills, T. 1981. The development of Annehurst School. *Educational Leadership 38*(7):569.

Parkay, F. W. 1986. *Implementing research on school effectiveness: Two inner-city case studies.* Paper presented to the annual meeting of the American Educational Research Association, San Francisco, April 20.

Parkey, S. C., and Smith, M. S. 1983. Effective schools—A review. *Elementary School Journal 83*:427–452.

Rosenholtz, S. J. 1985. Effective schools: Interpreting the evidence. *American Journal of Education 93*(3):352–388.

Rutter, M., Maughan, B., Mortimore, P., Ouston, J., and Smith, A. 1979. *Fifteen thousand hours: Secondary schools and their effects on children.* Cambridge, MA: Harvard University Press.

Sagor, R. 1991. What project LEARN reveals about collaborative action research. *Educational Leadership 48*(6):6–10.

Sagor, R. 1993. *How to conduct collaborative action research.* Alexandria, VA: Association for Supervision and Curriculum Development.

Schaefer, R. 1967. *The school as the center of inquiry.* New York: Harper and Row.

Schmuck, R. A., Runkel, P., Arends, J. H., and Arends, R. I. 1977. *The second handbook of organizational development in schools.* Palo Alto, CA: Mayfield.

Sohns, M. L. 1984. School readiness for staff development. Unpublished manuscript, Government Center, Hanford, CA.

Wayson W. W., DeVoss, G. G., Kaeser, S. C., Lasley, T., and Pinnel, G. S. 1982. *Handbook for developing schools with good discipline.* Bloomington, IN: Phi Delta Kappa.

Suggested Readings

Calhoun, E. F. 1993. Action research: Three approaches. *Educational Leadership 51*(2):62–65.

Calhoun, E. F. 1994. *How to use action research in the self-renewing school.* Alexandria, VA: Association for Supervision and Curriculum Development.

Houser, N. O. 1990. Teacher-researcher: The synthesis of roles for teacher empowerment. *Action in Teacher Education 12*(2):55–60.

Hubbard, R. S., and Power, B. M. 1993. *The art of classroom inquiry: A handbook for teacher-researchers.* Portsmouth, NH: Heinemann.

Russell, T., and Munby, H. (Eds.). 1992. *Teachers and teaching: From classroom to reflection.* London: Falmer.

Sagor, R. 1993. *How to conduct collaborative action research.* Alexandria, VA: Association for Supervision and Curriculum Development.

Part V

Conclusion

The purpose of Part V was to make instructional improvement and school success a realistic goal. We have looked at the five tasks of supervision that have direct impact on instructional improvement: direct assistance, group development, professional development, curriculum development, and action research. Emphasis was given on how the use of each task can unite teacher needs with organizational goals (see Figure V.1).

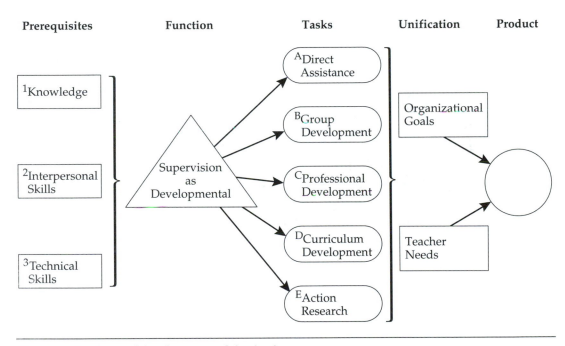

FIGURE V.1 *SuperVision for Successful Schools*

We were able to use prerequisites of knowledge, interpersonal skills, and technical skills to function in the realm of supervision and apply it to the five tasks. Chapter 16 examined clinical supervision, peer coaching, accessibility, arranged time, and delegation. Chapter 17 studied the supervisor's role in the group with attention to task and person behaviors, confronting dysfunctional members, resolving conflict, preparing for meetings, and lessening leadership control as the group becomes cohesive. Chapter 18 looked at professional development in terms of research findings of successful professional development, teacher concerns, conceptual and psychological states of teachers, and stages of professional development. Chapter 19 examined various issues in developing curriculum, the range of developers of curriculum, and degree of teacher involvement. Finally, Chapter 20 showed how teachers can become researchers on their own instructional problems. Such research integrates the four previous supervisory tasks and unifies teacher needs with organizational goals to promote collective action.

Part VI

Function of SuperVision

Chapter 2 looked at the obstacles to supervision. Those obstacles were listed as three propositions:

- Proposition 1: *Supervision cannot rely on the existing work environment of schools to stimulate instructional improvement.*
- Proposition 2: *Supervisors cannot assume that all teachers are reflective, autonomous, and responsible for their own development.*
- Proposition 3: *Supervisors will have to redefine their responsibilities—from controllers of teachers' instruction to involvers of teachers in decisions about school instruction.*

Chapter 3 introduced five research-based propositions about supervision:

- Proposition 1: *Supervision can enhance teacher belief in a cause beyond oneself.*
- Proposition 2: *Supervision can promote teacher sense of efficacy.*
- Proposition 3: *Supervision can make teachers aware of how they complement each other in striving for common goals.*
- Proposition 4: *Supervision can stimulate teachers to plan common purpose and actions.*
- Proposition 5: *Supervision can challenge teachers to think abstractly about their work.*

Chapter 4 detailed the need for looking at teachers in a developmental manner and proposed the following:

- Proposition 1: *Effective supervision responds to the principles of adult learning.* Teachers' learning should be related to their experiences, needs, and learning strengths; should include opportunities for collaborative action, reflection, and critical thinking; and should be directed toward teacher empowerment.

- Proposition 2: *Effective supervision responds to and fosters teacher stage development.* Teachers function at different stages of cognitive, conceptual, moral, and ego development and different stages of consciousness and concern. Teachers should not be treated as a homogeneous group. Rather, supervision should be matched to teachers' developmental stages. Supervision also should foster teacher growth toward higher stages of development.
- Proposition 3: *Effective supervision recognizes and supports different phases within teachers' life cycles.* It responds to young teachers' excitement and idealism, helps middle-aged teachers cope with life reassessment and reprioritizing, and provides opportunities for older teachers to consolidate achievements and identify remaining career objectives.
- Proposition 4: *Effective supervision helps teachers to understand, navigate, and learn from life transition events.* It provides special support and rewards for transitions from preservice to inservice teaching, probationary to tenured status, regular teaching duties to teacher leadership responsibilities, and employment to retirement.
- Proposition 5: *Effective supervision recognizes and accommodates teachers' various social roles.* It helps teachers to recognize the relationship of personal and family roles to their professional roles and to balance competing demands of all three roles.
- Proposition 6: *Effective administration and supervision foster teacher motivation.* Effective administration provides for Maslow's lower-level needs and Herzberg's hygiene factors. Effective supervision provides for Herzberg's motivating factors and Maslow's higher-stage needs, gradually increases teacher choice and decision making, and facilitates teachers' self-actualization.

Finally, Chapter 5 concluded Part II (prerequisite knowledge) with propositions about supervisory beliefs and actions:

- Proposition 1: *Supervisors should use a variety of practices that emanate from various philosophical and belief structures with developmental directionality in mind.*
- Proposition 2: *As supervisors gradually increase teacher choice and control over instructional improvement, teachers will become more abstract and committed to improvement, and a sense of ethos or a cause beyond oneself will emerge.*

The subsequent parts of the book explained the technical and interpersonal skills a supervisor needs to carry out the five tasks of supervision. Each task of supervision was carefully outlined with respect to how its delivery to teachers could help them move toward higher stages of development and collective action. This final part will examine the meaning of the function of development as it applies to supervision for school success.

21

SuperVision, Change, and School Success

Although not all change represents progress, progress—by definition—is not possible without change. Facilitating change necessary for instructional improvement is a supervisory function that cuts across all five tasks of supervision. Initiating a clinical supervision program (direct assistance), assisting teachers in deciding on schoolwide instructional improvement goals (group development), delivering a skill-development program in which teachers learn new models of teaching (professional development), moving from a discipline-based to an interdisciplinary curriculum (curriculum development), and assisting teachers as they conduct research on a new classroom management system (action research) are all examples of facilitating change. In this chapter, we will look at assumptions about change, change from the teacher's view, a developmental view of change strategies, creating a culture for change, changing the conditions of teaching, the role of supervision and supervisors in school improvement, and school success.

Assumptions about Change

After many years of research and reflection on change in schools, Michael Fullan (1991) proposed 10 assumptions about change. Our own experience with change efforts in schools leads us to agree with Fullan's assumptions:

1. Do not assume that your version of what the change should be is the one that should or could be implemented. On the contrary, assume that one of the main purposes of the process of implementation is to exchange your reality of what should be through interaction with implementers and others concerned. Stated another way, assume that successful implementation consists of some transformation or continual development of initial ideas....
2. Assume that any significant innovation, if it is to result in change, requires individual implementers to work out their own meaning. Significant change in-

volves a certain amount of ambiguity, ambivalence, and uncertainty for the individual about the meaning of change. Thus, effective implementation is a process of clarification....

3. Assume that conflict and disagreement are not only inevitable but fundamental to successful change....

4. Assume that people need pressure to change (even in directions that they desire), but it will be effective only under conditions that allow them to react, to form their own position, to interact with other implementors, to obtain technical assistance, etc....

5. Assume that effective change takes time. Unrealistic or undefined time lines fail to recognize that implementation occurs developmentally. Significant change in the form of implementing specific innovations can be expected to take a minimum of two to three years; bringing about institutional reforms can take five or more years. Persistence is a critical attribute of successful change.

6. Do not assume that the reason for lack of implementation is outright rejection of the values embodied in the change, or hard-core resistance to all change. Assume that there are a number of possible reasons: value rejection, inadequate resources to support implementation, insufficient time elapsed.

7. Do not expect all or even most people or groups to change. The complexity of change is such that it is impossible to bring about widespread reform in any large social system. Progress occurs when we take steps (e.g., by following the assumptions listed here) that increase the number of people affected....

8. Assume that you will need a plan that is based on the above assumptions and that addresses the factors known to affect implementation....Evolutionary planning and problem-coping models based on knowledge of the change process are essential....

9. Assume that no amount of knowledge will ever make it totally clear what action should be taken. Action decisions are a combination of valid on-the-spot decisions, and intuition....

10. Assume that changing the culture of institutions is the real agenda, not implementing single innovations. Put another way, when implementing particular innovations, we should always pay attention to whether the institution is developing or not. (pp. 105–107)*

Guskey's (1994, pp. 9–20) six guidelines for promoting professional development and change are consistent with Fullan's assumptions:

- Guideline #1: Recognize that change is both an individual and an organizational process
- Guideline #2: In planning and implementation, think BIG, but start SMALL (emphasis in original)
- Guideline #3: Work in teams to maintain support
- Guideline #4: Include procedures for feedback on results
- Guideline #5: Provide continued follow-up, support, and pressure
- Guideline #6: Integrate programs (integrate innovations into existing frameworks)

*Reprinted by permission of the publisher from M. Fullan, *The New Meaning of Educational Change* (New York: Teachers College Press, © 1991 by Teachers College, Columbia University. All rights reserved.)

Change from the Teacher's View

Gene Hall and Shirley Hord (1987) have extended the work of Frances Fuller (1969) on teacher concerns (discussed in Chapter 4) and described seven stages of concern about school innovations (numbered from stages 0 through 6). Figure 21.1 describes each of these stages. Note that awareness, informational, and personal concerns about the innovation relate to Fuller's self-concerns, management concerns about the innovation relate to Fuller's task concerns; and consequence,

FIGURE 21.1   *Stages of Concern about the Innovation*

Impact	6	REFOCUSING: The focus is on exploration of more universal benefits from the innovation, including the possiblity of major changes or replacement with a more powerful alternative. Individual has definite ideas about alternatives to the proposed or existing form of the innovation.
	5	COLLABORATION: The focus is on coordination and cooperation with others regarding use of the innovation.
	4	CONSEQUENCE: Attention focuses on impact of the innovation on student in his or her immediate sphere of influence. The focus is on relevance of the innovation for students, evaluation of student outcomes, including performance and competencies, and changes needed to increase student outcomes.
Task	3	MANAGEMENT: Attention is focused on the processes and tasks of using the innovation and the best use of information and resources. Issues related to efficiency, organizing, managing, scheduling, and time demands are utmost.
Self	2	PERSONAL: Individual is uncertain about the demands of the innovation, his or her inadequacy to meet those demands, and his or her role with the innovation. This includes analysis of his or her role in relation to the reward structure of the organization, decision making, and consideration of potential conflicts with existing structures or personal commitment. Financial or status implications of the program for self and colleagues may also be reflected.
	1	INFORMATIONAL: A general awareness of the innovation and interest in learning more detail about it is indicated. The person seems to be unworried about himself or herself in relation to the innovation. She or he is interested in substantive aspects of the innovation in a selfless manner such as general characteristics, effects, and requirements for use.
	0	AWARENESS: Little concern about or involvement with the innovation is indicated.

Source: Adapted from *Change in Schools, Facilitating the Process* edited by Gene E. Hall and Shirley M. Hord. Reprinted by permission of the State University of New York Press. © 1987, State University of New York. All rights reserved.

collaboration, and refocusing concerns about the innovation relate to Fuller's impact concerns. Teachers are not likely to move to higher stages of concern until their lower-stage concerns have been addressed.

To help us better understand stages of concern, Hord and associates (Hord, Rutherford, Huling-Austin, and Hall, 1987) have provided "expressions of concern" made by individuals at each stage of concern. Table 21.1 lists stages and expressions of concerns. The supervisor's role is to facilitate teachers' movement through stages of concern—*and* implementation of the innovation—by (1) assessing individual and group stages of concern and (2) meeting the needs of teachers and groups at various stages. The supervisor can assess teachers' stages of concern through conferencing, open-ended concerns statements, and questionnaires (see Hall and Hord, 1987).

Chaos Theory and Change

Chaos theory cuts across a wide number of disciplines, including biology, chemistry, mathematics, meteorology, and physics. The "new science" of chaos has two foci. The first is the exploration of the hidden order that exists within chaotic systems. The second is the study of how self organization emerges from chaos (Hayles, 1990). Chaos theory involves a number of related concepts, not all of which

TABLE 21.1   *Stages and Expressions of Concern*

Stages of Concern		*Expressions of Concern*
I M P A C T	6 Refocusing	*I have some ideas about something that would work even better.
	5 Collaboration	*I am concerned about relating what I am doing with what other instructors are doing.
	4 Consequence	*How is my use affecting kids?
T A S K	3 Management	*I seem to be spending all my time getting material ready.
S E L F	2 Personal	*How will using it affect me?
	1 Informational	*I would like to know more about it.
	0 Awareness	*I am not concerned about it (the innovation).

Source: S. M. Hord, W. L. Rutherford, L. Huling-Austin, and G. E. Hall, *Taking Charge of Change.* Alexandria, VA: Association for Supervision and Curriculum Development, 1987, p. 31. Reprinted with permission of S. M. Hord.

are relevant to change in schools and classrooms. Several aspects of chaos theory that have significance for educational change are reviewed here.

Nonlinearity

In a linear system simple cause and effect relationships exist; A causes B which causes C, and so on. A linear system is analogous to tipping over the first in a line of dominoes. The falling first domino knocks down the second, the second knocks down the third, and so on. A chaotic system is nonlinear. A nonlinear system is analogous to throwing a bowling ball toward a set of pins. Myriad variables come into play and interact with each other. The slightest variation in how the bowling ball is released may result in a strike in one frame, and a split or a gutter ball in the next.

Complexity

Chaotic systems take complex forms, making their precise measurement difficult if not impossible. Chapter Five's discussion on measuring the coast of Britain is an example of the problem with measuring complex forms; the method of measurement affects the measure. If one uses 200 mile-long rulers, the coast of Britain is 1600 miles long. If the rulers are 25 miles long, the length increases to 2,550 miles (Smith, 1995). As the length of the rulers becomes shorter, the length of the coast of Britain increases, on to infinity (Briggs and Peat, 1989).

Butterfly Effect

This phenomenon is technically known as *sensitive dependence on initial conditions.* This means that a small and seemingly unrelated event in one part of a system can have enormous effects on other parts of the system. Theoretical meteorologist Edward Lorenz made the term *butterfly effect* famous when he argued that a butterfly stirring its wings in Bejing today could unleash powerful storms in New York City next month. One implication of sensitive dependence of initial conditions is the impossibility of predicting not only next year's weather, but the long-term future of any chaotic system.

Fractals

A fractal is a geometric shape that is similar to itself at different scales. Mid-sized branches of a tree are remarkably similar in shape to the larger branches from which they come. Smaller branches, in turn, are the same shape as the mid-sized branches from which they come, and so on. Other examples of fractals include coastlines, mountains, clouds, rivers, weather patterns, and the human vascular system. Complex social systems can also reveal self-similarity on different scales: at each level of the system, specific patterns of organization and culture reappear.

Feedback Mechanisms

Chaotic systems contain feedback loops enabling outputs to feed back into the system as input. Feedback can bring stability or turbulence to a system. For example, a thermostat is a feedback mechanism that causes temperature stability. Conversely, when the sound from a loudspeaker feeds back through a microphone, it is rapidly magnified to create a disruptive shriek (Gleick, 1987). Feedback can also cause a system to move toward greater levels of complexity. Physicist Joseph Ford, for example, has referred to evolution as "chaos with feedback."

Turbulence

Turbulence can be caused from disturbances inside or outside of a system. Consider a river, flowing smoothly until it runs through a bed of rocks. The water is perturbed and becomes unstable. Turbulence can also be caused by a heavy rain that greatly increases the volume of water flowing through the river bed. The more complex a system is, the more subject it is to instability due to turbulence. If instability becomes great enough, a point of phase transition is reached; sudden, radical change takes place, resulting in either reorganization or disintegration.

Strange Attractors

Chaotic systems are not truly random. Rather, they possess patterns that are extremely complex and unpredictable, but that stay within certain parameters. Strange attractors are "deeply encoded structures" within chaotic systems (Hayles, 1990).

> The discovery that chaos possesses deep structures of order is all the more remarkable because of the wide range of systems that demonstrate this behavior. They range from lynx fur returns to outbreaks of measles epidemics, from the rise and fall of the Nile River to eye movements in schizophrenics. (Hayles, 1990, p. 10)

To summarize, chaos theory informs us that order and chaos are not opposites. Rather, in the words of Margaret Wheatley (1992) they are "mirror images, one containing the other" (p. 11).

Chaos Theory Applied to School Change

School improvement efforts traditionally have treated the change process as linear, with each step in the change effort affecting the next step in a simple cause and effect relationship. But, despite linear organization charts and improvement plans, schools are not linear systems; they are *nonlinear*, chaotic systems. An implication for this reality is that, rather than viewing a change effort as a blueprint to be drawn and followed, it should be viewed as an organic process:

Here the metaphor for change is the growth and development of a complex organism (for example a human being) rather than the operation of a simple machine. A complex organism begins life at a relatively small stage. Its development is not completely predictable. Its health requires interdependence, consistency, and balance among its various subsystems. Finally, organisms that flourish tend to be adaptable to changing environments. In fact, they are themselves in a constant state of change or "becoming" (Gordon, 1992, p. 73).

The fact that schools are nonlinear systems means that change cannot be controlled from above. It can only be nurtured by promoting a culture for change. The supervisor attempting to nurture such a culture needs to remember Fullan's admonition not to believe that the change the supervisor envisions is the one that should or even could be implemented. Rather it is the interaction of the supervisors ideas about change with ideas from other members of the school community—and the interaction of the change process with many other variables within the school culture—that will determine the direction of change.

The *complexity* of schools means that neither external research on effective schools, nor legislated standards, nor the results of standardized achievement tests can, by themselves, precisely measure improvement needs or the level of success of improvement efforts. Keedy and Achilles (1997) argue that local educators must ask the questions:

1. Why they want to change;
2. What they want to achieve; and
3. How to go about the change process (p. 116)

We would argue that local educators need to ask a fourth question as well: *how to measure success*. Keedy and Achilles recommend that supervisors and teachers reach consensus on these questions through collaborative, critical inquiry informed by awareness of the change process.

The *butterfly effect* apples to school change: it is impossible to predict the long-term effects of school improvement efforts. This does not mean that formal planning for school change should not take place. It does mean that a different type of planning is needed. Planning in a chaotic system like a school should be medium range (one to two years) rather than long range (five to ten years). It should emphasize general goals, broad guidelines, and built-in flexibility (Gordon, 1992). Formal planning in an unpredictable system needs to focus on process rather than product, with the goal of producing "a stream of wise decisions designed to achieve the mission of the organization" (Patterson, Stewart, and Purkey, 1986).

Like *fractals* in nature, schools reveal self-similarity in different scales. For example, a schoolwide staff development day, a department meeting, a classroom lesson, and a hallway interaction between a teacher and student might all reveal the same cultural characteristic. Thus reflective inquiry at the school, team, classroom, and individual level can help educators better understand their school culture, needed change, and pathways to improvement.

Once school improvement efforts are underway, feedback becomes essential for monitoring and assessing change. *Feedback mechanisms* need to be created and maintained. Feedback can take the form of student performance data, survey results, quality circles, third party reviews, and so forth. The important thing is that meaningful data on the results of change efforts be made available to teachers, and that they be given opportunities to reflect on the data and redirect their change efforts accordingly.

All complex systems experience *turbulence*, but efforts at change tend to increase its frequency and intensity. Turbulence is not always negative. Without some perturbance, the system would remain in a steady state and improvement would not be possible. However, too much turbulence (from outside or inside the school) can cause school improvement efforts to disintegrate. Keedy and Achilles (1997, p. 115) maintain that supervisors and teachers should construct a normative consensus—"a collective, critically-examined, and contextually-based agreement" of essential school norms that they can hold fast to during times of turbulence. He maintains that it is this normative consensus (referred to earlier in this text as a "cause beyond oneself") that can hold a school together during the change process.

Finally, *strange attractors*, those deeply encoded structures within chaotic systems, have implications for school change. Is it possible for supervisors and teachers to create strange attractors within schools that will—albeit in unpredictable ways—create permanent patterns leading to school improvement? Policy makers have attempted to do just that, mandating such structures as site-based management, shared decision making, and parent choice (Keedy, 1996). However, these structures have all failed to lead to patterns of improvement. Keedy (1995) maintains that the design that should be embedded throughout the social fabric of schools—for our purpose a "strange attractor,"—is *student-centered learning*. He also believes that embedding this design within traditional schools is an extremely difficult task, and that the best chance for making student-centered learning a school's underlying pattern is the design of new schools around that concept.

Implications of Chaos Theory at the Classroom Level

Chaos theory has implications beyond the school level. Classrooms and even individual students can be considered chaotic systems (the reader smiles and nods in agreement)! All joking aside, chaos theory is consistent with recent research that the brain learns in *nonlinear* ways. This calls into question a host of traditional classroom practices, including grouping students by age, separate subjects, a sequential curriculum, and discrete behavioral objectives (Rockier, 1990–1991; Tygestad, 1997). Nonlinearity supports constructivist teaching and learning as discussed in Chapter 5.

Complexity implies that student learning can take many different forms and can be expressed in different ways. This means that teachers should place less emphasis on any single indicator of student aptitude or achievement. It especially calls into question use of the standardized achievement test as the sole measure of student growth (Rockier, 1990–91). Complexity suggests the use of multiple measures of student learning, matching different assessment measures to different learning goals. It also supports the use of authentic assessment methods. Finally, complexity gives credence to the idea of allowing students to participate in planning assessment, and in making self-evaluation part of the assessment process.

The *butterfly effect* means that a wide variety of factors seemingly unrelated to a lesson plan (whether a student argued with a parent the night before, ate breakfast, or made a new friend on the school bus that morning) can lead to significant differences in what takes place in the classroom when the lesson is taught, and how the lesson affects an individual student's learning. The butterfly effect assures that no lesson will ever go completely as planned, or have the same effect on any two students. It indicates the need for teacher flexibility in teaching, as well as the need for individual attention to students, each of whom is experiencing a given lesson within his or her own personal context.

If the butterfly effect accounts for differences in classroom interactions and student outcomes, *fractals* are a metaphor for patterns that can be observed on different scales within the classroom. Systematic classroom observation can record behaviors and effects that cut across whole-class, small group, and individual levels. Additionally, patterned behaviors and interactions can be observed from lesson to lesson. Reflective inquiry into classroom practice, whether in the form of clinical supervision, peer coaching, or action research, can help the teacher to identify patterns that foster and hinder student learning, and to alter the learning environment accordingly.

Feedback mechanisms can have positive or negative effects on classroom teaching and learning. For example, high stakes testing (much to the chagrin of those who design the tests) can become a negative mechanism. In many cases, feedback on student performance on high stakes tests has led teachers to ignore curriculum not measured by the test, and teach to the test through "drill and kill" methods focused on practice test items. With all of the the unpredictability present in classrooms, beneficial feedback is critical for both teachers and students. For teachers, student performance data, direct student feedback, and classroom observation data can all assist teachers to improve classroom instruction. Skill at what Donald Schon calls "reflection in action" enables teachers to receive and analyze feedback and respond to that feedback while in the act of teaching. For students, feedback on their cognitive and affective performance—from teachers, parents, and peers—is an essential part of the learning process. The fact that in chaotic systems like classrooms output becomes input means that the artificial distinctions we often draw between learning and assessment need to be removed: in reality, learning and assessment cannot be separated.

Turbulence, like nonlinearity, supports constructivist teaching and learning. Trygestad (1997) points out that new knowledge, like turbulence, causes instability ("disequilibrium") before it is assimilated into a new conceptual scheme. The teacher's task is to first present perturbations that cause instability and activate conceptual change (Luffiego, Bastida, Ramos, and Soto, 1994), and then to support student reconstruction (Doll, 1986).

Finally, the improvement of teaching—like whole school improvement—is dependent on the ultimate *strange attractor,* student-centered learning. Additional patterns within the fabric of classroom practice can foster student-centered learning, including reflective inquiry, instructional dialogue, and collegial support. It is not possible to predict precisely how these embedded patterns will change classroom instruction in the long run. Rather, they are designed to facilitate a process of continuous improvement.

And so ends our brief journey into the world of chaos, a world that elicits different reactions from those who enter it.

> Those who feel comfortable with order and reason, with symmetry, equilibrium, and stasis, will find life in the world of dynamic complexity quite challenging. On the other hand, those who are comfortable with being in the process, the flow of the system, those who can see the larger patterns beyond the endless change and dynamisms, those who can tolerate ambiguity and unpredictability, those people will find being in a complex system at the edge of chaos to be stimulating and rewarding (McAndrews, 1997, p. 40).

Does not all that is said in the above quote about chaotic systems apply as well to modern schools and classrooms?

Creating a Culture for Change

The traditional literature on organizational culture treats culture and change as polar opposites, with one purpose of the culture being to *resist* change. Such resistance indeed seems to be part of the typical school culture. However, some school cultures actually foster positive change. What characteristics do these school cultures have that are not present in most schools? Those who have studied "cultures for change" have described very similar characteristics. Little (1982), Rosenholtz (1989), and Fullan, Bennett, and Rolheiser-Bennett (1990) all cite shared purpose, collegiality, and a spirit of continuous improvement. Simpson (1990) described sharing and collegiality, teacher empowerment, and participative/collaborative leadership. Leithwood (1992) described "transformational leadership" that fosters school reform through maintaining collaborative cultures, fostering teacher development, and improving group problem solving.

As one reviews the literature on the relationship between school culture and change, it is impossible to ignore a third concept that intersects with the first two: *teacher empowerment.* For example, let's review a list of "themes for empowerment" identified by Malenyzer (1990) in a study of middle school teachers:

1. Teachers sharing leadership
2. Teachers sharing in decision making

3. Teachers assessing the knowledge base
4. Trusting relationships and confidence in self and others
5. The extension of recognition and appreciation
6. Caring, sharing, a sense of community
7. Honest and open communication between teacher-teacher and between administrator-teacher
8. The maintenance of high expectations
9. Collegial and administrative support
10. Safeguarding what's important

These 10 characteristics of teacher empowerment sound very much like the characteristics of school cultures that support change! Although more research needs to be done examining the relationships of school culture, teacher empowerment, and change, it seems likely that one key to creating school cultures that foster needed change is to empower those individuals who make up the culture! Rather than viewing school culture as a wall impeding change, a better way to define it is as a set of commonly held beliefs, values, norms, and assumptions that can result in change being resisted *or* embraced. Empowered individuals and groups are more likely to develop beliefs, values, norms, and assumptions that are congruent with risk taking, experimentation, and continuous improvement rather than with the status quo. Given the many problems facing our schools today, creating a culture for change has become a critical imperative for supervision and supervisors.

Changing the Conditions of Teaching

Our times have witnessed considerable national concern with upgrading the teaching profession. Among the results have been (1) providing college scholarships to attract more intelligent and achievement-minded students into teacher education, (2) raising teacher salaries to compare more favorably with salaries in private industries, and (3) creating financial career ladders to pay teachers substantially higher salaries when they achieve certain plateaus (Darling-Hammond and Berry, 1988). The aim of these actions is to attract and keep more capable people in the profession by providing financial incentives. Such increases are long overdue. Teaching should be a more extrinsically rewarded profession. At the same time, national concern has resulted in more legislated requirements for schools. The result has been that even with more financial benefits, teachers' morale and satisfaction has been seriously eroded. Changing the outer conditions for teachers without making subsequent changes in the internal conditions in their work life will not substantially improve instruction. Improving the external conditions without improving the internal conditions is like baking a loaf of bread and having a beautiful, smoothly textured crust, only to bite into a moldy and unmixed core. Obviously, the teaching profession should be satisfying from both within and without.

The Carnegie Foundation survey of 13,500 teachers, directed by Ernest Boyer, addressed these internal conditions. "What the data shows is that teachers feel largely bypassed in the process. Regulations have added more paperwork and the bureaucracy has increased. Teaching conditions have gotten worse. And in the process, morale has gone down" (Boyer, 1988).

John Goodlad, upon completing the most comprehensive study of schools ever undertaken in the United States, concluded:

> In general the practicing teacher—to the degree we can generalize from our findings—functions in a context where the beliefs and expectations are those of a profession but where the realities tend to constrain, likening actual practice to a trade....A question arises as to whether the circumstances can be made conducive to developing in all teachers the behavior a profession entails. By its very nature a profession involves both considerable autonomy in decision making and knowledge and skills developed before entry and then honed in practice. The teachers in our sample, on the whole, went into teaching because of those inherent professional values. However, they encountered in schools many realities not conducive to professional growth. (1984, pp. 193–194)

Boyer and Goodlad, two of our most distinguished educators, concluded from their research in the 1980s that the work environment of schools was not conducive to the professional development of teachers and to the success of schools. Only when supervisors attend to individual differences in teachers and improve what Boyer (1983, p. 159) referred to as "the intellectual climate of the school" will teachers become more abstract in their thinking and committed to instruction for students.

As we enter the twentieth century, there are major efforts to change the conditions of education, teaching, and teachers. Many supervisors have made their schools centers of teacher inquiry, autonomy, and dialogue. There is certainly enough information available about supervision, interpersonal skills, technical skills, tasks, the nature of change, and the psychology of individual and group development to make all our schools better places. The door for improving internal conditions will never close; it's simply a matter of whether or not we care to step in and make a difference.

The Role of SuperVision and Supervisor in School Improvement

This book began by defining the key to successful schools as instructional supervision that fosters teacher development by promoting greater abstraction, commitment, and collective action. The aim of supervision is to bring faculty together as knowledgeable professionals working for the benefit of all students. The role of supervision is to change the attitude of many schools that a classroom is an island unto itself to an attitude that faculty is engaged in a common schoolwide instructional task that transcends any one classroom—a cause beyond oneself.

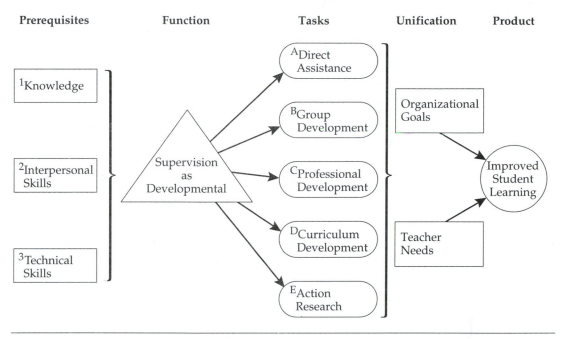

| Prerequisites | Function | Tasks | Unification | Product |

FIGURE 21.2 *SuperVision for Successful Schools*

Whether they are building-level persons such as school principals, department heads, instructional lead teachers, or master teachers; district personnel such as assistant superintendents, curriculum directors, subject area specialists, or consultants; or school-level generalists (early childhood, elementary, middle school, or secondary)—supervisors can play an important part in improving schools. The critical tasks for such improvement are direct assistance, curriculum development, professional development, group development, and action research. Each of these tasks can be planned to enhance teacher development and collective action. Districtwide and building-level supervisors can work together to implement such plans. An instrument that shows how a school or district can assess its current supervisory practice can be found in Appendix C. Rarely can one person do it all, but in almost any situation, supervisors concerned with instructional improvement can begin the work. We know that school success can be achieved when supervisors attend to those tasks that enable teachers to develop individually and collectively (Pratzner, 1984).

What Is School Success?

Ironically, the definition of school success has been left to near the end of this book. This has been done for a reason, however. The rationale for a school faculty making its own collective definition of school success should be apparent. In referring to studies of successful schools to support many of the propositions of this book, we mentioned schools that were achieving what they had set out to do, regardless of what those goals were. Some schools prioritize academic learning and achievement as their criteria for success. Some prioritize creativity and self-directed learning. Other schools prioritize problem solving, community involvement, and social cooperation as their criteria for success. Many schools want it all: they want to be successful in academics, creativity, self-directed learning, problem solving, community involvement, and social cooperation (Goodlad, 1984, pp. 33–60). Schools should strive to educate all students well, in ways consistent with education in a democratic society (Barber, 1993). Although we personally prefer schools that strive to have it all, that decision should be a local school matter. It is in the clarity of common purpose that action to improve instruction takes place.

With an understanding of what is meant by improved instruction and school success, we can fill in the remaining circle on the diagram of supervision for successful schools that has served as the map of this book (see Figure 21.2 on page 459).

Exercises

Academic

1. Find in the literature a description of an educational leader who has turned an unsuccessful school into a successful one. Which of the change strategies discussed in this chapter did the supervisor use? Report on actions related to each of the five tasks of supervision that he or she carried out while turning the school around.

2. If Boyer (1983, 1988) or Goodlad (1984) were asked to write a three-page paper on "What Makes Effective and Successful Schools," what would each of them say in his essay? Assume the role of one of these authors and, on the basis of reading their studies, write such a paper.

3. Prepare a report comparing and contrasting the views of three authors who have written about educational change.

4. Prepare a report on recent efforts by individuals and groups outside of education and government to provide concrete assistance to education and educators. What have they proposed, and what is being done?

5. Diagram your own model for effective supervision. Provide a written explanation of each component of your model. Explain the scope, arrangement, sequence, and relationship of model components.

Field

1. Interview a supervisor on practical problems that must be considered to bring about change within a typical public school system. Prepare a report on your interview. Include your own ideas on how appropriate knowledge, skills, roles, functions, processes, tasks, and strategies discussed in this book can be applied to overcome or reduce problems described by the interviewee.

2. Prepare a photo and/or written essay about schools, students, teachers, and super-visors that has as its theme "A Cause beyond Oneself" and that reflects the meaning this book attaches to this phrase. Share the essay with others.

3. Interview five teachers concerning a program innovation that is being proposed or introduced in their school. On the basis of the interviews, attempt to classify each teacher according to his or her stage of concern about the innovation.

4. Create a collage in which the key ideas of the text are represented. Share the collage with others who have read this text.

Developmental

1. Begin a file of newspaper, magazine, and journal articles describing ideas and efforts of individuals and organizations both in and outside of education for achieving success in education.

2. Use selected readings from other texts on educational supervision to compare authors' ideas on specific issues you consider crucial to your own education and development in supervision.

3. Use opportunities as they arise to test out this book's ideas on supervision within your own particular work setting. Through such exploration, determine which of the proposals and suggestions are of most value to your own development and that of others.

References

Barber, R. R. 1993. America skips school. *Harpers* 287(1722):39–46.

Boyer, E. L. 1983. *High school: A report on secondary education in America*. New York: Harper & Row.

Boyer, E. L. 1988. *Report card on school reform: The teachers speak*. Princeton, NJ: Carnegie Commission for the Advancement of Teaching.

Briggs, J., and Peat, F. D. 1989. *Turbulent mirror: An illustrated guide to chaos theory and the science of wholeness*. New York: Harper and Row.

Darling-Hammond, L., and Berry, B. 1988. *The evolution of teacher policy*. Santa Monica, CA: Rand Center for Policy Research in Education.

Doll, W. E. 1996. *Prigogine: A new sense of order, a new curriculum. Theory into practice*, 25(1), 10–16.

Fullan, M. G. 1991. *The new meaning of educational change*. New York: Teachers College Press.

Fullan, M. G., Bennett, B., and Rolheiser-Bennett, C. 1990. Linking classroom and school improvement. *Educational Leadership* 47(8):13–19.

Fuller, F. F. 1969. Concerns of teachers: A developmental conceptualization. *American Educational Research Journal* 6(2): 207–266.

Gleick, J. 1987. Chaos: *Making a new science*. New York: Penguin Books.

Goodlad, J. I. 1984. *A place called school: Prospects for the future*. New York: McGraw-Hill.

Gordon, S. P. 1992. Paradigms, transitions, and the new supervision. *Journal of Curriculum and Supervision*, 8(1), 62–76.

Guskey, T. R. 1994 *Professional development in education: In search of the optimal mix*. Paper presented at the annual meeting of the American Educational Research Association, New Orleans, April.

Hall, G. E., and Hord, S. M. 1987. *Change in schools: Facilitating the process*. Albany: State University of New York Press.

Hayles, N. K. 1990. *Chaos bound: Orderly disorder in contemporary literature and society*. Ithaca: Cornell University Press.

Hord, S. M., Rutherford, W. L., Huling Austin, L., & Hall, G. E. 1987. *Taking charge of change*. Alexandria, VA: Association for Supervision and Curriculum Development.

Keedy, J. L. 1995. Teacher practical knowledge in restructured high schools. *Journal of Educational Research*, 89(2), 76–89.

Keedy, J. L., and Achilles, C. M. 1997. The need for school-constructed theories in practice in US school restructuring. *Journal of Educational Administration,* 35(2), 102–121.

Leithwood, K. A. 1992. The move toward transformational leadership. *Educational Leadership* 49(58):8–12.

Liberman, A. 1992. *The changing concerns of teaching.* Chicago: University of Chicago Press.

Little, J. W. 1982. Norms of collegiality and experimentation: Workplace conditions of school success. *American Educational Research Journal* 19(3):325–340.

Luffiego, M., Bastida, M. F., Ramos, F., and Soto, J. 1994. Systemic model of conceptual evolution. *International Journal of Science, 16(3), 305–313.*

Malenyzer, B. J. 1990. *Teacher empowerment: The discourse, meanings, and social actions of teachers.* Paper presented at the Annual Conference of States on Inservice Education, Orlando, November. (ERIC Document ED 327 496)

McAndrew, D. A. 1997. Chaos, complexity, and fuzziness: Science looks at teaching English. *English Journal,* 86(7), 37–43.

Patterson, J. L., Purkey, S. C., and Parker, J. V. 1986. *Productive school systems for a nonrational world.* Alexandria, VA: Association for Supervision and Curriculum Development.

Pratzner, F. C. 1984. Quality of school life: Foundations for improvement. *Educational Researcher* 13(3):20–25.

Rockler, M. M. 1990–1991. Thinking about chaos: Non-quantitative approaches to teacher education. *Action in Teacher Education, 12(4), 56–62.*

Rosenholtz, S. 1989. *Teachers' workplace: The social organization of schools.* White Plains, NY: Longman.

Simpson, G. W. 1990. Keeping it alive: Elements of school culture that sustain innovation. *Educational Leadership* 47(8):34–37.

Smith, R. D. 1995. The inapplicability principle: What chaos means for social science. *Behavioral Science,* 40(1), 22–40.

Tygestad, J. 1997. *Chaos in the classroom: An application of chaos theory.* Paper presented at the Annual Meeting of the American Educational Research Association, Chicago, March.

Wheatley, M. J. 1992. *Leadership and the new science: Learning about organization from an orderly universe.* San Francisco: Berrett-Koehler.

Suggested Readings

Barth, R. S. 1991. *Improving schools from within.* San Francisco: Jossey-Bass.

Brandt, R. (Ed.). 1990. *Educational Leadership* 47(8). Theme issue on "Creating a Culture for Change."

Fullan, M. 1991 *The new meaning of educational change* (2nd ed.). New York: Teachers College Press.

Fullan, M. G., and Miles, M. 1992. Getting reform right: What works and what doesn't. *Phi Delta Kappan, 73:* 745–752.

Fullan, M. G. 1996. Turning systematic thinking on its head. *Phi Delta Kappan,* 77:420–423.

Glatthorn, A. A. 1992. *Teachers as agents of change.* Washington, DC: National Education Association.

Harvey, T. R. 1990. *Checklist for change.* Boston: Allyn and Bacon.

Joyce, B. R. 1995. School renewal: An inquiry, not a formula. *Educational Leadership, 52*(7): 51–55.

Larson, R. L. 1992. *Changing schools from the inside out.* Lancaster, PA: Technomic.

Patterson, J. L. 1993. *Leadership for tomorrow's schools.* Alexandria, VA: Association for Supervision and Curriculum Development.

22

SuperVision for Democratic Education

Returning to Our Core

Now that we are moving into the twenty-first century, it is appropriate to realign our understanding of education and supervision to its largest context. In discussions about educational improvement in our schools, we have heard much about voice and empowerment, while at the same time we have heard about standards, assessment, curriculum, and program alignment. Two processes for school reform dominate: One relies on grass-roots, site-based decision making, the other urges systemic, systemwide alignments. These approaches often are, in appearance and practice, at cross-purposes with each other. Taken to an extreme, systemic change, on the one hand, can result in a tightening of the regulatory mandates from which local educators and schools have for years been seeking some release. On the other hand, site-based decentralization, when poorly conceived and implemented, can become a laissez-faire abdication and balkanization of local schools from their district, state, and nation (Hargreaves and Macmillan, 1992; Darling-Hammond, 1993).

Educators, students, and parents in local schools need to participate as equals in the decisions about their school, school district, state, and national concerns. We need to create ways to move the exceptional aspects of democratic and powerfully active public schools into the mainstream of practice and put the antidemocratic and ordinary schools into the margins (Goodlad, 1992). All of our supervisory actions need to be taken in congruence with the higher principles of our American democracy. Successful educational improvement is most often a result of simultaneous bottom-up and top-down initiatives that converge into a clear, moral center (Fullan, 1991). In effect, the result of such change is that no one is coerced into doing what is wrong. Instead, everyone works toward what is believed by all to be right for students. What is right (or morally good) should never, in our democracy, be justified by power or status.

In the early 1970s, one of us was a principal of a school engaged in many of today's "innovations" and recalls listening intently to a professor speak about what needed to be done to sustain the open education movement. He presented well-reasoned ideas about teaching and curriculum, and the belief that these student-centered practices would continue to expand in influence. But the open education reform movement did not last. At its zenith, it is estimated to have affected at best 5 percent of the schools. It was torn down by its critics as well as by its proponents. The critics argued against any change that involved student participation or any digression from teaching as stand-up authority, using traditional, sequential basal textbooks. Many proponents often were guilty of poor planning and irresponsible practices and reinforced the critics' fear of chaos by pushing activity-centered, nongraded, team teaching practices on unknowing and ill-prepared teachers, administrators, and parents. In short time, walls that had been removed to allow large class groupings went back up, multiage groupings returned to lockstep grade levels, assessments based on accounts of student growth were surrendered to numerical grades and standardized testing, and, for the next 20 years, we saw an accumulation of prescriptive, sequential curriculum, textbooks, and evaluations.

Larry Cuban, a student of reforms that attempt to profoundly change the structure of educational experiences for students, found that most have a very short life (Cuban, 1992). Such efforts are activated by passionate reformers who impress impatient policy makers. The result is a quick surge in interest among previously dormant educators who always had felt that there were better ways to operate schools. But, as Cuban noted, such reforms eventually step on too many toes; they alienate too many people; they threaten too many existing job responsibilities; and the controversies become headaches for superintendents, school boards, and legislators. Eventually, the old structures of schools reclaim dominance. The name of the reform may stay but the spirit is lost. Of course, there are noticeable exceptions; some lasting, substantial, and positive educational changes have been institutionalized in some schools and school districts for 10 years or more. But the track record of substantial alteration of public education is not great. Now, why has this been the case and what do we do about it?

In the early 1970s, the most valid research of the time by such notables as Piaget, Bruner, Inhelder, Kammi, Vygotsky, Kohlberg, and others clearly supported activity-centered, developmental learning. Similarly, the research of the 1980s and 1990s by people such as Gardner, Slavin, Joyce, Resnick, and others supports the activity-centered, constructivist learning of today. The learning that we all retain, after school is over, is that learning that engaged, challenged, and involved us. But the fact that research has validated the case for learning as democratic engagement has had little influence on prevailing practice.

The education historian, Lawrence Cremin, in his book about attempts to transform the American school, wrote that the perennial issue of change is one of public education being a massive enterprise (Cremin, 1964). It takes great personal energy and commitment by highly intelligent, sensitive, and knowledgeable educators to move existing structures (Schlecty and Cole, 1992). In a sobering statement, Cremin wrote that the real question about structural reform in public education is whether the concept of public, by definition, means that a critical mass of energizers can ever exist. It is easier to propel reforms with a select group of 20 like-minded people in one school than with a work force of 2 million teachers and administrators in thousands of schools who have been reasonably secure in the prevailing system for their entire professional lives. This was what Gorbachev experienced in trying to change the government of the Soviet Union *with* the same people who were its perpetuators. So, the dilemma, according to Cremin, is whether any existing public institution with a large work force and clientele can ever become better than average.

We are, again, at another time in education when conventions are being rethought, substantial collaborations are taking place, and public education is being challenged by some to excel and by others to disappear. As current education is being criticized (often inaccurately through ignorance or design; see Berliner, 1993, Kirst, 1993, and Huelskamp, 1993), with that criticism has come proposals for reducing or eliminating public schools, school districts, and board responsibilities through vouchers, choice plans, performance contracts, and national standards and assessments (Darling Hammond, 1997; Kohn, 1999). Yet, at the same time, we find great positive publicity and reinforcing recognition given to public schools that differ dramatically from the conventional ones and that are—because of those differences—held up as good examples of profound, powerful, and successful learning for students. These schools that are praised for their differences can be found among schools that are part of various networks such as the Coalition of Essential Schools, the Accelerated Schools, the Effective Schools, the Outcomes Based Education Schools, the Comer Schools, and the League of Professional Schools. They also can be found operating in isolation in a multitude of districts and states as magnet schools, charter schools, Re-Learning Schools, next generation schools, America 2000 Schools, and similar pilot and demonstration schools. There are more schools involved in rethinking practice as part of school collaborations than ever before. But even so, as Marshall Smith, a leading proponent of systemic reform and Under Secretary of the U.S. Department of Education, noted in the fall of 1993, "The really fundamental issue here is that we've got to reach 110,000 schools and...networks only reach maybe one half of one percent of them. They (these committed schools) serve as terrific examples, but they are not going to meet the problems of kids throughout the nation" (O'Neil, 1993).

So, at last, we're back to the nub of supervision. How do we reverse the history of reform by causing schools that struggle to excel to be the definers of mainstream and how do we push the all too dominant number of ordinary, noninitiating schools to the margin? How should we go about this invigoration for excellence in our schools, communities, districts, states, and our nation? We've never succeeded before. Why do we think that we can succeed now? In this book, we've discussed how individual schools and districts can succeed. Now let us identify some broad actions we must take if extraordinary education is to become the norm in our land.

Systemic Reform around Purpose

Listen to the voices of teachers talking about the same group of regular students they have during the schoolday:

Mr. A: The kid here is where the problem is today. These kids are just unteach-able. There's nothing wrong with the curriculum.... If I could just get the right students, I could teach and everything would be wonderful.

Ms. B: These students are just not real smart, and they don't want to learn. They're just putting in time.

Mr. C: There are kids here who really want to do a good job, but they have seen so much and heard so much that they are often distracted. Their perspective is gone. But they are basically really good kids.

Ms. D: My guys. They're very, very clever and brave kids. It's amazing how they are always figuring out what is going on around them. It is a joy to keep up with their energy and channel it into learning experiences.

Without arguing over perception versus reality as reflected in those attitudes towards students, let us ask which views you heard are consistent with the founding principles of our society.

> All men (and women, now) are created equal, that they are endowed by their Creator with certain inalienable Rights; that among these are Life, Liberty, and the pursuit of Happiness; that to secure these rights, Governments are instituted among men, deriving their just powers from the consent of the governed, that whenever any Form of Government becomes destructive of these ends, it is the Right of the People to alter or abolish it. (Declaration of Independence, 1776)

Take those previous words by teachers about their students and change a few words and you have the central purpose of public education.

> All students are created equal; that they are endowed by their Creator with certain inalienable Rights; that among these are an education that will accord them Life, Liberty, and the pursuit of Happiness; that whenever any public school becomes destructive of preparing students for these ends, it is the Right of the People to alter or abolish it.

In essence, the reason we have public education is to enculturate students into the values of our democracy! To summarize Thomas Jefferson, public educa-tion has two corollary purposes: (1) to provide for an educated citizenry to partic-ipate in decisions about promoting the future good of our democratic society and (2) to allow for leadership in a democratic society to develop from the merits, abilities, and talents of the individual. Leadership in a democratic society should not be accorded based on family privilege, economic wealth, religion, race, or group privilege (see Lee, 1961).

Indeed, the Supreme Court has concluded that "The Constitution presupposes the existence of an informed citizenry prepared to participate in governmental affairs, and these democratic principles obviously are constitutionally incorporated into the structure of our government. It therefore seems entirely appropriate that the State use public schools to…inculcate fundamental values necessary to the maintenance of a democratic political system" (*Board of Education* v. *Pico,* 1982).

American schools are indeed better than they've ever been in reaching all students. But the challenge of American schools is not primarily that of achieving economic superiority in the world or of focusing on subject area achievement. The challenge is to rise to the far more demanding and crucially important standard of educating all students to be knowledgeable, proactive, resourceful, and responsible members of our democratic society.

In order to have systemic reform at a national level, we need to understand that the national goals of America 2000 are goals offered in reaction to an immediate, perceived crisis. The goals of America 2000 do not offer a proactive response to the fundamental purpose of our schools (Goodlad, 1992). In utilitarian terms, we will not achieve the immediate goals of American education and sustain educational advancements unless we direct our changes to the application of learning that gives relevance and competence to every student in becoming a valued and contributing citizen of his or her community. Such core purpose can give tremendous direction and sustaining power to what needs to be altered in educational practice. Without such purpose, what we do today in education will be simply a response to an alarm that, when media attention wanes, will be swallowed again by the deep structures of compliance, control, and complacency (McNeil, 1988). The struggle to engage and prepare students for proactive life in a democracy will always be our future challenge and *it will never be finished!*

What we need to understand is that the fundamental reform of public education is not to find a new vision of education but instead to refocus on the original vision—indeed, what should always be the SuperVision of education in our society. We are not creating something new (whether we call it "restructuring," "transforming," "outcome basing," "quality managing" or whatever). We must focus on the recentering of public education based on the principles of a democracy. Issues of work force preparation, subject-matter knowledge, and advancing to higher education are all important but secondary obligations of our schools. We run into trouble and the impossibility of attaining those secondary goals for all when we treat them as primary. For example, our concerns about the next generation not being able to advance economically and have a higher economic standard than the current generation misses the point of education. Our democracy is predicated on the belief that each generation will become more intelligent, more insightful, and more competent to decide on a better, more just, and more caring society. Such a democracy is most often realized in the small, day-to-day events and interactions between people.

Introducing and constantly reinforcing the concept that the good of a society translates into the rights and responsibilities of individuals is what Amy Gutman

(1987) referred to as the "central obligation" of American public schools. Public schools must ensure a democratic threshold of learning experiences that give all students the knowledge, skills, compassion, and understanding to participate in human affairs. It is these requisites for democratic living that we should be returning to in determining decisions about standards, assessments, curriculum, professional development, placement, and grouping of students, as well as the ways that adults themselves function with each other. The supreme irony of public schools is that the only institution in the United States with the explicit purpose of preparing students for a democracy often operates in ways that demonstrate the lack of belief in such collective participation. Most schools do not include faculty, students, and parents in democratic decision making. Indeed, in many cases, where formal leaders wish for such involvement, many faculty, students, or parents would rather not be involved. Schools in the United States all too often operate in accord with dependency and hierarchical relations, not democratic ones. How can we, as a country, continue to sacrifice the lives of young men and women to protect and extend democracy as the best way of determining the common good while we stand unwilling to use the same beliefs in how we make decisions about the education of our youth?

We keep masking the essential purpose of schools in neutral terms such as *site-based management, decentralization, collaboration,* and *participatory decisions.* Why do we find it difficult to say simply that our schools should be democratic and thus consistent with their mission?

Support for Hard and Unglamorous Work

There are many parallels that can be drawn between successful schools and successful businesses. Both types of organizations are marked by a three-dimensional, interrelated, moral framework that guides internal decisions (Glickman, 1993). Such schools have (1) a covenant or a SuperVision of principles, purpose, and goals; (2) a charter for decision making that is understood by all that activates the covenant, and (3) a critical study process for gathering information to inform decisions, accompanied by an action research process to assess whether such decisions are accomplishing the intended educational effects for students. The work of powerful schools is not prescriptive or linear; rather, it is based on a recursive stream of decisions that people make together over time to determine if the school is creating a better educational experience for students. This is all done with the full knowledge that whatever will be done at the moment will not be perfect and that ongoing incidents, calamities, and controversies will continue to arise.

The lessons about powerful schools need to be analyzed in comparison with the promotions from the education marketing industry that, for example, promise to deliver the "six magic steps" guaranteed for success if the school purchases its staff-development program complete with consultants and materials. If powerful schools are to become the norm rather than interesting and probably short-term exceptions, we all need to realize the realities involved in improving educa-

tion. School districts, boards, unions, states, and other agencies need to *provide capacity-building structures* to invite schools to become more democratic, flexible, responsive, and responsible.

Why Systemic Reform as Locally Derived?

How can this policy plan for inviting, encouraging, and supporting locally initiated and decentralized school renewal be consistent with the systemic reform world that exhorts national standards, assessment, and curriculum alignment? (See Clune, 1992; Fuhrman and Massell, 1992.)

To some degree, a middle ground can be found. Every time we exclude local educators from the decisions that they are expected to carry out, we rob them of the process of learning and the opportunity to develop commitment to the change. When national, state, or school district agencies develop policies, curriculum objectives, student tests, teacher tests, or other school requirements without local involvement, we create the conditions for what Seymour Sarason (1990) refers to as "the predictable failure of school reform." School district, state, and national educators, citizens, and policy makers should have the right to participate in the decisions about standards and systemic reform. However, realize that the right to participate in decision making about the local school is not the same as the authority to make the final decisions *for* local schools. Those who live and work in the schools almost certainly have better ideas of the needs and opportunities there. They should be free to make the decisions for that school.

What we need to do is to reshape our thinking about national, state, and school district decisions as the participation of all. It is not "they" who decide, but "we." We, as local people in our own local schools—teachers, administrators, parents, students, and community members—are entitled to be at the table for school district, union, state, and national decisions. When we talk about the district, we need to know to whom are we referring: Who is the district? Who does the district represent? Does the district represent all of us or just one school board or administrative cabinet that exerts influence over other weaker bodies? Does the state represent all of us or just one body of policy makers or legislators that excludes others? Are federal decisions made by *us* or *them?*

We believe that it is eminently reasonable for public education to have national standards around the core education of a democratic citizenry. All national standards and assessments should be in accord with the principles of our democracy. Our schools should ensure that all students can:

- Enjoy and exercise freedom of speech and accept the obligation to show respect for the rights of others.
- Understand the key importance of separation of church and state in governmental affairs.
- Know and be committed to the steps of due process prior to the deprivation of life, liberty, property, and the pursuit of happiness.

- Be knowledgeable and conversant about the issues of our society.
- Know how to reason well, consider various perspectives, test ideas, and form informed opinions.
- Practice and communicate the acceptance of equality of all humans.

None of these national standards is a vested interest of a special-interest group or the domain of a particular subject area, but these are the standards of what it means to be an educated American. Democratic standards certainly demand the ability to read and to write and to be knowledgeable in arithmetic, science, history, art, music, and skills adequate for employment and future educational pursuits. But school districts, unions, and states need to allow for local schools to determine the operations, curriculum, educational programs, and allocations of money to meet the essential standards of public education. Schools and districts should be under the legal obligation to demonstrate their success at meeting the democratic threshold of standards through student evidences of performances, exhibits, and demonstrations.

The existing and what appears to be perennial issues about education practices and school structure must find resolution from the fundamental, core purpose of public education. The disagreements that we have in regard to grade levels versus multiage grouping, authentic testing versus standardized testing, tracking versus nontracking of students, cooperative learning versus individualized learning, and phonics versus whole language will continue to be determined as they have been in the past—by those who have the political or marketing power of the time. That is, *unless* we attempt to answer the basic question about public education. The question is:

> What should we be doing in our schools, our curriculum, our placement and our scheduling of students, our allocations of resources, and our teaching to give every child his or her inalienable rights to life, liberty, and the pursuit of happiness. What is just, what is fair, what is democratic?

Such a fundamental question has many correct responses and yet such a question clearly provides a screen for what are wrong and intolerable responses. Grouping students in ways to label and limit their aspirations is wrong! Allocating more money to privileged students at the expense of underprivileged students is wrong! Keeping a student from advancing beyond his or her peers is wrong! Restricting teaching to a daily routine of compliance and passivity is wrong! Not allowing students to develop their abilities to think, reason, and problem solve is wrong! And allowing some students to deprive others of their rights to an education is wrong!

Appropriate responses are not situational and relativistic determinations. Our democracy is not a process of decision making always predicated on the rule of the majority. The rule of the majority can be tyrannical. We balance the rights of the majority with the rights of the minority. If necessary, we turn to the courts to interpret the Constitution and the correctness of decisions. We are an imperfect society. Our aspirations often are far removed from our practices, but our aspirations are what always should guide practice.

Conclusion

We realize the truly awesome responsibility that educators have taken upon themselves to lead a SuperVision of instruction. We cannot think of ourselves as first-grade teachers, high school mathematics teachers, middle school counselors, central office specialists, high school principals, or superintendents. These positions are reflections of where we locate our bodies to go to work, but the names don't reflect where we need to locate our minds and our hearts. Educators are the primary stewards of the democratic spirit. The total of our efforts is far greater than the particulars of our job (Glickman, 1988).

There is a tremendous, democratic impulse being played out in many schools, school districts, and networks throughout America. The unfettering of regulations and exhortations for change have allowed that impulse to grow. Now that the impulse has been activated, we must stay the course and see improving teaching and learning as simply the professional work of educators.

Thank goodness we live in a society that aspires to operate according to beliefs and actions that transcend a single person's thoughts. The democratic impulse for renewing education continues to resonate in the thoughts of many local teachers, parents, administrators, and citizens in schools throughout this country—perhaps among more people than ever before. However, schools blessed with such far-sighted people are still in the margin. The challenge to bring democracy as the guiding principle into public education is enormous. We have been here before and we might fall short once again. But, whether we succeed or simply keep the spirit alive, we will have let other generations of educators and citizens know that this is the most important fight in which to engage—the democratic education of our students for a just and democratic society.

References

Barber, B. R. 1993. America skips school. *Harpers* 287(1722):39–46.

Berliner, D. C. 1993. Mythology and the American system of education. *Phi Delta Kappan* 75(4): 632–639.

Board of Education v. *Pico.* 457 U.S. 853, 1982, p. 186.

Chubb, J. E., and Moe, T. N. 1990. *Politics, markets, and America's schools.* Washington, DC: Brookings Institution.

Clune, W. H. 1992. *The best path to systemic educational policy: Standard/centralized or differentiated/decentralized?* Wisconsin: University of Wisconsin-Madison, Wisconsin Center of Educational Research, School of Education.

Cremin, L. A. 1964. *The transformation of the school: Progressivism in American education.* New York McGraw-Hill.

Crowin, R. G., and Diana, M. R. 1993. What can we really expect from large-scale voucher programs? *Phi Delta Kappan,* 75(1):68–74.

Cuban, L. 1992. What happens to reforms that last? The case of the junior high school. *American Educational Research Journal* 29(2):227–251.

Darling-Hammond, L. 1997. *The right to learn: A blueprint for creating schools that work.* San Francisco: Jossey-Bass Publishers.

Darling-Hammond, L. 1993. Reframing the school reform agenda: Developing capacity of school transformation. *Phi Delta Kappan* 75(4): 753–761.

Etzioni, A. 1993. *The spirit of community: rights, responsibility and the communitarian agenda.* New York: Crown Publishers.

Fuhrman, S. H., and Massell, D. 1992. *Issues and strategies in systemic reform.* University of Wisconsin-Madison, the Policy Center and the Finance Center.

Fullan, M. G. 1991. *The new meaning of educational change* (2nd ed.). New York: Teachers College Press.

Glickman, C. D. 1998. *Revolutionizing America's schools.* San Francisco: Jossey-Bass.

Glickman, C. D. 1993. *Renewing America's schools: A guide for school-based action.* San Francisco: Jossey-Bass.

Goodlad, J. I. 1991. *Teachers for our nations schools.* San Francisco: Jossey-Bass.

Goodlad, J. I. 1992. On taking school reform seriously. *Phi Delta Kappan* 74(2):232–238.

Gutmann, A. 1987. *Democratic education.* Princeton, NJ: Princeton University Press.

Hargreaves, A., and Macmillan, R. 1992. *Balkanized secondary schools and the malaise of modernity.* Paper presented at the annual meeting of the American Education Research Association, San Francisco.

Holmes Group. 1986. *Tomorrow's teachers.* East Lansing, MI: Author.

Houston, P. D. 1993. School voucher: The latest California joke. *Phi Delta Kappan* 75(1):61–64.

Huelskamp, R. M. 1993. Perspectives on education in America. *Phi Delta Kappan,* 75(4): 718–721.

Kirst, M. W. 1993. Strength and weakness of American education. *Phi Delta Kappan* 75(4): 613–618.

Kohn, A. 1999. *The schools our children deserve.* Boston: Houghton Mifflin Co.

Lee, G. C. 1961. The precious blessings of liberty. In G. Lee (Ed.), *Crusade against ignorance: Thomas Jefferson on Education.* New York: Columbia University. (pp. 27–28).

Lieberman, A. 1992. The meaning of scholarly activity and the building of community. *The Education Researcher* 21(6):5–12.

Lightfoot, S. L. 1983. *The good high school: Portraits of character and culture.* New York: Basic Books.

McLaughlin, M. W., and Talbert, J. E. 1992. *Social constructions of students: Challenges to policy coherence.* Stanford University, Center for Research on the Context of Secondary Teaching, San Francisco.

McNeil, L. N. 1988. Contradictions of control. Part 2: Teachers, students, and curriculum. *Kappan* 69(6):432–438.

Meier, D. 1992. Reinventing teaching. *Teachers College Record 93*(4). Teachers College Press.

O'Neil, J. 1993. On systemic reform: A conversation Marshall Smith. *Educational Leadership 51*(1):12–13.

Sagor, R. 1993. Creating a level playing field. *Phi Delta Kappan* 75(1):64–66.

Sarason, S. 1990. *The predictable failure of school reform.* San Francisco: Jossey-Bass.

Sashkin, M., and Egermeier, J. 1992. *School change models and process: A review of research and practice.* San Francisco: Office of Educational Research and Improvement, United States Department of Education.

Schlecty, P. C., and Cole, R. W. 1992. Creating "Standard-Bearer Schools." *Educational Leadership 50*(3):45–49.

Shanker, A. 1993. Presentation to the IDEA Senior Fellows Academy. Claremont College, July 15.

Talbert, J. E., and McLaughlin, M. W. 1992. *Teachers' professionalism as negotiated order.* Stanford University, Center for Research on the Context of Secondary Teaching, San Francisco.

U.S. Department of Education, National Center for Educational Statistics; College Entrance Examination Board. (1993, August 22). An Encouraging rebound for many public schools. *The Atlanta Journal/The Atlanta Constitution,* p. A8.

Wohlstetter, P., and Buffett, T. M. 1992. Promoting school-based management: Are dollars decentralized too? In A. Odden (Ed.), *Rethinking school finance.* San Francisco: Jossey-Bass.

Suggested Readings

Darling-Hammond, L. 1997. *The right to learn: A blueprint for creating schools that work.* San Francisco: Jossey-Bass Publishers.

Elmore, R. F. 1990. *Restructuring schools.* San Francisco: Jossey-Bass.

Glickman, C. D. 1998. *Revolutionizing America's schools.* San Francisco: Jossey-Bass.

Glickman, C. D. 1993. *Renewing America's schools: A guide for school-based action.* San Francisco: Jossey-Bass.

Kohn, A. 1999. *The schools our children deserve.* Boston: Houghton Mifflin Co.

Murphy, J., and Hallinger, P. 1993. *Restructuring schooling.* Newbury Park, CA: Sage.

Reavis, C., and Griffith, H. 1992. *Restructuring schools.* Lancaster, PA: Technomic.

Sarason, S. B. 1991. *The predictable failure of educational reform.* San Francisco: Jossey-Bass.

Schlecty, D. D. 1990. *Schools for the 21st century.* San Francisco: Jossey-Bass.

Appendix A

What Is Your Educational Philosophy?

Instructions

Please check the answer under each item that best reflects your thinking. You may also want to check more than one answer for any one of the questions.

1. What is the essence of education?
   A. The essence of education is *reason* and *intuition.*
   B. The essence of education is *growth.*
   C. The essence of education is *knowledge* and *skills.*
   D. The essence of education is *choice.*
2. What is the nature of the learner?
   A. The learner is an experiencing organism.
   B. The learner is a unique, free choosing, and responsible creature made up of intellect and emotion.
   C. The learner is a rational and intuitive being.
   D. The learner is a storehouse for knowledge and skills, which, once acquired, can later be applied and used.
3. How should education provide for the needs of man?
   A. The students need a passionate encounter with the perennial problems of life; the agony and joy of love, reality of choice, anguish of freedom, consequences of actions and the inevitability of death.

Source: Patricia T. Jersin, "What Is Your EP: A Test Which Identifies Your Educational Philosophy," *Clearing House, 46,* pages 274–278, January 1972. Reprinted with permission of the Helen Dwight Reid Educational Foundation. Published by Heldref Publications, 1319 Eighteenth St., N.W., Washington, D.C. 20036–1802. Copyright © 1972. (You may note that Jersin has identified four philosophies. Since educational practice is reflected in three, we would subsume her philosophies in this way—Perennialism (belief in changeless knowledge) grouped with Essentialism, Progressivism as Experimentalism, and Existentialism as itself.)

   B. Education allows for the needs of man when it inculcates the child with certain essential skills and knowledge which all men should possess.

   C. The one distinguishing characteristic of man is intelligence. Education should concentrate on developing the intellectual needs of students.

   D. Since the needs of man are variable, education should concentrate on developing the individual differences in students.

4. What should be the environment of education?

   A. Education should possess an environment where the student adjusts to the material and social world as it really exists.

   B. The environment of education should be life itself, where students can experience living—not prepare for it.

   C. The environment of education should be one that encourages the growth of free, creative individuality, not adjustment to group thinking nor the public norms.

   D. Education is not a true replica of life, rather, it is an artificial environment where the child should be developing his intellectual potentialities and preparing for the future.

5. What should be the goal of education?

   A. Growth, through the reconstruction of experience, is the nature, and should be the open-ended goal, of education.

   B. The only type of goal to which education should lead is to the goal of truth, which is absolute, universal, and unchanging.

   C. The primary concern of education should be with the development of the uniqueness of individual students.

   D. The goal of education should be to provide a framework of knowledge for the student against which new truths can be gathered and assimilated.

6. What should be the concern of the school?

   A. The school should concern itself with man's distinguishing characteristic, his mind, and concentrate on developing rationality.

   B. The school should provide an education for the "whole child," centering its attention on all the needs and interests of the child.

   C. The school should educate the child to attain the basic knowledge necessary to understand the real world outside.

   D. The school should provide each student with assistance in his journey toward self-realization.

7. What should be the atmosphere of the school?

   A. The school should provide for group thinking in a democratic atmosphere that fosters cooperation rather than competition.

   B. The atmosphere of the school should be one of authentic freedom where a student is allowed to find his own truth and ultimate fulfillment through non-conforming choice making.

   C. The school should surround its students with "Great Books" and foster individuality in an atmosphere of intellectualism and creative thinking.

    D. The school should retain an atmosphere of mental discipline, yet incorporate innovative techniques which would introduce the student to a perceptual examination of the realities about him.

8. How should appropriate learning occur?

    A. Appropriate learning occurs as the student freely engages in choosing among alternatives while weighing personal responsibilities and the possible consequences of his actions.

    B. Appropriate learning takes place through the experience of problem-solving projects by which the child is led from practical issues to theoretical principles (concrete-to-abstract).

    C. Appropriate learning takes place as certain basic readings acquaint students with the world's permanencies, inculcating them in theoretical principles that they will later apply in life (abstract-to-concrete).

    D. Appropriate learning occurs when hard effort has been extended to absorb and master the prescribed subject matter.

9. What should be the role of the teacher?

    A. The teacher should discipline pupils intellectually through a study of the great works in literature where the universal concerns of man have best been expressed.

    B. The teacher should present principles and values and the reasons for them, encouraging students to examine them in order to choose for themselves whether or not to accept them.

    C. The teacher should guide and advise students, since the children's own interests should determine what they learn, not authority nor the subject matter of the textbooks.

    D. The teacher, the responsible authority, should mediate between the adult world and the world of the child since immature students cannot comprehend the nature and demands of adulthood by themselves.

10. What should the curriculum include?

    A. The curriculum should include only that which has survived the test of time and combines the symbols and ideas of literature, history, and mathematics with the sciences of the physical world.

    B. The curriculum should concentrate on teaching students how to manage change through problem solving activities in the social studies… empirical sciences and vocational technology.

    C. The curriculum should concentrate on intellectual subject matter and include English, languages, history, mathematics, natural sciences, the fine arts, and also philosophy.

    D. The curriculum should concentrate on the humanities; history, literature, philosophy, and art—where greater depth into the nature of man and his conflict with the world are revealed.

11. What should be the preferred teaching method?

    A. *Projects* should be the preferred method whereby the students can be guided through problem-solving experiences.

     B. *Lectures, readings,* and *discussions* should be the preferred methods for training the intellect.

     C. *Demonstrations* should be the preferred method for teaching knowledge and skills.

     D. *Socratic dialogue* (drawing responses from a questioning conversation) should be the preferred method for finding the self.

Scoring the Test

This test is self-scoring. Circle the answer you selected for each of the questions checked on the test (Table A.1). Total the number of circles below each column.

TABLE A.1 *What Is Your EP?*

	Progressivism	Perennialism	Essentialism	Existentialism
1	B	A	C	D
2	A	C	D	B
3	D	C	B	A
4	B	D	A	C
5	A	B	D	C
6	B	A	C	D
7	A	C	D	B
8	B	C	D	A
9	C	A	D	B
10	B	C	A	D
11	A	B	C	D

Implications

The four answers selected for each of the questions in this multiple-choice test represent positions on educational issues being taken by hypothetical advocates of the major educational philosophies heading each column—Progressivism, Perennialism, Essentialism, and Existentialism. If, in scoring your test, you find that a majority of your choices, no matter how much doubling up of answers, falls in a single column, you are selecting a dominant educational philosophy from among the four. For example, if you find your totals: Progressivism (9), Perennialism (1), Essentialism (3), and Existentialism (2); your dominant educational philosophy as determined by this test would be *Progressivism* (9 out of 15 choices being a majority). If you discover yourself spread rather evenly among several, or even all four, this scattering of answers demonstrates an eclectic set of educational values. Indecisiveness in selecting from the four positions could indicate other values and beliefs not contained within one of these major educational systems.

In all formal systems of philosophy, an important measure of the system's validity is its consistency. Your consistency in taking this test can be measured by comparing the answer you selected for item #1 that identifies *essence* with your other answers. The more of the remaining 10 responses you find in the same column where you circled item #1, the more consistent you should be in your educational philosophy. The fewer of the other 10 responses in the same column as item #1, the more you should find your responses contradicting one another—a problem inherent in eclecticism. Again, keep in mind, lack of consistency may also be due to valuing another set of educational beliefs, consistent in themselves, but not included as one of the possible systems selected for representation here.

Appendix B

Skill Practices Using Directive Control, Directive Informational, Collaborative, and Nondirective Approaches

B-1: Directions for Instructor and Participants
B-2: Skill Practice in the Directive Control Approach
B-3: Skill Practice in the Directive Informational Approach
B-4: Skill Practice in the Collaborative Approach
B-5: Skill Practice in the Nondirective Approach

B1: Directions for All Skill Practices

1. Each conference will have the same identical three phases.

Phase One: Goal Identification
Gathering information and descriptions of situation
Finding a focus for improvement
Stating a goal

Phase Two: Plan
Exploring alternative actions
Anticipating consequences for various alternatives
Selecting and specifying those actions likely to achieve the goal
Writing the plan

Phase Three: Critique
Supervisor asking for feedback on his or her behaviors

Discussing ways the supervisor could improve further conferences with supervisee

2. Each conference will produce a simplified plan of action to include:

   I. Goal to be achieved
   II. Specific actions to be taken

(A more detailed plan could include objectives, activities, resources, and evaluation.)

3. Each skill practice should be a *real* conference dealing with an *actual* professional concern, problem, or situation that the supervisee wishes to act on and that is *within* his or her control to do something about. Situations that are dependent on actions by persons outside of the supervisee's sphere of influence should not be used in these skill practices.

4. An authentic and original plan that will be implemented should be the outcome of the conference. Once again, supervisor and supervisees are not pretending to be somebody else—they are to be themselves, engaged in real professional discussion about goals and actions.

5. The only difference is that one person is responsible for conducting the conference according to a particular approach. The person conducting the conference is called the supervisor, responsible for moving through the three phases and seeing that an action plan is derived. The supervisee is the person who comes to the conference with a professional goal or concern for which he or she wishes to establish a plan.

6. At the conclusion of each skill practice, it is illuminating to ask the *supervisees*, in writing, to rate the value of their plans (how good is the plan for reaching your goal) on a scale from one (not of value) to ten (of great value) and then, also in writing, to describe with three adjectives the personal experience of having a (directive control, directive informational, collaborative, or nondirective) approach used. Ask the supervisor to describe with three adjectives the personal experience of using a (directive control, directive informational, collaborative, or nondirective) approach. Each person should write independently, and then the instructor can solicit responses to each question with the entire group. Some fascinating discussions about the use and misuse of a particular approach usually ensue, with an opportunity at the end to compare all four approaches.

7. Each skill practice session will need about 30 to 40 minutes for the actual conference and 20 to 30 minutes for debriefing—a total of 50 to 70 minutes for each approach.

8. It might help to reproduce the skill practice guides on the next two pages as overheads. Explain the approach to be used, ask participants to pair off, designate supervisor and supervisee, and time (announcing start and stop) through each step of the conference.

Conferences

Goal-Identification Phase
  Information and Descriptions
  Focus for Improvement
  Goal Statement

Plan Phase
  Alternative Actions
  Consequences
  Selecting and Specifying
  Writing Plan

Critique Phase
  Feedback on Supervisor's Behaviors
  Feedback on Ways to Improve Next Conference

Written Action Plan

Goal Statement

Actions to Be Taken

  1.
  2.
  3.

Signed _____

_____

B2: Directive Control Skill Practice

Directions: Review Chapter 8. (Remember that the supervisor assumes full responsibility for developing the plan. In this case, the supervisor already has information about the problem. The supervisor identifies the problem at the beginning of the conference, but allows teacher input before determining the best solution.)

  I. Goal-Identification Phase
    A. Supervisor identifies problem—2 minutes.
    B. Supervisor asks for supervisee input.
    C. Supervisor states goal, asks if teacher understands goal, and clarifies if necessary—3 minutes.
    D. Supervisor writes statement of goal—1 minute.
  II. Plan Phase
    A. Supervisor tells supervisee at least three expectations and rationale for each expectation—3 minutes.
    B. Supervisor asks supervisee for input into expectations—3 minutes.

     C. Supervisor modifies expectations, if necessary, and provides specific details of each expectation—6 minutes.

     D. Supervisor reviews and writes goal and expectations—4 minutes.

III. Critique Phase—3 minutes

     A. Supervisor asks, "What feedback can you give me on how I conducted this conference?"

     B. Supervisor asks, "What might we do next time to make these observations and conferences more helpful?"

     C. Supervisor summarizes what he or she has learned, for use in later conferences.

B3: *Directive Informational Skill Practice*

Directions: Review Chapter 9. (Remember that the supervisor is the source of information and direction in developing the plan. In this case, the supervisor does not have prior information about the situation or possible goals, so he or she gathers feedback to identify the goal. Eventually, the supervisor will provide the arena of choice for the supervisee in developing the final plan.)

  I. Goal-Identification Phase

     A. Supervisor tells supervisee, "Describe to me the situation that you are facing"—3 minutes.

     B. Supervisor asks for additional information about the situation—2 minutes.

     C. Supervisor asks questions to understand the supervisee's goal—2 minutes.

     D. The supervisor states his or her understanding of the goal and asks supervisee to react to the statement—1 minute.

     E. Supervisor writes statement of goal—1 minute.

  II. Plan Phase

     A. After writing the goal, the supervisor thinks of possible actions and says, "Based on my experience (knowledge), I believe that you might do the following…. The supervisor gives at least three specific actions and reviews the anticipated consequences of using each action—4 minutes.

     B. Supervisor asks supervisee to respond to the proposed actions: "What do you think?"—2 minutes.

     C. After hearing the supervisee's response, the supervisor now modifies, revises, or expands the alternatives and directs the choices. "These appear to be realistic actions that you might take. You could do the following…." Supervisor then asks "Which one of these makes the most sense to you?" and "Which will you use?"—4 minutes.

     D. After the supervisee makes his or her choices, the supervisor affirms, "I understand that you will do…" and writes actions on plan—4 minutes.

  III. Critique Phase—3 minutes

     A. Supervisor asks, "What feedback can you give me on how I conducted this conference?"

    B. Supervisor asks, "What might we do next time to make these observations and conferences more helpful?"

    C. Supervisor summarizes what he or she has learned, for use in later conferences.

B4: *Collaborative Skill Practice*

Directions: Review Chapter 10. (Remember that the supervisee and supervisor have equal influence in determining the goal and plan. So as not to exert undue influence, the supervisor should allow the supervisee to lead first in each phase of the conference. Before beginning, they should pick a topic of concern that is of mutual interest.)

  I. Goal-Identification Phase

    A. *Describe the situation* (both parties). Supervisor asks supervisee to explain the current situation that he or she wishes to improve. Supervisor paraphrases and checks for accuracy, and then explains how he or she sees the situation, asks for a paraphrase, and gives feedback on accuracy—7 minutes.

    B. *Ask for further information.* Supervisee asks questions of supervisor and supervisor asks questions of supervisee, to gather further information to determine a common goal—5 minutes.

    C. *State the goal.* Supervisor states the common goal, checks for accuracy and agreement, and writes it down on the first part of the plan—2 minutes.

 II. Plan Phase

    A. *Brainstorm possible actions* (let supervisee lead). Supervisor asks supervisee to brainstorm at least three possible alternative actions and then offers his or her own possibilities of actions—2 minutes.

    B. *Ask questions and discuss consequences.* Supervisor and supervisee question each other about consequences of various proposed actions and look for commonalities and differences—5 minutes.

    C. *Negotiate.* Supervisor and supervisee determine actions that they both agree will help reach the goal—2 minutes.

    D. *State a jointly agreed action.* Supervisor and supervisee specify the agreed upon actions so that each knows exactly:
Who will do what?
How will it be done?
When will it be done?
When will it be reviewed?—3 minutes.

    E. *Write the plan.* Supervisor writes the agreed-upon actions in the plan. (No action is recorded unless both parties fully agree to it.)—5 minutes.

III. Critique Phase—3 minutes

    A. Supervisor asks, "What feedback can you give me on how I conducted this conference?"

B. Supervisor asks, "What might we do next time to make these observations and conferences more helpful?"

C. Supervisor summarizes what he or she has learned, for use in later conferences.

B5: *Nondirective Skill Practice*

Directions: Review Chapter 11. (Remember that the supervisor's responsibility is to facilitate the supervisee's own thinking and decision making and not to impose his or her own ideas.)

   I. Goal-Identification Phase

      A. Supervisor begins, "Could you explain the current concern that you need to take action on?"
Supervisee talk—3 minutes
Paraphrase by supervisor—45 seconds
Accuracy of paraphrase (check by supervisor)—30 seconds

      B. Supervisor asks questions to gather further information—2 minutes.

      C. Supervisor states perceived goal and checks for accuracy. Supervisor writes goal on first part of plan—3 minutes.

  II. Plan Phase

      A. Supervisor asks supervisee to brainstorm possible alternative actions (at least three)—5 minutes.

      B. Supervisor asks supervisee to weigh pros and cons of alternatives—3 minutes.

      C. Supervisor asks, "What will you do?" Paraphrase: "Then I understand you will...."—2 minutes.

      D. Supervisor now writes a plan of action as dictated by supervisee (make sure actions are clear and specific)—3 minutes.

 III. Critique Phase—3 minutes

      A. Supervisor asks, "What feedback can you give me on how I conducted this conference?"

      B. Supervisor asks, "What might we do next time to make these observations and conferences more helpful?"

      C. Supervisor summarizes what he or she has learned, for use in later conferences.

Appendix C

Assessing School-Based Supervisory Practices for Promoting Instructional Improvement

Directions: For each item, please circle a number in the right column to indicate the degree to which the item describes the current supervisory practice in your school(s):

1. Definitely false
2. More false than true
3. More true than false
4. Definitely true

I. In the area of direct personal support in my school(s), leadership personnel provide:
   A. Assistance with identifying and obtaining resources for instruction   1 2 3 4
   B. Demonstration of teaching techniques in the classroom   1 2 3 4
   C. Consultation on instructional problems and concerns   1 2 3 4
   D. Conferences to schedule and plan observations   1 2 3 4
   E. Observations of classes for assistance in improving instruction (not for evaluation)   1 2 3 4
   F. Conferences after observations to discuss and analyze the lesson observed   1 2 3 4
   G. Opportunities to analyze teaching with audio or videotape   1 2 3 4

Source: Jean W. Jones, *A data collection system for describing research-based supervisory practices for promoting instructional improvement in a local school district.* Ed.D. dissertation, University of Georgia, 1986. Reprinted by permission of the author.

    H. Opportunities to observe and discuss classes taught by
       other teachers   1 2 3 4
    I. Genuine concern for teachers and students   1 2 3 4
    J. Supportive and helpful assistance   1 2 3 4
    K. Stimulation to think consciously about teaching skills   1 2 3 4

II. In my school(s), leadership personnel assist teachers with:
    A. Planning appropriate learning objectives   1 2 3 4
    B. Designing appropriate instructional activities   1 2 3 4
    C. Developing remedial and enrichment activities   1 2 3 4
    D. Developing activities for daily review and diagnosis   1 2 3 4
    E. Developing strategies for student team or group learning   1 2 3 4
    F. Developing learning activities for students who finish early   1 2 3 4
    G. Evaluating student progress   1 2 3 4
    H. Interpreting and using test scores from standardized
       or criterion-referenced tests   1 2 3 4
    I. Organizing and arranging the space and materials for instruction 1 2 3 4
    J. Increasing and maintaining student academic engagement time 1 2 3 4
    K. Stimulating learner interest during lesson presentation   1 2 3 4
    L. Managing student behavior (discipline)   1 2 3 4
    M. Clarifying classroom rules and procedures for students   1 2 3 4
    N. Giving clear directions and preparing for transitions in
       the classroom   1 2 3 4
    O. Using questioning techniques with students   1 2 3 4
    P. Involving all students during guided practice to increase
       success on objectives   1 2 3 4
    Q. Providing students with corrective feedback and praise   1 2 3 4

III. Structured learning opportunities such as workshops, in-service
    activities, or staff development programs in my school(s) include:
    A. Active support and clear direction by leadership personnel   1 2 3 4
    B. Opportunities for collaborative planning of in-service activities   1 2 3 4
    C. In-service activities that are consistent with clearly defined
       goals for instructional improvement   1 2 3 4
    D. Activities that present information or skills that have
       been shown to be effective   1 2 3 4
    E. Presentation of information and skills that are practical
       and useful   1 2 3 4
    F. Activities that are well organized and carefully developed   1 2 3 4
    G. Program leaders who have credibility and expertise   1 2 3 4
    H. Formal opportunities to learn, solve problems, and
       interact with small groups or teams   1 2 3 4
    I. Programs that extend over several sessions   1 2 3 4
    J. Presentations by a combination of instructional techniques   1 2 3 4
    K. Presentation of information or skills through modeling
       or demonstrations (live or taped)   1 2 3 4

    L. Planned opportunities to discuss usefulness of information
       or skills and to share instructional ideas   1 2 3 4
    M. Opportunities to apply and practice information or skills
        by direct experience during workshop or teaching situations   1 2 3 4
    N. Opportunities for observation and objective feedback
       between sessions to promote acquisition of information or skill 1 2 3 4
    O. Observations by leadership personnel to see if skills or
       information presented in inservice programs are being used 1 2 3 4
    P. Access to materials and resource people to help
      implement a program after formal inservice presentations
      have been completed   1 2 3 4

IV. Are there additional ways in which leadership personnel can support teachers in increasing and maintaining instructional effectiveness? Please comment:

Name Index

Note: Pages in *italic* locate the reference cited.

Subject Index